Macintosh

Microsoft Office 98 for Macintosh
The Comprehensive Guide

Ned Snell
Brian J. Little

Microsoft Office 98 For Macintosh: The Comprehensive Guide
Copyright © The Coriolis Group, 1998

All rights reserved. This book may not be duplicated in any way without the express written consent of the publisher, except in the form of brief excerpts or quotations for the purposes of review. The information contained herein is for the personal use of the reader and may not be incorporated in any commercial programs, other books, databases, or any kind of software without written consent of the publisher. Making copies of this book or any portion for any purpose other than your own is a violation of United States copyright laws.

Limits of Liability and Disclaimer of Warranty

The author and publisher of this book have used their best efforts in preparing the book and the programs contained in it. These efforts include the development, research, and testing of the theories and programs to determine their effectiveness. The author and publisher make no warranty of any kind, expressed or implied, with regard to these programs or the documentation contained in this book.

The author and publisher shall not be liable in the event of incidental or consequential damages in connection with, or arising out of, the furnishing, performance, or use of the programs, associated instructions, and/or claims of productivity gains.

Trademarks

Trademarked names appear throughout this book. Rather than list the names and entities that own the trademarks or insert a trademark symbol with each mention of the trademarked name, the publisher states that it is using the names for editorial purposes only and to the benefit of the trademark owner, with no intention of infringing upon that trademark.

The Coriolis Group, Inc.
An International Thomson Publishing Company
14455 N. Hayden Road, Suite 220
Scottsdale, Arizona 85260

602/483-0192
FAX 602/483-0193
http://www.coriolis.com

Library of Congress Cataloging-in-Publication Data
Snell, Ned
   Microsoft Office 98 for Macintosh: the comprehensive guide/by Ned Snell and Brian Little.
      p. cm.
   Includes index.
   ISBN 1-57610-279-3
    1. Microsoft Word. 2. Microsoft Excel (Computer file) 3. Microsoft PowerPoint (Computer file) 4. Microsoft Outlook. 5. Business--Computer programs. 6. Word processing. 7. Electronic spreadsheets. 8. Business presentations--Graphic methods--Computer programs. 9. Internet (Computer network) 10. Time management--Computer programs. 11. Personal information management--Computer programs.   I. Little, Brian. II. Title.
HF5548.4.M525L57   1998
005.369--dc21   98-3884
                                                                               CIP

Printed in the United States of America
10 9 8 7 6 5 4 3 2 1

an International Thomson Publishing company

Albany, NY • Belmont, CA • Bonn • Boston • Cincinnati • Detroit • Johannesburg • London • Madrid
Melbourne • Mexico City • New York • Paris • Singapore • Tokyo • Toronto • Washington

---

Publisher
Keith Weiskamp

Acquisitions
Stephanie Wall

Marketing Specialist
Jody Kent

Project Editor
Meredith Brittain

Production Coordinator
Jon Gabriel

Cover Design
Anthony Stock

Layout Design
April Nielsen

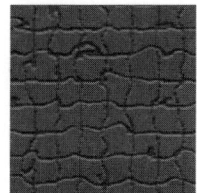

Dedication

I dedicate my portion of this work to five people:

- Steve Jobs and Steve Wozniak—The arrogant visionary and the inspired guru who built the most amazing computer, and the most amazing computer company, ever. Hoist the skull and crossbones over Cupertino!
- Lawrence Lessig—For standing up for what he believes is right.
- Guy Kawasaki—Who knows what the Mac can, and should, become, and speaks plainly about it.
- Lara Little—My wife, who reminds me on a regular basis that it is, after all, just a computer, and not nearly as much fun as playing Frisbee with Darwin the dalmatian.

Thanks to all of you. You're the best.

—Brian J. Little

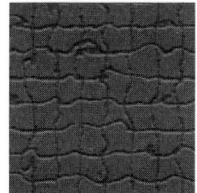

About The Authors

Ned Snell (Gotha, CA), an award-winning computer journalist, is the author of seven other computer books, including *The Comprehensive Guide to Office 97*, *Souping Up Windows*, and *Navigating the Internet with Windows 95*. In addition, he has written hundreds of articles for *Datamation* (for which he was also a contributing editor), *Software Magazine*, and others; he was also editor-in-chief for several national publications, including *Edge* magazine and *Art and Design News*.

Brian J. Little (Charlotte, NC) is a freelance technical editor and writer and a network systems administrator at the University of North Carolina at Charlotte. He has used every Macintosh since the Plus and has run just about every version of Word and Excel. Other books he has contributed to include *The System 7 Book*, *Voodoo Macintosh*, *The Microsoft Excel Power Toolkit*, and *Desktop Publishing with Word*.

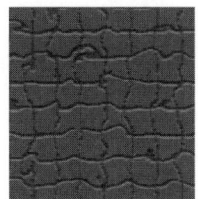

Acknowledgments

Many thanks to Meredith Brittain, Jennifer Mario, Diane Haugen, Stephanie Wall, Paula Kmetz, Jon Gabriel, Tony Stock, and all the other fine folks at Coriolis who put up with missed deadlines and irritable late-night email, and somehow still managed to smile. Thanks also to Chris Grams, late of Ventana Press, for his help in getting this started. Special thanks go to Ned Snell, the author of *The Comprehensive Guide to Microsoft Office 97*, for setting the groundwork for this book. Many thanks as well to my wife, for tolerating far too many of my long nights in front of the screen; to Gary Fisher Bicycles and Bungie Software, who manufacture the most excellent stress-relievers known to man; and to my cats, all five of them, for keeping my toes warm while I work. It's finished! Let's find the catnip.

—Brian J. Little

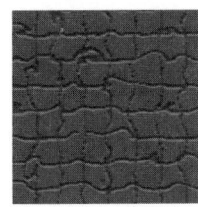

Table Of Contents

Introduction XVII

PART I: The Office Environment

Chapter 1
Discovering Office 98 3

What's Office 98, Anyhow?   3
About The Programs   7
Moving On   15

Chapter 2
Getting To Know The Office 98 Environment 17

Opening And Closing Office Programs   18
Choosing From The Menu Bar   20
Using Toolbars   21
Scrolling To See More   24
Dragging And Dropping   25
Control-Clicking To Use Contextual Menus   25
Understanding Dialogs   25
Understanding Dialog Defaults   28
Using Shortcut Keys   28
Using The Microsoft Office Manager   30
Using OfficeArt   34
Customizing Office Applications   39
Getting Help   40
About The Value Pack   48
Moving On   48

PART II: Word

Chapter 3
Getting Started With Word 51

Creating A New Word Document 52
Entering Text 52
Saving Documents 54
Closing Documents 62
Opening Documents 63
Controlling Word's Display 68
Jumping From Page To Page 73
Printing Your Document 74
Moving On 77

Chapter 4
Working With Text 79

Choosing Text To Work With 79
Changing Your Mind After Changing Text 81
Editing Text 83
Tracking Changes 89
Formatting Text 90
Applying Advanced Text-Control Options 95
Adding Symbols And Special Characters 100
Moving On 103

Chapter 5
Designing Pages 105

Understanding And Creating Sections 106
Setting Up The Document 108
Adding Headers And Footers 118
Working With Columns 122
Breaking Pages And Columns 124
Formatting Paragraphs 127
Formatting Lists 130
Working With Tabs 134
Moving On 138

Chapter 6
Adding Pictures, Tables, And Borders 139

    Adding Pictures To Documents   140
    Creating Text Boxes   153
    Overlapping Pictures, Text, And Boxes   155
    Making Tables   156
    Working With Borders, Shading, And Color   162
    Moving On   167

Chapter 7
Working Faster And Easier In Word 169

    Wizarding Up A New Document   170
    Working With Templates   173
    Working With Styles   176
    Browsing Through Text   183
    AutoCorrecting And Formatting Text   184
    Finding And Using Synonyms   196
    Finding And Replacing Text And Formatting   197
    Repeating And Copying Formatting   200
    Assembling And Printing Mailings   201
    Moving On   204

PART III: PowerPoint

Chapter 8
Getting Started With PowerPoint 207

    Creating A New Show   208
    Saving Presentations   215
    Choosing A View   216
    Modifying Wizards And Templates   221
    Checking Spelling   227
    Adding, Moving, And Removing Slides   228
    Moving On   230

Chapter 9
Designing Presentations 231

Opening Existing Presentations   231
Rearranging Slide Elements   233
Changing Slide Colors   236
Creating Notes Pages And Handouts   243
Choosing A Presentation Medium   245
Printing Transparencies   248
Making 35mm Slides   250
Taking A Show On The Road   252
Moving On   254

Chapter 10
Livening Up Your Presentations 255

Adding Multimedia To Slides   255
Creating Your Own Sound For Presentations   260
Adding Animation Effects   265
Adding Hyperlinks To Presentations   272
Setting Up And Running Electronic Shows   276
Using Speaker Options In A Presentation   280
Moving On   283

PART IV: Excel

Chapter 11
Getting Started With Excel 287

Managing Excel Workbooks   288
Printing A Workbook   297
Closing A Workbook   298
Exchanging Files With Other Programs   299
Opening Workbooks   299
Adding Add-Ins   304
Moving On   306

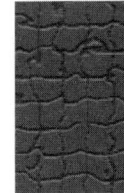

Chapter 12
Adding Data, Formulas, And Functions 307
    Entering Cell Data   308
    Adding Comments   313
    Editing Cell Data   314
    Working With Formulas And Functions   324
    Moving On   336

Chapter 13
Formatting Workbooks 337
    Fast Table Formatting With AutoFormat   338
    Formatting A Worksheet   339
    Working With Worksheets   342
    Inserting Pictures Into A Worksheet   352
    Formatting Pages   353
    Moving On   362

Chapter 14
Organizing, Analyzing, And Charting Data 363
    Creating Charts   364
    Managing Data   373
    Creating A Form   379
    Moving On   384

PART V: Outlook Express

Chapter 15
Communicating Via Outlook Express 387
    Installing Outlook Express   388
    Opening Outlook Express   390
    Configuring Outlook Express   391
    Learning The Outlook Express Interface   397
    Working With Folders   402

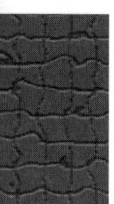

  Receiving And Reading Email 405
  Sending Mail 414
  Organizing Mail 424
  Working With Contacts 431
  Finding Email Addresses 439
  Using Newsgroups 440
  Moving On 450

PART VI: Getting It Together

Chapter 16
Collaborating And Integrating With Office 98 453

  Exchanging Information Between Programs 454
  Collaborating On Projects 462
  Moving On 467

Chapter 17
Office 98 And The Internet 469

  Publishing Native Office Documents Online 470
  Writing Web Pages With Office 478
  Authoring Web Pages With Word 481
  Building Web-Based PowerPoint Shows 490
  Adding Excel Data To Web Pages 493
  Publishing Your Web Page 494
  Learning More About Web Authoring 495
  Moving On 495

Appendix A
Installing And Configuring Office 98 497

  System Requirements 497
  Preparing For Installation 498
  Installing Office 98 499
  Installing The Microsoft Office 98 Value Pack 505

Appendix B
A Brief Introduction To Internet Explorer 509
- Installing Internet Explorer   510
- Getting Around In Internet Explorer   513
- Configuring Your Own Start Page   518
- Pay Dirt   526

Appendix C
Mac OS, Fonts, And Microsoft Office 98 529
- Recognizing A Font   529
- Types Of Fonts   530
- Installing And Removing Fonts   533
- Fonts And System Performance   534

Glossary 537

Index 545

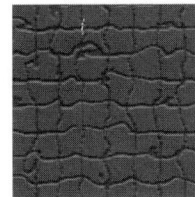

Introduction

Welcome to Office 98, Macintosh Edition! Come in, relax, have a snack. If you want to, kick off your shoes. It's always dress-down day here.

This is *Microsoft Office 98 for Macintosh: The Comprehensive Guide*, and although that sounds terribly lofty, the book you've picked up is lofty only when you count its pages. But if you're like most people, you won't use every page—you'll use just the parts you need. And the parts, friends, are simple, clear, and—when nobody's looking—fun.

Fun notwithstanding, this book is very serious about helping you accomplish whatever it is you plan to do in Office 98. To meet that end, the book follows a time-tested educational axiom: People learn best when you empower them with a little background and a few important skills, and then get the heck out of their way. As you'll learn if you take a quick read through this Introduction, this comprehensive guide aims to empower you, to give you skills and understanding to take you confidently in whatever direction that your own personal Office projects lead.

If we've done our job right, you shouldn't need this book for very long. You'll be much too busy working productively in Office to be flipping pages here. If you follow the approach outlined in this Introduction, you should be able to quickly acquire all the Office skills you need without wading through a lot of stuff that does not contribute directly to the skill set you seek. After that, you may want to keep the book around for reference or to explore one day any programs or features you skipped the first time around.

Ready to get started? Then read on. We'll start the countdown to the day you go solo.

Who This Book Is For

This book is for real people. And real people have work to do.

Real people don't set out to learn Office for its own sake. They want to learn Word because somebody put them in charge of the newsletter, or learn PowerPoint to prepare for a speech at an upcoming conference, or learn Outlook Express to make better use of email, or learn Excel to make straight sense of seemingly random information. They

don't want to learn every tiny technical detail, nor do they want to be treated like "dummies" and taught too little. They want to learn enough to get the job done—and done right. And because real people all have too much to do, they want the time they invest in learning a new skill to pay long-term returns by laying a foundation from which they can grow, easily adding to their skill set later as their needs evolve.

This book is written for real people who want to learn to use Office at a beginning-to-intermediate level, whether they're newcomers to Office or upgraders from a previous version. It is designed and organized to make you productive in your chosen Office applications as quickly as possible, while at the same time grounding you in essential concepts that equip you to build upon what you learn. Here and there, the book also contains a little humor, because real people have to laugh sometimes or else they'll get crusty.

To achieve all that, of course, the book has to leave something out. What you won't find here are advanced Office techniques that have less to do with getting something done and more to do with programming and with the administration of Office on a network. But even if you're a Mac guru, you'll find this book a useful guide to the general operation of Office. This book places no limits on the reader—it just limits the discussion to intermediate ambitions.

Which Office 98 Does This Book Cover?

This book covers all of the programs available in the Standard Edition of Office 98: Word 98, Excel 98, PowerPoint 98, and Outlook Express. (We'll also make brief mention of Internet Explorer, which is on the CD, but not really part of the Office suite.)

Another version of Office 98, the Gold Edition, contains Word, Excel, PowerPoint, and Outlook Express, plus several other Microsoft applications; although this book does not cover all of that edition, users of that edition will benefit from this book's coverage of Word, Excel, PowerPoint, and Outlook Express.

How To Use This Book Productively

The organization of this book is based on a fact of nature: Nobody will actually read it in order from beginning to end. In fact, virtually no one besides us and the copyeditors will read the whole book, in any order. And frankly, we can't even make any promises about ourselves.

That's because everyone comes to Office with a different agenda. Few Office users really use all of Office, at least not right away—so there's little incentive to approach the whole bailiwick start-to-finish. Every Office user has a primary application he or she wants to explore first. With a majority of users, that's Word—but with many others, it's some-

thing else. Also, folks upgrading from a previous Office version may want to go first to what's completely new—Outlook Express—before learning what's changed in their favorite Office programs.

With all of those different needs in mind, this book is designed so that you can jump directly to any part of the book to learn about a specific program—after first taking your Office orientation by reading the two short chapters in Part I. The book is really divided into three chunks:

- *Part I*—A quick orientation to Office, which all readers should visit before moving on to any other part of the book.

- *Parts II through V*—Program sections, each covering one of the main Office 98 application programs: Word, PowerPoint, Excel, and Outlook Express.

- *Part VI*—Semi-advanced material showing how you can use Office 98 programs collaboratively, integrate them, and use them in concert with corporate networks and the Internet.

The two short, easy chapters in Part I orient you by showing you what's in Office and how to do important stuff that pertains to all of Office, such as opening programs and using Help. After reading Part I, feel free to jump directly to any of the program sections. The final part, Part VI, is best left until you've already become familiar with whichever Office programs you will use regularly.

The four parts devoted to programs are self-contained; they don't require you to have read any of the other program parts. For example, after reading Part I, you may jump straight to Part V to begin learning about Outlook Express, then jump back to Part II to learn about Word.

You should be aware, however, that if you are interested in learning all of Office, there are rewards to following the parts in order. The order is designed to make the transition from one program to another simple. For example, Word comes first because it's the most used—and most intensively used—Office program for most folks. PowerPoint is the most "Word-like" of the other programs, so it comes hot on Word's heels, while Word is fresh in the reader's mind. Next, Excel introduces data management. Finally, Outlook Express is last because it has the least in common with the other programs.

While you needn't follow the parts of the book in order, the chapters within each part do build upon one another, so it's best to read the chapters within a part in order. The first chapter grounds you in the absolute basics of using the program—creating and saving files, getting around in the program, important terms and concepts, and so on. As the chapters progress, they cover more sophisticated activities; the most advanced (and least used) parts of a program are always covered in the final chapter of a part. Depending on

your needs, you may find that you've learned everything you want to learn before reaching the end of a part. That's OK—learn what you want, and leave the rest for a time when your needs expand.

If You're An Upgrader From Office 4.2.1...

If you're moving up from Office 4.2.1, you'll find much in Office 98 that feels familiar, and much more stuff that's new. Even such basic activities as saving a file work a little differently in Office 98 from the way they worked in Office 4.2.1. So although Office is not new to you, it's a good idea to read Chapter 1, "Discovering Office 98," and Chapter 2, "Getting To Know the Office 98 Environment," to become familiar with general changes to the Office 98 interface and other new Office-wide features before moving on to the program sections.

In the program sections, pay special attention to the first chapter in each part. There, you'll find not only new features governing the overall use of the program, but also essential upgrading information, such as instructions for converting your existing document or data files to Office 98 format.

Stuff You'll See Along The Way

As you go, you'll notice a variety of helpful sidebars, blurbs set off from the body of the page by a box or a different font. You'll quickly see that all of this stuff is self-explanatory, just like the sidebars you'd see in a magazine. But it is a longtime law of computer book publishing that anything self-explanatory be explained anyway, in the Introduction. (That's okay—for the rest of the book, we'll let the self-explanatory explain itself.)

You'll see three kinds of sidebars:

- *Fast Track*—A Fast Track tip describes a faster way to get something done or offers semi-advanced tips for performing the task at hand. Nothing you'll find in a Fast Track is essential, so you can skip 'em when you're not feeling ambitious.

- *FYI*—An FYI (For Your Information) sidebar offers expanded interesting and practical information related to the topic at hand—special considerations, problems to watch out for, ideas to muse upon. Atop every FYI, a title summarizes the FYI's main point, so you can easily decide at a glance whether to read the FYI or skip it.

- *Net Savvy*—A Net Savvy tip describes Internet-related activities involving the task at hand or tells where you can find related information and resources on the Internet. Like Fast Tracks, Net Savvys are never essential—they're just handy if you use the Internet. (Of course, lately, that means just about everyone.)

- *Walk-Through*—A Walk-Through sidebar offers step-by-step practice of a newly learned task. You'll find most explanations in this book clear and simple, so you should have no trouble going directly to Office and applying your new knowledge there. Again, the goal of this book is to empower you with skills you can apply in your own way, not to force you to memorize step-by-step procedures. However, when you work through a lot of new information, it sometimes sinks in better if you take a quick, hands-on practice run. That's what a Walk-Through offers.

Completely voluntary, a Walk-Through gives you a step-by-step, guided tour of the most important activities covered in the general vicinity where the Walk-Through appears. Every chapter in the program sections has two or three Walk-Throughs, each of which leads you through a series of practice steps to accomplish one or more important goals: formatting text, inserting pictures, sending messages, and so on.

Not everything you can learn from this book is covered in a Walk-Through—if it were, the book could cover Office only superficially, or it would have to be three times as long as it is. But the Walk-Throughs provided will give you enough hands-on practice to crystallize the rest of what you discover.

What You Need To Get Started

Starting with Chapter 1, this book assumes that Office 98 has already been installed (by you or someone else) on your Mac or local area network. If Office has not yet been installed on your computer, skip to Appendix A to install Office 98 before proceeding with the program sections. (You may want to visit Chapter 1, "Discovering Office 98," before installing, to learn which programs may be valuable to you.)

Note that the various CD files that make up Office—programs, add-ins, accessories, and so on—may be installed in different ways. The simplest method is a drag-and-drop installation, which moves the most commonly used parts of Office to your hard drive (or Zip disk, or whatever you're running Office from). There are also separate installers for the Value Pack files, Internet Explorer and Outlook Express. Finally, you can run a standard installer program for Office, which lets you select an Easy Install (similar in content to the drag-and-drop) or a Custom Install (where you choose the Office components you want installed). At any time after installation, you may open the Microsoft Office Installer program to add or remove Office programs and files or to customize your personal Office setup. (You learn how to do this in Appendix A.)

The drag-and-drop installation scenario has been designed to install all of the programs and files that the beginning or intermediate user will need (except for Outlook Express), while leaving advanced stuff on the CD to be installed later, if and when the user needs it. (If you purchased a Mac with Office pre-installed, it probably has the drag-and-drop installation.)

Throughout the book, the explanations assume that your Mac has been equipped with the drag-and-drop installation (or with a Custom Install that nonetheless includes at

least all of the drag-and-drop set's files) and with Outlook Express. We also cover a number of files that are not included in the drag-and-drop; when we do, we remind you that you may have to run the Microsoft Office Installer (as described in Appendix A) or the Value Pack installer to add the file if you want to use it.

What You Need To Run Office 98

If you have not yet purchased Office 98 (or purchased a Mac on which Office is pre-installed), it's important to know Office's system requirements:

- *Operating system*—Office 98 requires Mac OS 7.5 or better. System 7.5.5 or better is recommended.

- *Mac*—Office requires at least a PowerPC 601 (as in the Performa 6xxx, PowerMac 6xxx, etc.). A PowerPC 603 or 604 class machine with a minimum speed of 120 MHz is highly recommended. Office also needs at least 16MB of RAM to run programs independently. Simultaneous use of two or more programs will require 32MB or more of memory. As with other software, the more RAM and the faster your machine, the happier Office will be.

- *Hard disk space*—The amount of disk space you need for Office depends on which edition of Office you purchase and which installation scenario you select. This can run anywhere between 49MB and 120MB, but the average is around 90MB. In addition, the Value Pack options can add up to 58MB, and Internet Explorer requires 10MB.

  Note, however, that you should never allow your hard disk to come anywhere near full. For one thing, you would have no room on the disk for your creations. But more importantly, the Mac OS uses hard disk space as "virtual memory" to run programs that demand more memory than your Mac has available (although this is somewhat dependent on your particular system setup). Even on a Mac with 16MB of memory, the Office programs will perform better when there is plenty of free hard disk space available. For good Office performance, try to keep your hard disk at least 10 percent empty, or have at least 80MB of free space, whichever is greater.

- *CD-ROM drive*—A CD-ROM drive is required for installing Office (there is no option to purchase floppy disks). A CD-ROM drive is also useful for later adding programs and accessories, when needed, that may have been left out of the installation, or to take advantage of other files included on the Office CD-ROM, such as the Value Pack (see Chapter 1, "Discovering Office 98").

- *Monitor*—Your monitor should be capable of 16 grays or 256 colors at 640×480 (no sweat…this includes virtually every monitor made in the last four or five years).

- *Modem*—To take advantage of the Internet capabilities of Office 98, you'll need a modem (28.8 or better recommended) and a connection to the Internet (via an office LAN or your own service provider).

What If I'm New To Macintosh?

The explanations in this book do not assume you have any prior experience with Office or its programs, but do assume you know the basics of getting around the Mac OS. To get started, you need to be able to perform the basic actions listed below:

- Start up your Mac.

- Locate the Menu bar (across the top of your screen).

- Use your mouse (or other pointing device) to move the pointer to an object on the screen.

- Use your mouse button(s). You can perform most activities by pointing to an object, clicking the mouse button once, and releasing it immediately. (That's called single-clicking.)

- Open your hard drive and navigate among the files on it and/or your network by clicking on folders and drive icons.

If you can do just these five things, we'll take you the rest of the way, beginning in Chapter 2, "Getting To Know The Office 98 Environment," where a number of other Mac skills are covered. If you feel you should strengthen your Mac skills before proceeding with Office, start with the orientation materials—movies, help files and Apple Guide documents—that ship with every new Mac. Look through these materials and follow the tutorials until you feel comfortable. Don't worry—you'll catch on quickly.

Also, if you consider yourself a real newcomer and you're not sure where to start your Office education, we highly recommend beginning with Word in Part II (after reading Part I, of course). Of all Office programs, Word is the one that a true newcomer will most likely visit first. We have therefore provided in the Word chapters a little extra beginner's detail, such as how to type and make corrections on a computer keyboard.

Enough introducing already—go to Chapter 1 to begin your own Office journey. And by the way—thanks for taking us along.

PART I

The Office Environment

Discovering Office 98

Office? Hmmm….

In naming its all-purpose program suite, Microsoft implies that Office 98 is a traditional business tool, a one-piece replacement for the cubicle typewriter, meeting-room blackboard, mailroom, ledger book, and file cabinet. Maybe that's just a marketing thing—we don't see Office quite that way.

People use their Macs for an astonishing variety of jobs. (Brian knows of a guy who uses his Mac solely as a control center for his gigantic model train layout.) But no matter where and why people use computers, most people spend most of their time on Macs doing any of the following: writing and formatting documents, drawing pictures, adding up numbers, managing files of information (recipes, baseball cards, stock portfolios), exchanging email, browsing the Internet, and playing games. Office 98 does all of that—except the game playing, of course—and adds just one largely business-specific activity: presentation-making.

The bottom line is that Office is about more than the bottom line. It's a great tool to use around the office—there's no question about that. But truly, it's more flexible than that, more universal. Office is really an effort to package together the programs that most people need most often and to give those programs a common look and feel so that users can apply experience with one program to learn another. That's it.

In this chapter, you'll get a quick overview of the Office 98 programs and their suggested uses. We hope you'll see that choosing an Office program for any particular project has more to do with your goals than with the traditional "business" role of a program. Office 98 is a tool. How and where you use it is entirely up to you.

What's Office 98, Anyhow?

Office 98 is an *application suite*, a family of programs, each of which does a different job, but which together share a common appearance, some features, and the ability to exchange information with one another.

First and foremost, the Office applications are four separate programs which, 90 percent of the time or more, you will use separately. Each does something different, and for any given job you will open up the program that's best suited to the task at hand. The family relationship among the Office programs does have a benefit—consistency—even when you use the programs one at a time.

As much as possible, Word, Excel, and PowerPoint have been designed to look and act alike in many respects. Outlook Express, however, is a different story. The use of Outlook Express is so different from that of the other three Office programs that it simply can't fit the mold that Word, Excel, and PowerPoint share, although it tries. Among the other Office 98 programs, however, you will find the following consistencies:

- *Appearance*—Word, Excel, and PowerPoint have similar windows, menu text, toolbars, and other aesthetics (see Figure 1.1). This makes all Office programs feel familiar once you've learned one, providing you with the confidence to explore new programs more easily.

- *Menus*—The organization of the menus is very similar among the three programs. Each program has its own unique menus, but the File, Edit, View, Insert, Format, and Help menus have the same positions on the menu bar in each program and contain many of the same choices. (In this respect, Office 98 makes a huge improvement over Office 4.2.x in observing Macintosh menu conventions.) You'll also find that the three programs share Tools and Window menus, although their positioning and content differs.

- *Dialog boxes*—The dialogs on which you perform common tasks, such as saving or opening files, are nearly identical among the programs. Although there are subtle differences and unique options among the programs, by and large, once you know how to open, save, and print files in one Office program, you know how to open and save files in them all.

- *Standard toolbar*—Each application has a Standard toolbar (see Figure 1.2), which appears right below the menu bar. The Standard toolbars differ by program, but they all contain buttons for performing common activities such as opening, saving, and printing files. Those buttons are in the same position on every Standard toolbar and look the same, as well.

- *Formatting toolbar*—Each application also has a Formatting toolbar for formatting text. The buttons on the Formatting toolbars are almost identical program to program—so when you know how to pick a font from a toolbar in Word, you know how to pick a font anywhere.

- *Microsoft Office Manager*—All Office applications are available from the Microsoft Office Manager, an optional Office accessory that hangs out on

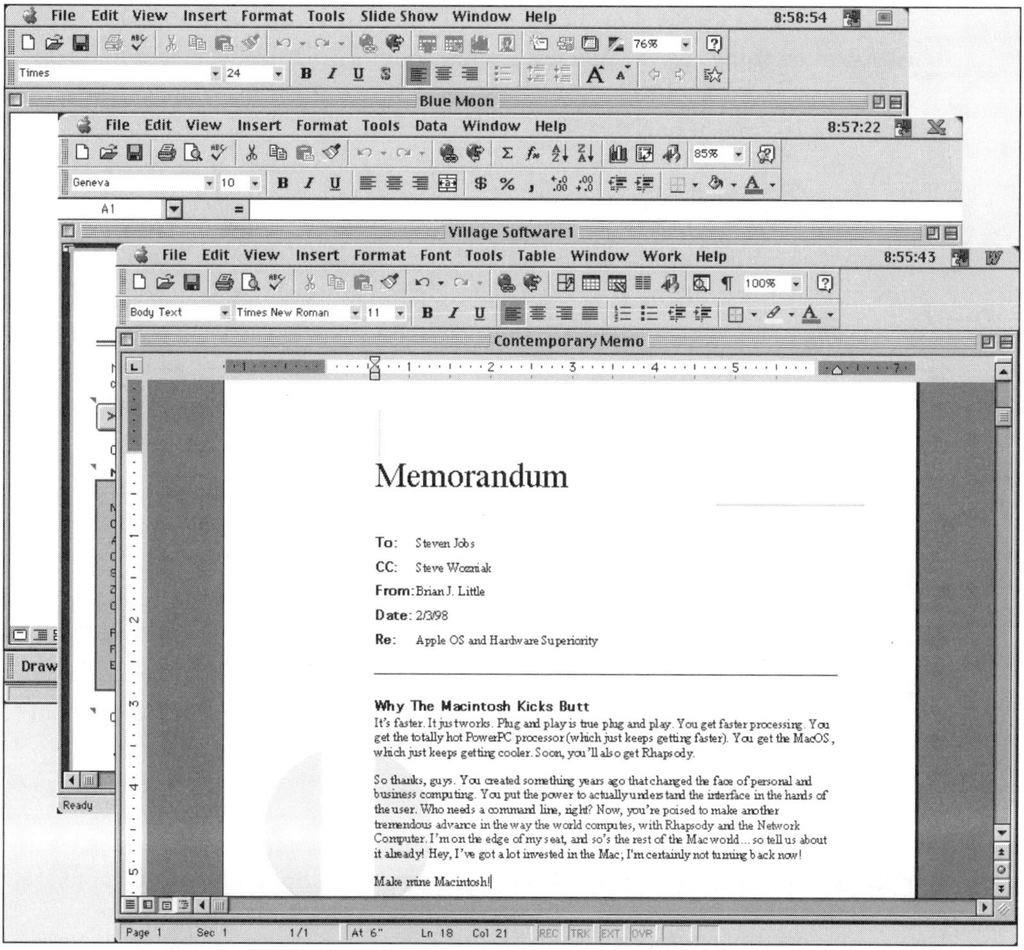

Discovering Office 98   5

Figure 1.1   Office programs share a strong family resemblance, which makes learning multiple programs easier. In fact, it's tough to tell in this figure which is which: Word is in front, followed by Excel, then PowerPoint.

Figure 1.2   Notice the similarities (and differences) among these Standard toolbars, each of which is from a different Office program. The PowerPoint toolbar is on top, followed by Excel, then Word.

your menu bar to give you quick access to Office programs, files, the Finder, or just about anything else. (You'll learn more about the Office Manager in Chapter 2.) Longtime Mac Office users may remember this Office Manager with some trepidation—at one time, it was notorious for causing system crashes. Never fear! The new Office Manager is rock solid and makes using Office (and your Mac) easier than ever.

- *Help options*—The Help facilities in all Office programs (except Outlook Express) work exactly the same way. In particular, Help features Help On The Web (for finding help and resources on the Internet) and the Office Assistant, a friendly, animated helper that butts in with advice related to what you're doing while you're doing it. (You'll learn more about Help and the Office Assistant in Chapter 2.)

In addition to these shared family traits, the Office 98 programs are designed to share information with one another. They do this in the traditional ways all Mac applications share information—by letting you cut or copy information from one program and paste it into another, drag and drop information between programs, use clippings, or link information in one program to a file in another. The Office programs also have their own, special level of integration. For example, you can generate form letters by merging a Word document with a list of addresses managed by Outlook Express, or you can click on a button on Word's toolbar to import a table or chart from Excel.

You'll learn how to use some of these integration features as you work through the parts of this book devoted to the different programs, and about others in Chapter 16.

Another important feature, especially for those of you who use PCs at work and a Mac at home (or vice versa), is the cross-platform compatibility of Office. Office for Macintosh will open and save all Office for Windows files (except Access files), and the controls are virtually identical. If you have to share files between home and work, Office makes it easy.

FYI: Is Office 98 "Built For The Internet?"

Office 98 is "built for the Internet," according to Microsoft. But what exactly does that mean?

Well, it means several things. First, it means that you can use all of the Office applications—except Outlook Express—in the creation of Web pages that you can publish online. Word is the principal Web-authoring tool, but the other programs can play a part.

Next, it means that you can configure all Internet addresses you see in Office files—whether in a Word document, a PowerPoint show, Excel worksheet, or Outlook Express message—as "live" hyperlinks—click on the address and Windows attempts to connect to it online.

Third, it means that the Help menus of all Office programs include Help On The Web, which cranks up your Web browser to show you a list of links to Microsoft's online help resources.

Finally, it means that Office includes two programs for interacting with the Internet: Outlook Express for exchanging email and Internet Explorer for browsing the Web. (Internet Explorer isn't really part of the suite, but it's on the Office CD anyway, to strengthen Microsoft's claim.)

You'll learn about Outlook Express's email capabilities in Part V and about all of Office's other Internet capabilities in Part VI. Internet Explorer is covered briefly in Appendix B, because it isn't really part of the Office suite proper.

About The Programs

The next several pages describe the major Office 98 application programs, their important features, and the types of projects to which you may want to apply them.

Word 98

The most widely used and versatile of the Office programs, the word processor Word provides a space in which you freely type text, edit that text, format the text to customize its appearance, and organize it into attractively designed pages. A true WYSIWYG (What You See Is What You Get) word processor, Word formats your work on the screen just as it will appear in print, so you can easily evaluate the appearance of your document as you work on it.

Word's primary function is producing attractive printed documents, such as letters, memos, resumes, reports, screenplays, and books. In keeping with the times, however, Word is evolving into an equally effective tool for formatting and editing text that you might never print, text that you might instead present online. In particular, Word's ability to help you write better—by correcting spelling, suggesting grammar and style improvements, and supplying alternative word choices (synonyms)—enhances your words no matter where you publish them.

Word's document formatting prowess extends to a level that was once the exclusive domain of desktop publishing programs. Word gives you precise typographic control of text, not only enabling you to choose the font (typeface) and size of your text, but also to control character spacing, line spacing, and the printing of kerning pairs. You can also easily incorporate pictures into pages, controlling the pictures' position, size, and appearance in various ways. The ability to incorporate pictures—along with such desktop-publishing capabilities as newspaper-style columns, borders, and shading—gives Word the formatting versatility to produce newsletters, advertisements, and magazine pages.

Of course, another beauty of Word is that the program's design makes ignoring its complexity easy. When you just want a place to bang out a quick, good-looking document—and you couldn't care less about kerning or columns—Word lets you get in, get the job done, and get out.

When Does A Job Call For Word?

Word is your program of choice when effectiveness, accuracy, and appearance of text are important, as well as the layout and appearance of the page as a whole (see Figure 1.3).

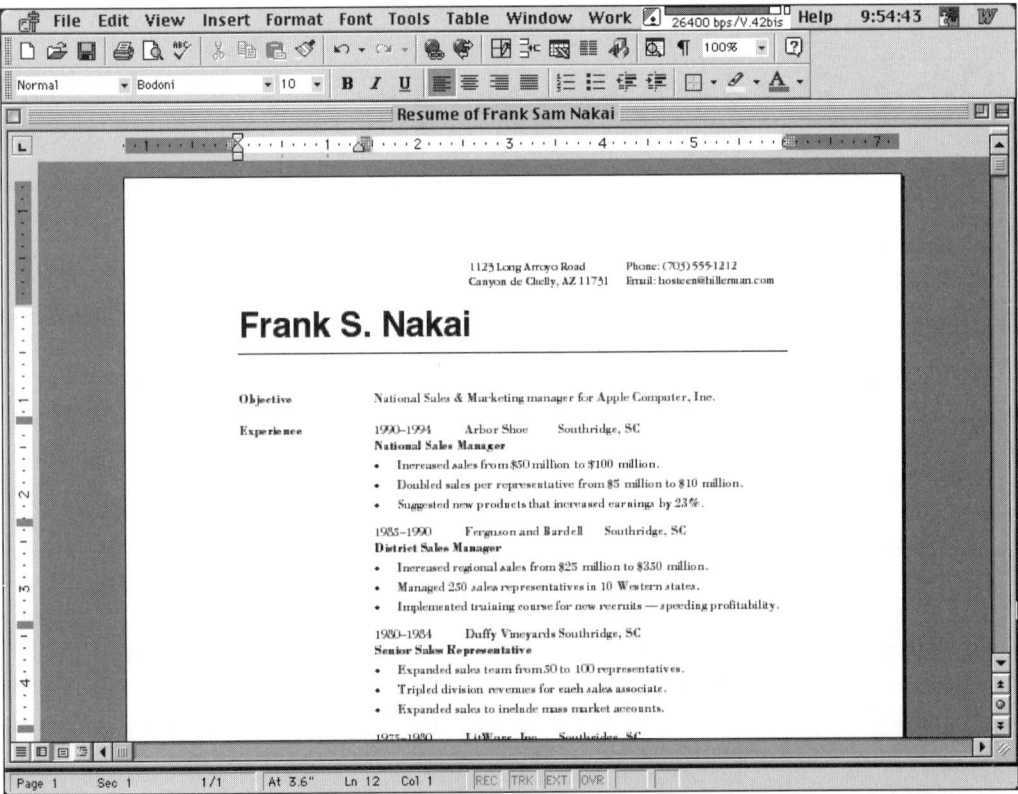

Figure 1.3 With Word, you can produce a limitless variety of formatted documents.

Key Word 98 Features

Among Word 98's most powerful, convenient, and surprising features are:

- Multiple view options that let you tailor the display according to the kind of work you're doing.

- Templates and wizards that preformat various types of documents to give you a head start.

- Easy text and paragraph formatting—including fonts, automatic numbered and bulleted lists, bold and italic text, and paragraph alignment and indentation—all accessible from buttons on the Formatting toolbar.

- Drag-and-drop editing, format copying, and other productivity tools to save you time and typing.

- Powerful tools for adding graphical impact to documents, including the ability to easily incorporate pictures, rules, borders, shading, and color.

- Automatic, as-you-go spelling and grammar checking, plus checking on demand.

- Instant, automatic correction of common typing mistakes.

- Automatic completion of words or phrases you type often, after you type only a few letters of the word or phrase.

- Mail merge capabilities that you can integrate with Outlook Express's contact management capabilities.

PowerPoint 98

Like Word, PowerPoint is about producing documents. But unlike the versatile Word, PowerPoint produces documents with a narrower purpose: to make a point, succinctly. (PowerPoint, get it?) PowerPoint organizes small dollops of text—usually just a title and a short paragraph or list of points—into dynamic, eye-catching slides. The slides are ideal as visual aids to accompany a speech or presentation, or they can serve as a self-running presentation, making their point without the aid of a speaker.

Often, people who must make presentations are not day-to-day Mac users, or even if they are, they're folks who must squeeze their presentation creation into a day otherwise filled with meetings, travel, and other commitments. Perhaps in recognition of that, PowerPoint is amazingly easy to use. You can put together a great-looking presentation of a dozen slides or so in an hour or two. Of course, when time and ambition allow, PowerPoint also gives you access to a host of advanced features for controlling and enhancing every aspect of the show.

PowerPoint can send its slides to any printer connected to your Mac, which you can load with transparency film to produce great-looking overheads. PowerPoint can also package its output for computer service bureaus that can quickly print your work on 35mm slides (for use in a regular slide projector) or on high-quality overheads.

Additionally, in the age of multimedia PowerBooks, LCD overhead panels, and big-screen monitors, many presenters never bother to "output" their slides to any medium, preferring instead to have a Mac show the slides electronically—and that's when PowerPoint really shines. PowerPoint not only helps you create, prepare, and display an electronic show, it also enables you to add exciting dimensions to your slides possible only in an electronic show, such as sound clips and music, recorded voice narration, animated text, transitions between slides, and even video clips.

When Does A Job Call For PowerPoint?

When your project must communicate through an eye-catching series of slides or pages, each containing only a small amount of text and (optionally) pictures, PowerPoint should be your program of choice (see Figure 1.4).

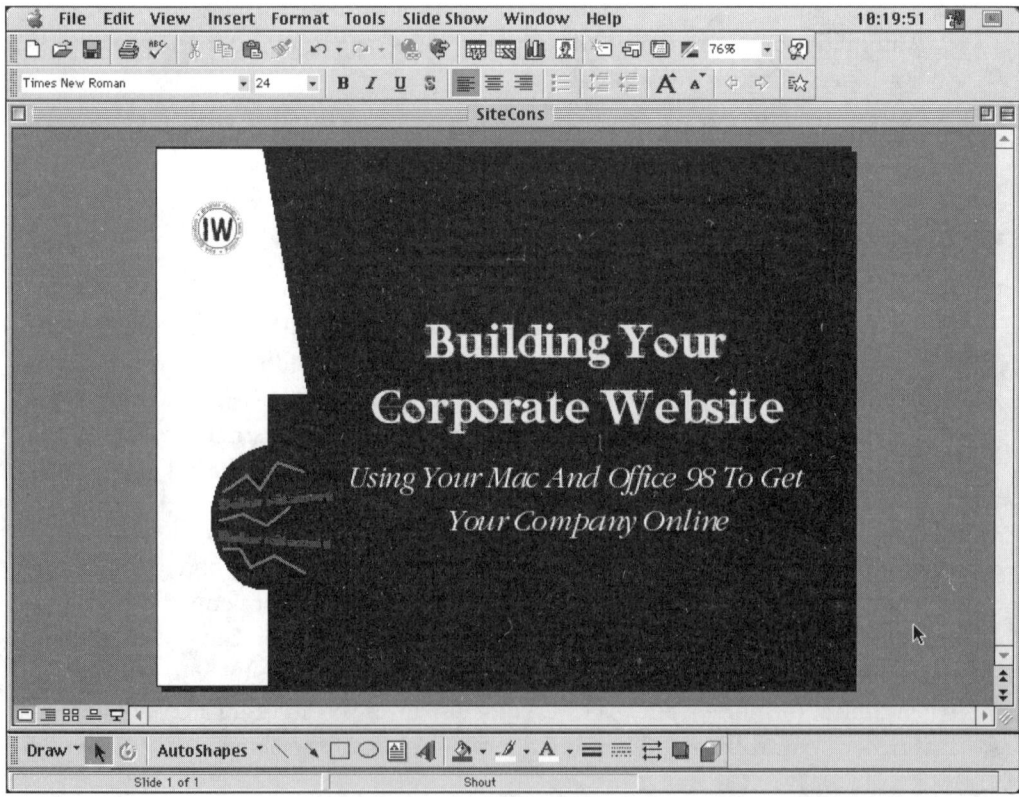

Figure 1.4 With PowerPoint, slides can back up a presentation—or even give the presentation on their own.

Key PowerPoint 98 Features

PowerPoint 98's most powerful points include:

- Easy creation of speaker notes and handouts to accompany a presentation.

- Multiple views that tailor the display to the kind of work you want to do.

- Full control of the color scheme, background, and slide design for great-looking shows.

- Full support of Mac multimedia for electronic shows, including the ability to play sound clips, narration, QuickTime clips, and audio CD tracks during a show.

- Easy-to-use animation features that make text and pictures move into slides in fun, eye-catching ways, and also animate the transitions between slides with wipes, dissolves, and other effects.

- Templates and wizards that preformat various types of slide shows (they can even supply some of the content of a show).

- An easy-to-use facility that prepares and sends your slide show to a popular service bureau via modem.

- Easy text and paragraph formatting with buttons on the Formatting toolbar.

- Automatic, as-you-go spelling and grammar checking, plus checking on demand.

- Style checking that suggests ways you can change your slides to communicate more effectively.

Excel 98

As the newest incarnation of one of the oldest categories of Mac application software—the spreadsheet—Excel is perhaps the most mature, time-tested application in Office 98. What's amazing about Excel is that all of the history and experience that went into its development have produced a program that's sophisticated when your needs are sophisticated and simple when your needs are simple.

In Excel, you work in a space called a *worksheet*, a grid of rows and columns. By entering information into the boxes formed at the intersection of rows and columns—cells—you automatically organize the information you type into neat tables. Excel automatically guesses the type of information you enter in a cell—ordinary text, a number to use in calculations, a date to use in time-based calculations, a dollar amount to use in financial calculations, and so on. Excel's primary concern is the data in your worksheet—not its appearance—but the program nonetheless provides you with an easy-to-use family of formatting tools for dressing up your tables and text and controlling how they look in print or online.

Once data is recorded in a worksheet, you can use it in powerful, creative ways. You can enter formulas that calculate new cell values by performing equations with existing cell data—for example, you can calculate row or column totals, determine statistical variances, or perform financial accounting operations. You can also use your cell data and formula results to generate a wide variety of great-looking charts and maps quickly and easily.

Any time you change the data in a worksheet, Excel automatically recalculates any formulas based on the data, updating the cells that show formula results and also any charts based on calculated values. That enables you to set up a worksheet and its formulas once and then produce quick, accurate results whenever conditions change. It also enables you to analyze and explore your data through "what-if" scenarios. As an experiment, you can change any value used in a formula and instantly see what the results would be.

Access is Microsoft's database program, but Mac users don't get, well, access to it. Fortunately, Excel doubles as an entry-level database manager, enabling you to create database tables—lists—in worksheets and then sort, filter, and perform other database operations on the records in the list.

When Does A Job Call For Excel?

Excel is your program of choice when you need to present information in an orderly table or when some values in the table must be calculated from others—especially when those calculations are financial. Excel is also the place to enter data and produce charts from that data that you can then import into a Word or PowerPoint document (see Figure 1.5).

Key Excel 98 Features

You'll excel by taking advantage of these Excel 98 features:

- Automatic formatting of cell entries, including assignment of number formats.

- Automatic fills (cell entries Excel creates for you by copying the data in a cell or by continuing a series you have begun).

- Quick, attractive formatting of tables through the AutoFormat facility.

- Tools for adding graphical impact to worksheets, including the ability to add pictures, rules, borders, shading, and color to your tables.

- Easy formatting of cell contents with buttons on the Formatting toolbar.

- Functions that enable you to easily perform sophisticated calculations within a formula.

- A Formula Palette that helps you type formulas and functions properly and check the results as you go.

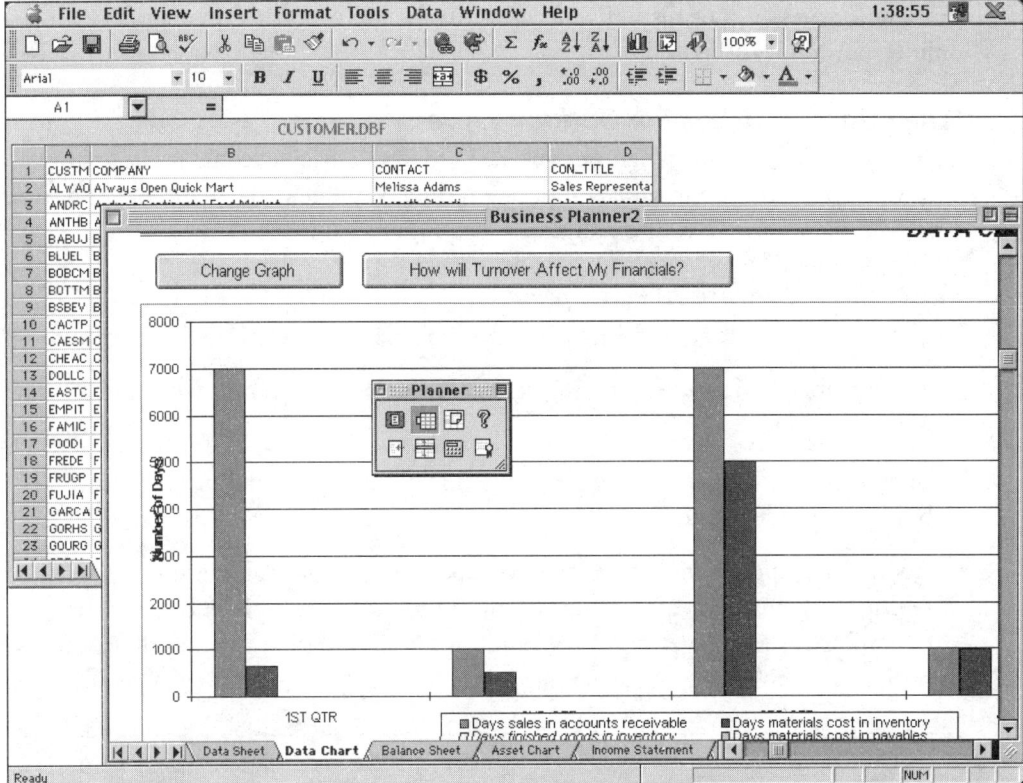

Figure 1.5 With Excel, you can easily organize information in attractively formatted tables or functional databases, and then use that information to produce calculation results, charts, and more.

- Easy creation of a wide variety of charts with the Chart Wizard, plus automatic generation of maps based on tables that contain place names.

- Automatic spellchecking.

- Simple, quick database management tools, such as Sort Ascending, Sort Descending, and AutoFilter.

- Special features for formatting worksheets as online or printed forms for collecting data.

Outlook Express

Outlook Express is the only new application in Office 98—well, it's new to the Mac, at least. Outlook Express is one program with three faces. In Outlook Express, you jump from a group of mail folders where you manage messages; to a Contacts folder where you record the names, addresses, and profile information of your contacts; to a newsreader for tracking your favorite Usenet newsgroups.

14 Chapter 1

Outlook Express is a fast, small, and easy-to-operate center for managing your online communications.

When Does A Job Call For Outlook Express?

Call on Outlook Express whenever you need to exchange electronic messages or keep track of names, addresses, and phone numbers in one convenient location. It's a single program for all your email needs (see Figure 1.6).

Key Outlook Express 98 Features

While you're discovering and exploring Outlook Express, be on the lookout for:

- Support for a variety of messaging services—including Internet Mail and Microsoft Mail.

- Support for Internet newsgroup reading, including automated filtering and binary image decoding.

- Room for keeping detailed information about each contact, including name, multiple mailing addresses, multiple email addresses, multiple phone numbers (including fax and pager numbers), and profile information, such as the contact's birthday, job title, or spouse's name.

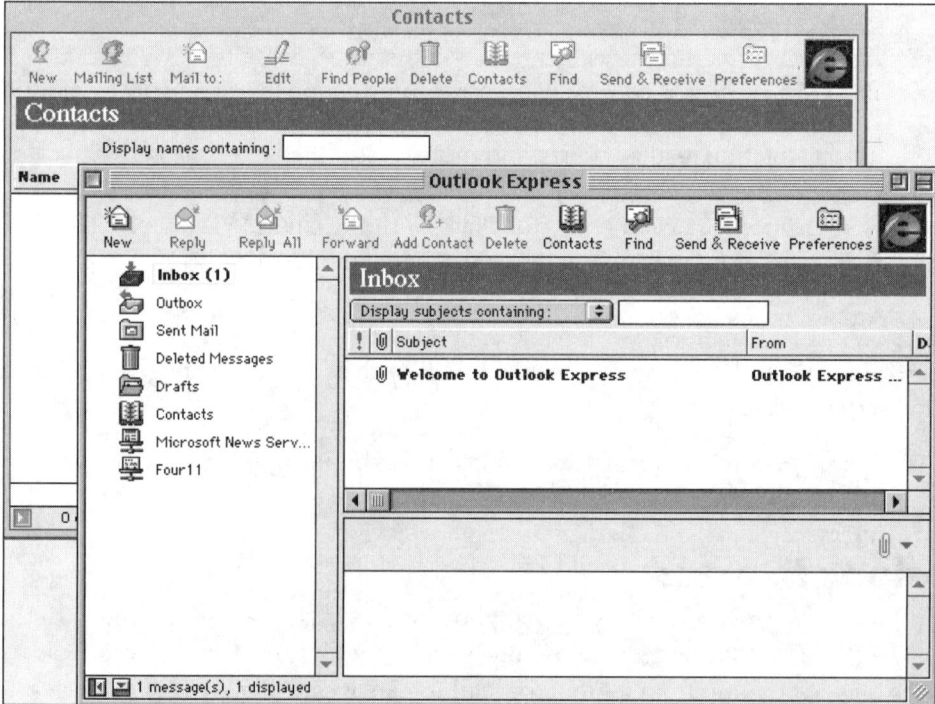

Figure 1.6 Outlook Express manages your email, contacts, and newsgroup messages—and the relationships among them.

Moving On

As you can see, the Office 98 suite is made up of four great programs that can do an awful lot among them. Except for playing games, you may never need a program that's not part of the Office family.

The capabilities of the programs tend to make them look overwhelmingly complex—but don't let that throw you. Each of the programs scales its difficulty level to your ambitions. Achieving easy goals—a quick letter, a simple presentation, a small table—is always pretty easy in Office. Harder projects are, well, harder—but if they weren't, you wouldn't feel so satisfied when you mastered them. And you will.

In Chapter 2, you'll pick up the basics of Office operation—the stuff that works the same in all Office programs. Though some of that stuff, such as drag and drop, falls under the heading of general Macintosh skills, some facilities—like the Office Assistant and the Drawing Tools—are so cool and powerful that they almost qualify as applications in their own right. Move on to Chapter 2 and check 'em out.

Getting To Know The Office 98 Environment

Ned grew up in Massachusetts, but never learned to ski. When he lived in Manhattan, he was surprised to discover that nearly every native New Yorker he met had never been to the Statue of Liberty or the top of the Empire State building, and most had never seen a Broadway show. And even though Brian grew up and still lives in the heart of NASCAR country, he's never once seen a stock car race. There's no denying it: *Length* of experience does not always equal *breadth* of experience, and vice versa.

Even among practiced users of the Macintosh, different folks have different gaps in their skill sets. We know experienced Mac users who had not yet discovered OS 8's contextual menus, or many of the ways you can use drag and drop, until we pointed these techniques out to them. Also, not all of us use the same names for the same stuff: What we call "dialogs" you might call "those box things that pop up."

Before we move into the meat of this book, we need to synchronize our watches and agree on a common vocabulary. In the program sections, you'll be instructed to perform actions by clicking on "toolbar buttons," opening "dialogs," choosing from "drop-down lists," and more. Though you may already know from your own experience how to do all of these things, you may not always recognize the words we use to describe them. Also, like most of us, you may have some of those lived-there-but-never-did-it gaps in your Mac background. If you can fill those gaps before moving forward, you'll gain much more from the rest of this book.

In addition to getting us all on the same Mac wavelength, this chapter introduces you to various utilities—such as the Office Drawing Tools and the Office Assistant help elf—that play a role not just in one Office program, but in several—if not all—of them. Because we have divided the books into parts so that you can read about each program separately, learning about these common elements now saves you from having to review them in each part to which they apply.

Take a quick scan through this easy chapter, and if you discover that you already know everything it covers, good for you. However, if you see anything new—and we bet you will—be sure to give it a good read. When you begin working with the Office programs in earnest, you'll be glad you did.

Opening And Closing Office Programs

As you learn the Office programs, you'll discover a variety of ways to open and close each program under various circumstances. But just to get you on your way, here's how to get into—and out of—any Office application.

The easiest way to open any Office program is to choose it from the Microsoft Office Manager. In the menu bar, click on the Office Manager icon (the puzzle piece just to the left of the Applications menu icon). In the menu that appears, you'll see a list of Office applications you can run (provided you've installed them all). Figure 2.1 shows the Office Manager menu—yours should look similar to this. (The Office Manager is not part of the regular Office installation—you have to install it from the Value Pack. See Appendix A for how to install the Value Pack. Normally, we wouldn't encourage jumping ahead, but the Office Manager is so convenient that it's well worth the risk.)

To open a program, select its name from the Office Manager menu. When the program opens, its icon appears on the Application menu at the top right of the screen (see Figure 2.2). For more information on using and configuring the Office Manager, see "Using The Microsoft Office Manager" later in this chapter.

If you've not installed the Office Manager, simply open the Microsoft Office 98 folder and double-click on the program icon of your choice, as you would with any other Macintosh application.

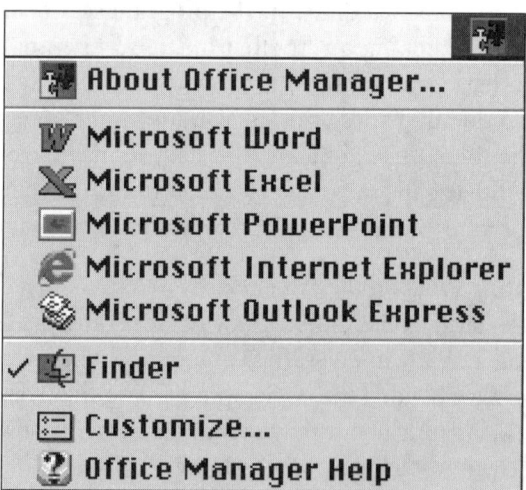

Figure 2.1 Click on the Microsoft Office Manager icon in the menu bar to reveal a list of Office applications to run.

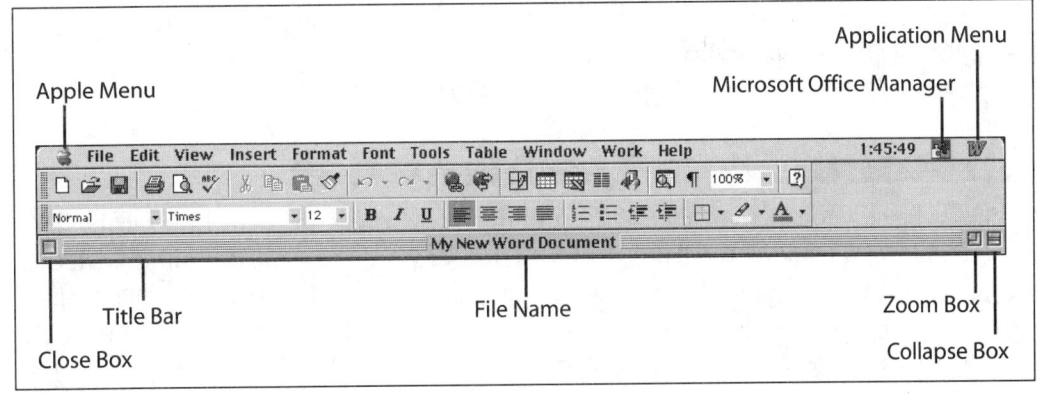

Figure 2.2 Use the Office Manager menu, Applications menu, and the window control widgets to identify, close, and scale a program window.

Usually, Office documents open *scaled*—that is, with the document window sized appropriately for the margins of the document—and that's generally the best way to use Office programs. If an Office program opens and the document window isn't sized correctly, click on the Zoom box to scale it so that all its contents fit. To return the window to its previous size, click on the Zoom box again.

If you'd just like to get a document out of your way for a while but not close it altogether, use the Collapse box. Clicking on the box will "roll up" your document window, leaving just the title bar on screen. Clicking on it again will roll the document window back down. You can accomplish the same effect by double-clicking on the title bar.

To close an Office document, click on the Close box at the upper left. Notice that this does *not* close the program. To do that, select File|Quit, as in other Mac programs.

Note that you don't have to close one Office program to open another. You can open another program from the Office Manager menu or from the Finder, and run the two applications simultaneously (provided you have the RAM). To see what programs are currently running, check the Applications menu—a list of current programs appears there, with a check by the one you're using now. You can also use the Office Manager menu (if you have it installed). In that menu, open programs are listed with a bullet, whereas the program you're using now has a check by it.

Depending on your work style, you may or may not prefer to leave multiple programs open at once. If you elect to keep several programs open, be sure you have enough memory installed in your Mac to do so (this isn't a problem with most newer machines). However, unless you're comparing files in different programs or moving or copying information from one program to another (as you'll learn to do in Chapter 16), there's rarely any technical reason to keep multiple programs open, and doing so can slow down the performance of the programs. Consider keeping just one Office application open at once to enhance your speed and performance. (See the Introduction or Appendix A to learn about memory requirements.)

Choosing From The Menu Bar

At the very top of your screen—next to the hexachrome (in English, "six-color") Apple logo marking the Apple menu—a row of words appears, beginning with the words File and Edit—the *menu bar*. Clicking on any word on the menu bar drops down a menu of choices, or *items*, as shown in Figure 2.3. If you click on one of these items, your Mac does one of the following:

- *Performs an action*—The action described by the menu item happens. Pow.

- *Opens a dialog*—A dialog box opens, on which you choose from among options that control how an action will be carried out. (See "Understanding Dialogs" later in this chapter.)

- *Opens a submenu*—If the item in the menu has an arrow next to it (see Figure 2.3), a *submenu*—a new menu to the right that presents you with even more choices—opens.

In the instructions you'll discover throughout this book, the precise menu items you need to choose to perform an action are shown in order, with vertical bars (|) between choices. The first item is always one of the main choices along the menu bar. For example, if you see the instruction "Choose Insert|Picture|Clip Art," you perform the action described by choosing Insert from the menu bar to open the Insert menu, then choosing Picture from the Insert menu to display the Picture submenu, then choosing Clip Art from the Picture menu.

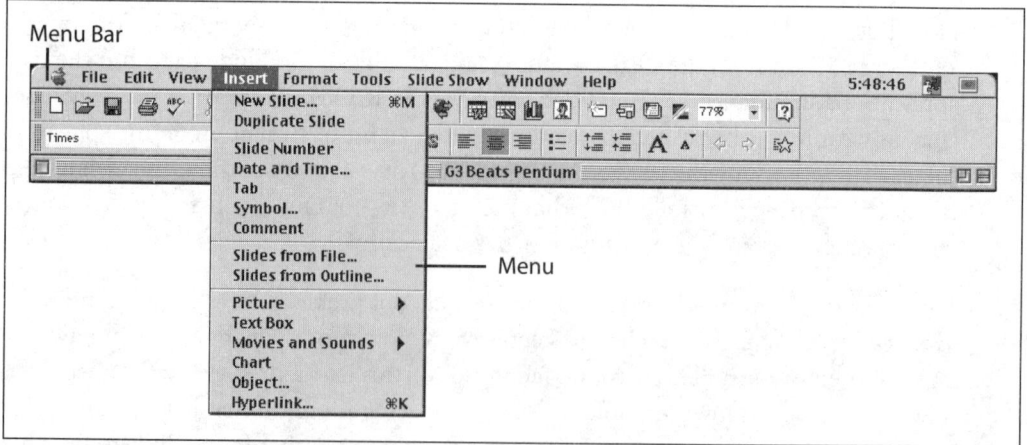

Figure 2.3 Click on any item on a program's menu bar to drop down a list of items you can click on to perform tasks.

Using Toolbars

Besides choosing from menus, you perform many actions in Office programs by clicking on the *buttons* (little squares with pictures on them) on *toolbars* (rows of buttons that usually appear right beneath the menu bar; see Figure 2.4). Note that toolbar buttons usually duplicate actions you can also perform by choosing from menus. The toolbar just provides a quicker way.

In addition to buttons, some toolbars have *drop-down lists* on them. You use a drop-down list to select from several options; for example, in Word, PowerPoint, and Excel, you can choose the *font* (typeface) of text by selecting from a drop-down list on the Formatting toolbar. You'll learn more about drop-down lists later in this chapter.

Finding The Button You Need

The pictures that appear on all toolbar buttons are designed to help you guess what the button does. For example, the Print button in every program's Standard toolbar has a picture of a printer on it; to print whatever you're working on, you click on the Print button. On Word's Formatting toolbar, the Bold button—which makes text bold—has a big, bold "B" on it, while the Italic button shows an italic "I," and the Underline button shows an underlined "U." In most cases, when you want to find and use a particular button, its appearance will help you identify it quickly.

If you ever have trouble finding a particular button on a toolbar or if you're just curious about what a particular button does, point to a button (but don't click), and allow the pointer to rest on the button for a moment. A *tooltip* appears (see Figure 2.5), telling you the name of the button you're pointing at. (To see not only the name of the button, but also a detailed description of what a button does, use Balloon Help, as described later in this chapter.)

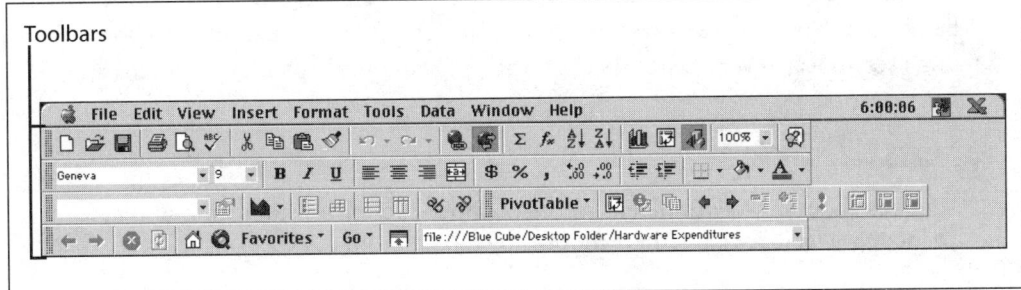

Figure 2.4 Toolbar buttons give you quick access to common activities.

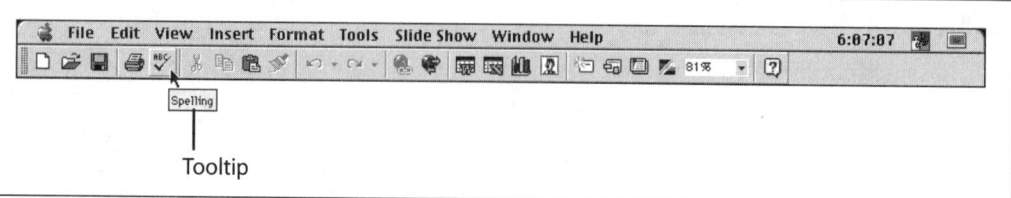

Figure 2.5 To learn the name of any toolbar button, rest the pointer on it for a moment without clicking.

Fast Track

You can take a tour of the tooltips on a toolbar to learn what each button does. Point to the leftmost button and wait a beat until its tooltip appears. Then move the pointer slowly to the right, through each button. As the pointer hits each new button, that button's tooltip appears.

Showing The Toolbar You Need

Each Office program has many different toolbars you can use, but they don't all appear at once. Instead, only the one or two toolbars containing the most-used buttons appear when you first open the program; each toolbar makes up one full row of buttons beneath the menu bar. If programs displayed all of their toolbars at once, the toolbars would take up the whole application window, and you'd have trouble seeing what you're working on.

In all Office programs, a toolbar called Standard appears by default; the Standard toolbar contains the buttons you're likely to need most often, such as those for opening a file, creating a file, and printing. You can choose to display other toolbars as you need them. To display any toolbar, choose View|Toolbars and then click on the toolbar's name in the menu that appears. Follow the same steps to remove a toolbar you don't want to see anymore. Once you display a particular set of toolbars, that same set appears every time you open the program until you change toolbars again.

Fast Track

Besides choosing View|Toolbars, you can Control-click on any toolbar to display a list of available toolbars; then, choose any toolbar from the list.

While they rest at the top of your display, the toolbars' names don't appear; but you can learn which toolbars are currently on your display by observing which names on the Toolbars submenu have check marks next to them. Also, note that you can move any toolbar from its spot atop the window—the toolbar area—by working with the vertical bar that appears at the extreme left end of every toolbar. (Depending on your display, it may look like one bar or like two or three rows of dots—either way, it's pretty obvious.) Double-click on that bar, and the toolbar jumps into the middle of the display as a floating toolbar (see Figure 2.6), which you can then drag anywhere you want to put it. (You restore a floating toolbar to the toolbar area by dragging it back to the spot where you want it and dropping it there—you'll see the toolbar's outline snap into its resting place as you drag.) Finally, you can change the order in which the toolbars appear in the toolbar area by clicking and holding on a toolbar's double bar and then dragging it where you want it. You can even choose to run your toolbars down the side of the screen by dragging them there, if you wish.

It's worth noting that a toolbar's title only appears on screen when it's displayed as a floating toolbar. Otherwise, you have to select View|Toolbars to see which bars are being displayed.

Fast Track

When you've torn a toolbar loose from the top of the screen, it can be treated like any other floating window. Double-clicking on the title bar rolls the toolbar's window up to save space. Double-clicking again expands the toolbar to its proper size.

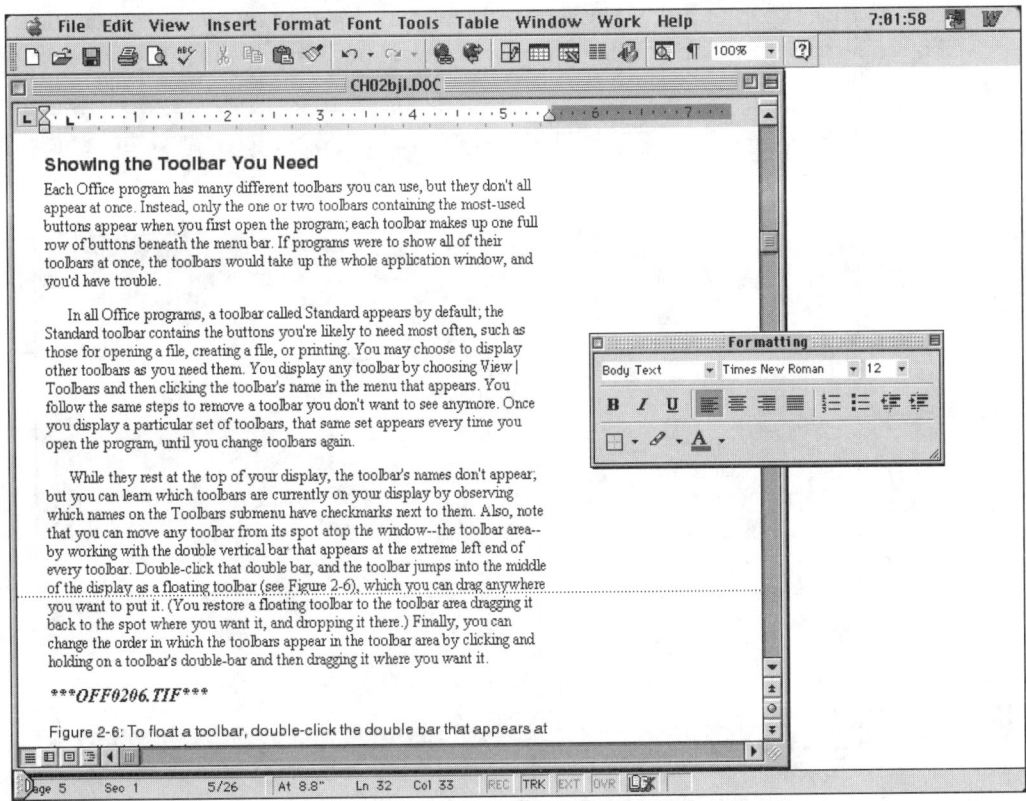

Figure 2.6 To float a toolbar, double-click on the bar that appears at the left end of the toolbar.

Scrolling To See More

When whatever you're working on—whether a file, a list of items, or anything else—is so tall or wide that you cannot view it all at once within the window, *scroll bars* appear (see Figure 2.7). When a vertical scroll bar appears along the right side of the window, there is more to see above or below what you're looking at. When a scroll bar appears along the bottom of the window, there is more to see at the sides (although in a normal document, this may be just white space).

It helps to think of the document window as a frame through which you view something that's larger than the frame. You use the scroll bars to shift the frame up and down or side to side to reveal the hidden parts above, below, or on the sides. Shifting the window this way is called *scrolling*.

Clicking on the single arrows that appear at each end of a scroll bar scrolls the window a short way in the direction of the arrow. To scroll a longer way, click and hold an arrow or drag the square box—the slider—that appears between the arrows. You can also click in the scroll bar itself—click above the slider to move up, and below it to move down, one screenful at a time. Also, any time you see a vertical scroll bar, pressing your PgDn or PgUp key scrolls the display down or up by one screenful. You can also use your Up and Down arrow keys to move line by line.

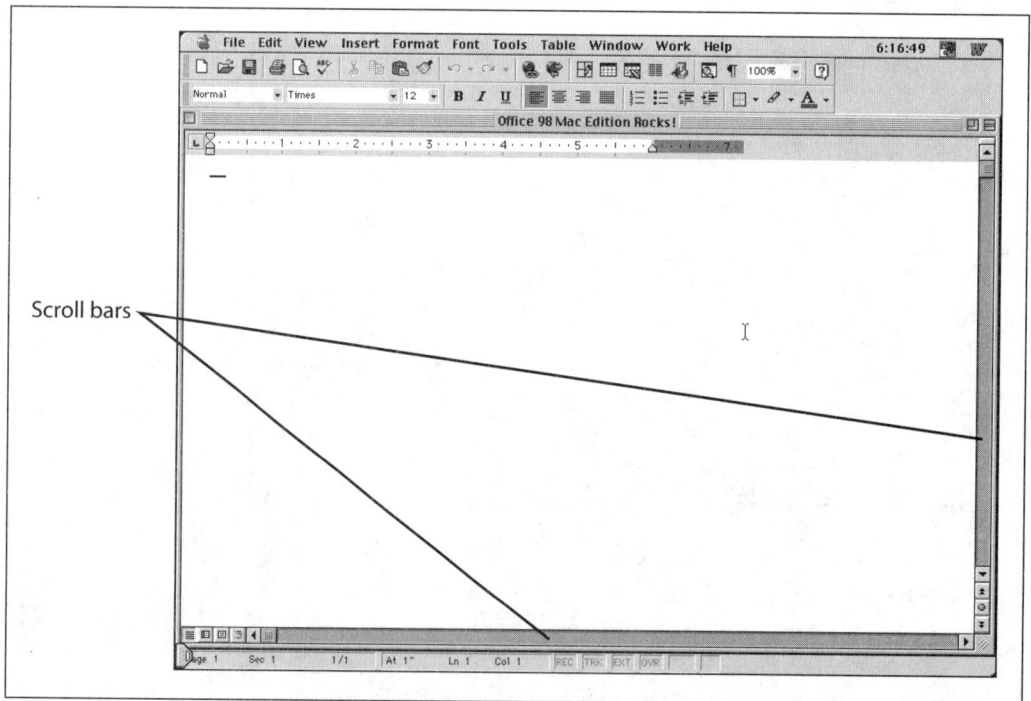

Figure 2.7 Scroll bars enable you to see more than what fits in a window.

Note that in Word and PowerPoint, you will see some specialized navigation buttons in the scroll bars—double-headed arrows and something called the Select Browse Object button. We'll cover those in more detail in Parts II and III of this book.

Fast Track

In most Office programs, selections on the View menu allow you to magnify or reduce the contents of the window, often reducing or eliminating the need for scrolling.

Dragging And Dropping

Dragging means clicking on an object, holding down the mouse button, then moving the mouse. You drag to move objects from one part of the screen to another, to operate scroll bars, to select text and objects, and much more. Throughout this book, you'll see specific instructions for things you can do by dragging.

When you drag an object to a particular place and then release it, you *drag and drop* it. The most familiar use of drag and drop on the Mac is to move files into folders by dragging a file icon to a folder icon, then dropping the file into the folder. Other familiar drag-and-drop operations are program launching, file trashing, and disk ejection. You'll discover some other helpful drag-and-drop uses in Office later on.

Control-Clicking To Use Contextual Menus

One of the most powerful, yet least-used, tricks in Mac OS 8 and higher is Control-clicking to display *contextual menus* (see Figure 2.8). A contextual menu is a list of items specifically related to the object or program you're working on. For example, if you point to the Desktop and Control-click, a contextual menu pops up, showing various operations you can perform from the Desktop.

Throughout this book, we'll alert you to the best opportunities to use contextual menus. But it's good to adopt a habit of instinctively Control-clicking on something you want to work with, to see whether the object's contextual menu provides you with a useful option. Control-clicking always either opens a contextual menu or does nothing at all—so you can't make a mistake or hurt anything by Control-clicking on it.

Understanding Dialogs

When you choose a menu item or click on a toolbar and a box pops onto your screen, that box is called a *dialog*. Dialogs allow you to supply details about an action you've started or choose from among options that affect how the action will be carried out. Each dialog has a name that appears in a title bar at the top of the dialog.

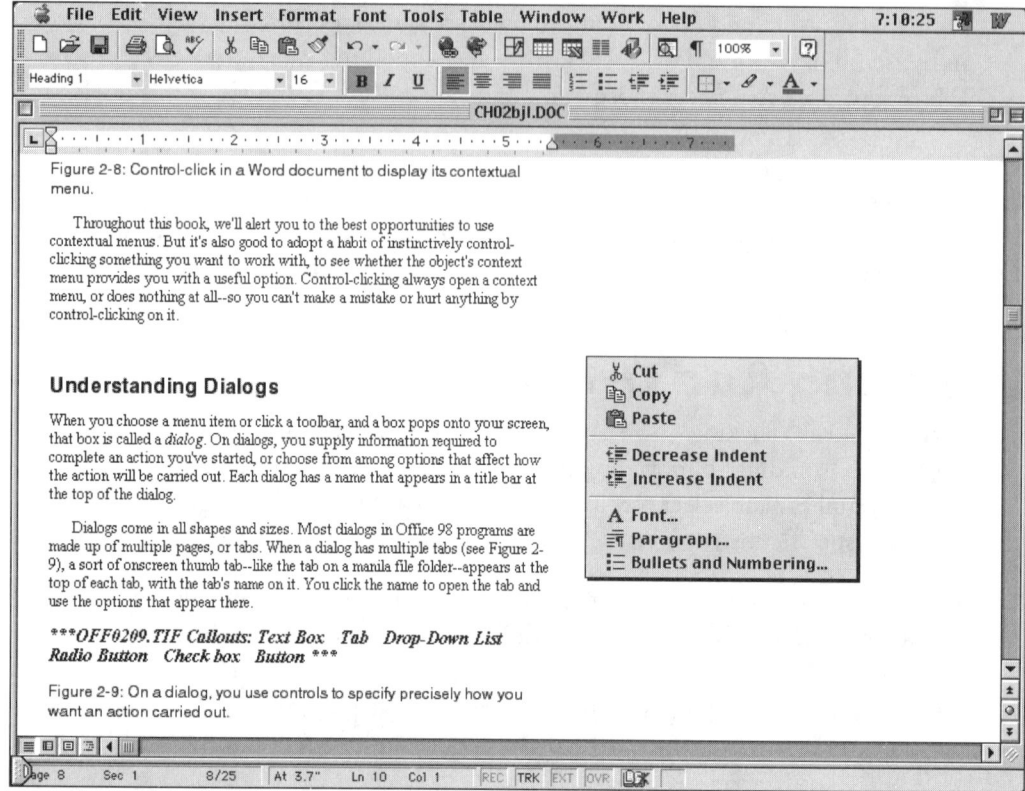

Figure 2.8 Control-click in a Word document to display its contextual menu.

Dialogs come in all shapes and sizes. Many dialogs in Office 98 programs consist of multiple pages, or *tabs*. When a dialog has multiple tabs (see Figure 2.9), a sort of on-screen thumb tab—like the tab on a manila file folder—appears at the top of each tab, with the tab's name on it. Click on the name to open the tab and use the options that appear there.

Using A Dialog

In dialogs and their tabs, you'll supply information and select from among options by using a variety of different controls (see Figure 2.9), including:

- *Text boxes*—A text box is a white rectangle in which you type something. For example, on the dialog you use to save a file, a text box is provided so you can type a file name. To use a text box, you simply click in it and type.

- *Drop-down lists*—A drop-down list looks like a text box, but has an arrow at its right end. If you click on the arrow, a list of options drops down so you can choose an item in the list by clicking on it. You can use many drop-down lists

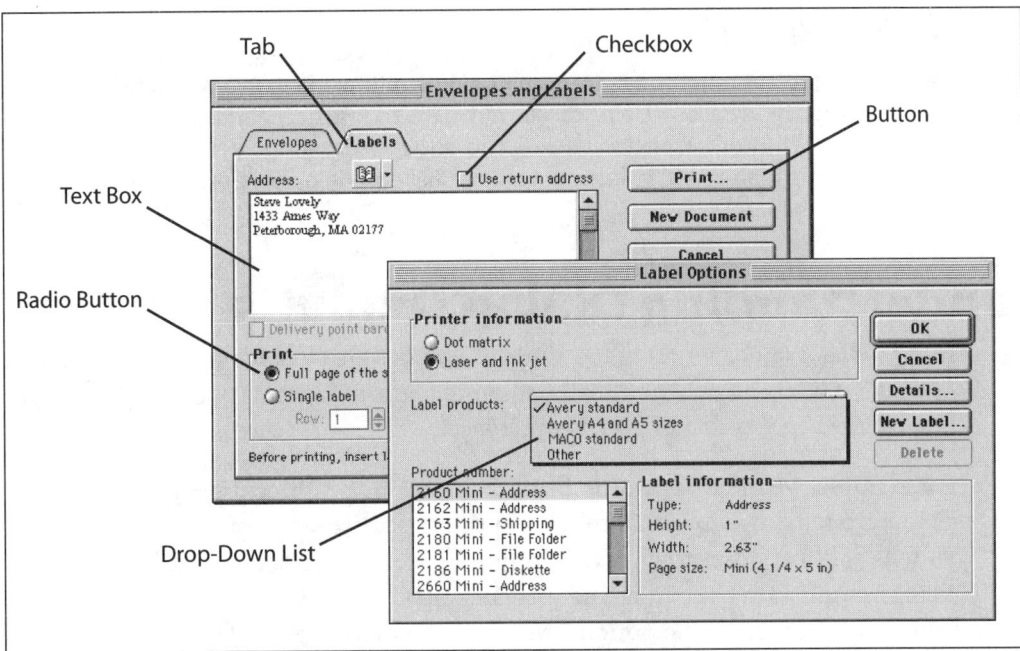

Figure 2.9 On a dialog, you use controls to specify precisely how you want an action carried out.

(but not all of them) in two ways: like a text box by typing your entry, or by dropping down the list and choosing from it.

- *Radio buttons*—A radio button is a small circle that indicates whether an option is selected or not. When the circle is white and empty, the option next to it is not selected. When the circle is full and black, the option is selected. Each time you click on an option that has a radio button next to it, you select or deselect the option.

- *Checkboxes*—A checkbox is a white square that contains a check mark when selected, but is empty when not selected. Each time you click on an option that has a checkbox next to it, you insert or remove the check mark. (Just as an aside, the difference between radio buttons and checkboxes is this—radio buttons are for selecting a *single* option, while checkboxes are for selecting *multiple* options. In other words, "choose one" usually implies a radio button, while "choose all that apply" would imply checkboxes.)

- *Buttons*—A button is a small, rectangular box with a name on it. You click on the button to perform the action the label describes. Buttons are used for a variety of actions. Most dialogs have at least two buttons: an OK button you click on to confirm that you're done choosing options on a dialog, and a Cancel button you click on to close the dialog without applying any changes you may have made.

Fast Track

A terrific—and often overlooked—accompaniment to working in any dialog is Balloon Help. Using Balloon Help, you can move the mouse over almost anything in a dialog—a button, an option, a box—and display a description of exactly what that item is all about. To learn how to use Balloon Help, see "Getting Help" later in this chapter.

Understanding Dialog Defaults

In most dialogs, most or all of the available settings are already made with defaults. A *default* is a setting or action that a program performs automatically, with no input from you, when you do not specify otherwise.

For example, when you open the Print dialog in most Office programs, you can choose from a drop-down list to select a printer to use, and you can use radio buttons and text boxes to choose to print only certain parts of a file. But if you change nothing on the dialog and just click on OK, the file is printed using default settings for all the options. Much of the time, these defaults will happen to be the choices you would have made anyway.

Default settings are terrific time-savers, because they match the settings most people are most likely to use. Because of defaults, you'll often find that even in a dialog containing many tabs and settings, you'll end up changing only one or two options—or none at all—because most options are already set the way you want them.

Using Shortcut Keys

Like any other Mac programs, Office 98 applications require a mouse, trackball, or other pointing device to get your work done. But in many instances, you can access a particular command or function from the keyboard using *shortcut keys*, key combinations that duplicate the actions of "mousy" work like choosing from menus.

Fast Track

Throughout this book, you'll see shortcut key combinations for accomplishing some tasks. When a shortcut key combination is given, it appears with a plus sign (+) in it to indicate that you hold down the first key, press the second, then release both. For example, to execute the key combination "Cmd+P," press and hold the Command key, press P, and release both keys. (The Control and Option keys are labeled as such, but the Command key is a bit obscure to the newcomer. You may also hear it called the clover key, the apple key, the open-apple key, the flower key, the splat key, etc. It's the one with the outlined Apple logo and a little flowery-looking thing on it. No, we don't know how they got that symbol for "Command," either.)

There are a number of special-purpose shortcut keys for performing common tasks; most of them require you to press and hold the Command key and then press another key. For example, Cmd+N creates a new file (N for New), Cmd+S saves a file (S for Save), and Cmd+P prints a file (P for Print). To help you learn and remember these shortcuts, they appear on menus, right next to the menu items whose actions they duplicate. For example, if you open the File menu in any Office program, you'll see Cmd+N listed right next to the New item on the menu. (The shortcut key combination is shown on the menu only for your education, not necessarily to be used right then; after all, by the time you've opened the menu, you've already done half of the shortcut key's job.)

Another type of shortcut key combo involves the Command key and the underlined letters that appear in certain dialog boxes when the Command key is held down. This method requires no memorization, and you can use it to shorten many tasks. To select an item or option, you press and hold the Command key, then press the underlined letter.

For example, pressing Cmd+F invokes the Find And Replace dialog. But if you look over the dialog for a moment, you'll notice that it has three tabs—Find, Replace, and Go To. To speed switching between these three tabs, press and hold the Command key. Now notice that one letter in each tab name is underlined, as are letters in many of the buttons and field names. Pressing the underlined letter while holding down the Command key will activate a button, jump you to a field, or switch you to a particular tab, depending on which function you invoke.

Besides shortcut keys, other ways to get around without a mouse include:

- *Scrolling*—Use PgDn, PgUp, and the arrow keys.
- *Moving among text boxes in a dialog*—Press Tab to jump to the next text box, Shift+Tab to jump to the previous one.
- *Choosing from lists*—Use a shortcut key or Tab to move to the list box, then press the Down arrow key to drop down the list.

Shortcut keys can be big time-savers, especially in Word, where you might work faster when you don't have to shift your fingers from keyboard to mouse. Nonetheless, a good pointer can be a great help, and Office knows it, having been built with many new ways to use drag-and-drop and other mouse-dependent techniques.

FYI: Improving Office's Accessibility

Though shortcut keys are not always the best way to perform most actions in Office programs, people with certain motor disabilities sometimes find key combinations easier to execute than pointing and clicking—especially when shortcut keys are used in tandem with the Mac's built-in Easy Access options. You enable these options from the Easy Access control panel.

Open the Apple menu and choose Control Panels|Easy Access to open the Easy Access control panel. In the control panel, you can enable or disable three options: Sticky Keys, Mouse Keys, and Slow Keys. Sticky Keys allows you to type shortcut key combinations like Cmd+P one key at a time. This is great for people with limited dexterity. Mouse Keys allows you to manipulate the cursor using the numeric keypad on your keyboard. On the keypad, use 5 as the mouse button, and use the surrounding keys to move the cursor. The period key locks the mouse button down, and the Clear key turns Mouse Keys off. (One note of caution: Using Mouse Keys requires an extended keyboard. You can't use the standard number keys to do this trick.) Slow Keys decreases the speed at which the system recognizes shortcut key combinations—a helpful feature for inaccurate typists.

In addition to using Easy Access options, users with vision disabilities may choose to adjust various *view* settings within each program to magnify the display. In particular, raising the Zoom percentage makes text appear larger and sharper on your screen. You'll learn about the view options for each program in the program sections. Further, every Macintosh has the built-in CloseView control panel. Open the Apple menu and select Control Panels|CloseView. With CloseView turned on, you can magnify the screen image from 2 to 16 times normal size, and invert the colors for easier reading. CloseView also pro-vides keyboard shortcuts for enabling and disabling magnification, and for changing the magnification percentage.

If you find that either CloseView or Easy Access is missing from your Macintosh, you can reload them from your Mac OS CD-ROM to activate them.

Using The Microsoft Office Manager

The Microsoft Office Manager is an optional menu/control panel that provides quick access to programs and files on your Mac—especially, of course, Office programs and files. To use the Office Manager, you must install it from the Value Pack on the Microsoft Office 98 CD-ROM (see Appendix A for more on using this installer). We highly recommend installing the Office Manager, because it makes life with Office even easier and faster.

The Office Manager lives in your menu bar, as Figure 2.10 shows. You access the items in the Office Manager menu just as you would the items in any other menu.

Getting To Know The Office 98 Environment   31

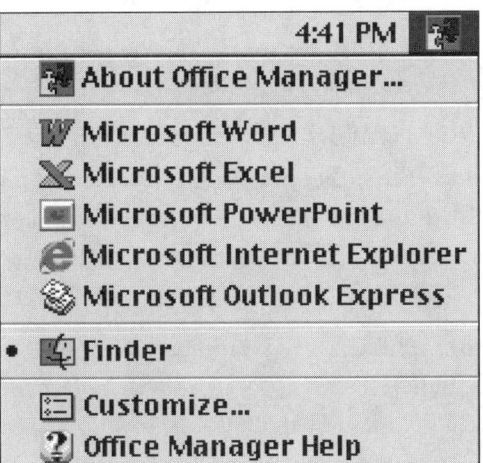

Figure 2.10   Microsoft Office Manager gives you access to Office programs and documents right from your menu bar.

Opening Office Programs From The Office Manager

The Office Manager is the handiest way to open Office programs. Simply open the Office Manager menu and select the program you want to run. The effect is the same as if you double-clicked on the program's icon in the Finder. The Office Manager simply provides you with a different way of going about it.

In the Office Manager menu, programs that are already open are listed with a check mark beside them. The program you are currently in is listed with a bullet.

FYI: Creating A Safe Place For Documents

Dialogs are not the only Office features that have defaults. Each Office program has a default folder where it wants to store everything you do in that program—the program's own folder.

When you save a new document, you have the option to store the document in any folder on any disk to which your Mac has access—including a shared network disk, if you have privileges there. But if you don't specify a storage location, the file goes in the program's resident folder automatically.

There are two ways to change this setting. First, from the Apple menu, select Control Panels|General Controls. In the lower right, you'll see a Documents section with three options. If you select Folder That Is Set By The Application, the default file-saving location is set to whatever folder the program you're using prefers (for example, the Word folder). If you select Last Folder Used By The Application, that's a little safer—provided that you saved somewhere safe last time. The best option is the Documents folder. Selecting this option creates a folder on your Desktop called *Documents*. From then on, every program you use, including the Office programs, will default to saving in this folder.

Second, you can set each Office program's preferences to point to a particular save location. This is handy if you like to divide your documents according to the program that created them. (See "Customizing Office Applications" later in this chapter.)

Why bother with a different save location anyway? Well for one thing, if you use the Documents folder, all your files will be in a single, central location. There's no scrabbling around in umpteen folders trying to remember where you saved something last week. More important, if you ever decide to uninstall or reinstall an Office program, you wouldn't want to accidentally dump your files along with the program—which might happen if you save your files in the program folder.

Using QuickSwitch

The Office Manager provides another neat trick for getting around. The QuickSwitch function allows you to jump between active programs with just a key shortcut. This isn't limited to only Office programs, either—it includes *any* active program.

To invoke QuickSwitch, press Cmd+Tab. A window will appear with a list of currently running programs. Press or hold the Tab key (while still holding the Command key) to select a program. When the one you want is highlighted, simply release the keys to change to that program. To move backward in the list, press Cmd+Shift+Tab. You can customize this key combination from the Microsoft Office Manager control panel (more on that shortly).

Modifying (Or Removing) The Office Manager

We have to tell you here and now that lots of people don't like the Office Manager, for one reason or another. Fortunately, it's very easy to customize or even remove. But why would you *not* want to run the Office Manager?

First, the Office Manager has a tainted history. Previous versions were the culprit behind a number of nasty system crash problems. That problem is long gone, but the stigma remains. Second, some people don't like having a cluttered menu bar—the Office Manager is just one more busy icon to them. Finally, it uses about 163K of RAM, and on a low-powered Mac, that might be the difference between just enough RAM and not enough.

If you have the Office Manager and you don't like something about it, click its icon in the menu bar and select Customize. A control panel appears with a variety of options for dealing with the Office Manager (see Figure 2.11).

First, you'll see the menu options—the items listed in your Office Manager menu. By default, the items listed are About Office Manager, a separator line, then items for Word, Excel, PowerPoint, Outlook Express, Internet Explorer, FrontPage, Outlook, Bookshelf, and Encarta. Then there's another separator, followed by an item for the Finder. Finally, after yet another separator, there's a selection for Office Manager Help. To show or hide any of these items, enable or disable the checkbox next to its name. To alter the order in which the list appears, select an item and click on the up or down Move arrow to shift its position.

You can also make more radical changes to the menu. For example, suppose you prefer a different Web browser than Internet Explorer. Rather than have the IE item cluttering up your menu, why not put your browser of choice on the menu instead? First, make sure Microsoft Internet Explorer is unchecked, so it won't appear in

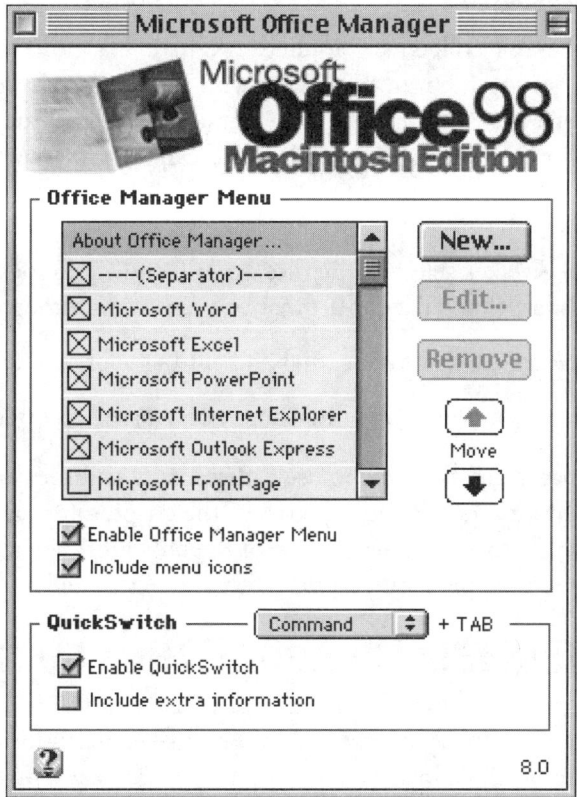

Figure 2.11 Open the Microsoft Office Manager control panel to customize your Office Manager and QuickSwitch functions.

your Office Manager menu. Then click on New. Navigate to the program you prefer, select it, and click on Add. Your new program will appear in the list, and you can shift its order as you like. If you change your mind later, use the Edit button to alter the program your item points to, or click on Remove to delete it entirely. You can use this same method to add documents, control panels, or just about anything to the Office Manager menu.

From the control panel, you can also enable or disable the Office Manager menu, and you can show or hide menu icons in the Office Manager menu. Finally, you can enable or disable QuickSwitch, change the key combination that invokes it, or opt to show "extra information." This means that when you invoke QuickSwitch, its window will show not only the active programs, but also the amount of memory each is using, the total amount of available memory, and the total memory currently in use.

When you've finished customizing your Office Manager menu, close the control panel to enable your new settings.

Using OfficeArt

OfficeArt is the name collectively applied to Office 98's built-in tools for creating pictures and inserting them in documents you create with Word, PowerPoint, and Excel. (OfficeArt is not available within Outlook Express. But then, there's really nothing to do in Outlook Express that would call for art, anyway.)

The OfficeArt tools include:

- *Clip Gallery*—Makes selecting picture, sound, and video files easy. Office 98 includes a library of popular clip art that you can access through the Clip Gallery.
- *Drawing toolbar*—A tool for creating and editing your own drawings.
- *WordArt*—Turns ordinary text into snappy text-based pictures.

The next few pages describe how to use OfficeArt. It's a little early in the game for you to dive right into these tools; this part of the chapter is designed to familiarize you with OfficeArt so you'll have a sense of the possibilities when you begin working in the programs themselves. Feel free at that time to come back here and review.

Picking Multimedia Files From The Clip Gallery

The Clip Gallery (see Figure 2.12) indexes pictures, sound clips, and movie clips by subject to make it easy to select any of these objects—collectively known as multimedia files—and insert them in an Office document. *Multimedia files* is a 50-cent phrase for pictures, sounds, and movies. Using multimedia can add sizzle to your PowerPoint presentation and spice to your Word newsletter. Never substitute spice and sizzle for substance, though. In other words, use the multimedia stuff sparingly.

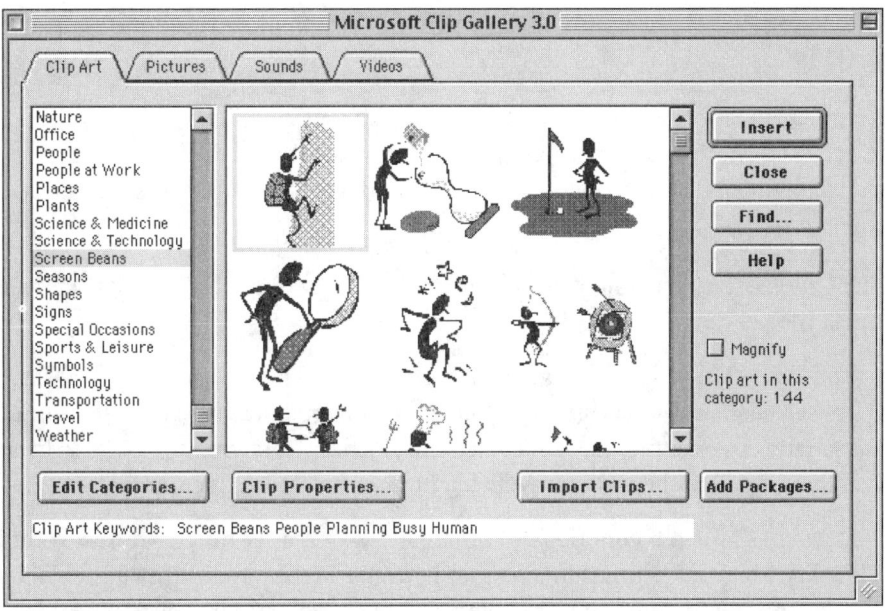

Figure 2.12 The Clip Gallery provides a way to find and insert multimedia files organized by category.

FYI: Can I Use My Own Pictures, Sound Clips, And Video?

Yes indeed. All you need to do is create the file. You can use paint programs, scanners, or digital cameras to produce bitmap pictures, and you can use drawing and charting programs to create vector graphics. You can create movies using video capture boards, or record sounds with the SimpleSound utility.

It really doesn't matter how you get the file; that's because Office 98 programs can use—import—virtually all popular picture, sound, and video file formats. After creating the file, you insert it into your document according to instructions you'll find in the program sections in this book.

Note that Office programs all share a common library of converters and filters that prepare files you want to use in Office. Though the converters and filters for most common file types are included in the drag-and-drop installation, not all of the converters and filters on the Office 98 CD-ROM are included. If you follow the instructions in the program sections for importing files into your documents, and the program won't accept the file, the filter for importing that file type has not been installed in Office. See Appendix A to learn how to add converters and filters from the CD.

In the programs that support it, you open the Clip Gallery by choosing Insert|Picture|Clip Art.

Note that most of the clip art that comes with Office 98 stays on the CD, but can be accessed there by the Clip Gallery. Always insert your Office 98 CD into your CD-ROM drive before opening the Clip Gallery to ensure access to the widest range of files.

The Clip Gallery has four tabs, each of which contains a different type of multimedia file:

- *Clip Art*—This tab includes drawing objects, also known as *vector graphics*. These images—generally very graphical in style and appearance—are in the same file format as the picture you can create with Office's Drawing tool, and you can edit and manipulate them in many different ways in Office documents.
- *Pictures*—This tab contains *bitmap* images, such as scanned photos or high-quality artwork. Bitmap images can be more lifelike than drawing objects, but you cannot edit them in as many ways in Office programs as you can drawing objects.
- *Sounds*—This tab contains sound clips, represented in Office documents by a speaker icon. Sound clips are used chiefly in PowerPoint presentations, but you can also use them in Word documents designed for online presentation.
- *Videos*—This tab includes video clips, represented in Office documents by a frozen image of the first frame of the clip. Like sound clips, video clips are used chiefly in PowerPoint presentations and online Word documents.

To choose a file from the Clip Gallery, select a tab, then choose an index category from the column on the left side of the tab. The tab shows only the files that match the category you selected. (Choosing the category "All Categories" shows all files in the tab.) Scroll down to see all the files in the tab; in the Clip Art and Pictures tabs, you'll see small thumbnail versions of each picture to help you choose. In the Sounds and Videos tabs, click on any file icon and then click on the tab's Play button to evaluate the selected sound or video clip. When the selected file is the one you want, click on Insert to copy it into the document.

To add your own files to the Clip Gallery, open the appropriate Clip Gallery tab, then click on the Import Clips button. A dialog opens, which you use to navigate to and select the file you want to add. After you select the file, another dialog opens, where you choose which Categories you want the new file to appear in.

Net Savvy

If you can't find the picture, sound, or video you want in the Clip Gallery and you don't want to create it yourself, your next best bet is to look in the many multimedia clip libraries on the Web. There you can select from among thousands of multimedia files, download what you want, and either add it to the Clip Gallery or insert the file in a document just as you would insert a file you created.

There are far too many clip sources on the Web to list here; instead, here's the address of two Yahoo! directories containing links to good file sources:

- For pictures, try the links at **www.yahoo.com/Computers_and_Internet/Multimedia/Pictures/Clip_Art/**

- For sounds and video, try the links at **www.yahoo.com/Computers_and_Internet/Multimedia/Archives/**

Before using downloaded clips, be sure to read any copyright notices on the page where you download them from, to be sure you're not violating copyrights. And if you're ever in doubt about whether a clip is copyrighted, don't use it.

Drawing Pictures

From within Word, PowerPoint, and Excel, you can create your own drawing objects to decorate your documents. These can be as elaborate as you want them to be, or they can be as simple as lines or arrows connecting text or other pictures in the document.

To draw in any of the supporting programs, display the Drawing toolbar (see Figure 2.13) by clicking on the Drawing button that appears on each program's

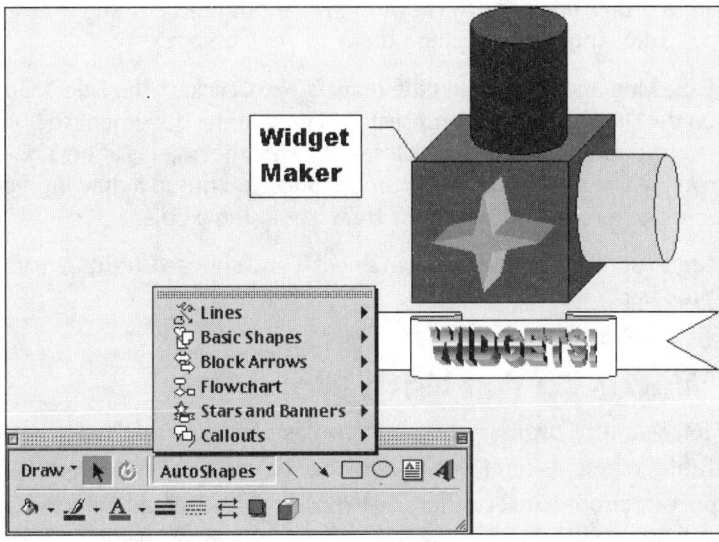

Figure 2.13 Use the tools on the Drawing toolbar to create your own drawing objects.

Standard toolbar. (Note that the Drawing toolbar, unlike most toolbars, plants itself at the bottom of the display, not the top. But you can move it, or float it, like any other toolbar.) To draw a simple object, click on the Line, Arrow, Rectangle, or Oval button. Then click and hold in the document, drag to create the object, and release the mouse button. Besides these simple shapes, you can also insert more complex shapes by dropping down the AutoShapes list from the Drawing toolbar.

Once you've inserted the basic shapes in your document, you can manipulate them. Begin by clicking on your drawing object to select it; when you do, its handles appear, little white squares you can click and drag to change the size or shape of the object. (You'll learn more about handles in the rest of the book.) Once an object is selected, you can:

- Click and drag the object to change its position.
- Click on the Free Rotate button to rotate the object to a different angle.
- Click and drag a handle to edit the size and shape of the object.
- Click on the Fill Color button to fill in ovals and rectangles with a selected color.
- Click on the Line Color button to choose a color for lines and shape outlines.
- Click on the Shadow and 3D buttons to add a three-dimensional look to your shapes.

Fast Track

You create complex drawings by drawing the various lines and shapes that make up the drawing, then grouping them into one object.

Begin by drawing and positioning the objects. Next, click on the Select Objects button on the Drawing toolbar and click and drag in the document to pull a dashed box around the objects, which selects all of the objects at once. Finally, drop down the Draw list and choose Group. Once you group a drawing, you can move it, change its size, and otherwise treat it as a single object.

If you need to ungroup it later, you can select it and choose Ungroup from the Drawing toolbar.

Turning Words To Art With WordArt

WordArt lets you turn ordinary text into cool, stylized, word-based artwork, like the fun and funky text and logos you see in ads. To create WordArt in the programs that support it, choose Insert|Picture|WordArt. The WordArt Gallery opens (see Figure 2.14), where you can choose from among the many available WordArt styles.

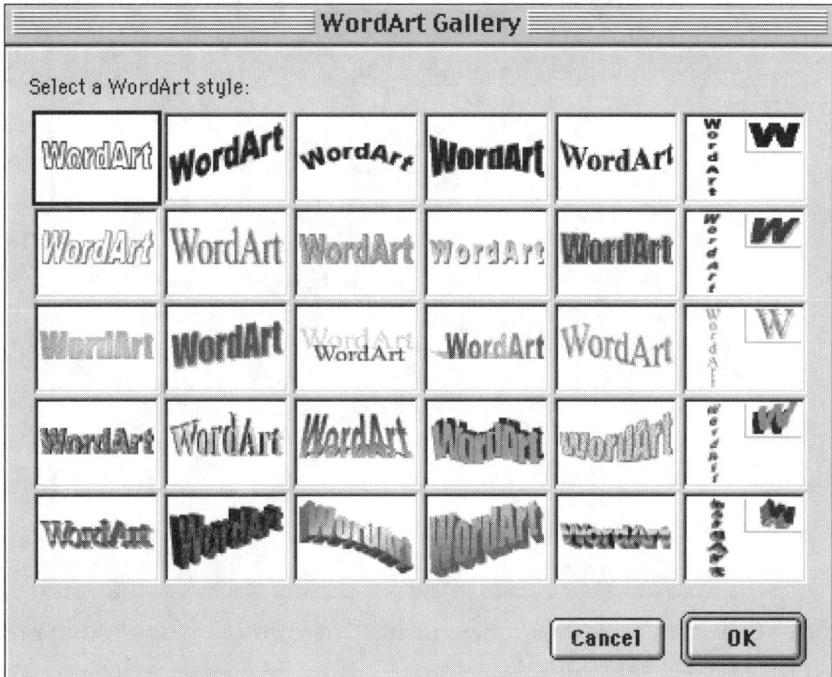

Figure 2.14 Choose a WordArt style to create highly stylized text that you can manipulate as a picture.

After you choose a style, another dialog opens in which you type the words you want to use.

When you finish, the new art appears in your file, along with a WordArt toolbar. You can drag the art to position it, change its size and shape by clicking and dragging its handles, or edit it in other ways by using buttons on the WordArt toolbar.

Customizing Office Applications

Every Office application program has its own Preferences dialog (see Figure 2.15), and in every Office program you open it the same way: Choose Tools|Preferences. The Preferences dialog contains an assortment of tabs on which you can change the appearance and behavior of the program.

In the rest of this book, you'll learn how to use some of the more important settings on each program's Preferences dialog. The Preferences dialogs simply contain too many options for us to discuss each in detail. The defaults on each program's Preferences dialog have been carefully selected to configure the program in a way most users will prefer, so while you're learning a program, you're usually better off leaving

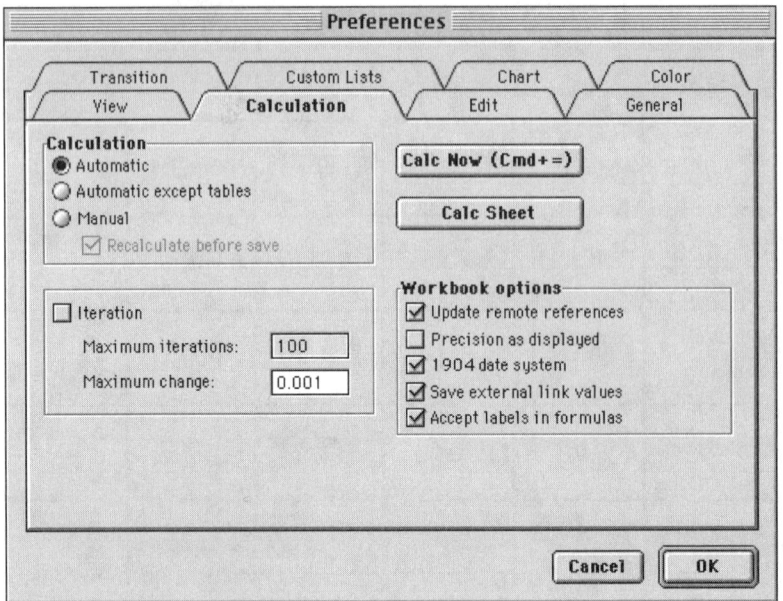

Figure 2.15 Choosing Tools|Preferences in any Office program opens that program's Preferences dialog.

its Preferences dialog alone. However, as you gain experience, you may find that you don't like the way some aspects of the program look or behave. When you get to that point, you can modify the program to your liking by changing settings on the Preferences dialog.

When you feel ready to change preferences, be sure to use Balloon Help (described in the next section, "Getting Help") to learn what a setting does before you change it.

Getting Help

The Office 98 programs offer a richer, more versatile set of help options than most Mac programs. In particular, they add Office Assistant—which you may find either hugely helpful or assertively annoying—to the standard Mac help facilities, as well as a whole bagful of Help On The Web links that may or may not hook you up to more help online.

The Office Assistant

Perhaps the single most radical new feature of Office 98 is the Office Assistant (see Figure 2.16), an animated cartoon character that pops up to offer help. By default, the Office Assistant pops up immediately when you open any Office program, offering a list of options—in a comic-style word balloon—to help you get started. The Office Assistant character starts out as an animated Macintosh Plus with legs, but you can

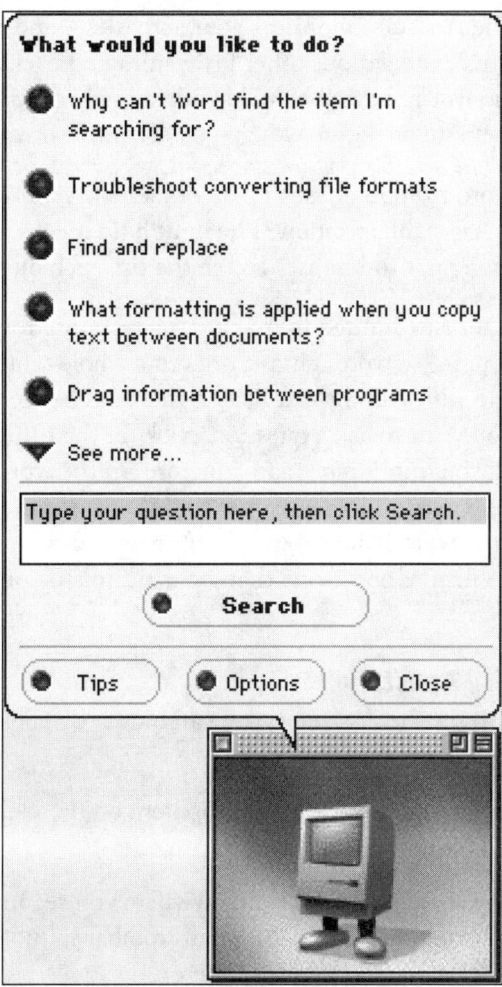

Figure 2.16 The Office Assistant watches over your shoulder and offers help when it thinks you need some.

change the character and customize the Office Assistant in other ways, too. (If you don't know what a Macintosh Plus is, or was, don't worry—it was a *long* time ago, in computer years.)

When the Assistant offers you a list of help items in its word balloon, you can click on any item to read whatever help the Office Assistant has to offer, or press Esc to close the balloon and go back to work. When you display the help text the Office Assistant suggests, what you see is generally the same help text you'd see if you navigated to a help topic in the traditional help facility, Contents And Index.

As you work, the Office Assistant stays open in a corner of your screen; you can drag it anywhere on the screen if it's in your way. Also, if you don't use it for a few minutes, it becomes smaller by about half, making itself less conspicuous.

While it's open, the Assistant monitors your activities—and paces around, does a Rubik's Cube routine, and various other little animated tricks, just to show off. If the Assistant senses you're having trouble with something, the word balloon opens, offering a list of help items that may help you accomplish what you're trying to do.

Sometimes, the word balloon doesn't open, but a little yellow light bulb appears within the Office Assistant's window. The light bulb means the Assistant has a tip for you, but it's trying not to impose. To see the tip, click on the bulb.

The Office Assistant isn't limited to making suggestions. You can ask it a question by typing a search term—a word, phrase, or even a whole sentence describing something you want help with—in the text box on the word balloon. (If the word balloon isn't open when you want to ask a question, click on the Office Assistant.) For example, in Word, you might type "add a picture" in the word balloon's text box when you want help with adding a picture to a Word document. Then click on the Search button in the word balloon, and the Assistant displays a list of help topics related to your problem. Choose one that looks promising or try a different search term.

Hiding The Office Assistant

If you don't want to see the Assistant, you can hide it by clicking on its Close box. You can redisplay it at any time by:

- Choosing Help, and then choosing the top item on the Help menu. (The wording of that item will differ from program to program.)

- Clicking on the Office Assistant icon anywhere you see it. The icon appears as a button on the far right end of the Standard toolbar in most Office 98 programs, and also shows up in dialogs here and there.

We should point out that a lot of people don't like the Office Assistant, considering it either too intrusive or too "cutesy." For your own sake, though, we advise you to leave it open, at least for the first week or two you use Office. If you find you don't use it, then by all means hide it. But once you get used to it, you may find it handy. And if you don't give it a chance to prove itself to you, you'll never know what you're missing. (Besides which, some of the animations are just too cool to pass up—watch the default Assistant character, Max, when you use the Quack beep sound.)

Customizing The Office Assistant

On the Office Assistant dialog (see Figure 2.17), you can choose the Assistant character and also control the way it behaves. To open the Office Assistant dialog, first insert your Office 98 CD into your CD-ROM drive (it contains the various characters you can select). Then click on the Options button that usually appears in the Assistant's word balloon (refer back to Figure 2.16).

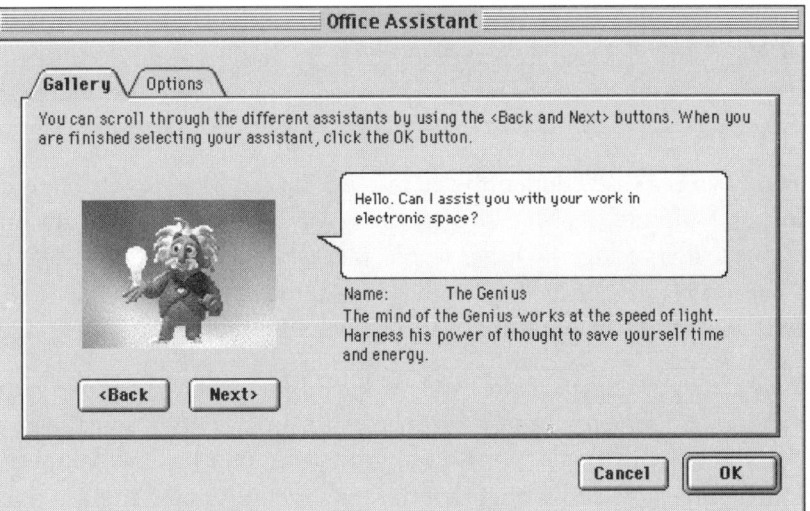

Figure 2.17 Use the Office Assistant dialog to choose a new personality for the Office Assistant.

Click on the Gallery tab to choose a character. On the tab, click on Next or Back to move through the nine available characters, including Albert Einstein, William Shakespeare, two dogs, Bosgrove the butler, and a group of more abstract choices. When you see the character you want, click on OK, or move on to the Options tab. Note that changing the character changes only the Assistant's appearance; you still get exactly the same help from it. (Einstein is no smarter than Scribble.) On the Options tab, check or clear checkboxes to control how and when the Assistant offers help, and when it should leave you alone.

FYI: Don't Confuse The Assistants

"Assistant" is also the term Apple uses for a couple of miniature programs that ship with every new Mac: the Mac OS Setup Assistant and the Internet Setup Assistant. These two programs are normally stored in an Assistants folder at the top level of your hard disk. They have *nothing* to do with Office 98, so don't confuse them for the Office Assistants, which are stored inside the Microsoft Office 98 folder.

Fast Track

If you Control-click on the Office Assistant, a contextual menu appears, offering items that close the Office Assistant (Hide Assistant), show tips (See Tips), open the Options dialog (Options), and more. The contextual menu also includes an

Animate button that you can click on to send the Assistant into a brief spasm of rapid animation for no apparent reason.

Balloon Help

Balloon Help is a vastly underutilized resource on the Mac. It's been around for a while now, built into the Mac OS, but the way most programs take advantage of it makes some users cringe (in other words, there hasn't been much help to be gained with Balloon Help). Office 98, though, comes through with an excellent implementation of Balloon Help—just about anyone will find it useful at some stage.

Balloon Help pops up a cartoon-style word balloon when you move your cursor over an item on screen (not just any item—the programmers must have enabled a balloon for an item, or you won't see anything). In that balloon, you'll typically find the item's name and a brief description of what it does. You can point to almost anything—a toolbar button, a menu item, an option in a dialog, a dialog's title bar—to learn more about how you use it (see Figure 2.18). Balloon Help is a great way to learn more about the various options on a dialog while making choices there, or to learn what different toolbar buttons do.

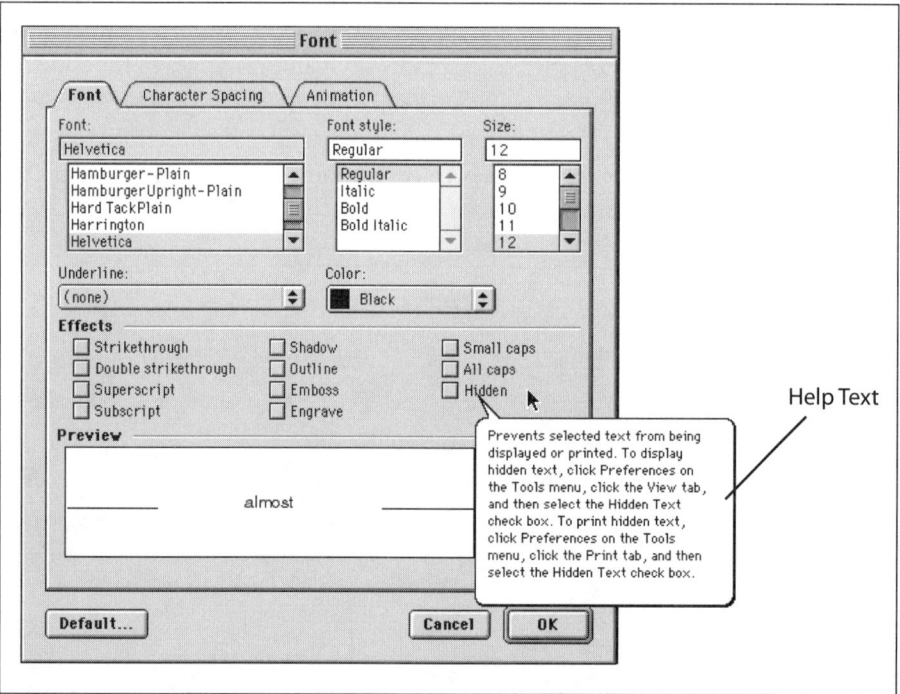

Figure 2.18 When you have Balloon Help enabled, move the mouse over almost anything to learn more about it.

You can get the Balloon Help by selecting Help|Show Balloons. To turn it back off, select Help|Hide Balloons. Once you've got the help you need, you'll almost always want to switch the balloons back off—they can get annoying after a bit.

Contents And Index

The standard Help facility in Office, Contents And Index, provides the most complete access to a program's Help resources. In all Office 98 programs, you open Contents And Index by choosing Help|Contents And Index.

The Contents And Index dialog (see Figure 2.19) has four buttons:

- *Contents*—A table of contents to the whole help system. Entries that have little book icons next to them represent multiple help topics grouped by subject; click on the book to display the individual help topic entries, which have little question mark icons next to them.

- *Index*—An alphabetical index to help topics. Type a word or phrase in the text box at the top of the tab, and the index scrolls to the appropriate help topic. When you've found the entry you want, click on the Show Topics button to display a

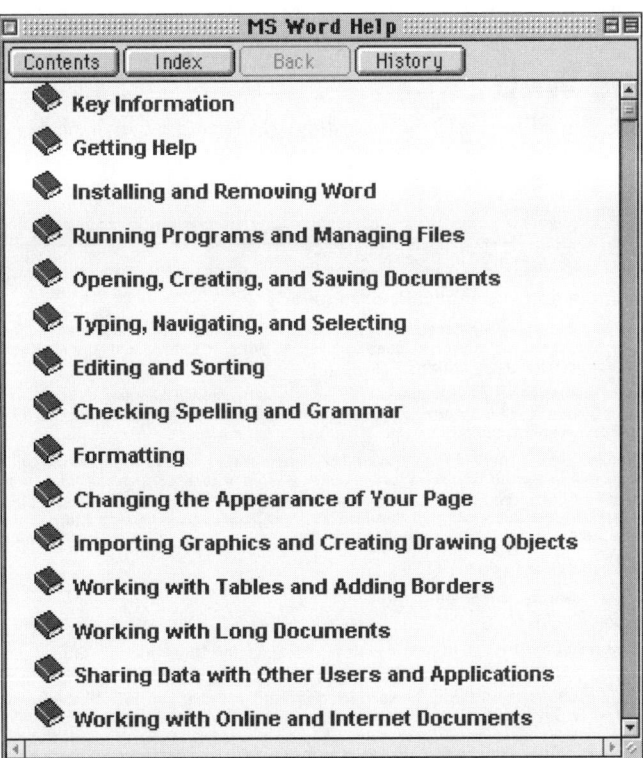

Figure 2.19 The Contents And Index help facility lets you find a help topic by subject or alphabetically.

list of individual help topics in the lower window. Then select the topic you want and click on Go To.

- *Back*—The Back button lets you navigate backward to the last window you looked at (handy if you selected a subtopic that didn't quite answer your question).

- *History*—Clicking on History shows a list of all the help topics you've visited in this session and allows you to jump directly to any of them. This is most helpful if you're engaged in a long search for a specific item and need to backtrack a bit.

Note that all these options lead to the same help topics—they just provide you with three different ways of looking for what you want. When you reach a help topic, it appears like the one in Figure 2.20.

Usually, a help topic simply tells you how to do something step by step. But within a help topic, you may also see a number of objects that can supplement the help:

- *Underlined words*—Click on any work underlined with dashes to see a definition for that word.

- *A gray button with double angle marks (>>)*—Click on this button to jump to a related help topic.

Help On The Web

In the Help menu of every Office application (except Outlook Express), you'll see the item Help On The Web. When you click on that item, your Web browser

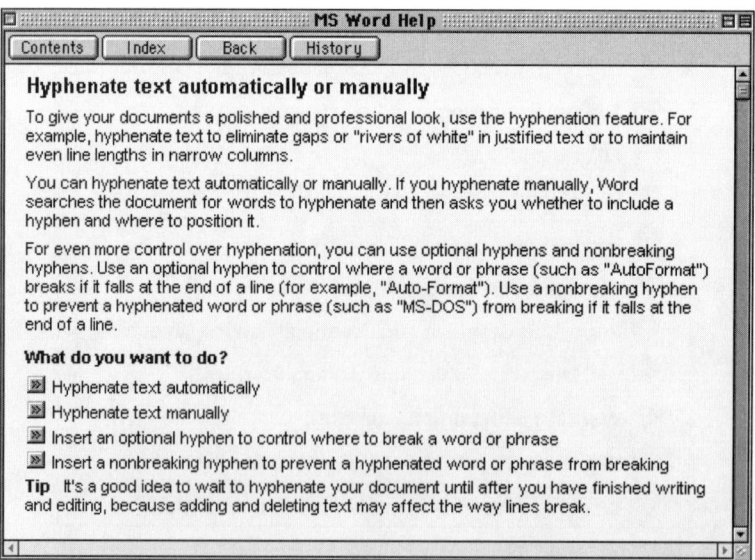

Figure 2.20 Help topics supply the explanations you've requested through the Office Assistant or Contents And Index.

launches, opening a file on your hard drive called WebHelp.htm (see Figure 2.21). Each link on this page points to a help document on the Microsoft Web site.

To use these links, you must have the following:

- *An Internet connection*—A dial-up connection (made through a modem) or through a local network server.

- *PPP Autoconnect enabled*—Internet resources initiate the connection procedure. To enable automatic connections for a typical Mac Internet setup, open the PPP control panel, click on the Options button, click on the Connection tab, and check the checkbox for Connect Automatically When Starting TCP/IP Applications. If you are not using Apple's PPP control panel (lots of Internet service providers use FreePPP or other control panels), consult the documentation that came with your Internet setup software.

- *A default Web browser specified*—Opens automatically whenever a Web resource is requested. Most Web browsers—including Internet Explorer and Netscape Navigator—allow you to make them the default browser automatically when you install them.

If you have all of this, clicking on any of the Help On The Web links initiates the Internet connection and displays the help at Microsoft's Web site. (Depending on your Internet configuration, you may be prompted to type your Internet password while your Mac is connecting to the Internet.)

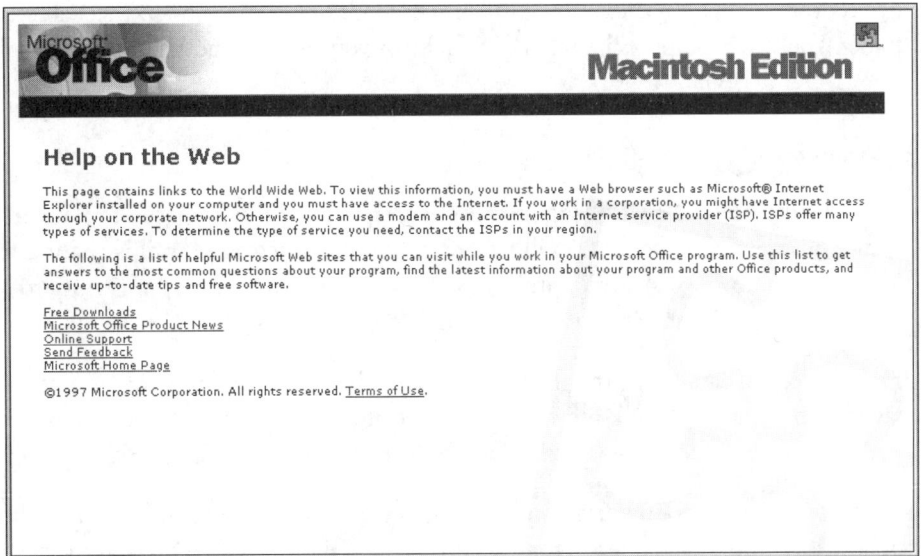

Figure 2.21 If you have the right configuration, Help On The Web takes you directly to resources on Microsoft's Web site.

Web help is a good idea, and by all means you should try it. But depending on your available memory and other factors, you may find accessing help text this way unreliable, even to the point where it brings your Mac to a screeching halt. The combination of Office applications, a Web browser, and network protocols all open and working together is a huge load on some Macs.

Instead of taking your chances with Web help, you may instead want to simply browse the Web directly. Listed below are the principal Web page addresses where you can learn more about Office. We must warn you, however, that at this writing these pages offer surprisingly little actual help. With luck, by the time you read this, these pages will have more to offer:

- General Office information and reference: **www.microsoft.com/macoffice/**
- Free Office add-ins and accessories: **www.microsoft.com/macoffice/freestuff/**
- Office Technical Support: **support.microsoft.com/support/**

About The Value Pack

The Office Value Pack is a library of additional templates, add-ins, sample files, and other useful stuff that is not installed in the typical drag-and-drop setup. Instead, it sits on your Office CD until you need it. From time to time in the program sections, we'll direct you to files on the Value Pack that you may find helpful.

To check out the Value Pack yourself, insert your Office 98 CD in your CD-ROM drive, double-click on the Microsoft Office 98 CD icon, then open the Value Pack folder. You can explore each area individually or you can run the Value Pack installer (see Appendix A).

Moving On

If you have a feel for everything in this chapter, you're fully prepared to take on any Office program you like. Don't worry if anything you discovered in this chapter feels fuzzy to you now—it'll come into focus as soon as you have an opportunity to apply it for real. This chapter is just orientation, not graduation.

From here, you can jump straight to any part of the book to learn the specifics of your favorite (or what you think might be your favorite) Office program. Be sure to begin the part you choose with its first chapter to learn the lay of the land in that program.

If no particular program beckons you, we suggest that you simply move forward from here straight on to Chapter 3, for Word may be the only Office program that's used by virtually everyone who has Office.

PART II
Word

Getting Started With Word

For most people, having Word is sort of like having a car that can go 140 mph. You'll never actually drive that fast (we hope), but somehow you enjoy knowing you *could* go that fast.

Because Word can do so much and has so many capabilities, few users apply even a fraction of what Word can do. (Take a look at Word's toolbar—it has more switches and lights than the Space Shuttle.) And that makes perfect sense; you use Word not to give its feature set a workout, but to produce precisely the document you want. If that document is a simple one, you'll produce it simply in Word, easily ignoring any extraneous power tools. If the document is elaborate, well, Word has all the gadgets you need to produce precisely the document you want, from a book to a brochure to a Web page. You have to put into Word only as much as you want to get out of it.

In keeping with that principle, Part I of this book proceeds from the very simplest of techniques—those that are applied in virtually any document—to more advanced, less-used features in the later chapters. In this first chapter about Word, you get the absolute basics: creating a new Word document, basic typing, saving the document, and finally printing it. And if you're upgrading from an earlier version of Word, here you'll learn how to upgrade your existing Word documents—and documents in many other word processing formats—to Word 98, and vice versa.

You can find all of the toolbar buttons described in this chapter on Word's Standard toolbar, shown in Figure 3.1. If you don't see the Standard toolbar on your screen, point to any spot on any visible toolbar and Control-click (or choose View|Toolbars from the menu bar), then click on Standard. To display the name of any button on the toolbar, rest the pointer on the button for a moment.

Figure 3.1 Word's Standard toolbar. You'll click on the buttons on this toolbar in many of the activities in this chapter.

Creating A New Word Document

The simplest way to create a new Word document is to let Word do it for you. Just select Word from the Office Manager menu, wait for it to start, *et voila*—a new document appears.

Of course, you can also create a new document manually. Select File|New, then double-click on the icon for Blank Document. (Instead of Blank Document, you may select any of the other template files that appear as Word—rather than Excel or PowerPoint—icons. But stick with Blank Document for now—you learn all about templates in Chapter 7.) After you double-click on the template icon, Word opens, and the new, blank document opens within Word, ready to accept whatever you type.

When Word is open, you can create another blank document at any time simply by clicking on the New button on Word's Standard toolbar.

Your new document does not yet have a real name—it's called *Document1* in the title bar. When you save the document (as described later in this chapter), you should also name it. (Saving something as "Document1" won't help you remember that you put your letter to the editor in there, so be descriptive.) You can save your new document immediately after creating it (even before you type anything), or after you've worked on it for awhile, or any time you feel like it. Once the document has been saved, its new name appears in the title bar.

Entering Text

The *edit cursor* always appears automatically in the upper-left corner (the top) of any newly created document (and also in any existing document that's just been opened). The edit cursor is a simple vertical bar that's a little taller than the surrounding letters. It also flashes on and off, so it's easy to see when it rests deep within a forest of words.

The edit cursor is ground zero, the hotspot, the place where anything you do on the keyboard happens within the document. If you press any letter key, the letter appears in the document exactly where the edit cursor was, and the edit cursor moves one place to the right (where the next letter you type will appear).

FYI: Cursors And Pointers In Word

Any time you create or open a document, you'll actually see two "cursors"—the edit cursor *and* the regular Mac mouse pointer.

The edit cursor always starts at the top of the document, whereas the mouse pointer may appear anywhere on your screen. The mouse pointer moves whenever you move your mouse, whereas the edit cursor moves when you press an arrow key.

When the mouse pointer is within the document window, it looks like a vertical I-beam; elsewhere, it appears just as it usually does on the Mac screen, usually as an arrow. You can use the I-beam pointer to relocate the edit cursor quickly. Point the I-beam pointer to the spot where you want to work, then click. The edit cursor jumps to that spot.

To enter text in a Word document, all you have to do is type away. As you type, the edit cursor moves to the right and jumps down to the start of the next line automatically when you reach the end of a line. Keep going. Let the genius fly from your fingertips. Go nuts.

You'll learn much more about ways to enter and format text in the upcoming chapters. If you've ever typed before—even on a typewriter—most of this stuff is second nature to you already. But here are a few essentials to get you started, in case you're new to typing:

- To type a blank space, press the spacebar.

- To break a paragraph and start a new one, or to insert a blank line, press Return. (Press Return only to break a paragraph or insert a blank line; don't use it to end a line within a paragraph. Unlike a typewriter, a word processor breaks the lines within a paragraph for you.)

- To type an *uppercase*—capital—letter (or the upper character that appears on a key that shows two characters), press and hold the Shift key, then press the letter key.

- To fix a mistake, use your arrow keys or pointer to move the edit cursor to the mistake, then press the Delete or Backspace key (depending on your keyboard), or the Del key (if you have an extended keyboard). Backspace or Delete erases the character to the left of the edit cursor; Del deletes the character to the right of the edit cursor. When the error is gone, type your correction.

Walk-Through: Creating A Document And Entering Text

Follow the steps below to practice creating a Word document and entering text into it.

1. Open the Office Manager menu and select Microsoft Word. Word opens with a new, empty document ready for your text. The edit cursor appears at the top of the document.
2. Press Return twice, to create two blank lines. The edit cursor jumps down a line each time you press Return.
3. Type a paragraph of your choosing, at least two lines long. Don't worry about fixing mistakes; just keep going.
4. At the end of the paragraph, press Return once to start a new paragraph.
5. Type a second paragraph of your choosing, at least two lines long.

When you are finished, leave the document open to save yourself a few steps if you plan to move on to the next walk-through. If you're quitting Word now so you can snag the last few chocolate chip cookies before someone else does, choose File|Quit. Word asks whether you want to save the document. For now, click on No.

Saving Documents

Unless you're brand new to computers, you know how important it is to save your work. When you create a new document, it exists only in your Mac's memory until it's saved on your hard disk (or a diskette). As you make changes to the document, those changes exist only in memory (not on disk) until you save the document again. If you accidentally switch off your Mac—or if a power outage shuts off your Mac for you—you may lose a document completely if you've never saved it, or you may lose the changes you've made to a document since the last time you saved it.

While saving is important, forgetting to save is not as dangerous as it once was. The Mac OS and Word 98 work together to protect you from accidentally losing work by failing to save. Suppose you're working on a document and have either never saved it or have made changes since the last time you saved it. If you attempt to close that document, exit Word, or shut down your Mac (using the Special|Shut Down command), Word immediately displays a prompt asking whether you want to save your work before exiting. Click on Yes, and the work is saved. Click on No, and it's history. So unless you simply switch off your Mac (or your Mac is shut down by a power outage) while unsaved work is open in Word, you almost can't make the old mistake of forgetting to save.

But saving isn't only about loss prevention. When you save, you make decisions that affect the way you may work with the document thereafter: the document's name, its storage location, and other important defining characteristics.

The precise steps involved in saving a document are different the first time you save it from every time afterward. In the next few pages, you discover how to save the first time and subsequently. You also learn variations on saving, including saving your document under a new name and converting your document to another word processing format.

Saving A Document The First Time

To save the document you're working on, click on the Save button on the Word Standard toolbar (or choose File|Save from the menu bar). The Save dialog opens, as shown in Figure 3.2. As the top of the figure shows, a folder, Documents, has been preselected as the save location.

The list box in the Save dialog shows all files and subfolders in the folder, so you can see which files your new file will share a folder with. Near the bottom of the Save

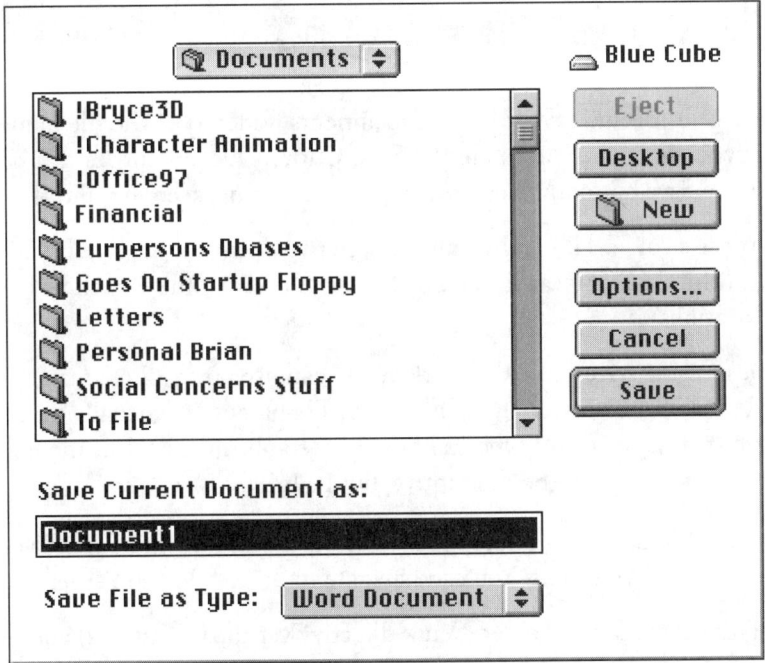

Figure 3.2 The Save dialog, where you save, copy, and convert documents.

dialog, the Save Current Document As text box appears. If you have already typed some text in your document, Word has automatically entered the first few words of your document in the file name box, on the assumption that you may want to use those words as the file name. (If you haven't typed anything yet, the default file name is Document1.) When you first arrive at the Save dialog, the entry in the Save Current Document As text box is highlighted. While the entry remains highlighted, whatever you type next replaces it.

FYI: Why "Documents"?

Brian set up a default folder called *Documents* for saving files on his Macintosh. You can create this type of folder through the General Controls control panel (see the FYI section "Creating A Safe Place For Documents" in Chapter 2). When you use Documents as the folder for your work, you don't have to bother choosing a folder when saving. Also, when you want to open the document later, you won't have to do any navigation in the Open dialog to get to it. However, you always have the option to save a document in any folder you wish, or on the Mac Desktop, or in a new folder you create right from the Save dialog.

Rather than using the General Controls control panel, you can also use the File Locations tab of Word's Preferences dialog (see Chapter 2) to set up a folder specifically for documents saved from Word.

To name your file and save it in the Documents folder, type the file name you wish (as you type, the name appears in the Save Current Document As text box), then click on the Save button. When creating your file name, keep in mind the following:

- Don't use a colon. This is the only character you can't use, in fact. If you try to type one, nothing will appear in the box (it has to do with the way the Mac OS tracks file locations).

- If you're using Mac OS 8.0 or earlier, you can use up to 32 characters. For users of Mac OS 8.1 or better and HFS+, your file names are virtually unlimited in length (really, you could type an entire paragraph, almost). But there's no sense getting carried away—be descriptive, but be brief.

To save the document in a folder other than the default, use the Save dialog to navigate to the folder you want. You can navigate to other folders in several ways:

- Drop down the Drive/Folder menu (directly over the file list box) and select from the list. At the bottom of the list is Desktop, which you may select to save the document on your Desktop. You may also select any Desktop folder from the list. To reach the Desktop more quickly, click on the Desktop button.

- On the Desktop, you can see any disk drives to which you have access, including drives on your local network. Double-click on a drive to see its contents. In the list of folders, double-click on a folder to see its contents (folders and files). To move back up one level, use the Drive/Folder menu and select the next level up (you can move more than one level this way).

- You can also navigate using the Command key and your arrow buttons. Use Cmd+Down Arrow to move into a selected folder or drive. Use Cmd+Up Arrow to move up one level. Cmd+Left Arrow and Cmd+Right Arrow select the previous available *drive* and the next available drive (handy if you're on a network, or have multiple hard drive/removable media drives attached to your Mac).

- To create a new, empty folder in which you'll save your document, click on the New Folder button in the Save dialog. When you click on New Folder, the new folder is created within the folder that appears in the file list box.

- If you're working with a removable drive (floppy, Zip, SyQuest, etc.) and you need to put another disk in that drive, select the current disk in the drive and click on Eject. This kicks out the current disk so you can put in another, the contents of which will automatically be shown in the dialog.

- The Options button opens a dialog which allows you to set a number of preferences related to the way Word saves your files. You can also change these preferences by selecting the Save tab in the Tools|Preferences dialog.

- Cancel does just that—cancels the save operation and drops you back into Word.

When the file list box shows the name of the folder you want, click in the Save Current Document As text box, type a file name, and click on the Save button. Be sure to remember how to find the folder—you'll need to navigate to it again when you open the file for another editing session.

FYI: Extra Rules For Files That Move

If for any reason the document you're saving may be copied later to a computer running Windows or MS-DOS, don't use any punctuation or spaces in the file name, and keep the file name to eight characters or fewer (not including the three-character extension). Windows 3.1 and MS-DOS generally choke on file names longer than eight characters, and Windows 95 isn't known for being nice about translations. Furthermore, all versions of Windows burp if you use certain punctuation characters—it's better to use none at all. If you use a longer file name, you can later create a copy of the file (using Save As, as described later in this chapter) and give the copy a DOS-friendly name.

Net Savvy

If the document you're working on will be a Web page, don't click on Save. Instead, choose File|Save As HTML, and don't use spaces or punctuation in the file name. To learn more about composing Web pages in Word 98, see Chapter 17.

Saving A Document After The First Time

Once you've named and saved your document for the first time, you needn't fuss with the Save dialog again. In fact, the Save dialog appears automatically only the first time you click on the Save button (or choose File|Save) for any particular document. Any time you click on Save thereafter, Word simply saves the document, with no further input from you—after all, Word already knows the file's name and storage location. While saving the document (which usually takes only a moment or two), Word displays a message in the status line, reporting that it is saving the document.

FYI: Word Saves You From Yourself

After the first time you save a new document, Word's AutoRecover feature engages. AutoRecover automatically saves a temporary copy of all your open documents every 10 minutes. Should catastrophe strike (lightning kills the power, a kid or co-worker yanks your power plug, you unplug a live SCSI device…), don't panic. The next time you open Word, the documents that were open at the time of the catastrophe are re-created from the temporary copies made the last time AutoRecover did its thing. You'll never lose more than the last 10 minutes of your labor.

As you work, when AutoRecover does its thing, it doesn't tell you about it, except for a message that appears briefly in the status bar. Unless you happen to notice your hard disk cranking away unexpectedly, you may never notice that AutoRecover is on the job.

To change how often AutoRecover saves the document, or to shut off Auto-Recover altogether, change the AutoRecover options on the Save tab of Word's Preferences dialog (Tools|Preferences).

Copying A Document In Word

From time to time, you may want to copy a document. For example, you may need to create several different versions of the same document, or several different documents that are very similar to one another. By saving a previously saved document under a different name (or under the same name, but in a different location), you effectively create a separate copy of that document. Later, you can edit each copy independently.

To save an existing document with a new name or location, force the Save dialog to appear by choosing File|Save As. The Save dialog opens just as it did when you first saved the document—only now the save folder isn't necessarily the same. Depending on your system settings, it may be the same folder, or the last folder where the current document was saved, or the last folder where you saved a document from Word.

In the Save dialog, you can:

- Change the entry in the Save Current Document As text box to save a copy of the document, under a new name, in the same folder as the original.

- Change the folder listed in the Save dialog to save a copy of the document in a new location.

- Change both the file name and the location to save a copy under a new name in a different folder.

- Change the file type listed under Save File As Type to save in a format other than Word 98. See "Converting A Document For Use Beyond Word" later in this chapter.

Make any changes you like in the Save dialog, then click on the Save button to create the copy. (Note that, if you change nothing at all in the Save dialog and then click on the Save button and okay the replacement of your original file, you accomplish the same thing you would have if you'd just clicked on the toolbar's Save button in the first place—you save the original document, using its original name, in its original location. No copy is created. You've wasted time you could have spent learning about bad B movies from the Cinemania CD-ROM.)

FYI: *What To Watch Out For With Save As*

When you use Save As, keep two slightly tricky issues in mind:

- After you click on the Save button in the Save dialog, the dialog closes and you return to editing in Word. However, the document now open before you is not the original document—it's the copy you just created. (Look at the title bar, and you'll see the name of the copy.) Since you just created the copy, Word assumes you want to work on it instead of the original. If you want to work on the original, just open it as you learn to do later in this chapter.

- A copy you create with Save As is a completely independent document. Changes you make to it do not affect the original document, and vice versa. (If you want to link two separate documents so that changes in one affect the other, you'll learn to do so in Chapter 16.)

Walk-Through: Creating And Saving A New Document

Follow the steps below to practice saving a new Word document (if the document you created in the preceding walk-through is still open, you can skip Step 1):

1. Create a new document and type anything you want (your personal manifesto, a list of friends or enemies, a love poem).
2. Click on the Save button on the toolbar (or choose File|Save). The Save dialog opens.
3. Make sure the entry in the Save Current Document As text box is highlighted. If it isn't, press Tab once to highlight it.
4. Type the file name "Walkthrough 2". Make note of the folder in which you save this file (if you've turned on the Documents folder option in your General Controls control panel, this shouldn't be a problem).
5. Click on the Save button in the Save dialog. The file is saved.
6. Add a few words to your document.
7. Click on the Save button on the toolbar. The document is saved again, without further input from you.
8. Choose File|Save As. The Save dialog opens.
9. Click on the Desktop button.
10. Click on Save. A copy of Walkthrough 2 appears on your Desktop.

Converting A Document For Use Beyond Word

Word includes a family of *filters* that can convert a document from Word 98 format into another file format. If all you ever want to do is write in Word, edit in Word, and print from Word, you don't need to worry about filters. But suppose you need to share a document you've created in Word with a friend or colleague who uses WordPerfect, or Microsoft Works, or maybe some word processor you've never even heard of. What then? At such times, you can convert any document from Word 98 format to other file formats for which you have filters.

After conversion, the document may or may not look and behave exactly as it did in Word. If the Word document contained formatting or other features that are not also provided in the other program, those aspects of the file are lost in the conversion. For example, if you convert a document from Word 98 to Word 2.0, the document loses any characteristics based on features included in Word 98 but not in Word 2.0. Ultimately, unless the document you're converting is very simple, its appearance (but not its words) will change in the conversion, and it will probably require some cleanup editing in the other program. But you won't have to retype it or totally reformat it, and that saves a lot of work.

To convert a file, open the Word file you want to convert, then choose File|Save As to open the Save As dialog. At the bottom of the dialog, open the list for Save File As Type (see Figure 3.3).

That list shows all of the filters currently installed on your system. Choose the file format you want, change the name to distinguish the new file from the old one, and click on Save. Word makes a copy of the document and saves it in the selected format.

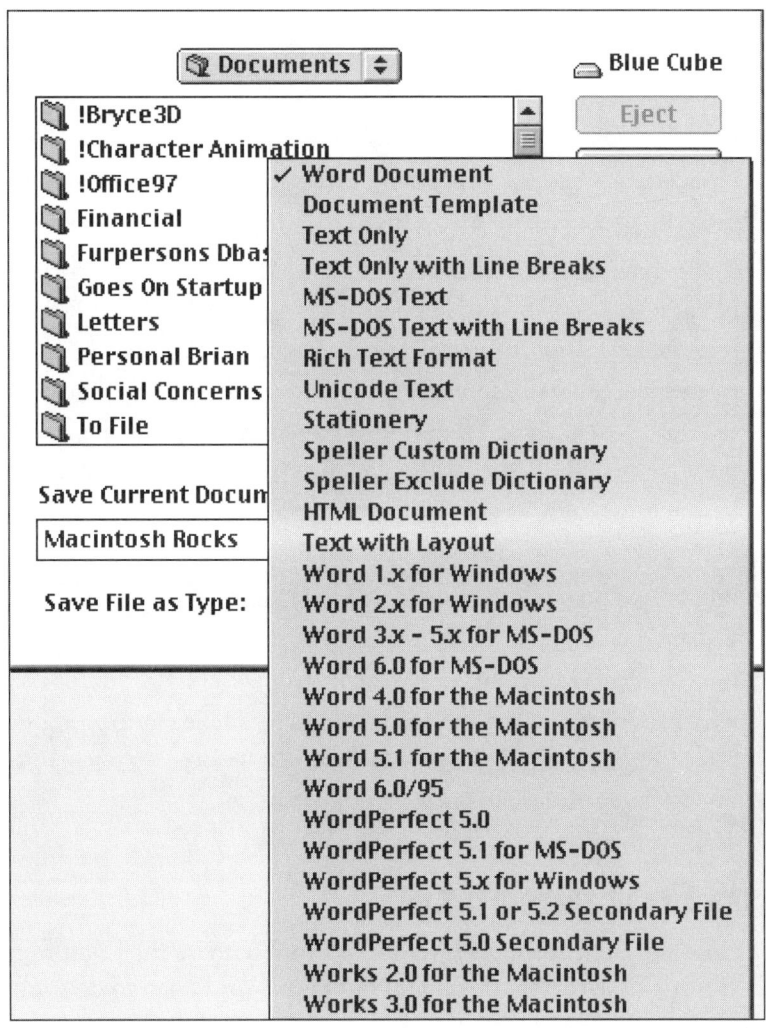

Figure 3.3 The Save File As Type list, showing the whole range of possible file formats (including those based on filters from a custom install).

FYI: Tips For Fuss-Free Conversions

Before attempting to convert a file, it's a good idea to find out the precise type of file you need to wind up with. For example, if you need a WordPerfect file, in which version of WordPerfect will the file be used?

Note that not all of the filters on the Office 98 CD are installed automatically in the drag-and-drop installation. If you don't see a filter you need on the Save File As Type list, you may be able to add it from the CD (see Appendix A).

If you can't find or add the precise filter you need, consider the following strategies:

- Check whether the program you want your file to be saved in can also convert, or *import*, documents from other sources. If so, you may choose to use that program to convert the Word file to its own format.

- Some converters in the Save File As Type list produce a file format that can be easily imported by a wide variety of programs. Rich Text Format (RTF) preserves much of the formatting in a document but makes the file easy for many other programs to import. The various other "text" converters (for example, Text Only or MS-DOS Text) remove most or all formatting, but preserve all of the text of the document—which makes the document easy to import not only by almost any word processor, but by many other types of programs, as well. The text can be reformatted, if necessary, in the other program.

- Finally, if you get really stuck, remember that almost every Mac made in the last couple of years comes equipped with MacLink Plus for file conversions. This handy little utility is able to convert a list of file types as long as your arm. Odds are, you can do what you need there. Check your system documentation for more on MacLink.

Closing Documents

You can close a document simply by quitting Word (choose File|Quit from the menu bar). To close just the current document but keep Word open to do something else, choose File|Close.

If you're finished not just with the document, but with the Mac itself (and ready for a nice sandwich), you can shut down the computer while Word (and any documents) is still open. To shut down, choose Shut Down from the Special menu. The Mac OS

FYI: *Don't Touch That Switch!*

Never switch off your Mac without first using the Shut Down routine. Not only does Shut Down help protect you against accidentally losing unsaved work, but it also performs a number of important, unseen housekeeping chores that the Mac OS needs to perform to run reliably.

automatically closes your documents, closes Word 98, and closes any other open applications or files, then shuts itself down.

No matter which method you use to close, Word always checks whether any open documents contain changes that have not been saved; if Word finds any unsaved work, it displays the prompt shown in Figure 3.4. To save the document, click on Save; to close without saving, click on Don't Save. To cancel closing the document and instead return to work on it, click on Cancel (this will even cancel the Shut Down process).

If you click on Don't Save, you lose all changes you made to the document since the last time you deliberately saved it, even if AutoRecover has saved the document in the meantime. In other words, if you last clicked on Save an hour ago, and you click on Don't Save when prompted to save before closing, you lose all changes you made in the last hour, even though AutoRecover may have done its thing five minutes ago. AutoRecover rescues you from unexpected shutdowns, not deliberate ones.

Opening Documents

If you're at all like Brian (and if so, heaven help you), you don't create most of your documents in one sitting, print them, and be done. You work awhile on a document, then shut down and watch *South Park*...again. Then you open the document on another day, rework what you've already written, add some more, then go make pizza. The document evolves across a series of writing and editing sessions until either 1) It's perfect, or 2) You run out of time. (Most of the time, it's 2.) When either 1 or 2 happens, the document is said to be "done," whatever that means.

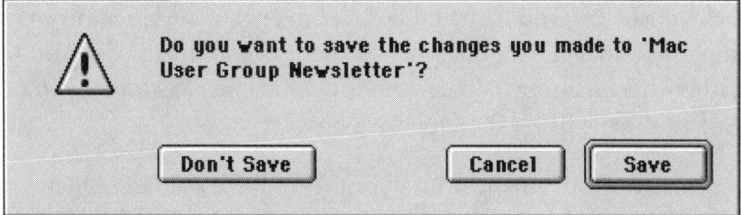

Figure 3.4 Word makes sure you don't quit without saving (unless you want to).

To work on a document through multiple editing sessions, you'll need to locate and open it—and you have a surprising number of ways to do that. Perhaps more important, you can apply some of the available opening methods to the task of importing documents that were originally created in other programs—earlier versions of Word, WordPerfect, Microsoft Works, and others.

Fast Track

Word remembers the names and locations of the last 10 documents you've edited, and lists and numbers them at the bottom of the Word 98 File menu. Number 1 is the last document you worked on; number 2 is the document you worked on before number 1, and so on. To open any of the last 10 documents you've worked on, open Word, choose File from the menu bar, then select the document you want (or press its number). The file names may have a long string of text in front of them separated by colons. This indicates the disk your file is on, followed by each folder and subfolder. The file name proper is all the way to the right. (This usually applies to files not saved in Word's native format.)

Also, you may find the last several documents you've worked on listed in your Apple menu's Recent Documents subfolder (provided you have this feature enabled). Go to the Apple menu and choose Recent Documents. If you see the document you want to edit listed there, select it. After Word opens (if it's not open already), the selected document opens.

Opening A Word Document

The easiest way to open an existing Word document is not to open Word at all, but to open the document itself. To open any document—whether it's a Word document, Excel worksheet, saved Web page, or any other file type—double-click on its file icon.

Double-clicking on a document's file icon works no matter where you find the icon: on your Desktop, in any folder, or in a Find dialog. If Word is closed when you open the document this way, Word opens automatically. If Word is already open, the Mac OS makes Word the active program. Either way, the document you opened appears in Word, ready to be edited or printed.

In some circumstances, you may find it easier to open a document from within Word. For example, you may have a document stored several folders deep on your hard drive. Rather than opening a dozen windows on your Desktop, it is much simpler to navigate to the file using the Open dialog.

To open an existing document from within Word, click on the Open button on the Standard toolbar (or choose File|Open from the menu bar). An Open dialog like the one in Figure 3.5 appears. In the dialog, use the file list box exactly as you would

Getting Started With Word 65

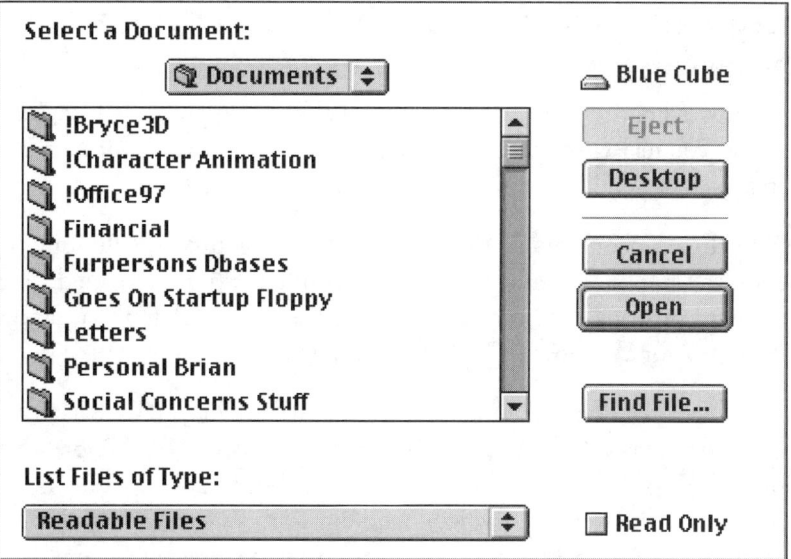

Figure 3.5 The Open dialog, where you select files to open.

use the one in the Save dialog: Click your way to any folder, or to the Desktop. The file list shows all subfolders and readable files stored in the currently selected folder.

When you have navigated to the folder containing the file you want to open, double-click on the file, or select it and then click on the Open button. Either way, the Open dialog closes, and the selected document opens in Word, ready to be edited.

Fast Track

You can open several documents at once in Word to compare documents or to copy text from one document to another. To open multiple documents, just keep opening documents without bothering to close any that are already open. To switch among your open documents, open the Window menu and select from the numbered list of open documents at the bottom. You'll learn more about working with multiple documents in Chapter 4.

FYI: Word 98 Usurps Earlier Versions

If you have an earlier version of Word still installed on your Macintosh, note that all of your Word documents—including those you created with an earlier Word version—now open automatically in Word 98, despite the availability of the older version. (See the next section, "Opening And Saving Documents From Earlier Word Versions.")

Opening And Saving Documents From Earlier Word Versions

If you're upgrading from an earlier version of Word, you probably have some documents that you revise from time to time, or use as boilerplates for new documents you create. If so, you'll be editing these documents in Word 98.

Opening these documents is no problem. Using any of the techniques described earlier (in the section "Opening A Word Document"), you can open documents from earlier Word versions, including versions 2.0 through 6.0.1 for Mac, and versions 2.0 through 7 for Windows. The file opens just like any other Word document.

When you save the document after editing it in Word 98, you have a choice to make. Word 98 documents are stored in a file format that is incompatible with all earlier versions of Word (but is cross-compatible with Word 97 for Windows). When you click on Save while working with a document from an earlier version of Word, the dialog shown in Figure 3.6 opens (or, if you have the Assistant open, the question shows up in the Assistant's balloon). If you intend to edit the document in Word 98 from now on, click on Yes. If you want to preserve the file's original file format so that you can edit it in either Word 98 or in a previous version, click on No. If you've changed your mind completely, click on Cancel.

If you click on No to preserve the file's original format, note that any changes you've made in Word 98 that require Word 98 will be lost. All text entries survive just fine—you never lose any of the text of your document when saving in an earlier Word format. But if you've applied some of Word's advanced formatting and automation features—such as engraved or shadow text effects (see Chapter 6) or animated text (see Chapter 17)—the results of your efforts may be lost in the conversion.

Fast Track

If you install Office 98 but also elect to keep an earlier version of Word on your Macintosh (instead of replacing it with Word 98), you can still edit Word 98

Figure 3.6 Word asks you to choose a format in which to save a document that was created in an earlier Word version.

documents in your previous version (say, Word 6.0.1). To do this, either save your document from Word 98 in a previous version format, or download and install Microsoft's import converter (located at **www.microsoft.com/macoffice/**). This converter will allow Word 6.0.1 to read your Word 98 documents (although it won't keep any of Word 98's bells and whistles).

Opening And Saving Documents From Other Word Processors

The filters installed in Word 98 not only enable you to convert your Word 98 documents to other formats, but also let you open documents from other programs within Word 98 and then save those documents in Word 98 format.

As a rule, you can't open a non-Word document in Word by double-clicking on its file icon. Instead, open Word, then choose File|Open to display the Open dialog (see Figure 3.5, earlier in this chapter). From the Open dialog, you locate and open a non-Word file exactly as you would open a Word file.

By default, the Open dialog is set to show all readable files in the file list. To make the Open dialog show only the type of file you want to open, go to the List Files Of Type menu (see Figure 3.7) and choose the appropriate file type from the list. If you're not certain of the exact file name extension, choose All Files from the menu. When the document you want to edit appears in the file list, double-click on it, or click on it and then the Open button.

When you attempt to save the file after editing it, you'll see a dialog similar to the one shown earlier in Figure 3.6. In that dialog, you can choose to save the file either in Word 98 format or in its original file format.

Fast Track

Want to have Office open your document from, say, ClarisWorks, without all that tedious fiddling in the Open dialog? No problem. Just open your Microsoft Office 98 folder so you can see the Word program icon (or just place an alias for the program on your Desktop). Now find the document you want to open, drag it over to the Word icon—or its alias—and hold it for a second. If the Word icon highlights, Word can probably open the file, so go ahead and drop it there—just release the mouse button. Word will try to open almost anything, even if it isn't a word processor file. If the Word icon doesn't highlight, you don't have the correct converter installed, or Word simply can't read the file. (You can still try to force the issue by selecting All Files in the Open dialog—sometimes that will at least get you enough text to work with.) You should also try using MacLink Plus. For more on that, see the sidebar "Tips for Fuss-Free Conversions" earlier in this chapter.

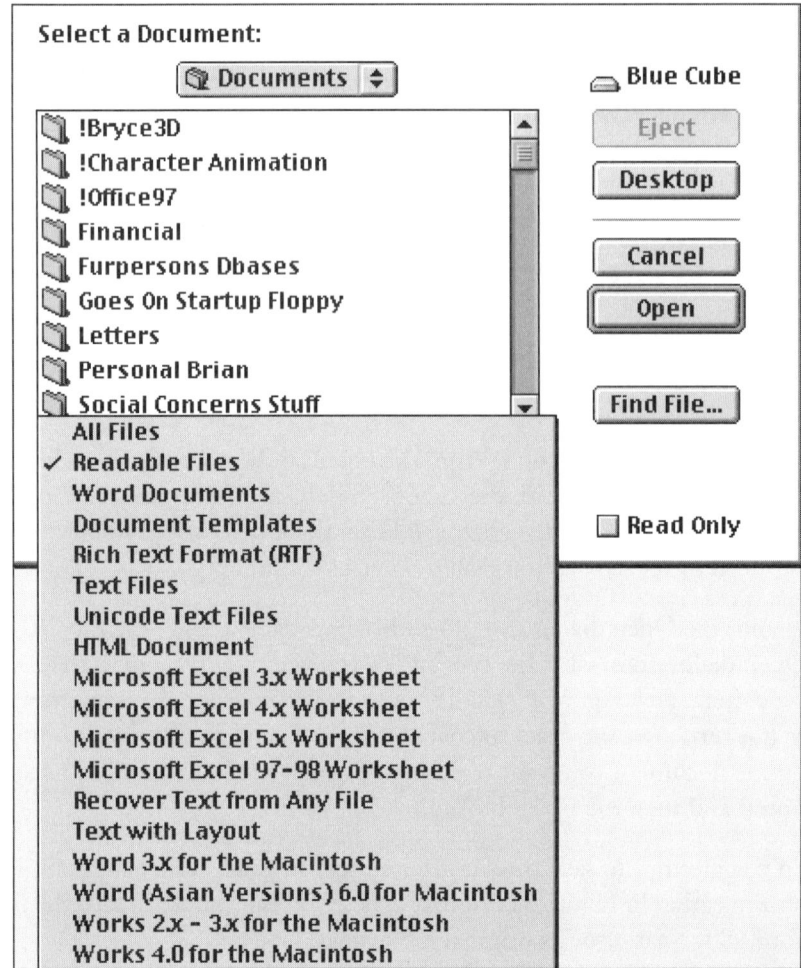

Figure 3.7 The Open dialog's List Files Of Type menu, where you choose the type of file you want to open.

Controlling Word's Display

In Chapter 1, you learned that Word is a WYSIWYG (What You See Is What You Get) word processor, one that shows your document on screen exactly as it will appear when printed. While that's valuable, it's not always efficient. By making a few simple selections, you can ask Word to sacrifice perfect WYSIWYG to make your editing work easier.

Keep in mind that none of the display-control options that follow have any actual effect on your document or the way it will look when printed. These options simply change the way Word represents that document on screen, to help you work more efficiently. Since changing your display options can't hurt your document, feel free to experiment with them. Try out different combinations of views, zooms, and so on—it's good practice.

Choosing A View

The *view* describes the extent to which you want Word's display to mimic the final, intended result of your document. You can choose among several different views; each is appropriate for a different kind of editing session. Choose a view by selecting an option from the View menu or by clicking on one of the view buttons (see Figure 3.8) at the bottom of the Word document window, immediately to the left of the horizontal scroll bar.

By default, most of the time you work in Word, you work in Normal view. In Normal view, the text of your pages appears as you intend it to, including all text and paragraph formatting and the correct margins (see Chapters 4 and 5). However, if you've added headers or footers to the document, they appear only on the first page, not on every page, as they would in print. Page breaks in Normal view are represented by simple dotted lines between pages. Also, if you've formatted newspaper-style columns (see Chapter 5) in your document, each column appears in its proper width in Normal view, but the columns don't appear side by side as they will when printed.

The Page Layout view, on the other hand, attempts to represent your document on screen exactly as it will appear when printed, including headers and footers (in gray), pictures, and actual page breaks that make each page appear to be a piece of paper on your screen (see Figure 3.9).

Because it does not visually break pages or fill space with repeated headers and footers, Normal view is the most convenient view to work in during the text entry and editing phase of document creation. You'll find that getting around in your document, particularly scrolling from page to page, is quicker and easier in Normal view. Depending on the speed of your hardware, you may also notice that Word performs most quickly when in Normal view. As you near completion of your document (and shift your focus from content to appearance), switch to Page Layout view to fine-tune the document's printed appearance.

Figure 3.8   Buttons for changing the view, found to the left of the scroll bar at the bottom of Word's document window.

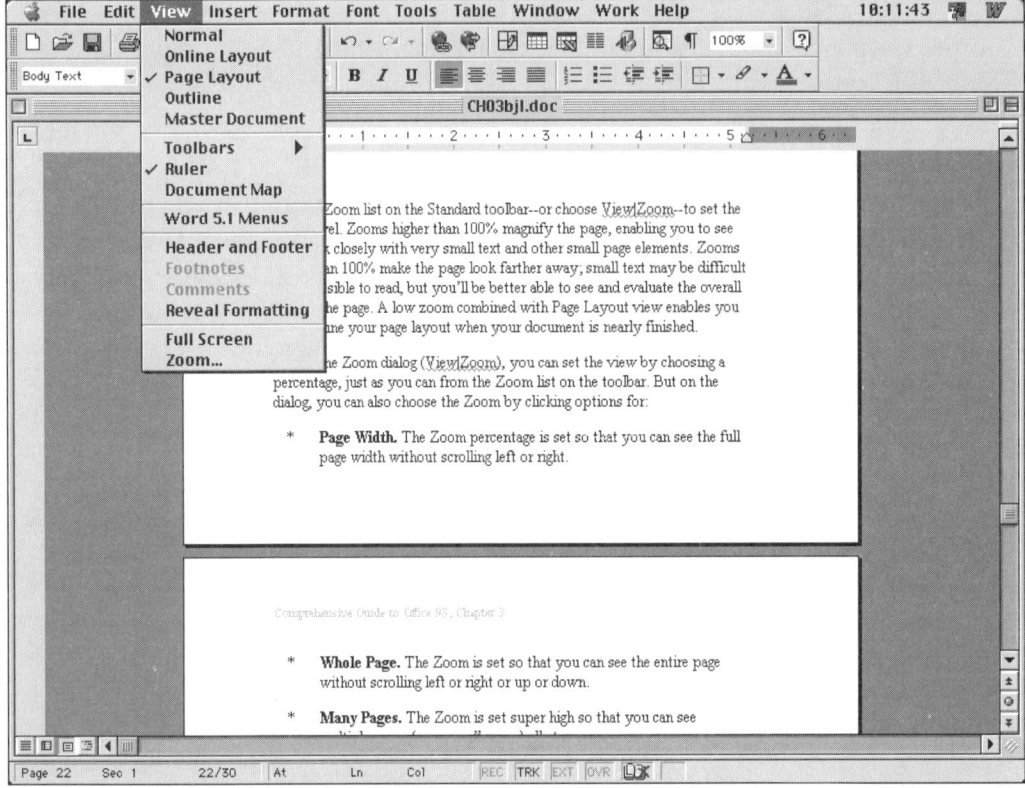

Figure 3.9 Word in Page Layout view, showing page breaks and headers.

In addition to Normal view and Page Layout view, you have four more view options:

- *Online Layout (View|Online Layout)*—This view is optimized for sharing the editing of the document across a network (see Chapters 16 and 17).

- *Outline (View|Outline)*—This view organizes your document in outline form, to help you evaluate and fine-tune the structure of a long, complex document (see Chapter 7). (You must be in Page Layout view to use this setting.)

- *Master Document (View|Master Document)*—This view shows you the *master document* for the multifile document on which you're working. A master document is a special document used to pull together several separate files into a cohesive single document. (You must be in Page Layout view to use this setting).

Fast Track

When you're evaluating your document's appearance, instead of using Page Layout view, you can display the Print Preview. Choose File|Print Preview to display your document in Print Preview.

In Print Preview, Word shows an entire page—or two pages at a time—so you can accurately predict how the page will appear when printed. However, although you can edit your document in Print Preview, doing so is a little tricky and cumbersome.

Fine-Tuning Word's Display

Three other adjustments to Word's display can help you deal with a variety of tricky circumstances: Zoom, Show/Hide, and Full Screen.

Zoom

Use the Zoom list on the Standard toolbar—or choose View|Zoom—to set the zoom level. Zooms higher than 100 percent magnify the page, enabling you to see and work closely with very small text and other small page elements. Zooms lower than 100 percent make the page look farther away; small text may be difficult or impossible to read, but you'll be better able to see and evaluate the overall look of the page. A low zoom combined with Page Layout view enables you to fine-tune your page layout when your document is nearly finished.

On the Zoom dialog (View|Zoom), you can set the view by choosing a percentage, just as you can from the Zoom list on the toolbar. But on the dialog, you can also choose the Zoom by clicking on options for:

- *Page Width*—The Zoom percentage is set so that you can see the full page width without scrolling left or right.

- *Whole Page*—The Zoom is set so that you can see the entire page without scrolling left or right or up or down.

- *Many Pages*—The Zoom is set super high so that you can see multiple pages (very *small* pages) all at once.

Show/Hide

Click on the Show/Hide button on the Standard toolbar to display all of the *nonprinting characters* in your document (see Figure 3.10). Nonprinting characters are characters you type that are invisible (until you click on Show/Hide), but they still affect the text around them—for example, spaces, tabs (see Chapter 5), and paragraph breaks (what you type when you press Return).

Show/Hide is useful when you're having formatting troubles that you think may be related to the placement of nonprinting characters. For example, showing the nonprinting characters can reveal whether you've used two spaces or one after a period, or whether you've pressed Tab twice in a place where only one tab character was called for. When you've solved your problem, just click on Show/Hide again to hide the nonprinting characters.

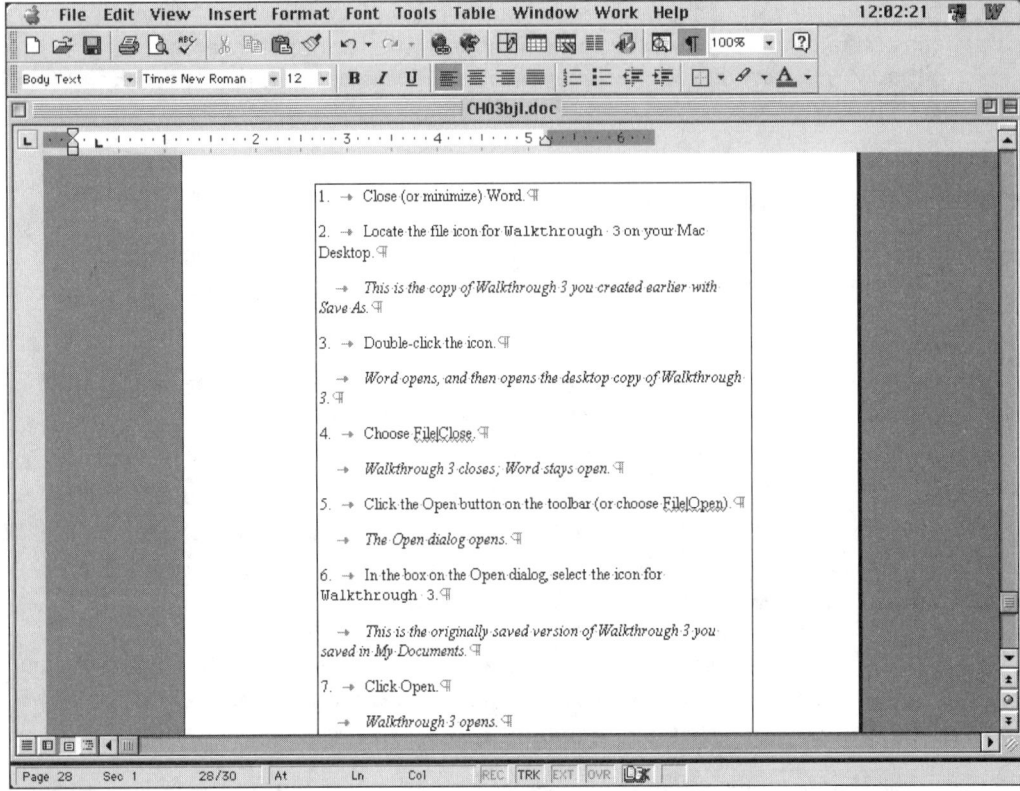

Figure 3.10 Nonprinting characters—paragraph breaks and spaces—appear when you click on Show/Hide.

Note that, like the other display-control options (views, Zoom, Print Preview), Show/Hide has no effect on the printed appearance of your document. Even if you print the document while Word is displaying the nonprinting characters, the nonprinting characters don't show up on paper.

Full Screen

Choose View|Full Screen to enter Word's Full Screen mode, which allows your document to fill up virtually the whole display by hiding almost everything but your document. Word's menu bar, status bar, scroll bars, and toolbars all vanish so that your document can fill up your screen completely. You may find Full Screen mode valuable if you have a small display (as on a PowerBook) or if you find the clutter of Word's tools distracting.

If you edit in Full Screen mode, use shortcut keys instead of toolbars—for example, you can save the document by pressing Cmd+S—or just use the menus. To get around without scroll bars, use your arrow keys or PgUp and PgDn.

The only thing you see in Full Screen mode besides your document is a small dialog with a single button: Close Full Screen. To exit Full Screen mode and restore all of Word's paraphernalia, click on the button, or press Esc.

Jumping From Page To Page

In Chapter 2, you discovered the principal ways you can get around in an Office document: scroll bars, PgUp, and PgDn. And most of the time you work in Word, you'll use those same methods to move from page to page, while using your mouse or arrow keys to relocate the edit cursor within a page.

When you're working in a long document, however, and you need to get from page 3 to, oh, page 129, you'll get there pretty slowly by scrolling or pressing PgDn. When you need to jump directly to a specific spot anywhere in your document, rely on the Go To tab of the Find And Replace dialog. (Note that you'll learn about the other tabs of this dialog in Chapter 7.)

FYI: *Where Am I?*

If you're just getting started, you're probably not thinking too much about how many pages make up your document. But as your skills develop and your documents become more complex, you'll need to know how many pages are in your document, and on what page you are.

When Word's status bar isn't busy telling you something else (like letting you know AutoRecover has engaged), it reports the precise location of the edit cursor to let you know where you are within your document. In the leftmost box of the status bar, Word reports (from left to right):

- The page number.
- The section number (see Chapter 5).
- The number of the current page within the total number of pages. For example, if the status bar reports 26/42, the current page is number 26 out of a total of 42 pages in the document.

To go straight to the Go To tab (see Figure 3.11), choose Edit|Go To or press Cmd+G. By default, the choice in the Go To What list is Page, so you can simply type a page number in the Enter Page Number box. When you type the page number, the Next button changes to a Go To button. When you click on the Go To button, your desired page appears in the document window, with the edit cursor positioned at the top of the page. If you're certain that's the page you want, close

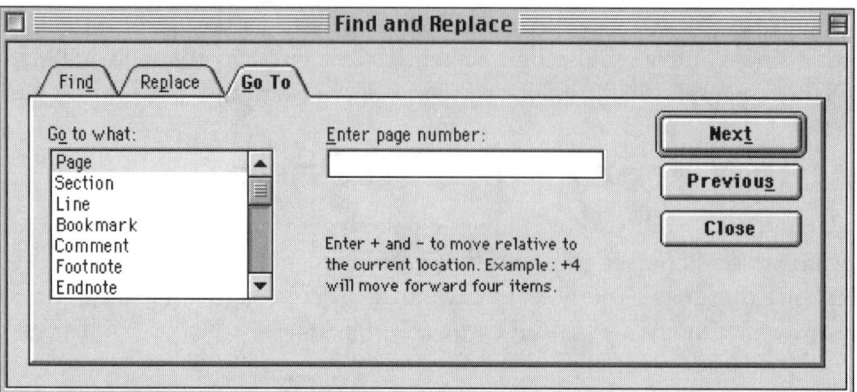

Figure 3.11 The Go To tab of the Find And Replace dialog.

the Find And Replace dialog and resume working. Otherwise, try another page number—the dialog remains open until you close it.

Fast Track

As Figure 3.11 shows, you can also use the Go To dialog to jump to a particular part of your document by choosing Section, Comment, or another choice in Go To What. After making your choice, use the text box to the right to enter whatever identifying information Word requests: section number, the text of the comment, and so on. (Don't worry if you don't yet know what all the choices in the Go To What list mean; you'll learn about most of them in upcoming chapters.)

Perhaps the most useful choice is Bookmark. By choosing Insert|Bookmark, you can create an invisible Bookmark anywhere in your document to mark a specific spot; for example, you might leave a bookmark where you quit the day's editing session. When you begin the next editing session, you can use the Go To tab to jump directly to the Bookmark and pick up right where you left off.

Printing Your Document

Like so many other things about Word, printing is as easy or as hard as you choose to make it.

Here's the easy method: To print all pages of the current document on your default printer, make sure the printer is switched on and loaded with paper, then click on the Print button on Word's toolbar. When the Print dialog appears, hit Print. That's it. Generally, the Print dialog's default settings work just fine, and no further input from you is required (provided you have your printer correctly selected in the Chooser).

So why do more? Word's Print dialog allows you to control how your document prints. For example, you can choose to print only selected pages of the document rather than the whole thing. And if your Mac is connected to more than one printer (as it might be if you use a local network), you can select which printer to use.

In the Print dialog (see Figure 3.12), you can choose a printer from the printer list, enter a range of pages to print, and more (depending on your printer). Most of what you can do on the Print dialog comes into play only when you're working on a long or complex document.

WYSMNBWYG (What You See May Not Be What You Get)

Theoretically, the printout of your document should be identical in every way to the on-screen version. But when you print, check your printouts very carefully, and prepare to discover some variation between the two versions—in fact, the pages may not even break at the same points they do on screen. (As a rule, the better your printer, the more accurate its results.)

This isn't really Word's fault, or the Mac's; rather, it's the result of your particular printer's inability to accurately print what the Mac tells it to. The variations are rarely serious, and you can usually fix their effects by making minor adjustments in your document. Also, the more elaborately you format your document, the greater the likelihood of variation between on-screen and printout versions. Throughout this book, we'll let you know which techniques are known to baffle

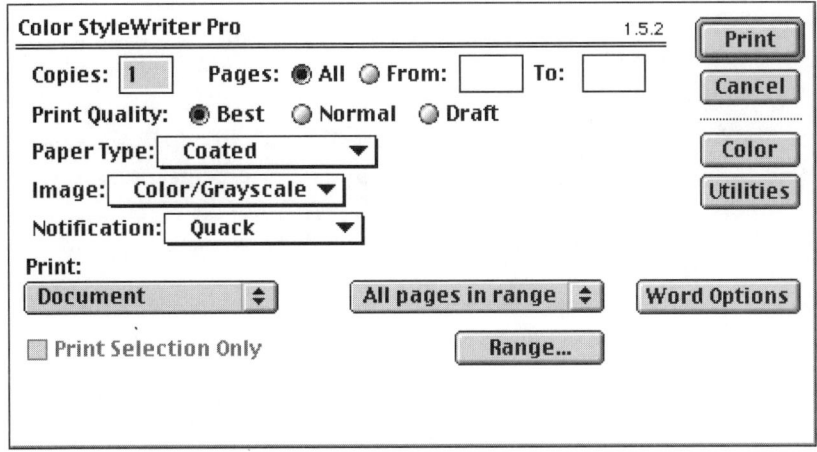

Figure 3.12 The Print dialog setup for Brian's default printer, an Apple Color StyleWriter Pro.

some printers. But there's really no way you can predict the outcome; through experience with your printer, you'll learn what it does well, and what it goofs up.

Also, keep in mind that different printers produce different results. Among reasonably new laser or ink jet printers, the variation is likely to be slight. But if you print your draft copies on one printer and then intend to print a final copy on another printer, be sure to check the final copy carefully and edit the document as necessary to adjust for any surprises.

Fast Track

If you have a fax modem attached to your Mac and configured correctly, you can use the Print dialog to fax the document to someone instead of printing it. Where the Mac is concerned, most fax modems behave as if they're printers. To fax a document instead of printing it, choose the fax modem from the Print dialog as if it were a printer. (Make sure your fax software is set up correctly first, though—you may have to make some adjustments in the Chooser.)

Walk-Through: Opening And Printing Documents

Follow the steps below to practice opening and printing a Word document.

1. Close (or hide) Word.
2. Locate the file icon for Walkthrough 2 on your Desktop. This is the copy of Walkthrough 2 you created earlier with Save As.
3. Double-click on the icon. Word opens, and then opens the Desktop copy of Walkthrough 2.
4. Choose File|Close. Walkthrough 2 closes; Word stays open.
5. Click on the Open button on the toolbar (or choose File|Open). The Open dialog opens.
6. In the Open dialog, select Walkthrough 2. This should be the version of Walkthrough 2 you originally saved in the Documents folder (if you saved it in a different folder, be sure Word is pointed to the correct location).
7. Click on Open. Walkthrough 2 opens.
8. Choose File|Close. Walkthrough 2 closes; Word stays open.
9. Click on the Open button on the toolbar (or choose File|Open). The Open dialog opens.
10. Drop down the Disk/Folder list, and choose Desktop. The box in the Open dialog shows all of the available documents on your Desktop.

11. Double-click on Walkthrough 2. The Desktop copy of Walkthrough 2 opens in Word.
12. Add a few words to Walkthrough 2.
13. Click on the Print button on the toolbar, then click on the Print button in the dialog to print Walkthrough 2.
14. Choose File|Quit. Word asks if you want to save Walkthrough 2 before exiting.
15. Click on Yes. Word saves the Desktop copy of Walkthrough 2, then closes.

Moving On

In one short chapter, you've become a fully functioning Word 98 user. You can create documents, enter paragraphs, save your work, and print it. In the grand scheme of things, there's not much else to it.

You discovered a number of other powerful techniques here—Save As, for example—but you probably won't use those techniques often. If you can create a new document, type in it, save it, and print it, you're already on the downslope of the learning curve.

What's left? Well, in this chapter you discovered the absolute basics of entering text into your new document. In Chapter 4, you'll learn not only how to edit that text in a variety of powerful ways, but also how to *format* that text and change its appearance and style. After you discover how to format text in Chapter 4, you'll move on to formatting the overall look of your pages in Chapter 5.

Working With Text

Some people in this world (those extreme right-brain types) want to fiddle with the layout and design of a document before supplying its content. In fact, Word does offer you ways to define how your document will look before you type a word of it—you'll learn how in Chapter 7. But for practical reasons, it makes more sense to first learn how to enter and edit the text of your document, then to deal with how your document will look. (If you think we're being too linear, well…Ned's wife agrees with you. That's what a liberal arts education does to you.)

In this chapter, you'll build on the skills from Chapter 3 by getting deeper into text entry and editing. You'll discover such essential editing skills as selecting text and undoing mistakes, plus time-savers like copying text. In the second half of this chapter, you'll begin a transition from left brain to right—from content to style—by learning how to *format* text (change its appearance and personality). That done, you'll be prepared to format the overall look of your pages—full right-brain stuff—in Chapter 5. (Man…Ned's wife is right.)

In the first half of this chapter, you'll discover still more stuff you can do with Word's Standard toolbar, which you first met in Chapter 3. In the second half, you'll begin working with Word's Formatting toolbar. Before beginning, it's a good idea to make sure both toolbars are on your screen and ready to go (see Figure 4.1). If you don't see one or both of these toolbars, point to any spot on any toolbar and Control-click (or choose View|Toolbars), then click on Formatting or Standard. To display the name of any button on either toolbar, rest the pointer on the button for a moment.

Choosing Text To Work With

Many of the activities in this chapter require *selecting text*—highlighting one or more characters so that the next action you perform affects the entire group of highlighted characters, known as a *text block*.

The simplest and most natural way to select text is to use your mouse. Point to the very beginning of the block you want to select, and click and hold the mouse button. Drag the mouse to the right (to select only part of a line) or down (to select multiple

Figure 4.1 Word's Standard (top) and Formatting (bottom) toolbars, which contain buttons for many of the activities in this chapter.

lines). As you drag, you highlight all text in the pointer's path (see Figure 4.2). When you reach the end of the block you wish to highlight, release the mouse button. The block remains highlighted, ready to accept whatever action you choose to perform on it.

If, after you've selected a block, you decide that you do not want to make any changes to that block, you can *deselect* it (remove the highlight) simply by clicking your mouse button once anywhere on the page or by pressing any of the arrow keys.

Besides dragging your mouse, you can select text in a variety of other ways, including:

- To select a word, double-click on the word.

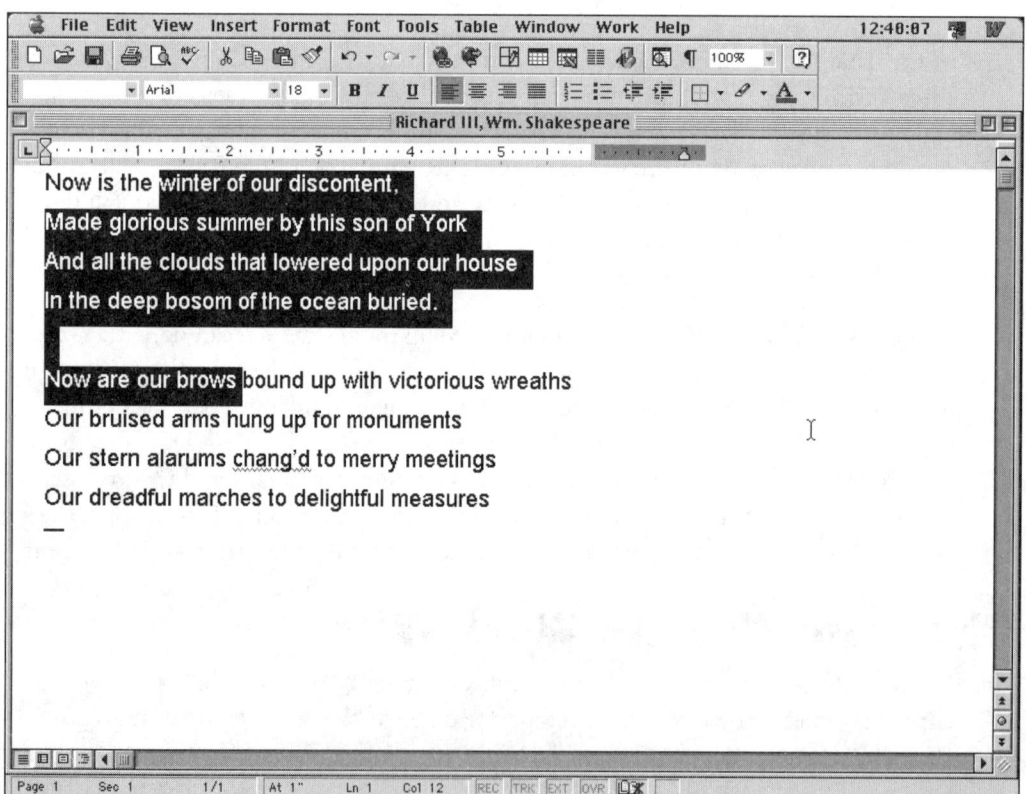

Figure 4.2 Selected text.

- To select a whole line, triple-click on the line. (To triple-click, click your mouse button three times quickly. Repeating "There's no place like home" is optional.)

- To select a whole paragraph, quadruple-click on the paragraph.

- To select an entire document, choose Edit|Select All.

- To select a sentence, press and hold the Command key, then click on the sentence.

- To highlight a selection that begins at the position of the edit cursor and ends wherever you release the arrow key, press and hold the Shift key, then press and hold an arrow key. Shift + Right arrow selects to the right, Shift + Down arrow selects multiple lines down, and so on. (This selection method is convenient if you prefer not to use a mouse.)

FYI: *Make Your Next Move Carefully*

Once a block is highlighted, do not press any key or click on anything with the mouse except to perform the specific action you want to perform on that block. For example, if you type anything—even a single character—while a block is highlighted, the entire block is instantly deleted and replaced by what you type. That's actually a handy editing feature, as you'll learn later in this chapter. Still, you don't want a careless keystroke to wipe out a block of text that you intended merely to format, not replace.

If you accidentally replace or delete a highlighted block—or do anything else to a selected block that isn't what you intended—you can restore the block to its previous state by clicking on the Undo button immediately after deleting (as described in the next section).

Changing Your Mind After Changing Text

The principle behind the Undo button is rather simple: When you click on Undo, the very last thing you did is undone, as if it had never happened. You'll find Undo (and its partner Redo) on the Standard toolbar.

Fast Track

If you're in a hurry, you can undo by pressing Cmd+Z.

If you click on Undo immediately after performing some action to a selected block of text, that block immediately returns to its exact state before you performed the action, and also remains selected, to make performing the desired action simple. For example, if you press Delete, you delete the selected block. If you then choose Undo, the selected block is restored and highlighted—ready for the correct action.

Predicting what Undo will do is pretty simple when what you're undoing is a deletion (the deletion is restored) or any action to a selected text block (the text reverts to the way it was before the last action). But Undo is a little trickier when it comes to typing.

When you click on Undo after typing something, undo deletes everything you've typed since the last time you did something besides typing. In other words, if you type three paragraphs in a row without stopping to format something or perform some other nontyping activity, clicking on Undo deletes all three paragraphs—it undoes the last uninterrupted typing session. If you type three paragraphs, then go back to fix a mistake, *then* type one more sentence, Undo deletes only that last sentence.

In those really confused moments, you may undo something and then decide that you liked it better before you undid it. For those occasions, the Redo button is available. Redo reverses the action of Undo—restoring, essentially, the changes that you thought were mistakes when you clicked on Undo. Note that Redo does nothing unless you've already used Undo—without an undo, there can't be a redo.

Fast Track

Sometimes you don't discover a mistake until you've already performed several other actions following your goof. For such times, Word offers the Undo list, which you display by clicking on the down arrow on the Undo button.

The Undo list catalogs the last several actions you performed. If the mistake happens to appear among those actions, select it on the list. Word undoes the error—*and* everything you have done since making that mistake. In effect, the Undo list is a time machine that takes your document back to the time just before your last screw-up. (Instead of using the Undo list, you can achieve the same effect by clicking on Undo several times in a row. Each click moves you back one level in the Undo list.)

If you value the work you did between making the mistake and discovering the mistake, you might not want to use the Undo list. Instead, simply do whatever is necessary to repair the error. That way, you don't also undo later actions you want to keep.

Walk-Through: Select And Undo

Follow these steps to practice selecting text, typing to replace a selection, and undoing an error:

1. Open or create any document containing text. (Walkthrough 2—which you created in Chapter 3—will do fine, but you can use any document you don't mind fooling around with.)
2. Point to the very beginning of a paragraph.
3. Click and hold your mouse button, drag to the end of the paragraph, and release. The paragraph is selected.
4. Click anywhere in the document window. The highlight disappears. The paragraph is deselected.
5. Select the paragraph again.
6. Type "This text replaces the selection." The selected paragraph is replaced by your typing.
7. Click on Undo. The original highlighted paragraph is restored.
8. Click anywhere in the document window. The highlight disappears.

Editing Text

As you learned in Chapter 3, you can easily edit your text as you go along by using the Delete and Del keys:

- Pressing Delete once deletes one character to the left of the edit cursor.
- Pressing Del once deletes one character to the right of the edit cursor.
- Pressing and holding either key deletes multiple characters until you release the key.

After removing a mistake, you can simply type a correction. But while this technique is effective for fixing typooos (uh, typos), it's not an efficient way to make major changes, such as rearranging paragraphs, making careful insertions within a sentence or paragraph, or making big cuts. In the next few pages, you'll discover Word's powerful editing tools.

Fast Track

Every document you create will require some manual editing using the techniques described in this chapter. However, Word also includes a family of automated editing tools that can fix your spelling and grammar, apply consistent formatting, and do much more to make editing more accurate and less time-consuming.

You'll discover automated editing in Chapter 7—but don't jump there yet. Word can do a lot automatically, but it can't do everything. To edit in Word effectively—and to properly apply the automatic tools you'll discover later—you need to understand the basics of manual editing.

Inserting And Overwriting Text

When you type, you can type in either of two modes:

- *Insert mode*—Your typing pushes the text out of the way, so that no existing text is overwritten.

- *Overtype mode*—Your typing *overtypes*—replaces—any text ahead of it as you go along, just as if you had "typed over" what was there.

The Insert mode (which is the default mode) allows you to move the edit cursor to a typo, delete the typo, and type a correction. To switch to Overtype mode, you must locate the OVR indicator in the status bar (see Figure 4.3).

In the right portion of the bar, a bank of four three-letter abbreviations appears: REC, TRK, EXT, OVR. When you're in Insert mode, the OVR indicator is grayed out. To switch from Insert to Overtype mode, double-click on the OVR indicator. It changes from gray to black to indicate that you're in Overtype mode. To return to Insert mode (and return the OVR indicator to gray), double-click on the OVR indicator again.

Copying, Moving, And Cutting Text

Word enables you to delete ("cut"), copy, and move the text contained in any selection very easily, using the Mac's clipboard. Note that Undo can reverse any cut, copy, or move operation you perform.

No matter whether you want to cut, copy, or move, always begin by selecting the text with which you want to work. With the text selected, you can:

- *Copy the selection*—Click on the Copy button on the Standard toolbar, move the edit cursor to the spot where you want the copy to appear, then click on the Paste button on the Standard toolbar. To insert another copy, position the cursor and

| Page 6 | Sec 1 | 6/25 | At 4.8" | Ln 15 | Col 3 | REC | TRK | EXT | OVR | |

Figure 4.3 A black OVR in the status bar indicates Overtype mode.

Working With Text 85

click on Paste again. You may insert as many copies as you want, at any time, until the next time you use Copy or Cut.

- *Move the selection*—Click on the Cut button on the Standard toolbar (the selection disappears, as if it had been deleted), move the edit cursor to the spot where you want the text moved, then click on the Paste button on the Standard toolbar. After moving, you may insert another copy of the moved text by positioning the cursor and clicking on Paste. You may insert as many copies as you want, at any time, until the next time you use Copy or Cut.

- *Remove the selection*—Click on the Cut button on the Standard toolbar. The selection disappears. (Note that pressing the Delete key has the same effect, and like Cut, Delete can be reversed by Undo. However, you may use Delete in place of Cut *only* when you intend to delete the selection, not move it. If you plan to move the selection, you must use Cut, not Delete.)

Fast Track

The actions of the Copy, Paste, and Cut buttons can all be duplicated with menus or keystrokes. You can copy with Edit|Copy or Cmd+C, paste with Edit|Paste or Cmd+V, and cut with Edit|Cut or Cmd+X.

FYI: Paste Always Inserts, Never Overtypes (Except…)

When you use Paste in a move or copy operation, the text is always inserted at the edit cursor position—it doesn't overwrite nearby text, even if you are in Overtype mode.

However, if you select something immediately before pasting, the text you paste replaces the selection.

Moving Or Copying Text Among Documents

By opening multiple Word documents in the same session, you may copy or move text from one document to another. The steps are exactly the same as the copy and move steps you just learned, except that after clicking on Copy (for copying) or Cut (for moving), you must switch to the document into which you want to paste.

For example, suppose you want to copy a paragraph from a Final Notice to a Pay Up Now letter. First, select the paragraph in Final Notice and click on Copy. Then switch to Pay Up Now, position the edit cursor at the desired spot in Pay Up Now, and click on Paste. *Voila.*

Fast Track

You can make copies quickly and neatly without ever using the Copy or Cut commands. Open both documents so you can see them on screen. Next, in the document you are copying *from*, select the text to be copied. Click and *hold* in your selection, and drag it to the other document's window. After a second, a small cursor will appear, indicating the spot where the dragged selection will be dropped. When you get to the right spot, release the mouse button. That's a drag-and-drop copy operation. (This trick also works for moving text within a single document.)

The only tricky part is deciding how you intend to switch among documents. If you plan to make only a single copy or move between two documents, you may find it simplest to close the first document after clicking on Copy or Cut, then open the second for the Paste. However, if you plan to move back and forth several times to make multiple cuts or copies, or if you need to copy or move text among three, four, or more documents, you'll find it more convenient to keep all documents open until you're finished.

Begin by opening the first document. Without closing the first, open the second—it takes over the document window, appearing to have closed the first document. But in fact, the first document remains open. Continue opening documents until you've opened all the files you need.

To switch among your open documents, open the Window menu (see Figure 4.4). All open documents are listed there, in alphabetical order. To switch to any document, choose it from the menu. When you finish with a document, close it—the others remain open until you close them.

Fast Track

If you want to insert the entire contents of a document—formatting and all—into another document, you needn't fiddle with opening multiple documents and

```
Window
  New Window
  Arrange All
  Split
  Show Clipboard
✓ 1 Brian's Paragon O' Pez
  2 CH04bjl.DOC
  3 master list.rtf
  4 Richard III, Wm. Shakespeare
  5 Vet Survey
```

Figure 4.4 The Window menu, from which you may switch among open documents.

making a copy or move. Instead, open the document into which you want the other document's contents inserted and position the edit cursor at the spot where you want the inserted file's contents to appear.

Choose Insert|File to open the Insert File dialog, which, except for the name, is identical to the Open dialog. Using the same techniques available in the Open dialog (see Chapter 3), navigate to the file whose contents you wish to copy, select it, and click on OK.

Changing Capitalization

Ideally, you'll type uppercase (capital) letters when you want uppercase letters, and lowercase when you want lowercase. But if later you must make broad, generalized changes to the ways you've capitalized certain words, doing so manually can be a pain.

For example, suppose you had used ALL CAPS for the headings in your document and then decided to use initial caps (uppercase only on the first letter of each word, as in the heading for this section). You could retype all of your headings. But Word offers a much more convenient option: the Change Case dialog (see Figure 4.5).

To use the Change Case dialog, select the text whose case you want to modify, then choose Format|Change Case. Choose the radio button next to the style of capitalization you want. The choices are:

- *Sentence case*—Word capitalizes the first letter of the first word of all sentences in the selection.

- *lowercase*—Word makes all letter characters in the selection lowercase.

- *UPPERCASE*—Word makes all letter characters in the selection uppercase.

- *Title Case*—Word capitalizes the first letter of each word in the selection, as in a title or heading. Note that Title Case does its thing to every word in the selection, including articles (a, the) prepositions (of, by) and other short words that are often left all lowercase in titles and headings, except when they're the first word.

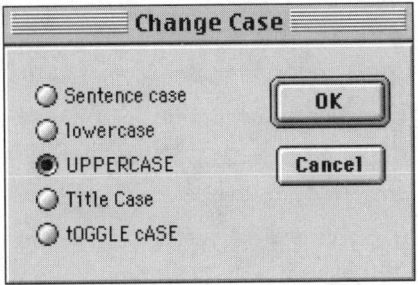

Figure 4.5 The Change Case dialog.

- *tOGGLE cASE*—Word automatically reverses the case of each letter in the selection. GORILLA becomes gorilla, lake becomes LAKE, Bob becomes bOB, NaCl (sodium chloride) becomes nAcL (nothin').

Observe two important points about Change Case:

- Each of the choices on the Change Case dialog is capitalized in a way that represents its effect.
- Change Case affects letter characters only—numbers and punctuation are unaffected.

Had you already guessed these?

Walk-Through: Insert, Overtype, Copy, Move

Follow these steps to practice inserting, overtyping, copying, and moving blocks of text in Word:

1. Open or create any document containing text. (Walkthrough 2—which you created in Chapter 3—will do fine.)
2. Position the edit cursor in the middle of a sentence.
3. Type a few words. The words are inserted within the sentence, without overtyping any existing text.
4. Select the words you just typed.
5. Click on the Cut button on the Standard toolbar. The selection vanishes.
6. Position the edit cursor at the very end of the document.
7. Click on the Paste button on the Standard toolbar. The cut selection appears at the bottom of the document. You have moved the selection.
8. Select any paragraph.
9. Click on the Copy button on the Standard toolbar.
10. Position the edit cursor at the very top of the document.
11. Click on the Paste button on the Standard toolbar. A copy of the selected paragraph appears at the top of the document.
12. Click on Paste twice more. Two more copies of that paragraph appear.
13. Position the edit cursor in the middle of any sentence.
14. Double-click on the OVR indicator in the status bar. The OVR indicator in the status bar turns from gray to black, signifying that you're in Overtype mode.
15. Type a few words. Your words replace existing text as you type them.
16. Double-click on the OVR indicator in the status bar. The OVR indicator in the status bar turns gray, signifying that you've returned to Insert mode.

Counting Words

You know that by printing your document or by checking the status bar, you can learn at any time how many pages you've created. But for many school, office, and professional projects, you need to know the number of words in your document. ("Class, for Monday please write a 500-word essay. Topic: Yeast: the Brewer's Friend.")

To find out how many words your whole document contains, make sure nothing is selected, then choose Tools|Word Count. A dialog like the one in Figure 4.6 appears, reporting not only the number of words, but also pages, characters, and other statistics.

To find out how many words a particular portion of your document contains, select that portion before choosing Tools|Word Count.

Tracking Changes

Let's say you just spent three days writing a document for work, and your boss asks to see it. After you provide your boss with the Word file, he or she then makes a few "minor" changes and returns it. Unless you have a really good memory or you have the time to compare this new, changed document with your original, you won't even know what was changed, right? Wrong! Word provides an excellent tool that allows you to make revisions plainly visible, so that another reader can see exactly what is new—what has been added, deleted, moved, and so on. Tools|Track Changes|Highlight Changes opens the Highlight Changes dialog box, in which you are presented with several choices:

- *Track Changes While Editing*—This feature makes any changes stand out from normal text. On the screen the changes appear in color—red, blue, green, even pink. (If you have a preference, the Options button allows you to choose the color.)

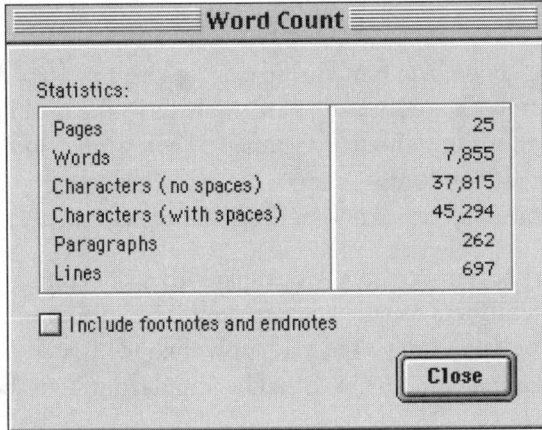

Figure 4.6 The Word Count dialog, showing statistics for the current document or selection.

Any new information will appear with an underscore, and any deleted material will appear with a strikethrough. If several users make changes, each person's color is unique. So you can tell if John from Accounting deleted that important financial information, or whether it was Mary from Legal. If this box was left unchecked when revisions were being made, you're out of luck. You won't be able to tell by looking at the document on screen or in print what changes have been made, or by whom. If you're going to share a document with people who have a penchant for making changes, be sure to leave this box checked before giving it to them so that you can see exactly what they do. (As an aside: If you have Track Changes While Editing enabled, you can only work in Insert mode—Overtype is disabled.)

- *Highlight Changes On Screen*—This feature, when checked, makes any changes that are made to a document appear on screen. If unchecked, the revisions that someone has made in a previous session will appear as normal text, rather than colored and underscored. Deletions will not appear at all.

- *Highlight Changes In Printed Document*—This feature, when checked, allows these revisions to appear when you print the document. If unchecked, revisions will appear as normal text, rather than colored and underscored; like Highlight changes on screen, deletions will not appear in the printed document.

Formatting Text

A *font*, as you probably already know, is a particular typeface, the general style in which your words appear both on screen and when printed. Every font has a name, such as Arial, Courier, or Fajita (see Figure 4.7). The font determines the style of your text, but you must also choose a size for the text in that font. In Word, the size is expressed in *points* (one point = 1/72 of an inch) and describes the height of the letters, or rather, the height of the capital letters. In 12-point type, a capital X is 1/6 of an inch high.

In Word, you can choose the font and size for any text in your document. You can even change fonts in the middle of a paragraph, or in the middle of a word. Or you may use a single font throughout a document. Professional-looking documents generally use at least two fonts—one for big type (headings, titles, and so on) and one for the general-purpose text, sometimes known as *body text*.

In general, try to use fonts creatively but sparingly. A document that incorporates four or five different fonts usually appears sloppy and disorganized. Choose two or three fonts that look good together, and apply them consistently throughout the document; for example, use font A for all headings, font B for body text, and font C for page numbers.

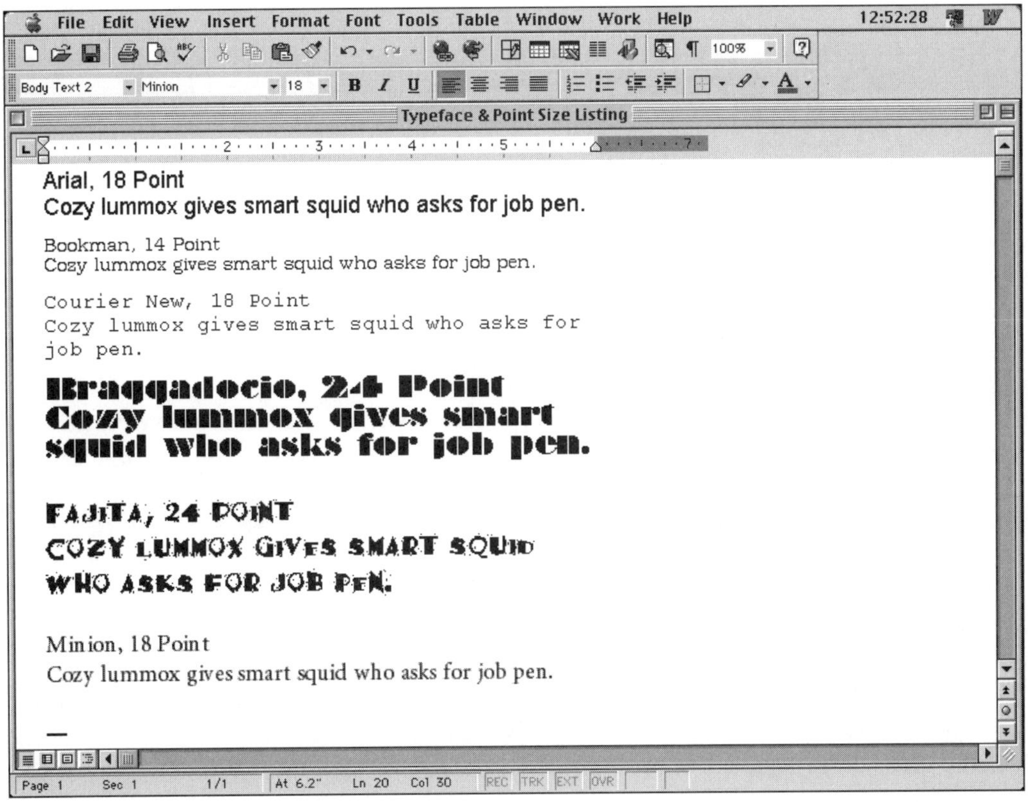

Figure 4.7 A sampling of fonts and sizes.

Net Savvy

When you're creating a Web page with Word, the level of text formatting you can perform—particularly the use of fonts—is much more restricted than for a document intended for printing. See Chapter 17 to learn why you may want to keep your text formatting very simple in your Web pages.

The fonts available to you in Word are installed not in Word, but in the Mac's System folder, and are thus available for text formatting in any Mac application that deals with text—including Word, Excel, and PowerPoint. The Mac OS comes with a varied selection of fonts you can use, and a few more are added by Office 98. To see all of the fonts available on your computer, drop down the Font list on the Formatting toolbar and scroll through the list. Brian's Font list is shown in Figure 4.8; yours probably has different fonts in it, since Brian collects fonts the way velvet collects cat hair.

The fonts you'll see come in two flavors: PostScript and TrueType. PostScript fonts are more sophisticated (technically, not visually) and require a PostScript-compatible

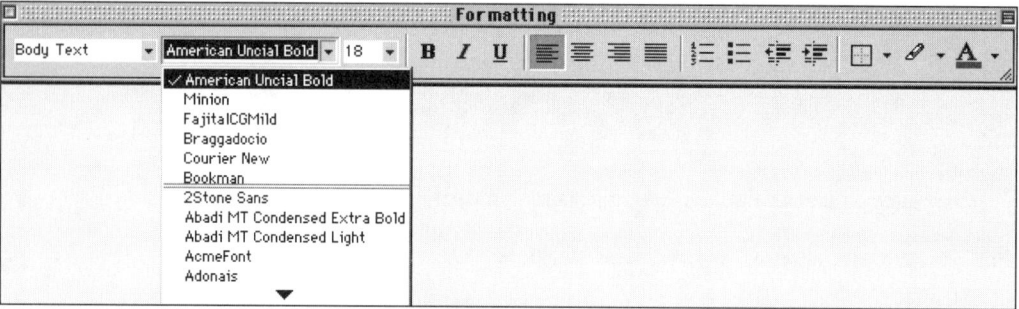

Figure 4.8 The Font list in the Formatting toolbar.

printer (usually a laser printer). TrueType fonts, which are a little more versatile, can be printed clearly on just about any printer—except possibly older dot-matrix printers. If you have a non-PostScript printer (this includes most middling to low-end ink jets), you may still be able to print PostScript fonts—they'll just be kind of blocky looking.

Although your Mac probably has a good selection of fonts to get you started, note that you can add fonts any time you want. Font files are available in commercial software packages, as shareware, and from professional font houses. You can learn how to add fonts to your system in Appendix C.

Net Savvy

TrueType, PostScript, and other fonts are widely available for downloading from the Web. You'll find them at many Web sites, but good starting places include:

- Microsoft's Typography page at **www.microsoft.com/truetype/fontpack/**
- Yahoo!'s Fonts directory at **www.yahoo.com/Computers_and_Internet/ Desktop_Publishing/Fonts/**

Choosing Fonts And Sizes

When you begin typing in a new, blank document, you're already using a font; the name of the font appears in the Font box on the Formatting toolbar, and the size of the type appears to the right, in the Font Size box. This font and size are preselected by the template you happen to be using. (Don't worry about templates for now.)

It really doesn't matter what font comes out when you type—you can always change it to any font and size available. To change the font of existing text, select the text you want to change, then drop down the Font list from the toolbar and select a font. To change the type size, leave the text selected (or select it again, if it has been de-selected), drop down the Font Size list, and select a point size. Note that the range of

Working With Text 93

available sizes differs from font to font. In general, TrueType fonts allow more point sizes that are clearly printable than PostScript fonts.

Keep in mind that font and font size work completely independently. For example, let's say you select a block that contains text in several different fonts and sizes—for example, some text in 12-point Arial and some in 10-point Courier. If you then choose Bookman from the font list, all of the text in the block changes to Bookman, but the sizes remain unchanged—you wind up with some 12-point Bookman and some 10-point Bookman. Conversely, if you select a multifont, multisize block and change only the size, all text in the block changes to the size you selected, but the fonts are unchanged.

FYI: Know Your Font Types

Stylistically, fonts are divided into two basic groups: *monospaced* fonts and *proportional* fonts.

```
In a monospaced font, such as Courier, every character
occupies the exact same amount of space; the letter i
is given as much space on the line as m. Monospaced
fonts have a typewriterish look to them. Monospaced
fonts that may be on your Font list include Courier
and Courier New.
```

In a proportional font, the space *between* the characters remains consistent, while each character takes up only as much space as it needs—i gets a little space, m gets a lot. Proportional fonts are dressier and are used much more often today than monospaced fonts. Most of the fonts on your Font list—including Arial, Bookman, Century Schoolbook, and Times New Roman—are proportional, unless your default printer happens to be incapable of printing proportional fonts. (Any laser or ink jet printer, and most modern dot-matrix printers, can handle proportional fonts. But some older dot-matrix printers, particularly high-speed line printers in many office environments, print only their built-in, monospaced printer fonts.)

Applying Bold, Italic, And Underlining

On the Formatting toolbar, to the right of the Font Size button, appears a bank of three buttons. These buttons change the look of text without actually changing the font. What they do is change the *attributes*, or style, of the text within the selected font. The buttons available are:

- *Bold*—Makes text **bold**.
- *Italic*—Makes text *italic*.
- *Underline*—<u>Underlines</u> text.

Fast Track

Instead of clicking on the attribute toolbar buttons, you can use the keyboard to create the same effect: Cmd+B = **bold**, Cmd+I = *italic*, and Cmd+U = <u>underline</u>.

These buttons all work in the same way, doing their bit to selected text. To apply an attribute to text, select the text, then click on the desired button. To apply an attribute to text as you type it, click on the button, then type. (Click on the same attribute button again when you're done).

Note that you can combine attributes. Highlight a word, click on the Bold button, then click on the Italic button, and the text becomes *bold and italic*. **<u>Bold and underlined</u>**, *<u>italic and underlined</u>*, and ***<u>bold and italic and underlined</u>*** are also possible. However, combining attributes in this way is generally considered overkill. A little emphasis—a single attribute—goes a long way. Also, italics are generally considered more professional looking than underlining (a move away from typewriter days, when the *only* way to emphasize something was to underline it).

To remove an attribute, highlight the text, then click on the attribute button again; for example, if the highlighted text is already bold, clicking on the Bold button removes the bold.

Fast Track

At the far right end of the Formatting toolbar appear three more buttons—Outside Border, Highlight, and Font Color. While in effect, these buttons also apply attributes; their proper use is related more to the application of graphics and color than to text formatting. Along with all of the other graphics- and color-related activities, these buttons are covered in detail in Chapter 6.

Walk-Through: Fonts, Sizes, And Attributes

Follow these steps to practice formatting text by applying fonts, font sizes, and attributes:

1. Open or create any document containing text. (Walkthrough 2—which you created in Chapter 3—will do fine.)

Working With Text 95

2. From the menu bar, choose Edit|Select All. The entire document is highlighted.
3. From the Formatting toolbar, drop down the Font list and choose Arial. All text in the document is set in Arial.
4. Select any text in the document (but not the whole document).
5. Drop down the Font list and choose Courier New. The selected text changes from Arial to Courier New.
6. Position the edit cursor at the very top of the document, type a title for your document, and press Return.
7. Select the new title you just created.
8. From the Formatting toolbar, make the following selections: Font list = Century Schoolbook; Font Size = 28; Bold button. The title at the top of your page is set in 28-point Century Schoolbook, bold.
9. Experiment with fonts, trying out each of the fonts in your list. While viewing them, think about what types of documents you might use each font for.

Applying Advanced Text-Control Options

Using the toolbar to change fonts, sizes, and attributes is a snap, as you have seen up to this point in the chapter. But you can control the appearance of text to a much finer degree through the Font dialog.

Before opening the Font dialog, select the text you want to format. Then open the Font dialog by choosing Format|Font. The dialog shown in Figure 4.9 opens, with its Font tab preselected.

Observe that the Font tab—like all the tabs on the Font dialog—includes a Preview pane near the bottom. As you make changes in the tabs, the Preview pane updates automatically to show you the effect you're building. When the Preview pane shows the full effect you're after, click on OK.

Fast Track

The Font dialog includes three tabs: Font, Character Spacing, and Animation. The first two tabs are described in this section. The third, Animation, is used only for dressing up documents that will be published online. Online publishing—including animation effects—is discussed in Chapter 17.

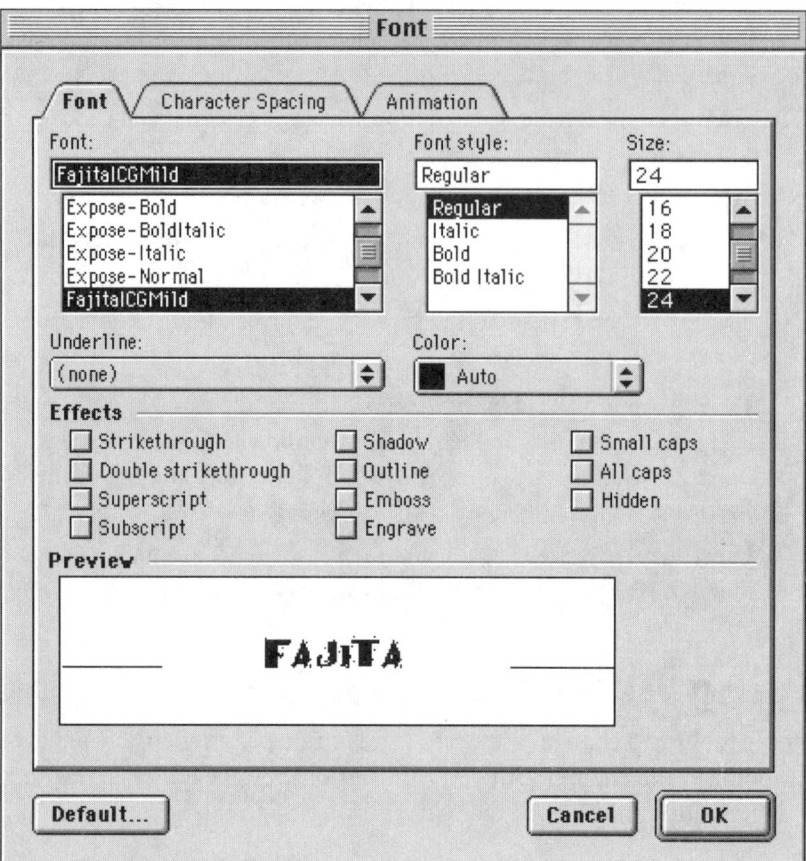

Figure 4.9 The Font dialog.

Using The Font Tab

On the Font tab of the Font dialog, the top three items—Font, Font Style, and Size—duplicate precisely the font-control activities you have performed with the Formatting toolbar. You use Font and Size exactly as you use their toolbar namesakes (the Font and Font Size boxes), whereas Font Style stands in for the actions of the Bold and Italic buttons (and the combination of those buttons, bold italic). Choosing Regular from the Font Style list removes any bold or italic effects.

Below the top row you'll find ways to do things you cannot do on the toolbar. For example, the Underline button on the toolbar simply applies a solid, unbroken underline under the entire block of selected text (including all words and the spaces between them). By choosing an option from the Underline list on the Font tab, you can achieve a wide variety of underlining effects. Figure 4.10 illustrates the effects of some of the choices on the Underline menu. (To test the effect of any item on the list, choose it and observe the Preview pane.)

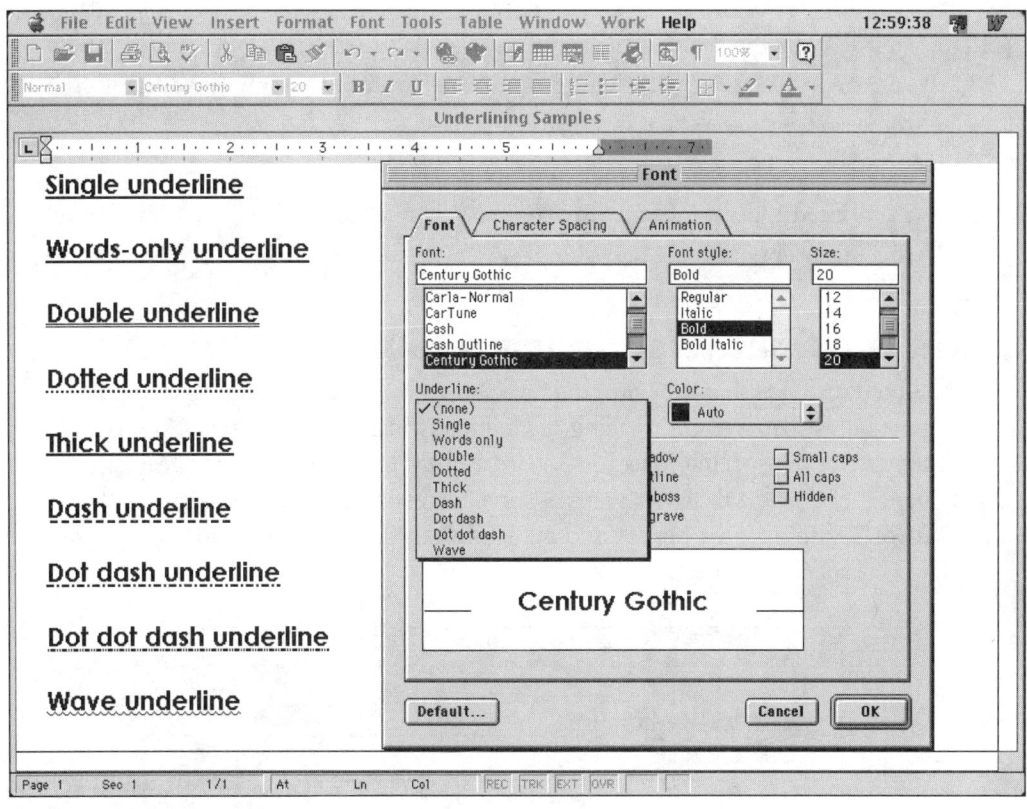

Figure 4.10 Underline options on the Font tab.

Fast Track

The Color list, to the right of the Underline list on the Font dialog, controls the color of text. Using color in your documents requires balancing many considerations, such as where and how the document will be published—online, on a laser printer, on a color printer, and so on. These issues—including the use of the Color list—are covered in Chapter 6.

The set of Effects checkboxes above the Preview pane enables you to apply a wide variety of special text effects, from Strikethrough to All Caps. Many of these may be used in combination. To experiment with the Effects until you achieve the effect you want, click on the checkboxes and observe the change in the Preview pane.

FYI: *Watch Out For Effects Overload*

When you're working with the Effects on the Font tab—particularly those in the center column such as Shadow, Outline, Emboss, and Engrave—keep in mind that such effects are notorious for looking much worse on paper than they do on your screen, even if you use a good laser printer. Similarly, any of the adjustments you can make on the Character Spacing tab (covered next) may be difficult for some printers to produce successfully.

Any time you choose to get fancy with text effects or spacing, be sure to evaluate the printed appearance carefully. You may wind up simplifying your text formatting once you see how it looks on paper.

Using The Character Spacing Tab

The Font dialog's Character Spacing tab (shown in Figure 4.11) enables you to make minute adjustments to the spacing of characters in the selected text. As a rule, font designers set the spacing for a font very carefully, to achieve an eye-pleasing effect. Unless you're a type designer yourself, or a professional graphic designer, odds are that you'll diminish the beauty and readability of the type if you fiddle with the character spacing needlessly.

Figure 4.11 The Font dialog's Character Spacing tab.

Still, you may choose to change the spacing to achieve a special effect. For example, you may want to s p r e a d o u t s o m e w o r d s in a title or heading to give it a unique appearance. (Advertisers do that a lot these days with product names and slogans.) Or you may choose to squeeze characters closer together to make a particular block of text fit within a restricted space.

Fast Track

You can open the Font dialog from a contextual menu. Select the text you want to format, Control-click the selection to open the contextual menu, and choose Font.

You can adjust the spacing of the selected text in three ways on the Character Spacing tab (note that you can use any of these in combination):

- *Spacing*—Spacing adjusts the space between the characters. When the default choice, Normal, is in place, the characters are spaced normally and no entry is necessary in the By box to the right. Instead of Normal, you may select Expanded from the list to increase the amount of space between characters, or choose Condensed to squeeze the characters closer together. Your entry in the By box determines the number of points (72nds of an inch) by which to adjust the spacing. A higher number in the By box always amplifies the effect (makes expanded text more expanded, condensed text more condensed).

- *Position*—Position adjusts the vertical spacing of the selected text in relation to the *baseline*, the invisible line on which the text sits. (*Descenders*—the dangly parts of letters like lowercase y and j—hang below the baseline.) In the Preview pane, the two horizontal lines jutting in from the sides of the pane indicate the baseline. When the choice in Position is Normal, all text sits on the baseline (except the descenders). Choose Raised to raise the text above the baseline or Lowered to lower it below the baseline. The entry in the By box determines the number of points by which the text is raised or lowered.

- *Kerning*—When font designers design a proportional font, they carefully select the uniform spacing between characters for the best overall effect. Unfortunately, when text is set at larger sizes, some character combinations begin to look like they're too far apart. For example, lowercase f and lowercase i may begin to look too far apart because of the way they're shaped. It's a trick of the eye—the characters are no farther apart or closer together than any others. Still, font designers have found a way to compensate for this phenomenon: kerning pairs. The type designer picks out the particular pairs of letters that begin to look oddly spaced at larger point sizes and builds into the font kerning instructions—spacing guidelines for kerning pairs.

By checking the checkbox next to Kerning For Fonts, you instruct Word to automatically apply spacing adjustment guidelines to any kerning pairs in the selected text. Because kerning is generally unnecessary and sometimes unattractive at smaller point sizes, you must also select a point size in the box preceding Points And Above. For example, if you check the Kerning For Fonts checkbox and select 18 in the Points And Above box, kerning will be applied to any text in the selection that is 18 points or larger; any text in the selection below 18 points will not be kerned.

Adding Symbols And Special Characters

In many documents, you may require special characters that appear nowhere on your keyboard. Examples of the more commonly used special characters appear in Figure 4.12, but in fact, hundreds of special characters are available. While many such characters are graphical in appearance, they are not graphics; they are text, and as such, you can set them within a line of text and format them in most of the ways you can format any other text.

Word groups these characters into two groups. Each group is represented on a separate tab of the Symbol dialog:

- *Special Characters*—Common text characters that do not appear on the keyboard, such as a long (em) dash, the copyright symbol, and so on.

- *Symbols*—Unusual characters, such as Greek letters, arrows, and others that are not used often and do not appear on the keyboard, but are part of the character

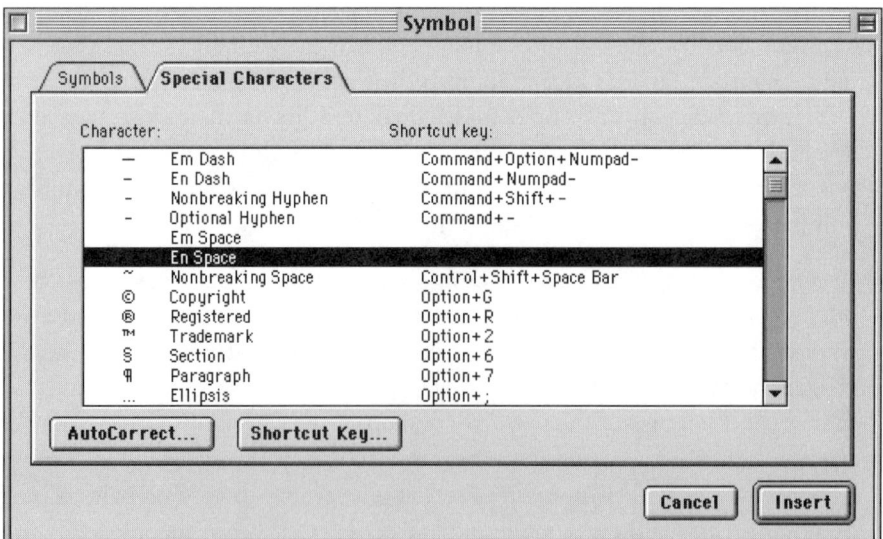

Figure 4.12 The Symbol dialog, where you can find all those funky characters you can't find on the keyboard.

sets of some fonts. Symbols also include characters from special "symbol" or "dingbat" fonts—fonts made up completely of icons and symbols rather than letters and number characters. These symbols are used in typing equations or non-English words, or to create fun and funky list bullets and other page dressing.

To insert a symbol or special character, first position the edit cursor in your document at the spot where you want to insert the character. Then open the Symbol dialog (shown in Figure 4.12) by choosing Insert|Symbol.

To insert any of the common special characters, choose the Special Characters tab, select the character you want from the list, and click on Insert. The character appears in the document, in the same font and size as the surrounding text.

Inserting a symbol takes a little more effort than a special character. First, click on the Symbols tab (see Figure 4.13). Then choose a Font from the list; when you do, the dialog displays all of the available characters for that font, including letters, numbers, punctuation, and any other special characters. To insert a character, click on it (it appears enlarged after clicking, so you can get a better look at it), and click on Insert.

If on the Symbols tab you choose the top selection in the Font list (normal text), the dialog displays a list of characters that are available for virtually any of the regular text fonts you may be using in your document. Usually, choices you make from the normal text list are, like the choices on the Special Characters tab, font-independent, and appear in your document in the same font as the surrounding

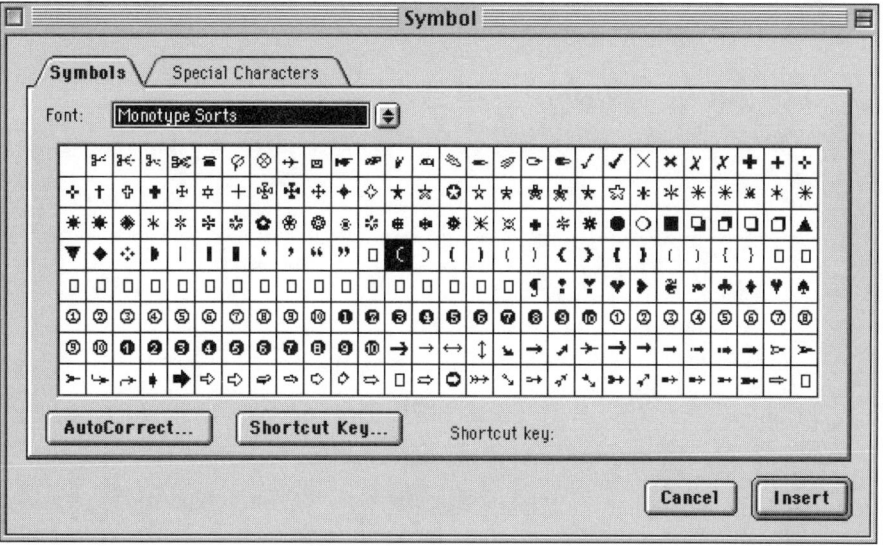

Figure 4.13 Use the Symbol dialog's Symbols tab to insert special characters from symbol fonts, such as Monotype Sorts.

text. Below normal text, the remaining choices on the Symbols tab's Font list are all special symbol or dingbat fonts, populated entirely with symbols (and in the case of dingbat fonts, such as Wingdings or Giddyup Thangs, funky little pictures). Symbols you choose in these fonts are font-dependent.

FYI: Symbols May Not Like Font Changes

The two groups of symbols—Special Characters and Symbols—overlap; some characters may appear in both groups. When that's the case, you're always better off choosing from among the Special Characters than from the Symbols.

Why? Well, the Special Characters are pretty much *font-independent*; that is, if you insert a copyright mark in a line of Arial text, you get an Arial copyright mark. If later you change the font of the line to Courier, the copyright mark changes to a Courier copyright mark. Selecting your symbols from the Special Characters list ensures that if you change the font of a text block that contains a symbol, the symbol changes font, too—but it remains the correct symbol.

Conversely, many (but not all) of the choices you may make from the Symbols tab are font-dependent. The inserted symbol will appear, at first, just as you want it to, but if you change fonts later, the symbol may change unexpectedly to an entirely different character.

Whichever tab you choose from, it's smart to recheck any inserted symbols carefully any time you change the font of a block containing symbols.

Walk-Through: Symbols

Follow these steps to practice inserting symbols and special characters in a Word document:

1. Create a new document.
2. Type "New—The 1998 Ford Econolux".
3. Select what you just typed, and set it in 18-point Arial.
4. Position the edit cursor at the end of the line.
5. Choose Insert|Symbol. The Symbol dialog opens.
6. Click on the Special Characters tab.
7. Select the trademark symbol from the list of special characters and click on Insert. "Econolux" is now trademarked.

8. Select the double dash (--) following "New". (Look out—Word's AutoCorrect feature may have changed your double dash to an em dash already. Don't worry—just select the em dash and proceed as usual.)
9. Choose Insert|Symbol.
10. Click on the Special Characters tab.
11. Select the em dash from the special characters list and click on Insert. The selection (a double dash) is replaced by an em dash.
12. Position the edit cursor just after the "E" in "Econolux".
13. Press Backspace to delete the "E".
14. Choose Insert|Symbol.
15. Open the Symbols tab and choose "(normal text)" in the Font list.
16. Find the character "È" and click on Insert. "È" now begins "Èconolux".
17. Select the word "Èconolux", including the copyright symbol.
18. Choose Format|Font.
19. In the Font tab, click on the checkbox next to All Caps.
20. Click on the Character Spacing tab, and choose Spacing Expanded By 3 points. Click on OK. How do you like the results? Too much? Not enough?

Moving On

You're in charge of your words now. You know how to funnel words from your brain into a Word document, make corrections and revisions, and edit, manipulate, and polish your writing by selecting text blocks and applying powerful time-savers like copy, move, and undo. You also know how to shape the look and feel of your words to an exacting degree. Gutenberg himself would be astonished at what you can do. Congratulate yourself—you're a *font* of knowledge, a *bold* pioneer, a *special character*, a *symbol* of excellence…. You get our 1/72nd of an inch (our *point*, get it?) Okay, I'll stop.

That's it for words—now the problem is pages. What should your pages look like? What size paper will your document be printed on, how wide are the margins, how many columns does it have? Are paragraphs indented? Are there headers or footers on the pages? Page numbers? You'll learn how to answer all of these questions, and more, all in the course of Chapter 5.

Designing Pages

When you speak, it isn't your words alone that communicate your meaning—it's how you say them. Your vocal inflections, pacing, facial expressions, and even your body language work together with your words to get your ideas across. In the same way, the formatting of your text and pages work together with the words to communicate their meaning more effectively. How your words and pages look is as important as what they say.

Open your eyes a little wider, and take in the whole page you're reading right now. Observe the various fonts and sizes, the occasional use of text attributes, the indenting of paragraphs, the width of the margins, the headers, and other aesthetic choices. All of this formatting was carefully selected to make this particular document attractive, easy to read, and professional looking. It was designed to help you learn.

What do you want *your* document to look like? Think about who your intended reader is. A friend? A potential customer? Your boss? All three? Do you want it to be a fun, crazy document, or a sober, businesslike one? The formatting choices you make determine your document's personality, and they dramatically affect how your readers perceive your words—and you.

If you've been through Chapter 4, you already know how to control the look of your text. That leaves three remaining activities that determine your document's appearance:

- *Page layout*—Choosing the geometry and organization of the page: paper size and orientation, margins, headers and footers (text automatically repeated at the top or bottom of each page), columns.

- *Paragraph formatting*—Choosing the look and behavior of paragraphs within the page layout: alignment, indenting, automatic list formatting, tab settings.

- *Graphical formatting*—Adding pictures, tables, borders, color.

We'll save the graphics for Chapter 6. Here, under the catchall of page design, you'll discover both layout and paragraph formatting (a.k.a. "the chicken and the egg," because of the way these two phases of page design are inextricably linked). You can best judge your indents, tabs, and other paragraph stuff only within the space allotted to those paragraphs by the page layout, so laying out pages first makes sense. On the other hand, performing both text and paragraph formatting before laying out pages allows you to play around with the page layout and accurately assess the overall impact of any changes to margins, header space, and so on. So it's a crapshoot.

Now, if we're anything, we're flexible. Live and let live, we always say. Don't snap like an oak, we say—bend like bamboo. So we hope you'll interpret our approach to this conflict—namely, "tell 'em how to do page layout and paragraph formatting without saying which comes first"—as evidence of open-mindedness and a desire to empower you (rather than as ambivalence and cowardice, which is, of course, the frank truth).

In this chapter, you'll learn how to complete the formatting of your document, paragraphs and pages together. Which you do first is your business. Once you've tried a little of both activities, I'm sure you'll discover an approach that feels natural to you. Trust your instincts. The Force will be with you—always.

Net Savvy

Laying out an online document or a Web page is an entirely different can of worms from laying out a printed document, with an entirely different set of rules and limitations. While the material in this chapter is essential to controlling the look of a printed document, little in this chapter has any relevance to online documents. You'll learn about the layout of online "pages" in Chapter 17.

Understanding And Creating Sections

For short, simple documents, you may want to lay out pages one way and have that layout apply to every page in the document. But more often than not, you'll want to use different layouts for different parts of the document. For example, you may want the *header* or *footer*—repeated text that appears at the top or bottom, respectively, of every page—to change with each major part of the document. Or you may want to create a title page or introductory pages for each part of the document, with an entirely different look from the rest of the document—different margins, headers, footers.

To accomplish this, you could break the document up into multiple files, then give each file its own layout. This approach makes a lot of sense for especially long or complex documents, as you'll discover in Chapter 7. But it's an inconvenient way to vary the layout in shorter documents. A better way is to break a single document file into multiple *sections*. To each section, you can apply unique page formatting—margins, headers and footers, page orientation—without affecting the rest of the document.

To start a new section within your document, you must insert a *section break*. First, position the edit cursor in your document immediately preceding the material that belongs in the new section. Choose Insert|Break from the menu bar to open the Break dialog shown in Figure 5.1. From the Break dialog, choose one of the four options listed under Section Breaks:

- *Next page*—A *page break* is inserted at the edit cursor position, and the new section begins with the very top of that new page.
- *Continuous*—The new section begins at the edit cursor position, with no page break.
- *Even page*—The new section begins on an even-numbered (left-hand) page. One or two page breaks are inserted automatically to force the new section to the top of an even-numbered page, creating a blank odd-numbered page, if necessary.
- *Odd page*—The new section begins on an odd-numbered (right-hand) page. One or two page breaks are inserted automatically to force the new section to the top of an odd-numbered page, creating a blank even-numbered page, if necessary.

Fast Track

If you click on the Continuous radio button, the layout settings from the preceding section—including the top, left, and right margin settings, and the header—will still apply to the page on which the new section begins. On that page, only elements following the section break—such as the footer and bottom margin—are affected by any layout changes you make.

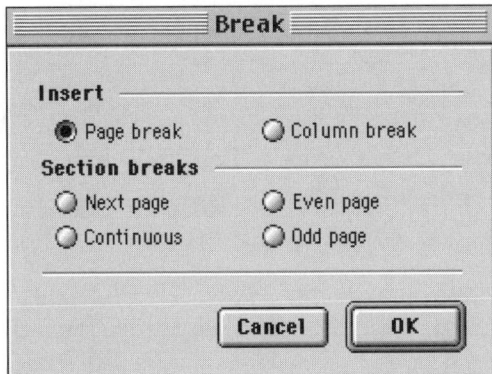

Figure 5.1 The Break dialog, where you make section breaks, page breaks, and column breaks.

The most common application of Continuous is to change the number or layout of columns within a page. For example, the top half of a page may have two columns, but the bottom half (following the section break) may have only one. See the "Working With Columns" section later in this chapter.

Whichever starting point you choose, the new section begins at that point and continues to the next section break, or, if you create no more sections, to the end of the document.

Once a section is created, you apply layout settings to it by locating the edit cursor anywhere within the section and then changing the Page Setup dialog as described in the next several pages.

Setting Up The Document

By "setting up the document," we mean defining the geometry of your final printed document by determining such things as the width of the margins, the size of the paper your document will be printed on, and more. The phrase "setting up the document" is meant to help you remember the name of the dialog on which you do all this stuff—the Document dialog (you'll also use the Page Setup dialog—which can be accessed conveniently from the Document dialog).

Choose Format|Document to open the dialog (see Figure 5.2). Then modify any entries you wish in the two tabs of the Document dialog, and any items you wish in the Page Setup dialog, according to the instructions you'll find on the next several pages. Note that defaults are supplied for all Document and Page Setup entries. You needn't change everything—just change what you want to.

FYI: Entering Measurements

In many of the activities in this chapter, you'll need to enter measurements in text boxes. For example, you'll need to supply measurements for the width of the margins.

On most text boxes that collect measurements, you'll see an up arrow and a down arrow on the right side of the box; you can click on the arrows to increase or decrease the measurement. Still, you may need to type a measurement in such a box, so it's important to learn how right now.

Type all measurements in inches, using decimal fractions when necessary (.5" = 1/2 inch; .75" = 3/4 inches; 1.25" = one and one-quarter inches, and so on). Don't bother including the quote mark (") to indicate inches; Word fills in the quote mark for you.

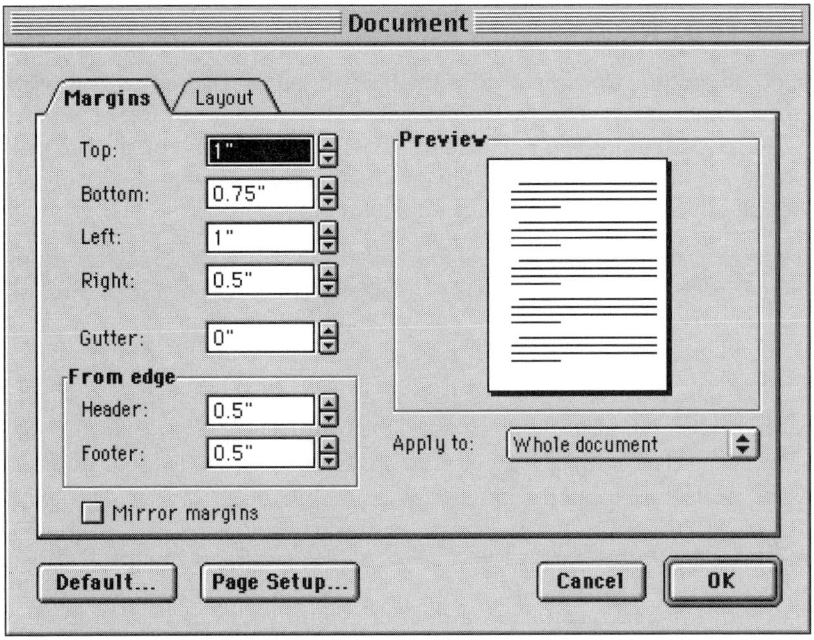

Figure 5.2   The Document dialog.

Fast Track

In Normal or Page Layout view, you can also open the Document dialog by double-clicking on a margin area of the ruler that appears below the title bar of your document. A margin area appears at each end of the ruler, colored gray. (If you don't see the ruler, select View|Ruler to switch it on.)

Both tabs in the Document dialog have a Preview pane. Any time you make a change, the Preview pane immediately displays how that change affects your pages.

Also on both tabs, the Apply To list appears. From this list, you'll choose which portion of the document will be affected by your changes. The choices are:

- *Whole Document*—Changes you make to the Document dialog affect the whole document.

- *This Section*—Changes you make to the Document dialog affect only the section that now contains the edit cursor. (This option is available only if you have split your document into sections.)

- *This Point Forward*—Changes you make to the Document dialog affect the page containing the edit cursor and all pages that follow it. Pages preceding the one containing the edit cursor are unaffected.

Fast Track

On both tabs of the Document dialog, you'll also see the Default button. Clicking on the Default button changes the *template* of the current document to match the Document settings you've chosen. The new setup is then applied not only to the current document, but also to all new documents you create from then on using the same template as the current document.

Using a template, the Document dialog, and the Default button, you can quickly change the layout of a whole family of related documents. See Chapter 7.

Margins

On the Margins tab (see Figure 5.2), you set the margins of the page, including not only the left and right margins you may think of first, but also top and bottom margins, plus special margin adjustments to dress things up.

In the Top, Bottom, Left, and Right boxes on the tab, enter margin widths in inches.

In the From Edge box, you choose the position of your header and footer (both of which you learn how to create and format later in this chapter). If you don't intend to use headers or footers in your document, you can ignore the From Edge box.

If you intend to create headers or footers, use the From Edge box to choose the distance from the edge of the paper (top edge for header, bottom edge for footer) to the header or footer itself. Note that these settings are entirely independent of the top and bottom margin settings.

The remaining options on the Margins tab—Gutter and Mirror Margins—make special adjustments that are required only for documents that will be bound in some way and printed on both sides of each page. The adjustments are necessary for two reasons:

- The edge of the page that goes to the binding—the *inside* edge, or *gutter*—tends to lose a quarter inch or so of readable space, because of the binding. (Unless you're one of those evil people who open books so wide that the binding breaks—and if so, you must use the same public libraries we do.)

- What makes a bound document look attractive isn't consistent left and right margins, but consistent inside and outside margins. As in this book, the outside edge is the right side of a right-hand page, but it's the left side of a left-hand page. So unless you enter identical measurements for the left and right margins, the inside margin will change from page to page, as will the outside margin.

The Gutter box solves the first problem. By entering a measurement in the Gutter box, you instruct Word to automatically add that measure to the margin on the gutter side of the page. For example, if you choose 1" margins for both Left and Right, then enter ".25" in Gutter, Word automatically adds an extra .25" to the inside margin (the right margin of all left-hand pages and the left margin of all right-hand pages) to add a little breathing space for the binding.

FYI: Top And Bottom Margins Include Headers And Footers

When you're deciding on top and bottom margins, consider the margin to be the space between the edge of the paper and the space allotted for the regular text of your document—*not* the space between the edge of the paper and any header or footer you may create.

The header or footer can appear within the space allotted to the margins, while all of the other text in your document is forced out of that space. For example, if you have a 1" top margin, the top line of text in your document will begin 1" below the top edge of the paper, but the header may sit just 1/2" from the edge.

While headers and footers don't obey top and bottom margins, they do obey left and right margins.

Mirror Margins solves the second problem. If you check the checkbox in Mirror Margins, Word changes the Margin tab. Where once you could enter measurements for "Left" and "Right" margins, you'll see instead boxes for defining "Inside" and "Outside" margins. The Inside margin setting is applied to whichever margin faces the binding (in addition to any measurement in Gutter), and the Outside entry is applied to the edge opposite the binding. This makes all outside margins the same, and all inside margins the same from page to page. (Note that Mirror Margins is irrelevant if the measurement in Inside is the same as that in Outside, or if Left matches Right.)

Fast Track

In Page Layout view or in Print Preview mode, you can use the ruler to adjust margins. The horizontal ruler appears just below the toolbars, and the vertical ruler appears to the left of the page. (If you don't see the rulers, choose View|Ruler.)

The gray areas on the ends of the rulers indicate the current margins. Point carefully to the spot where the gray margin meets the white part of the ruler. The pointer becomes a double-pointed arrow, and a tool tip appears, reporting which margin—Left, Right, Top, Bottom—you're about to adjust. Click and drag to change the margin, then release.

FYI: *Don't Upset Your Printer*

When you're choosing margins and From Edge settings, keep in mind the mechanical limits of your printer. For example, most laser printers cannot print within .25" of any edge of the page (they grab the paper in that quarter-inch). When using such a printer, all of your margin settings (and your From Edge settings, if you use headers or footers) must be .25" or greater.

If you choose margins that exceed your printer's capabilities, Word automatically warns you with a special dialog. On that dialog, you can click on Fix to automatically set all margins to the minimum required by your printer. Or, if the printer's limitations don't matter to you—if, for example, you will print the document on a printer other than the one defined as your default printer—choose Ignore on the dialog to instruct Word to accept whatever margins you choose.

Layout

The Layout tab (see Figure 5.3) is a lie—almost everything on the Margins tab pertains to page layout, too, so just who does this Layout tab think it is, anyway? In fact, the Layout tab would more properly be labeled the Miscellaneous tab, but

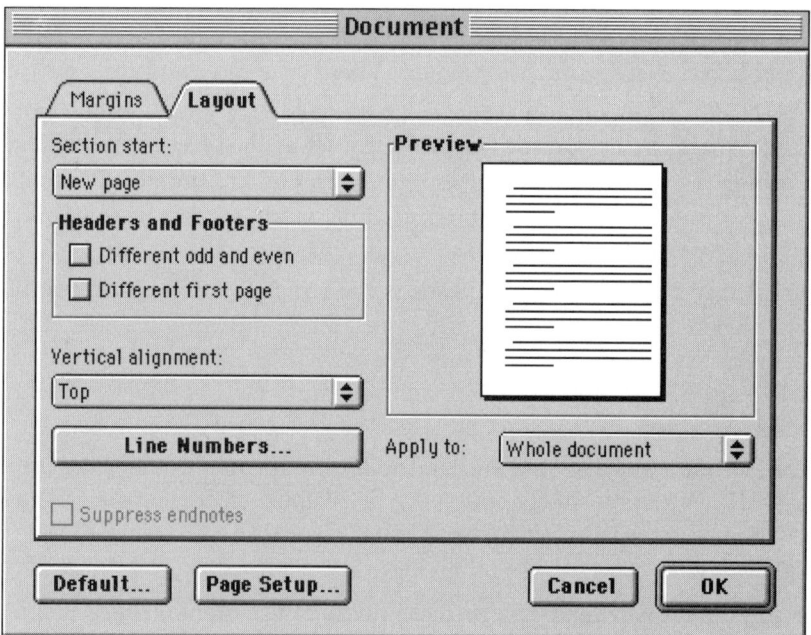

Figure 5.3 Use the Layout tab to control a few miscellaneous aspects of the page layout.

"Miscellaneous" doesn't fit easily in the space provided. On the Layout tab, you define a few final, optional aspects of your page layout.

The Section Start list lets you start a new section, to which the current page setup will be applied. Selecting from the Section Start list has the same effect as using Insert|Break to start a new section (see "Understanding And Creating Sections" earlier in this chapter), and includes the same options.

By default, the header or footer you enter is repeated throughout a document (or section) identically on every page (see "Adding Headers And Footers" later in this chapter). You can change this behavior in two ways using the entries in the Headers And Footers box:

- *The Different Odd And Even checkbox*—By checking the Different Odd And Even checkbox, you instruct Word to permit you to enter two headers or two footers—one header or footer for right-hand pages, a different one for left-hand pages (as in this book). Using different odd/even headers in this way is common in long documents; for example, you may wish to put the document title in the header on left-hand pages, and a chapter or section title on right-hand pages.

- *The Different First Page checkbox*—By checking the Different First Page checkbox, you instruct Word to permit you to enter a header or footer on the very first page of the section or document that's different from the header or footer in following pages.

Fast Track

You may use the checkboxes in the Headers And Footers box to eliminate headers or footers from selected pages. For example, to omit the header from the first page, check Different First Page and then don't bother to type a first-page header. To omit footers from left-hand pages, check Different Odd And Even, then don't type a header for the even-numbered pages. See "Adding Headers And Footers" later in this chapter.

Finally, the Vertical Alignment box on the Layout tab allows you to specify how Word should spread the lines of text vertically within the page. In general, the vertical alignment has no effect on any page that is full—top to bottom—of text, including paragraph breaks. But on pages that aren't full, Word can align the text within the page three ways:

- *Top*—The text starts at the top of the page and stops wherever it stops, leaving some empty space at the bottom. This is the default choice, and also the best choice except when you're going for an unusual effect.

- *Center*—The text is centered vertically within the page, leaving equal amounts of empty space above the text and below it. Center provides an easy way to perfectly center a title within a title page.

- *Justified*—Extra space is automatically inserted between lines to spread out the text so that it always completely fills the page, top to bottom. Justified causes the line spacing to vary from page to page, and creates truly weird results when a page runs more than a few lines short of a full page.

FYI: Printing Line Numbers In Your Document

> If you need line numbers printed in your document (as is required in some types of contracts and other legal documents), click on the Line Numbers button in the Layout tab. A small dialog opens in which you can define where (how far from the text) and how (numbered consecutively throughout the document, restarting at every page, and so on) you want line numbers to appear. (If you want to number only a portion of the document, select that portion before opening the Document dialog and choosing your line numbering.)

Page Setup

The Page Setup dialog handles a number of formatting options related to the way your selected printer handles paper and how your document will translate to that paper. It's a pretty straightforward setup process—with one hitch: Your page setup may look nothing like ours. That's because the Page Setup dialog box changes, depending on your printer driver. So, for example, if you're using the LaserWriter 8 driver to print to your HP LaserJet, you're going to see something quite different from your neighbor, who's using the default driver for her old StyleWriter ink jet printer.

For the sake of complete explanation, we're going to show you pictures taken on a Macintosh using the PSPrinter driver (a fairly standard office network setup). If you're using a different setup (which you probably are), you'll see many of the same options—but probably not all of them. Don't worry, nothing's broken. You may have the same option in a different place, or your printer might not be capable of something we show. Just roll with it—you'll be printing in no time.

If you've already got the Document dialog open, just click on the Page Setup button to invoke the Page Setup dialog. Otherwise, select File|Page Setup. You'll see a number of options, starting with the Paper list at the top.

Choose your paper size from the Paper drop-down list (see Figure 5.4). Standard sizes include US Letter, US Letter Small, US Legal, A4, and so on. (You can also

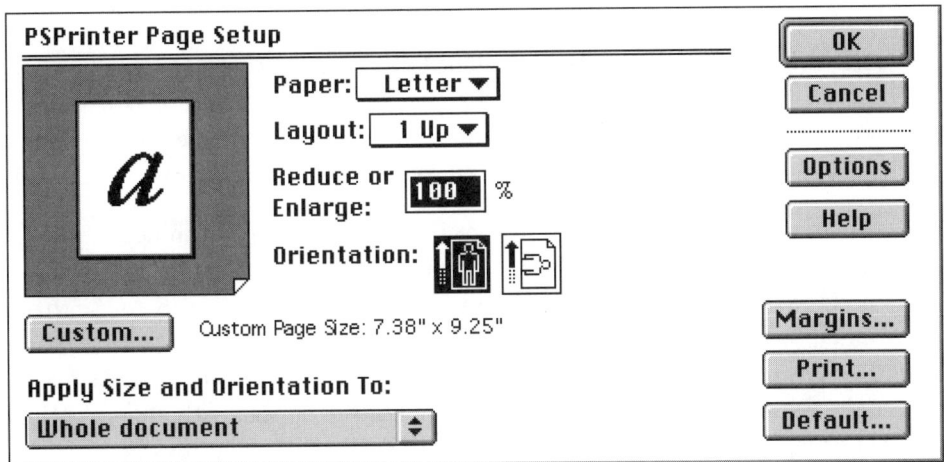

Figure 5.4 The PSPrinter Page Setup dialog.

select a custom size—more on that in a minute). "Paper size" describes the dimensions of a page of your document in its finished form—i.e., when it comes out of your printer. These dimensions are figured into the formatting of your documents within the margins. For example, if you tell Word that the paper is 7" wide, and you've set 1" margins left and right, Word formats your text within a 5" column (7" minus the margins).

It's important to understand that your document's dimensions do not have to match the actual size of the paper on which you will print the document. For example, you may print your document on regular letter-size paper (8.5" × 11") but intend to trim it, after printing, to 5" × 7". Or you may print on letter-size paper for draft copies, intending to later print the final copy on smaller paper, perhaps on a different printer. By defining your intended page in the Page Setup dialog, you instruct Word to properly format the document for its intended page size, regardless of the actual paper used to print it.

You'll also need to select a layout for your document, from the Layout drop-down list. This refers to how many document pages you want printed on a sheet. In other words, if you have a 16-page file in Word and select the 1 Up Layout setting, you'll wind up with 16 printed pages. If you choose 4 Up, though, each printed sheet will contain 4 miniature images of your pages, so you'll get 4 total printed pages. (This setting is most useful if you need a quick "thumbnail" proof of a file.)

Next, tell the program if you want to enlarge or reduce your document. For most documents, you'll want to keep this setting at 100 percent, but you can change this if you need to. For example, if you've set up a tabloid (11" × 17") document, and you need to print a proof on letter-size paper, set Reduce Or Enlarge to about 60 percent to fit your document on the smaller sheet.

Now select your document's Orientation by clicking on one of the two icons provided. If the pages of your document will be taller than they are wide (like this book), choose the vertical orientation. If pages are wider than tall (like a bank check or a computer screen), choose the horizontal orientation. Check out the preview pane as you choose your Orientation—it will show you how your final document will print.

Clicking on Custom invokes the Custom Paper Size dialog. If you need to set up a special, nonstandard paper size, open this dialog, check the Custom Paper Size box, and provide the correct width and height figures. Then click on OK to use that size to print. (The dialog warns you that if you have Custom Paper Size checked, it will override any other paper size options in the Page Setup dialog.) Now take a look at the right side of the dialog, where a column of buttons appears. OK and Cancel will accept or reject any changes you've made in the dialog. The Options button calls up a set of checkboxes for settings related specifically to PostScript-capable printers. If your printer is non-PostScript, these options won't be available. Most are fairly self-explanatory, so let's just run down the list. Notice the preview window on the left of the dialog is back—this time it's even more helpful in figuring out what these settings do (see Figure 5.5).

First you have the Visual Effects choices:

- *Flip Horizontal*—Prints your document with the document's left side on the printed page's right side, and vice-versa. In short, it prints a mirror image of what you see on your screen.

- *Flip Vertical*—Prints an upside-down mirror image of your document.

- *Invert Image*—Causes the white areas of your document to print black, and the black areas to print white.

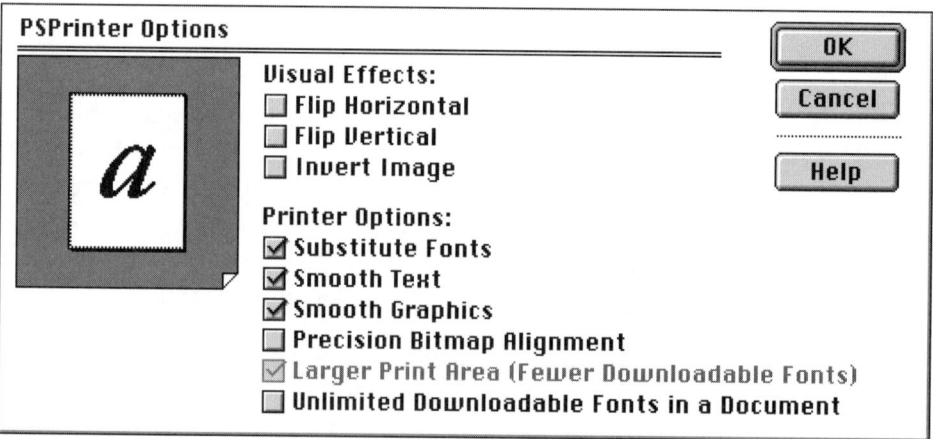

Figure 5.5 The PSPrinter Options area of the Page Setup dialog.

Then come the Printer Options:

- *Substitute Fonts*—Certain fonts on your Mac are meant only for on-screen use and look really atrocious when printed. This option overcomes that problem by substituting Times for New York, Courier for Monaco, and Helvetica for Geneva. (As type design goes, these might not necessarily be more attractive than the originals, but at least they print better.)

- *Smooth Text*—Improves the appearance of your document's text by *anti-aliasing* the edges, resulting in a smoother, more rounded appearance.

- *Smooth Graphics*—Does the same thing as Smooth Text, except it works on graphics.

- *Precision Bitmap Alignment*—Sometimes, printing can create minute distortions in certain graphics. Check this option to compensate for those distortions (you'll probably never notice the difference, really).

- *Larger Print Area*—This allows you to print to a greater area of the page, which requires more of the printer's memory. The trade-off is that you can use only a limited number of fonts. Unless you've really gone font-crazy, though, you can normally check this option without interfering with your print.

- *Unlimited Downloadable Fonts*—If your document uses a large number of fonts, enable this option so they will all print correctly. One catch: Using this option can dramatically increase your print time.

The Help button on the PSPrinter Page Setup dialog opens a small help screen, which explains very briefly what each setting in the Page Setup dialog does. This is handy for quick reminders.

The Margins button at the right invokes the Margins tab of the Document dialog, which we've already discussed. The Print button invokes the Print dialog if you're ready to commit your work to paper, and the Default button works just like the Default button in the Document dialog, making your current settings the default for all new documents.

Finally, there's the Apply Size And Orientation To menu. You can select Whole Document, which does just what it says—applies the settings you've just selected to your entire document. You can also choose This Point Forward, which applies your settings only to the rest of the document. All pages prior to the one that currently contains your edit cursor will stay as they are. This is handy for documents with multiple page types, allowing you to contain both vertical (portrait) and horizontal (landscape) pages in the same file.

Walk-Through: Page Layout

Follow these steps to practice setting up pages:

1. Open or create any multipage document you're comfortable experimenting with. (If necessary, use Save As to make a copy you can play around with while not affecting the original.)
2. Print the document.
3. Choose Format|Document. The Document dialog opens.
4. On the Margins tab, double the width of all four margins.
5. Click on OK.
6. Print the document again and compare it to the earlier printout, paying special attention to differences in the width of the text and in the places where pages break.
7. Choose Format|Document.
8. Go to the Layout tab.
9. In Section Start, choose Continuous.
10. In Vertical Alignment, choose Center.
11. Click on OK.
12. Print the document again, and compare it to the earlier printout, paying special attention to the space above and below the text of each page.

Adding Headers And Footers

In the Document dialog, you decided where to put your headers and footers (from the Margins tab), and whether to enable different headers and footers for odd and even pages or for the first page (from the Layout tab). Now's a good time to make 'em.

To review, a *header* is any text you want to appear regularly at the very top of every page (or every other page, if you've used the odd/even option in the Layout tab). A *footer* is text you want to appear at the very bottom of the page (or every other page). You should choose all of your header and footer options in the Document dialog before adding the headers and footers themselves.

If your settings in the Document dialog enable multiple headers and footers within the document, you must supply each different header and footer separately (see "Working With Multiple Headers And Footers", next). If your page setup does not permit multiple headers or footers, you can enter your header and footer on any page in the document, and Word will automatically repeat it on every page.

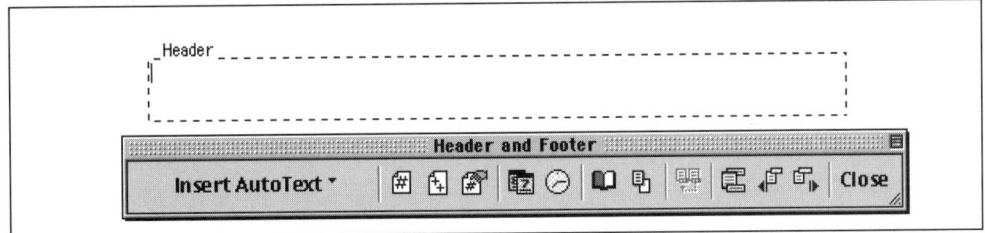

Figure 5.6 Header And Footer dialog.

To add a header or footer, choose View|Header And Footer. As Figure 5.6 shows, three things happen:

- The view switches to Page Layout view (if you were not already in Page Layout view).
- The Header And Footer dialog opens.
- Above the dialog, a dashed box labeled Header appears—the *header space*. The edit cursor appears within the header space.

Fast Track

When you're already in Page Layout view, your headers and footers appear in gray on each page of the document. You can open the Header And Footer dialog and edit the header or footer by double-clicking on the gray header or footer on any page.

To add a header, type your header into the header space and apply any formatting you wish, including text formatting—font, font size, attributes, and so on—and paragraph formatting (see "Formatting Paragraphs" later in this chapter).

To add a footer, click on the Switch Between Header And Footer button on the Header And Footer dialog. A dashed box labeled Footer opens (the *footer space*). Type your footer and format it any way you wish.

Working With Multiple Headers And Footers

By now you know that your headers and footers can change within a document. You can define a different header and footer for each section in your document, and within a section or document, you can use different headers or footers for odd and even pages. You can even have the header or footer on the first page differ from those used in the rest of the section or document.

That's a confusing tangle of possibilities, so here's a simple way to deal with it. You need remember only one basic rule to use multiple headers and footers: Identify all pages or sections that are permitted to have a unique header or footer, and supply one there. For example:

- If your document has multiple sections, add a header and footer on any page within each section; Word automatically repeats that header or footer throughout the section.

- If the page setup permits different odd and even headers and footers (Layout tab), add a header and footer on any odd page, and add a header and footer on any even page. Word automatically repeats the headers and footers on their respective odd/even pages throughout the section or document to which the page setup applies.

- If the page setup uses the different first page option (Layout tab), go to the first page of the section or document to which the setup applies and enter a header and/or footer there, then go to any other page to supply the header and footer for the rest.

Of course, you can always choose not to supply a header or footer and leave the header space or footer space blank. For example, if you don't want the first page of a section to have a header, use the Different First Page option, then don't add a header on the first page. To print footers on odd pages, but no footers on even pages, use the Different Odd And Even option—add a footer on any odd page (it will repeat on all odd pages), but add no footer to any even page.

Finally, you may have places where you're permitted to have a different header or footer, but nevertheless want to continue the header or footer from the previous page or section. If so, go to the section or page where you're required to supply a new header or footer, open the Header And Footer dialog (and jump to the footer space, if adding a footer), then click on the Same As Previous button on the Header And Footer dialog. The header or footer from the preceding page or section is copied to the new page or section.

Fast Track

If a required new header or footer will be only slightly different from the preceding one, you can save yourself some typing and formatting. Go to the page or section where you must enter the new header or footer, use the Same As Previous button to copy over the previous header or footer, then just edit the copy to create the new, unique header or footer.

Adding Page Numbers And Other Stuff To Headers And Footers

You can easily add page numbering, the current date, and other useful information in the header or footer through the buttons on the Header And Footer dialog. These buttons don't insert just text, but also *field codes* (see Chapter 7), special coding that allows Word to update changeable information in your document automatically. For example, page numbering will automatically change as necessary if you add pages to or delete pages from your document; Word will also update dates automatically as the days go by.

The easiest way to use this feature is to click on the Insert AutoText button on the Header And Footer dialog. A list of choices drops down; each choice is a predefined header or footer. For example, if you open the header space and then choose the Author, Page #, Date option from the Insert AutoText list, you get a one-line header in which your name appears on the far left, the page number is centered, and the current date appears on the far right.

Fast Track

Some of the information AutoText uses is pulled from the document's Properties dialog, which you can open by choosing File|Properties. Some items in the Properties dialog are filled in for you (for example, on the Summary tab, Word names you as the author if Word is registered in your name), but you can add to and edit the information in the Properties sheet, as you'll learn in Chapter 16.

After adding a header or footer from the Insert AutoText list, you can change the text formatting—fonts, font sizes, and attributes—to whatever you want. However, it's best to restrict your changes to formatting—don't try to edit the text of the header itself. If you do, you may scramble the coding so that it no longer works properly, and you'll have to create your header all over again. If you don't like any of the AutoText choices as written, you're better off creating your own header or footer.

Instead of using AutoText, you may use the other buttons in the Header And Footer dialog to insert field codes into your own text. For example, type the word "Page" and a space, then click on the Insert Page Number button on the Header And Footer dialog. A field code for the page numbering is inserted following "Page". Word automatically replaces that code with the correct page number.

Fast Track

If all you want in a header or footer is page numbering, you needn't fiddle with the Header And Footer dialog. Just choose Insert|Page Numbers to open the Page Numbers dialog. In that dialog, you can choose whether you want the page number to appear in either the header or the footer, and whether you want it to be centered, flush left, flush right, and so on.

Working With Columns

Despite assertions to the contrary, all documents have *columns*. The document you're reading right now isn't column-free—it's a one-column document. The text is organized in one fat column, running from margin to margin.

But when folks talk about columns, they're usually describing newspaper-style columns (sometimes called *snaking columns*) that divide your text into two or more vertical strips. The columns automatically snake, or wrap, so that when your text reaches the bottom of a column, it continues at the top of the next column. Columns are a great way to give your document a snazzy, periodical look that is most appropriate for newsletters, magazines, or brochures—and less so for instructional documents or lengthy documents, such as books. Not surprisingly, column-formatted documents work best when pictures are incorporated into the layout. (See Chapter 6.)

To define columns, choose Format|Columns to open the Columns dialog (see Figure 5.7). The simplest and most effective way to define columns is to double-click on any of the five Presets, all of which have been carefully predesigned to produce attractive results:

- *One*—A single column (like this book) from margin to margin. (If you don't like the way your document looks in multiple columns, you can use the One preset to switch it back to one column.)

- *Two*—Two columns of equal width, .5" apart.

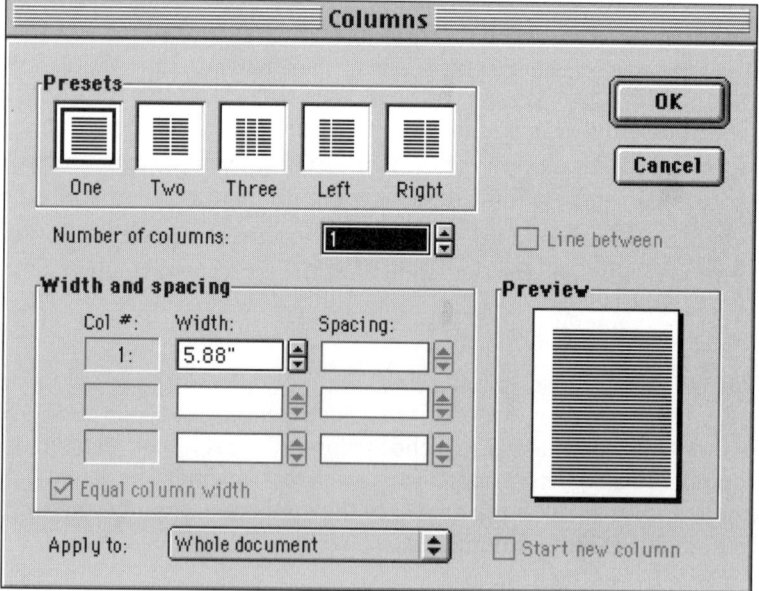

Figure 5.7 The Columns dialog.

- *Three*—Three columns of equal width, .5" apart.
- *Left*—Two columns—a narrow column on the left and a right column twice as wide—.5" apart. This preset (and the Right preset, as well) provide two columns but visually divide the page by thirds—2/3 on one side, 1/3 on the other.
- *Right*—Two columns—a narrow column on the right and a left column twice as wide—.5" apart.

FYI: With Columns, The View Makes A Big Difference

When you use two or more columns, all columns appear in Page Layout view just as they would appear when printed. In Normal view, however, you see only a single column, not multiple columns. (The spots where columns break are indicated with dashed lines labeled Column Break.) The single column you see in Normal is the proper width—you can see how each column will look, you just can't see columns side by side.

In general, you'll find heavy editing easier in the one-column Normal view. Switch to Page Layout when the text is almost final, and the layout takes precedence.

Fast Track

You can change the number of columns in the middle of a page by inserting a Continuous section break and then changing the column settings following the break. For example, you may create a newsletter-style layout with two columns on the top half of the page and one below.

If you want more than three columns, or if you want to fine-tune the width and spacing of columns, enter a Number Of Columns, then enter the Width And Spacing for each column in inches (or check the Equal Column Width checkbox to automatically make all columns equally wide).

Finally, to dress up a document with two or more columns, check the Line Between checkbox. A vertical line appears in the exact center of the space between any two adjacent columns.

Fast Track

To create from one to four equal-width columns in a hurry, click on the Columns button on the Standard toolbar. A four-column picture drops down from the button. To choose two columns, point to the second column (from the left) in the picture, then click. To choose three or four columns, click on the picture's third or fourth column. To change a multicolumn document or section to a single column, click on the picture's leftmost column.

Breaking Pages And Columns

Throughout your document, Word breaks pages and columns automatically whenever the text reaches the bottom margin. These automatic breaks are called *soft breaks*, because they move within the text automatically whenever necessary. If you add half a page of text to a document, Word automatically changes soft breaks to accommodate it.

As your document nears completion, you'll want to nail down the page and column breaks, making sure each major part—section, chapter, and so on—begins on a new page, and making sure that columns break where you want them to. To do that, you insert *hard breaks*—page breaks and column breaks that always break the page or column at the same spot in the text, regardless of subsequent changes. Also, Word can automatically dress up your document by making some smart decisions about where to apply its automatic page breaks. For example, you can instruct Word never to automatically break the page in the middle of a paragraph.

You'll learn to add hard breaks and also to control Word's soft breaks in the next few pages.

Inserting And Removing Hard Breaks

To break a page or column, position the edit cursor where you want the break to happen, then choose Insert|Break from the menu bar. The Break dialog opens (shown earlier in Figure 5.1), from which you can select either a Page Break or a Column Break. In Normal view, hard breaks appear as dashed lines labeled "Page Break" or "Column Break." In Page Layout view, the breaks appear as they will print.

To delete a hard page or column break, run a selection through the break (starting before the break, ending after the break) and press the Delete key (or click on the Cut button on the Standard toolbar). Instead of first selecting the break, you may position the edit cursor immediately after the break, then press Backspace.

Controlling Line And Page Breaks

Line And Page Breaks is a tab on the Paragraph dialog. While you'll learn about using the rest of that dialog later in this chapter, the Line And Page Breaks tab is important here because it sets the rules for how and when Word inserts its automatic soft breaks. You can modify the rules, and by doing so enable Word to place its soft breaks intelligently, so that more of the breaks in your document can be Word's automatic soft breaks instead of the hard breaks you insert manually.

Why are soft breaks preferable, other than the fact that you needn't insert them yourself? Experience teaches us that a document is never finished when we think it is. We'll polish it up, put the hard breaks right where we want them, and then suddenly realize that we want to make changes.

The more hard breaks your document contains, the more likely it is to fall apart when edited. Previously perfectly positioned page and column breaks are suddenly all wrong after the edits, and you must carefully delete and reposition them all, one by one. Certainly, if a major section of your document must always begin on a new page, a hard break is one way of ensuring that it does so (though not the only way, as you'll see). But other breaks you may insert, for aesthetic reasons, to manage breaking points almost always end up wrong as soon as you make even minor changes. To the extent that you rely on Word to properly format your document with soft breaks, the document will reformat itself after any edits. You may need to make only minor clean-up changes to the breaks, or even none at all.

To use the Line And Page Breaks tab, select the portion of the document to which you want the rules you choose to apply. Choose Format|Paragraph, then click on the Line And Page Breaks tab. The whole tab (see Figure 5.8) is checkboxes. Check a box to enable a particular policy. The choices are:

- *Widow/Orphan Control*—When you permit Word to break pages in the middle of a paragraph, two unattractive things can happen: The paragraph breaks right before its very last line, so that the last line appears all by itself on the top of the next page (a *widow*), or it breaks right after its very first line, so that the first line appears all by itself at the bottom of the page (an *orphan*). A check in this checkbox forces Word to break the page immediately before the paragraph to prevent an orphan, or to move the break a few lines up in a paragraph to prevent a widow.

- *Keep Lines Together*—A check here prevents Word from inserting a soft break in the middle of a paragraph. If the bottom of the page is reached mid-paragraph, Word breaks the page immediately before the paragraph.

- *Keep With Next*—Instructs Word to never insert a break between the selection and the paragraph that follows it. Use this checkbox to ensure that particular paragraphs always share a page.

- *Page Break Before*—Ensures that the page always breaks immediately before the selection. For elements that you want always to begin on a new page, this is a good alternative to a hard page break. If a full page precedes the selection, Word doesn't add an extra break. If the preceding page is not full, Word puts in a soft break.

- *Suppress Line Numbers*—If you've instructed Word to print line numbers (as described earlier in this chapter), this checkbox prevents the numbering for the selection.

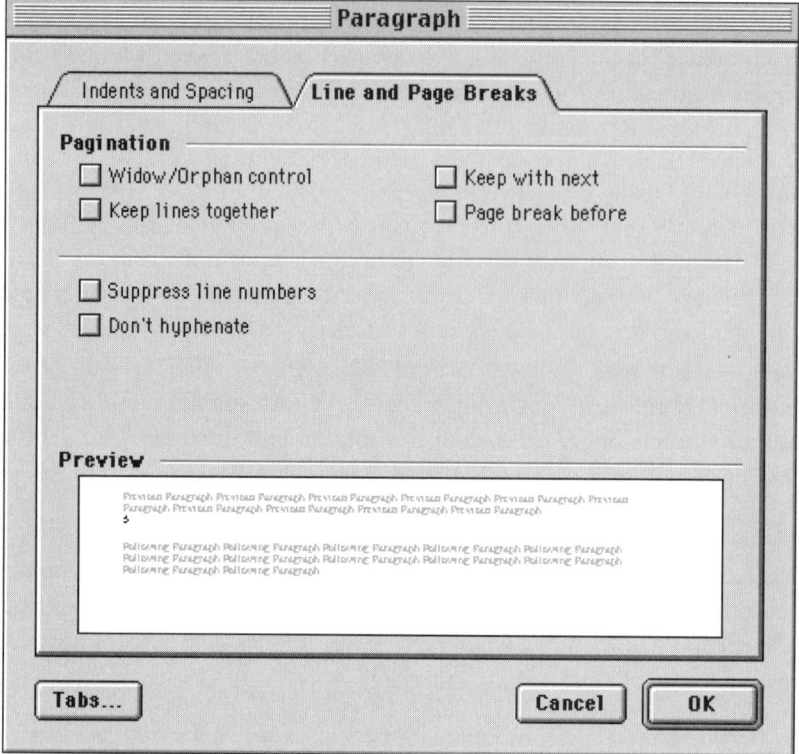

Figure 5.8 The Paragraph dialog's Line And Page Breaks tab.

- *Don't Hyphenate*—By default, at the end of a line Word breaks and hyphenates words according to accepted conventions about when to break a word and where in the word the break can occur. If you'd prefer that Word not hyphenate, but rather always break all lines between two words, check this box.

Walk-Through: Headers, Footers, And Columns

Follow these steps to practice working with headers, footers, and columns:

1. Open or create any multipage document you're comfortable experimenting with. (If necessary, use Save As to make a copy you can play around with while not affecting the original.)
2. Position the edit cursor somewhere near the middle of the document.
3. Choose Insert|Break. The Break dialog opens.
4. Under Section Breaks, choose Next Page, then click on OK. On the page following the edit cursor position, a new section begins.

5. Without moving the edit cursor, choose View|Header And Footer. The Header And Footer dialog opens, and the edit cursor appears in the header space.
6. Choose any header you wish from the Insert AutoText list. The AutoText header appears in the header space.
7. Click on the Switch Between Header And Footer button on the Header And Footer dialog. The edit cursor appears in the footer space.
8. Type and format any text you wish in the footer.
9. Click on the Close button in the Header And Footer dialog.
10. Choose Format|Columns. The Columns dialog opens.
11. Click on the Three preset.
12. Make sure the entry in Apply To is This Section, then click on OK. The section containing the edit cursor is reformatted to three columns.
13. Observe the section number reported in the status bar, and scroll forward until the section number changes. The edit cursor is in the section you created in Step 4.
14. Add a new header and footer for the new section.
15. Print the document (or review it in Page Layout or Print Preview). How is the document different now?

Formatting Paragraphs

First off, it's important to be clear on what a "paragraph" is—to Word, anyway. A paragraph is any block of text not interrupted by a paragraph break. A paragraph can be a single character, a word, a sentence, a group of lines, or pages and pages of text—as long as no paragraph breaks interrupt the flow of the text, it's a single paragraph, even if it runs across multiple pages or columns. Any place you've pressed Return (which inserts a paragraph break), one paragraph ends and another begins—even if the return appears after a single character.

That understood, the next several pages describe ways you can control the look and feel of the paragraphs in your document.

Fast Track

To apply paragraph formatting, you need not select the whole paragraph. You need only locate the edit cursor anywhere within the paragraph, then choose your paragraph formatting from the toolbar or menu bar. The formatting is automatically applied to the whole paragraph, even though you didn't select anything. You cannot apply paragraph formatting to only part of a paragraph.

To apply paragraph formatting to multiple paragraphs, hold down and drag your mouse to highlight anywhere within the first paragraph to anywhere within the last one. All parts of all paragraphs that have any part of them selected will take on the formatting you choose—including the unselected portions of the first and last paragraph.

Aligning Paragraphs

Alignment describes the way the lines of a paragraph are organized on the page. There are four alignment buttons on the Formatting toolbar; each applies one of the four types of alignment. The four types are described below and illustrated in Figure 5.9:

- *Left (the default)*—All lines of the paragraph align evenly on the left side (flush left), while the right ends of the lines are permitted to break at their natural break points to create an uneven, or *ragged*, right side. In a left-aligned paragraph, the first line is often indented by a tab, and so does not line up exactly with the lines that follow. But the paragraph is still said to be left-aligned.

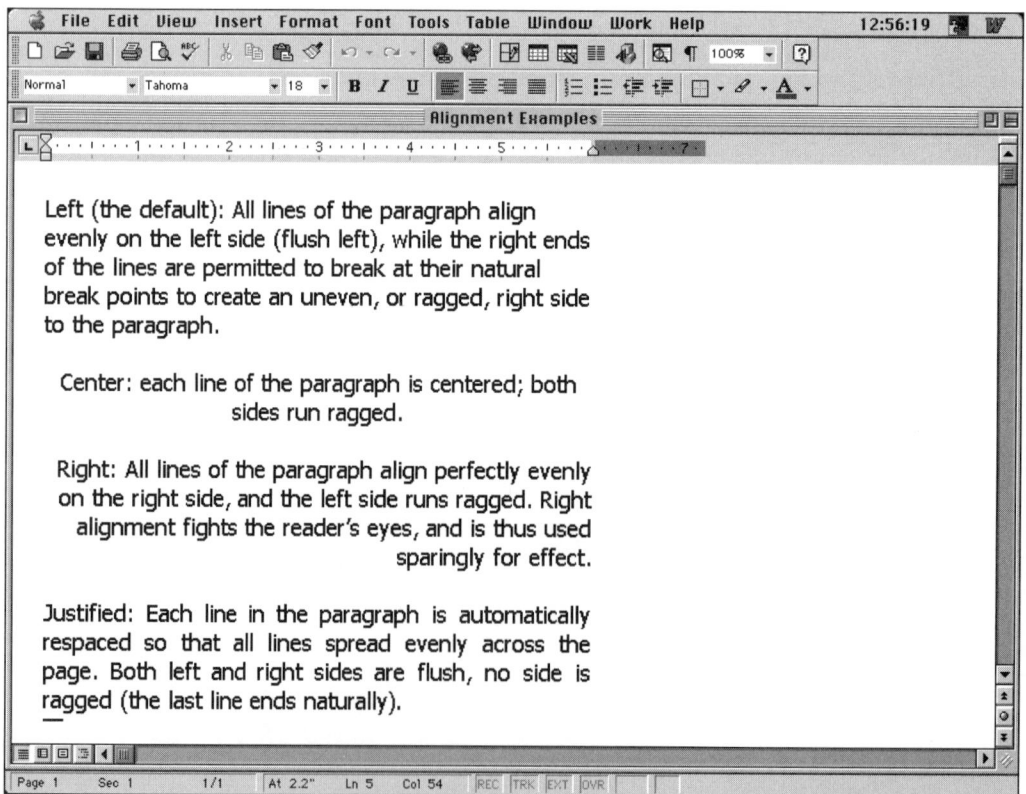

Figure 5.9 Ways you can align paragraphs.

- *Center*—Each line of the paragraph is centered; both sides of the paragraph run ragged. Except for special effects—such as poems or ad copy—center alignment is rarely used for multiline paragraphs, and is generally used for centering titles, headings, or other text elements less than one line long.

- *Right*—All lines of the paragraph align evenly on the right side, and the left side runs ragged. Right alignment fights the reader's eyes—which are trained to always jump back to a consistent left side to start each new line—and is thus used sparingly for effect, not as a standard paragraph format.

- *Justified*—The spacing between words in the paragraph is automatically adjusted so that each line spreads completely across the page. Both left and right sides are flush; no side is ragged. Justified alignment can create a dressy look, but with certain fonts or narrow columns, some lines may appear unnaturally spaced out or squeezed together.

To change the alignment, locate the edit cursor anywhere within the paragraph, then click on the appropriate button—Align Left, Center, Align Right, or Justify—on the Formatting toolbar.

Fast Track

Instead of clicking on toolbar buttons, you may change a paragraph's alignment by positioning the edit cursor within the paragraph, then pressing Cmd+L (for left), Cmd+R (for right), Cmd+J (for justified), or Cmd+E (for center). Yes, we know—one might expect center to be Cmd+C, but that key combo is already taken by Copy. See Chapter 4.

Indenting Paragraphs

When you *indent* a paragraph, you push it away from the margin on one side. Most of the time folks indent, they *left indent*—push the paragraph in from the left margin, as shown in Figure 5.10. While the left side of the paragraph is pushed in, the right margin prevents the right end of the paragraph from moving to compensate; indenting makes the paragraph narrower, and usually longer.

To make a quick and easy *left indent*, position the edit cursor anywhere within the paragraph you want to indent, then click on the Increase Indent button on the Formatting toolbar. The paragraph is indented to the first *tab stop* (see "Working With Tabs" later in this chapter). Click on Increase Indent again to indent the paragraph further, to the next tab stop. To shift the indent back one tab stop, click on Decrease Indent.

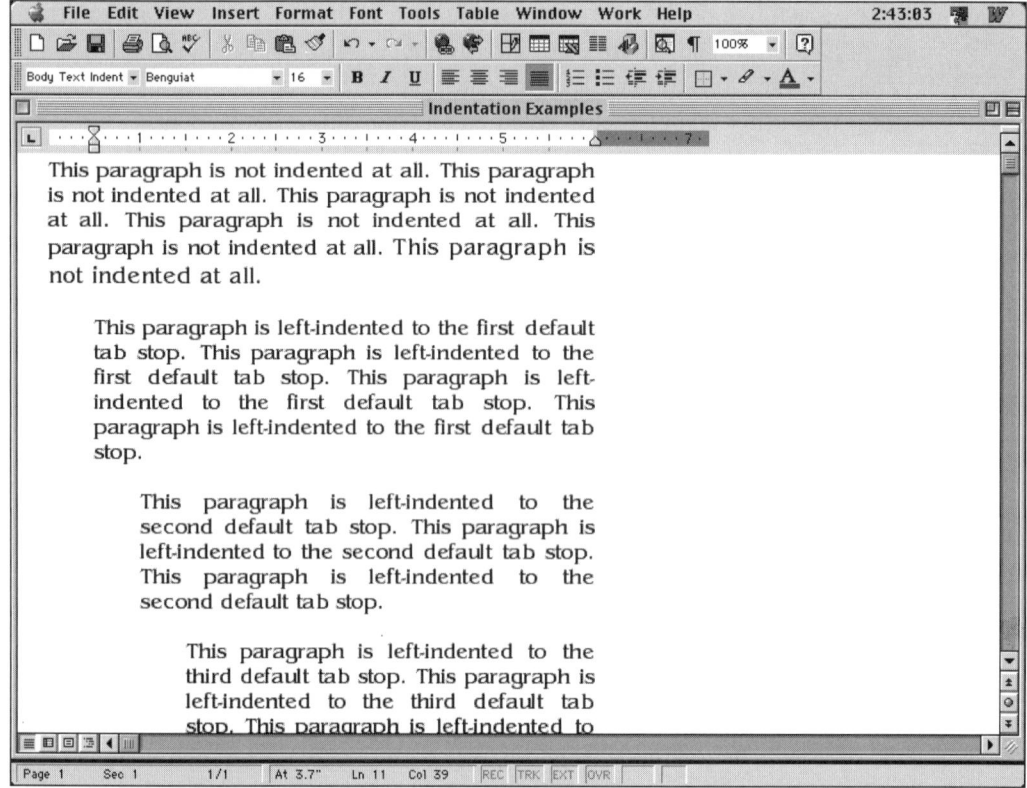

Figure 5.10 Before and after indenting.

Fast Track

To control left indents even more precisely and create special types of indents (such as right indents and hanging indents), choose Format|Paragraph to open the Paragraph dialog. The Indents And Spacing tab on the Paragraph dialog includes controls for precise indenting, plus fine control of other aspects of paragraph formatting, such as line spacing.

Alternatively, the horizontal ruler includes triangular slides that control indents. To learn how to use them, consult Word's Help index under *indentation, with ruler*.

Formatting Lists

If you really wanted to, there's no reason you couldn't simply type your lists and then dress them up with indenting. But Word's list formatting tools do the job much more conveniently, and better, for two reasons:

- Word automatically creates two types of lists: bulleted and numbered (see Figure 5.11). In a bulleted list, an attractive bullet symbol flags each list item. For numbered lists, Word automatically adds the number to the beginning of each

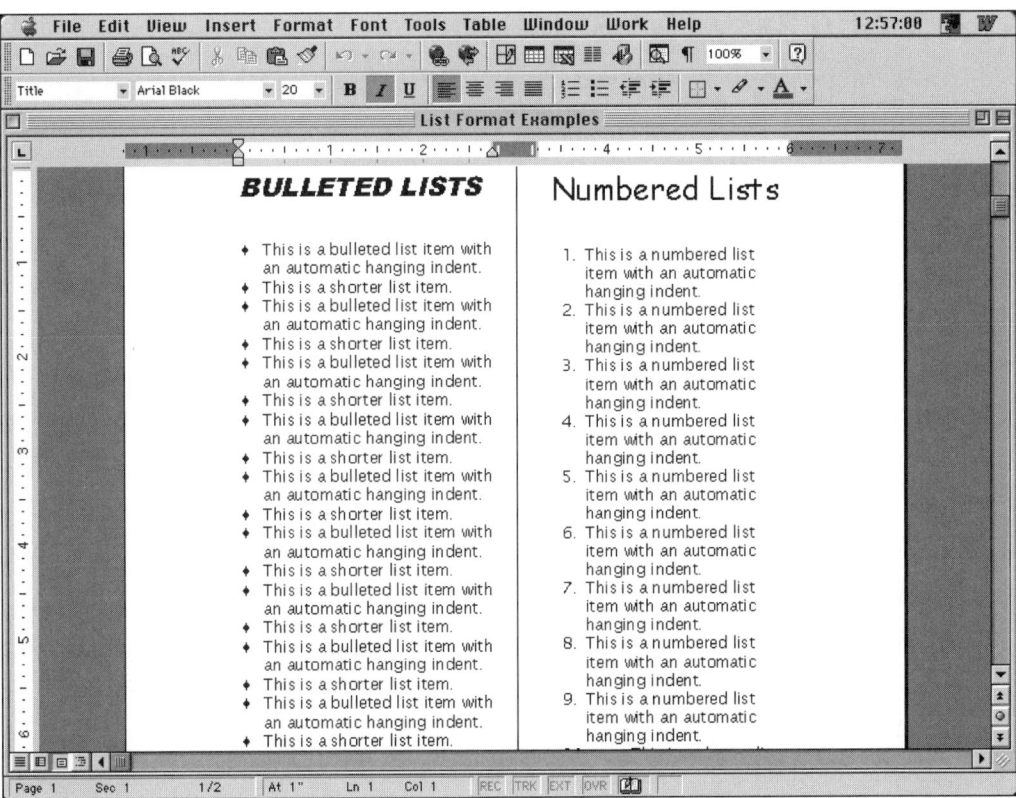

Figure 5.11 Types of lists.

list item, numbering the items consecutively. More important, Word automatically renumbers the list for you if you later add or remove any items.

- Word automatically formats lists with hanging indents. In a *hanging indent*, the whole paragraph is indented, except for the first line, which isn't indented. The first line "hangs" back from the rest of the paragraph. This nice touch allows the bullets or numbers to line up in their own column on the left while the text of each list item appears indented.

Each item in a list is a separate paragraph—whether the item is a single word or a dozen lines of text. That's important to keep in mind, because when you create lists, you're always applying list formatting to multiple paragraphs. Generally, it's easiest to type your whole list first, without worrying about formatting it as such. Just type out each list item, pressing Return once between each item so that each is its own paragraph. (Don't bother typing the numbers or trying to insert the bullets—Word takes care of that.) When you're finished typing the list, select all of its paragraphs (select from anywhere within the first list item to anywhere within the last), and then choose your desired list formatting as described next.

Quick And Easy List-Building

Once your list items are all typed and the list has been selected, format the list by choosing a button on the Formatting toolbar:

- To create a bulleted list, click on the Bullets button.
- To create a numbered list, click on Numbering.

That's it. Once your list is created, you can change it in a number of ways:

- Click on Increase Indent or Decrease Indent to adjust the hanging indent.
- Add list items. Position the cursor between two list items, and press Return. A new bullet or number is added automatically, and you can type the item. (If it's a numbered list, the rest of the list is automatically renumbered to accommodate your additions.)
- Customize the bullet style, numbering scheme, or other aspects of the list using the techniques described next, in the "Advanced List Formatting" section.

To undo list formatting (revert list items to normal paragraphs), select the items and click on the toolbar button (Bullets or Numbering) you used previously to create the list.

Fast Track

If you make extensive changes to the text of a list after formatting it, eventually the formatting may get a little scrambled, with some items formatted like regular paragraphs or with the numbering messed up. This happens when your edits break the list in such a way that Word thinks it's not one list, but several separate lists.

To straighten out the list, just select the whole list again, and apply the desired list formatting. Word reinterprets the selection as a single list and applies the formatting consistently.

Advanced List Formatting

To control the appearance of your lists more precisely, select the list (before or after applying any list formatting with the toolbar) and choose Format|Bullets And Numbering. The Bullets And Numbering dialog opens (see Figure 5.12).

The Bullets And Numbering dialog has three tabs. Any changes you make on these tabs—or on a few other dialogs you can reach through buttons on these tabs—reformat the selected list or make the selection into a list. By experimenting with the selections on these tabs, you'll discover many ways to dress up your lists. Here's a tour through the most important:

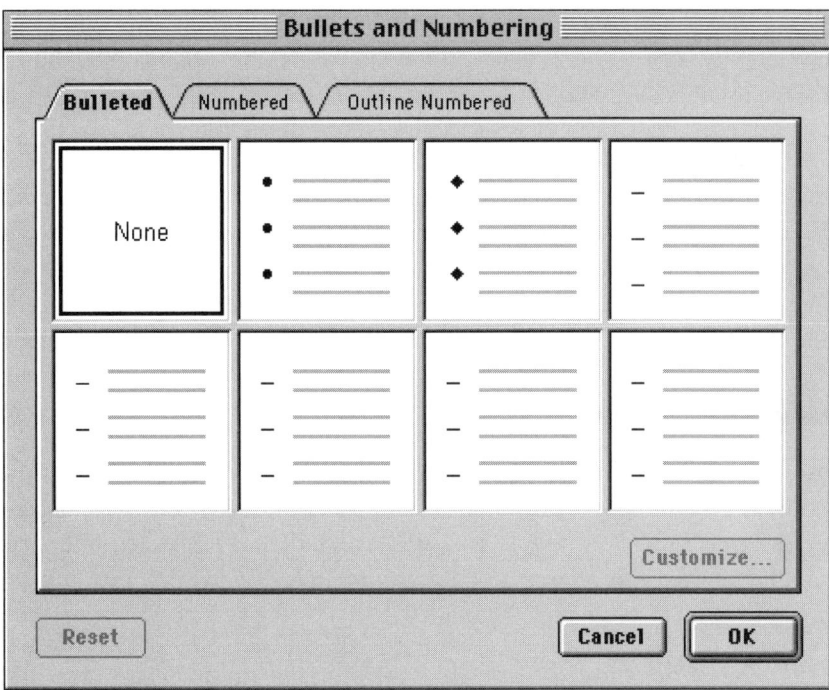

Figure 5.12 The Bullets And Numbering dialog.

- *Bulleted tab*—Click on any of the boxes shown to choose a new bullet style. If you don't care for any of the choices, or if you want to fine-tune the indent of the list, click on Customize to open the Customize Bulleted List dialog. That dialog features a few more bullet choices to select from, and a Bullet button that opens a dialog from which you may choose any symbol to use as a bullet (see Chapter 4 to learn more about working with symbols).

- *Numbered tab*—Just like the Bulleted tab, the Numbered tab offers a selection of different numbering styles, plus a Customize button that opens a Customize Numbered List dialog. On that dialog, you choose among different numbering styles and fine-tune the indents (Number Position and Text Position). You can also select a Start At number or letter, if you wish to begin at a later spot than the default (1, A, i, or a).

Fast Track

In rare circumstances, you may choose to restart the numbering somewhere in the middle of a list. For example, you may want the list to be numbered from 1 to 10, then to start over again at 1 on the 11th item.

Position the edit cursor anywhere within the list item at which numbering should start over. Then choose Format|Bullets And Numbering, click on the Numbered tab, and click on the radio button next to Restart Numbering. If you change your mind later, you can restore the old numbering scheme by clicking on the button next to Continue Previous List.

- *Outline Numbered tab*—This tab creates a type of list you can't create from the toolbar. An outline numbered list has multiple levels, as an outline does (see Figure 5.13). Word can automatically number such lists, applying a different number style to each level and restarting the numbering where appropriate. When typing such a list, choose the level of each item by pressing Tab before the item until it is indented to the desired level.

Working With Tabs

Tabs play many roles in Word. They can indent the first line of a paragraph, line up items in a list, or automatically align a column of numbers. Like indenting, tabs can push text away from the margins. But unlike an indent, a tab affects only one line of text. A tab at the beginning of a paragraph indents just the first line, not the whole paragraph.

Every time you press the Tab key while working in your document, you insert a tab character into your text. Like a space or paragraph break, a tab is a *nonprinting character*. A tab pushes the character next to it in a particular direction.

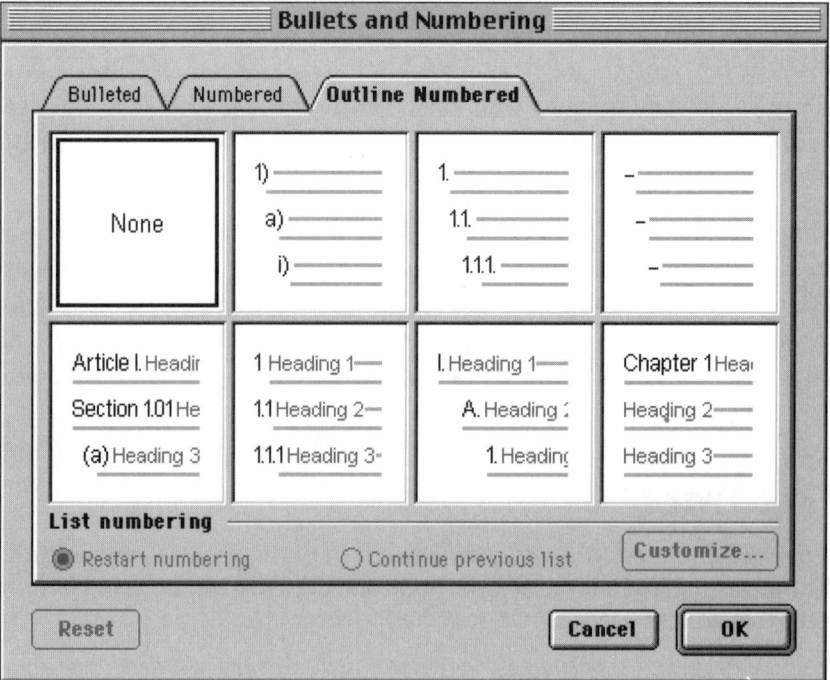

Figure 5.13 Choosing a format on the Outline Numbered tab.

Fast Track

Ordinarily, you don't see the actual tab character in your document; you just see its effect. But sometimes you may want to see exactly where your tabs (and other nonprinting characters) are actually placed in your document. To display all nonprinting characters in the document, click on the Show/Hide button on the Standard toolbar.

Setting Tab Stops

A tab character aligns the text it precedes to a preset point, called a *tab stop*. Typically, multiple tab stops are spread out along the width of the document. Starting at the left margin, pressing the Tab key once moves the text to the first tab stop (from the left), pressing Tab twice moves the text to the next tab stop, and so on.

Tab stops come in four different types. The most commonly used, a left tab stop, does exactly what you expect from tabs: The tab pushes the text away from the left margin, aligning the character following the tab with the tab stop. The three other types are:

- *Right tab stop*—Pressing Tab when the next tab stop is a right tab pushes the text away from the right margin, aligning the character following the tab with the tab stop.

- *Center tab stop*—Pressing Tab when the next tab stop is a center tab centers the text following the tab character around the tab stop.

- *Decimal tab stop*—Pressing Tab when the next tab stop is a decimal tab pushes a number following the tab until its decimal point (or its presumed decimal point, if it doesn't contain one) aligns with the tab stop. Decimal tabs are used to align a column of numbers properly.

In a document that has no specific tab stops set, Word assumes *default tab stops*—all left tab stops—at every .5" from margin to margin. Each time you press Tab, the text to the right of the edit cursor is pushed half an inch to the right. Press Tab three times, and you push the line to the right by 1.5 inches. Note that the default tab stops are also used by the Increase Indent and Decrease Indent buttons on the Formatting toolbar to determine how far to indent a paragraph.

By setting your own tab stops, you can replace the default tab stops with tab stops of your choosing, and set any type of tab stop, as well. The best way to choose tab stops is with the Tabs dialog. Begin by selecting the paragraph(s) to which you want the tab settings to apply. Then choose Format|Tabs to open the dialog (see Figure 5.14).

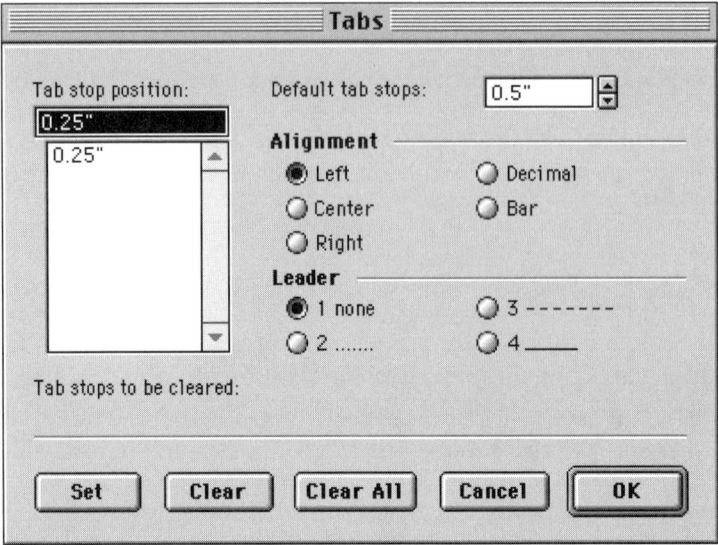

Figure 5.14 The Tabs dialog.

In the Tabs dialog, you can enter a measurement in Default Tab Stops to determine the amount of space between each of the default, left tab stops. Alternatively, you can define and set specific tab stops, one by one. First, in Tab Stop Position, enter the distance from the left margin (regardless of the tab type you're creating); for example, enter "2.5" to create a tab stop 2.5" from the left margin. In Alignment, choose the type of tab stop, then click on the Set button. The position of the new tab appears in the box beneath Tab Stop Position. You may then set another tab stop by choosing a new position and alignment, or click on OK to close the dialog.

To remove a tab stop, highlight its position in the list beneath Tab Stop Position and click on the Clear button.

Instead of using the Tabs dialog, you can set tab stops on the horizontal ruler. Begin by selecting the paragraph(s) to which you want the tab stops to apply. Point to the spot along the ruler where you want to put a left tab stop, and click. A left tab stop marker appears on the ruler. You may click back in the document and continue editing, or click on another spot on the ruler to add another left tab stop.

To add a right, center, or decimal tab stop, you need to change the tab stop type in the square at the extreme left end of the ruler. By default, the left tab stop symbol appears in the square. Each time you click on the square, the type changes. See Table 5.1 for a description of each symbol.

To remove a tab stop from the ruler, simply drag it off the ruler, and it will disappear. Be careful, though—if you've formatted text with that tab stop, you may misalign all your carefully aligned work.

Table 5.1	Alignment symbols on the ruler.
Symbol	Description
	Left tab
	Center tab
	Right tab
	Decimal tab

To insert a tab stop, click on the square until your desired tab stop type appears there, then point to the spot on the ruler where you want to insert the tab stop, and click. The tab stop marker deposited on the ruler matches the type you selected.

FYI: Leader Characters

The Tabs dialog lets you optionally select *leader* characters. Leader characters fill any empty space on the line created by the tab with a dotted line, dashed line, or solid line. (The default choice, None, inserts no leader characters.)

The most common use of leader characters is to run dotted lines in a table of contents—an effect you can achieve by aligning page numbers to a right tab stop and using a dotted leader character.

Walk-Through: Paragraph Formatting

Follow these steps to practice applying paragraph formatting:

1. Open or create any multipage document you're comfortable experimenting with. (If necessary, use Save As to make a copy you can play around with while not affecting the original.)
2. Locate (or create) any group of three paragraphs in a row.
3. Position the edit cursor within the first paragraph.
4. Click on the Center alignment button on the Formatting toolbar. The paragraph is centered on the page.
5. Position the edit cursor within the second paragraph.
6. Click on the Increase Indent button on the Formatting toolbar once. The paragraph is indented to the first tab stop.
7. Click on the Decrease Indent button on the Formatting toolbar once. The paragraph is not indented.

8. Select from anywhere in the first paragraph to anywhere in the third.
9. Click on the Justified alignment button on the Formatting toolbar. All three paragraphs are justified.
10. Click on the Bullets button on the Formatting toolbar. The three paragraphs become a bulleted list.
11. Click on the Bullets button on the Formatting toolbar. The list formatting is removed.
12. Choose Format|Tabs. The Tabs dialog opens.
13. Click on Clear All. All tab stops for the selected paragraph are removed.
14. Enter ".75" in Tab Stop Position.
15. Click on Set, then OK.
16. At the very beginning of each of the three paragraphs, press Tab. Each paragraph has an indented (tabbed) first line.

Moving On

There's so much to page design—a zillion little settings, options, and controls. Fortunately, it's usually just the big stuff that really counts—margins, headers and footers, columns. The rest is largely fine-tuning, and you may be able to ignore most of it unless 1) you're working on a document that requires great precision, or 2) you're obsessive-compulsive. In either case, even complex page design isn't so tough if you approach it by making the broad strokes first, then selectively fiddling with any other settings that appear to require your attention.

It's fitting, though, that you understand all of the ways you can dress up your document with nothing but page design and text formatting. For you see, in Chapter 6 you'll discover the cool stuff—pictures, tables, borders, and color. While all of the cool stuff has a dramatic impact on the look of your document, a lot of folks get so wrapped up in that stuff that they shortchange the page design. They wind up with documents whose graphical pizzazz is undercut by bland, careless text and page formatting.

You, on the other hand, know how to create a snappy page with nothing but a few fonts, some carefully composed headers, and a loving heart. So when you get into graphics, you'll apply them as an enrichment of a good design, not as a cover-up for a poor one.

Adding Pictures, Tables, And Borders

The basic mechanics of adding pictures, tables, and borders to your Word documents are amazingly simple—so simple, in fact, that if you're even a moderately experienced Mac user you could probably figure them out yourself over lunch.

The problem with all this graphical stuff is that getting it into your document is only half the battle. The real challenge in adding graphics is sorting among, and applying, the unbelievably varied array of options for how those graphics can look. For example, inserting a clip art file in your document is a snap—a few clicks and it's done. *Then* all you have to do is decide whether text should flow around, over, or under the picture; whether the picture should move with the text it's next to or stay in the same spot on the page no matter what happens to the text; whether it needs a border or shading, and what type of border or shading; whether it's the proper size and orientation…you get the general idea.

You'll find all this to be simpler if you think of graphics as mere content, just as the text you type is content. Whether the object at hand is text or graphics, the job always takes two steps:

1. Put the raw content into the document.

2. Format the content by applying any of a wide range of options to it.

In this chapter, you'll discover all the ways you can add graphical impact to your Word documents. Although the most obvious example is adding pictures, related techniques such as defining borders and creating text boxes are equally important to making your document appealing. And though a table may at first seem like text, when you think about it, a table is a graphical way of treating text—so you'll learn about table-making here, plus a few final surprise visual tricks Word 98 puts into your bag.

In the course of doing all this, you'll encounter two toolbars you haven't seen before—Picture and Tables And Borders (see Figure 6.1). Unlike the Standard and Formatting toolbars, these graphics-related toolbars open automatically

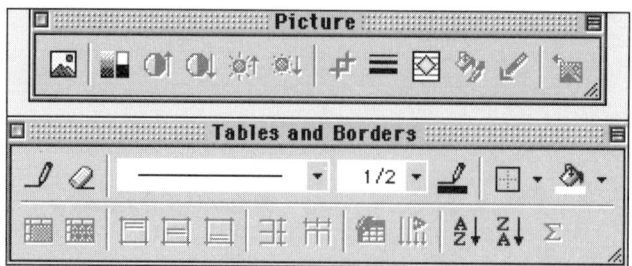

Figure 6.1 The Picture and the Tables And Borders toolbars.

whenever you do something that may require their help, and close when you're finished—so you needn't choose to display them all the time. However, if you want to display them (even if only to check 'em out), choose View|Toolbars and then choose the name of the toolbar you want to display.

Adding Pictures To Documents

Before adding a picture to your document, you must:

- Decide roughly where in the layout of the document the picture belongs.
- Know where the picture file is stored on disk.

Inserting A Picture

To insert a picture, begin by positioning the edit cursor roughly where you want the picture positioned in your document. (Don't worry about creating an empty space for it or positioning it exactly—that stuff comes later.) Choose Insert|Picture. A submenu like the one in Figure 6.2 appears.

> ### *Fast Track*
>
> To insert a picture into a header or footer, position the edit cursor in the header space or footer space as explained in Chapter 5. Then choose Insert|Picture. This is a great way to dress up a document by displaying a company logo or other picture at the top or bottom of every page.
>
> To select the picture for formatting (see "Formatting A Picture" later in this chapter), first open the header or footer space containing the picture, then click on the picture.

From the Picture submenu, choose Clip Art to insert a picture from the Clip Gallery (as described in Chapter 2), or choose From File to insert any type of picture file you have on disk.

Adding Pictures, Tables, And Borders 141

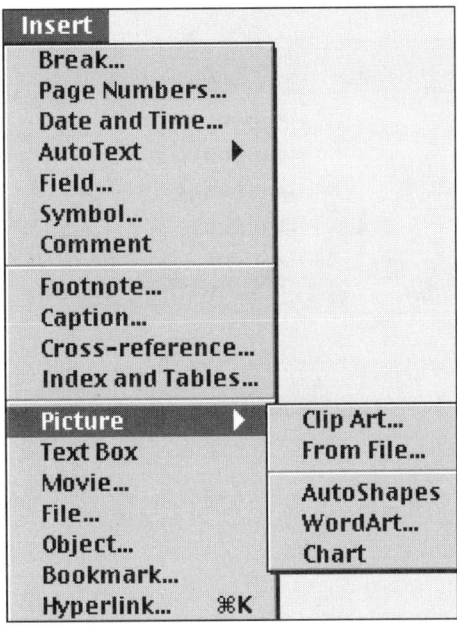

Figure 6.2 The Picture submenu.

If you choose From File, the Insert Picture dialog opens (see Figure 6.3). By default, the dialog opens in the Office 98 Clip Art folder. You're free to choose any of the clip art pictures from the Insert Picture dialog, although if it's Office clip art you want, you'll find using the Clip Gallery more convenient than using the Insert Picture dialog. The Insert Picture dialog shows you just one file at a time, while the Clip Gallery allows you to preview not only many files, but many *kinds* of files at once.

FYI: Get Pictures In Chapter 2, Use Them Here...

The Office environment provides a variety of powerful graphical tools, including OfficeArt (the Clip Gallery and Drawing Tools), WordArt, and an optional Photo Editor for advanced editing. These tools are considered part of the Office environment because you use them the same way whether in Word, Excel, or PowerPoint.

In Chapter 2, you not only learn about using these tools, but you also learn about the many other ways you can acquire and create picture files. To learn how to incorporate those pictures into a document, consult the appropriate chapter:

- *Word*—This chapter
- *PowerPoint*—Chapter 9
- *Excel*—Chapter 13

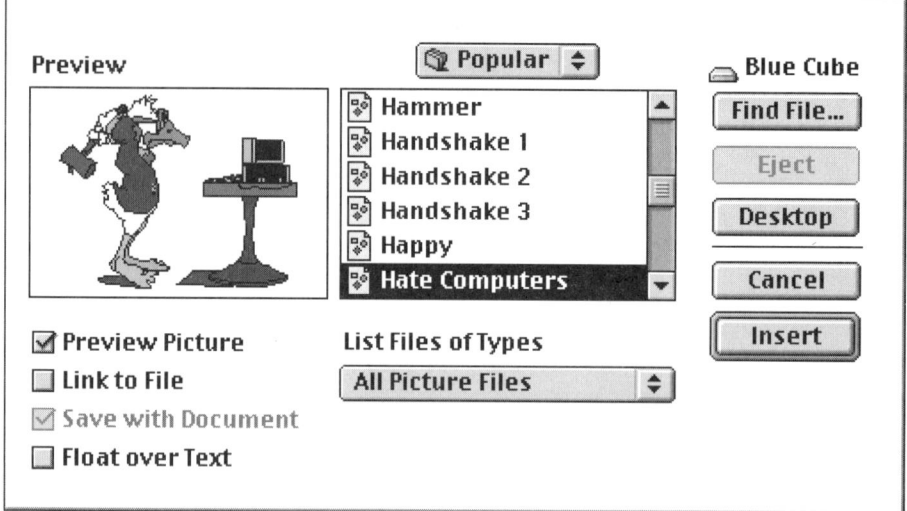

Figure 6.3 The Insert Picture dialog.

FYI: Understanding Color

To a varying degree, almost everything you do in this chapter allows you to add color to your document. For example, you may add a color picture, or you may lay a transparent, colored highlight over selected text.

Although Word exerts no limitations over how you may work with color, when you're working with color you must keep in mind how your document will be published. If the document is intended for online publishing, either in native Word format or as a Hypertext Markup Language (HTML) file (Web page format), you can pretty much do anything you want to color-wise—although you must consider a few compatibility issues you'll learn about in Chapter 17.

When your document is intended for printing, however, you must consider how well—if at all—your intended printer handles color. Whereas a good printer will reproduce the same colors you see (green on screen will be green in print), subtleties of color—the precise hue and saturation—will almost always differ.

Net Savvy

When you publish a document on the Web in the standard file format (HTML), all pictures in the document should be in one of the two standard file types supported by Web browsers: GIF or JPEG. GIF, which stands for Graphics Interchange Format, is supported by all graphical browsers. JPEG, which stands for

Joint Photographic Experts Group, is supported by fewer browsers than GIF, but by all market leaders (including Netscape Navigator and Internet Explorer).

When you save a Word file in HTML format, Word automatically converts all picture files—including OfficeArt—to GIF format, except for JPEG images, which are left in their native format. That frees you to use any pictures you wish—OfficeArt, scanned photos, and so on—in a Word document that will wind up on the Web.

To navigate to the folder that contains the picture file, begin by dropping down the drive/folder list to choose a folder, disk, or the Desktop. When the file you want appears in the file list box, click on it to select it. A preview of the picture appears in the Insert Picture dialog's Preview pane, so you can verify that the file you've selected contains the picture you really want. If the file is a type that you must convert before it can be inserted, the Preview pane displays a message that the preview is unavailable. In addition, note that the Preview pane may not show the picture at its full size. (Also note that if you've unchecked the Preview Picture option, you won't see a preview—sure, it's a simple thing, but easy to forget if you're in a hurry.)

Clicking on Insert plugs the picture into the document and closes the Insert Picture dialog. Before you click on Insert, however, you may want to choose from among the three optional checkboxes that appear along the left-hand side of the Insert Picture dialog:

- *Link To File*—When this checkbox is checked, the picture file doesn't actually become part of the Word document file. Instead, the picture is kept separate but is linked to the Word file so that the picture appears to be part of the document when you display or print it. Linking has certain advantages and disadvantages over *embedding* (making the picture part of the Word file), as you'll learn in Chapter 16.

- *Save With Document*—When this checkbox is checked (it's available only when Link To File is checked), Word automatically copies the picture file to the same folder as the document (if the picture file was not in that folder to begin with). This option helps you keep a Word file and its linked pictures together.

- *Float Over Text*—When this checkbox is checked, the picture "floats" on the page so that you can position it anywhere, without regard to text or other elements on the page. Floating enables you to precisely position the picture on the page and to control how text wraps around it. If you leave the option unchecked, the picture is inserted as an *inline* picture, one that's essentially part of the flow of the text and cannot be positioned except by paragraph formatting options such as left, center, or right alignment. You'll learn more about floating later in this chapter.

When you click on the Insert button to insert the picture, two things happen:

- The picture appears in your document at the edit cursor position.
- The Picture toolbar appears.

You may now adjust the picture's formatting or its position within your document. See "Formatting A Picture" and "Positioning A Picture," coming up next.

FYI: Which Comes First—Picture Format Or Picture Position?

After you insert a picture, it doesn't really matter whether you format the picture's appearance and then adjust its position on the page, or position first, then format. However, some formatting changes—especially changing the size and shape of a picture or cropping it—inadvertently change the picture's position, too. So you'll usually save yourself some jumping back and forth between formatting and positioning if you format first, then position.

Fast Track

When you're working with larger pictures, you may find formatting and positioning the picture most convenient if you reduce the Zoom percentage by choosing from the Zoom list on the Standard toolbar.

Formatting A Picture

Immediately after you insert a picture, it is automatically *selected* for editing. Unlike selected text, a selected picture isn't highlighted; instead, the perimeter of the image is marked by tiny squares called *handles* (see Figure 6.4), and the Picture toolbar appears. (If you see handles but don't see the Picture toolbar, choose View|Toolbars|Picture.)

The handles enable you to use your mouse to change the size and shape of the picture or *crop* it (trim the sides to remove parts you don't want). The Picture toolbar enables you to fine-tune a picture's contrast level, brightness, and other characteristics, much as you might adjust your TV's picture. In the next few pages, you'll learn how to use handles and the Picture toolbar to change an inserted picture's appearance.

Although a picture is preselected immediately after you insert it, you don't have to work on it right away. You can always go back later and select and format the picture while editing the document that contains it. Begin in Page Layout view. Point to the picture (when the pointer is over a picture, it changes to a four-pointed

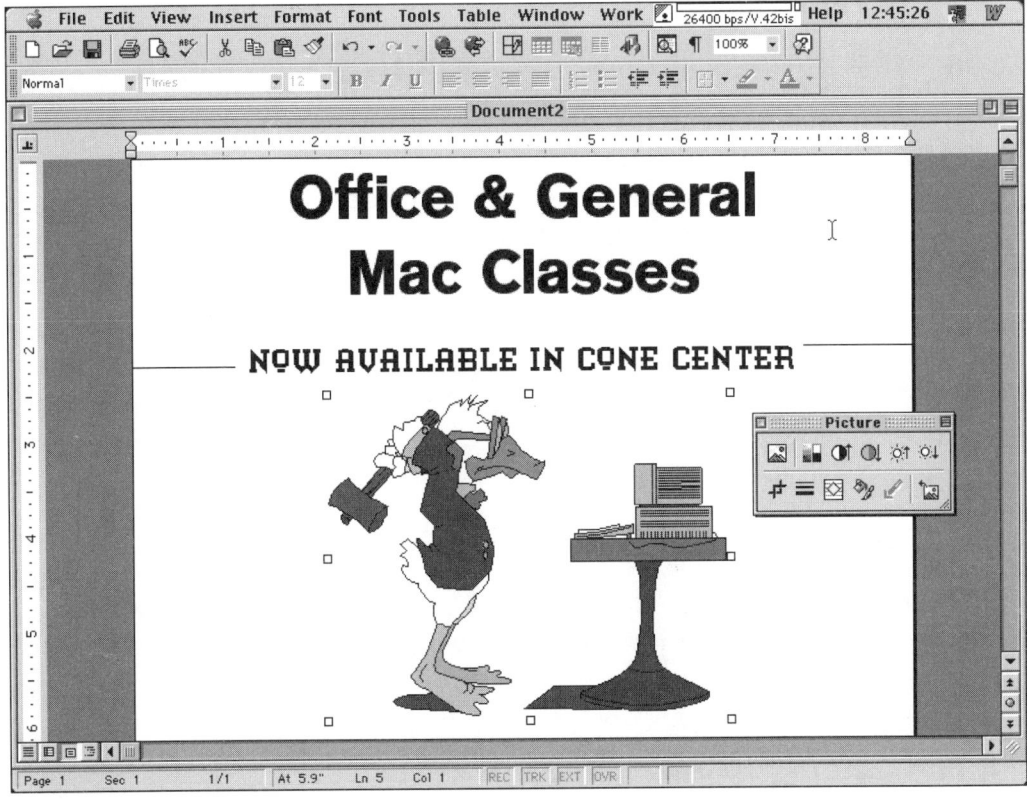

Figure 6.4 Selected picture showing handles and the Picture toolbar.

arrow) and single-click; the handles and Picture toolbar appear. (Should the toolbar fail to appear, select View|Toolbars|Picture.)

When you finish formatting a picture, deselect it by clicking anywhere in the document except on the picture. The handles and Picture toolbar disappear, and you may return to working with the text and page design of your document. If you were working in Normal view, notice that Word leaves you in Page Layout view, so you'll have to switch back manually.

Fast Track

You can apply most of the formatting and positioning techniques you'll discover in the next several pages to any type of picture, whether an OfficeArt file (clip art or drawing object) or a bitmapped file. However, when you're working with OfficeArt you have additional options, including ways to group separate drawing objects together so that you can format and position them as if they were a single picture. See Chapter 2.

Sizing A Picture

To change the size of a picture (*scale* it), point to a handle that appears at a corner. When the pointer is resting on a corner handle, it changes to a two-pointed arrow that points directly toward and away from the center of the image. Click and hold the mouse button and drag to resize the picture—drag away from the picture's center to enlarge it, or drag toward the center to reduce the picture. When the picture is the size you want, release the mouse button.

You can change the overall geometric shape of a picture in the same way that you scale it—by grabbing and dragging a handle. However, although dragging a corner handle scales a picture, dragging any of the other handles changes the picture's *shape*. For example, dragging the top or bottom handle away from the center of the picture stretches the height of the picture without affecting its width; dragging the top or bottom handle toward the center shortens the picture.

Note that when you change a picture's shape, you distort the original proportions of the image; for example, if you drag up the top handle on a picture of a person, the person will appear unnaturally thin (like the actors on *Friends*). Playing with the shapes of pictures this way is best left to abstract (rather than natural) subjects, unless you're going for an unusual or unnatural effect.

FYI: Undoing Picture Formatting

You can undo any type of picture formatting in any of three ways:

- Use Undo to reverse formatting you've done within your last few edits in Word. (To learn more about Undo, see Chapter 4.)
- Click on the Reset Picture button on the Picture toolbar to remove all formatting and restore the picture to its original appearance when first inserted.
- Apply new formatting that's the opposite of the old; for example, if you've shrunk a picture, enlarge it.

Cropping A Picture

Cropping a picture means cutting off a slice of the image on one or more sides to remove an unwanted portion. For example, if a scanned photograph shows both Steve and Gil, but you want to show only Steve in your document, you can crop out Gil.

To crop, click on the Crop button on the Picture toolbar. The pointer changes to a crop pointer, which looks just like the icon on the Crop button. Point to a handle, click, drag toward the center of the picture to crop, then release. What you crop depends on which handle you click on:

- To crop just one side (top, bottom, left, or right) of the picture, point to a handle on that side and drag inward.

- To crop the top or bottom while also cropping a left or right side, point to a corner handle. When you drag toward the center, the sides that meet at the selected corner are cropped together. By dragging at different angles, you can crop more or less of each side involved. Try it!

- To crop opposite sides of the picture, or three or four sides, just do multiple crops.

To remove cropping (restore a cropped portion of an image), just crop again, but drag away from the center of the image rather than toward it. You may also use Undo to undo cropping.

Controlling Brightness, Contrast, And Color

Four buttons on the Picture toolbar—More Contrast, Less Contrast, More Brightness, Less Brightness—allow you to fine-tune the contrast and brightness levels of a picture. As a rule, there's no point fiddling with these controls until you see the picture printed out, so you can see whether the printed contrast and brightness are appropriate. If not, you can adjust the picture with the buttons.

Each time you click on one of the buttons, the picture changes by a small increment. By clicking on a button several times, you can make a noticeable change. For example, clicking on More Brightness once makes the picture a tiny bit brighter. Clicking on More Brightness five or six times makes it a lot brighter. The tiny increments give you subtle control over contrast and brightness.

Positioning A Picture

When you insert a picture, you place it in the general vicinity where you want it to appear. However, careful page design usually dictates that you'll have to carefully adjust a picture's position, especially after formatting. Also, after inserting and formatting a picture, you need to select among a group of options that determine how you want the text around that picture to flow in relation to the picture.

You can choose to lock a picture into a spot on the page so it stays in that spot no matter what happens to the text around it. Alternatively, you can anchor the picture to a paragraph so that it always stays with its paragraph, wherever that paragraph may move in response to changes in the document.

To position a picture anywhere you want and to control how text wraps around it, you must *float* the picture. If, when inserting a picture, you uncheck the Float Over

Text checkbox in the Insert Picture dialog, the picture is *inline*—that is, it's part of the text.

An inline picture moves with the text and responds to paragraph formatting; for example, if you apply center alignment to a selection containing an inline picture, the picture will be centered on the page.

By default, all pictures imported into Word float. You have to tell Word if you want them set inline. You can distinguish a floating picture from an inline picture by the handles that appear when you select it—floating pictures have hollow handles, while those on an inline picture are solid black, connected by a line.

You can apply any of the picture formatting tools described earlier—scaling, shaping, cropping, brightness, and contrast—to an inline picture, but you cannot apply any of the positioning techniques discussed in this section, such as text wrapping.

FYI: *Formatting Can Scramble Pictures*

Different picture file formats respond differently to various kinds of picture formatting. Whereas OfficeArt files retain their image quality no matter how you format them, many bitmapped pictures may develop severe *artifacts*—unattractive flaws—when scaled, and especially when shaped. Cropping, brightness/contrast adjustments, and other kinds of formatting are less likely to create artifacts, but may still create unattractive results in some circumstances.

Unfortunately, we can't offer a reliable way to predict which types of bitmap files respond poorly to what formatting. A wide range of factors determines the effect of formatting on a picture. These include not just its file type, but also the number of colors or levels of gray it incorporates, the presence or absence of certain textures or line patterns, the amount of scaling or other formatting applied (and in what combination), and others.

Try to acquire picture files that require as little formatting in Word as possible—ones that are the proper size and shape to begin with. When you create a picture yourself with a paint program or scanner, perform any necessary scaling or other manipulation within the paint or scan program before inserting the file in Word. And whenever possible, favor OfficeArt pictures—whether clip art or drawing objects you create—over bitmaps, so you can format all you like without worrying about artifacts.

To change a picture from inline to floating, Control-click on the picture and choose Format Object to open the Format Object dialog (which is identical to the Format Picture dialog shown in Figure 6.5), choose the Position tab, and check the checkbox next to Float Over Text.

To position a picture in your document, point to the picture, click and hold the mouse button, then drag to the desired spot and release. Once the picture has been positioned, select options from the Position tab of the Format Picture dialog to control how the picture responds to changes in the document. To open the Format Picture dialog, select the picture (if it is not already selected), then click on the Format Picture button on the Picture toolbar. (Alternatively, you can Control-click on the picture and choose Format Picture from the contextual menu, or select the picture and choose Format|Picture from the menu bar.)

After the Format Picture dialog opens, choose the Position tab (see Figure 6.5). On the Position tab, the entries in the boxes for Horizontal and Vertical (and their respective From boxes) have been preselected for you by Word, based on where you dragged the picture to. These boxes are used to locate the picture at a precise spot

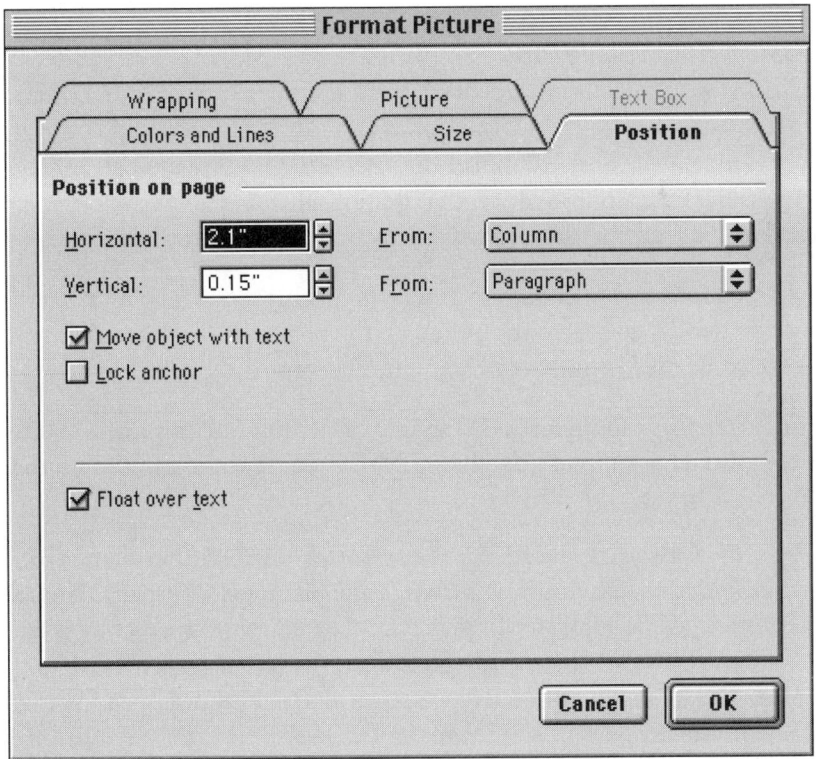

Figure 6.5 The Position tab.

within the page by recording the distance between the picture and a horizontal page element (such as a paragraph) and between the picture and a vertical element (such as a column). In general, you needn't fiddle with these boxes, though you may use them to fine-tune the distance between the picture and the adjacent margin, paragraph, or column.

The meat of the Position tab is in two of the checkboxes: Move Object With Text and Lock Anchor. When neither of these is checked, the picture remains in the same position on the page, regardless of what happens to the text around it. For example, let's say you position a picture at the bottom of the page and then add text to the page. The new text doesn't "push" the picture onto the text page; some of the text that was above the picture jumps to the next page instead, so the picture can stay where it is.

If you check Move Object With Text, the picture's position is tied not to the page, but to the adjacent paragraph. The picture always maintains its position relative to the paragraph and column, but moves up and down on the page—and from page to page—as the text moves. If you check Lock Anchor, the picture not only moves with the text, but also stays on the same page as the text it is anchored to no matter where that text moves.

Choosing How Text Wraps

The final step in integrating a floating picture into your page is determining how text wraps around it. You can accomplish this most easily by selecting the picture and then clicking on the Text Wrapping button on the Picture toolbar. A list of Wrapping Options—each one a button that graphically illustrates a way text can wrap in relation to the picture—drops down, so you can select your desired wrapping style.

For more options and finer control of wrapping, visit the Wrapping tab of the Format Picture dialog. To do so, Control-click on the picture and choose Format Picture from the contextual menu, then choose the Wrapping tab (see Figure 6.6).

On the Wrapping tab, choose a Wrapping Style from the top row of buttons. Note that two of the buttons—Through and None—don't wrap text around the picture, but run text through the picture:

- *Through*—OfficeArt objects may have "empty" areas within them. (Bitmapped pictures do not have empty areas; when the picture is a bitmap, Through has the same effect as the Tight wrapping style.) For example, if a picture is created by the grouping of two objects, space between the two objects may be considered empty. The Through option wraps text around the picture (just like Tight), but also runs the text within any empty areas.

- *None*—The text doesn't wrap at all—it runs straight through the picture. Whether the text runs on top of the picture or is covered by it depends on whether the

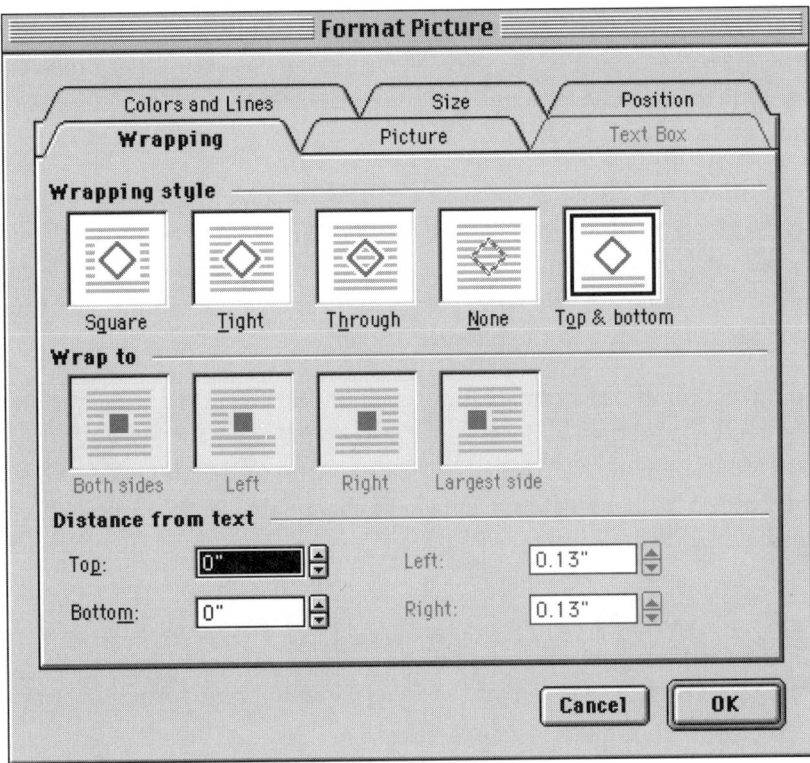

Figure 6.6 The Wrapping tab.

picture is configured to be in front of text or behind text. See "Overlapping Pictures, Text, And Boxes" later in this chapter.

If you select any of the first three Wrapping styles—Square, Tight, or Through—you may also choose a Wrap To option from the second row of buttons. The default Wrap To option—Both Sides—allows text to wrap on both sides of the picture (provided there's room between the picture and the margins). The Left and Right Wrap To options each prevent wrapping on one side, while the Largest Side option allows text to wrap only on the side of the picture where there's the most room.

Finally, the Distance From Text boxes at the bottom of the Wrapping tab enable you to increase or decrease the white space between the picture and the text on any side. If you think there's too much or too little white space between the picture and the text around it, decrease or increase the measurements in Distance From Text until you get the effect you want.

Changing The Wrap Shape

When you're using the wrapping options that wrap text tightly around the edges of a picture, the results may not always be what you expect. Sometimes irregularly shaped pictures include an invisible, rectangular background, to which the text will wrap instead of wrapping to the parts of the picture you see. Other times, the wrapping around irregular shapes looks uneven—the text appears too close to the image at some spots, too far at others.

You can fix either of these problems by editing the picture's *wrap points*, invisible points that form an outline around the picture. When Word wraps text, it wraps not to the picture, but to the invisible wrap points, which loosely follow the contours of the picture. By adjusting the wrap points, you reshape the outline, and thus change the way text wraps around the picture.

To edit wrap points, select the picture, click on the Text Wrapping button on the Picture toolbar, and then choose Edit Wrap Points from the list. A dashed outline appears around the picture, dotted by black squares at the corners. Grab and drag any part of the line, or any black square, to change the shape of the outline. When finished, deselect the picture.

Walk-Through: Insert, Format, And Position The Picture

Follow these steps to practice inserting, positioning, and formatting a picture:

1. Open a document containing text.
2. Choose Insert|Picture|From File. The Insert Picture dialog opens.
3. In the list of folders, double-click on Popular. The box lists picture files in the Popular folder.
4. Scroll down the list and select the file Flower. A rose appears in the Preview pane.
5. Click on Insert. The Insert Picture dialog disappears, and the rose appears in your document.
6. If the Zoom level is higher than 50 percent, drop down the Zoom list on the Formatting toolbar and choose 50 percent. The Zoom level drops to 50 percent, to make seeing and working with the picture easier.
7. If the picture is not already selected, point to it and click on it to select it. The handles and the Picture toolbar appear. (If the Picture toolbar does not appear, select View|Toolbars|Picture.)
8. Point to the handle at the lower right corner of the picture. The pointer becomes a two-pointed arrow.
9. Click and drag the pointer about halfway toward the center of the image, then release.
10. Point to the picture so that the pointer becomes a four-pointed arrow.

Adding Pictures, Tables, And Borders   153

11. Click and drag the picture over any paragraph, then release it.
12. Control-click on the picture and choose Format Picture from the context menu. The Format Picture dialog opens.
13. Choose the Wrapping tab.
14. On the Wrapping tab, choose Tight as the wrapping style, then click on OK. The text wraps tightly on all sides of the picture.

Creating Text Boxes

A *text box* is exactly what it sounds like: a box containing text. The beauty of a text box is that, although it contains text, it can be treated much like a picture. You can scale a text box, change its shape, or apply borders and shading to it. Most important, you can drag a text box to any spot on your page and control how text wraps around it, just like a picture. Also like a picture, a text box can float—so it can sit on top of text, a picture, or another text box, or lay behind them (see the section "Overlapping Pictures, Text, And Boxes" later in this chapter).

To create a text box, choose Insert|Text Box. The pointer becomes a crosshair, and the Text Box toolbar opens (see Figure 6.7). To create a small, square text box (you

Figure 6.7   A text box floating on top of a picture.

can change its size and shape later), click where you want the text box to go. To create a text box of a particular size and shape, point the crosshair to the spot where you want to position the upper-left corner of the text box. Click and hold, then drag downward and to the right. When the box is the shape and size you want, release the mouse button.

Once your text box is created, you can do any of the following:

- *Select the text box*—Click on the text box. Handles appear, along with a hashed border around the entire box, to indicate that the box is selected.

- *Enter and format text*—Click inside the box so that the edit cursor appears there, then type or edit as you wish. You can apply any text formatting or paragraph formatting you wish to the text within the box.

- *Size the text box*—Select the text box and drag its handles exactly as you would to scale or shape a picture.

- *Enter tables and pictures*—Click inside the box to move the edit cursor there, then insert a picture or table as you normally would. Note that while the inserted graphic will automatically resize itself to fit the text box, resizing the text box later on has no effect on the size, shape, or format of a table or picture inside the text box.

- *Position the text box*—Select the text box, then point to the hashed border (the pointer becomes a four-pointed arrow). Click and drag to move the box, then release.

- *Choose text wrapping and other options*—Select the text box, then point to the hashed border (the pointer becomes a four-pointed arrow). Control-click on the border and choose Format Text Box from the context menu. Use the dialog that appears—Format Text Box—exactly as you would use the Format Picture dialog to format a picture (in fact, formatting a text box works almost exactly like formatting a picture, so this should be easy if you've been following along).

Fast Track

You can change the *text direction* of the text in a text box, turning normal text (running left to right, like other text in the document) sideways so that it runs top-down or bottom-up. Select the text box, then click on the Text Direction button on the Text Box toolbar until you get the text direction you want.

Overlapping Pictures, Text, And Boxes

Floating pictures, text boxes, and text can overlap one another in Word documents. The ability to overlap objects can be quite useful. You can, for instance, overlap a text box with the corner of a picture to create a graphical caption (refer back to Figure 6.7). But if you decide to overlap objects, you'll need to control the order of overlapping elements—what's on top of the stack, what's at the bottom of it, what's in between. Begin by positioning your floating pictures and text boxes and choosing Wrapping Options without regard to order. Then find any improperly ordered overlaps and change the order of each element by Control-clicking on the element and choosing Order from the contextual menu. A list of choices appears as shown in Figure 6.8. Notice the small icons in the menu that help you determine the outcome of your selection.

To put the selected object on top of any it overlaps, choose Bring To Front. To put the object under any it overlaps, choose Send To Back. When more than two objects are involved, use Bring Forward and Send Backward to change the selected object's place in the stack one level at a time.

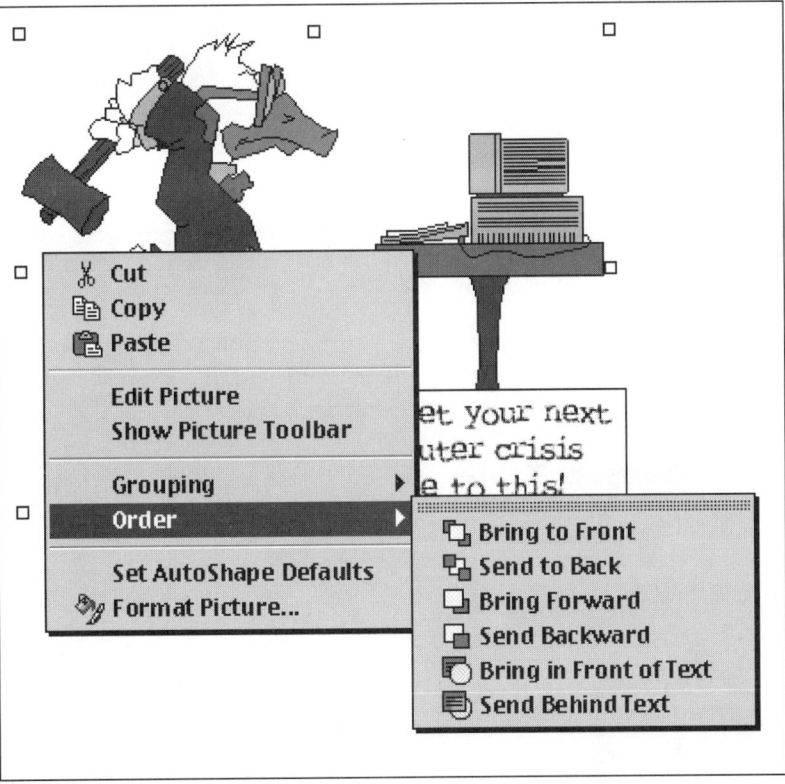

Figure 6.8 The Order submenu.

To make an object cover text (when the Wrapping Style for the object is None), choose Bring In Front Of Text. To allow text to run over the object, choose Send Behind Text.

If you don't want objects to overlap one another, be careful not to overlap elements when positioning them, and don't use the None text wrapping style when choosing Wrapping Options for pictures and text boxes.

Making Tables

As with so many things in Word, making tables is a two-part job. First comes format (defining the rows and columns of the table), then comes content (creating and formatting the contents in each box or *cell* within the table).

There are two basic types of tables: simple and complex (see Figure 6.9). A simple table is just what you would expect: a grid of rows and columns wherein each column has the same number of rows. A complex table is one in which some columns have more rows than others, or vice versa. Most tables are simple, so that's the type you'll

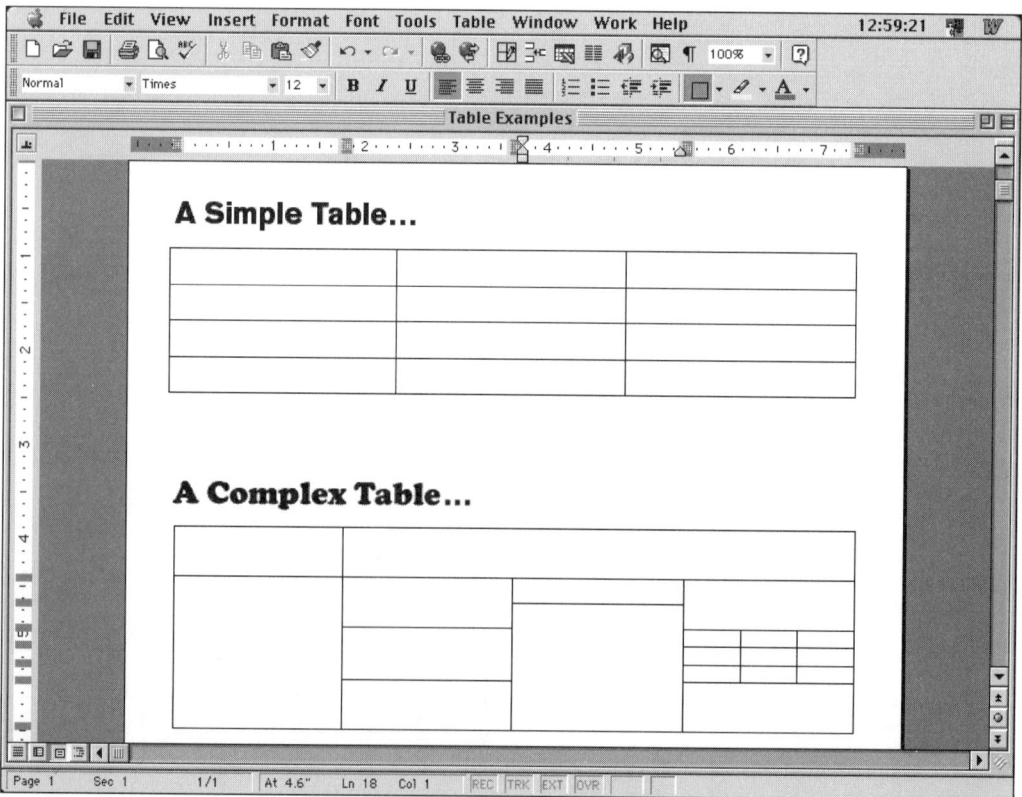

Figure 6.9 Examples of simple and complex table types.

learn to create first in this section. Following simple tables, you'll learn how to enter table content, then how to create complex tables with Word's Draw Table function.

When you're creating tables, keep in mind that the initial table you create need not match exactly the table you'll end up with—in fact, it probably won't. When you create a table, you create a rough repository for the table's contents, just a place to put stuff. As the table evolves, you can adjust its column widths and row heights, customize its borders, add shading, and much more.

Fast Track

Two Office 98 applications can create tables: Word and Excel. Since you can import an Excel table into Word, you may choose to create a table for a Word document in either application.

Which application should you use for tables? That depends a lot on which program you're comfortable with. Even when Excel is the ideal tool for a given table, you may want to use Word anyway if Excel isn't your bag. However, all things being equal, here are the rules of thumb:

If The Table Requires…	Use…
Fancy text formatting (lists, hanging indents, fine control of spacing, etc.)	Word
Fancy calculations, data analysis, or charts generated from table data	Excel
Table contents automatically generated by searching and sorting a database	Excel

Also, when you need a table in a PowerPoint presentation, you'll find importing it into the presentation easiest if you create the table in Word.

To learn about importing an Excel table into a Word document, or a Word table into PowerPoint, see Chapter 16.

Creating A Simple Table

To create a simple table, position the edit cursor where you want the table to appear, then click on the Insert Table button on the Standard toolbar. A grid of boxes opens (see Figure 6.10); move the pointer down to highlight the number of columns in the table, then across to choose the number of rows. Click to insert the table.

The largest table you can create with the Insert Table button is four rows by five columns. To create a larger simple table, choose Table|Insert Table. The Insert Table dialog opens (see Figure 6.11). Choose the number of columns and the number of rows. Then choose an option in Column Width. The default option, Auto, creates

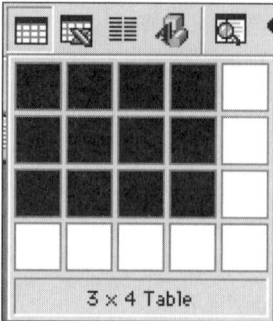

Figure 6.10   A simple table grid created by the Insert Table button.

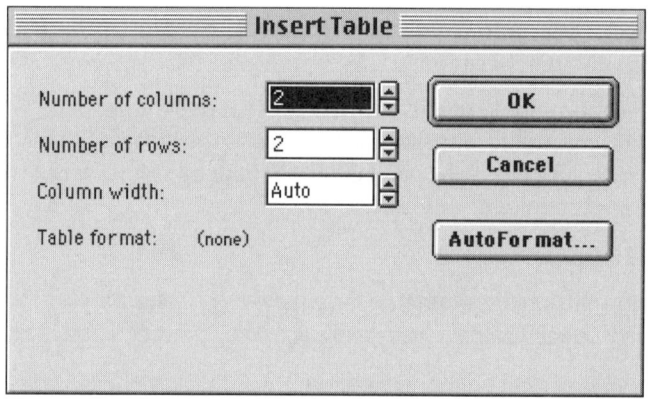

Figure 6.11   The Insert Table dialog.

a table that runs the full width of the page (margin to margin) made up of equally wide columns. Alternatively, you can select a measurement for the columns in Column Width. (Remember that you can always fine-tune column widths later.)

Creating And Formatting A Table's Contents

Once your table is set up, point to a cell and click to supply that cell's contents. You can type in a cell to enter text, or click in the cell and choose Insert|Picture to put a picture in the cell. To move to another cell, click in the cell you want to go to, or press Tab to jump from the current cell to the next one (to the right). If the content you provide requires it, the height of the row automatically increases to accommodate it.

You can format the text in a cell exactly as you would anywhere else in the document. (See Chapter 4.) You can select text and apply character formatting, including fonts, font sizes, attributes, and symbols. You can also apply paragraph formatting, but it works a little differently than it does outside of a table cell. For paragraph-formatting purposes, a cell acts like a whole page. For example, if you position the edit cursor within a paragraph in a cell, then click on the Center Alignment button on the Formatting toolbar, the paragraph is centered within the cell (not within the page as a whole). The other alignment, indenting, and list buttons all do their regular thing, too, but relative to the cell, not the page.

Fast Track

In addition to applying regular text-formatting techniques to text in cells, you may also apply a few formatting options available from the Tables And Borders toolbar.

Begin by selecting the cells you want to format (see the next section, "Selecting Tables And Cells"). Then click on a button on the Tables And Borders toolbar:

- The Align Top, Center Vertically, and Align Bottom buttons let you format the contents of the selected cells to vertically align at the top, center, or bottom of the cell. (You can control the horizontal alignment in the cell with the regular Left, Center, and Right Alignment buttons on the Formatting toolbar.)

- The Change Text Direction button tilts text in the selected cells so that it runs top to bottom or bottom to top, rather than left to right. You might use this option, for example, to create column headings whose text runs bottom to top.

- The Sort Ascending and Sort Descending buttons rearrange the selected cells so that their contents appear in alphabetical or numerical order (ascending) or reverse alphabetical or numerical order (descending).

Selecting Tables And Cells

By selecting a group of table cells, you can conveniently perform a variety of actions that affect all cells in the selection. The most natural way to select table cells is to click in a cell and drag across other cells until all desired cells are selected. Other ways to select table cells include:

- *To select a single cell*—Click on the left edge of the cell.

- *To select a row or column*—Place the edit cursor within the desired row or column, then choose Table|Select Row or Table|Select Column.

- *To select a whole table*—Place the edit cursor within the table and choose Table|Select Table.

Once you've selected the cells to work on, you can:

- Apply text formatting to format the text in all selected cells the same way.

- Choose Table|Merge Cells (to merge two or more cells into one) or Table|Split Cells (to split each cell into two). You can use this technique to turn a simple table to a complex one, or vice versa.

- Apply borders or shading to only the selected cells. For example, you can highlight column headings in a table by selecting the cells containing the headings and applying a heavier border or shading to them than to the rest of the table.

- If you select a row or column of cells, you can choose Table|Delete Cells to remove a portion of the table and all of its contents.

Finally, if you select the whole table, you can use copy and paste (to copy the table) or cut and paste (to move the table). See Chapter 4.

FYI: Delete Cuts Content, Not Cells

When you select cells and the press the Delete key, only the cell contents are deleted—the empty cells remain. To delete the cells themselves, or rows or columns from a table, select the cells and choose Table|Delete.

Drawing A Complex Table

Using Word's Draw Table facility, you can "draw" a simple or complex table. Click on the Tables And Borders button on the Standard toolbar (or choose Table|Draw Table). The Tables And Borders toolbar opens (see Figure 6.12) and the pointer becomes a pencil. The pencil draws the grid lines of the table when you click and drag.

To create a column, point to where you want the top of the column to appear and drag downward; as you drag, a dashed line appears to indicate the line you're drawing. When you reached the end of your desired column, release the mouse button. To create a row, point to where you want the left end of the row to appear, then drag to the right. You can split rows or columns into smaller rows or columns by clicking on their grid lines and then dragging new grid lines within them. To erase a row or column, click on the Eraser button on the Tables And Borders toolbar, click on a line in the offending table element, drag to highlight the portion to erase, then release.

When you're finished drawing your table, click outside the table to restore the regular pointer. Then enter the table's contents or adjust its format as desired.

Adjusting Column Width And Row Height

As you develop your table and add its contents, you'll inevitably want to adjust the column widths. The row heights change automatically to accommodate your cell entries, but you may decide to adjust row heights manually, as well.

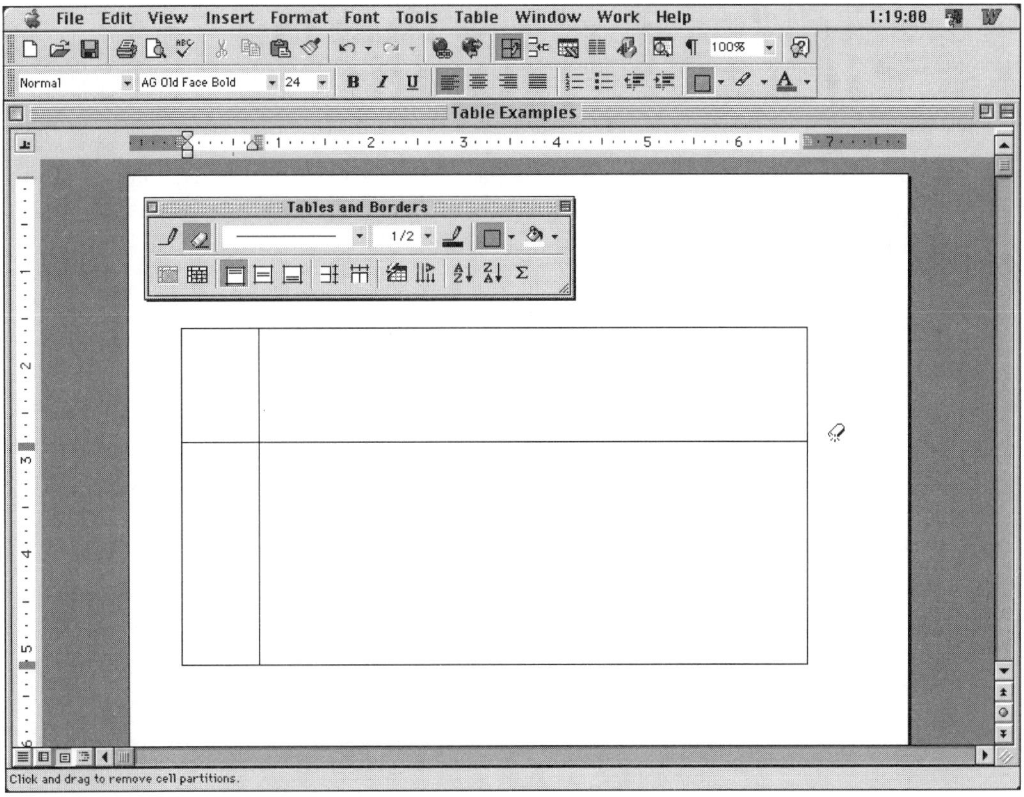

Adding Pictures, Tables, And Borders   161

Figure 6.12 Drawing a complex table.

The most natural way to adjust column widths and row heights is to drag the grid lines of the table. If you point very carefully to a vertical grid line in a table, you'll see the pointer change to a vertical double bar with a horizontal arrow on each side. To change the column's width, click and drag to the right or left. You can adjust row height in the same way by dragging the horizontal grid lines up or down. To change the height or width of selected cells, rather than whole rows or columns, first select the cells, then click and drag the grid lines within the selection. Note that the width or height of the selected cells will no longer match up with the rest of the row or column.

Word can automatically resize a selected group of rows or columns to make them all of equal width or height. To create equal-width columns, select the columns and choose Table|Distribute Columns Evenly. To create equal-height rows, select the rows and choose Table|Distribute Rows Evenly. (Instead of using the Table menu, you can also select the rows or columns and use the Distribute Columns Evenly button or the Distribute Rows Evenly button on the Tables And Borders toolbar.)

Working With Borders, Shading, And Color

A *border* is a rectangular box that can appear around almost anything in a Word document: a picture, a text box, a table, a paragraph, selected text within a paragraph, or even a whole page. Within a border—which may be visible or invisible—you can add *shading*, a color or pattern (or both) that lends extra emphasis or visual variety to your document.

You control the look of borders and shading by selecting from among the following characteristics:

- *Line Color*—The color of the border lines.
- *Line Style*—A straight line, squiggly line, zigzag, dashed line, and so on.
- *Line Weight*—The thickness of the line (expressed in points, just like font size).
- *Sides/Grid Lines*—On which sides of the selected object (or on which grid lines in a table) the border appears.
- *Fill Color*—The color of the shading.
- *Pattern*—A line pattern or dot pattern that adds texture to the shading (a pattern may be used in combination with fill color).

Now, to make borders and shading as confusing as possible, Word offers four different ways to apply them. Having options is terrific, but the benefit of having four ways to do borders and shading is undercut by three problems:

- No type of object (text, pictures, tables, etc.) works with all four methods.
- Only one method, the Borders And Shading dialog, gives you complete control over all characteristics of the borders and shading.
- Terminology is used inconsistently from method to method. For example, fill color is called "fill color" in one method, "highlight color" in another, and "shading color" in another.

Fortunately, there's one part of this job that's reliable: You always begin by selecting the object to which you want to apply borders and shading. Once the object is selected, you can apply borders and shading with the method that meets your needs.

On the next several pages, we describe each of the four ways you can apply borders and shading—including to which objects you can apply each method and which characteristics you can control.

FYI: Tables Carry Extra Border Options

Border lines can appear on any or all of the four sides of a picture, text box, paragraph, page, or selected text. However, a table isn't a single box—it's many boxes, because each cell is a box unto itself.

You can select a whole table and apply borders and shading to it. When you do, you can use the Outside Border button on the Tables And Borders toolbar, or the Preview pane of the Borders And Shading dialog, to selectively apply or remove the border line from any grid line on the table. (When a table grid line has no border line applied to it, it appears gray on your display and will not appear at all in print.)

Alternatively, you can select part of a table and apply borders and shading only to that part. For example, you might apply shading to a single row to make it stand out, while not shading other rows.

Formatting Toolbar

This option allows you to quickly apply simple borders or colored highlights to selected paragraphs, text, text boxes, and tables (but not pictures). Here are two ways to use it:

- Click on the arrow on the Outside Border button of the Formatting toolbar. A box of options appears, from which you can choose the sides to which you want to apply borders. This option provides no control over line weight, style, or color.

- Click on the arrow on the Highlight button of the Formatting toolbar. A box of options appears, from which you can choose the color of the shading. This option provides only a fraction of the shading options available with other methods.

Colors And Lines Tab

This option applies a border on all sides, or shading, to a selected picture or text box. On the tab, shading is called *fill color*; a fill color shades a text box in the selected color or shades empty areas of a picture.

To open the tab shown in Figure 6.13, Control-click on a picture and choose Format Picture from the contextual menu (or Control-click on a text box and choose Format Text Box). Then click on the Colors And Lines tab.

Choose a color (in the Fill area of the tab) to apply a fill color to the selection, or choose the top item in the color list—an empty box—to apply no shading. (Check the Semitransparent checkbox to allow items behind the picture or text box to be seen through a fill color.) In the Line section of the tab, choose among options for the border's color, style, and weight.

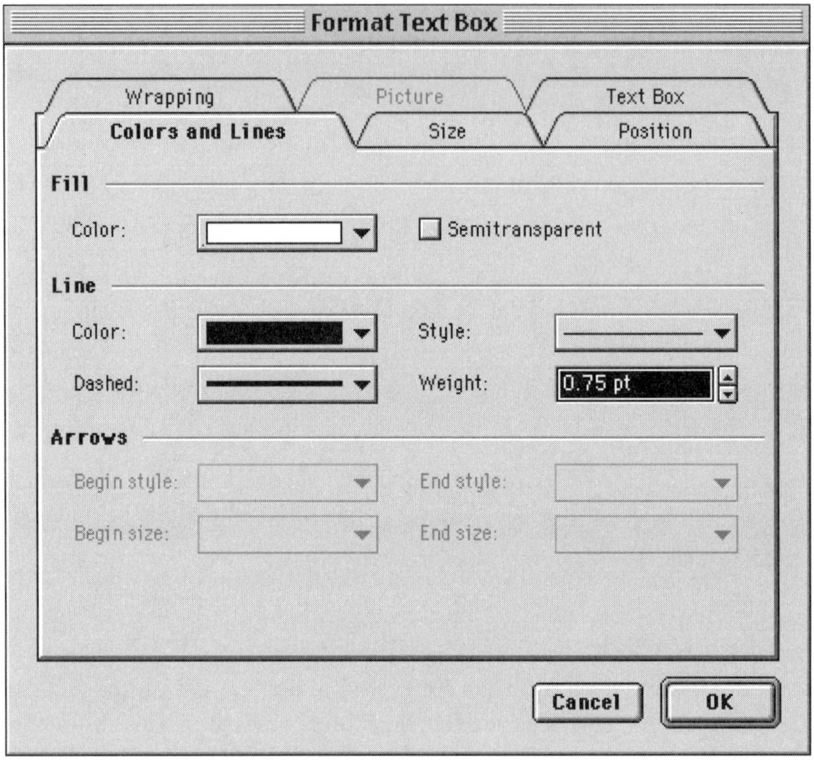

Figure 6.13 The Colors And Lines tab.

Fast Track

To create a cool solid line—a horizontal *rule*—under a header or over a footer (or to apply shading to a header or footer), apply borders and shading to the text of the header or footer.

For example, to create a rule under the header, open the header space (choose View|Header And Footer), select the header text, then apply a border using the Formatting toolbar or the Borders And Shading dialog (covered later in this chapter).

Tables And Borders Toolbar

This option allows you to apply any of several types of borders or fill colors to a table. Select all or part of the table, then open the Tables And Borders toolbar (choose View|Toolbars|Tables And Borders). Choose the sides and grid lines to which you want to apply a border by clicking on the Outside Border button (which works just like the Outside Border button on the Formatting toolbar) and choosing from the list. Note that you can achieve better control of which grid lines get borders by using the Borders And Shading dialog instead of the toolbar.

Customize the line by selecting from the toolbar's lists for Line Weight, Line Style, and Border Color. Choose any desired fill color from the Shading Color button.

Borders And Shading Dialog

This option applies the widest available range of border and shading options and is available for selected text, paragraphs, text boxes, and tables (not pictures).

Begin by selecting the object, then choose Format|Borders And Shading. The Borders And Shading dialog opens, as shown in Figure 6.14. On the Borders tab, choose the overall look of the border under Setting, then fine-tune the look of the lines by choosing from the Style, Color, and Width (weight) lists. To selectively add or remove the border from any side of the object, click on a side of the image in the Preview area.

To shade the selection with a fill color or pattern, click on the Shading tab and select from among the fill color and pattern options provided.

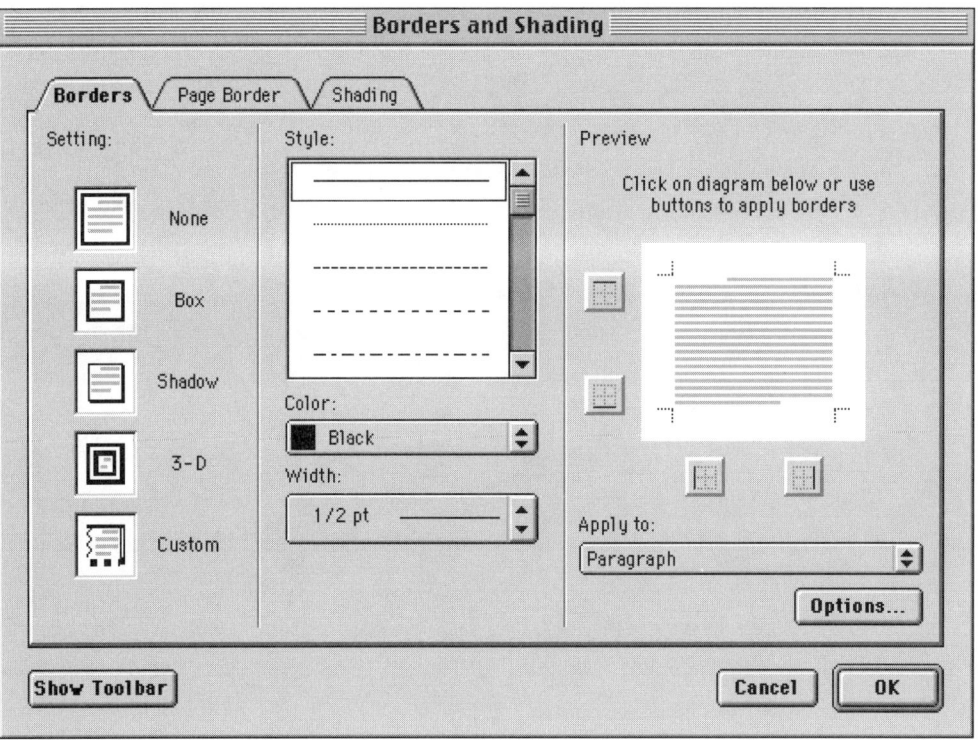

Figure 6.14 The Borders tab.

Fast Track

You can put a border around a selected page, all pages in a section, or all pages in a document. First, locate the edit cursor anywhere in the page, section, or document on which you want to put a border. Then choose Format|Borders And Shading and click on the Page Border tab.

Choose from among the options on the Page Border tab, which are identical to those on the Borders tab. When you're finished, choose an item from the tab's Apply To list to apply the page border to the whole document, the current section, just the first page of the current section, or all pages in the current section except for the current page.

Walk-Through: Tables And Borders

Follow these steps to practice working with tables and borders:

1. Open or create any document.
2. Position the edit cursor in the document and click on the Insert Table button on the Standard toolbar. The grid of table columns and rows drops down.
3. Move the pointer down and to the right to highlight three rows by four columns (3 × 4).
4. Click. A simple 3 × 4 table appears in the document.
5. Click in any cell(s) you wish and practice entering and formatting text.
6. Click in any cell (but don't select the cell) and choose Format|Borders And Shading. The Borders And Shading dialog opens.
7. On the Borders tab under Setting, choose All.
8. In Width, choose 3 pt, then click on OK. A three-point border appears on all lines of the table.
9. Click in any cell along the top row of the table.
10. Choose Table|Select Row. The top row is selected.
11. Choose Format|Borders And Shading. The Borders And Shading dialog opens.
12. In Width, choose 6 pt.
13. Choose the Shading tab.
14. In Style, choose 20 percent.
15. Click on OK. The top row of the table has a border twice as thick as the rest of the table and is shaded with a 20 percent gray pattern.

Moving On

The applications included with Office 98 cover a lot of different activities, but curiously, serious computer graphics creation isn't one of them. There's no shortage of such programs outside of Office 98, including such animals as Macromedia FreeHand and Adobe Illustrator, if you need more advanced graphics tools than those accessible through Word.

In practice, creating pictures is one discipline and integrating them into documents is another—that's why many companies have both graphic artists and desktop publishing pros on staff. Still, Word gives you a level of control over the formatting and positioning of pictures that until very recently was the exclusive province of desktop publishing software and beyond the toolset of an ordinary word processor. And yes, through Office's Clip Gallery and Drawing toolsets, you can provide your own pictures, to a limited extent. Nevertheless, that stuff is really extracurricular as far as Word is concerned. Word doesn't care where the picture comes from or how it was created; Word's job is to fit the picture within the page, and it does that well.

Again, you'll find working with pictures in Word easier if you mentally separate the job into two parts:

1. Get the picture into the document (a quick trip to the Insert Picture dialog or Clip Gallery).

2. When necessary, fiddle with its formatting and positioning (beginning with the buttons on the Picture toolbar), to create precisely the effect you want.

Tables, similarly, are a two-part job:

1. Map out the rows and columns.

2. Enter the contents of each cell.

Now that you know how to add graphical flair, you know how to do just about everything that you can do to a Word document. So why does another chapter about Word remain? Well, we must confess that for many of the activities you've already learned how to perform—and a few you haven't—Word offers a faster, easier, or more powerful way to get the job done. Don't get mad—we had a really good reason for dragging you through the hard way first. We'll explain everything right at the start of Chapter 7.

Working Faster And Easier In Word

"It's the last chapter about Word," you may say, "and *now* you're telling me how to do stuff faster and easier than I did it in earlier chapters? Is this some kind of cruel joke?"

No joke. We had a really, *really* good reason. See, you're probably one of two types of readers: a complete newcomer to Word, or an upgrader from a previous version. If you're an upgrader, you probably haven't read all of the preceding chapters; you've just skimmed the stuff that's new and worked your way here quickly, so your patience hasn't been taxed. And besides, as a user of an earlier Word version, you already knew that a number of time savers were available to you.

But if you're new to Word, then it's important that you know the mechanics of a document before you turn those tasks over to an automated helper. For example, a *template*—which you learn how to use in this chapter—can automatically apply page formatting like margins and paper size, so you don't have to bother. But unless you already know something about page formatting and how it's applied, how can you determine if a template's settings are right for you? More importantly, if you decide you want to use the template, but you also need to modify some of the formatting it applies (as most users of templates inevitably do), you have to know how.

By first showing you the nuts and bolts of document creation and formatting, we've given you the tools to control every aspect of your documents, so you can produce exactly the look you want or need. In this chapter, you'll discover a number of shortcuts that can make creating, formatting, editing, or producing some types of documents quicker and easier. But make no mistake—nothing you learn in this chapter is a replacement for knowing the techniques you picked up in Chapters 3 through 6, just as the availability of a spellchecker (which you'll also learn about here) doesn't mean you can ignore spelling as you type.

No shortcut is perfect. Knowing the nuts and bolts enables you to enjoy the shortcuts when they apply, but not to be dependent on them. We want you to control Word—not the other way around.

FYI: More Ways To Use What You Learn...

The first two sections in this chapter cover two types of files that help you create and format new documents more quickly and easily: wizards and templates.

Many of the wizard files and template files included with Office 98 are copied to your Mac in the drag-and-drop installation—but some aren't. If you want to install other templates that are included with Office, run the Microsoft Office Installer (see Appendix A) and choose Custom Install. From the list that appears, drop down Microsoft Word and select Wizards And Templates. Make sure no other items are selected, then proceed with the install.

Finally, a few more wizards and templates are included in the Value Pack folder on the Office 98 CD. Choose Value Pack, then Templates, then Word to open a folder of additional wizards and templates. Copy any you like to your Templates folder as described later in this chapter. You can also install these items by running the Value Pack Installer. Select Custom Install, open the Templates item, and select Additional Word Templates and/or Word For Windows templates, then click on Install. You'll then have access to all the templates available from the Value Pack. (Incidentally, Word For Windows templates don't require Word For Windows. They just came over from that program. They'll work fine on your Mac.)

Wizarding Up A New Document

Word includes a family of *wizards* for quickly producing any of several common types of documents, including letters, faxes, resumes, mailing labels, and many more. Wizards are similar to Mac assistants. If you've installed Mac OS 8, or if you've recently bought a new Mac, you probably used the Mac OS Setup Assistant and the Internet Assistant. A wizard is simply a miniature software program of sorts, meant to take you through a process step by step. For instance, Word's wizards step you through the process of creating certain types of documents. (Wizards are different from templates, though. Templates are ready-made documents into which you plug your information. They don't actually walk you through anything.)

You use a Word wizard simply by starting it up and then doing whatever the wizard tells you to do. To begin, click on File|New to open the New dialog. (Don't click on the New button on the toolbar; it creates a new document without opening the New dialog.) In the tabs of the New dialog, you'll see two kinds of files—wizards (which are so labeled), and templates (anything that doesn't say wizard in the name).

Browse among the tabs to locate a wizard whose name suggests that it might fit what you want to produce. For example, if you intend to write your resume, open the Other Documents tab and choose Resume Wizard. The Preview pane in the New dialog shows you a sample of the kind of document the selected wizard produces (see Figure 7.1). When you've selected the wizard you want, click on OK to start the wizard.

A wizard dialog opens, as shown in Figure 7.2, offering instructions for using the wizard. Click through the wizard's dialogs as instructed, choosing among options or supplying text when the wizard tells you to. To advance to each new dialog, click on the Next button; to go back to an earlier dialog to make a change, click on Back. Like the Resume Wizard shown in Figure 7.2, many wizards offer a sort of index along the left side of the dialog. The index helps give you a sense of what the wizard will require of you; it also enables you to jump directly to any dialog in the wizard simply by clicking on any entry in the index.

When you've supplied the wizard with all of the entries it requires, click on the Finish button (or click on Finish at the bottom of the index). The wizard generates the document, opens the document in Word, and then the wizard closes. You may edit or expand the wizard-produced document however you like, save it, or print it.

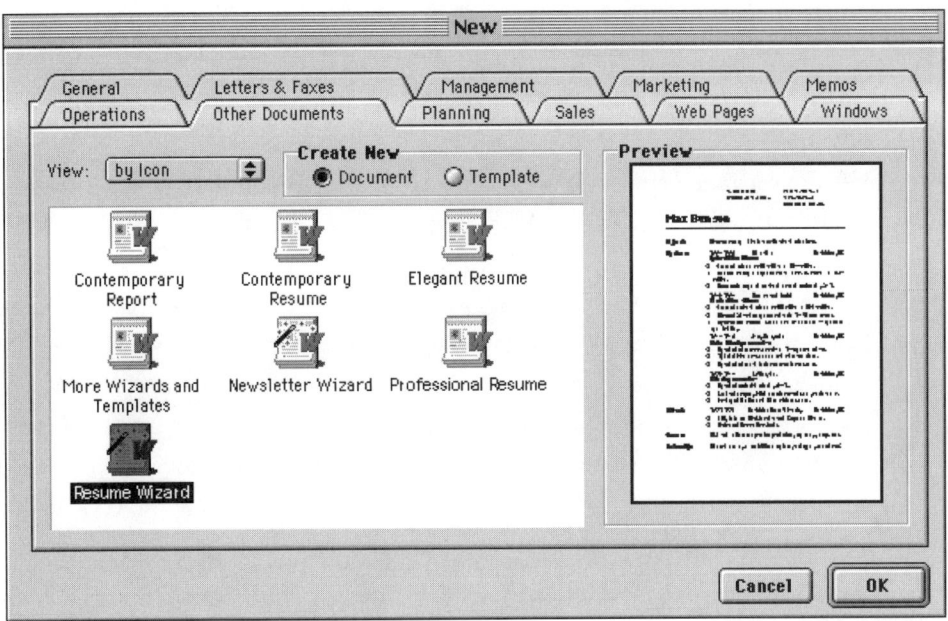

Figure 7.1 You can select a wizard file (and see a preview of it) in the New dialog (the extra tabs you see are from installing the Value Pack templates).

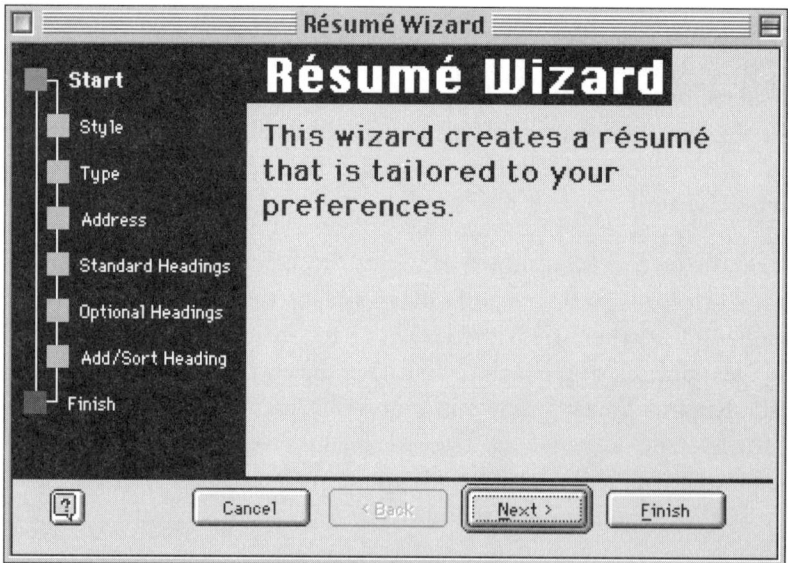

Figure 7.2 A Word document wizard leads you step by step through creating the document.

FYI: *Letter Wizard*

On the assumption that letters are the most frequently composed documents for most Word users, Microsoft has included a special Letter Wizard in Word 98 that doesn't behave like other wizards.

You can start the Letter Wizard in two ways: from the New dialog, or by choosing Tools|Letter Wizard. (There are several letter-making wizards among the wizards in the Templates file, but they're not the same as the Letter Wizard.) It's worth noting that there is an inconsistency in the ways you can start the Letter Wizard. Choosing Tools|Letter Wizard simply opens the Letter Wizard's dialog. But choosing Letter Wizard from the New dialog's tabs offers you the option to send a letter to one recipient or to multiple recipients. If you open the Letter Wizard this way, choose one recipient for the moment. Choosing multiple recipients initiates the Mail Merge Helper, and we're not ready to cover that yet. (Hopefully, Microsoft will resolve this minor inconsistency soon.)

If you use Word with the Office Assistant, whenever you do something in a new document that suggests you may be composing a letter—for example, typing an address or starting a line "Dear Lara", Office Assistant asks whether you want help with writing a letter. If you say you do, the Assistant opens the Letter Wizard.

The other way the Letter Wizard differs from other wizards is that it isn't really

> a wizard—it's just a four-tab dialog. On the dialog, you choose options defining the style and layout of the letter, and also enter such standard letter elements as the recipient address, salutation, and closing. A Preview pane in the Letter Wizard shows you the letter you're creating as you go.

Working With Templates

A *template* is a prefab document, a head start on a document you'll create.

The template contains settings for page layout, paragraph formatting, character formatting, headers and footers, and more, so you don't need to define all of these elements yourself. In fact, a template may even contain some of the text of the document, or pictures. When you use a template, all you have to do is supply whatever the template doesn't supply—usually just the text—and you're finished. Instead of both writing and formatting your document, you just plug your writing into a preformatted shell.

Using a template has two benefits. The first and most obvious is that a template saves you time when you create a new document. But another, less obvious benefit comes into play when you create a group of documents that share common formatting or portions of text in common. By basing all of the documents on the same template, you ensure that they're formatted consistently and have common elements—including any common text they may share—defined in advance.

Net Savvy

You can download new wizards and templates from the Microsoft Word Free Stuff page. If you have a default Web browser set up (using Internet Config or the Internet Setup Assistant), open Word and choose Help|Microsoft On The Web|Free Stuff. Or point your browser to **www.microsoft.com/OfficeFreeStuff/Word/**.

When you're downloading new templates or wizards, be sure to save them in your Templates folder (or move them there after downloading). For most Office users, the Templates folder is inside your Microsoft Office program folder. There are a number of subfolders—pick the one most appropriate for your new template or wizard. If your Mac is on a local network, the Templates folder may be called User Templates or Workgroup Templates.

Using An Existing Template

The easiest way to use a template is to select it when creating a new document. You can choose a template from Word's New dialog (File|New).

In the New dialog (see Figure 7.1, earlier in this chapter), click among the tabs and locate a template whose tab and file name suggest a close match for the type of document you want to create. Single-click on the file icon to select the template; the Preview pane in the New dialog shows you a sample of the kind of document the selected template produces.

When you've found the template you want to use, check the top center of the window to make sure that Document (not Template) is selected under Create New, then click on OK. A new document, based on the template, opens in Word. Add to and edit the document any way you want, and save it or print it as needed.

Note that some templates include built-in instructions, prompting you to "Click here and type…" something or other. For example, at the top of the document that appears when you open Elegant Letter (in the Letters & Faxes tab), you'll see the line "CLICK HERE AND TYPE COMPANY NAME." When you click on that text, the whole line is automatically selected, and whatever you type replaces the instruction and is formatted as a letterhead.

Finally, some templates have sample text built into them to help you visualize the document. For example, if you create a new document based on the template Elegant Resume (in the Other Documents tab), you'll see that the template is a resume for somebody named Rich Andrews. Unless you're him, you'll need to replace the content of his resume with yours.

FYI: Templates Aren't Married To Their Docs (Part I)

When you're working on a document that you created with a template, you can change anything you want to change in the document—including the stuff the template contained. For example, if the template contained margin settings, you may nevertheless change the margins in the document; if the template contains text, you may edit, reformat, or even delete the text in the document.

Changes you make to the document have no effect on the original template or to other documents based on the same template. You can edit the document all you like, and the template remains the same. Also, if you move or copy the document, you needn't move or copy the template along with it. The document is fully independent of the template.

Obviously, the more you change stuff that was part of the template, the less useful the template has been to you. Still, it's important to remember that the template really just helps you start a document. Once the document is open, you can do anything you want with it—it's just a document like any other.

Creating Or Editing A Template

To create a template, all you need to do is create a document that contains all of the stuff you want to include in the template. A template can include:

- Text
- Pictures
- Page layout (see Chapter 5 for a discussion of settings on the Page Setup dialog)
- Styles for paragraph and character formatting (see "Working With Styles" later in this chapter)

Begin by creating your document, just as you would any other document. As you work, you may save the document, just as you would any other. You can even begin with an existing document and edit it to create the document that will become the template.

When the document contains all of the elements you want featured in the template, open the Save As dialog by choosing File|Save As. In the File Name box, give your new template a name that describes the type of document it creates. In the Save File As Type list near the bottom of the dialog, choose Document Template; the entry in Save In automatically changes to the Templates folder. Choose (or create) a subfolder within Templates in which you want to store the template, and click on the Save button. The template is now available for creating a new document; you can get to it from the New dialog. (You can save a template anywhere—it needn't live in the Templates folder. However, the Templates folder is as good a place as any, and if you use it, you'll locate the template more quickly when you need it.)

Instead of creating a new template from scratch or from an existing document, you can edit a template—whether one included with Office or one you created yourself. To edit a template, open it as you would an existing document—choose File|Open, navigate to the Templates folder, and choose a template. (The Templates folder is usually called Microsoft Office 98/Templates. If your Mac is on a local network, the Templates folder may be called User Templates or Workgroup Templates.) Make any changes you want, then save the template.

By default, the template is saved as a template file. If you wish, you may use the Save As dialog to change the file name (to create a new, edited copy of an existing template), but be careful not to change the entry in Save File As Type—it must be Document Template.

Fast Track

When you create a new document but don't choose a template, Word automatically uses a template called Normal. The new, blank document based on the Normal template appears whenever you open Word, click on the New button on the Standard toolbar, or choose Blank Document from the Open dialog.

By editing the Normal template, you can change the formatting of this default document. For example, if you'd like to be able to click on the New button and instantly begin work on a document that has 1-inch margins all around and uses Arial as its default font, simply edit the Normal template to match these settings.

You'll find the Normal template in your Templates folder. You can edit the Normal template any way you wish, but don't move it from the folder where you find it. When you create a new, blank document, Word looks for the Normal template in your Templates folder. If Word can't find it there, Word automatically creates a new Normal using its default settings.

FYI: Templates Aren't Married To Their Docs (Part II—The Sequel)

Just as changing a document does not affect the template on which it's based, changing the template does not affect any documents previously created with that template. Changes you make to a template affect only the documents you create with it *after* you've changed it.

There's one little exception to this rule: If you make changes to the *styles* the template contains, you can optionally instruct Word to update the styles in documents based on the template. See the next section, "Working With Styles."

Working With Styles

A *style* is a collection of formatting characteristics—including both character formatting (fonts, font sizes, attributes) and paragraph formatting (alignment, indentation, line spacing, list formatting)—that define how you want a block of text treated.

By creating and using styles in Word, you can conveniently format whole blocks of text without the bother of separately applying each formatting characteristic. Styles not only save formatting time, but also help you make formatting consistent within a document—all headings use a Heading style, the body text is always formatted with the Body Text style, and so on.

More important, by using styles you can make sweeping formatting changes to entire documents easily, because changing the formatting of a given style automatically changes the format of every text block of that style. For example, if you've formatted all of your chapter headings with a style called Heading 1, and then decide you'd like all of your headings to appear in Arial font, you simply change Heading 1 so that it applies the new font, and presto, all of your headings will then appear in the new font.

There are two basic types of styles: paragraph and character. A paragraph-type style can apply both paragraph formatting and character formatting, and always affects an entire paragraph, even if only a portion of the paragraph is selected when you apply the style. A character-type style includes only character formatting, and may be applied to all or part of a paragraph.

Fast Track

The styles saved with the Normal template are automatically available for use in any document, even if the document is based on another template instead of Normal. You can make a new style you create accessible from within any Word document by adding that style to Normal.

Applying A Style

All of the styles available in the current document are available from the Style list on the far left side of the Formatting toolbar (see Figure 7.3). The styles available in any document include:

- All styles that are part of the template on which the document is based.
- All styles in the Normal template.
- Any new styles Word has created for you as you've developed the document.
- Any new styles you have created for the document (if any).

To apply a style, select the text to which you want the style applied and then choose the style from the Style list. Observe that each item on the Style list is formatted to approximate the look that the style applies. To the right of each style entry in the list, you will find a small gray block with several icons in it. The first indicates the style's text alignment setting (using the same indicators as the alignment buttons in the Formatting toolbar). If the style is a paragraph-type style in the list, a paragraph symbol appears (¶); if the style is a character-type style, an underlined letter "a" appears. Finally, for the paragraph-type style elements, you'll see a line listing the point size of your style.

If the style is a paragraph-type style, and you want to apply it to a single paragraph, just position the edit cursor anywhere within the paragraph and choose the style. If

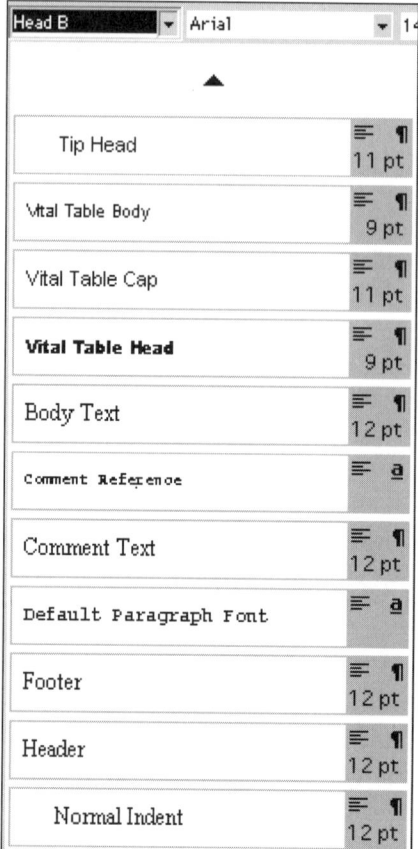

Figure 7.3 Apply a style by choosing from the Styles list on the Formatting toolbar.

the desired style is a character-type style, or if you want to apply a paragraph-type style to more than one paragraph, select the text to which the style should be applied, and choose the style.

To preview the look of a style before applying it, select the text you want to format, then choose Format|Style. The Style dialog opens as Figure 7.4 shows, with previews of the paragraph and character formatting the style applies. Beneath the preview, a somewhat cryptic description of the style appears; if you look at it carefully, you'll see that it includes a font name, font size, and other information. In the Styles list, choose the style you want to preview. When you find the style you want to use, click on the Apply button.

Fast Track

If you make manual formatting changes to a selection, and then decide you preferred the way the selection was originally formatted, you can always revert it to

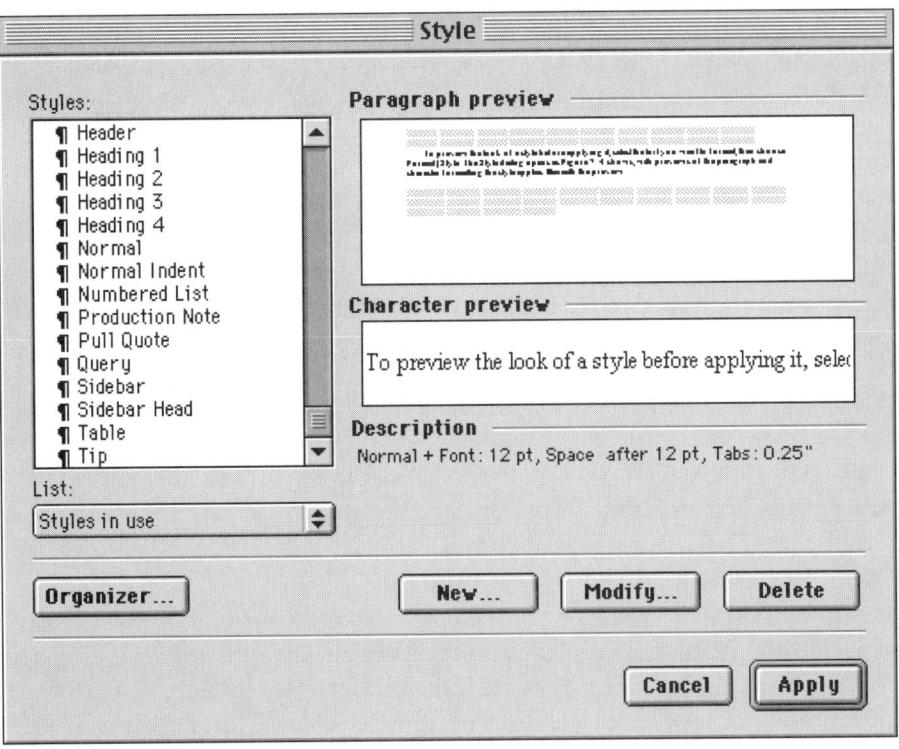

Figure 7.4 In the Style dialog, you may select and preview a style, modify or delete styles, or create new ones.

its old appearance with Undo. But you may find it easier to simply reapply the selection's original style.

Choose the style from the Style list, and a dialog appears, asking whether you want to update the style to match the selection's formatting (see "Changing A Style" later in this chapter), or reapply the style's original formatting to the selection. Click on the radio button next to Reapply, then click on OK.

Creating Or Changing A Style

As you format text blocks in Word, Word automatically creates new styles. For example, if you center a line of text at the top of a document and format it in a large font size, Word will guess that the line is a title, and will create a new style called Title based on the formatting you applied. The styles Word comes up with may or may not be useful to you.

You can deliberately create new styles and add them to the current document or template. If you add a new style to a document, it's available only in that document. If you add it to a template, it's available in any document based on that template. If you add a style to the Normal template, it's available in all documents, regardless of the template on which they're based.

Making A Paragraph Style The Easy Way

The easiest way to create a new paragraph-type style is to format a paragraph in the way you want the style to format your paragraphs, then create the style from that formatting.

First, select your preformatted paragraph. Click in the Style box on the Formatting toolbar, but instead of selecting a style from the list, type a name for the new style and press Return. The new style name is added (alphabetically) to the Style list, and the paragraph you used to create the style now has that style officially applied to it. You may apply your new style anywhere in the document.

If you save the document as a template, any new paragraph styles you've created using this method become part of the template and may be applied in other documents based on the template. If you save the document as a Word document, the new styles you've created are available only within the document.

Defining A New Character Or Paragraph Style

To create a character-type style (with no paragraph formatting), choose Format|Style to open the Style dialog, then click on the New button on the Style dialog to open the New Style dialog (see Figure 7.5). In the New Style dialog, you can create not only a character-type style, but also a paragraph-type style and apply to it optional controls that are unavailable with the easy method described earlier.

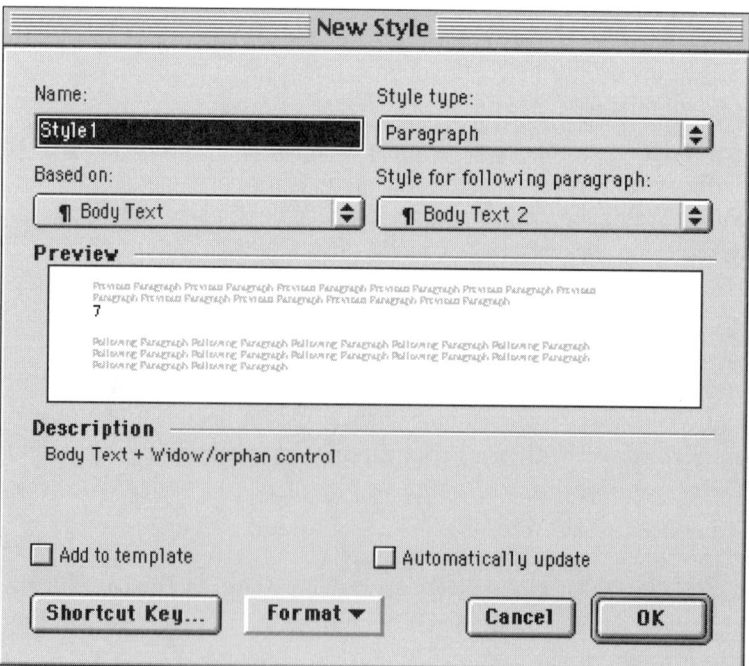

Figure 7.5 Define a new style by choosing options in the New Style dialog.

In the New Style dialog, begin by giving the style a name, and choose a Style type (Paragraph or Character). In the Based On list, you can select an existing style that's a close match for the one you want to create, to save yourself some work defining the style. For example, if the only difference between an existing style called "Heading" and the one you want to create is the font size, choose Heading in Based On. If no existing style is close to your desired style, choose the top entry in the Based On list, which is No Style for paragraph-type styles or Underlying Properties for character-type styles.

With the Style For Following Paragraph option (which is available only when you've selected Paragraph as the Style Type), you may choose an existing style to be automatically applied to any paragraph that follows a paragraph using the style you're creating. For example, when you create a style for headings, you may specify that you always want to use a Body Text style for the paragraph following a heading. Using this option applies the style automatically to the following paragraph, but you can, if you want, apply a different style or formatting to that paragraph within the document.

You're finally ready to select the formatting for the new style. Click on the Format button at the bottom of the New Style dialog to drop down a list of formatting options—Font, Paragraph, and so on. Selecting any one of these brings up the regular dialog used for that type of formatting; for example, choosing Font brings up the Font dialog so you can choose the font, font size, and character spacing. Using any of the available dialogs, apply whatever formatting you want to. Each time you complete a formatting dialog, you automatically return to the New Style dialog, where the Preview shows you how the style looks with the changes you've made so far.

Fast Track

Near the bottom of the New Style dialog appear two checkboxes you can use to control two optional aspects for applying the style:

- If you check the Add To Template checkbox, the new style is added not only to the current document, but also to the template on which the document is based.

- If you check the Automatically Update checkbox, Word changes the style definition automatically if you change the formatting of text to which the style has been applied. This option enables you to change style definitions on the fly from within a document, but it also creates a potential for accidentally changing whole style definitions when you merely wanted to change the formatting of a paragraph.

When you finish formatting and the Preview pane shows what you want to see, click on OK on the New Style dialog. The new style is then added to the Style list on the Formatting toolbar.

Changing A Style

To change a style, choose Format|Style to open the Style dialog, then click on the Modify button to open the Modify Style dialog. The Modify Style dialog is identical to the New Style dialog (see "Defining A New Character Or Paragraph Style" earlier in this chapter); just change whatever you want to on the dialog and use the Format button to edit the formatting. When you're finished, click on OK on the Modify Style dialog.

After you change a style, you can make the changes effective in existing documents. This allows you to change the formatting in one or more documents automatically, simply by making changes to styles applied in those documents. Begin by changing the style, and be sure to check the Add To Template checkbox on the Modify Style dialog.

After opening any document based on the template, if you want the style changes applied in the document, choose Tools|Templates And Add-Ins. In the Templates And Add-Ins dialog that opens, check the checkbox for Automatically Update Document Styles. The style modifications become effective in the current document, and any new styles you've added to the template become available in the current document.

Fast Track

To change styles on the fly, select a block of text to which the style has been applied, then change its formatting to match what you want the style to do. Then choose the style from the Style list and a dialog appears, asking whether you want to update the style to match the selection's formatting or reapply the style's original formatting to the selection. Click on the radio button next to Update, then click on OK. The style definition is changed, and all text in the document formatted with that style changes to match the new formatting.

Walk-Through: Templates And Styles

Follow these steps to practice working with templates and styles:

1. Choose File|New. The New dialog opens.
2. In the New dialog, click on the Other Documents tab.
3. Click on the template Elegant Resume. A preview of the Elegant Resume template appears.

4. Click on OK.
5. Select the name (RICH ANDREWS, whoever that is) at the top.
6. Type your name (note that you needn't press Shift; the name is capitalized automatically by the style).
7. Under OBJECTIVE, click on the instruction that appears.
8. Type a brief description of your life goals.
9. Position the edit cursor anywhere within your name at the top of the resume.
10. Drop down the Style list and choose Document Label. The name is reformatted in the Document Label style. (You may have to fix its capitalization now.)
11. Save the resume, for practice. Don't actually submit it anywhere unless you happen coincidentally to have been a salesperson for Arbor Shoe.

Browsing Through Text

Sometimes you need to locate specific parts of your document—for example, after giving your file to someone else for editing, you might want to see just the comments when you get it back. In cases like this, it's handy to have a fast way to skip from point to point, looking at just those things you need to see.

Word includes a handy Browse By feature for just this situation. In the lower left of every document window below your vertical scroll bar, you'll see two sets of double-arrows and a button between them with a ball on it. The Browse By function is operated from the "ball" icon—the Select Browse Object button. Clicking on this button opens a table that lists several objects. Selecting one of these objects automatically moves your cursor to the next appearance of that type of object. For instance, if you select the table, your cursor moves to the next table in your document.

Once you've selected a browse object, the double arrows come into play. Clicking the double up arrows jumps to the previous object (following our example, this would be the previous table). Similarly, clicking on the double down arrows jumps to the next object.

You can browse by a variety of objects: tables, graphics, headings, edits, pages, section, comments, endnotes, footnotes, and fields. The Select Browse Object table also has Find and Go To selections, which open the Find dialog and the Go To dialog, respectively.

AutoCorrecting And Formatting Text

When you think of using a word processor to automatically check your work, you probably think first of spellchecking. Word indeed will spellcheck the living daylights out of your documents, and check your grammar for good measure—as you'll learn in the section "Checking Spelling And Grammar" later in this chapter.

But first you'll discover a group of handy tools called AutoCorrect features, for lack of a better word. Unlike spellchecking—which you fire up as needed—most of the AutoCorrecting features are on duty all of the time, checking and correcting your typos, cleaning up certain types of text formatting, and even finishing words and phrases for you when you type just the first few letters. That's more "AutoHelpingYouOut" than "AutoCorrecting," but that's names for ya.

Using Word's AutoCorrect Features

All of the AutoCorrect features depend upon Word's ability to know—and, in a few cases, guess—how you want certain types of errors and other text handled. Thus the most important step in using AutoCorrect is choosing among the many options on the AutoCorrect dialog to tell Word what you want done and what you want left alone.

To begin, open the AutoCorrect dialog by choosing Tools|AutoCorrect. Consult the next several pages to learn how to complete each of the four tabs of the AutoCorrect dialog.

As you learn about AutoCorrect, keep in mind that choosing the exact options you want to apply takes some experience, some trial and error. If you were to check every checkbox on the AutoCorrect dialog—instructing Word to fix every mistake it thinks it sees—you might find that Word keeps trying to fix things that you want left alone. Through experience, you'll learn how to fine-tune the AutoCorrect dialog to match the way you work.

Fast Track

In the next few pages you'll learn how to customize and operate Word's AutoCorrect features, but the four tabs of the AutoCorrect dialog contain so many correction/formatting options that not all can be described in detail here. If you want to know specifically what an option on a tab does, just choose Help|Show Balloons, then point to the desired option and click. An explanation of the option's effect appears.

AutoCorrect

On the AutoCorrect tab (see Figure 7.6), choose the errors you want Word to fix automatically. Note that Word makes AutoCorrect changes instantly and

Figure 7.6 The AutoCorrect tab—where you control how Word makes automatic fixes—is the first of four tabs in the AutoCorrect dialog.

automatically, and does not prompt you or otherwise inform you when making a change. For example, if the top checkbox in the AutoCorrect tab, Correct TWo INitial CApitals, is checked, when you type "GOdzilla," Word automatically changes the word to "Godzilla" the moment you finish typing it.

In the top three checkboxes of the AutoCorrect tab, check the checkbox for any of the three common capitalization errors listed if you want Word to correct such errors automatically. Note that Word is pretty smart about how it applies these capitalization repairs. For example, the fix for two initial capitals comes into effect only when the word has three or more letters, and only when you capitalized the first two letters, but not all letters. Thus, mistakes like "DOg" get fixed, but Word doesn't prevent you from typing "TV" or "VCR."

Fast Track

If your AutoCorrect settings are preventing you from applying some special capitalization you require—for example, if you really want to use two initial caps on a word, as you might with some unusual company names—you have three options. First, of course, you can open the AutoCorrect dialog and uncheck the checkbox that is thwarting you. Alternatively, you can select the characters you want to control capitalization for, choose Format|Change Case, and choose a case for the selected characters. Change Case settings override AutoCorrect. Finally, you can open the AutoCorrect dialog, click on Exceptions, go to the INitial CAps, and add your exceptions to the list. This makes a permanent exception for words you enter here (in fact, Brian had to do it so he could type the name of the Correct TWo INitial CAps checkbox).

When the fourth checkbox on the AutoCorrect tab, Replace Text As You Type, is checked, all of the items in the list below the checkbox go into effect. In each case, Word automatically replaces text you type—specified in the left column of the list—with different text or a special character.

If you scroll through the long list, you'll see that the predefined entries insert a number of commonly used special characters when you type their standard typewriter-based equivalents. When you type "(c)", a real copyright symbol is in-serted in its place. Beneath the special characters in the list are entries for dozens of the most common typing errors; there's a list entry to change "adn" to "and," "mesage" to "message," and so on. (Note that AutoCorrect doesn't actually check your spelling—it simply makes the replacements in the list. To learn how to check spelling as you type, see "Checking Spelling And Grammar" later in this chapter.) Fixes for a few especially common grammatical errors appear in the list, as well.

Net Savvy

By default, Word's AutoCorrect feature turns most *smileys*—the little faces made of characters that are used to express emotions on the Internet—into neat little graphical faces that show the same emotion (provided you have the right fonts installed—in this case, the Wingdings font that ships with Office).

You can edit or delete any entry in the list you don't want, and more importantly, you can add your own new entries. Odds are that the mistakes you make often are already there (Ned's big one, typing "comapny" for "company," is there), but if you want to change the list, here's what you do:

- To add a new entry, click in the Replace box and type the error, then click in the With box and type its correct replacement. Click on the Add button to add the new entry to the list.

Working Faster And Easier In Word   **187**

- To delete an existing entry, select it from the list and click on the Delete button.
- To edit an existing entry, select it from the list, edit it in the Replace and With boxes as desired, then click on the Replace button (which appears in place of the Add button when you edit an existing entry).

Fast Track

If there's a long or difficult word you type often, you can add an entry to the AutoCorrect list to make Word automatically type the word for you.

For example, suppose you work for McGillicuddy, Inc., and must type that long and tricky name often in your documents. In the Replace box, enter a short nonsense word—a word you know you'll never type for any other purpose, such as "mgc." Then enter "McGillicuddy, Inc." in the With box and click on Add. Whenever you type the word "mgc" in a document, Word automatically replaces it with the full company name.

You can achieve a similar result with AutoComplete (see "AutoText [And AutoComplete]" later in this section). But AutoCorrect is more convenient for this purpose than AutoComplete because with AutoCorrect, Word makes the change automatically, whereas with AutoComplete, Word prompts you to accept or reject each entry.

AutoFormat

AutoFormat works a lot like AutoCorrect, except that it applies certain types of paragraph formatting and special character formatting instead of correcting. You actually have two different AutoFormat facilities in Word:

- *AutoFormat As You Type*—As soon as you type anything AutoFormat is programmed to format, Word applies the formatting, just as AutoCorrect automatically applies its changes.
- *AutoFormat On Demand*—Word AutoFormats nothing while you're typing. Instead, when you want Word to AutoFormat, you choose Format|AutoFormat to open the AutoFormat dialog and instruct Word to work through the document, applying the formatting as it goes. Also, unlike AutoFormat As You Type, the on-demand flavor optionally enables you to approve or reject each change.

Each AutoFormat flavor has its own tab in the AutoCorrect dialog (the AutoFormat As You Type tab appears in Figure 7.7; the AutoFormat tab is similar). You do the same thing in both dialogs: Check the checkboxes for formatting you want applied. You needn't work as if you had to select checkboxes on either one tab or the other; you may want some types of changes applied as you go along, and others applied selectively on demand.

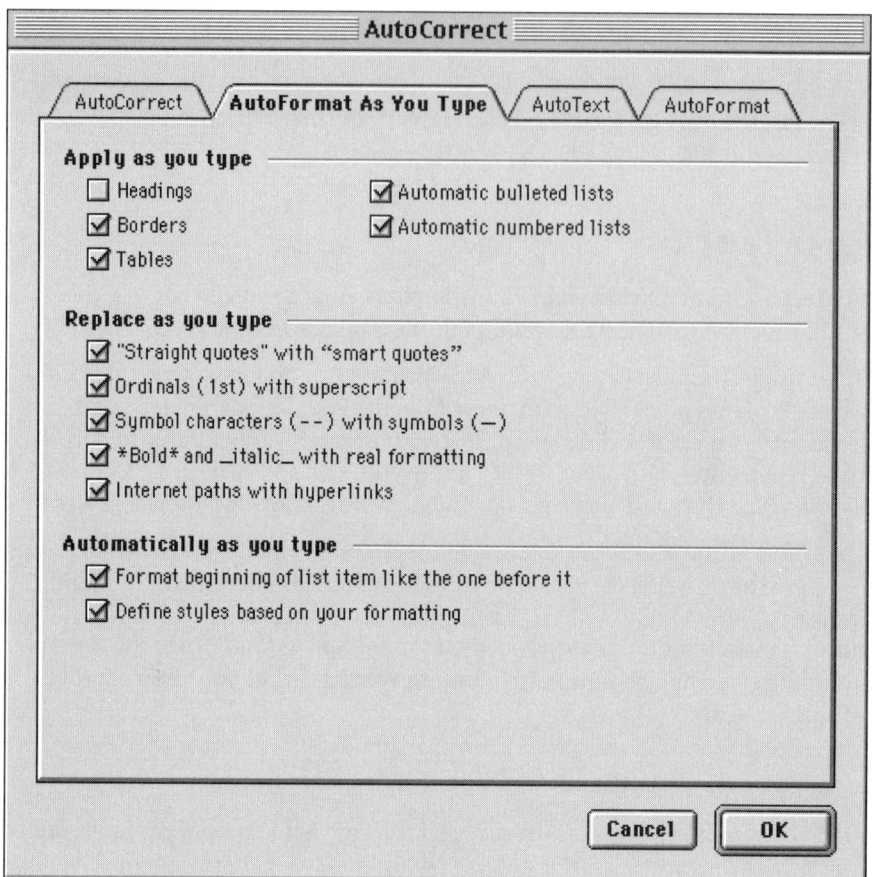

Figure 7.7 Choose formatting options from the AutoCorrect dialog's AutoFormat As You Type tab.

How Word decides what to format depends on a system of intelligent guesses. For example, if at the beginning of a line you type a dash or asterisk, then a space or tab, then some text, Word guesses that you're starting a bulleted list and formats the line accordingly (if Automatic Bulleted Lists is checked). If a number and a space or tab starts the line, Word guesses you're typing a numbered list and applies numbered list formatting.

After you've checked your checkboxes, the selections on the AutoFormat As You Type dialog are applied automatically as you work. To apply the formatting selected on the AutoFormat tab, choose Format|AutoFormat to open the AutoFormat dialog (see Figure 7.8). Here's what you can do on this dialog:

- To AutoFormat the entire document with no further input from you, choose AutoFormat Now and click on OK.

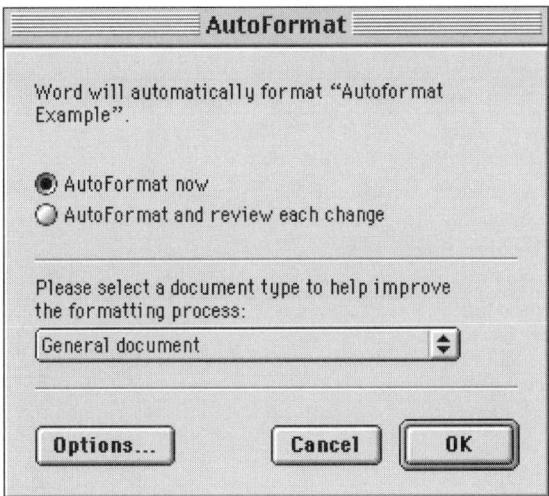

Figure 7.8 Use the AutoFormat dialog to initiate "on-demand" automatic formatting.

- To AutoFormat the entire document and then review changes, select AutoFormat And Review Each Change and click on OK. Word AutoFormats the entire document, then opens a dialog you can use to review each change, accept or reject changes, and edit the styles Word has applied.

AutoText (And AutoComplete)

"AutoText" is Word's way of describing words and phrases that are used often in documents. Because you are likely to use such phrases as "To Whom It May Concern," "Best wishes," or even your own name in your documents, Word maintains a list of such items and offers you two ways to insert them in your documents without actually typing them.

A long list of AutoText entries is predefined in Word; you can review the list by scrolling through it on the AutoText tab (see Figure 7.9). When you select any item in the list, you can preview its effect by watching the tab's Preview pane. To add a new entry of your own, simply type it in the box under Enter AutoText Entries Here and click on the Add button. To delete an AutoText entry, select it in the list and click on the Delete button.

In your document, you can insert items from the AutoText list in either of two ways:

- *AutoText toolbar*—Click on the Show Toolbar button on the AutoText tab (or choose View|Toolbars|AutoText) to show the AutoText toolbar (see Figure 7.10). Any time you need an AutoText entry, position the cursor in your document where you want the insertion made, then click on All Entries on the AutoText toolbar. A list of categories drops down; choose a category, then choose an entry from the list that appears.

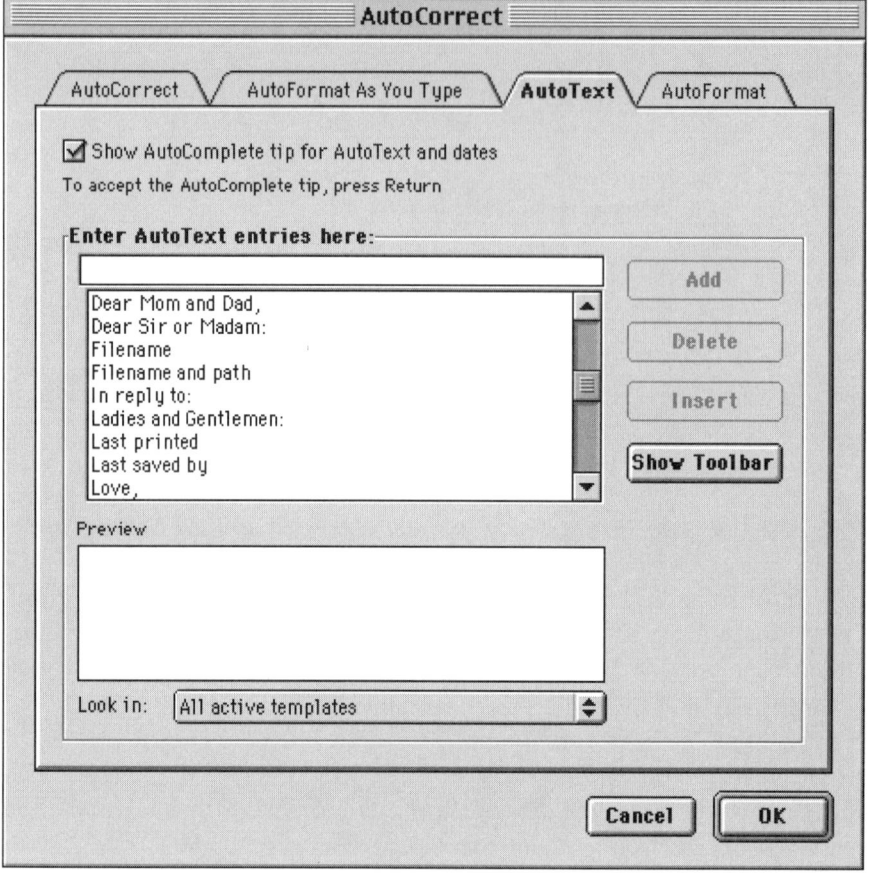

Figure 7.9 Use the AutoCorrect dialog's AutoText tab to create and modify shortcuts to many different types of text entries.

- *AutoComplete*—Check the checkbox at the top of the AutoText dialog to enable AutoComplete. When AutoComplete is enabled, any time you type the first several characters of an AutoText entry, AutoComplete guesses what you're trying to type and displays a tip box (see Figure 7.11). To accept AutoComplete's suggestion, press Return; to reject it, just keep typing.

Note that the number of characters you must type before AutoComplete kicks in varies. In some cases, you need to type only the first four characters. In other cases, you must type enough of the word or phrase for AutoComplete to distinguish what you're typing from among several possibilities in the list. For example, you must type "Best w" before AutoComplete suggests "Best wishes." Until you type the "w," AutoComplete must wait to see whether you're aiming for "Best wishes" or "Best regards."

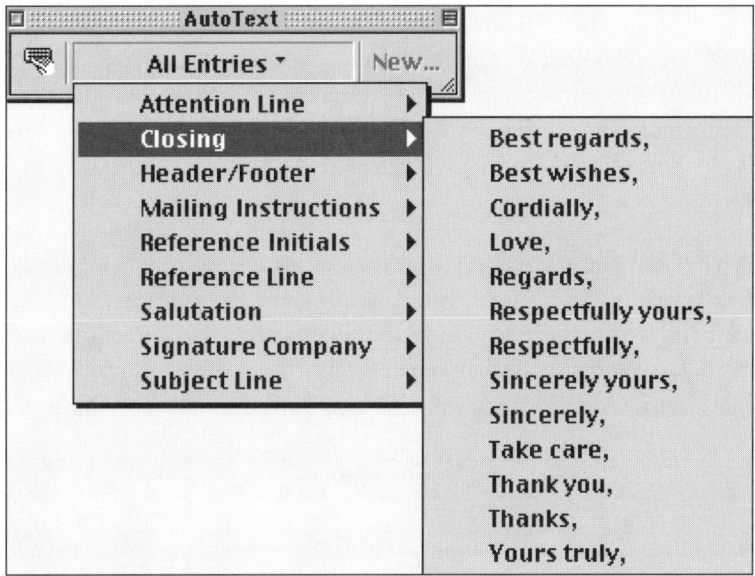

Figure 7.10 You may insert any of your AutoText entries by choosing from the AutoText toolbar.

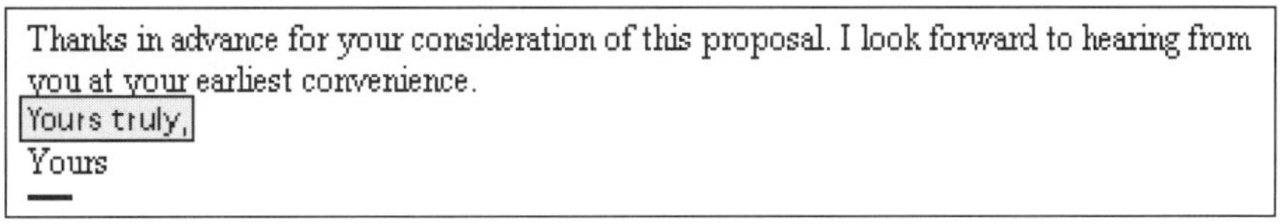

Figure 7.11 Press Return to accept changes suggested in an AutoComplete tip.

Checking Spelling And Grammar

Spellchecking is a great benefit and also a trap. The trap is that sometimes you may pay too little attention to spelling when writing or reviewing your document because you know you'll spellcheck it later. As you know if that trap has ever caught you, spellcheckers are terrific at locating obviously misspelled words, but incapable of discovering when you've used the wrong word—"to" for "two," "your" for "you're," "lose" for "loose," and so on.

That's why Word's grammar checker—which works just like its spellchecker—is so important. For casual correspondence, you may not care whether you've ended a sentence with a preposition or split an infinitive. But the grammar checker is also quite adept at using the structure and context of a sentence to determine when you've used the wrong word. Grammar checking is great when you're unsure of your grammar, but just as important as an adjunct to spellchecking.

Word's spellchecking and grammar checking can both do their thing on the fly as you type, or on demand. You'll learn both methods in the next few pages.

Fixing Spelling And Grammar As You Go

To instruct Word to check your spelling and grammar automatically as you type, choose Tools|Preferences to open the Preferences dialog, then choose the Spelling & Grammar tab (see Figure 7.12). There you'll find checkboxes for Check Spelling As You Type and Check Grammar As You Type, along with a variety of other options.

If you've checked these checkboxes, Word automatically runs a red zigzag underline beneath words and phrases whose spelling and/or grammar are suspect. If you don't want the word or phrase corrected, just ignore the underline; it doesn't show up in print. To solicit Word's help with fixing the spelling or grammar of a zigzag-underlined item, Control-click on it. A contextual menu (see Figure 7.13) opens,

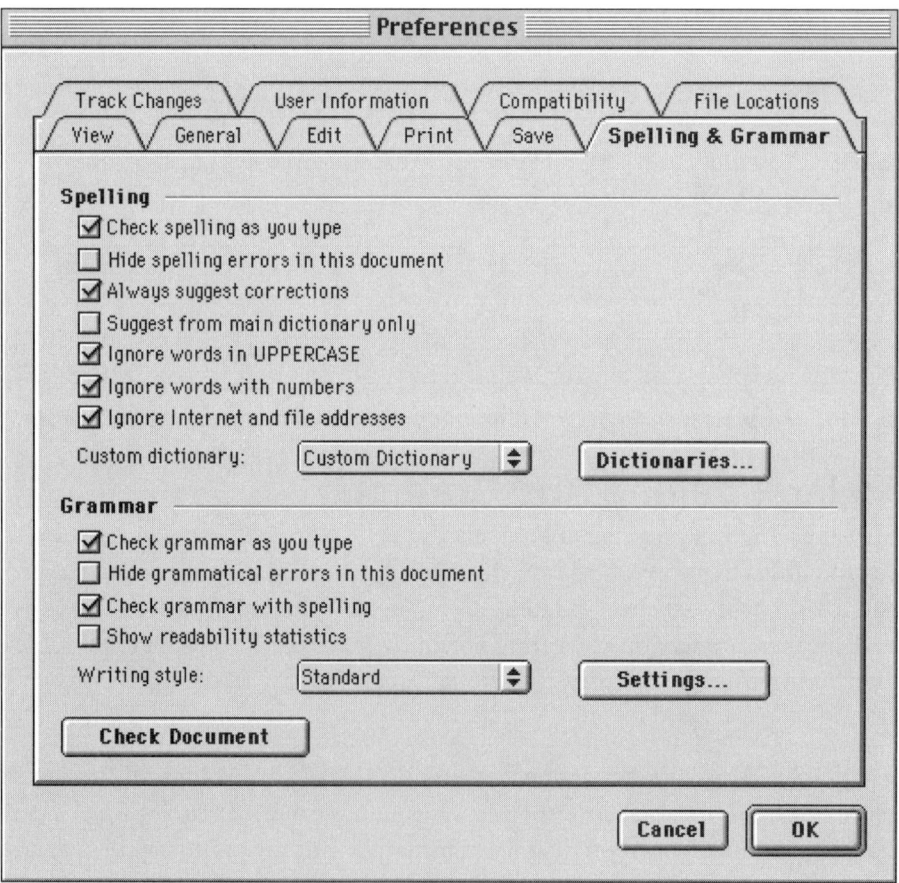

Figure 7.12 Control how and what Word checks by making choices on the Spelling & Grammar tab of Word's Preferences dialog.

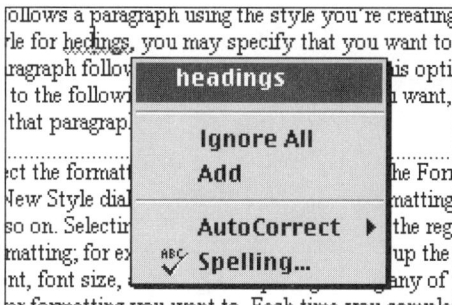

Figure 7.13 To fix spelling and grammar on the fly, Control-click on items Word underlines with a zigzag.

suggesting alternatives (in bold, if any suggestions are available) to the item. From the contextual menu, you can:

- Replace the zigzag-underlined item with a suggested alternative by clicking on an alternative.

- Instruct Word to stop interpreting the underlined item as an error by choosing Ignore All. Word will no longer zigzag underline the word anywhere it appears in the document.

- Apply other options from the Spelling And Grammar dialog (see the next section, "Spell And Grammar Checking On Demand") by clicking on Spelling or Grammar (one of the two options appears on the contextual menu, depending upon the nature of the error).

FYI: Tell Word Which Grammar Matters

Different writers and different types of documents require different levels of grammatical precision. For example, in a letter to a client or customer, you may care whether you've properly hyphenated compound words; in a letter to your Uncle Sal, you may not (after all, Uncle Sal won't know the difference).

To help Word decide how strictly to watch the grammar in your writing, open the Spelling & Grammar tab of the Preferences dialog, then click on the Settings button to open the Grammar Settings dialog. At the top of the dialog, you'll find a list from which you can select a writing style to tell Word what general sorts of grammar rules to apply. Beneath the writing style is a complete list of the grammar and style errors Word can identify. By checking the checkbox for an item in the list, you tell Word to spot such errors; by leaving a checkbox blank, you tell Word not to be picky about the error.

> Three lists at the bottom of the Grammar Settings dialog control how Word treats three common punctuation policies. By picking from each list, you may instruct Word to enforce a rigid policy for each (for example, to require that final series comma, a.k.a. the Harvard comma) or to ignore these issues so you can apply your own judgment.

Spell And Grammar Checking On Demand

To spellcheck (and, optionally, grammar check) a document, click on the Spelling And Grammar button on the Standard toolbar or choose Tools|Spelling And Grammar. The Spelling And Grammar dialog opens (see Figure 7.14), showing the first detected mistake following the edit cursor position. (You needn't go to the top of a document before starting the spellcheck; if you begin in the middle of a document, the spellcheck begins there, checks through the end of the document, then jumps to the top of the document and continues checking until it comes full circle.)

If you want Word to check both grammar and spelling, make sure that the checkbox at the bottom of the dialog, Check Grammar, is checked. If you usually want to check grammar and spelling together, click on Options on the Spelling And Grammar dialog and make sure Check Grammar With Spelling is checked in the dialog that appears. If you do that, the Check Grammar checkbox on the Spelling And Grammar dialog is checked by default, but you can uncheck it any time you don't want grammar checked along with spelling.

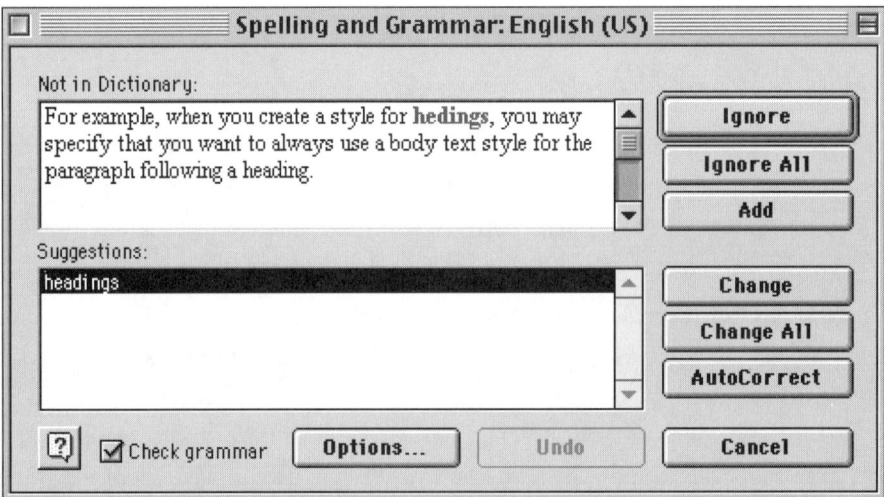

Figure 7.14 Use the Spelling And Grammar dialog to choose how (or whether) Word fixes errors it finds.

Two boxes appear in the dialog. The top box shows the error Word has found; the box's label changes to describe the type of error found—Capitalization, Not In Dictionary, and so on. The bottom box shows corrections Word suggests, if Word can come up with any. For each error located, you can do any of the following:

- Select one of the suggestions and click on the Change button to replace the error with the suggestion (or Change All to replace all instances of the error in the document with the replacement), then move ahead to the next error. (If no suggestions appear, the error is such that Word can't guess what the correction might be.)

- Click on the Ignore All button to ignore this particular error throughout the document. Note that Ignore All doesn't affect variations of the same word. If "Saab" is picked out as a mistake and you choose Ignore All, Word no longer considers "Saab" an error in this document, but continues to hit on "Saabs" and "Saab's" as errors.

- Click on the Ignore button to ignore this particular instance of the error, but still identify the same word as an error if it comes up elsewhere in the document.

- Click on the error in the top box and edit it to correct it, then click on the Change button to replace the error with your correction (or Change All to replace all instances of the error in the document with your correction), then move ahead to the next error.

Fast Track

After choosing a suggestion or typing/editing a change, but before clicking on Change, you can click on the AutoCorrect button on the Spelling And Grammar dialog to add the error and its correction to the AutoCorrect list. Word can then fix that mistake automatically any time you commit it in the future. See "Using Word's AutoCorrect Features" earlier in this chapter.

- Click on the Add button to add the error to the dictionary so that it will no longer be identified as an error in this or any other document using the same dictionary. Add is a good choice when the word is a name you may type often, but one that Word doesn't recognize.

After you've spellchecked a document, Word remembers the words and phrases it thought were errors but you told it to ignore. The next time you run the spellchecker, Word will ignore those errors automatically.

Finding And Using Synonyms

Word includes a built-in thesaurus to help you write more effectively. Using the thesaurus, you can find synonyms or antonyms to many words to vary the vocabulary in your document or to apply a more interesting (or more descriptive) word than the first word you thought of. Judicious application of a thesaurus can make your writing more colorful (bright, vivid, brilliant, resplendent, cool…).

To find a synonym, Control-click anywhere within the word for which you want a synonym or antonym. From the contextual menu that appears, select Synonyms, then pick the word you want (see Figure 7.15). For antonyms, select Tools|Language|Thesaurus. In the dialog, use the list on the left to choose from among the various meanings of the selected word. In the list on the right, a list of synonyms to that meaning appears. (To see a list of antonyms on the right, choose Antonyms from the Meanings list.) Choose a synonym or antonym from the Replace With list and click on the Replace button to replace the selected word with the synonym or antonym.

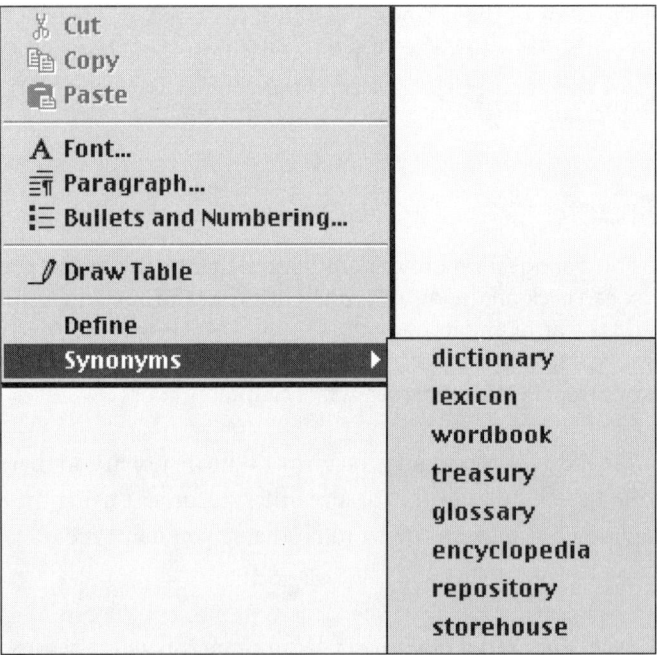

Figure 7.15 Use Word's Thesaurus to pick a word that's better…improved… superior… more suitable….

Finding And Replacing Text And Formatting

Word's find and replace capabilities enable you not only to locate specific text anywhere within your document and replace it with different text of your choosing, but also to locate and replace formatting. For example, you could replace any <u>underlining</u> in your document with *italics*, or make all instances of a selected word **bold**. Perhaps most importantly, you can find and replace instances of a style, so you can replace one style with another everywhere it's applied in the document.

Fast Track

Three items on Word's Edit menu—Find, Replace, and Go To—all open the same dialog, Find And Replace, although each opens to a different tab. Choosing Edit|Replace is the quickest option for the task at hand, since that goes straight to the Replace tab. But in practice, you can use any of the three ways to open the dialog, then just choose the tab you want.

To use find and replace, begin by opening the Find And Replace dialog (choose Edit|Replace). When you first open the Replace tab, only the top two text boxes show, and the tab features a button labeled More. You can perform very simple text replacement operations with the basic tab, or click on More to reveal advanced options (see Figure 7.16). (If you reveal options with the More button, clicking on the Less button hides them again.)

The Find And Replace dialog has three tabs: Find, Replace, and Go To. The Find tab is used simply for finding stuff without changing it; you use Find exactly as you use the Find portions of the Replace tab, described next. (To learn about the Go To tab, see Chapter 3.)

On the Replace tab, to find and replace text only, click in Find What and type the exact text you want replaced. Then click in Replace With and type the replacement. Click on Find Next; Word locates the first instance it can find of the Find What text and stops there.

To handle the replacement, you can:

- Click on Replace to replace the text and automatically jump to the next instance Word can find.

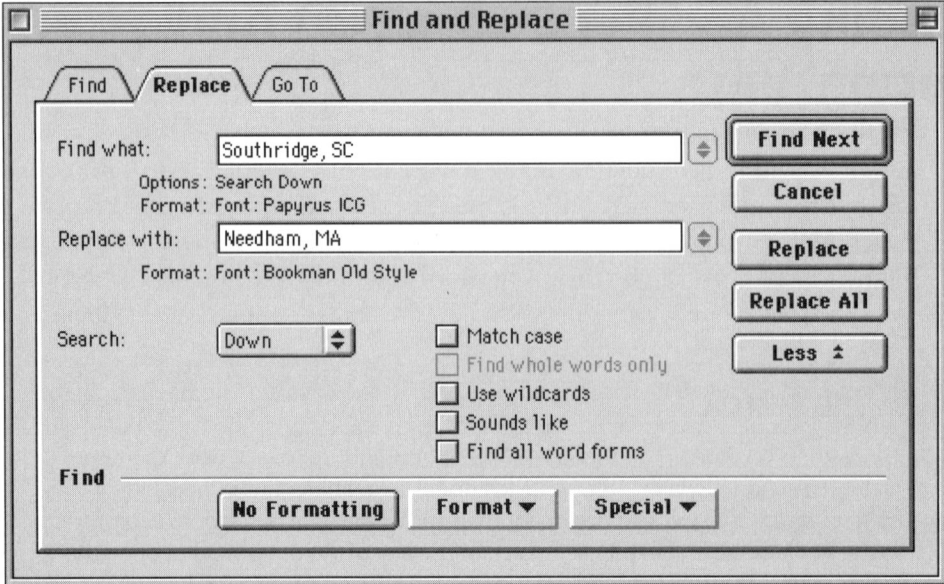

Figure 7.16 Clicking on the More button reveals all of the Replace tab's options.

- Click on Replace All to instruct Word to replace every instance of the text found in the document without prompting you again.

- Click on Find Next to leave the current instance of the Find What text unchanged and move on to the next.

Note that when you replace text this way, the changes do not affect formatting in any way—the replacement is formatted exactly as the original was. Unless you check the Match Case checkbox (discussed next), capitalization is ignored when finding the word—if you type "John" in Find What, Word finds John, john, and JOHN. When replacing, Word capitalizes the replacement text the same way that the original was capitalized.

Fast Track

To find and replace only within a portion of a document, select the portion before opening the Find And Replace dialog. Word will first perform the find and replace within the selection only. When finished with the selection, Word displays a dialog asking whether you want to continue finding and replacing for the rest of the document.

To perform more sophisticated searching and replacing, click on the More button on the Replace tab. The tab expands to reveal advanced search and replace options you enable by checking their checkboxes. For example:

- Check the checkbox for Match Case to force Word to find only words that match the text *and* the precise capitalization of the entry in Find What. If the entry in Find What is John, Word finds John, but not john or JOHN. Also, when this option is checked, the replacement is inserted exactly as you typed it, with no changes to its capitalization. Using Match Case, you can easily repair a capitalization error throughout the document.

- Check the checkbox for Find Whole Words Only to prevent Word from finding the Find What text when it is part of another word. For example, if you type "John" in the Find What box, Word finds "John," but not "Johnny" or "John's."

Fast Track

Check the Find All Word Forms box to instruct Word to find not only the Word in Find What, but also other forms of the same word, and to replace with the appropriate form of the word in Replace With. For example, if you replace "run" with "walk" and have the Find All Word Forms checkbox checked, Word replaces "run" with "walk," "ran" with "walked," "running" with "walking," and so on.

For this to work, of course, the Find What and Replace With entries must both be the same part of speech. This is a powerful option, but it can be tricky. Use it sparingly, and proof carefully after using it. The grammar checker can help you locate any errors you may inadvertently create by using this option.

The Format and Special buttons at the bottom of the dialog let you find and replace formatting and special characters. You can find and replace formatting or special characters wherever they occur, or you can use formatting or special characters to modify a text-replacement operation. For example:

- To replace underlining with *italic*, click in the Find What box, click on the Format button, choose Font, and choose the Underline formatting in the Font dialog. Then click in the Replace With box and follow the same steps to put italic in the Replace With box. (Observe that text appears beneath each box to describe formatting you're finding or replacing.)

- To replace the phrase "Misty Jones" in Arial font with "Mr. James" in Courier, type "Misty Jones" in Find What and then select Format|Font to choose Arial. In Replace With, type "Mr. James" and select Format|Font to choose Courier font for the Replace With box. Word will find "Misty Jones" when that text is set in Arial, but ignore it when it's in another font. When you choose to replace, the replacement will be "Mr. James" in Courier font.

Walk-Through: Replace

Follow these steps to practice replacing text:

1. Create a new document based on the Elegant Resume (in the Other Documents tab of the Templates).
2. Choose Edit|Replace. The Find And Replace dialog opens, with the Replace tab showing.
3. In Find What, type "Southridge, SC".
4. In Replace With, type "Needham, MA".
5. Click on Replace All. All instances of Southridge, SC are replaced.
6. Your Mac will beep, and a dialog appears telling you how many replacements have been made. Click on OK to dismiss the dialog. Can you find examples of Southridge that weren't replaced, because they didn't include "SC"?
7. Clear all text from Find What and leave the edit cursor there.
8. Choose Format|Font to open the Font dialog.
9. Choose Italic in Font style, and click on OK to close the Font dialog.
10. Repeat the gist of Steps 7, 8, and 9 to clear the Replace With box and put bold italic formatting there.
11. Click on Replace All. All italic text in the document becomes bold italic.
12. Click in the Find What box, and click on the No Formatting button to clear the formatting instructions from Find What.
13. In Replace With, type "Needham".
14. Click in the Replace With box, and click on the No Formatting button to clear the formatting instructions.
15. Choose Format|Highlight to add a highlighting instruction to Replace With.
16. Click on Replace All. Needham is highlighted throughout the document.

Repeating And Copying Formatting

Creating and applying styles really is the best way to apply the same formatting to various text blocks spread throughout your document. But in case the need arises, you should be aware that Word offers two ways to quickly copy formatting.

The first way, Repeat, works sort of like Undo in reverse. When you press the Repeat key (Cmd+Y), Word repeats the last action you performed. (You can also select Edit|Repeat.) Repeat may be most useful when you need to format separate paragraphs the same way throughout a document. Format the first paragraph as desired, then move the edit cursor to the next paragraph requiring the same formatting and press Repeat. You can use Repeat to repeat a single formatting operation—applying a style, a font, a font size, and so on.

The second method, Format Painter, copies all of the formatting from one block to another. It's less convenient than Repeat, but whereas Repeat can repeat only a single formatting instruction at a time, Format Painter copies all of the formatting instructions—style, font, font size, attributes, and paragraph formatting—from one block to another. To use Format Painter, select the text whose format you want to copy, then click on the Format Painter button on the Standard toolbar; the pointer becomes a paintbrush. Point to the text you want formatted and click (to format the whole paragraph) or click and drag (to format a selection within the paragraph, or multiple paragraphs).

Assembling And Printing Mailings

Word provides two great ways to help you with mailing tasks.

First, when all you want to do is to print a few envelopes or format some mailing labels, Word provides the Envelopes And Labels dialog (Tools|Envelopes And Labels). The dialog has two tabs: Click on the Envelopes tab (see Figure 7.17) to choose an envelope size and type the address, or click on the Labels tab to choose a label size and style and supply the address. The Envelopes And Labels dialog saves

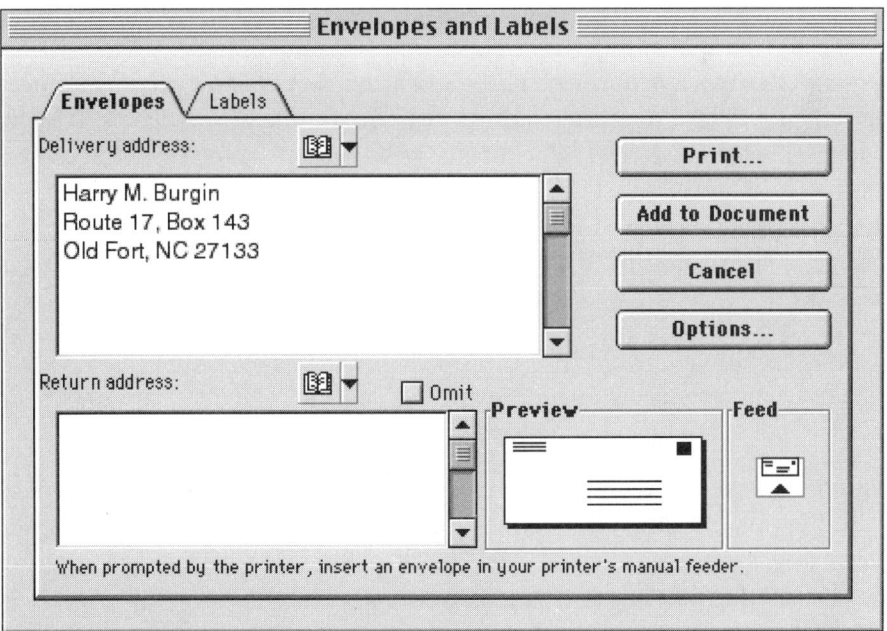

Figure 7.17 The Envelopes And Labels dialog makes quick work of creating and formatting addressed materials.

you the trouble of defining the page layout for envelopes and labels, which can be a tricky proposition.

Fast Track

On each tab in the Envelopes And Labels dialog, you'll see an Address Book button. Click on the button to quickly copy names and addresses from your Outlook Express Address Book.

For more complex mailing projects, Word offers *mail merge* facilities. Mail merge, as you may already know, is a word processor's way of automatically combining a document—a form letter or other document intended for multiple recipients—with a file of names and addresses to crank out a separate document for each addressee, ready to mail. Mail merge is a four-step job. You must:

1. Create the form letter or other document.

2. Choose the *data source*, the file of addresses or other information you want plugged into the document.

3. Compose the document, inserting *fields* where mail merge will plug in information from the data source.

4. Instruct Word to run its mail merge routine to produce the final documents by plugging each entry from the data source into a separate copy of the document.

Word 98 provides a Mail Merge Helper—which is sort of like a wizard, only not quite as helpful—to take you through these steps. To use the helper, choose Tools|Mail Merge. The Mail Merge Helper opens, as shown in Figure 7.18. You can call on the helper at any point while working on a mail merge document—even when you started without its help. (In fact, after many of the actions you perform on the Mail Merge Helper dialog, the dialog disappears. If you need more help from it, just re-open it.)

To create your mail merge document, click on the Create button. A list of different types of mail merge documents—Form Letter, Mailing Labels, and so on—drops down. Choose the type that best matches what you want to create.

For the data source, Word can use a variety of different types of data files. Perhaps most importantly, Outlook Express's Address Book is available as a data source for Word's mail merge, so you can automatically address Word form letters, envelopes, or labels to the folks in your Outlook Address book.

Working Faster And Easier In Word 203

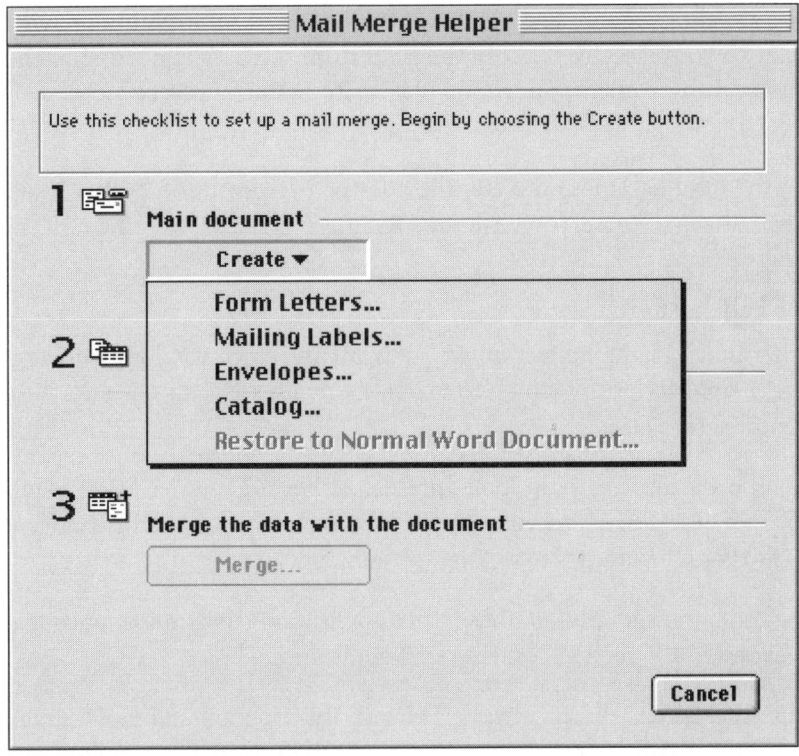

Figure 7.18 The Mail Merge Helper takes you through the steps of merging a mailing list with a document.

Click on the Get Data button in the Mail Merge Helper dialog to display a list of options for the data source. Then choose:

- Create Data Source to display a dialog you use to type your data now.

- Open Data Source to open an existing Word data file (one you created previously with Create Data Source).

- Use Address Book to use an Outlook Address Book as the data source.

After choosing the data source, you're ready to compose and edit the form letter. Click on the Edit button in the Create Document section of the Mail Merge Helper. The document appears, along with the Mail Merge toolbar. Enter the text of the form letter and format it as you wish.

In the document where you want the Mail Merge data plugged in, position the edit cursor where you want the data to go, then click on the Insert Merge Field button on the Mail Merge toolbar. A list of fields—for example, First Name, Last Name, and so on—drops down. The list includes all types of information included in the data source you selected. Choose the field from the list. The name of the field appears in the document, surrounded by double angle marks (<< >>), as shown in Figure 7.19.

When the form letter is complete, click on the Merge button on the Mail Merge Helper dialog or choose Tools|Merge Documents.

Moving On

Whither now? That's a question we can't answer, since we don't know which Office 98 applications you plan to use (nobody uses 'em all—we don't care what Microsoft says).

If you have a hankering to do some Internet authoring, you may want to jump ahead to Chapter 17 to learn how you can use Word to compose Web pages, send email, and link Word documents to online text and data.

Or you can jump ahead to another Office application—beginning, of course, with the first chapter in the section covering that application.

Failing other plans, you can always stay with the program and move straight ahead to Chapter 8, the first of three chapters about the presentation-maker PowerPoint. In fact, there's some logic to doing so, because PowerPoint is the most Word-like of the other Office 98 applications. In fact, if you've already grappled with most of this Word section, you'll find PowerPoint refreshingly simple. Take a peek.

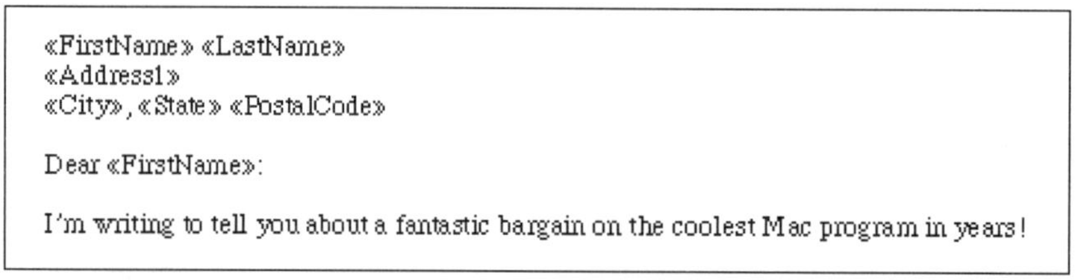

```
«FirstName» «LastName»
«Address1»
«City», «State» «PostalCode»

Dear «FirstName»:

I'm writing to tell you about a fantastic bargain on the coolest Mac program in years!
```

Figure 7.19 Mail merge data fields appear surrounded by double angle marks (<< >>).

PART III

PowerPoint

Getting Started With PowerPoint

There's no business like show business. And make no mistake, PowerPoint is a show-biz program—Office 98's own Flo Ziegfeld.

Think about it: If all you wanted were some boring old transparencies to help your audience get a nice afternoon nap, you could easily write 'em up in Word and save yourself the learning curve and hard drive space a presentation program demands. But making an effective presentation means sparking audience neurons with audio-visual stimuli, and it also means making the presenter (whom we assume is you, but needn't be) look polished and professional—a class act. PowerPoint helps you create and perform such shows.

Learning to use PowerPoint is a lot like learning to cook. There are so many possible projects that if you set out to understand it all at once, you'd quickly turn in your spatula. However, creating any one specific show—or recipe—is a pretty straightforward activity, a step-by-stepper. You'll find the whole topic easier to deal with if you first gain an overview of PowerPoint's capabilities and starting points, then deal with the details of show-making. That's what this chapter offers.

In this quickie chapter, you'll pick up an understanding of what you can create with PowerPoint and of how to present each type of show that PowerPoint produces. You'll also learn the ropes of getting PowerPoint going and getting around within it. Armed with these basics, you'll be well prepared to move on to Chapter 9, where you'll learn how to produce your show. In Chapter 10, you'll learn how to use advanced features to enhance your show.

Before beginning, note that you learn to perform several activities in this chapter from PowerPoint's Standard toolbar (see Figure 8.1). PowerPoint comes preconfigured to display the Standard toolbar, but if you don't see its buttons on your display, open PowerPoint and choose View|Toolbars|Standard.

Figure 8.1 You will use PowerPoint's Standard toolbar to perform many of the activities in this chapter.

Creating A New Show

Which comes first in a PowerPoint show—the words? Or the slides on which the words appear? Well, in practice, they evolve in tandem.

1. You typically begin by jotting down some, but not all, of the words.

2. Then you format those words in their slides.

3. Next, you expand and edit the text in the slides.

4. Thereupon you tweak the look of the slides some more or add new ones.

Unless you're a frighteningly well-structured human being, creating a PowerPoint show usually requires a lot of hopping back and forth between dealing with text—or rather, content—and dealing with appearance.

When you launch PowerPoint, a special sort of startup dialog opens automatically, as shown in Figure 8.2. (Note that if this is the first time you've used PowerPoint, the Office Assistant will appear and ask if you want help with PowerPoint. Tell it you want to continue using PowerPoint. If you don't see the four-button startup dialog, quit PowerPoint and start again—then we'll all be on the same page.) On the dialog, you may select any of the three radio buttons under Create A New Presentation Using to start a new show; the details of all three approaches are covered in Chapter 9. By selecting the bottom radio button, Open An Existing Presentation, you

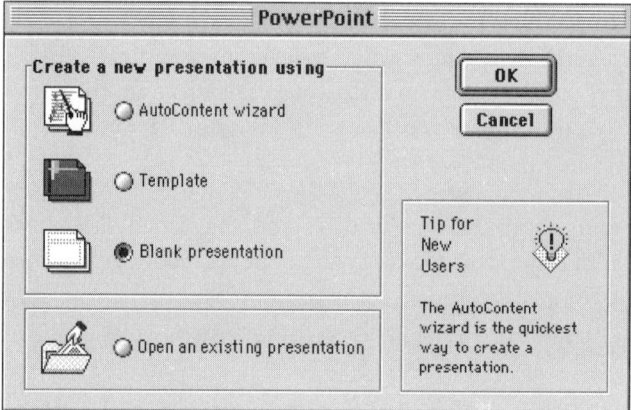

Figure 8.2 Get productive quickly by choosing a starting point from PowerPoint's handy all-purpose startup dialog.

Getting Started With PowerPoint

bring up the Open dialog so you can open an existing presentation file. (You learn how to use the Open dialog in "Opening Existing Presentations" at the beginning of the next chapter.)

Although the startup dialog in Figure 8.2 may help you get started on the day's PowerPoint session, there's nothing in it that you can't also accomplish from PowerPoint's regular menus. On the dialog, you can click on Cancel, or press Esc, to close the dialog and begin working in PowerPoint any way you wish.

To get started, you needn't know all the words you are going to use on your slides, but you do need to address the overall look and structure of your presentation before trying to nail down the details of content and formatting. PowerPoint has two ways of helping you accomplish this:

- The AutoContent Wizard
- Templates

Whichever way you get started, you wind up with what we call a *proto-presentation*—a collection of fully formatted slides populated mainly with suggestions for content where your words must go. You complete your presentation by replacing the suggestions with your own text and by changing the slide design or adding, moving, or removing slides however your fancies dictate.

In the next few pages, you'll learn how to create your proto-presentation with the AutoContent Wizard or with a template. Following this section, you learn how to turn your proto-presentation into your own show, beginning with the section "Editing Text."

Jump-Starting With AutoContent Wizard

When you open PowerPoint, you can jump straight into the AutoContent Wizard by choosing it from the opening dialog. If you've already cleared the opening dialog, but want to use the AutoContent Wizard, choose File|New to open the New Presentation dialog. In the dialog, click on the General tab, then double-click on the file icon for AutoContent Wizard.

However you open it, the AutoContent Wizard starts you off with the dialog shown in Figure 8.3. Beginning with this dialog, you'll click your way through just five dialogs to tell the AutoContent Wizard a little about the presentation you're trying to create. To advance to each new dialog, click on the Next button. To go back at any time to dialogs you've already visited, click on Back. Or, instead of using Next and Back, you can jump directly to any dialog in the AutoContent Wizard by clicking on an item in the index that always appears along the left side of the dialog.

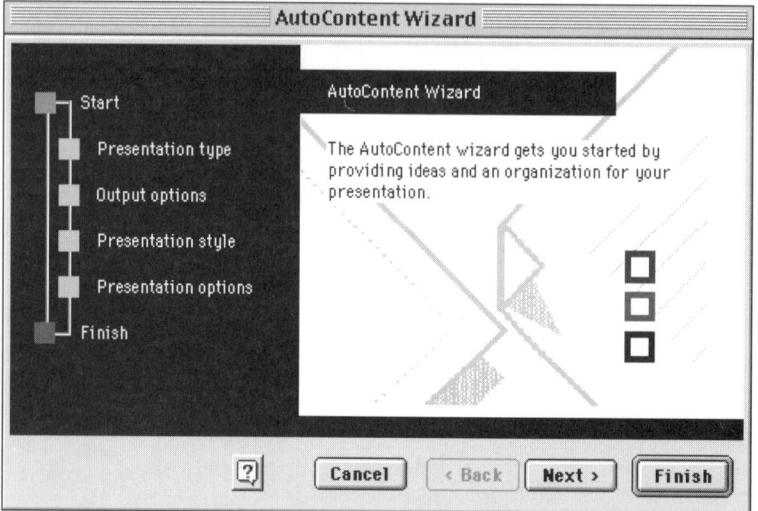

Figure 8.3 The AutoContent Wizard helps you start a new presentation.

When you're finished filling in the dialogs (described next), move to the Finish dialog, then click on the Finish button. The proto-presentation opens in PowerPoint, ready for you to begin editing the text.

Presentation Type

In the Presentation Type dialog, you choose a presentation on which yours will be modeled. We've chosen the Marketing Plan type of presentation, as Figure 8.4 shows. The presentation you choose need not be exactly what you want to create—you'll

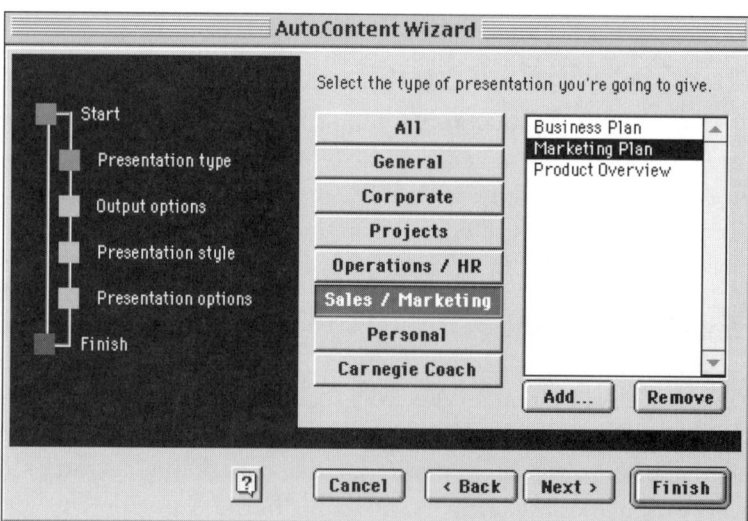

Figure 8.4 In the AutoContent Wizard, you can select a presentation type.

Getting Started With PowerPoint

edit the results later. But the more closely your choices on this dialog match what you want to produce, the less work you'll have to do later.

Begin by clicking on the button that most closely matches the general type of presentation you plan to create. After you click on a button, the list in the dialog offers a collection of different presentations of that type. By selecting Sales/Marketing, the Business Plan, Marketing Plan, and Product Overview presentation types appear. (The All button lists all of the presentations available from the other buttons combined. The Carnegie Coach button lists presentations based on Dale Carnegie sales training techniques.) Choose your best match from the list, then click on Next to move ahead.

Output Options

In the Output Options dialog, click on one of the radio buttons to choose how the presentation will be shown. The AutoContent Wizard chooses some of the formatting options and other elements based on the choice you make here. More importantly, the AutoContent Wizard uses your choice on this screen to determine which options to offer on the next dialogs.

Presentation Style

The Presentation Style dialog (which is not available, or necessary, if you choose Internet|Kiosk from the Output Options dialog) lets you choose from among the various methods you may use to present a show of the type you selected in Output Options. You can select from Onscreen Presentation, Color Overheads, Black And White Overheads, or 35mm Slides.

Presentation Options

The options you see on the Presentation Options dialog (see Figure 8.5) vary depending on the choices you made in the Output Options and Presentation Style dialogs. Typically, this dialog offers you an opportunity to create some of the text of the presentation. For example, this dialog may include text boxes for your presentation title, your name, and other information. The AutoContent Wizard may use this information for creating your title slide or for creating slide headers or footers that include the title and/or your name. Although filling in the Presentation Options dialog may make your proto-presentation more finished at the start, consider this dialog optional—it really doesn't offer anything you can't add yourself later.

Using Templates

In case you hadn't already guessed, all the AutoContent Wizard really does is help you choose a template, add a little text to it, and select from among a few options. If you're confident in your ability to choose a template for yourself, you may want to forego the AutoContent Wizard and simply create your proto-presentation by choosing a template.

212   Chapter 8

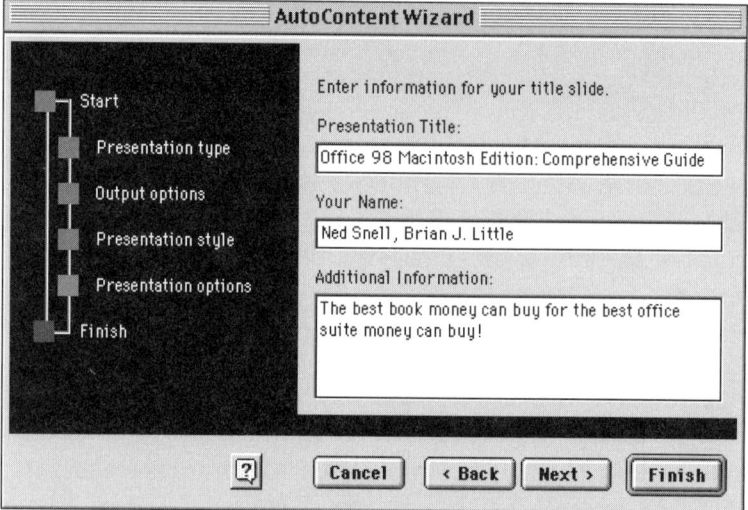

Figure 8.5 The AutoContent Wizard's Presentation Options dialog lets you define your new show more specifically.

Begin by choosing File|New. The New Presentation dialog opens, as shown in Figure 8.6. The template files are grouped into tabs:

- *General*—Typically, the General tab provides only one template, Blank Presentation, a very basic, no-frills design for no-frills shows, along with the AutoContent Wizard.

- *Presentation Designs*—The templates in this tab are designs only—they offer no sample text or content suggestions. You may want to use one of the Presentation

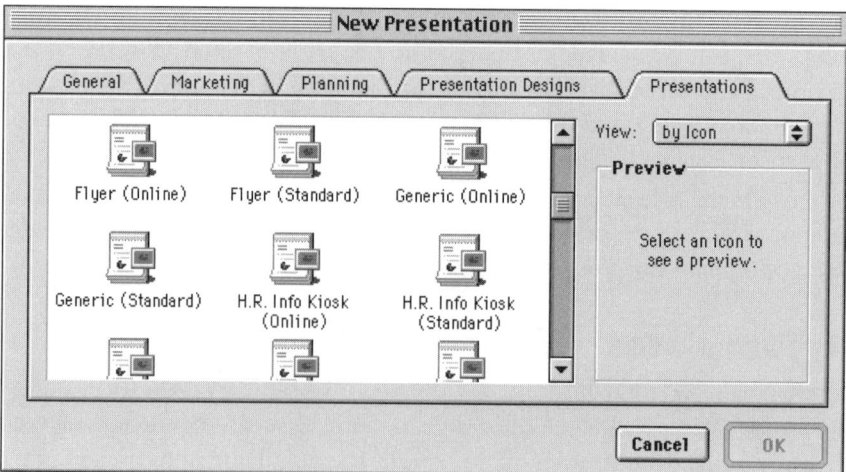

Figure 8.6 Choose File|New to see the templates you can use to create a new show.

Designs templates when you want a template's help with slide design, but not with content.

- *Presentations*—Each template in this tab includes both slide design and suggested content. The Presentations templates not only provide you with a prebuilt design, but also give you a head start on the structure and content of your show. These are your best bet when you want a template's help with the look of your slides and with their content. Note that the Presentations templates are the same ones offered by the AutoContent Wizard.

If you're upgrading from Office 4.2.1, you may see other tabs, like Marketing or Planning. These tabs contain presentation designs brought over from your previous version of PowerPoint, and they have a different icon than PowerPoint 98 templates. You can still use them, but when you open the template, you will see a dialog telling you that PowerPoint is converting the template from a previous version. Simply wait for the template to open, then continue as usual.

Fast Track

The names of some of the templates in the Presentations tab include the word "Online" in parentheses. For each "Online" template there is another template in the Presentations tab that has the same name, except that "Online" is replaced by "Standard." The online template includes features that can be used only if the show will be presented electronically; for example, the template may feature on-slide buttons so the viewer can control the show interactively. The standard version omits such techno-frills so that you have the option of presenting it electronically or in print, slides, or transparencies.

To choose a template, find one whose name suggests that it may be a close fit to what you want to produce. Remember that you won't find a perfect fit—you're going to do some editing, no matter which template you choose. But the closer your choice, the less work you'll have to do later. Click on the icon for a template to see a preview of its appearance in the Preview pane.

When you've selected the template you want, click on OK. What happens next depends on which tab you chose from:

- If you chose from the Presentations tab, the first slide of the proto-presentation opens in Slide view. You may begin by replacing the template's content suggestions with your own content, as described in the "Editing Text" section later in this chapter.

- If you chose from the Presentation Designs tab, or chose Blank Presentation from the General tab, the Slide Layout dialog opens so you can select a layout for the first slide in the presentation. Choose one that includes all of the types of objects—text, pictures, and so on—you intend to include on the first slide. After you make your choice, the proto-presentation opens, containing one simple slide in the layout you selected. You may build your presentation from there by adding slides, text, a background, and so on.

FYI: Taking Text From Elsewhere

If you already have an outline of your presentation typed up in Word—or if you prefer to compose your text in Word—you can easily convert that outline into slide text.

Begin by formatting your Word document. To get the best results, pick out each slide title in your Word outline and apply the style Heading 1 to it. As you work, keep in mind that slides look best when you limit the contents of each to a few lines.

When finished with your Word outline, save it, then switch to PowerPoint. Choose File|Open to display the Open dialog. In the List Files Of Type list, choose All Outlines. Navigate to the Word file containing the outline and double-click on it. The Word outline opens in PowerPoint as a new presentation, in Outline view. Each line that used the Heading 1 style is the title of a new slide.

In Chapter 16, you'll discover other ways to move information from Word—and other Office 98 programs—into PowerPoint.

FYI: Slides Are Populated With Placeholders

Each object that can appear in a PowerPoint slide appears in its own *placeholder*, an invisible box. Different kinds of objects have different placeholders with different properties—there are text placeholders, picture placeholders, chart placeholders, and so on.

Placeholders enable you to easily rearrange and compose the various objects in a slide, as you'll learn in Chapter 9. If you've read Chapter 6, you'll soon notice that text placeholders in PowerPoint work just like Word's text boxes and that other placeholders behave like picture outlines.

In addition to the text placeholders that hold the sample text, some of the Presentations templates include other types of placeholders. For example, the first slide of the template Product Overview includes a picture placeholder for a photo of your product. When a template you choose includes such placeholders, you may either fill them with what they're designed to hold or delete them.

Saving Presentations

Of course, as you work on your presentation, you need to save it from time to time. If you attempt to exit PowerPoint without first saving your work, a dialog appears, asking if you want to save the file; click on Yes to open the Save dialog (see Figure 8.7). Despite this safeguard, it's smart to save often while developing a show. You can save as soon as you create a show and any time you feel like it thereafter.

To save, click on the Save button on the Standard toolbar or choose File|Save. The first time you save, the Save dialog opens so you can give your show a name and select a folder in which to store it. After that first Save, clicking on Save or choosing File|Save simply saves your file without opening a dialog.

In the Save dialog, the drive/file list at the top shows the folder in which the file will be saved. By default, that folder is your Documents folder (provided you've set your Mac to use one), but you can drop down the drive/folder list to choose a different folder. The file list box beneath the drive/file list shows the presentation files that are already stored in the folder.

When the dialog shows the folder you want to use, click in the Save As box and type a name for your presentation. After supplying a file name, click on Save to save the file. The Save dialog closes, and you can return to work on the presentation.

Fast Track

To save a file in PowerPoint Show format, choose PowerPoint Show from the Save File As Type list.

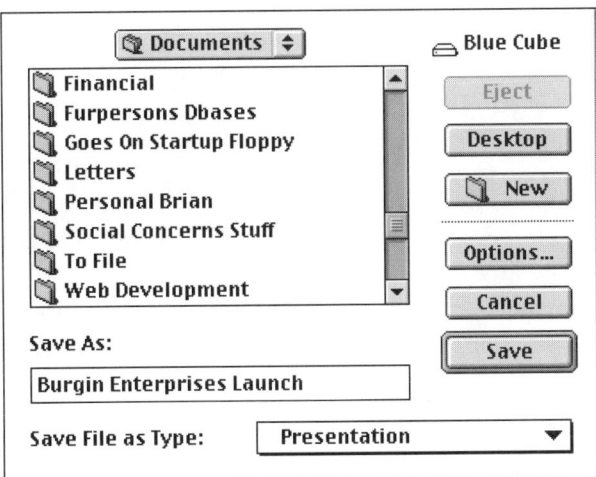

Figure 8.7 Use the Save dialog to choose a file name and storage location for your show.

Choosing A View

Perhaps the most important part of dealing productively with a presentation is choosing the right *view* to work in for a given task. Throughout this PowerPoint part of the book, we'll always tell you which view works best for the task at hand.

You can switch easily among the views in either of two ways. First, all views are available from the View menu on PowerPoint's menu bar. Also, a row of tiny View buttons appears in the lower left corner of the PowerPoint window (see Figure 8.8). As with toolbar buttons, these view buttons feature tooltips—rest the pointer on a button for a moment to display a label telling you which view that button opens.

In addition to the views described here, there's another, special-purpose "view" that's not included among the View buttons or in the same section of the View menu with the others: Black And White. See "Printing Transparencies" in the next chapter to learn about this view.

Slide View

Slide view is just what it sounds like. You see one slide, big and lovely, in the PowerPoint window (see Figure 8.9). The number of the slide you're viewing appears in the left end of the PowerPoint status bar at the bottom of the window.

Slide view gives you the best look at individual slides and is best suited to fine-tuning the text and design of individual slides as the show nears completion. When you're in Slide view, you can edit the text of the slide you see, edit the design and layout of that slide, and even apply some types of slide formatting—such as a new background or color scheme—to the presentation as a whole. You can also run the spelling and style checkers for the whole presentation while in Slide view.

To move from slide to slide while in Slide view, press PgDn (to advance forward in the presentation), PgUp (to move toward the beginning of the show), or scroll up or down in the show with the vertical scroll bar.

To see and work with minute details of a slide, you can increase the Zoom percentage to "zoom in" closer to the slide, magnifying its details (see Figure 8.10). Choose View|Zoom to open the Zoom dialog and choose a percentage, or drop down the Zoom box in the Standard toolbar. (The Standard toolbar appears in PowerPoint by default, but if you don't see it, choose View|Toolbars|Standard.)

Figure 8.8 The View buttons let you switch quickly among PowerPoint's views.

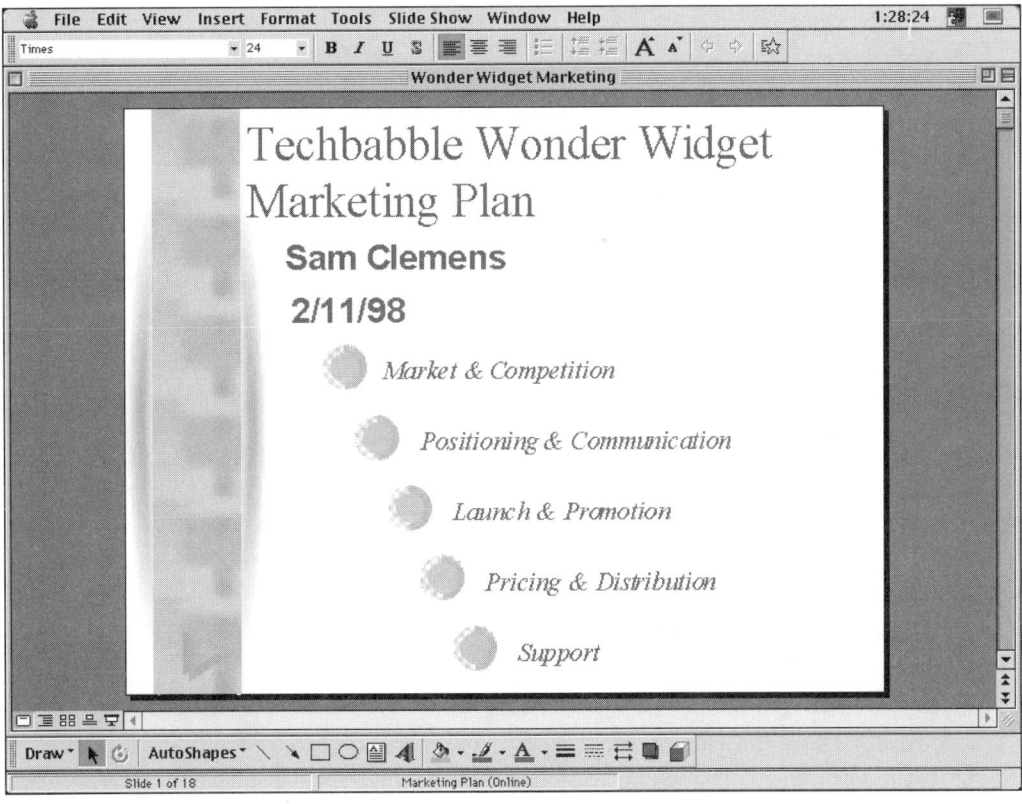

Figure 8.9 In Slide view, you work with one slide at a time.

Outline View

In Outline view, you can focus on writing and editing the text of your presentation. Outline view shows the entire presentation as a text outline (see Figure 8.11). This not only makes navigating among slides while editing text easier, it also lets you evaluate the general organization and flow of your show without the distraction of the slide designs. To the left of each slide title appears the slide's number.

Of course, Outline view doesn't completely ignore the aesthetics of your slides. First, the text in the outline appears fully formatted, exactly as it will appear on the slides, including the selected fonts, sizes, and more (everything but color). Also, the *slide miniature* appears, as Figure 8.12 shows. The slide miniature shows you a thumbnail version of the slide in which you're working in the outline.

To see the miniature for a particular slide, click on the slide icon that appears next to the slide number, or just click anywhere in the slide's text to move the cursor there. The slide miniature shows you the slide's appearance. (If you don't want to see the slide miniature, just click on its Close box.)

Figure 8.10 Raise the Zoom percentage to magnify the slide for detailed work.

Fast Track

While working in Outline view, you can instantly display any slide in Slide view by pointing to the slide's icon (between the slide number and title) and clicking on it.

Slide Sorter View

Slide Sorter view (see Figure 8.12) is best applied to evaluating the structure and flow of your show and changing that structure by adding, deleting, or moving slides. The number of each slide appears beneath it.

You can't edit or format text or make manual slide layout changes in Slide Sorter view, although you can perform most slide-formatting tasks, such as changing the background or color scheme of slides. To open any slide you see in Slide Sorter view, point to it and double-click.

The number of slides you see at one time depends upon the Zoom percentage. By default, the Zoom is set at 66 percent, and 12 slides appear on one full-screen window. If you increase the Zoom percentage (through the Zoom list on the Standard

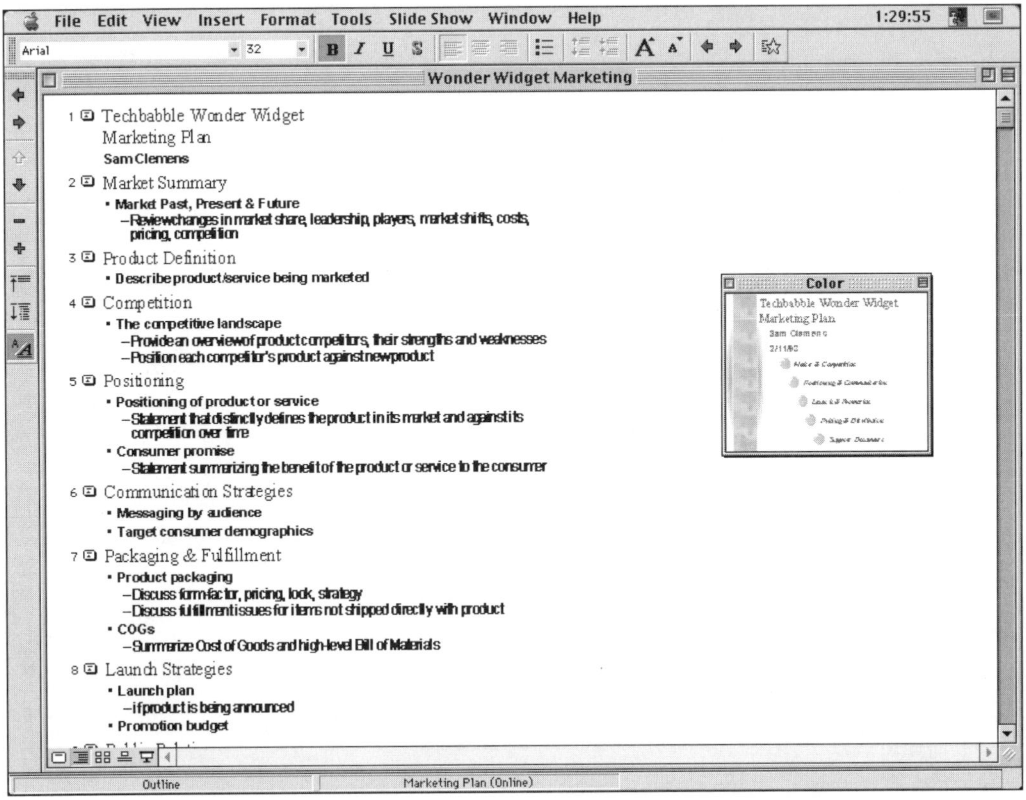

Figure 8.11 Enter, review, and organize the text of your whole show in Outline view.

toolbar or by choosing View|Zoom), fewer slides appear per screen, but those that do appear are larger and easier to read. If you reduce the Zoom, more slides appear at once, but each slide is smaller.

If the Zoom you choose to work in can't show all of your slides on one screen, use the vertical scroll bar to scroll the window to see more slides.

Slide Show View

The look of Slide Show view depends on whether you've configured the show as a full-screen (presenter-run or kiosk) show or as a windowed, viewer-run show. A full-screen show takes over the entire display (see Figure 8.13). A windowed view displays the show in a window, with the Web toolbar available to help the viewer navigate.

In Slide Show view, you can step through the slides just as you would when giving the presentation (or as a viewer does in a kiosk or windowed show). This view plays two important roles, enabling you to:

- Present a show electronically.

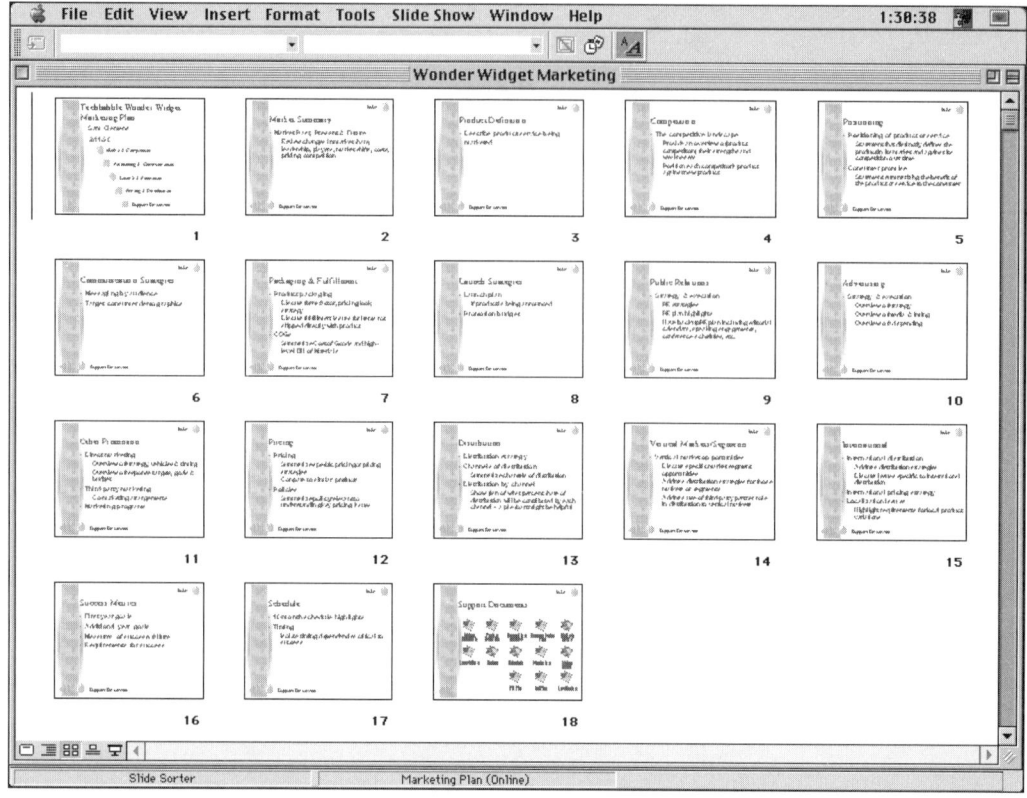

Figure 8.12 Work with the order of slides in Slide Sorter view.

- Evaluate and practice a show that will later be output to transparencies or slides. Slide Show view helps you ensure that your show is finished and ready to go before you prepare slides or transparencies.

You can start Slide Show view from the View menu or View buttons, like any other view. However, when you're in Slide view, or when you have selected a particular slide in Outline or Slide Sorter view, the two options work slightly differently. View|Slide Show always starts the slide show from the very first slide. The Slide Show button starts with the current slide (in Slide view) or with the selected slide (in Outline or Slide Sorter view).

In Slide Show view, you can:

- Advance to the next slide in the show by pressing PgDn, the Down arrow key, or the Right arrow key.

- Back up to the previous slide in the show by pressing PgUp, the Up arrow key, or the Left arrow key.

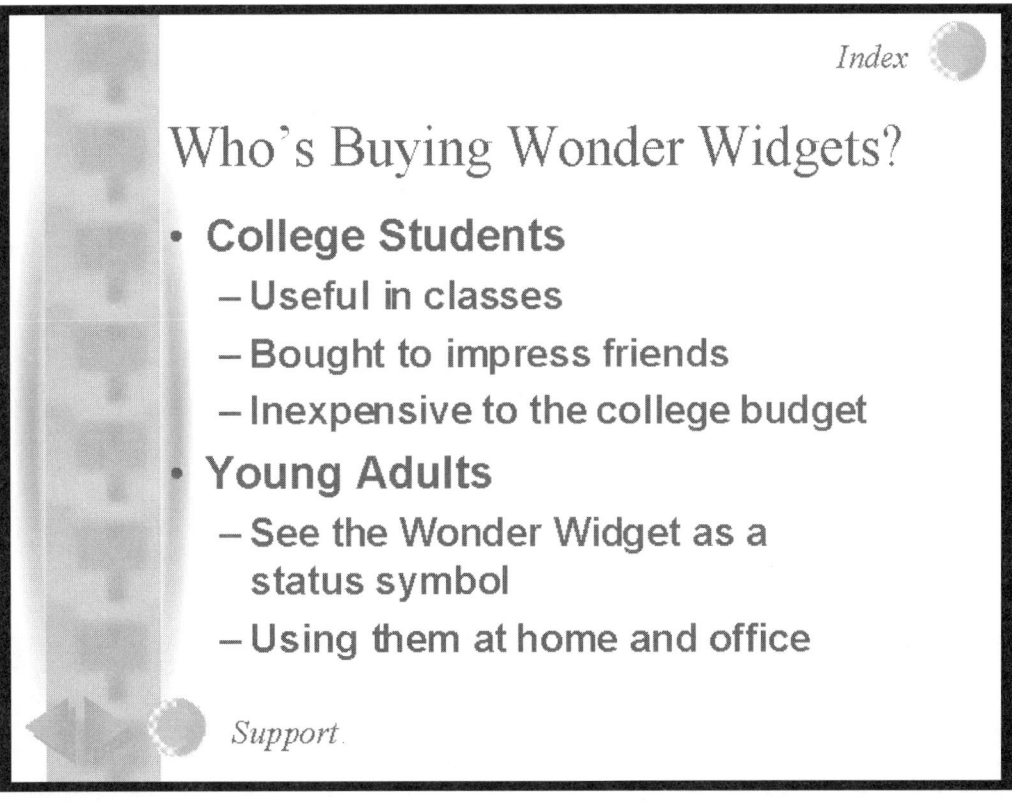

Figure 8.13 Review, rehearse, or present your show in Slide Show view.

- Point and click to activate any on-screen buttons or links you've created in an electronic presentation.
- Press Esc to close Slide Show view and return to the previous view.

Modifying Wizards And Templates

Substantial text editing requires *selecting* the text on which you want to work. As you probably know, you can select text in almost any Mac program—PowerPoint included—by pointing to the beginning of the selection, clicking and holding the mouse button, dragging to the end of the selection, and releasing the button. However, we recommend a different selection strategy when doing the big replacement job of changing a proto-presentation into your own show.

You can work with your text on the slides themselves (in Slide view) or in Outline view. We recommend doing most of your heavy-duty text entry and editing in Outline view, in part because these tasks are easier in Outline view, but also because working in Outline view helps you better manage the structure and flow of your show. Outline view also forces you to focus on the real content of your show without the distraction of the visuals. Once your text is complete, you can then work with it in Slide view to fine-tune its appearance.

Editing Text

To edit in Outline view, simply select and edit at will. You can work with the outline very much as you would in any word processor. To add a new item to a list, position the edit cursor at the very end of a list item line and press Return. To delete any line, select it and press Delete.

The same selecting and editing techniques apply in Slide view—with one difference. Before you can edit text, you must click on it to open the text placeholder that contains the text. Often, the text in a slide will actually appear in multiple placeholders—for example, one for the title and another for the bullets.

When you click on any text in Slide view, a hashed outline appears around the text, showing the borders of the placeholder (see Figure 8.14). The edit cursor appears

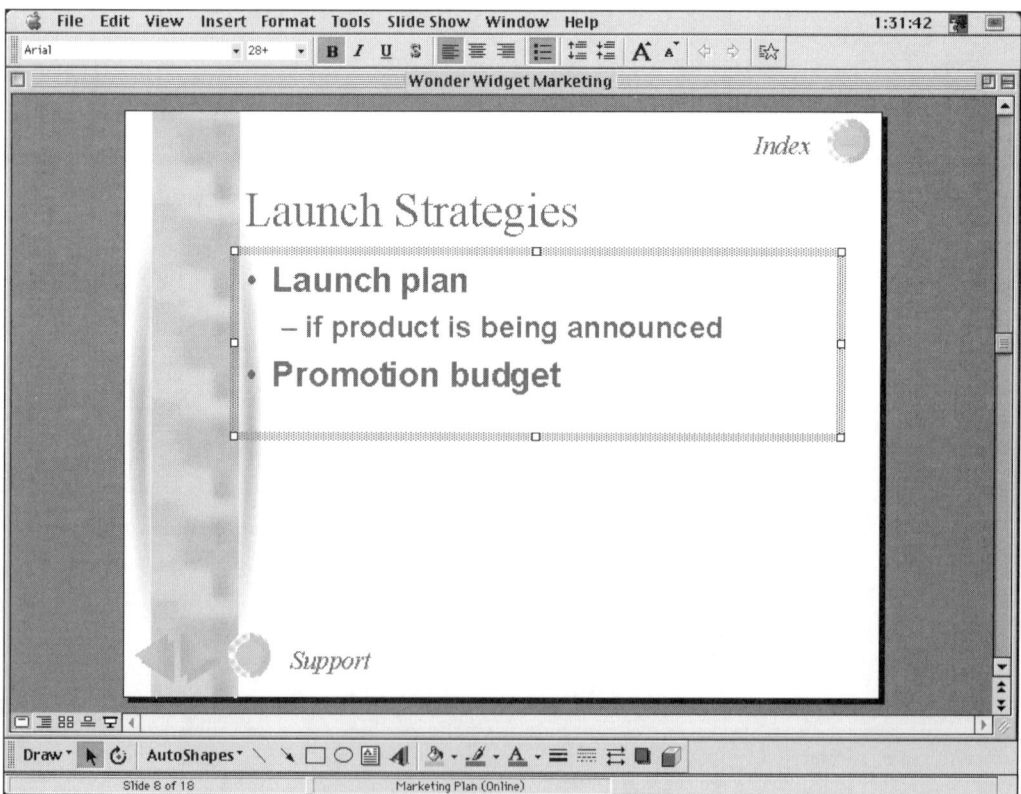

Figure 8.14 Slide text is contained in *text placeholders*.

within the text at roughly the spot where you pointed. Within the selected placeholder, you may select and replace text exactly as you would in Outline view. You can double-click to the right of a line to select it and then type a replacement or delete the line. You can point and click—or use your arrow keys—to move the edit cursor within a line and make edits.

When you've finished editing the text in a placeholder, click on another text placeholder to edit its text, or simply deselect the placeholder by clicking in the empty part of the screen to the left or right of the slide.

Walk-Through: Starting A Show, Editing Text

Follow these steps to learn about setting up a show and working with text on a slide.

1. Choose File|New. The New Presentation dialog opens.
2. Click on the Presentations tab.
3. Click on Marketing Plan (Standard). A preview appears in the Preview pane.
4. Click on OK. The first slide of the proto-presentation appears.
5. Switch to Outline view (click on the Outline View button in PowerPoint's lower left corner or choose View|Outline).
6. Point just to the right of the title (Product Name) and double-click to select the title.
7. Type a name for your product.
8. Point to the right of the first bullet (Market Past, Present) and double-click to select it.
9. Type any new text to replace the first bullet line.
10. Click at the end of the first bullet line to position the edit cursor there, and press Return. A new bullet line begins.
11. Type some bulleted text.
12. Double-click on the slide icon for Slide 4 to see Slide 4 in Slide view.
13. Point to the very end of the last bullet line, then click. The text placeholder appears, and the edit cursor appears at the end of the line.
14. Press Return to start a new bullet line.
15. Type some text.

Changing Text And Attributes

There's a science to the presentation and organization of text in presentations. And as pedestrian as it may seem, the pattern followed in most of the slides produced by PowerPoint templates works—a bold, big slide title stating a main point, followed by bulleted items supporting or expanding on that point. We alert you to this not to inhibit you, but to let you know that you're likely to get a pretty effective presentation if you stick pretty close to what the template gives you. If you fiddle too much with the text formatting, you may detract from it, and in doing so, make your show less effective than it might otherwise be.

That said, PowerPoint gives you complete control over the appearance of the text in your slides. You can choose the *font* (typeface) of text and its size, make text bold or italic, and more. You can turn lines of text into a bulleted list (or vice versa) and align text to the left side, right side, or center of the text box that contains the text. All of the controls required for this formatting are featured on the Formatting toolbar, shown in Figure 8.15. If you don't see the Formatting toolbar, choose View|Toolbars|Formatting.

Fast Track

In "Character Formatting," next, you learn how to change the way your text looks in all of the available ways but one: color. The color of text is determined by the color scheme. See "Changing Color Schemes" in the next chapter.

Character Formatting

You can apply character formatting—font, size, or attributes (bold, italic, underline, shadow)—to any group of characters you wish, from a single character, to a word, to a whole slide or group of slides.

Begin by selecting the text you want to format. Use the same selection techniques you use to edit text, in Outline or Slide view. In addition, you have a few extra ways to select text for applying character formatting:

- When no text is selected, any character formatting you apply affects the whole word in which the edit cursor appears.

- To select a whole slide so that any character formatting affects all text in the slide, single-click on the slide's icon in Outline view.

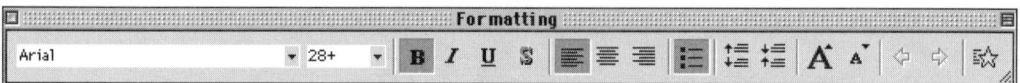

Figure 8.15 Change the look of your show easily with the buttons on the Formatting toolbar.

After making your selection, apply your desired formatting from the Formatting toolbar. To change the font and font size, drop down the Font list and select from among the fonts installed on your Mac, and drop down the Font Size list to select a size for your text. (To learn more about fonts, see Chapter 4.)

To change the attributes of selected text, click on the Bold, Underline, Italic, or Shadow button. Note that you can click on any combination of these buttons to combine their effects—bold italic, italic shadowed, and so on. To remove attributes, click on the button again; for example, to revert bold text to regular text, select the text and click on the Bold button.

Fast Track

To quickly increase or decrease the size of selected text without fiddling with the Font Size list, click on the Increase Font Size button or the Decrease Font Size button on the Formatting toolbar.

Paragraph Alignment And Spacing

In PowerPoint, all of the text before a paragraph break is called a *paragraph*, even though most paragraphs in slide shows are only one line long or less. The slide title is a paragraph, and each item in a list is also a paragraph, even if the item contains only a single word.

Unlike character formatting, paragraph formatting—alignment and spacing—always affects entire paragraphs. If you select nothing before applying the formatting, the paragraph containing the edit cursor gets the formatting. If you make a selection within a paragraph, the formatting still affects the whole paragraph. If you start a selection in one paragraph and run it through several others, the formatting affects all paragraphs that have any part of them selected.

The alignment buttons on the Formatting toolbar—Left, Center, and Right—align a selected paragraph or paragraphs within their placeholder. For example, click on Center to center the selected paragraph within the placeholder. Pay special attention to the fact that alignment is relative to the placeholder, not the slide as a whole. If you want to center text on the slide, use the Center button to center it in the placeholder. Then position the placeholder so that it is centered on the slide (see "Rearranging Placeholders" in the next chapter).

To increase or decrease the space between paragraphs, select the paragraphs you want to modify, then click on Increase Paragraph Spacing or Decrease Paragraph Spacing on the Formatting toolbar.

Bulleted Lists

PowerPoint understands that most presentations are made up mainly of slide titles followed by bulleted lists. That's why most templates and slide layouts format your show that way, and that's also why PowerPoint helps you format lists easily.

To turn any paragraph into a bulleted list item, position the edit cursor in it and click on the Bullets button on the Formatting toolbar. To change a group of paragraphs into a bulleted list, run a selection from anywhere in the first paragraph to anywhere in the last, then click on Bullets. (To change a bulleted item back into an ordinary paragraph, select it and click on the Bullets button.)

PowerPoint supports *nested lists*—lists that contain other lists, which may contain other lists, and so on (see Figure 8.16), as in a table of contents or structured outline. As in an outline, each new hierarchical level in the list is distinguished by being indented farther to the right and by a unique bullet character.

Once you've formatted a paragraph as a bullet list item, you can easily change its level by positioning the edit cursor in it and clicking on Promote or Demote on the

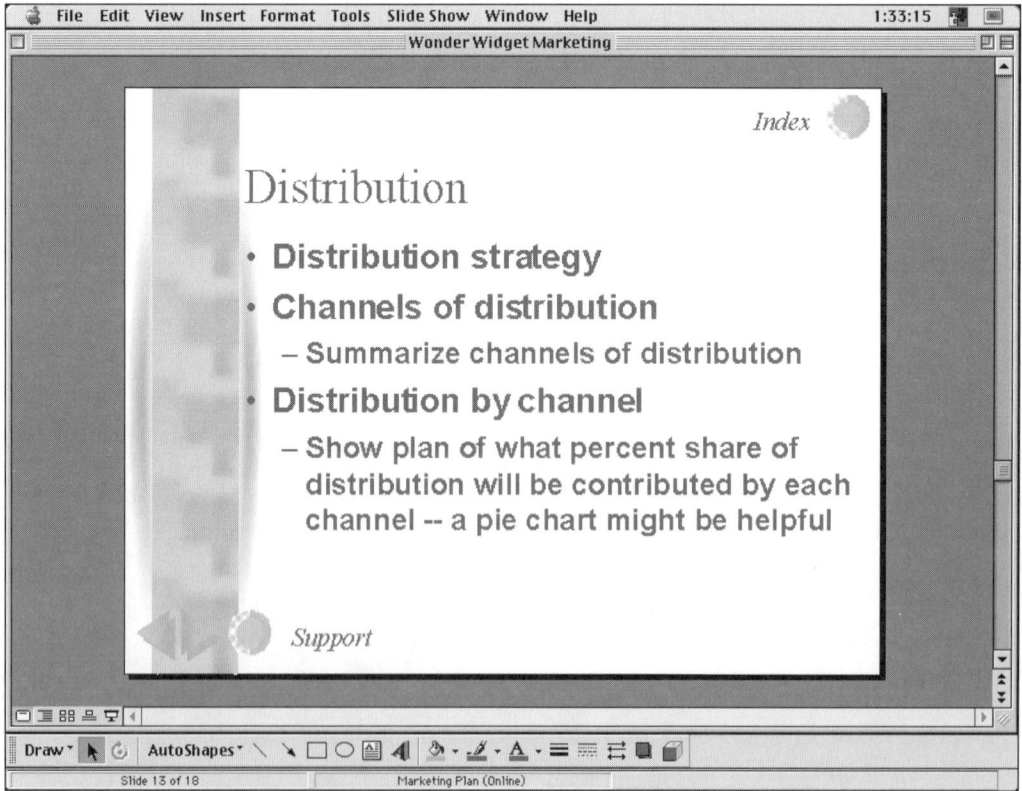

Figure 8.16 When your lists contain lists, you've got *nested lists*.

Formatting toolbar. Each time you click on Demote, the item is indented farther to the right and automatically takes on the bullet character of the level it occupies. Promote has the opposite effect, moving an item or items higher up in the list structure. You can select multiple bulleted items and then Promote or Demote them together.

Although PowerPoint does a great job of automatically assigning unique bullet styles to all levels in lists, note that you can apply a different bullet character, color, and size to selected list items. Select the items, then choose Format|Bullet to open the Bullet dialog.

In the Bullet dialog, click on the bullet character you want to use. By default, the choice in Bullets From is Normal Text, which applies the same basic bullet regardless of the font in which the bullet text is set. But if none of the bullet characters shown appeal to you, choose a font from the Bullets From list to see more bullet character choices. (A default Office font in the list, Wingdings, has some great bullet choices, as does the Mac standard font Zapf Dingbats.) You may also choose a special color or size for the bullets from the lists provided.

Fast Track

To create a nicely formatted list that doesn't have bullets, select all paragraphs that make up the list (and click on Bullets if the list has not already been bulleted), then open the Bullet dialog and clear the Use A Bullet checkbox.

Checking Spelling

If you've given—or seen—many presentations, you know how humiliating misspelled slide text can be. Ned once saw a sales presentation in which the product name was misspelled on every slide. (It was one of those old computer product names like "PCcalcX2.5," so nobody knew the difference. But still....)

PowerPoint checks your spelling to help you avoid embarrassment. To check spelling, choose Tools|Spelling. (Note that you can check spelling from any view.) When PowerPoint locates a suspect word, you'll see the dialog shown in Figure 8.17.

If the word is incorrect, review the Suggestions box to see whether Word has suggested a correct replacement. If so, click on the correct suggestion. If not, edit the word in Change To to correct it. After clicking on a suggestion or editing Change To, click on Change.

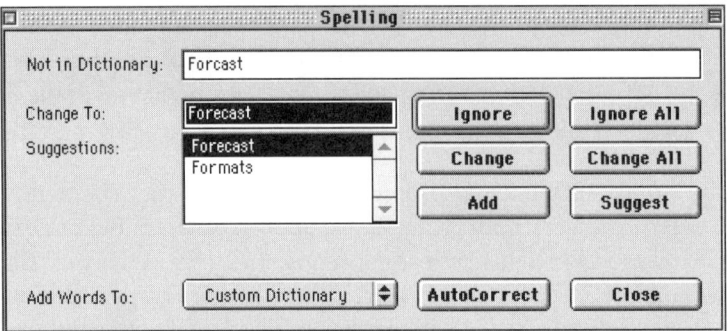

Figure 8.17 Use the spellchecker to fix spelling.

Adding, Moving, And Removing Slides

Changing the order of slides and adding or deleting slides is easiest to do when you're in Slide Sorter view. Note that when you make any of the changes described below, the slides in your presentation are renumbered automatically, as necessary.

As you begin to apply what you learn in this section—particularly deleting a slide—keep in mind that you can use Undo to undo any slide addition, removal, or relocation. (Click on the Undo button on the Standard toolbar or choose Edit|Undo.)

Begin by switching to Slide Sorter view (click on the Slide Sorter view button in PowerPoint's lower left corner or choose View|Slide Sorter). Your options are as follows:

- *To add a slide*—Click between slides where you want to insert a new slide. (You may click to the left of the first slide, or to the right of the last, to add a slide at the beginning or end.) A vertical bar appears where you clicked. Click on the New Slide button on the Standard toolbar (or choose Insert|New Slide). The New Slide dialog opens (see Figure 8.18), showing the available slide layouts. Click on an AutoLayout to select it, then click on OK.

Fast Track

If you want to add a slide that will contain text or formatting that's very similar to an existing slide, select the slide you want to duplicate, then choose Insert|Duplicate Slide. An exact copy of the selected slide appears immediately following it in the presentation. You can edit the duplicate any way you wish or move it elsewhere in the show.

- *To delete a slide*—Click on the slide to select it (a black border appears around the slide to show that it is selected). Press the Delete key.

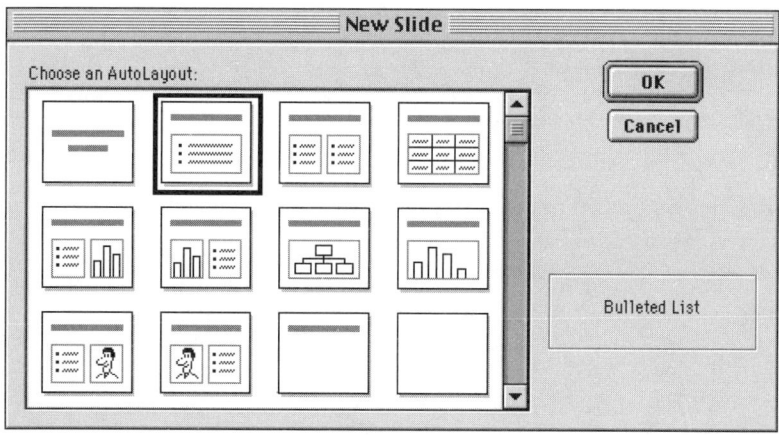

Figure 8.18 Choose an AutoLayout when adding a new slide.

- *To move a slide*—Point to the slide. Click and hold, then drag the slide over the slide whose spot you want the moved slide to take. When you release the button, the slide is moved.

Walk-Through: Formatting Text, Adding/Moving/Removing Slides

Follow these steps for hands-on experience in working with text on slides and manipulating the slides themselves.

1. After choosing File|New to open the New Presentation dialog, go to the Presentations tab and create a new presentation based on the template Project Overview (Standard).
2. Switch to Outline view.
3. Highlight the title of the first slide (Project Overview).
4. On the Formatting toolbar, click on the Increase Font Size button twice. The size of the title text increases by 10 points.
5. In the second slide, beneath the bullet list item "Ultimate Goal Of Project," add two new items:
   - Short-term
   - Long-term
6. Start a selection anywhere in Short-term, and run it to anywhere in Long-term.
7. On the Formatting toolbar, click on Demote to indent the new bullet items and change their bullet format.

8. With the new bullets still highlighted, choose Format|Bullet to open the Bullet dialog.
9. Pick a fun and funky bullet style and click on OK.
10. Switch to Slide Sorter view.
11. Click on Slide 6 to select it, then press Delete. Slide 6 disappears, and the following slides are renumbered.
12. Click and hold on Slide 4, drag it on top of Slide 7, and release. Slide 4 becomes Slide 7, and other slides are renumbered as necessary.
13. Click in between Slides 2 and 3.
14. On the Standard toolbar, click on New Slide. A new Slide 3 appears, and other slides are renumbered as necessary.

Moving On

Got a feel for PowerPoint? Feeling creative? Okay then…move ahead to Chapter 9, where you'll learn how to create presentations quickly and beautifully. Nearly all of what you learn in Chapter 9 is medium-independent—that is, you apply the same techniques whether the presentation you're making is destined for transparencies, slides, or electronic presentations.

In Chapter 10, you'll supplement your authoring skills by learning how to use all of the electronic gadgetry PowerPoint supports, including animation, movies, sound, and much more. You'll also learn the ins and outs of configuring and presenting an electronic extravaganza.

Designing Presentations

The last time Ned had to produce a PowerPoint presentation, he had been invited to speak at a conference in Bermuda. Of course, he was very excited to be going to Bermuda, and he knew about the conference months in advance. So he really can't explain why he didn't start working on his presentation until the day before his departure. (He wanted it to seem fresh?)

He's not trying to wriggle off the hook, but we know that his behavior was more the rule than the exception. Most people who must author their own presentations do so not as part of their daily responsibilities, but in addition to them—in crisis preparation for the "Big Sales Meeting," or customer confab, or what have you. And though we all start out hoping to create a state-of-the-art slide show, in the end we're often grateful to have a dozen colorful text slides with only one typo each.

We designed this chapter in recognition of that reality. We'll help you create a good-looking presentation as quickly as possible by first covering the basics. You can move through just the first few sections of this chapter to produce an attractive show fast. After that, call the airport—if your flight has been delayed, you can proceed ever deeper into this chapter, discovering how to fine-tune your show and customize it precisely to your tastes, needs, or whims.

Opening Existing Presentations

PowerPoint remembers the file names of the last four files you've opened and lists them at the bottom of the File menu. To quickly open any of the last four presentations you've worked on, choose File, then click on the presentation's file name on the File menu.

If the file you want isn't on the File menu, you can open it from PowerPoint's Open dialog (Figure 9.1), which you can display in any of three ways:

- On PowerPoint's Startup dialog, choose the radio button next to Open An Existing Presentation and click on OK.

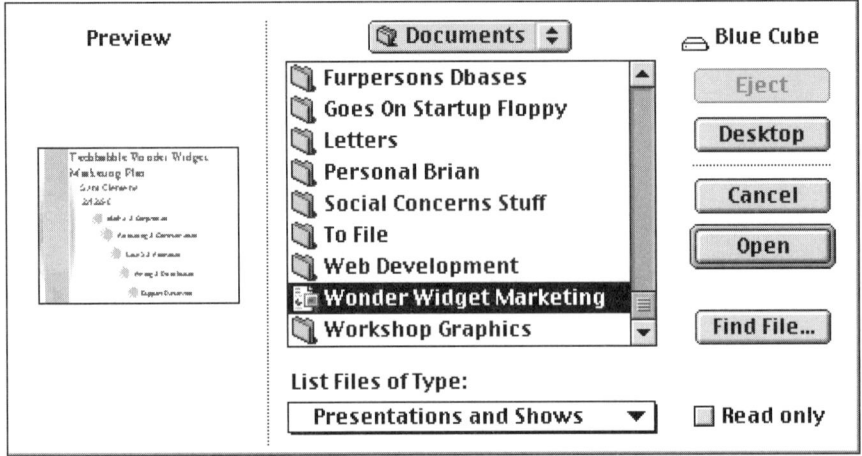

Figure 9.1 Use the Open dialog to navigate to and open an existing presentation.

- Click on the Open button on PowerPoint's Standard toolbar.
- Choose File|Open.

In the Open dialog, the drive/folder list names the current folder, and the file list box lists all of the presentation files in the current folder. Drop down the drive/folder list and use it to navigate to the folder containing the file you want to open. When the file you want appears in the list, click on it once to select it; an image of the selected file's first slide appears in the Preview box on the left side of the dialog. When you're sure you've found the file you want, click on Open.

Fast Track

When you open a PowerPoint show file by double-clicking on its icon in the Finder, the show opens automatically in Slide Show view. However, when you open a show file from the Open dialog, it opens for editing in Slide view, exactly as a presentation file does.

Besides opening PowerPoint from the Office Manager menu, you can also open the program by opening any PowerPoint file (just like other Mac programs). You open a file from any window—the Desktop, a folder, or Find Results—by double-clicking on its file icon.

Although opening any PowerPoint file opens PowerPoint, things happen a little differently depending upon which of the three basic PowerPoint file types you open. Table 9.1 describes the types of PowerPoint files and explains what happens when you open each. (Examine the icons carefully. All are similar, but each is slightly different. The extensions list will help you share files with Windows users—if you're sending a file

Table 9.1 PowerPoint files and their actions when opened.

File Icon And Extension	Description	What Happens When You Open It
.ppt	A PowerPoint presentation.	PowerPoint opens in Slide view so you can work on your presentation (see "Choosing a A View" in Chapter 8).
.pps	A PowerPoint presentation configured to open in Slide Show view.	PowerPoint opens in Slide Show view. Other than opening in Slide Show view, a show file is just like a presentation file. You can watch the show, or choose another view to edit the presentation.
.pot	A PowerPoint template, used to get a head start on creating a presentation.	PowerPoint opens, and a new presentation is created based on the template file.
.pwz	A PowerPoint wizard, which leads you step-by-step through a PowerPoint activity. (The only PowerPoint wizard included with Office 98, AutoContent Wizard, helps you start a new presentation by selecting a template for you.)	PowerPoint opens, and the wizard opens to prompt you through the task.

to someone on a Windows machine, use the correct extension. Alternately, if you're receiving a file from a Windows box, knowing the extension will tell you the file type.)

Fast Track

To quickly find and open any of PowerPoint's template or wizard files, use the New dialog. The Presentations and Presentation Designs tabs include only PowerPoint files. The General tab holds your Blank Presentation and AutoContent Wizard files. Also, consider adding aliases of frequently used templates to your Office Manager or Apple menu for quick and easy access.

Rearranging Slide Elements

Text formatting and *slide formatting*—choosing the colors, background, layout, and other aesthetics of the slide—go hand in hand. After changing the text formatting, you'll often want to fiddle with the slide formatting, and vice versa. Each changes your perception of the other.

For example, if you make text larger, the larger text may suddenly seem too close to another object on screen, and you'll want to reposition the placeholders to restore the compositional balance of the slide. Changing the background fill of a slide may make text harder to read, so you'll want to change the font, enlarge the text, or apply attributes to it to help it stand out against the new background.

Fast Track

To radically change the look of an existing presentation, you can apply a new design template to it. Applying a different design template does not affect the content of your presentation, but it may change much of the text formatting as well as many of the slide formatting options that follow.

Note that if you feel you need the radical overhaul of a new design, the template you chose was probably a bad fit for what you wanted to create. If you've not put much effort yet into the content of your presentation, you may be better off starting over and choosing a different template from the Presentations tab.

To apply a new design to an existing show, click on the Apply Design button on the Standard toolbar, or choose Format|Apply Design. A dialog opens, showing a list from which you may choose (and preview) any of PowerPoint's Presentation Designs templates. Alternatively, you can use the dialog to navigate to one of your own presentations and copy its design to the current show.

The arrangement of placeholders on a slide is called the slide's *layout*. PowerPoint has 24 predefined AutoLayout options, each containing a different layout.

When you create a presentation with the AutoContent Wizard or from a template on the Presentations tab, an AutoLayout is assigned to each slide for you. When you use a Presentation Designs template or Blank Presentation, the AutoLayout dialog opens so you can choose an AutoLayout for the first slide. When you add slides, you're always prompted to choose an AutoLayout.

You can change the layout of a slide in either of two ways: You can pick a new AutoLayout, or you can manually rearrange the placeholders. Both techniques are described next.

Changing The Slide Layout (AutoLayout)

To change the slide layout, select the slide you want to change, then click on the Slide Layout button on the Standard toolbar (or choose Format|Slide Layout). The Slide Layout dialog opens.

In the thumbnail pictures of the available layouts, the horizontal gray bars represent placeholders for title text, whereas the other boxes feature tiny graphics to help you understand the types of placeholders they contain—a cartoon face for a picture placeholder, a film clapper for a movie clip, and so on. Click on any layout option to see a description in the box on the right side of the dialog. When you've clicked on the layout you want, click on Apply.

If the selected slide contains placeholders that are not included in the AutoLayout you select, don't worry—all of your objects remain on the slide. For example, if the slide has a picture placeholder and the AutoLayout has no picture but does have a chart placeholder, your slide will wind up with both a picture and a chart. However, since the AutoLayout has no built-in spot for the extra placeholder, you'll need to rearrange the placeholders manually (as described next) to make everything fit.

Rearranging Placeholders

To reposition, resize, and reshape any placeholder, begin by clicking on it to select it and reveal its border (see Figure 9.2). Along the placeholder border, you'll notice little squares—called *handles*—on all the sides and corners.

- To reposition the placeholder, point to any part of the border *except* a handle. The pointer becomes a four-pointed arrow. Click and hold the mouse button, drag the outline to the new position, and release to drop it there.

- To change the size of the placeholder without changing its shape, point to a corner handle. The cursor becomes a two-pointed arrow. Click and hold, then

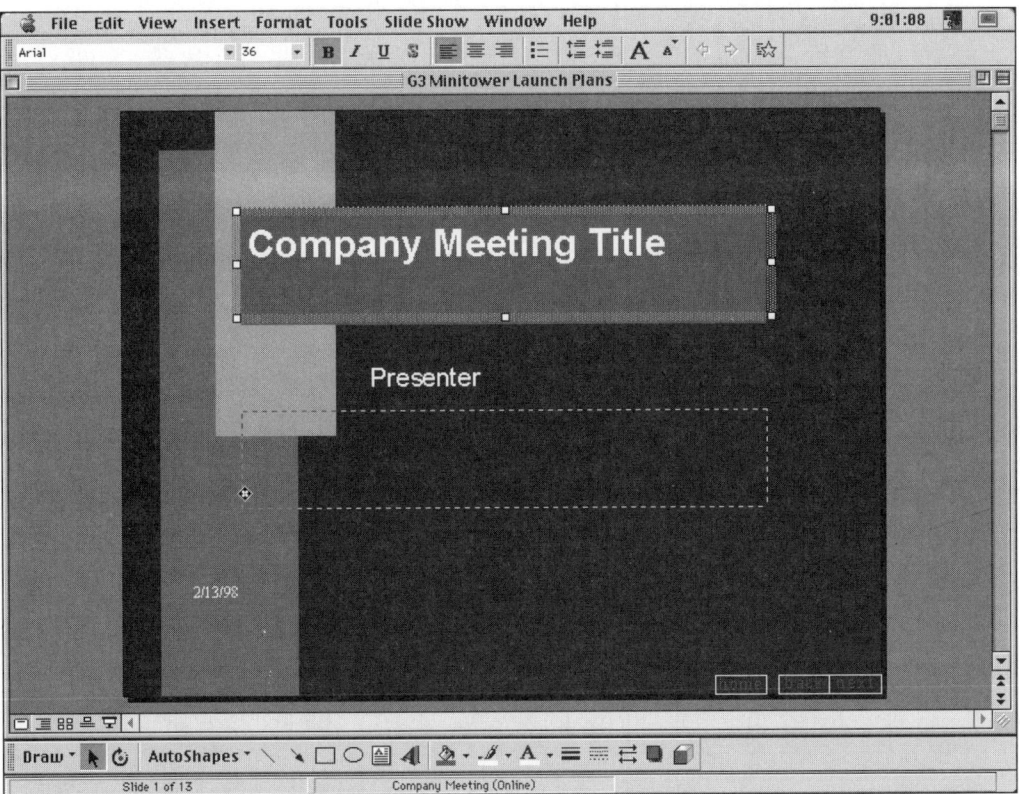

Figure 9.2 Use drag and drop to rearrange placeholders.

drag toward the center of the placeholder to shrink it. Drag toward the outside of the placeholder to enlarge it.

- To change the placeholder's width (without affecting its height), point to a handle on either side (but not on a corner). The cursor becomes a two-pointed arrow. Click and hold, then drag toward the center of the placeholder to make it narrower or drag away from the center to widen it.

- To change the placeholder's height (without affecting its width), point to a handle on the top or bottom (not on a corner). The cursor becomes a two-pointed arrow. Click and hold, then drag toward the center of the placeholder to shorten it or drag away from the center to make it taller.

Dealing With Overlapping Objects

When objects overlap—as they often may, accidentally, when you change the AutoLayout of an existing slide—you can always adjust size and position to make everything fit without overlapping.

Of course, sometimes you *want* placeholders to overlap. For example, to place a small caption on top of a picture (as you learn to do in Chapter 10), you must lay a text placeholder atop a picture. You can also create fun designs by overlapping multiple picture placeholders.

The trick with overlapping objects is choosing the *order* of each—whether an object is *in front* (covering all others), *in back* (behind all others), or somewhere between front and back when three or more objects overlap. To choose the order of a placeholder that overlaps others, Control-click on it. The placeholder is selected, and a contextual menu opens (see Figure 9.3). From the contextual menu, choose Order, then the position that you want the selected object to hold.

Changing Slide Colors

The *color scheme* is the combination of different colors used in slides. The scheme assigns a different color to each element in the slide—one color for the background, another for the text, and so on. Each template includes one or more predefined color schemes, designed so that the colors complement one another and suit the style of the show the template is designed to support.

Changing Color Schemes

You can change the color scheme for selected slides or for an entire presentation. Begin by selecting the slides you want to change (if you plan to change the scheme for the whole show, it doesn't matter which slides you select). Choose Format|Slide Color Scheme to open the Color Scheme dialog shown in Figure 9.4. (Each template has its own color schemes, in addition to certain "standards.")

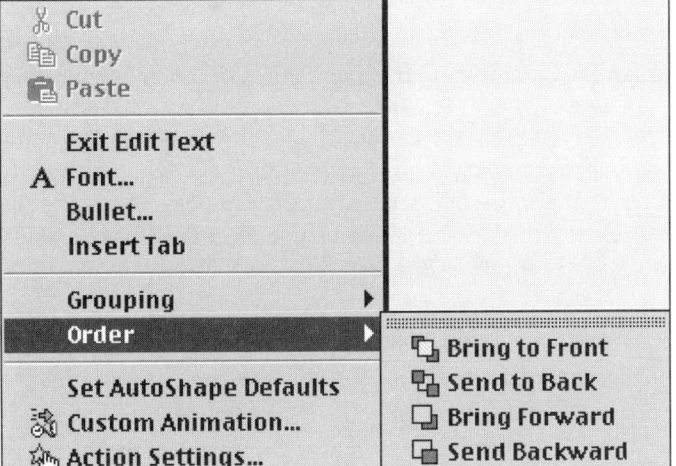

Figure 9.3 Control-click on objects and choose Order from the contextual menu to choose the order of overlapping objects.

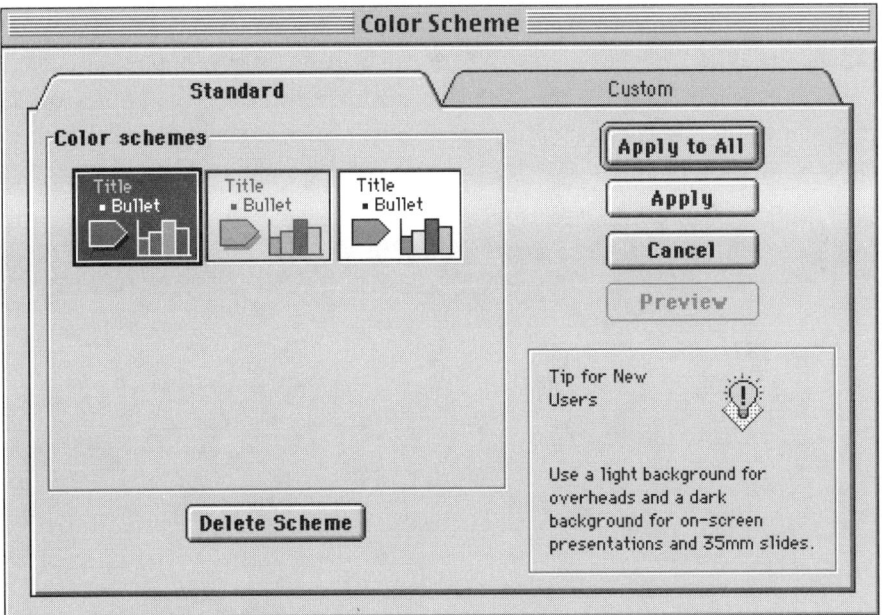

Figure 9.4 Use the Color Scheme dialog to pick the color of each element in a slide.

To use one of the schemes included with the template, select one of the schemes shown in the Standard tab, then click on Apply to apply the scheme only to selected slides, or Apply To All to apply the scheme to the whole presentation.

Fast Track

The little thumbnail examples of the Standard color schemes may not provide you with a full sense of how the scheme will appear in your slides. To get a better idea, click on the Preview button on the Color Scheme dialog. The current slide takes on the selected color scheme—just temporarily. (You may have to drag the dialog out of the way—or just use the Collapse box—to see the slide.) Note that the Preview is just that—no change is actually made to your slides unless you click on Apply or Apply To All.

To create a new scheme, click on a scheme in the Standard tab that's closest to the scheme you want to create, then click on the Custom tab (see Figure 9.5). The color squares next to each slide element in the list of Scheme Colors show the color from the scheme you chose in the Standard tab. For any element whose color you want to change, click on the element's color box, then click on the Change Color button. A dialog opens like the one shown in Figure 9.6. Although this dialog looks the same no matter which slide element you selected, observe that its name varies depending on what you're choosing a color for—Shadows Color, Background Color, and so on.

In the dialog, the big, bug-eye hexagon shows the full range of colors you can choose, and the group of little hexagons beneath the big one offer various shades of gray, from white (the leftmost hexagon) to black (the rightmost). To choose any color or gray, point to it and click. The tiny hexagon you click on is outlined in white. In the square that appears in the lower right corner of the dialog, the bottom of the square

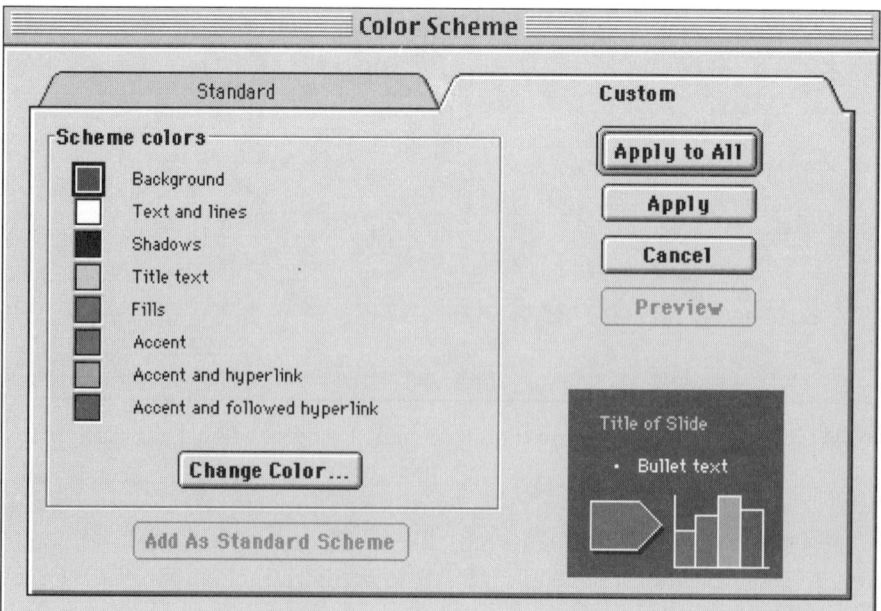

Figure 9.5 Click on the Custom tab to create a new color scheme.

Designing Presentations 239

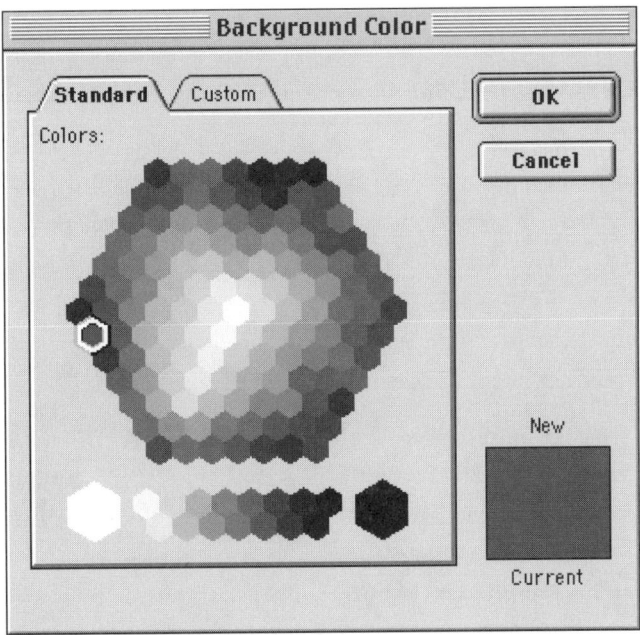

Figure 9.6 To choose a color, click on a hexagon.

shows the Current color (the one you're changing), and the top shows the New color (the one you've selected).

When you're happy with your choice, click on OK to return to the Color Scheme dialog. You may proceed to change the color of another element, click on Preview to see the custom scheme applied to a slide, or click on Apply or Apply To All to apply the scheme.

Fast Track

After creating a custom scheme, click on the Add As Standard Scheme button on the Custom tab to add the new scheme to the Standard tab, so you can easily apply it again in the future.

FYI: Working With "Masters"

A *master* is a slide or page whose contents and formatting affect all other slides or pages in a show. Every presentation has four masters:

- *Slide Master*—Controls the appearance of all slides in the show.
- *Title Master*—Controls the appearance of just the title slide, so it can differ from the rest of the show.

- *Notes Master*—Controls the appearance of all notes pages in the show.
- *Handout Master*—Controls the appearance of all handouts in the show.

A master establishes default formatting for the show and can also include text or pictures that can appear on every slide (or page). In other words, any text, pictures, or formatting in the master affects everything else. You can even put a company logo or special background in a master, and it will automatically appear on all slides—except those you specifically change. Also, whenever you apply a new design template, the masters are changed automatically. To view or edit one of the masters, choose View|Master, and then choose the master you want from the Master submenu.

When you specifically change the background, color scheme, or other slide formatting, you break the bond between slide and master, and make that slide follow its own individual format. But when you do not make these changes to a slide, the slide retains the formatting from the master. When you make any changes to the master of an existing show, the rest of the slides change to match the master—except any slides whose bond to the master you have broken with custom formatting.

In general, you don't have to think about the masters if you don't want to—you can just format slides as you wish. But when you're creating an especially long show and you want it to have a consistent look and feel throughout, a master is a handy tool.

Changing Backgrounds

You can choose a background color by choosing or creating a new color scheme as described in the preceding section. However, there's more to backgrounds than color. Using the Background dialog, you can change not only the color, but also the *fill* of the background—a pattern, texture, or picture that dresses up the slide.

Begin by selecting the slides whose background you want to change (if you plan to change the background for the whole show, it doesn't matter which slides you select). Choose Format|Background to open the Background dialog. In the dialog, the Back-ground Fill box shows the current background settings. Drop down the list in the Background Fill box (see Figure 9.7) to reveal options for changing the background.

As Figure 9.7 shows, you can choose Automatic to have PowerPoint pick an appropriate background color for you, or click on one of the squares beneath Automatic to choose any color in the current color scheme. If you don't like any of the colors

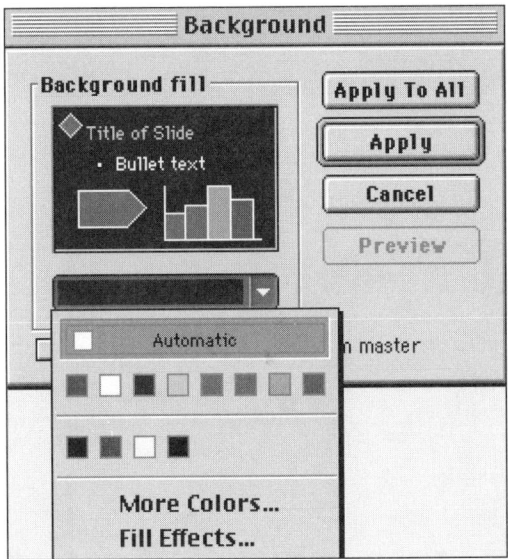

Figure 9.7 Choose Format|Background to change the slide background.

that appear, choose More Colors. A dialog just like Figure 9.6 (shown earlier in "Changing Color Schemes") appears. Choose a color from the dialog just as you would to pick a color for a custom color scheme.

To change the fill pattern or texture, choose Fill Effects. A dialog opens like the one in Figure 9.8. The first three tabs—Gradient, Texture, and Pattern—offer a wide range of different fill effects you can select for your background. The fourth tab, Picture, opens a file dialog from which you can navigate to and select a picture file to use as the background. (To learn more about pictures, see Chapter 10.) Make a selection on any tab, then click on OK to return to the Background dialog.

After choosing your background color and fill, click on Apply to apply the background only to selected slides, or Apply To All to apply the background to the whole presentation.

FYI: One Fill To A Customer

Throughout a presentation, you can apply as many different background fill effects as you like. However, any given slide can have only one of the four options in its background. In other words, a slide cannot have both a background picture and a pattern, or both a texture and a gradient. When using the Fill Effects dialog, complete one—and only one—tab to add a fill effect.

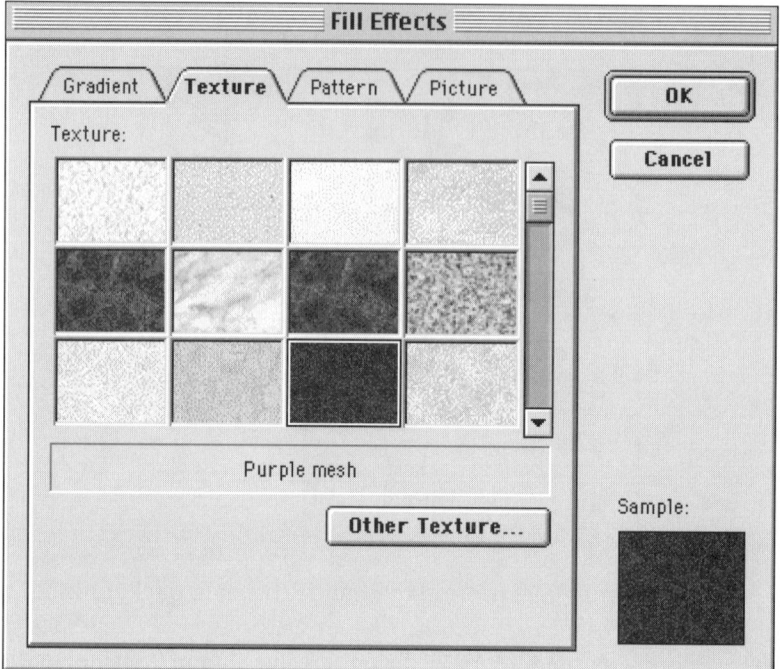

Figure 9.8 You can apply a *background fill*, a color or pattern for the background.

Walk-Through: Changing Slide Elements

Run through this exercise once to get some practice changing placeholders to actual usable elements:

1. After choosing File|New to open the New Presentation dialog, go to the Presentations tab and create a new presentation based on Marketing Plan (Standard).
2. Switch to Slide Sorter view.
3. Double-click on Slide 6 to open it in Slide view, and click on Slide Layout on the Standard toolbar.
4. On the Slide Layout dialog, choose the layout from the third row, first column, called Text & Clip Art.
5. Click on Apply. The text placeholder containing the bullet items is squeezed into a left-hand column and a placeholder for clip art appears to the right.
6. Choose Format|Background.
7. On the Background dialog, drop down the list in Background Fill, and choose Fill Effects.
8. On the Gradient tab, click on the upper right square under Variants, then click on OK.

9. On the Background dialog, click on Apply. A new gradient fill is applied to Slide 6.
10. Click on the Save button on the Standard toolbar. In the Save dialog, click on Desktop, name your file, and save it to your Mac's Desktop.

We'll be using this presentation as an example for the next walk-through.

Walk-Through: Opening a Presentation, Views

Follow these steps to practice opening presentations and working with views:

1. Open PowerPoint.
2. Choose File|Open.
3. Click on the Desktop button.
4. In the file list box, locate the presentation you saved from the last walk-through. Double-click on it to open the file.
5. Press PgDn to advance to Slide 2, and again to advance to Slide 3.
6. Switch to Outline view (click on the Outline view button or choose View|Outline).
7. Switch to Slide Sorter view (click on the Slide Sorter view button or choose View|Slide Sorter).
8. Double-click on any slide to view it in Slide view.
9. Choose Slide Show|View Show. The show begins at Slide 1.
10. Practice using the mouse and the arrow keys to move through the presentation. Clicking moves forward one slide, Command-clicking moves back one. The Right and Down arrow keys will advance one slide, whereas the Up and Left arrow keys will step back one.
11. When you feel comfortable navigating the presentation, Control-click on any slide, and from the contextual menu select End Show to return to Slide view.
12. Choose File|Close to close your test presentation.

Creating Notes Pages And Handouts

Notes pages are printed pages, each of which shows one of your slides plus any notes you've typed relating to that slide. You may want to create notes pages for either of two purposes:

- *For yourself (speaker notes)*—To use during the presentation as a guide to what you planned to say or do during the display of each slide. The notes beneath the slide image should include a more detailed outline of what you planned to say during the display of the slide.

- *For your audience*—To provide your listeners with a picture of each slide as well as notes expanding upon that slide (or empty space to jot their own notes).

If you want to give your audience copies of slides—but no notes—you can also create *handouts*. Handouts cannot include notes, but they can feature two, three, or six slides per page—enabling you to fit the slide images for a whole presentation in just a few handout pages.

Typing Slide Notes

To type the notes for a slide, open the slide in Slide view, or select the slide in Outline view or in Slide Sorter view. Then choose View|Notes Page. The notes page for the selected slide opens as shown in Figure 9.9.

The whole area beneath the slide image is a big text placeholder you use like any other. Click in it and type to add text. Format text by selecting the text and choosing buttons from the Formatting toolbar.

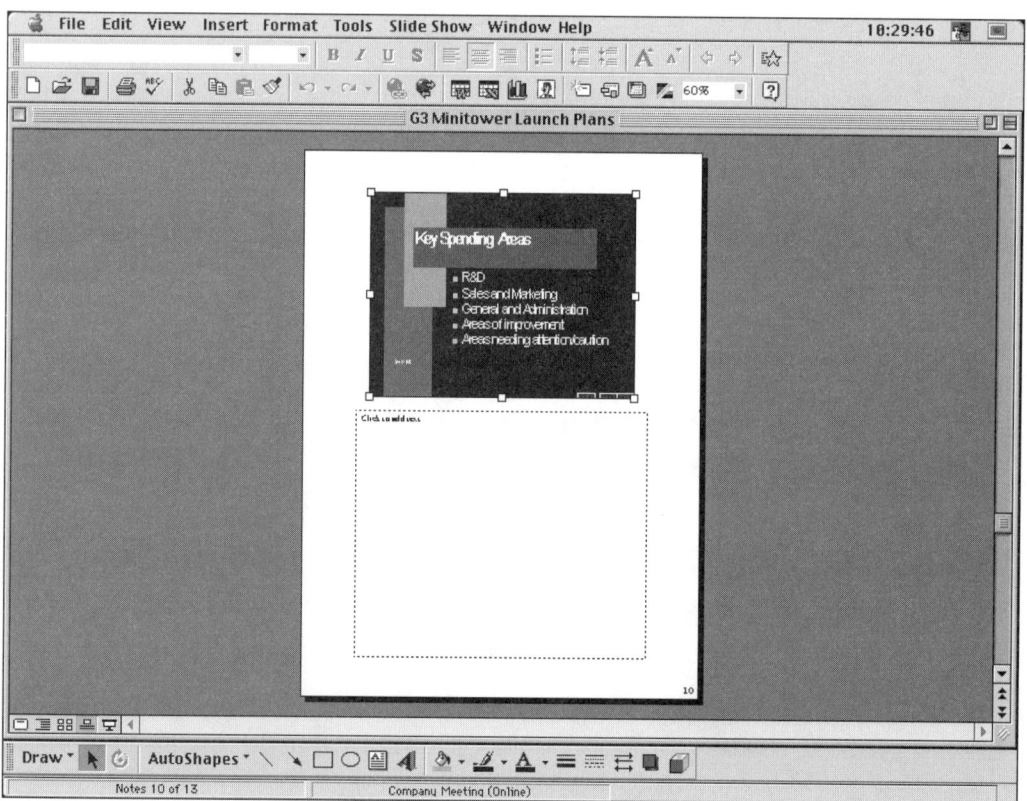

Figure 9.9 Type your speaker notes in Notes Page view.

When the Notes Page view opens, it shows you the whole page by default. That's helpful, because then you can see the slide you're writing about. However, you may have trouble seeing your typing when the whole page appears—your text will be too small. To see better (without having to get new glasses), click on the Zoom box on the Standard toolbar and raise the Zoom percentage to 100 percent or so. When typing notes, scroll up the page whenever you need to refer back to the slide.

Printing Notes And Handouts

To print notes or handouts, begin by opening the presentation for which you want to print notes or handouts, then choose File|Print to open the Print dialog. Near the bottom of the dialog appears a list labeled Print What (see Figure 9.10). Note that here, as in many cases with Office, you may not see the same options shown in the figure (it's dependent on your printer driver). If you don't see what the figure shows, look for a drop-down menu with a Microsoft PowerPoint item. That part of the dialog probably holds the notes and handouts options. To print handouts, drop down the Print What list and choose one of the three Handouts options—two slides per page, three per page, or six per page—and click on OK. To print notes pages, drop down the Print What list and choose Notes Pages, then click on OK.

Choosing A Presentation Medium

As you begin creating your show, decide up front how and where you will present it. PowerPoint supports the full range of presentation media, from simple transparencies, to animated multimedia presentations, to Web pages. The great part is that the

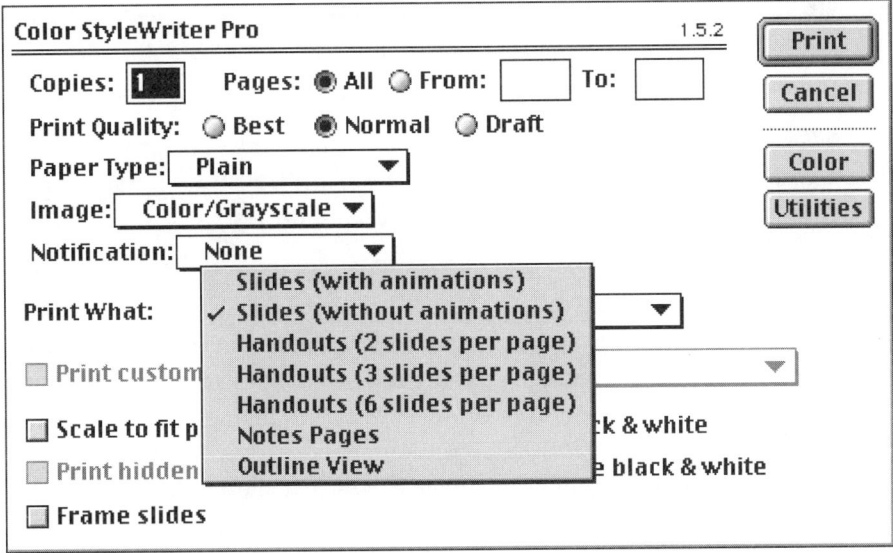

Figure 9.10 Choose from the Print What list to print notes or handouts from the Print dialog.

steps required to create your show are essentially the same, no matter where and how it will be shown. Of course, the one important difference is that, when you present your show on a Mac, you can apply a family of multimedia features that you obviously can't use on a slide or transparency.

Special content you can include in your Mac-presented show—known as an *electronic presentation* in PowerPoint parlance—includes:

- *Animation*—PowerPoint's animations are easy-to-apply animation effects that reveal text in a slide, make fun transitions between slides, and more. Animations are the quickest, easiest way to add real sparkle to a show.

- *Sound*—You can attach sound effects or other sound clips to events within your show—such as slide transitions—or record and play slide narration for a self-running show. You can also instruct PowerPoint to play a CD in the background, or to dynamically compose and play an electronic soundtrack—automatically—to underscore the show.

- *Movies*—Mac video files in QuickTime format can be embedded in slides and played during your show.

- *Hyperlinks*—You can configure text on a slide as a link so that clicking on it opens something new. When clicked, a link can open a new slide, a Word document, or even a page on the Web.

- *Action buttons*—These attractive, on-screen buttons can do all of the same things links do.

Also, when a presentation is destined for Mac play, you have an extra set of options that customize the show for presentation in different venues and circumstances. Using these options, you can set up any show to play on a Macintosh as:

- *A full-screen, speaker-driven presentation*—The slides take up the whole screen, hiding PowerPoint behind them. The speaker controls the show, moving from slide to slide and activating any links or action buttons.

- *A windowed, viewer-driven presentation*—The slides appear in a window with the Web toolbar along the top so that the viewer controls the presentation. (The Web toolbar is really just a set of buttons for moving around in the show; it's called "Web" not because it's used for Web presentations, but because it's used just the way the navigation tools on Web browsers are used, taking advantage of skills many viewers already possess.) This option provides individuals or small groups with self-training presentations or similar shows that allow viewers to move along at their own pace.

- *A kiosk presentation*—A viewer-controlled show that appears full-screen (hiding PowerPoint). Unlike a speaker-driven full-screen show, in a kiosk show access to PowerPoint navigation and editing tools is completely cut off—the viewer can get around by clicking on any links or access buttons in slides, but cannot otherwise control the show or access PowerPoint. Kiosk mode is designed to support kiosks at trade shows or other venues where unsupervised viewers may approach the Mac and explore the show on their own. An example of a kiosk presentation is shown in Figure 9.11.

- *A self-running presentation*—You can configure any of the preceding types of shows as self-running shows that move from slide to slide all by themselves, with no viewer or speaker control. You get to select the *timings* for self-running shows—the number of seconds PowerPoint displays each slide before proceeding to the next. Whereas the most obvious place for a self-running show is a kiosk, some speakers prefer this option to advancing the slides manually, as long as their shows are carefully timed and rehearsed.

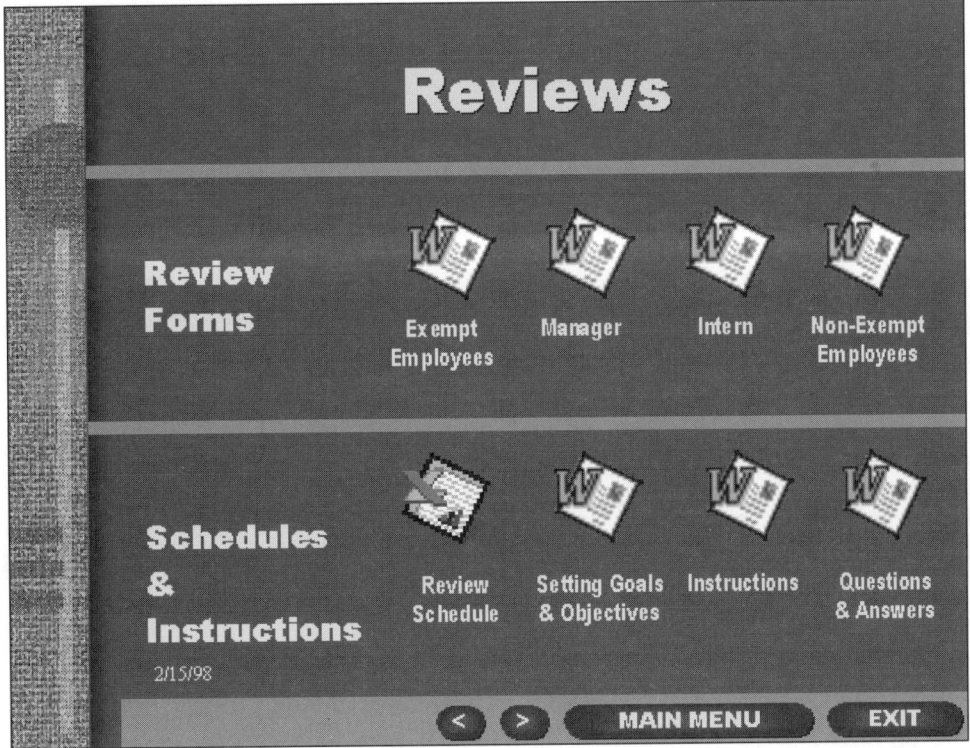

Figure 9.11 In a kiosk show, you can add on-screen buttons to enable viewers to move from slide to slide.

- *An online presentation*—Finally, PowerPoint presentations may be shown over a network so that viewers in different cities—or countries—may take part. PowerPoint supports several ways to create online presentations, including saving shows in HTML (Web) format for universal support of Internet and intranet environments, and running a "Presentation Conference" in which multiple viewers in different cities can simultaneously view and participate in a single presentation. To learn more about online presentations, see Chapter 17.

Printing Transparencies

Printing overhead transparencies is as simple as printing a document from Word or from any Mac application. Open the presentation you want to print (don't worry about the view you start in; view doesn't affect printing) and choose File|Print. The Print dialog opens (see Figure 9.12). To print all slides in the presentation using the default printer and options, simply click on OK. (Note that the figure shows Brian's printer, which offers a special option for printing transparencies as well—your printer may not offer this.)

Fast Track

If you don't want to make your own transparencies, or if you don't have access to a good color printer that accepts transparencies, you can order high-quality overhead transparencies from many of the same service bureaus that can create 35mm slides from your PowerPoint files. See "Making 35mm Slides" later in this chapter.

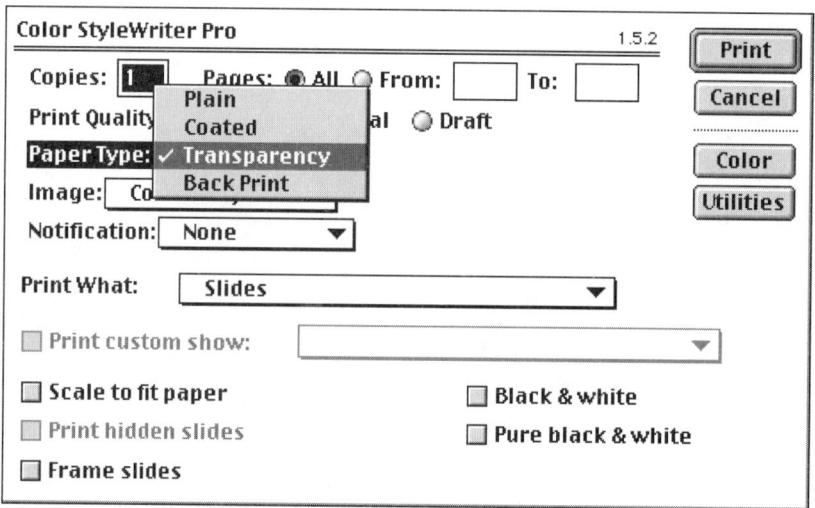

Figure 9.12 Printing transparencies is as easy as printing on paper.

Of course, before clicking on OK on the Print dialog, you have a variety of options to choose from that affect the printout. The most important are:

- *Printer name*—The Print dialog lists your currently selected printer. Depending on your printer and driver, you might have the option of selecting a different printer directly from the Print dialog. If not, open the Chooser from your Apple menu and select the appropriate printer (if necessary).

- *Options button*—Again, the presence and function of this button and the dialog it invokes vary with your printer. For laser printers, you can usually set print density, resolution, color/grayscale preference, and how the printer reports print errors to you. Ink jet printers usually have variable print-quality settings (from ink-stingy economy quality to ink-eating high quality), color dithering options, and more. By checking out and (if necessary) modifying the printer properties, you ensure that your printer produces the best-looking transparencies possible.

- *Print range*—By default, the print range radio button next to All is selected, so all slides in the current presentation print. But if you need to print only one or some of the slides (for example, if you corrected a single typo in a show you'd already printed), you can save time, ink, and transparencies by choosing to print a select range of pages (slides). To print a single slide, Slide 3 for instance, tell your printer to print from page 3 to page 3. Similarly, a range of five slides would be from page 3 to page 7.

- *Copies*—Enter a number of copies to print. If you check the Collate button (if one is offered), your printer produces one copy of all selected slides at a time. (When you're printing the whole presentation, the result should be slides in the proper order, ready to go. However, note that many color printers stack printed pages face up, not face down. If yours does that, you still have to reshuffle each set of copies to collate the set properly.) If you leave the checkbox blank, your printer produces all copies of the first selected slide, then all copies of the next, and so on.

- *Print What list*—By default, the entry in this list is Slides (without animations). But note that you may use this list to print handouts or notes pages with speaker notes for your reference. (See "Creating Notes Pages And Handouts" earlier in this chapter, for more information on this subject.)

FYI: Plain Ol' Black And White—Making It Work

Color is so important to making an effective presentation that it's hard to imagine anyone choosing to create black-and-white output from PowerPoint. But some folks just don't have access to a color printer. And even when you print your slides in color, you may want to print handouts or notes pages in black and white. When you want to print in black and white, check either of the two checkboxes in the lower left corner of the Print dialog:

- Black & White optimizes the formatting of your color slides to make them look their best when printed on a good printer that's capable of producing a good range of gray levels.
- Pure Black & White optimizes your slides for true monochrome printing: just black, no gray. Use this option when your printer (or paper stock) produces grays poorly.

If after trying these options you're still not happy with the look of your slides in black and white, you can edit the black-and-white appearance of your slides without making any change to their appearance in color. When you're formatting slides, click on the Black And White View button on the Standard toolbar. In that view, PowerPoint shows you your slides as they'd appear when printed in black and white. Any changes you make to the slide formatting while in Black And White view—such as removing background fills to make text easier to read—have no effect on the color versions of your slides, but may dramatically improve the slides' look when they're printed in black and white.

Making 35mm Slides

To make 35mm color slides from a PowerPoint presentation, the file must be output to a device called a *film recorder*. Film recorders are cheaper than they used to be, so companies that make a lot of slides often have one somewhere in house. If you have access to a company film recorder, the person who runs it will know how to make your slides. Typically, a film recorder is attached to a Mac; the operator simply moves through your slide show in PowerPoint, one slide at a time, and clicks on a button to record each image on 35mm film.

Lacking a film recorder of your own, you'll need to provide your presentation files to a service bureau, a company that records the slides on its own film recorder, develops them, and returns them to you, ready to pop into a projector. To find a service bureau near you, check the Yellow Pages under Computers/Graphics, Photo-finishing, or Photographic Services. You may also ask your local copy/print shops if they make slides—many do. Note that some service bureaus can make not only slides from your PowerPoint files, but also high-quality overhead transparencies, posters, and who knows what else. (T-shirts? Coffee mugs?)

When you've located the service bureau you intend to use, ask what you must supply to have your slides made. Typically, you send your PowerPoint file to the service bureau via modem, or copy your show to diskettes that you can take to the service bureau. Also popular is transfer via one of the small removable drives that almost all service bureaus have (Zip, Jaz, SyQuest, SyJet, etc.—check with your bureau to be sure they have the drive you use).

Finally, some high-volume service bureaus can accept your files via modem or mail, make your slides, and send them back to you, often all within 24 hours. PowerPoint includes a wizard that takes you through all of the steps required to send your files to Genigraphics (the largest slide service bureau, serving all of North America), along with payment information and return shipping instructions. If your Mac has a modem and phone connection, you may use the wizard to order slides in a jiffy. Keep in mind, however, that Genigraphics has no monopoly on making PowerPoint slides—you can use any service bureau you want to.

To use the Genigraphics Wizard, you must first make sure it is installed on your Mac (it's not included in the drag-and-drop installation). In PowerPoint, choose File|Send To, and look at the bottom of the submenu that appears. If the Genigraphics item that appears there is grayed out, you need to install the Genigraphics Wizard from your Office 98 CD-ROM (it's part of the Value Pack). You can learn how to add Office 98 programs in Appendix A of this book. When you run the Value Pack Installer, you'll find the Genigraphics Wizard listed under the options for Custom Install.

Once the Genigraphics Wizard is installed, begin by opening the presentation you want to send. Then choose File|Send To|Genigraphics. The Genigraphics Wizard opens with a dialog explaining the steps you'll perform to place your order. Click on Next to begin filling out your order instructions. A dialog like the one in Figure 9.13 opens, prompting you to select the type of output—slides, transparencies, and so on—you want made from your PowerPoint files. Note that this dialog contains a very important button—Display Pricing Information—that shows complete pricing information, not just for slides, but for costly extras such as rush delivery.

Work your way through the Genigraphics Wizard's dialogs, completing each and clicking on Next to move forward. If you fail to make any required selection, the Genigraphics Wizard displays a message when you click on Next, telling you what you need to do. Note that Genigraphics's toll-free number appears in the lower left corner of the Genigraphics Wizard, so you can call them if you run into any problems or have questions about pricing or policies (you can also take a gander at the Genigraphics Web site at **http://www.genigraphics.com**).

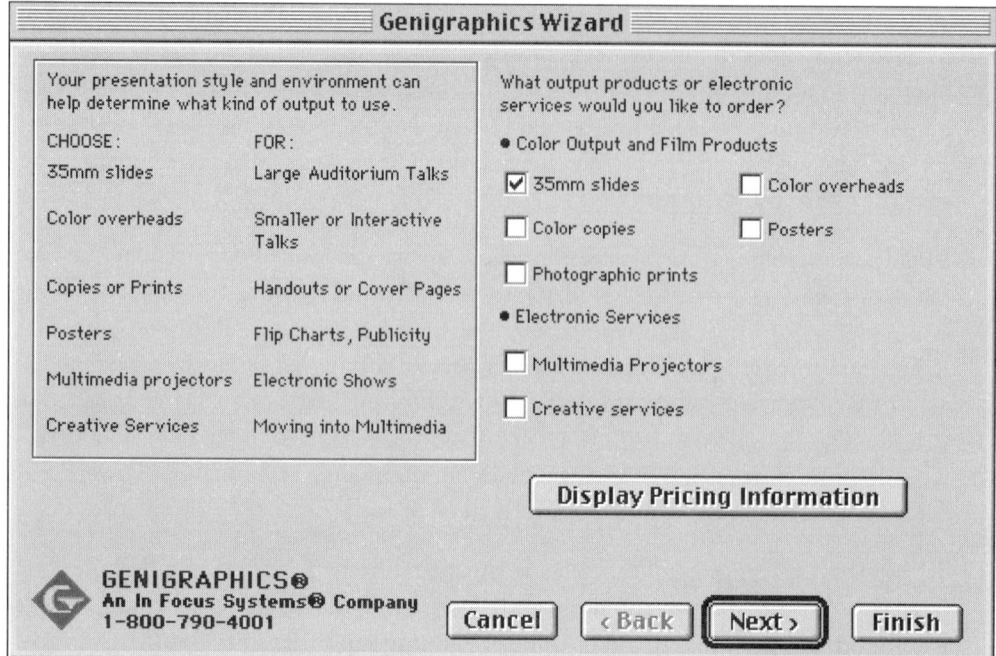

Figure 9.13 The Genigraphics Wizard prepares and sends your show files to a major service bureau to be printed on 35mm slides or transparencies.

Taking A Show On The Road

Frequent presenters these days often carry their Macs with them—as PowerBooks—so that they can run their shows from their own hardware, and that's a terrific advantage. If you're not so equipped, and you must present your show somewhere that you can't take your own Mac, you'll need to copy your show to disk and take it with you.

You'll need to make sure that the Mac you'll use to put on your show—let's call it the "presentation Mac"—is equipped to display PowerPoint files. If the presentation Mac has PowerPoint installed, you're all set to go. If the Mac does not have PowerPoint, you'll need to bring along the PowerPoint viewer to teach the presentation Mac how to show a PowerPoint file.

In the next few pages, you'll learn how to prepare and package everything you need to take it all with you.

Packing Up A Show

A short presentation's file will fit easily on a diskette—so in some cases, you can simply copy your file onto a diskette and take it with you. However, you should consider a few things before packing up:

- Be sure that you bring along all of the files your selected show needs. For example, when you pack up a show containing multimedia and links, you need to pack up not just the presentation file, but also linked files and multimedia files. You'll also need to have the correct fonts along.

- Be sure that the presentation Mac can read the media to which you're saving the presentation. For example, if you have a large presentation with many links, and you need a Zip disk to hold everything, be sure the presentation Mac has a Zip drive installed. If not, carry yours along.

- When you copy your files to a disk, be sure to store them all in the same folder, so your presentation won't lose its links.

Fast Track

Mac fonts aren't easy to master, but you'll need to have the right ones along to make your presentation run correctly. Here's a quick rundown of the various formats (all fonts installed on your machine can be found in the Fonts folder, which resides inside the System folder):

- *TrueType*—When you view a TrueType font by icon, its icon shows three A's. These fonts have only one associated file, and that's the one you're looking at. Copy their suitcase to your disk.

- *PostScript*—PostScript fonts are more complex and are split into two files—a *screen font* and a *printer font*. When viewed by icon, screen fonts are usually in a suitcase and have only one A. In addition, somewhere in your Fonts folder you'll find another file with a similar name, but a different icon. This is the printer font. Make sure you pack both.

Learn more about Macintosh fonts and how to handle them in Appendix C of this book.

If your presentation Mac doesn't have PowerPoint installed, you'll need the PowerPoint viewer (don't take your Office 98 CD along and "temporarily" install PowerPoint—you've only got a license for one machine). Unfortunately, at press time, the PowerPoint viewer was not yet available. To retrieve it when you need it, select Help|Help On The Web, and click on the Free Stuff link to jump to Microsoft's downloads page. You should find it there.

Setting Up And Running Your Road Show

Once you reach your destination, you have a couple of options. You can run your presentation from the diskette, or you can copy it to the hard disk of your presentation Mac. Which should you do? Well, it depends.

If you have your presentation on diskette, copy the presentation and all associated files to the presentation Mac's hard disk—floppies are notoriously slow, and can hamper the speed of your presentation. Be sure to install your fonts in the Fonts folder on the presentation Mac.

If you're using a larger removable medium—Zip, SyJet, etc.—it's up to you. You'll still need to copy your fonts to the presentation Mac's Fonts folder, but you should test your presentation to see if the removable medium is speedy enough to run it. If so, run it from your disk. If it stutters or hesitates at all, copy it to the hard disk.

To run your presentation:

- *In PowerPoint (where available)*—Open PowerPoint, open the presentation file, and choose Slide Show|View Show.

- *In the PowerPoint viewer*—Drag the icon for your presentation over the viewer's icon and release it. The viewer will start and run your presentation.

Moving On

In two chapters—8 and 9—you've discovered how to create and present elegant, professional-looking presentations, and to produce useful accessories—notes and handouts. That's a lot of presentation power for just a little work.

However, at this point your slides contain just text. That's okay—90 percent of all presentations contain nothing more, and one well-organized text-based presentation is more effective than a dozen poorly organized light shows. Then again, smartly applied, a little flash never hurt a presentation. That's where Chapter 10 comes in. There you'll learn not only how to add pictures to your show, but also how to create knockout effects with easy-to-apply animation, sound effects, recorded narration, video clips, and more.

Livening Up Your Presentations

It's no secret that a presentation with color makes a stronger impression than one without, and that a picture here and there helps spice up a show, keeping your audience attentive. But if that's true, how much *more* persuasive might the show be if charged up with animation, music, sound effects, and even movie clips?

In this chapter, you'll discover the exciting ways you can impact a presentation—sorry…give your presentation more *impact*—by adding the full thrust of Macintosh multimedia to your PowerPoint slides. Since most multimedia plants us squarely in the realm of electronic presentations, you'll also discover in this chapter the ins and outs of creating, configuring, and presenting electronic shows.

Note that although pictures can appear in slides whether the show is presented electronically or traditionally (on 35mm slides or transparencies), the steps for inserting pictures in slides logically belong in this chapter because those steps are essentially the same as those for inserting other media types—sound and movie clips.

So without further ado—on with the show!

Adding Multimedia To Slides

Adding multimedia to slides can be as simple or as complicated as you want it to be. As you'll discover throughout this chapter, PowerPoint offers a few quick, easy ways to add visual and aural interest to your show by choosing from among its own pre-made multimedia options and files from the Office 98 Clip Gallery. The more specific—and more personal—your multimedia needs, the more work you have to do, because you can't rely on PowerPoint to supply the media for you. Still, adding even custom multimedia is a pretty straightforward job.

Working Objects Into The Slide Layout

Just as the text on slides is contained within flexible placeholders, so are any other objects, including all types of media files. Even the speaker icon for a sound clip is contained within placeholders. Any time you add a new object to a slide, you add a placeholder. To fit the newly inserted element within the layout, you usually must reposition its placeholder, and sometimes edit the placeholder's size or shape, to make everything fit.

Adding multimedia to slides can be as simple or as complicated as you want it to be. As you'll discover throughout this chapter, PowerPoint offers a few quick and easy ways to add visual and aural interest to your show by allowing you to choose from among the Office 98 Clip Gallery's pre-made multimedia options and files. The more specific—and more personal—your multimedia needs are, the more work you have to do, because you can't rely on PowerPoint to supply the media for you. Still, adding even custom multimedia is a pretty straightforward job.

As you discover the ways to add multimedia, keep in mind that inserting the media is usually not the end of the job. There are still a few things you should keep in mind:

- After inserting any object, you usually must fiddle with its size, shape, and position to make it fit attractively within the slide layout.

- By default, all objects on a slide appear when the slide does. But you can animate any object on a slide so that it materializes in the slide later—when you advance the show or after a preset number of seconds—in any of a wide range of fun, funky ways. See "Adding Animation Effects" later in this chapter.

FYI: Other Stuff You Can Insert In Slides

Like its Office 98 sisters (brothers? cousins?), PowerPoint 98 can use charts produced by Microsoft Chart and the many types of pictures you can create with the OfficeArt drawing tools. To learn more about OfficeArt and Chart, see Chapter 2. To create and insert these objects from within PowerPoint, choose Insert|Chart (for a chart) or choose Insert|Picture and select one of the drawing options.

You can also import a Word table or Excel worksheet right into a PowerPoint slide, where you can work it into the layout exactly as you would a picture. To learn about importing tables and worksheets, see Chapter 16.

Fast Track

When you use a template to create a new show or apply one of PowerPoint's AutoLayouts to create the slide layout (see Chapter 9), some slides may have empty placeholders in them, with instructions to "double-click" to add the object. When you double-click on the empty placeholder, a dialog opens that allows you to add the particular type of object the placeholder wants. For example, if the note in the placeholder says "Double-click to add clip art," the Office 98 Clip Gallery opens.

Although the empty placeholder may be perfectly positioned within the layout, when you fill the placeholder with an object, the placeholder's size and shape may change to conform to the object you inserted. So you still must fine-tune the shape, size, and position of the placeholder, even when that placeholder was supplied by the template or AutoLayout.

FYI: Working With Movies And Sound

As you do with pictures, charts, and tables, you must also work movie and sound clips into the layout. By default:

- A movie clip appears in the slide layout as a still image of the first frame of the video—it appears to be an ordinary picture, and you can size, shape, and position it just like a picture.

- A sound clip appears in the layout as a tiny speaker icon. You can size, shape, and position the icon.

During the presentation, the clips play when clicked on. However, you can configure a clip's custom animation settings to play automatically, or to hide the icon or clip picture until the clip plays. See "Customizing Animations" later in this chapter.

Inserting Media From The Clip Gallery

The easiest and best way to add pictures, movies, and sounds to slides is to borrow them from Office 98's Clip Gallery. Not only is the Clip Gallery easy to use, but the pictures and movies in the Gallery retain their appearance after being worked into a slide layout. You can use the Clip Gallery's Find feature to selectively browse for pictures to add to your slides, or you can just poke around and see what you find.

Fast Track

You can use the Clip Gallery to insert art into any Office 98 document; you can also customize and add to the Clip Gallery. To learn more about the Clip Gallery, see Chapter 2.

Choosing Art From The Gallery

Begin by opening in Slide view the slide to which you want to add art. Then click on the Insert Clip Art button on the Standard toolbar (or choose Insert|Picture| Clip Art). From the tabs in the Clip Gallery, choose the art you want to use, then click on Insert.

Note that you can add anything from the Clip Gallery this way—a clip art image, picture, sound, or video clip. Alternatively, you can open the Clip Gallery by choosing Insert|Movies And Sounds, then choosing Movie From Gallery or Sound From Gallery. But it really doesn't matter how you open the gallery—once you're there, you can choose any form of art from the gallery.

Fast Track

Whenever you insert and select a picture—whether from the Clip Gallery or from a file—the Picture toolbar appears automatically (see Chapter 6). You can use the Picture toolbar to crop the picture or change its brightness, contrast, or other characteristics. To close the Picture toolbar, press Esc. (If for some reason the toolbar doesn't appear, select View|Toolbars|Picture.)

However, it's often wisest—especially when using professionally created artwork—to avoid manipulating the image with the Picture toolbar. The image has been designed to look its best under a variety of circumstances, and any change might detract from its appearance.

Placing Other Types Of Media Objects

If the Clip Gallery doesn't have the media you want, you can insert many types of picture, sound, and movie files in PowerPoint slides. PowerPoint includes built-in support for popular sound, image, and video file formats, including:

- *Pictures*—JPEG, PICT, Painting (PNTG), PNG, BMP
- *Sound clips*—QuickTime, Macintosh System 7 Sound, WAV
- *Movie (video) clips*—QuickTime, QuickTime VR, MPEG, AVI

In addition to these file types, you can insert other types for which Office 98 *filters* have been installed. See Appendix A to learn how to install optional filters from your Office 98 CD-ROM.

To insert a media file, open the slide in which you want to insert the media, in Slide view. From the Insert menu, you have several choices:

- To insert a picture, choose Insert|Picture|From File.
- To insert a sound clip, choose Insert|Movies And Sounds|Sound From File.
- To insert a movie clip, choose Insert|Movies And Sounds|Movie From File.

Whichever medium you choose, a dialog similar to the one in Figure 10.1 opens. Use the file/folder list to navigate to the folder containing the media file. When you see the file you want, click on its name, then click on Open. If you're not sure which

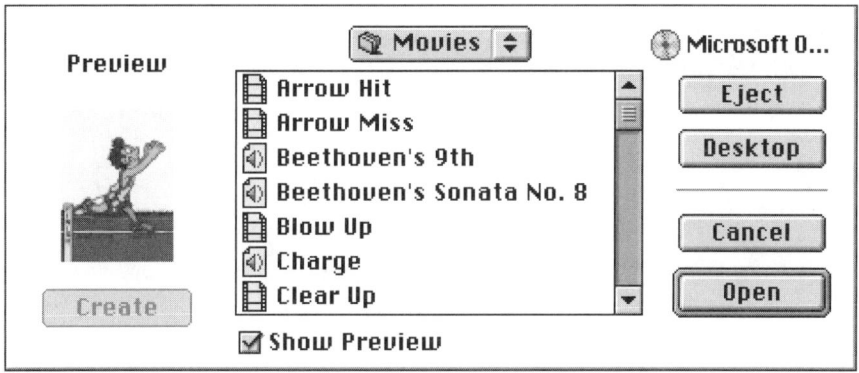

Figure 10.1 To insert a media file, navigate to the file and select it.

file you want, check the left side of the Insert dialog. When you click an item, it will be previewed in this area. Movies show the first frame, and sounds show a speaker icon and a Play Sound button. Click on the button to listen to the sound and be certain it's what you want. If you don't see a preview for a movie, click on Create, and one will be made if it's possible.

The picture, still movie clip, or sound file icon appears in the slide. If you inserted a picture file, the Picture toolbar appears—so if you want, you can fine-tune the picture's appearance.

If you're working with sounds, keep in mind one other thing—they may need to be converted. Mac OS sound files (the ones with the speaker icon in the Finder) aren't cross-platform, so PowerPoint will convert them to a QuickTime movie sound for you (don't worry about the technical bits here—this all happens in the background). When you select a sound in the Insert dialog, PowerPoint knows if it needs to be converted. If it does, you'll see the Open button change to Convert. Click on it, and you'll get a Save dialog. Pick a name and location for the new file, and remember where you put it for later. Then, go about your merry way—your sound is now cross-platform compatible.

Walk-Through: Inserting Objects In Slides

Follow these steps to practice inserting objects in slides:

1. Open or create a presentation (in Slide view).
2. Choose a slide in which there's room for a picture. If that slide contains some text besides the title, change the shape and position of the text placeholder to leave open an area large enough to put a picture. (Be sure to deselect the text placeholder when you're finished.)
3. Make sure your Office 98 CD is in your CD-ROM drive.

4. Click on the Insert Clip Art button on the Standard toolbar (or choose Insert|Picture|Clip Art).
5. Click on the Clip Art tab, click on any image you like, and click on Insert. The clip art appears in the slide, with its placeholder selected.
6. Point to the picture's placeholder border, then click and drag the picture to position it in the area you set up for it.
7. Click and drag the placeholder's handles as necessary to make the picture's shape and size conform to the area allotted to it.
8. Press Esc to deselect the picture.
9. Click on the New Slide button on the Standard toolbar (or choose Insert|New Slide). The New Slide dialog opens, showing the AutoLayouts.
10. Scroll down the list of AutoLayouts, choose one that contains a picture of a movie clapper, and click on OK. The slide layout changes, and a placeholder prompts you to "Double-click to add media clip."
11. Double-click as instructed. The Insert Movie dialog opens.
12. Click on Desktop. In the file list box, double-click on the Microsoft Office 98 CD.
13. Open the Value Pack folder, then the Clip Art folder, then Multimedia, then Movies.
14. Click on Clock, then click on OK. A clock image—the frozen first frame of a clock movie—opens in the placeholder.
15. To test the clip, click on the Slide Show view button, then click on the clock.

Creating Your Own Sound For Presentations

When you want a sound that's truly personal or specific to the show, you need to record it yourself, then attach it to a slide. You can do that easily, all from within PowerPoint.

Recording New Sound Clips

Open the slide in which you want to insert a recorded sound in Slide view. Then choose Insert|Movies and Sounds|Record Sound. The Record Sound dialog opens, as shown in Figure 10.2.

On the dialog, the Record and Play controls mimic those on a VCR or tape deck. The leftmost button (with the big dot on it) is the Record button. The "thermometer" bar at the bottom shows how long you've been recording. The leftmost number is 0, or the starting point, and the rightmost number will vary. This number indicates

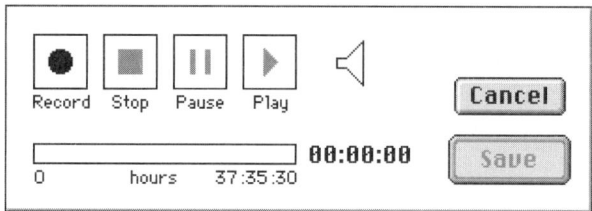

Figure 10.2 Choose Insert|Movies and Sounds|Record Sound to record a new sound clip.

the maximum length of the sound file you can record, based on the disk space you have to store it.

When you're ready to start recording your sound, click on the Record button, then speak, whistle, play a tape, or otherwise make the sound you want to record. When you're finished, click on the Stop button (the middle button with the square on it). Then do any of the following:

- To hear your new sound, click on the Play button (the button with an arrow on it).

- To record over the sound (in case you don't like your first try), click on Record.

- To stop recording altogether, click on Cancel.

- To save your sound and insert it in your slide, click on Save, enter a name in the Sound Name dialog, then click on OK.

FYI: Microphone Basics

In case you hadn't thought about it, you should remember that recording a sound requires a microphone or other sound input (such as a line input from a tape player) attached to your Mac. Most Macs, both PowerBooks and desktop machines, ship with a basic microphone, but for professional presentation, we suggest you consider purchasing a better-quality microphone. Also, desktop Mac microphones sitting on the computer, and any PowerBook mikes, will pick up hum and buzz from the hard drive, fans, and other components. You should hold the mike in your hand and get as far away from the computer as is practical. (Consider standing a few feet from the Mac and having a partner work PowerPoint for you.)

Narrating Slides

You can record narration for a specific slide in the same way you would record any new sound. But if your plan is to record narration for an entire show, you're better off firing up PowerPoint's Record Narration dialog. Record Narration enables you to step through your slides—just as if you were presenting them—and narrate as you go, so you can record all of your slide narration in a single session. More importantly, with Record Narration, you can automatically set the timings of slide changes for a self-running presentation (see "Setting Up And Running Electronic Shows" later in this chapter).

Before recording narration, you should do the following:

- Finish creating and editing the rest of the presentation, including adding any animation effects. You want to avoid making changes that would affect the timing of the presentation after you've already recorded narration.

- Script your narration, then rehearse it—while watching the slide show—until you can perform it smoothly.

- Connect a good external microphone to your Mac.

When you're ready to start recording your narration, open the presentation and choose Slide Show|Record Narration. The Record Narration dialog opens (see Figure 10.3). The current settings for recording quality appear on the dialog.

Note that the Record Narration dialog recommends that you link narration to the presentation file by checking the Link Narrations In checkbox. That's always a good idea. If you do link and later take your presentation on the road, be sure to pack the narration file along with the presentation. (To learn more about linking, see Chapter 17.) Now you're ready to record. Take a deep, relaxing breath, then click on OK. The slide show begins with Slide 1. Speak your narration for Slide 1, and when you finish, click on the slide to advance to Slide 2 and continue your narration.

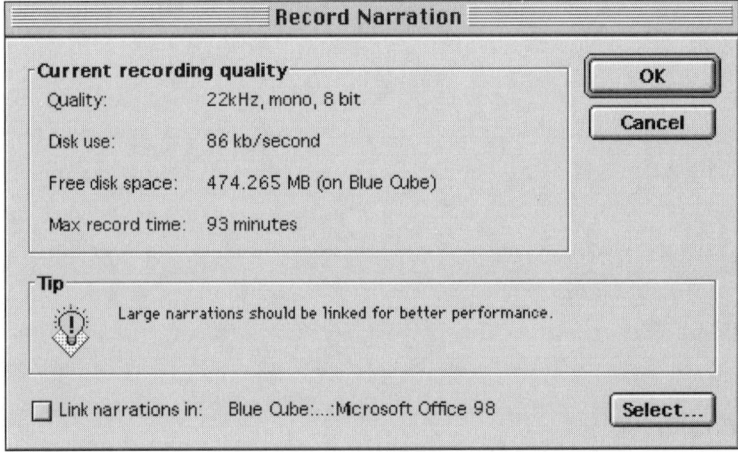

Figure 10.3 You can record narration slide by slide with the Record Narration dialog.

Continue through the show until you reach the end, then press Esc. A dialog opens, informing you that the narrations have been saved, and asking whether you'd like PowerPoint to save slide timings (for a self-running show; see "Setting And Rehearsing Slide Timings" later in this chapter) based on the "performance" of the slide show you just gave. Click on Yes to save the timings and close the slide show, or No to discard the timings. If you click on Yes, you'll be asked if you want to review your timings. At this point, you may either review the timings or cancel the process to continue and save.

FYI: Sound Quality Vs. Disk Space

Most sound cards can record at several different quality levels, from scratchy-sounding "telephone" quality, to serviceable "radio" quality, to "CD" quality, the highest-quality audio.

The higher the quality of the recording, the more disk space it takes up per minute. Though you may be tempted to record your narration at CD quality, you should be aware that a mere 10 minutes of CD-quality narration requires over 100MB of disk space. At radio quality, you can fit around 80 minutes of narration in 100MB. (Obviously, even at radio quality, recording complete narration is practical only for relatively short shows.)

The Record Narration dialog shows how much hard disk space will be used for each second of narration at the current quality level (Disk Use) and the maximum length of narration you can record based on the available disk space. Currently, the default setting for recording is 22kHz, or "radio quality." At press time, Microsoft had not provided a way to manipulate this setting (hopefully, this will change).

Playing A CD In The Background

To accompany your show, you can play an audio CD from the presentation Mac's CD-ROM drive. You can attach any track or cut from a CD to a slide, or you can start a CD from any slide and have it play continuously through successive slides.

Note that, for you to use this feature when presenting, the presentation Mac must be equipped with a CD-ROM drive and speakers, and must be capable of playing an audio CD (most, but not all Macs can—certainly any Macintosh running Office 98 should be able to).

Begin by inserting the audio CD in your CD-ROM drive. In Slide view, open the slide on which you want the audio to play (or begin playing), and choose Insert|Movies And Sounds|Play CD Audio Track. The Play Options dialog opens (see Figure 10.4).

Figure 10.4 Play your favorite CD during a show.

On the dialog, choose the number of the Start and End tracks (by default, Start shows Track 1 and End shows the number of the last track on the CD). To start or end at a particular moment within a track, enter the time index in the Start At or End At field. (Use the display on your CD player, or the AppleCD Audio Player program, to find the time index settings for the moment you want to start or end.) If you want the track to repeat itself if it finishes before the slide is advanced, click on Loop Until Stopped. Click on OK.

A CD icon appears on the slide. You can edit the CD icon's placeholder like any other to change its position, size, or shape. When you view the show, click on the CD icon to play the CD track. If you advance the slide before the CD track finishes playing, play stops automatically.

To change the settings on the Play Options dialog later, Control-click on the CD icon and choose Edit Sound Object from the contextual menu.

Fast Track

To configure the CD audio to play automatically, or to play through multiple slides, change its Custom Animation settings (see "Customizing Animations" later in this chapter).

Adding Animation Effects

Animation effects are a great (and easy!) way to add the visual kick of motion—and often sound, too—to your show. Animation changes the way an object in a slide makes its way onto the screen.

For example, without animation, a picture on a slide appears at the same time the slide does. But if you animate that picture, the slide at first appears without the picture. Then, when you advance the presentation or when a selected number of seconds passes, the picture animates its way into the slide—it may slide in from the side, explode from nowhere, or materialize like it was transported from the starship *Enterprise*. Usually, the animation effect is accompanied by a sound effect, which just makes it more fun.

You can animate anything that appears on a slide—the title, bullet text, pictures, charts, tables, or movies. More important, you can animate multiple objects on a slide. A slide can appear with nothing but a title—then, one by one, the words and pictures come flying, wiggling, and sliding in. In addition to animating objects in slides, you can animate the way the slide itself shows up. Animating a slide's arrival is called animating its *transition*.

In the next few pages, you'll learn how to animate any slide object, customize the way the animation behaves, and animate slide transitions.

Applying El Quicko Animations

The easiest way to animate is to apply one of PowerPoint's Preset Animation effects. In Slide view, click on the object you want to animate to select it. Choose Slide Show|Preset Animation. A list of animation options appears, as shown in Figure 10.5. (The list is too long for us to describe what each choice does—and besides, an animated picture is worth a thousand words. Try 'em and see what happens.)

After you select a Preset Animation, you return to Slide view. To see your selected animation in action, click on the Slide Show view button; the current slide opens in Slide Show view. By default, a slide containing animation appears at first without any of the animated objects on it; advancing the show—by clicking, pressing PgDn, or pressing the Right arrow key—starts the animation and brings the object onto the slide.

Note that when you apply animation to a placeholder containing multiple paragraphs—such as a bulleted list—each item in the list is animated separately. In

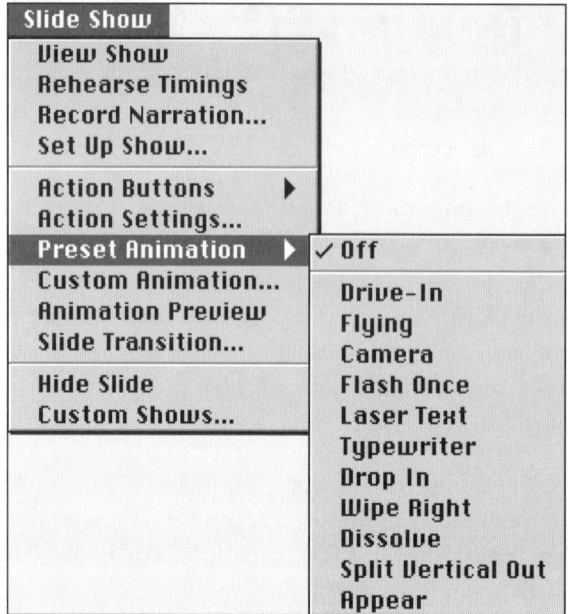

Figure 10.5 You can add Preset Animation options in a snap from a submenu.

other words, when you advance, only the first paragraph or list item in the placeholder animates its way on screen. When you advance again, the next item appears, and so on. (You can change this behavior; see the next section, "Customizing Animations.")

Also, you can animate multiple placeholders on a single slide. When you run the slide show, the objects appear one at a time—one object each time you advance. The objects appear in the same order in which you assigned Preset Animation to them. For example, if you apply animation to the title, then to a picture, the title appears the first time you advance, then the picture appears the second time you advance. You can change the animation order by reapplying the Preset Animation in a new order or by changing the order in the Custom Animation dialog.

Customizing Animations

The Custom Animation effects are not really different from the preset ones. What's different is the level of control Custom Animation gives you over the order of animations on a slide, the timing of their appearance, and other aspects of slide animation. You can use the Custom Animation dialog to apply new animations, change the behavior of existing ones (including preset animations you've applied), and change the animated behavior of charts, movies, and sounds.

To apply or edit custom animation, open the slide whose animation you want to customize in Slide view (you don't need to select a placeholder). Choose Slide Show|Custom Animation to open the Custom Animation dialog (see Figure 10.6).

In the dialog, the Animation Order list shows any objects in the slide that are already animated and shows them in the order in which they'll make their appearances. To change an object's order, select it in the list (when you select, the Preview pane on the right shows the placeholder for the object you've chosen). Click on one of the arrows to the right of the list—up to make the object appear earlier in the animation order, down to make it appear later.

The Timing tab lists any objects on the slide that are not currently animated. To animate any object listed, select it, then click on the radio button for Animate. The object appears in the Animation Order list; you may change its order and customize its animation just like any other animated object.

To customize the animation of an object, select it in the Animation Order list, then change the settings on the four tabs. After making any change, you can click on the Preview button to see the effects in the Preview pane—with one important exception. The Preview pane automatically runs through all animations on the slide, without

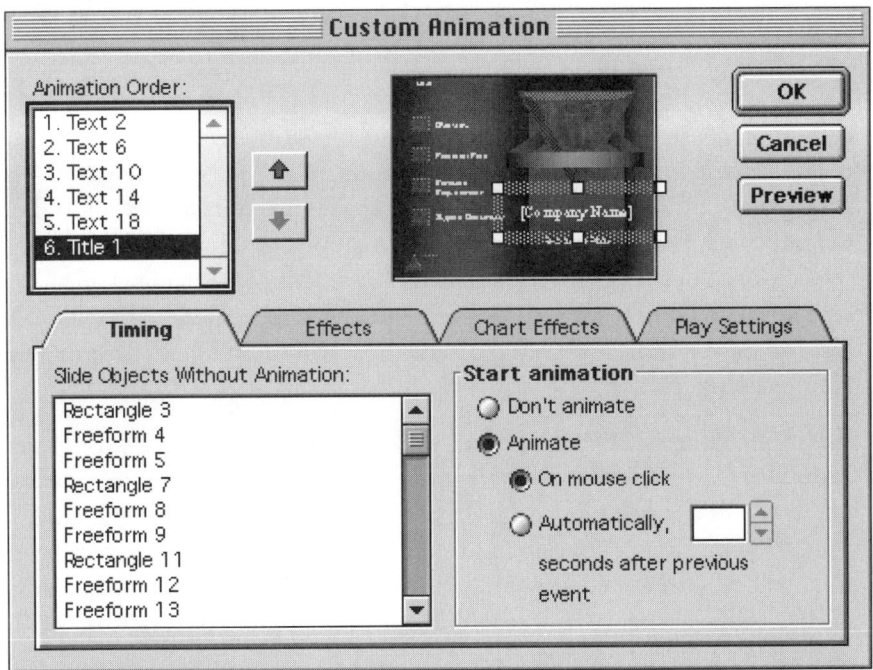

Figure 10.6 Choose the timing for animation on the Timing tab of the Custom Animation dialog.

your having to advance the slide. (To better test the real-life appearance of an animated slide, click on OK to close the Custom Animation dialog, then click on the Slide Show view button.)

Fast Track

To change the animation settings for a specific object faster, select that object in Slide view before opening the Custom Animation dialog. When the dialog opens, that object is preselected for customizing.

You can also do the same thing by Control-clicking on the object, then choosing Custom Animation from the contextual menu.

Important settings in the Custom Animation dialog include:

- *Timing tab (see Figure 10.6)*—For animated objects, choose On Mouse Click to specify that the object appears only when you advance the slide (whether by mouse click, PgDn or the Right arrow key). Choose Automatically and a number of seconds to enable the object to appear a few seconds after the previous event without any action from you. If the selected object is Number 1 in the animation order, it appears the set number of seconds after the slide appears. If it is Number 2 or later, it appears the set number of seconds after the preceding object in the animation order.

- *Effects tab (see Figure 10.7)*—On this tab you can choose from lists to select an animation effect (from a much wider array of options than the Preset Animations) and a sound effect to go with the animation (or No Sound). In After Animation, choose how an object should appear when its animation is done and the next object appears. For example, if you open this list and click on one of the color squares it offers, the selected object "dims" to that color when the next animated object arrives. This is a great way to help viewers focus on new ideas as they appear. For example, when a new item in a bullet list materializes, the preceding items dim.

    When the selected object contains text, you can drop down the list under Introduce Text to make each paragraph (or bullet item) animate its way onto the screen in a single block (All At Once), or a word or letter at a time. By default, a checkmark appears in Grouped By, so that each paragraph in the placeholder is animated separately, requiring its own advance to appear. If you uncheck the checkbox, all text within the placeholder appears at once—bullet items don't materialize separately.

    If you leave the checkmark in Grouped By, you can select how the various levels appear within nested lists (see Chapter 9). By default, lists are grouped

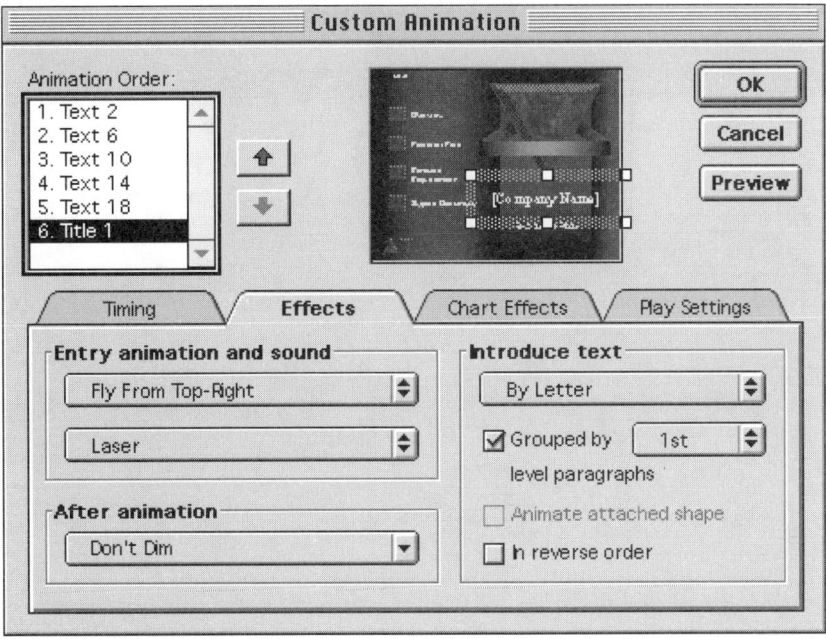

Figure 10.7 Change what the animation does on the Effects tab of the Custom Animation dialog.

by 1st-level items for animation. In other words, at each advance, one 1st-level bullet *plus* any bullets indented beneath it—2nd level, 3rd level, and so on—appear. If you change the Grouped By entry to 2nd level, at an advance one 1st-level item appears, not any 2nd- or 3rd-level items beneath it. At the next advance, the first 2nd-level bullet (and any 3rd-level bullets beneath it) appears.

- *Chart Effects tab*—Here you can customize the effects for an animated chart, including selecting different effects for different elements of the chart, and After Animation effects (see Effects tab). You can also animate a chart's grid and legend separately from the chart by checking the checkbox provided.

- *Play Settings tab (see Figure 10.8)*—Here you customize the play of sound files, movie clips, or CD audio tracks you've inserted in the slide. The Play Using Ani-mation Order option configures the object to play automatically at its spot in the Animation Order list, instead of waiting for you to click on it. If you check that checkbox, you can apply further options in the same part of the tab. For example, to configure a sound clip or CD audio track to continue playing even after the slide is advanced, choose Continue Slide Show, then choose After Current Slide and select the number of slides through which you want play to continue.

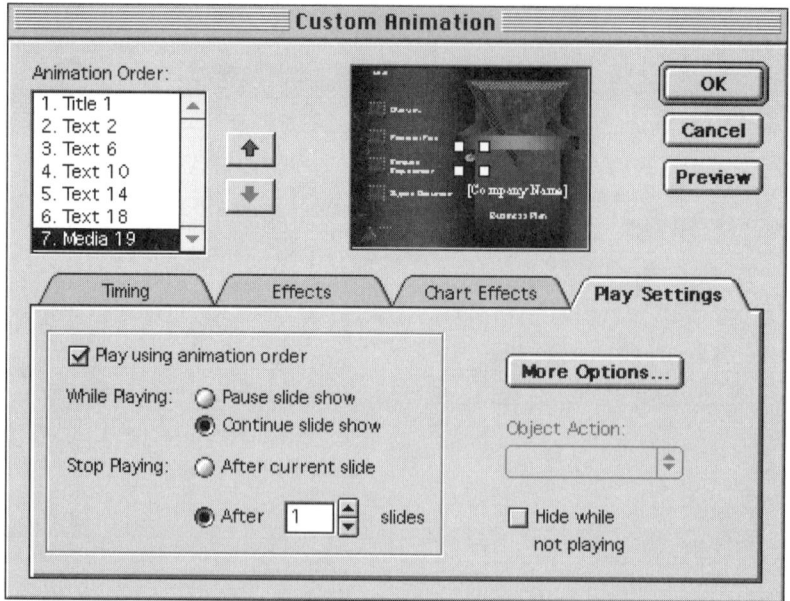

Figure 10.8 Control how sound, movies, and CD tracks play on the Custom Animation dialog's Play Settings tab.

Walk-Through: Animations

Follow these steps to practice adding animation to slides:

1. In Slide view, open (or create) a slide containing a bulleted list and a picture.
2. Click on the list to display its placeholder.
3. Choose Slide Show|Preset Animation|Drive-In.
4. Click on the picture to display its placeholder.
5. Choose Slide Show|Preset Animation|Flying.
6. Click on the Slide Show view button. The slide appears without the list or picture.
7. Advance the slide (click once). The first list item "drives in" and makes a squealing rubber sound.
8. Advance through the rest of the animations.
9. Return to the slide in Slide view.
10. Choose Slide Show|Custom Animation.
11. In Animation Order, choose Text 2. The list will be selected in the Preview pane; if not, select a different text entry in the list until you see the list highlighted in the preview.
12. Click on the Effects tab.

13. Drop down the After Animation list and click on a color square.
14. Click on OK to save the custom animation.
15. Switch to Slide Show view and advance through the animations. What's different?

Animating Slide Transitions

In addition to animating what's on a slide, you can animate the way the slide itself materializes on the screen—the *slide transition*. By default, all slide transitions are simple "cuts"—one slide vanishes, the next appears. To choose a more creative transition, open (in Slide view) the slide whose transition you want to change. (You edit the way the selected slide makes its way on screen, *not* the way the selected slide makes way for the next.)

Choose Slide Show|Slide Transition to open the Slide Transition dialog (see Figure 10.9). The little preview picture is not your show, but a two-slide example (a dog and a key—make up your own story for it!) that automatically demonstrates any effect you choose from the list beneath it. (The example also plays the selected transition any time you click on it.) Choose an effect from the list and click on a radio button to choose whether the animation of that effect should be Slow, Medium, or Fast. (To choose no effect, choose Cut, or No Transition, from the list of effects.)

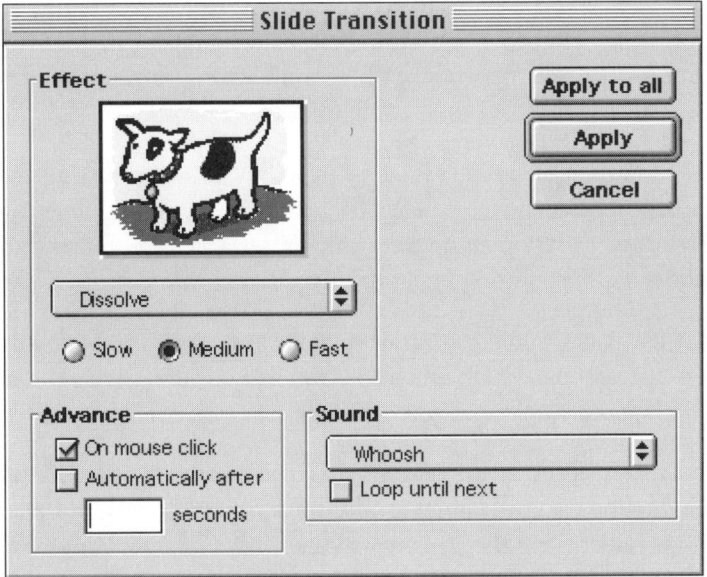

Figure 10.9 Choose Slide Show|Slide Transition to add an animated transition between slides.

Under Advance, choose On Mouse Click to display the transition effect only when you arrive at the slide. If you choose Automatically After and enter a number of seconds, the transition effect repeats itself every time the set number of seconds passes (the transition effect repeats automatically, but the show doesn't advance to the next slide).

Under Sound, select a sound to accompany the transition. If you check the Loop Until Next checkbox, the selected sound plays over and over until another sound plays.

When you've finished configuring the transition, click on Apply to apply the transition to just the selected slide, or Apply To All to apply the transition to every slide in the show.

Fast Track

To preview the animation and transition for a slide without starting the show, open the slide in Slide view and choose Slide Show|Animation Preview. The slide miniature opens and shows the transition and all animation (without waiting for advances between animations, even if they are required). To see the animation again, click on the miniature.

Adding Hyperlinks To Presentations

A *hyperlink* is anything in a slide—text, a picture, a chart, or table—that takes the presentation somewhere else when you click on it (or point to the link). A link can lead to another slide in the presentation or to a custom show, or it can even open a Word document, Excel spreadsheet, or other type of file. To make a hyperlink more obvious for the benefit of kiosk users and others who must run a show for themselves, PowerPoint includes an assortment of "action buttons," attractive buttons you can easily insert in any slide and then configure as hyperlinks.

During a show, when the pointer is over a hyperlink (whether text, an action button, or other type), the regular cursor changes to a hand with a pointing finger, just as it does in a Web browser when it's on an Internet link. When a viewer—rather than a presenter—controls the show, the pointing finger helps the viewer locate and activate the hyperlinks.

In the next few pages, you'll learn how to make any object in a slide into a hyperlink and how to specify where each link leads. You'll also learn how to add action buttons to your slides and how to configure them.

Although hyperlinks and action buttons are obvious candidates for windowed and kiosk shows (see "Setting Up And Running Electronic Shows" later in this chapter), you should also consider using them in your speaker-driven shows. For example, suppose a Word document is available that elaborates on or supports a bullet item on a slide. If that bullet is a link to the Word file, and someone in the audience asks you to expand on the bullet, you can call up the Word file in a heartbeat—how's that for interactive?

Net Savvy

In addition to pointing to local resources, a hyperlink in a slide can contain a Web page address. If the Mac on which the show is run has a default Web browser and Internet access, clicking on the link automatically opens the browser, connects to the Internet, and opens the specified Web page online. For more, see Chapter 17.

Creating A Hyperlink

To add a hyperlink, open the slide in Slide view and select the object you want to make a link. If the object is a picture, simply clicking on the picture to display its placeholder is enough to select it. If you want to make just some of the text within a placeholder or table into a link, select the text just as you would to edit it (see Chapter 9). For example, to configure one bullet item in a list as a link (but not the others), select the placeholder containing the text, then double-click to the right of the bullet item.

With the object or text selected, choose Slide Show|Action Settings. The Action Settings dialog opens (see Figure 10.10). The dialog has two tabs:

- *Mouse Click*—The action you specify on this tab happens when the link is clicked on.

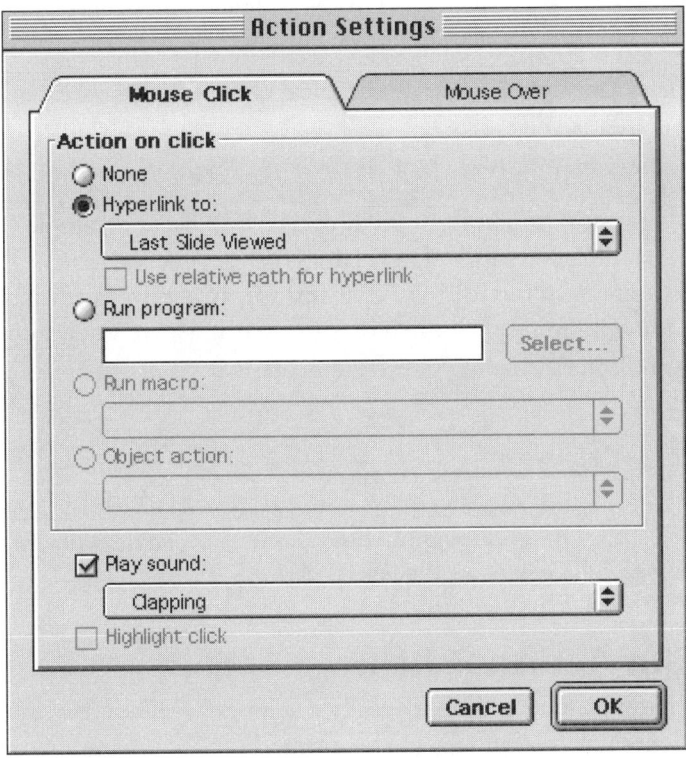

Figure 10.10 Use the Action Settings dialog to determine where a link leads.

- *Mouse Over*—The action you specify on this tab happens when the pointer simply rests on the link for a moment; no click is necessary.

You can specify an action on just one tab, or complete both tabs to assign two separate actions to one link: one action that happens when the pointer moves to the link (Mouse Over), another that happens when the link is clicked on (Mouse Click).

To specify where the link leads, choose the tab for which you want to define the link, then click on the radio button next to Hyperlink To. Drop down the Hyperlink To list and choose one of the options (note that choosing some options in the Hyperlink To list brings up another dialog so you can further define the action):

- *Custom Show*—This option brings up a list of custom shows based on this presentation so you can select the one you want to link to. (For more on custom shows, see "Setting And Rehearsing Slide Timings" later in this chapter.)

- *Slide*—This options brings up a list of the slides in the current show so you can select one.

- *URL*—This option opens a dialog so you can enter the full Internet URL (Uniform Resource Locator); for example, **www.microsoft.com** (see Chapter 17).

- *Other PowerPoint Presentation*—This option opens a dialog very much like PowerPoint's Open dialog, so you can navigate to and select a file.

- *Other File*—This option brings up a typical Open dialog so you can navigate to and select a Word document, Excel worksheet, or other file. The "other file" can also be a picture, sound clip, or video clip that you want to appear when a link is clicked on.

After making your selection from the Hyperlink To list and completing any dialog that opens, you return to the Action Settings dialog. A description of the hyperlink's destination appears in the list box. Click on OK to return to editing the slide. If you made the link from text, notice that the text in the presentation now appears underlined and in a different color from other text.

Fast Track

Near the bottom of the Action Settings dialog appears a checkbox called Play Sound. If you check the checkbox and then choose a sound from the list, the selected sound plays whenever the link is used.

Creating An Action Button

An action button is no big deal; it's really just an extra-handy, button-shaped hunk of clip art whose mission in life is to be a hyperlink. Action buttons are attractive and convenient, but actually you can insert any button-like images you want and use them as buttons, just by making them into hyperlinks. Action buttons, however, have one additional trick: When clicked on, their borders change shading, creating a sort of 3D imitation of a button being depressed. It's up to you to decide whether you think that's cool or not.

To insert an action button, open (in Slide view) the slide in which you want the button to go. Choose Slide Show|Action Buttons to open the Action Buttons submenu (see Figure 10.11). There are 12 buttons in the submenu.

Fast Track

The first selection on the Action Buttons submenu, Custom, is a button backing to which you may add a picture to define your own, custom-designed button.

In general, try to use the buttons for their designated purposes, since their designs match icons and buttons used for similar purposes in software and electronics. In a kiosk or windowed show, applying the buttons in their intended roles will help your viewers intuitively guess each button's purpose from its appearance. However, the buttons' actions are not predefined—you're free to assign any action to any button.

Click your chosen button, and the pointer changes to a big crosshair. The crosshair enables you to position and, optionally, size the button. To simply insert the button in the slide in its default size, point the crosshair pointer to the desired spot and click. To size and shape the button as you insert it, point the crosshair pointer to the area where you want to insert the button, click and hold, drag to form an outline of

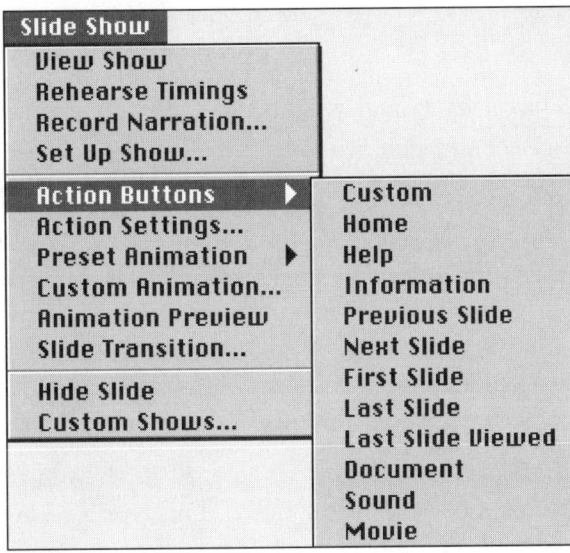

Figure 10.11 Choose an action button from the Action Buttons submenu.

the size and shape you want, then release. (If you don't get the size, shape, or position just right, don't worry—you can edit the size, shape, and position of an action button just like any other picture.)

When you insert the button, the Action Settings dialog opens automatically so you can define the button's hyperlink destination and sound.

Setting Up And Running Electronic Shows

Once everything else in your electronic show—the slides, the text, the pictures and multimedia, the hyperlinks and action buttons—is done, it's time to configure a few final options that control how your show operates when it's running. For example, you must select whether the show will be presented by a speaker, be browsed in a window, or be browsed at a kiosk—since each of these affects the options available during the running of the show.

Also, you may choose to configure the presentation as a *self-running* show, one that just keeps cranking through the slides with no input from you or the viewer. If you create a self-running show, you'll need to select *timings* for the show—the length of time between each slide change, or between animations.

In this final section on PowerPoint, you'll discover how to configure your show for the precise venue and other circumstances in which it may appear.

Choosing The Presentation Type

On the Set Up Show dialog, you select how you want your electronic show presented. To open the dialog, choose Slide Show|Set Up Show (see Figure 10.12).

Under Show Type, choose from among options for how the show will appear when viewed in Slide Show view, when run by View Slide Show (on the Slide Show menu), or run in the PowerPoint viewer:

- *Presented By A Speaker*—Select this type (the default, traditional show type) to present your show full-screen, hiding everything—PowerPoint (or the PowerPoint viewer), the menu bar, and so on—but the slides. The presentation appears to take over the Mac, but the speaker still has access to all of PowerPoint's editing features underneath, so the speaker can make changes in a pinch. The speaker may also access a number of mid-show tools, such as a pen for scribbling notes on screen (see "Using Speaker Options In A Presentation" later in this chapter).

- *Browsed By An Individual*—This type presents the show in a window, accompanied by navigation tools (the Web toolbar). This type is ideal for presentations the viewer will run him- or herself—such as internal computer-based training sessions. The viewer can advance slides and activate hyperlinks, and can even

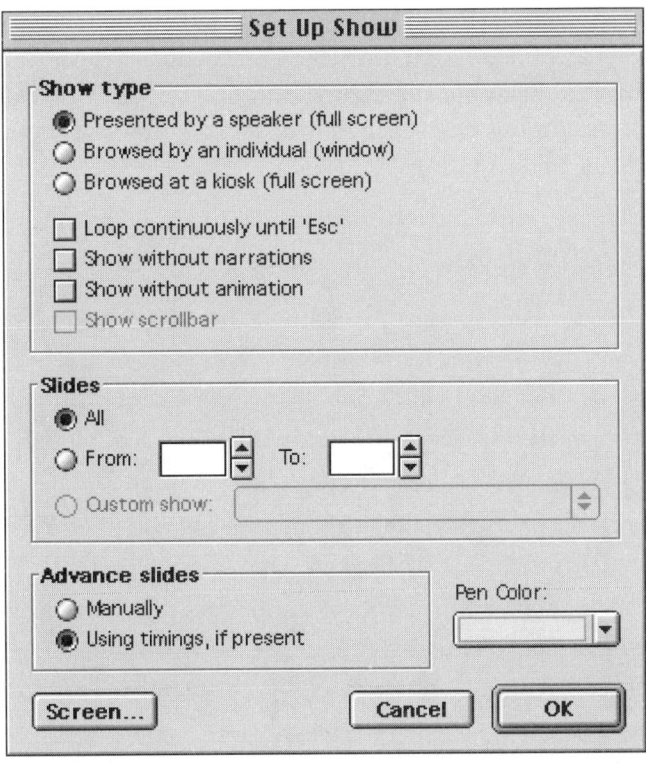

Figure 10.12 Use the Set Up Show dialog to control how your show will be presented.

change the size and shape of the window. The viewer can also run other applications while viewing the show.

- *Browsed At A Kiosk*—This type takes over the whole screen—just like the top menu choice—but prevents the viewer from accessing PowerPoint or changing the presentation. Viewers can activate links.

After you choose a Show Type, everything else on the Set Up Show dialog is optional. But you'll find a number of options for fine-tuning the behavior of the presentation, beginning with the checkboxes in the Show Type section. You can choose to show the presentation without animation (slides containing animation appear as if all animations have already been completed) or without narration, if you have recorded it. These options are useful for creating alternate, lower-tech versions of a multimedia-rich presentation when the right equipment may not be available for playing the show in its full glory.

In the Slides section, you can choose to present only a portion of a show by entering slide numbers in From and To. When you next present the show, it will begin with the slide in From and end at the slide in To. To present a show made up of slides in the current presentation in any order you wish, choose one of your Custom shows.

Finally, in the Advance Slides section, choose Manually to allow slides to be advanced at will by the presenter or viewer (except for kiosk shows), or choose Using Timings to make the show a self-running one in which slides advance automatically according to a schedule you set (see the next section, "Setting And Rehearsing Slide Timings").

FYI: Kiosk Behavior

A show presented in kiosk mode looks just like one in speaker mode, but behaves differently in the following important ways. These differences—which are based on the assumption that the kiosk may include a mouse or other pointing device but does not include a keyboard—must be taken into account in the design, structure, and testing of a kiosk show:

- Slides can be advanced only by the actions of hyperlinks (or action buttons), or automatically advanced by timings (see the next section, "Setting And Rehearsing Slide Timings"). If you intend for the viewer to advance the slides or navigate the presentation, then the slides must include all of the links required to get around. PgUp/PgDn and other advancing methods are disabled.

- The show can be stopped only by the Esc key. Until Esc is pressed, the show loops automatically—when the timings or the viewer advance past the last slide, the show starts over at Slide 1 automatically.

- When the show is not self-running, and five minutes pass during which the viewer does not click on a link, the show automatically returns to the first slide (it assumes the previous viewer has left, so it resets itself for a new viewer).

Fast Track

To prevent the PowerPoint window from appearing after the last slide in a show, go to Tools|Preferences, choose the View tab, and check the checkbox for End With Black Slide.

Setting And Rehearsing Slide Timings

The *timings* of a show are the fixed amounts of time PowerPoint stays on a slide, or between animations, before advancing automatically in a self-running show. If you record narration for your show, you can automatically apply the timing of your narration session to the show. Otherwise, you'll need to set the timings.

Fast Track

Some folks use timings not just for self-running shows, but also to prepare very tightly timed speaker-driven presentations. By setting timings, you give yourself a sort of time budget, with a certain amount of time allotted to each slide or topic. By rehearsing the show as a self-running presentation, you can tailor your own performance to fill precisely the amount of time you wish. When you present for real, you can use the timings or trust that your rehearsal has conditioned you to time the show precisely.

To set timings, first work through the presentation several times to develop a good sense of what the timing should be like. When you're ready, choose Slide Show| Rehearse Timings. The show begins at Slide 1, and a time-tracking button appears (see Figure 10.13). The button shows a counter that tracks the total time you've spent on the current slide.

Clicking on the button advances to the next animation or slide. Wait the desired length of time between slides and animations, then click on the button to advance. As you go, the timing is recorded. Each time you advance to a new slide, the counter starts over at 00:00:00.

When you're finished, press Esc. A message appears, asking whether you want to save the timings you just recorded. Click on Yes to save them. Before running the show, open the Set Up Show dialog (Figure 10.12) and make sure the Using Timings radio button is selected.

FYI: Custom Shows

Sometimes, you may want to present a variation on an existing show. For example, if you have a long show you perform for different groups, you may want to shorten the show, or change the order of slides, to customize it for a particular group.

A great way to do that is to create a *custom show*—a new show constructed by reshuffling slides from an existing show. To create a custom show, open the show you want to customize, then choose Slide Show|Custom Shows. A dialog opens, from which you may select existing custom shows for editing. To create a new one, click on New. The Define Custom Show dialog opens, showing a list of slides in the current presentation.

Figure 10.13 Use the time-tracking button to time your slide changes.

> To create the custom show, select desired slides from the list, and click on Add to copy them into a list of slides in the custom show. In the list of slides you create, you can change the order of the slides any way you like. Note that the slides bring along their animation, multimedia, and narration.
>
> To present a custom show, choose it from the Set Up Show dialog (refer back to Figure 10.12).

Using Speaker Options In A Presentation

By now, you understand the basics of running your electronic show: Fire it up in PowerPoint (or the PowerPoint viewer), start the slide show (switch to Slide Show view or choose Slide Show|View Slide Show), and advance through the slides and animation by pressing PgDn or the Right arrow key. If that's all you want to do, you're all set.

But just in case you want to get fancy, you should be aware that you can do more during a slide show than just step through slides. You can jump directly to a selected slide, draw right on the slides as if they were transparencies, take notes during a meeting, and more. In this section, you'll learn how.

Note that the stuff you learn how to do on the next few pages is available only when:

- The Slide Setup dialog for the current presentation shows Presented By Speaker as the Show Type.

- The slide show is being presented in the PowerPoint viewer or in PowerPoint in Slide Show view.

During a show, you can call up a contextual menu of activities available in mid-show. The menu appears when you Control-click anywhere on the display except on a hyperlink. Alternatively, as soon as you move the mouse while viewing any slide, a little control button appears in the lower left corner of the slide; click on the button to open the contextual menu (see Figure 10.14).

Much of what's on this contextual menu is self-explanatory; for example, Next and Previous advance and move backward within the show, and Go opens further submenus for navigating in the presentation. You can choose Go|By Title to jump to any slide by picking its title from the list that appears.

Meeting Minder (see Figure 10.15) opens a dialog on which you can make notes while presenting in a meeting or small conference. You can record the minutes of a meeting on the Meeting Minutes tab and build a list of "action items"—the stuff people promise in meetings they'll do later—on the Action Items tab.

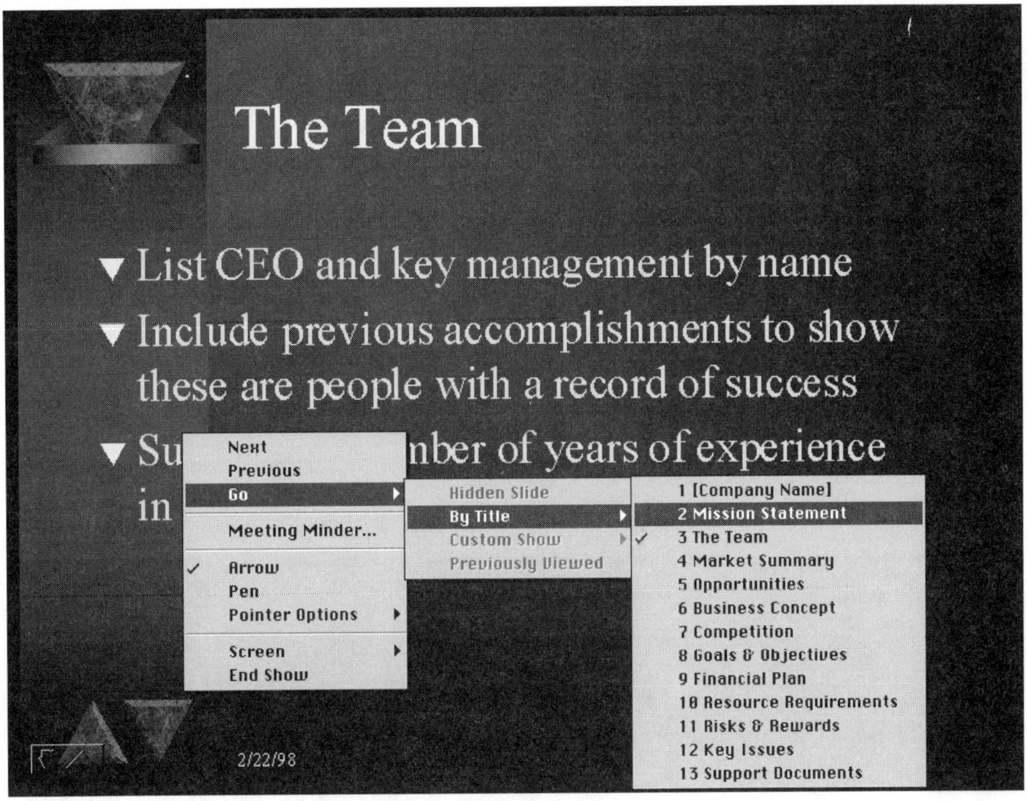

Figure 10.14 During a show, Control-click on a slide to choose from among display and navigation options.

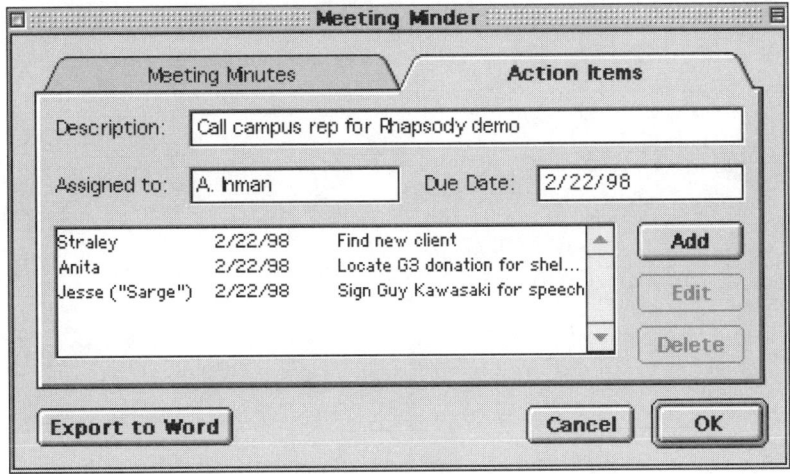

Figure 10.15 Use the Meeting Minder to keep notes during a meeting.

The Pen item on the contextual menu changes the standard Mac pointer into a pen pointer. While the pointer is a pen, you can draw on the screen as you would on a blackboard—circling important items, checking off items in a list, crossing out items (see Figure 10.16). To draw with the pen, point to where you want to begin drawing, click and hold the mouse button, draw your line, and release.

After you draw, the pointer remains a pen, in case you want to draw some more. To revert the pen back to the regular pointer, press Esc. (Be careful to press Esc only once, since pressing Esc twice would close the show.) To erase drawing on a slide, open the contextual menu and choose Screen|Erase Pen.

Finally, the Pointer Options item on the contextual menu opens a submenu on which you can choose to hide the pointer (so it doesn't distract in a show where it's not used) or choose a new Pen Color, in case the color of your on-screen drawings isn't showing up well.

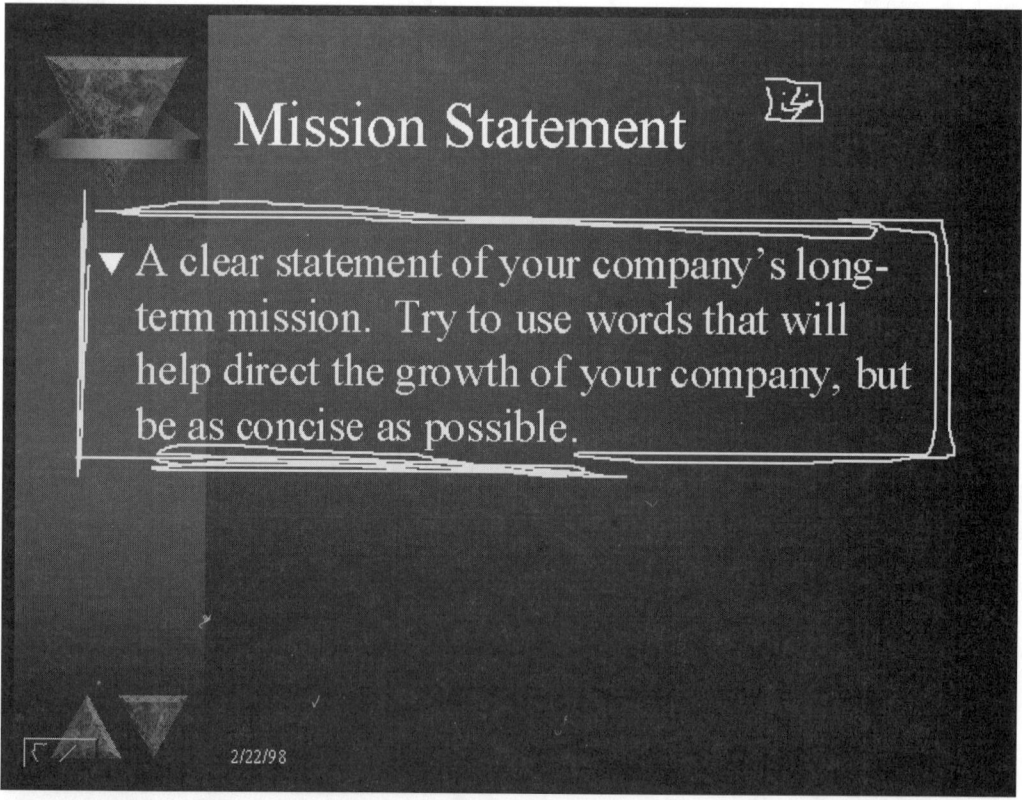

Figure 10.16 Using the pen, you can draw on slides without getting ink on your cuffs.

Moving On

That's it for PowerPoint. If you want to explore further, and find new artwork or animation you can download for free, explore the PowerPoint resources available on the Web. A good place to start is Microsoft's Free Stuff page (Help|Help On The Web|Free Stuff).

Of course, if you've had your fill of PowerPoint, move ahead to Chapter 11 and Microsoft Excel.

PART IV

Excel

Getting Started With Excel

11

The first time Ned used Excel, he had been hired by a publisher to manage—among other things—the master schedule that tracked the progress and deadlines of all books underway. Because this was in the days before sophisticated work scheduling programs, he was supposed to record all of the projects and deadlines in an Excel worksheet. He could then print and distribute the worksheet at staff meetings to give everyone a visual aid in appreciating how desperately late everything was.

Not having had previous experience with spreadsheets, Ned was happy to discover that when a document consists mainly of a big table, Excel is a much better tool for the job than Word is. Organizing projects, deadlines, and other information in a clear, well-formatted table was a snap in Excel. Soon he made another discovery: By inserting *formulas*, he could make the schedule update itself in response to changes. For example, when an author turned in a manuscript a month late (authors are *so* unreliable), Ned could change just one date in his schedule, and other dates would change automatically to estimate new deadlines for editing, page production, and printing. Ned had found a way to make extra time in his day for putting out fires, which is really the only thing a publishing manager does, anyway.

Upon discovering his creative application of Excel formulas, Ned's boss quickly put a stop to it. A tenet of publishing, she explained, is to stand firm on impossible deadlines, because extending schedules to accommodate delays alleviates panic, and employee panic is the lubricant of a productive publishing empire. (So Ned quit.)

By now, despite appearances to the contrary, you know that Ned's anecdotes all have a point. The point here is twofold: 1) Even if you use Office, you can't please everybody, and 2) Excel isn't just a bean-counter, an accountant's plaything. Excel is a terrific document-maker when the document you need is table-like—*tabular*—in nature. More important, tables usually include information—*data*—and data has a habit of changing. Excel helps you keep changeable data current, and it can manage, analyze, chart, and graph that data quicker than the Rain Man counts spilled toothpicks.

Figure 11.1 You'll use Excel's Standard toolbar to perform many of the activities in this chapter.

You can find most of the toolbar buttons described in this chapter on Excel's Standard toolbar, shown in Figure 11.1. If you don't see the Standard toolbar on your screen, point to any spot on any visible toolbar and Control-click (or choose View|Toolbars from the menu bar), then click on Standard. To display the name of any button on the toolbar, rest the pointer on the button for a moment. Note that the controls on the Standard toolbar for Excel differ a bit from those in Word. Word has buttons for inserting tables, handling borders, and so on, but Excel's Standard toolbar focuses on manipulating data.

Managing Excel Workbooks

An Excel file is a *workbook*, which itself is a collection of *worksheets*. A worksheet is a single set of rows and columns, a big table you fill in with your data. Sometimes it helps to think of worksheets as pages and the workbook as the book in which the pages are bound. But keep in mind that a worksheet may or may not correspond exactly to a printed page; a large worksheet might take up many printed pages.

Creating A New Workbook

Each time you open Excel, you create a new, blank workbook automatically. You may begin by making entries in cells, formatting the workbook, or saving it (see "Saving a Workbook" later in this chapter). While Excel is open, you can create another blank workbook at any time simply by clicking on the New button on the Standard toolbar. Alternatively, you can create a new, blank workbook by choosing File|New to open the New dialog, then choosing the Workbook icon from the General tab.

Your brand-new workbook does not yet have a real name—it's called Workbook1 in the title bar (see Figure 11.2). You'll have the opportunity to name the workbook when you save it (as described later in this chapter). You can save your new workbook immediately after creating it (even before you type anything), or after you've worked on it for awhile. Once the workbook has been saved, its new name appears in the title bar.

The new, blank Excel workbook that you see when you open Excel (see Figure 11.3) contains three worksheets to get you started—Sheet1, Sheet2, and Sheet3. You can add and delete worksheets from the workbook as needed. A workbook can hold a single worksheet, or many. Near the bottom of the Excel window, you'll see a tab for each worksheet in the current workbook file.

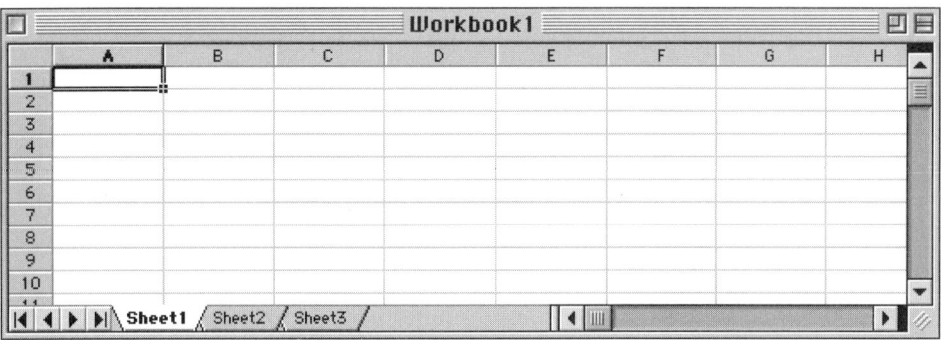

Figure 11.2 Each new workbook is given the generic moniker Workbook1.

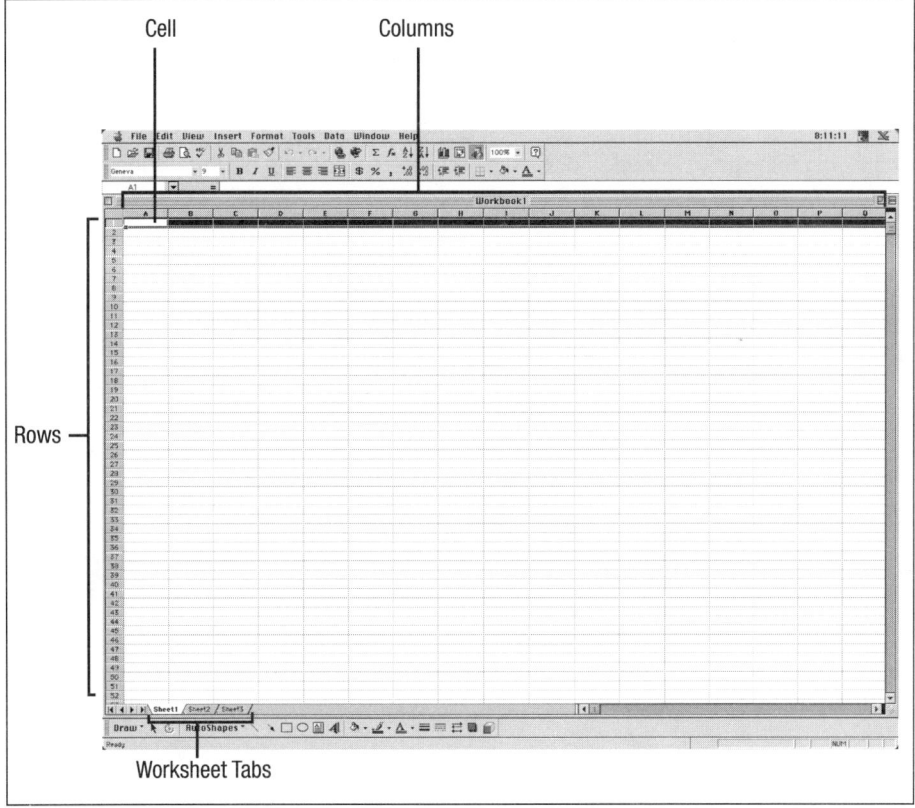

Figure 11.3 An Excel file is a workbook that contains one or more worksheets.

Understanding Cells

Like any table, a worksheet consists of horizontal rows and vertical columns. Columns are labeled with letters, left to right—the leftmost column is Column A, the next to the right is B, the third is C, and so on. Similarly, the rows are numbered—the top row is Row 1, the next down is Row 2, and so on. In a worksheet, you can see the column letters across the top of the workspace, and the row numbers along the left side of the worksheet.

Each of the boxes is called a *cell*. Each cell has its own unique *address* that describes the cell's location within the worksheet (see Figure 11.4). The address is made up of the letter of the column in which the cell appears, followed by the row number. For example, the leftmost cell in the top row is cell A1. To the right of A1 is B1. Below A1 is A2. Cell addresses become important when you do something in one cell that affects others. For example, you may insert an equation in a cell that adds up numbers from other cells.

Fast Track

When you click on any cell, you can read the cell's address in the Name Box on the Formula bar. (To learn more about the Formula bar, see Chapter 13.) Also, the Row number (along the left edge of the sheet) and the Column letter (along the top) of the clicked cell both turn bold.

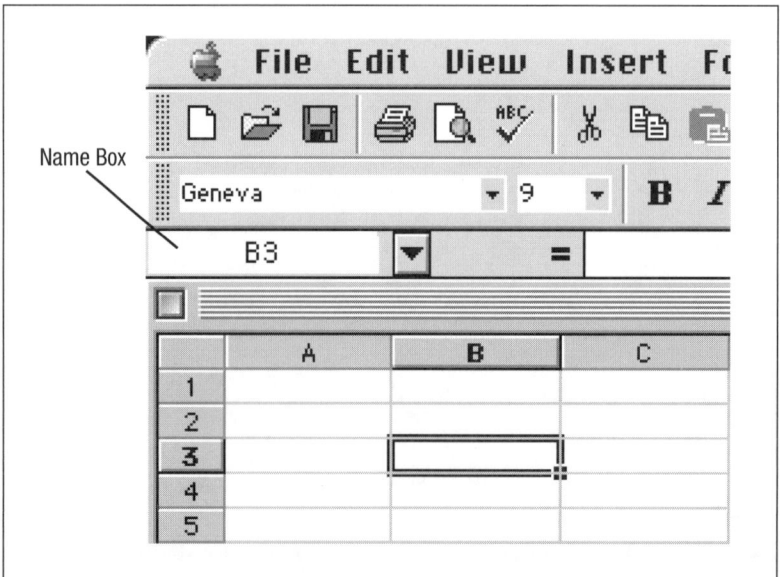

Figure 11.4 The selected cell's address is B3.

Getting Around In A Workbook

Here's how to get around within an Excel workbook:

- To move from worksheet to worksheet, click on the worksheet tabs at the bottom of the Excel window.

- To move around within a worksheet, use the horizontal and vertical scroll bars (see Chapter 2). You can also move around in the worksheet by using the arrow keys, PgUp, and PgDn.

When you've filled out many cells in a worksheet, you may have to do a lot of scrolling to see and work with the whole sheet. You can minimize scrolling two ways: Zoom and Full Page.

Use the Zoom list on the Standard toolbar—or choose View|Zoom—to set the Zoom level. When the Zoom is set to its default, 100 percent, the worksheet is supposed to appear on your screen at roughly the same size it would appear in print—although, due to size differences among monitors, 100 percent is never quite 100 percent. Zooms higher than 100 percent magnify the worksheet, enabling you to see and work closely with very small text and with a smaller number of cells on the screen. Zooms lower than 100 percent make the page look farther away and show more cells on the screen at once. At low zooms, small text may be difficult or impossible to read, but you'll be better able to see and evaluate the overall look of the worksheet and move from cell to cell without scrolling.

Choose View|Full Screen to enter Excel's Full Screen mode. Full Screen mode hides almost everything but your workbook, allowing it to fill up the whole display. The menu bar remains, but the status bar, scroll bars, and toolbars vanish so that your workbook can fill up your screen completely. You may find Full Screen mode valuable if you have a small display (as on a PowerBook) or if you find the clutter of Excel's tools distracting. To move around in a worksheet without the scroll bars, use your arrow keys or PgUp and PgDn.

Besides your workbook and menu bar, all you see in Full Screen mode is a small dialog box with a single button: Close Full Screen. To exit Full Screen mode and restore all of Excel's paraphernalia, click on the Close Full Screen button.

Using Excel Templates

A *template* is a head start on a new workbook, a way to provide yourself with a pre-formatted workbook you can then edit to create one of your own. If you use a template that's similar to the workbook you want to wind up with instead of creating your workbook from scratch, you'll save yourself some effort.

Note, however, that a template is not a replacement for knowing how to create a workbook on your own. Even if you use a template, you'll need the skills you pick up in this chapter—and in Chapters 12 and 13—to effectively edit the template and understand any formulas or other special elements it contains.

If you're familiar with templates from Word or PowerPoint, you may be surprised to discover that Excel—out of the box—is much less template-rich than either Word or PowerPoint, offering far fewer templates and no wizards to assist you with using templates. Office 98's drag-and-drop installation gives you only a single template—Invoice—for creating formatted invoices. (There is also the Workbook icon, which just makes a new, blank workbook, and the Village Software template, which is basically an advertisement for a maker of custom Excel solutions.) Using the Microsoft Office Installer, you can optionally install two more templates, and you can pick up still more templates from the Office 98 Value Pack and from the Internet. Finally, you can easily create your own templates. You'll learn how to do all of this in the next few pages, along with creating a new workbook from a template.

Creating A New Workbook From A Template

To create a new Excel workbook from a template, choose a template file in Excel's New dialog. Excel template files use a file icon similar to workbook files, but whereas the workbook icon is a document with a turned-down top right edge, the template icon is a stationery pad, with a turned up lower right edge.

The templates installed by Office Setup are stored in the Templates folder, which itself is stored in your Microsoft Office folder. You can easily use any of the templates in your Templates folder by opening Excel and choosing File|New. The New dialog opens (see Figure 11.5). The dialog includes two tabs:

- *General*—This tab includes only the Workbook template, which creates the blank workbook that appears automatically when you open Excel (and isn't really a template, at that).

- *Spreadsheet Solutions*—This tab includes any Excel templates installed with Office 98.

Note that the New dialog also has a drop-down View menu that allows you to select the view you prefer: By Icon, By Small Icon, or By Details. Changing this selection works just like changing the View selection in the Finder.

Fast Track

If you're upgrading from Office 4.2.1, you may see a variety of other tabs in the New dialog. These hold Excel templates carried over from your previous version. You can open and use them just like you would any Excel 98 template.

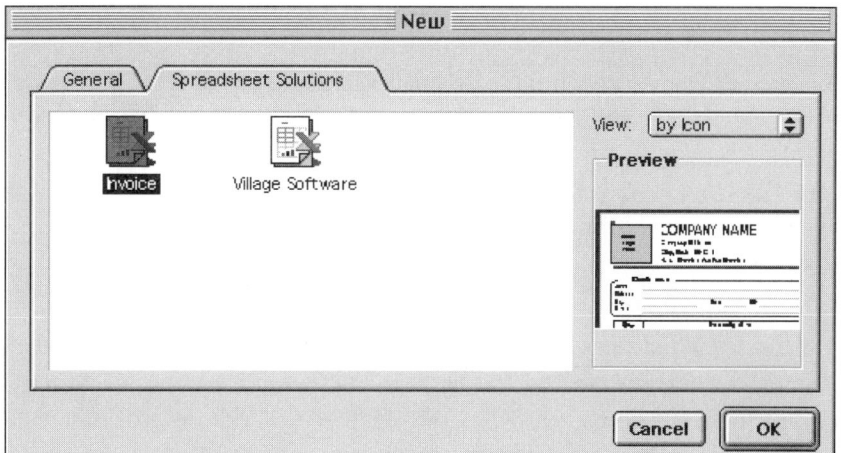

Figure 11.5 Choose File|New to open the New dialog and choose a template.

To create a new workbook based on a template, click on the template's file icon once to select it. A preview of the selected template appears in the New dialog's Preview pane. Click on OK to create the workbook. The new workbook opens in Excel, ready for your changes. (You may get a dialog warning you about macros in the template. Simply instruct Excel to enable macros by clicking the appropriate button, and proceed—we'll cover macro disabling later). The new workbook file has a temporary name based on the name of the template from which it was created, but you can use the Save As command to give it a new name.

Note that when you choose a template in the New dialog, you are not opening the template file itself. Rather, you are creating a new workbook file with contents and formatting that are based on those in the template file. Changes you make to your new workbook have no effect on the template file.

Picking Up More Templates

The drag-and-drop install gives you only a meager selection of templates, but you can pick up more templates easily. On the Office 98 CD-ROM, the Value Pack folder includes another seven templates, including a Personal Budgeter, a Timecard template, and a Loan Manager. To locate the Excel templates on the CD, open the Value Pack folder, then the Templates folder, then the Spreadsheet Solutions folder.

To use the Value Pack templates or any other templates you acquire or create, you must copy them to the Office Templates folder (which, on most computers, is in the folder Microsoft Office 98/Templates). The Templates folder contains a special folder for Excel templates: Spreadsheet Solutions. Copy your templates from the CD to this folder to make them available in the New dialog.

Net Savvy

From time to time, Microsoft posts new templates on Excel 98's Free Stuff page. To review and download the available templates, connect to the Free Stuff page.

In Excel, choose Help|Help On The Web|Free Stuff, or point your Web browser to the Free Stuff page at **www.microsoft.com/msdownload/** or the Office 98 Online Catalog at **www.microsoft.com/off98cat/**.

Creating Templates

To create a new template, simply save a workbook in template format. Begin by creating the workbook and including in it any data, formatting, or other elements you want included in the template. (To create the workbook, you can even use an existing template, then edit it to create a new template.)

When the workbook is ready, choose File|Save As. On the Save dialog, drop down the Save File As Type list and choose Template. In the file list box, navigate to the Spreadsheet Solutions folder, then click on Save.

The new template will be available from the Spreadsheet Solutions tab of the New dialog the next time you choose File|New. (To learn more about Save As, see the next section, "Saving a Workbook.")

Saving A Workbook

After working on your new workbook, you must save it to make your changes permanent. Note that unlike Word, Excel has no built-in automatic saving capability, although you can add this capability (see "Adding Add-Ins" later in this chapter).

To save an open workbook, click on the Save button on the Excel toolbar (or choose File|Save from the menu bar). The first time you save a new workbook, the Save As dialog opens so you can choose a name and storage location (see Figure 11.6). This happens even though the workbook file already has a temporary name: Workbook1. If the workbook has been saved before, clicking on Save saves the file, with no further input from you. To change the workbook's name or storage location, use Save As. Note that using Save As creates a second copy of the workbook, so make sure you can distinguish it from your prior save.

At the top of the Save As dialog, the Save In box shows the name of the folder in which Excel will store the workbook. The default (if your computer is so configured) is the Documents folder, but you can drop down the drive/folder list to choose any folder. The file list box shows all files and subfolders in the folder.

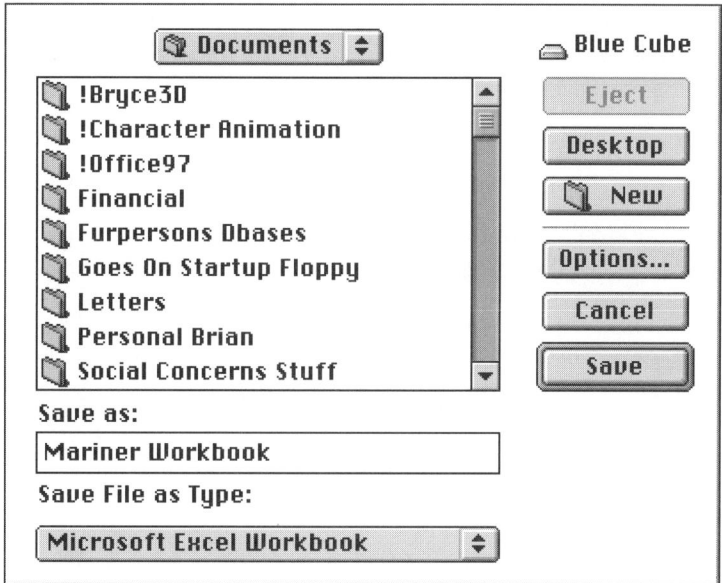

Figure 11.6 Use the Save As dialog to name a workbook and choose its storage location.

Fast Track

Among its optional *add-ins*, Excel includes AutoSave, which automatically saves open Excel workbooks according to a schedule you select. (To install AutoSave and other Excel add-ins, see "Adding Add-Ins" later in this chapter.)

After installing AutoSave, you can choose how often AutoSave saves, and other options, by choosing Tools|AutoSave.

FYI: Naming Workbook Files

To name your file, click in the File Name box and type a name. When phrasing your file name, keep in mind the following:

- You can enter long file names, more than 218 characters (if you're running the latest Mac OS). But short, simple names are more convenient to work with.

- If the workbook you're saving might be copied later to a computer running Windows 3.1 or MS-DOS, you should stay within the file-naming restrictions of Windows 3.1 and MS-DOS. Don't use any punctuation or spaces in the file name, and keep the file name to eight characters or less (not including the three-character .xls extension).

To save the workbook in a folder other than Documents, use the Save As dialog's drive/folder list and file list box to navigate to the folder you want. You can navigate to other folders in several ways:

- Drop down the drive/file list and select from it. At the bottom of the list is Desktop, which you can select to save the workbook on your Macintosh Desktop.

- Click on Desktop, and in the file list box, navigate to any drive connected to your Macintosh: removable media, network drives, floppies, and so on.

- To create a new, empty folder in which you'll save your workbook, click on the New Folder button. When you click on New Folder, the new folder is created within the folder currently open in the file list box.

- When you've finished choosing a name and storage location for your workbook, click on the Save button on the Save dialog.

FYI: Copying A Workbook

From time to time, you may want to copy a workbook. For example, you may need to create several different versions of the same workbook or several different workbooks that are very similar to one another. By saving a previously saved workbook under a different name (or under the same name, but in a different location), you effectively create a separate copy of that workbook, which you can then edit in any way you wish.

To create a copy, use the Save As command to save the existing workbook with a new file name. When the Save dialog closes, the open workbook in Excel is the copy—not the original (the copy's name appears in the Excel title bar).

Walk-Through: Creating And Saving A New Workbook

Follow these steps to practice creating, saving, and closing an Excel workbook.

1. Open Excel. A new workbook, Workbook1, opens in Excel.
2. Click on the Save button. The Save dialog opens.
3. Click in the File Name box and type "My Workbook".
4. Click on the Save button. The file My Workbook is saved to your hard drive.
5. Click on the Save button on the Standard toolbar. The file is saved with no further input from you.
6. Choose File|Close.
7. Choose File|New. The New dialog opens.

8. Choose the Spreadsheet Solutions tab, then click on Invoice. A preview of the Invoice template appears in the Preview pane.
9. Click on OK. A dialog appears with a warning about macro viruses.
10. Click on Enable Macros. A new workbook, Invoice1, opens.
11. Choose File|Quit. Excel asks whether you want to save Invoice1 before exiting Excel.
12. Click on No. Excel closes without saving Invoice1.

Printing A Workbook

When you format your worksheets, as you'll learn to do in Chapter 13, you can choose a print area—the portion of a worksheet that you want printed. By default, when you print, only the print area prints; the portion of a worksheet outside of the print area is ignored. That's sensible, because the whole worksheet area is much, much larger than most of the creations made within it.

To print, choose File|Print to open the Print dialog (see Figure 11.7). From the Print dialog, you can choose a printer from the printer list, enter a range of pages to print, and more.

Fast Track

Instead of choosing File|Print, you can simply click on the Print button on the Standard toolbar to print a worksheet. Note that clicking on the Print button does not open the Print dialog, but simply prints immediately using the default print settings.

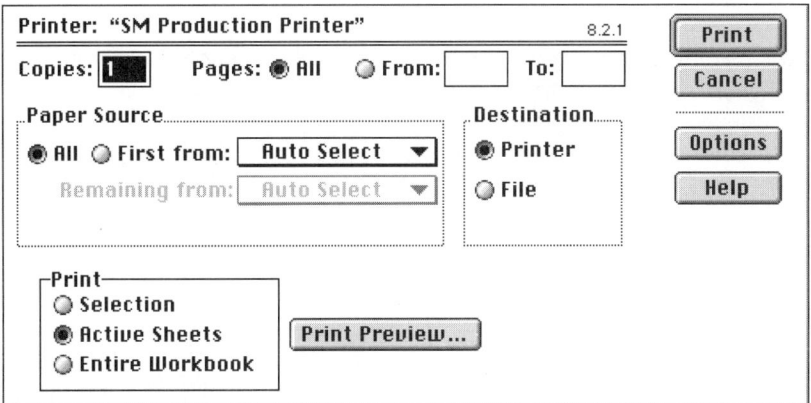

Figure 11.7 Use the Print dialog to control printing options.

On the Print dialog, under Print, you have several items to choose from:

- *Selection*—Only the cells in the worksheet that are currently selected print (you'll learn how to select cells in Chapter 13). This option enables you to print only a portion of the print area of a worksheet, or even selected cells outside the print area.

- *Active Sheets (the default setting)*—All selected worksheets print. (If you have defined a print area for any sheet, only the print area prints.) Usually, only the current worksheet is selected, and this option is a great way to print the current worksheet without printing the whole workbook. However, you can select multiple worksheets (before opening the Print dialog) by holding down the Control key and clicking on the tab for each sheet you want to print.

- *Entire Workbook*—All sheets in the current workbook print, except blank sheets (those containing no data). If you have defined a print area for any sheet, only the print area prints.

After choosing any options on the Print dialog, click on OK to print.

Fast Track

Before printing, you can choose File|Print Preview to see an on-screen representation of the way your worksheets will appear when they are printed with the default settings. To see a preview of the way worksheets will print with settings other than the defaults, open the Print dialog, choose any print options, then click on the Preview button on the Print dialog.

Closing A Workbook

You close a workbook simply by exiting Excel (choose File|Quit from the menu bar). To close just the current workbook but keep Excel open to do something else, choose File|Close.

If you're finished not just with the workbook, but with everything on your Mac (and ready for a nap), you can shut down your machine while Excel (and any workbooks) is still open. To shut down, choose Shut Down from the Special menu (in the Finder). Excel automatically closes your workbook and quits; then the Mac OS closes any other open applications or files and shuts itself down.

No matter which method you use to close, Excel always checks to see whether any open workbooks contain changes that have not been saved. If Excel finds any unsaved work, it displays the prompt shown in Figure 11.8. To save the workbook, click on Yes; to close without saving, click on No. To cancel closing the workbook and instead return to work on it, click on Cancel.

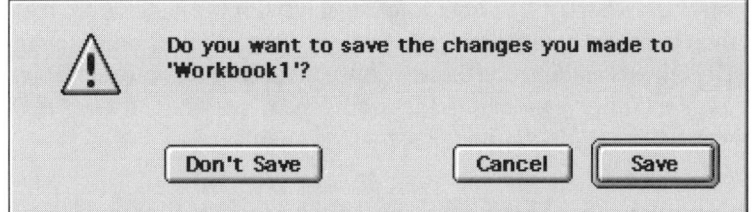

Figure 11.8 Excel makes sure you don't close a workbook or quit without saving, unless you really want to.

FYI: Don't Touch That Switch!

Never switch off your Mac without first using the Shut Down command (or the Shut Down accessory in the Apple menu). Not only does Shut Down help protect you against accidentally losing unsaved work, it also performs a number of important, unseen housekeeping chores the Mac OS must perform to run reliably.

Exchanging Files With Other Programs

Excel includes a family of file converters that enable you to work with files from other programs in Excel and prepare Excel workbooks for use in other programs.

Note that not all of the available converters are installed in the typical Excel setup. If a converter you need does not appear to be available in Excel, use the Office 98 Setup program to check for and install other converters.

Opening Workbooks

Like PowerPoint, Excel remembers the names and locations of the last four files you've edited and lists them at the bottom of its File menu, numbered 1 through 4. Number 1 is the last workbook you worked on; number 2 is the workbook you worked on before number 1, and so on. To open any of the last four workbooks you've worked on, open Excel, choose File from the menu bar, then click on the workbook you want (or press its number).

Fast Track

You'll probably find the last several workbooks on which you've worked listed in Recent Documents (under the Apple menu). Click on the Apple menu and select Recent Documents. If you see the workbook you want to open listed on the menu, click on it. Excel opens (if it's not open already) and the workbook opens in Excel.

If you don't have a Recent Documents folder, select Control Panels from the Apple menu, then click on Apple Menu Options. Under Recent Items, enter the numbers of Documents, Folders, and Servers you want to show up in your Apple menu, then close the Control Panel. From that point on, your recently used files will appear in your Apple Menu under Recent Documents.

To open an existing workbook that's not among the last four you've edited, choose it from Excel's Open dialog. Click on the Open button on the Standard toolbar (or choose File|Open from the menu bar). An Open dialog like the one in Figure 11.9 appears. In the dialog, use the drive/folder list and the file list box just as you would in the Save dialog: Click your way to any folder or to the Desktop. The file list box shows all of the Excel files (or rather, all files *readable* by Excel, including those created in other programs) currently stored in the folder selected in the drive/folder list.

When you have navigated to the folder containing the file you want to open, double-click on the file, or single-click on it and then click on the Open button. Either way, the Open dialog closes and the selected workbook opens in Excel, ready to edit.

From outside of Excel, you can open a workbook—and open Excel at the same time—by opening the workbook file from the Finder. You open any file in the Finder by double-clicking on its file icon wherever you find it: on the Desktop, in a folder, or in Results in the Find dialog. If Excel is closed when you open the workbook this way, Excel opens automatically. If Excel is already open, the active application switches to Excel. Either way, the workbook you opened appears in Excel, ready to edit or print.

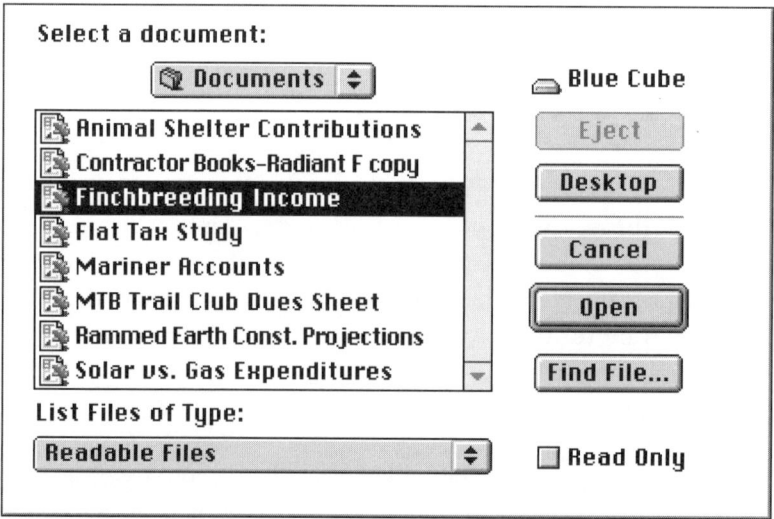

Figure 11.9 Use the Open dialog to navigate to and open an existing workbook.

When you're opening Excel files from their file icons, be careful to open workbooks and not templates. Double-clicking on a template file usually opens the template for editing instead of creating a new document based on the template.

Working With Earlier Excel Versions

If you used an earlier version of Excel, you probably have some workbooks you'd like to continue using. Opening these workbooks is no problem. Using any of the techniques described earlier in this chapter under "Opening Workbooks," you can open workbooks from earlier Excel versions just as you would an Excel 98 workbook.

After editing a file that was created in an earlier version of Excel, you have a choice to make when saving. Excel 98 workbooks are stored in a file format that is incompatible with all earlier versions of Excel. If you save the file as an Excel 98 workbook, the file cannot be used in earlier Excel versions. You have the option of saving the file in its original format. When you click on the Save button to save the workbook, the dialog box shown in Figure 11.10 opens. If you intend to edit the workbook in Excel 98 from then on, click on Yes. If you want to preserve the file's original file format, click on No. If you click on No to preserve the file's original format, note that any changes you've made in Excel 98 that require Excel 98 will be lost.

You can also convert an Excel 98 workbook into an earlier format, using the same techniques you use for converting workbooks to other programs, such as Works or dBase. See the next section, "Working With Other Spreadsheet Programs."

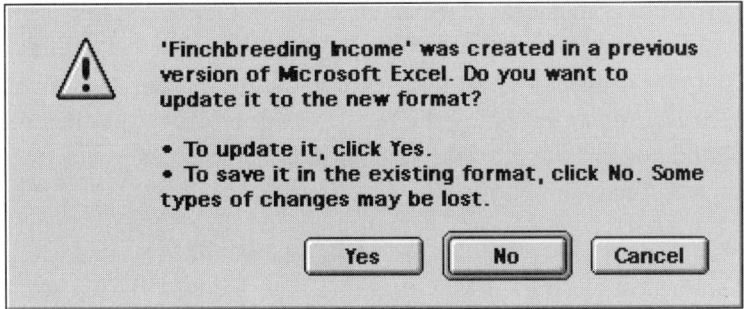

Figure 11.10 When you save a workbook that was created in an earlier version of Excel, you can choose whether to convert the document to Excel 98 format.

Fast Track

In the Save dialog's Save File As Type list, one choice—Microsoft Excel 98 & 5.0/95 Workbook—saves the workbook in a special dual file format compatible with both Excel 98 and Excel 5.0/95. You can edit the file in either program, although features and formatting unique to Excel 98 will be disabled when the file is opened in Excel 5.0/95. However, when the same file is reopened in Excel 98, the unique features remain intact. The dual file format lets you move a file back and forth between Excel 98 and Excel 5.0/95 as often as you want to without having to convert it each time it moves. (This feature is especially handy for sharing files with Windows-based colleagues.)

Working With Other Spreadsheet Programs

Among Excel converters are several that can convert a workbook to Excel 98 from another file format, such as Works or dBase. The same converters also do the reverse: They can save an Excel 98 workbook in a different file format for use by another program.

Fast Track

Among its optional add-ins, Excel includes the File Conversion Wizard, an add-in that leads you through the steps necessary to quickly convert a group of files to Excel format. (To install the File Conversion Wizard and other Excel add-ins, see "Adding Add-Ins" later in this chapter.)

Converting A File To Excel

To convert a file from another format, choose File|Open in Excel, just as you would to open an Excel worksheet. In the Open dialog, drop down List Files Of Type and choose the type of file you want to open. Use the file list box and drive/folder list to navigate to the folder containing the file you want to convert. When the file icon for the workbook you want to edit appears in the box, double-click on it, or click on it and click on the Open button.

When you attempt to save the file after editing it, you'll see a dialog box similar to the one shown earlier in Figure 11.10. From that dialog, you can choose to save the file either in Excel 98 format or in its original file format.

Converting An Excel File To Another Program

To convert an Excel 98 file to a format used by another program, open the Excel file and choose File|Save As. In the Save dialog, drop down the Save File As Type list (see Figure 11.11). The Save File As Type list includes all of the file formats in which you can save the file. Choose the format you want, and click on Save.

Getting Started With Excel   303

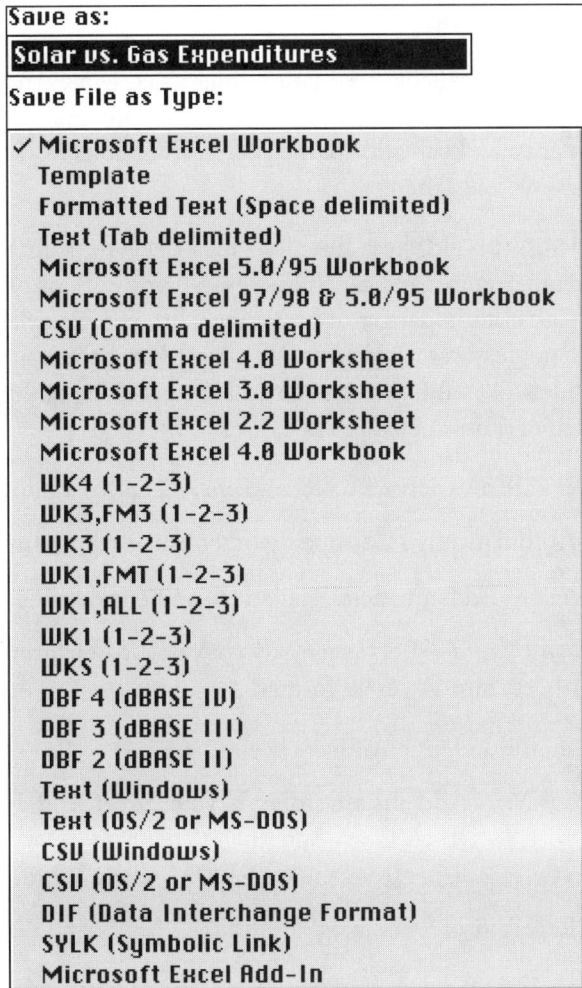

Figure 11.11   In the Save dialog's Save File As Type list, you can choose to convert a file to a new format.

When you open the file in the other program, note that it may not look or behave exactly as it did in Excel. If the Excel workbook contained formatting or other features that are exclusive to Excel, those aspects of the file are lost in the conversion.

Fast Track

If the format you need does not appear on the Save File As Type list, and you've run the Microsoft Office Installer to check the CD-ROM for the converter you need, try choosing SYLK from the Save File As Type list. SYLK (which stands for "Symbolic Link") is a file format that most spreadsheet and database programs import easily.

Adding Add-Ins

You can expand Excel's capabilities by installing its add-ins. An *add-in* is a program that adds new functionality to Excel, such as new commands, toolbar buttons, or menu items. After you add an add-in, the add-in's functions work seamlessly in Excel, as if they had always been there.

Why didn't Microsoft build these functions into Excel to begin with? Well, Excel already has so many features and capabilities—so many options on every menu, toolbar, and dialog—that it's in danger of becoming a little unwieldy and overwhelming. By packaging some features as add-ins, Microsoft keeps the core Excel product manageable while still enabling users to add any special capabilities they want or need (and to ignore those they don't need).

Office 98 comes with a variety of Excel add-ins, including (among others):

- *AutoSave*—Automatically saves open workbooks at regular intervals.
- *Analysis ToolPak*—Adds financial, statistical, and engineering analysis functions.
- *File Conversion Wizard*—Lets you easily convert a whole group of files from other spreadsheets into Excel 98 format.

To use an add-in, the add-in must have been:

- Copied to your Mac. Add-ins are stored in your Excel Add-Ins folder (usually in Microsoft Office 98/Office/Excel Add-Ins). When you install Office 98, the setup program copies add-ins from the CD-ROM to the Library folder.
- Installed in Excel's Add-Ins dialog.

Some add-ins are installed automatically in Excel; others you must select from the Add-Ins dialog (see Figure 11.12). To open the dialog, choose Tools|Add-Ins. The dialog shows all Add-In files currently in your Office Library folder and has check marks next to those that are already installed. Check the checkbox of any add-in you want to add to Excel or clear the checkbox of any add-in you want to remove.

Fast Track

Note that not all of the add-ins on the CD-ROM are copied to your hard disk in the drag-and-drop Office installation. To see and install other add-ins on the CD-ROM, run the Value Pack Installer program (see Appendix A), then examine the options for Excel.

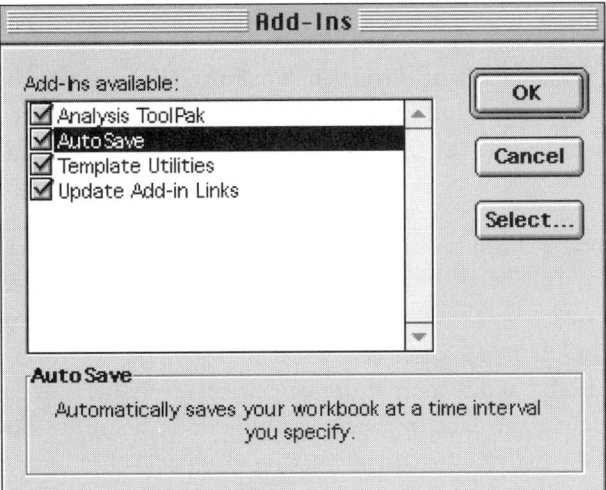

Figure 11.12 Choose Tools|Add-Ins to install any add-ins that have been copied to your Mac and stored in your Office Library file.

Walk-Through: Opening And Printing Workbooks

Follow these steps to practice opening and printing an Excel workbook.

1. If Excel is already open, close it.
2. In the Finder, locate the practice workbook you saved earlier, called *My Workbook*.
3. Double-click on the file icon for My Workbook. Excel opens, and My Workbook opens within it.
4. Choose File|Close to close My Workbook.
5. Choose File, and locate My Workbook in the list on the File menu.
6. Click on My Workbook in the File menu. My Workbook opens.
7. Close My Workbook.
8. Choose File|New, and create a new workbook from the Invoice template on the Spreadsheet Solutions tab. (If you feel adventurous, click on any area in the invoice and type—just to see what happens. Make any changes you like in this way.)
9. Save the new workbook, giving it any name you wish.
10. Choose File|Print. The Print dialog opens.
11. Click on OK to print the invoice.

Moving On

Now you know the basics of Excel—not just the all-important functional skills, such as creating, saving, and converting workbooks, but also the *conceptual* basics: workbooks, worksheets, cells. Those three concepts are the foundation for all that follows.

First, in Chapter 12, you'll discover how to create and edit the contents of cells. You'll learn not only how to enter and edit text and numbers in cells, but also how to exploit the real power of Excel by using formulas and functions to make calculations in cells. In Chapter 13, you can take a step back from cell-centric thinking and learn how to design and format entire worksheets. Finally, in Chapter 14, you'll discover how to use the data, formulas, and functions in your worksheets to organize and analyze data and produce great-looking charts.

Ready? Put on your clerk's green eyeshade and flip to Chapter 14 to discover the wonderful world of putting data in cells.

Adding Data, Formulas, And Functions

There's the trees, and there's the forest. In Excel, the forest is the worksheet: its size, shape, background, and other formatting characteristics.

Well, you can forget about all that for now, 'cause here we're talkin' trees (psych!), or more specifically, *cells*. In this chapter, you'll learn how to put stuff in cells—words, numbers, dates, equations, and so on. You won't be distracted by what those cells look like or what the worksheet as a whole looks like (all that will come later, in Chapter 13). Instead, here you'll be thinking like...well, like a computerized spreadsheet. You'll plug data into a grid, determine what the data means, and specify how different chunks of data interrelate. You don't need to worry about what it looks like, for the moment.

Planting trees in Excel is easier than it sounds. Most of the time, all you'll need to do is simply type words, numbers, and dates in cells—Excel is excellent at guessing what you want done with that information. But you'll soon move beyond just entering data in cells. You'll start using that data to create new cell values automatically: totals, averages, sums, and the rest. That's where the real power of Excel comes into play. Also in this chapter, you'll learn all about the mundane (but handy) housekeeping tools that help with entering and managing data in cells, such as spellchecking and copying data from one cell to others.

You'll use the Formula bar to do a lot of the activities in this chapter (see Figure 12.1). The Formula bar is sort of like a toolbar except that it's not included in the list of toolbars you can select by choosing View|Toolbars. If you don't see Excel's Formula bar (right above the worksheet and below Excel's toolbars), choose Tools|Options, click on the View tab on the Options dialog, and check the checkbox next to the Formula bar.

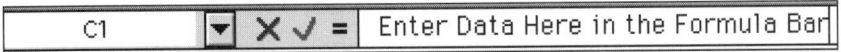

Figure 12.1 You enter and edit cell contents in the Formula bar.

Entering Cell Data

Regardless of what you put in a cell, you'll generally follow the same procedure to get it there. As this chapter proceeds, you'll learn how to phrase cell contents for various purposes. But for the next few pages, you can pick up the basics of entering data in a cell and begin to explore what Excel does with the different kinds of data you give it.

Typing Data In Cells

As you move your mouse around while you're in Excel, you'll notice that the pointer changes, depending upon what it's resting on:

- When it's resting over cells, the pointer is a big cross—the Excel *cell pointer*.

- When it's resting over menus, toolbars, and other controls, the pointer looks like the regular Mac pointer.

To enter anything into a cell, you must first select the cell by pointing to it with the cell pointer, then single-clicking. A heavy border appears around the cell to show that it is selected. On the left end of the Formula bar, Excel's Name Box shows the address of the cell you have selected.

When a cell is selected, anything you type appears in two places simultaneously: within the selected cell, and also in the Formula bar (see Figure 12.2). To enter data, you simply select a cell and type. When you finish typing your cell entry, move on in one of three ways:

- Press Return to record the cell entry and jump down to the next cell in the column. Return is useful when you want to enter a whole column of cells.

- Press Tab to record the cell entry and jump to the right, to the next cell in the row. Tab is useful when you want to enter data in a whole row of cells.

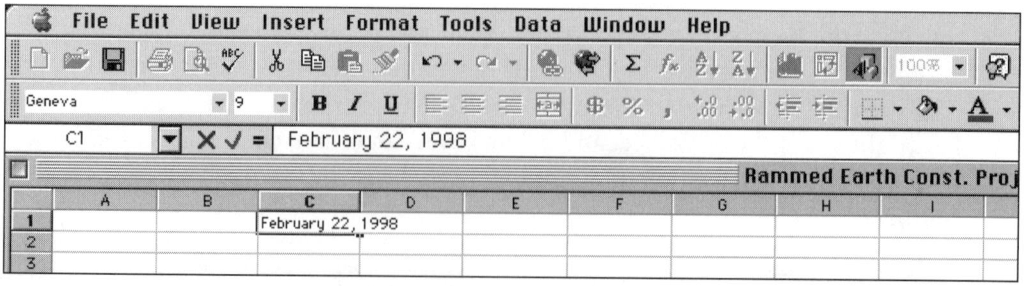

Figure 12.2 As you type a cell entry, the entry appears in the Formula bar.

- Press Esc to discard the entry you just typed—to *clear* the cell. The empty cell remains selected, so if you want to, you can type a new entry. Note that you can press Esc at any time while you're entering data in a cell to clear the cell and start over. (This only works while you're still in the cell—you can't come back to it later and try this trick.)

FYI: What If My Entry Won't Fit In The Cell?

In a single cell, you can enter up to 255 characters. When you type an entry that's too wide to fit in the cell, Excel accommodates your entry in one of two ways, depending upon whether the next cell to the right is empty or contains data:

- If the next cell is empty, Excel simply widens the cell containing your wide entry to cover as many empty cells as necessary to display all the data you typed.
- If the next cell has data in it, Excel doesn't widen the cell, to avoid covering up other data. (It does widen the cell as you type, but when you change cells, things snap back to the correct size.) The cell holding your wide entry appears at its regular size, and you see only the portion of the data that fits. However, the long entry is stored in its entirety in the cell; you simply can't see all the data in the worksheet. To see the full entry, click on the cell and read the Formula bar.

Either way, keep in mind that Excel's adjustments to cells are just temporary, to help you enter data effectively. When you format the worksheet (as you'll learn to do in Chapter 13), you'll adjust column widths, row heights, and other formatting so that all of your cell data is visible and rows and columns are neatly aligned.

Understanding Number Formats

To perform equations, update dates, and do the other cool stuff it's famous for, Excel must know the *number format* of each cell. The number format describes the type of data the cell contains: ordinary text, a date, a dollar amount, and so on.

Consider this: Suppose we type "10" in a cell. We might just want the "10" to appear there as a word, not as a value for Excel to use in calculations. Or that "10" may be one entry in a row or column of numbers we want Excel to add up or average—in which case, Excel must interpret our entry as the number 10, not the word 10. The "10" may also mean 10 dollars, 10 percent, or October (the tenth month). Each of these different meanings for "10" is a different Excel number format.

Excel is pretty smart about guessing your intended number format from your entry. For example, if you type "$10", Excel knows the number format is Currency. If you type "10-24-61", Excel knows it's a date, and records it in Date number format. When Excel can't guess the number format automatically from what you enter, it chooses "General" number format—a special format that treats any text in the cell as ordinary text, but still permits you to use the numbers in the cell in calculations.

In most cases, the number format affects not only the way Excel "thinks" of the cell entry, but also the way the data appears in the worksheet. Entries in any of the *numeric* data formats—Number, Currency, Date, Time, Percentage, and so on—are displayed according to rules set in the Number tab of the Format Cells dialog. For example, if the default currency format includes two decimal places, Excel automatically adds ".00" to the end of any whole dollar amount you enter in a cell; if you enter "$12", you'll see "$12.00".

These formats keep the presentation of each type of information consistent throughout the worksheet, even if you type them inconsistently. However, you can selectively change this formatting for any cell, group of cells, or a whole worksheet. (See "Editing Cell Data" later in this chapter.)

Typing Text

Excel determines that a cell entry is text when no other format seems to apply; in other words, if Excel knows your entry is not a number, date, or time (or a formula), it treats it as text and assigns it the number format "General." By default, text is left-aligned in the cell, but you can change the alignment by formatting the cell, as you'll learn to do in Chapter 13.

The only tricky part about entering text comes into play when you enter a number, date, or time that you want treated as text, not as numeric data, so that you can preserve the way you typed it and also omit it from any calculations. To treat a number as text, you must assign it the Text number format, which you can do in either of two ways:

- In the cell, precede the number with an apostrophe (').

- Select the cell containing the number and use the Format Cells dialog to assign Text format to it (make sure you've entered the number by pressing Return first).

Typing Numbers

By default, whenever you type a number in a cell that does not appear to be a date or time—and you do not precede the number with an apostrophe (') to force Text format or an equals sign (=) to indicate a formula—Excel considers the entry to be a number and records it as such. In general, Excel automatically right-aligns numbers in cells, but as always, you can change alignment.

Adding Data, Formulas, And Functions

You can type whole, positive numbers into cells without using any special symbols, such as decimal points or dollar signs. When you type a number and don't use a symbol, Excel automatically considers it a positive, whole number, and assigns it General number format. General format applies no special formatting to the data, so it appears in the cell exactly as you typed it. However, any numbers that are recorded in General format can be used by formulas.

To indicate special types of numeric data—a negative number, a dollar amount, and so on—use the symbols shown in Table 12.1 when typing the data in the cell.

Fast Track

When typing numbers or dates, you can either include commas (for example, 16,586,000 or Feb. 14, 1998) or leave the commas out. Excel doesn't care, and interprets the value the same whether you include the commas or not.

Typing Dates And Times

When you type a date or a time, Excel records the cell in Date or Time number format, respectively. In general, Excel automatically right-aligns dates and times, but you can change the alignment.

You can type the date or time in almost any of the ways dates and times are commonly represented; but note that the way Excel presents the value in the cell depends on how you type it. Table 12.2 shows the default formatting Excel applies to date and time values, based on what you enter in the cell.

While you're reviewing the table, observe two important points about entering dates and times:

- *Dates*—When typing dates, you can use either hyphens (-) or slashes (/) to separate the month, day, and year when using numbers alone to represent a date. Excel recognizes month names from their abbreviations.

Table 12.1 Symbols used with numeric data.

Symbol	What It Indicates	Example
-	The number that follows is a negative number.	-45
( )	The number within is a negative number.	(45)
.	The numbers that follow are decimals.	14.25
$	The number that follows is a dollar amount.	$14
%	The preceding number is a percentage.	45%

Table 12.2 How Excel displays your date and time entries.

If You Type	Excel Displays
9/15/98	9/15/98
9-15-98	9/15/98
Sep 15	15-Sep
September 15	15-Sep
September 15, 1998	15-Sep-98
Sep 98	Sep-98
4:20 am	4:20 AM
16:20	16:20
4:20:10	4:20:10

- *Time*—When typing times, you can type "AM" or "PM", or use values based on a 24-hour clock. If you use AM or PM, be sure to type a single space between the time value and the AM or PM; for example, 5:00 AM. Note that if you don't type "AM" or "PM", the value is assumed to be based on the 24-hour clock; an entry of 5:00 with no AM or PM is assumed to be 5:00 AM.

You can enter a time and date together in a cell; for example, 9/15/98 4:20 PM. When entering a date and time together, be sure to type a single space between the date and time.

FYI: What About The 21st Century?

When you type only two digits for the year in a date—for example, 8/18/98—Excel automatically determines—somewhat arbitrarily—the century portion of the year:

- When you type a year value from 30 through 99, Excel assumes the year is in the 20th century; for example, Excel interprets 98 as 1998.

- When you type a value from 00 to 29, Excel assumes the year is in the 21st century (or in 2000, the final year of the 20th); for example, Excel interprets 07 as 2007.

The only time this might present a problem for you is when you want to enter a year earlier than 1930, or later than 2029. (That's not that unusual—pretty soon, an amortization table for a new 30-year mortgage will run to 2030! Think about it.) In such cases, just enter the whole four-digit year to make Excel record the desired century.

FYI: *What's A ZIP Code—A Number Or Text?*

Postal ZIP codes always make trouble in spreadsheets. When you type a ZIP code—especially when you type it by itself in a cell—Excel thinks it's a real number. Not only will Excel use the ZIP code in calculations as if it were a number (when ZIP codes should be ignored in calculations), but also Excel removes the zero from the beginning of ZIP codes that begin that way. If you type the ZIP code "02192" (Needham, Massachusetts) in a cell, Excel instantly reformats it to 2192.

What to do? Well, whenever you enter a ZIP code, use the Format Cells dialog to apply the special ZIP code number format. On the Number tab, choose Special from the Category list. From the list of further options that then appears on the right, choose Zip Code or Zip Code+4.

Adding Comments

A *comment* looks like a little sticky note that records information related to a given cell. You can see your comments when you rest your pointer on them, but otherwise they're invisible and they don't show up in the final printed or online workbook.

To attach a comment to a cell, select the cell and choose Insert|Comment from Excel's Standard tool bar. A text box opens in the worksheet (see Figure 12.3), with your name at the top. Your name appears in the comment to show who wrote the note; this feature is useful in a workgroup, where several users may comment on the same worksheet. (You can delete the name, if you wish.) The edit cursor also appears inside the comment box, so whatever you type next will appear there. Type anything you want to—unlike cells, comments even permit you to press Return to break a paragraph and start a new one.

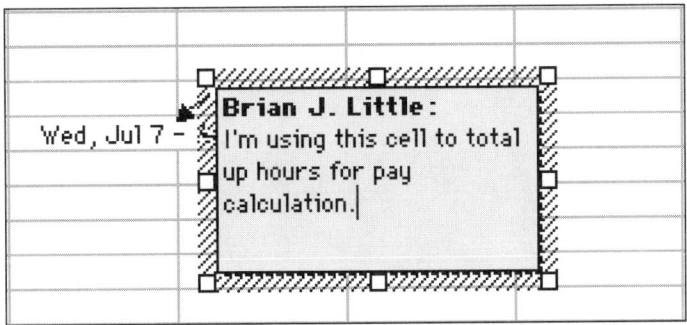

Figure 12.3 Comments are like sticky notes attached to cells.

When you've finished typing your comment, click anywhere on the worksheet. The comment vanishes, but a tiny red triangle appears in the cell's upper-right corner, to indicate that the cell has a comment attached to it. Any time you point to the cell or select it, your comment appears. To edit a comment, select the cell to which the comment is attached, then choose Insert|Edit Comment.

Editing Cell Data

Just as you can enter data one cell at a time, you can *edit* it cell by cell as well. You'll learn over the next several pages that you can perform a variety of editing and entry jobs more quickly by selecting a block of cells (see Figure 12.4). For example, you can change the number format of a whole group of cells by first selecting the cells, then applying the format.

The easiest way to select a block of cells is to point to the upper left cell of the block you want to select, click and drag to select cells, then release when you see the whole block highlighted. Dragging down highlights rows, dragging to the right highlights columns, and dragging diagonally highlights rows and columns together.

If you want to deselect a selection, click anywhere in the worksheet. The cell where you click is selected, but the earlier selection is deselected. Note that in Excel, at least one cell is always selected.

Clicking and dragging is usually the most effective method to select cells, but you can also select cells in a variety of other ways:

- *Using arrow keys*—Click on one cell to select it, then press and hold the Shift key while pressing an arrow key to extend the highlight to other cells.

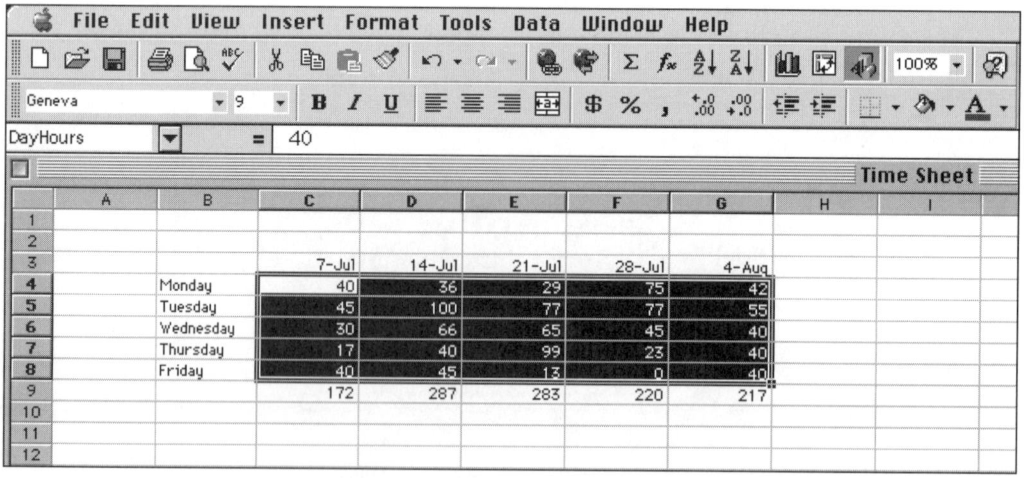

Figure 12.4 To work on a group of cells all at once, select the whole block.

- *Selecting the entire worksheet*—Locate the empty square that appears at the junction of the column headings and row numbers (the square directly above the row label *1* and to the left of the column label *A*), and click on it to select the entire worksheet.

- *Selecting rows or columns*—Click on a column heading to select all cells in the column, or click on a row heading to select all cells in the row. You can click, hold, and drag on a row or column heading to select multiple rows or columns.

- *Selecting noncontiguous cells*—To select *noncontiguous* cells, blocks of cells, rows, or columns that don't touch (see Figure 12.5), make your first selection, then press and hold the Command key while making all the other selections. For example, to select noncontiguous columns, select the first column, then press and hold Command, and click on any other desired column headings (or make any other type of selection).

Changing The Number Format And Formatting

To change the number format or formatting of selected cells, choose Format|Cells to open the Format Cells dialog, then choose the Number tab (see Figure 12.6).

From the list under Category, choose the type of data the selection represents. Depending on your category selection, further options may appear to the right of the Category list. For example, if you choose Date format in Category, a list of different types appears, each showing a different way of presenting a date. Choose from among the options and click on OK.

Editing Cell Contents

To completely replace a cell entry with new data, single-click on the cell and type your new entry. Your entry immediately deletes the existing entry.

To make changes to data without removing or replacing it, double-click in the cell. The *edit cursor*—a vertical bar—appears within the cell (see Figure 12.7). Use your

	7-Jul	14-Jul	21-Jul	28-Jul	4-Aug
Monday	40	36	29	75	42
Tuesday	45	100	77	77	55
Wednesday	30	66	65	45	40
Thursday	17	40	99	23	40
Friday	40	45	13	0	40
	172	287	283	220	217

Figure 12.5 To make noncontiguous selections, make your first selection, then press and hold Command while making the rest.

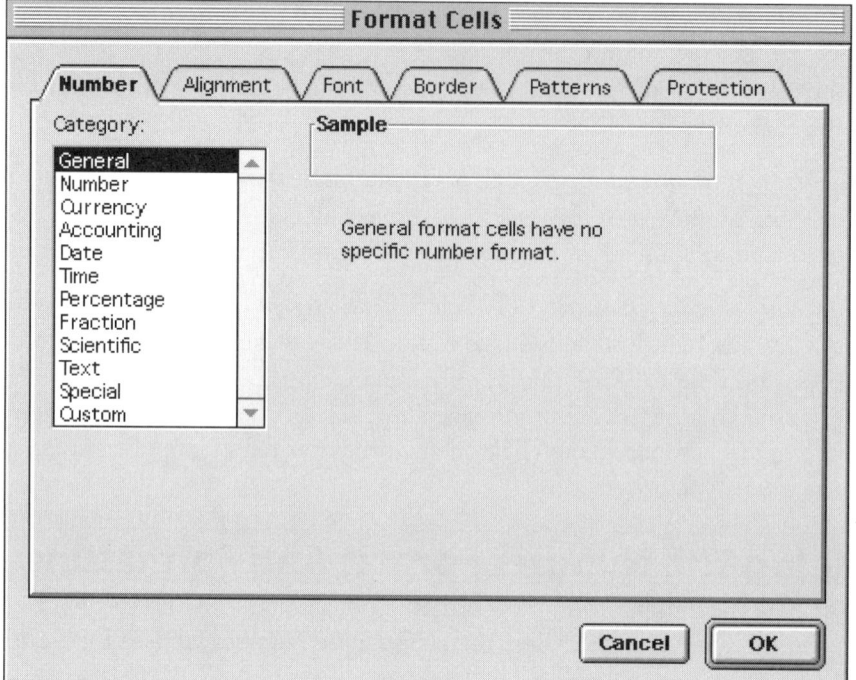

Figure 12.6 Change number formats and formatting in the Number tab of the Format Cells dialog.

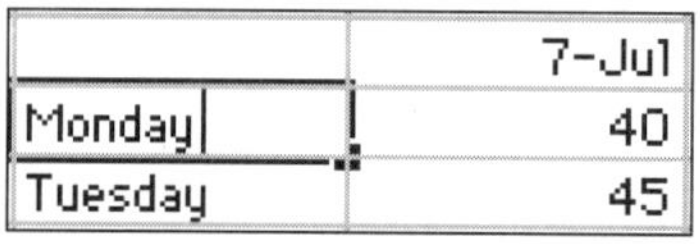

Figure 12.7 Double-click on a cell to put the edit cursor within the data, ready to make changes.

arrow keys to move the edit cursor to the spot where you want to make a change, then make your change as desired:

- To insert characters at the spot where the edit cursor appears, type the characters.

- To "type over" characters so that each character you type replaces a character, select the characters you want to type over, then begin typing.

- To delete characters to the right of the edit cursor, press the Del key.

- To delete characters to the left of the edit cursor, press the Delete key.

After making your changes, press Return or Tab to record the changes and move on to another cell, or press Esc to discard your changes and restore the original cell entry.

Adding Data, Formulas, And Functions   317

FYI: Data Looks Different When You Edit

When you double-click on a cell to edit its contents, the presentation of the data may change temporarily while you edit. For example, when you double-click on a cell containing a dollar amount, the dollar sign disappears, and only the amount remains. When you double-click on a cell containing a date, the date appears in MM/DD/YY format (for example, 10/24/61), regardless of how it appeared in the cell before you double-clicked.

Don't worry—you haven't changed the cell formatting. When you edit a cell entry, Excel assumes you're only interested in changing the value, not the formatting (you do that on the Format Cells dialog). Excel presents the value to you in the way that's most convenient to edit; for example, it strips the dollar sign out of a cell because when you're editing a dollar amount, you want to change numbers, not symbols. When you press Return or Tab to leave the cell after making changes, the data's original formatting is restored.

This handy habit of Excel's has one pitfall. Although Excel assumes you're only changing a value, if you change the value in a way that suggests a new number format, Excel makes the number format change for you; for example, stick a dollar sign in front of a number, and Excel changes the Number format to Currency. However, when you make a change for which Excel can't deduce a new number format, the old format remains.

For example, if you replace a dollar value with "Shirley," the cell remains in Currency format. That's not a big deal—you'll still see "Shirley" in the cell. But in a complex worksheet, you could wind up with problems down the road. Be careful when you're changing the type of data in a cell, and when in doubt, check the number format in the Format Cells dialog.

Clearing Cells

To *clear* a cell—delete its contents—select it and press the Delete key. Note that clearing a cell in this way deletes the cell entry, but leaves the formatting—number format, font, and so on—in the cell, so that the next entry you put in the cleared cell takes on the formatting automatically.

To clear formatting, choose Edit|Clear to display the Clear submenu. Then choose from among the options you see there:

- *All*—Allows you to delete cell contents, formatting, and any attached comments.

- *Formats*—Allows you to delete cell formatting, but leave contents and comments intact.

- *Contents*—Allows you to delete cell contents, but leave formatting and comments intact.

- *Comments*—Allows you to delete any comments attached to selected cells, but leave the cells' contents and formatting intact.

Filling Cells Automatically

Excel features a handy capability called data *fills*. Using one or more entries you've already made in cells, fills can do two things:

- Copy the data from one cell into a series of cells in a row or column.

- Fill a row or column with cell entries that continue a *series*, a trend started by your entries in selected cells. For example, if you've filled two cells in a row with "January" and "February," respectively, Excel can automatically fill in the next 10 cells in the row with the remaining months of the year.

To make fills happen, you drag the *fill handle*, the tiny box that marks the lower right corner of a selected cell or block of cells. When you point to the fill handle, the pointer becomes a cross. Click and hold on the fill handle and drag, and you automatically fill the cells you drag across. As you drag along, a tiny box pops up at each cell to tell you what Excel will deposit in that cell. When you release the mouse button, the cell entries appear.

For example, to fill a row of cells to the right of a selected cell, click and hold the cell's fill handle, drag across the row to select as many cells as you wish, and release to fill the cells. To fill a column of cells beneath a selected cell, click and hold the cell's fill handle, drag down to select as many cells as you wish, and release.

What does Excel put in the cells? That depends on what's in the cell or cells whose fill handle you drag:

- To simply copy the contents of a cell into the other cells, select the cell and drag its fill handle (see Figure 12.8).

- To fill cells with data deduced from a series, begin by making at least two cell entries that establish the trend, then select those cells and drag the fill handle (see Figure 12.9). For example, if you fill the first cell with 2 and the next cell with 4, then select both cells and drag the fill pointer, Excel fills in the next cells with 6, 8, 10, 12, and so on.

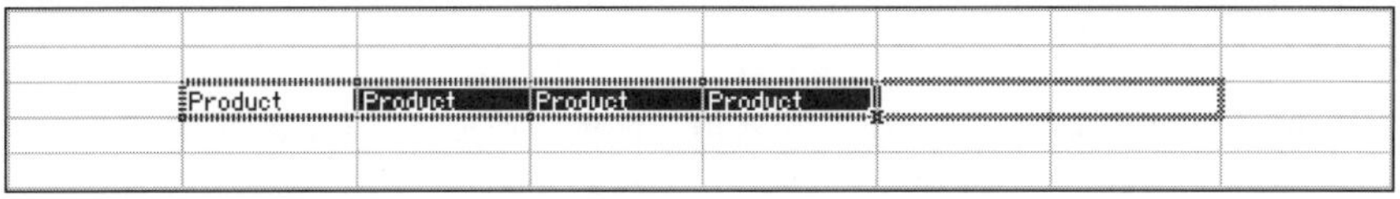

Adding Data, Formulas, And Functions   319

Figure 12.8 Drag a cell's fill handle to automatically fill cells with data copied from a selected cell.

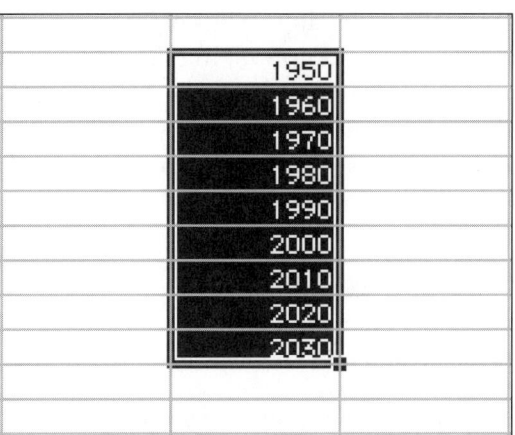

Figure 12.9 To fill cells with continued entries in a series, select two cells that establish a trend, then drag the fill handle.

Fast Track

When a cell entry is obviously part of a series—a month or day of the week, for example—you do not have to create or select two entries. For example, if you enter Monday in a cell, dragging that cell's fill handle automatically fills in successive days of the week.

To prevent Excel from following the series in such cases (when you just want to copy the data cell to cell), press and hold Control while dragging the fill handle. Watch out, though. This doesn't work the same way with numbers (see the next Fast Track section).

Excel is pretty smart about deducing the trends. For example, you can enter two dates a certain number of days apart, select them, and drag the fill handle to continue the trend. Also, note that Excel can extend a series in both directions. For example, suppose you enter "June" in a cell. You can drag the fill handle to the right or down to fill in July, August, and so on. But you can also drag the fill handle to the left or up to fill in May, April, March, and so on, all in their proper series positions.

Fast Track

If the trend you want to use for a fill is in increments of 1 (for example, 5, 6, 7...1998, 1999, 2000), you needn't set up two cells to establish the trend. Instead, fill in just one cell, press and hold the Option key, drag the fill handle, and release. Each cell in the fill increases by 1.

It's also possible for a cell to contain two bits of information that can be serialized. For example, your cell may read April-98. In this instance, you can easily tell Excel which part to serialize—the month or the year. As you drag the fill handle to select your range, hold down the Control key. When you release your selection, a contextual menu will appear. Simply select the data you wish to serialize by choosing the appropriate item—in this case, Fill Month or Fill Year.

Moving And Copying Data

Excel enables you to copy or move cell data from one cell to another easily, using the same toolbar buttons, menu items, and keystrokes that work in Word.

No matter whether you cut, copy, or move, you always begin by selecting the cell or cells you want to work with. With the cells selected, you can:

- *Copy the cells*—Click on the Copy button on the Standard toolbar; a marquee appears around the selected cells. Then point to the cell where you want the first cell (the top left cell of the selection) to appear, and click to select the cell. Click on the Paste button on the Standard toolbar to copy the cells.

- *Move the cells*—Click on the Cut button on the Standard toolbar; a marquee appears around the selected cells. Then point to the cell where you want the first cell to appear, and click to select the cell. Click on the Paste button on the Standard toolbar to copy the cells.

- *Cut the cells*—Choose Edit|Clear|All. The selected cells clear.

Fast Track

You can duplicate the actions of the Copy, Paste, and Cut buttons with menus or keystrokes. You can Copy with Edit|Copy or Cmd+C; Paste with Edit|Paste or Cmd+V; or Cut with Edit|Cut or Cmd+X.

You can copy and move cells not only within a worksheet, but also from worksheet to worksheet and from workbook to workbook, as well. The steps are exactly the same as the copy and move steps you just learned, except that after clicking on Copy (for copying) or Cut (for moving), you must switch from the current worksheet or workbook—the *source*—to the worksheet or workbook into which you want to paste—the *target*.

Adding Data, Formulas, And Functions   321

To move or copy cells to another workbook, begin by opening the source workbook. Without closing the source, open the target workbook—both workbooks are now open in Excel, although you see only one at a time. Choose Window, then select the source workbook from the Window menu to switch to it. Select the cells, then click on Copy (or Cut, to move). Choose Window, then select the target workbook from the menu to switch to it. Click on the tab for the worksheet to which you want to paste, select a cell, and paste.

Fast Track

When you move or copy a cell containing a formula, any cell addresses that are part of the formula may change to accommodate the cell's new position. To learn more, see "Working With Formulas and Functions" later in this chapter.

Undoing Mistakes

If you've followed this book from the beginning, you already know all about Undo, which fixes recent mistakes by undoing an action. But just in case you started with Excel, let us fill you in about Undo: When you click on Undo, the very last thing you did is undone, as if it had never happened. You'll find Undo (and its partner Redo) on Excel's Standard toolbar.

If you click on Undo immediately after performing some action to a selected block of cells, that block returns to its exact state before you performed the action and also remains selected, to make performing the desired action simple. For example, if you clear a block of cells, then click on Undo, the cell data is restored, and the cells remain highlighted—ready for the correct action.

If you undo something and then decide that you liked it better before you undid it, you can click on the Redo button, which reverses the action of Undo—restoring the effects of the action that you thought was a mistake. Note that Redo does nothing unless you've already used Undo—without an undo, there can't be a redo.

Spellchecking

Yes, we know—worksheets are about numbers, not spelling. Still, there's an awful lot of text in some worksheets, and worksheets may be incorporated as tables into company reports and other documents where a misspelling might be embarrassing. So why not make sure everything's spelled correctly?

Excel's spellchecker works exactly like Word's, except that Excel's lacks a grammar checker. (If you think your worksheet needs grammar checking, you're probably using the wrong program for what you're creating. Switch to Word.) Note that the spellchecker checks only one worksheet at a time; to check a whole workbook, you must spellcheck each of its worksheets individually.

To spellcheck a worksheet, first press Esc to make sure only one cell is selected. (If two or more cells are selected, the spellchecker checks only the selected cells, not the rest of the worksheet.) Then click on the Spelling button on the Excel toolbar. The spellchecker searches for words it doesn't recognize; when it finds one, the Spelling dialog (see Figure 12.10) opens, describing the error at the top of the dialog. Read the error carefully.

For each error found, you can deal with the error in several different ways:

- *Ignore/Ignore All*—If the word is actually correct (as it may be if it's just a name the spellchecker doesn't recognize), click on Ignore (to ignore just the current instance of the word) or Ignore All (to ignore the word throughout the worksheet).

- *Suggestions box*—If the word is incorrect, review the Suggestions box to see whether Excel has suggested a correct replacement. If so, click on the correct suggestion. If not, edit the word in the Change To box to correct it. After clicking on a suggestion or editing Change To, click on Change.

After you change or ignore an error, the spellchecker continues checking the worksheet until you have resolved all of the errors it finds.

Fast Track

Excel shares Word's AutoCorrect facility. AutoCorrect enables Excel to automatically fix a long list of the most common typing and spelling errors, particularly common capitalization errors. The changes are made automatically and instantly, as you type. If you type an entry, and it seems to change capitalization or spelling

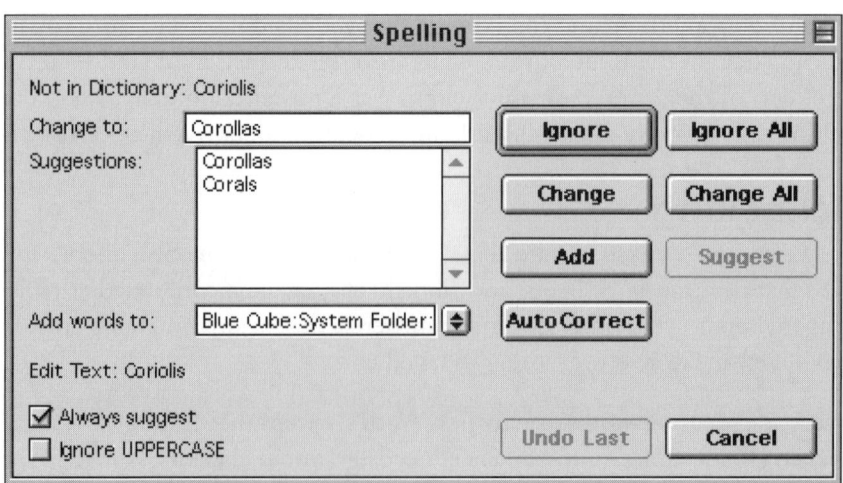

Figure 12.10 Use the Spelling dialog to check the spelling of your Excel worksheet.

all by itself, AutoCorrect is probably doing its thing (although you can attribute certain changes to automatic number formatting). To learn more about Auto-Correct, see Chapter 7.

Automatically Replacing Cell Entries

Excel features a no-nonsense Replace facility that works just like Word's, except that it has fewer options. Using Replace, you can quickly change all instances of a particular cell entry (or only selected instances) to a different entry. Like the spellchecker, Replace works on only a single worksheet at a time, not the whole workbook.

To use Replace, first press Esc to make sure only one cell is selected. (If two or more cells are selected, Replace does its thing only within the selection and ignores the rest of the worksheet.) Choose Edit|Replace to open the Replace dialog (see Figure 12.11). Click in the Find What box, and type the cell entry you want to replace. Then click in the Replace With box and type the replacement.

After making your Find What and Replace With entries, you have two options:

- Choose Find Next to locate the first instance of the Find What text. Replace moves to the first instance and highlights it in the document. You can then click on Replace (to replace the instance with the Replace With text and then move on to the next instance) or Find Next (to skip an instance of the Find What entry without replacing it).

- Choose Replace All to replace all instances of the Find What text with the Replace With text throughout the worksheet.

Also on Excel's Replace dialog, you can choose from the Search list to conduct the search By Rows (top to bottom) or By Columns (left to right). You can check the whole worksheet either way; the only difference between the two options is the order in which Excel locates and shows you the instances of the Find What entry.

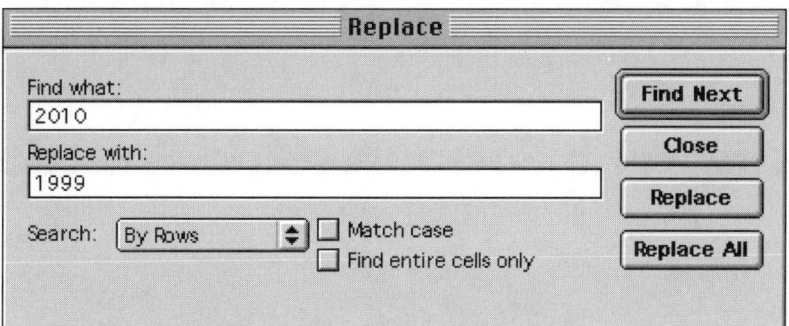

Figure 12.11 Choose Edit|Replace to find and replace specific data in a worksheet.

Walk-Through: Entering And Editing Data

Follow these steps to practice entering and editing cell data in Excel:

1. Open a new, blank document in Excel.
2. Click on Cell C3. Cell C3 is highlighted.
3. Type "Work Hours" and press Return. The words "Work Hours" are entered in the selected cell, and then Cell C4 is selected.
4. Type "40", and press Return. The number 40 is entered in the selected cell, and then Cell C5 is selected.
5. Repeat Step 4 four times, filling in four cells with any values you want and pressing Return after each entry.
6. Click on Cell B4 and type "Monday". Cell B4 is highlighted and "Monday" appears in the cell.
7. Point to Cell B4's fill handle, click on it, drag downward through Cell B8, and release. Cells B4 through B8 are filled with the days of the workweek.
8. Click on Cell D4, type a number value, and press Tab to finish. The number is entered in Cell D4, and then Cell E4 is selected.
9. Repeat Step 8 until you have filled through Cell G4.
10. Practice data entry by completing all rows of the table you have created. You can either work by rows, pressing Tab after each entry, or by columns, pressing Return.
11. Click on Cell C3 and press Delete to clear the cell. Cell C3 is empty.
12. In Cell C3, type "July 7", then press Tab. Your entry is reformatted to 7-Jul.
13. In Cell D3, type "July 14", then press Tab.
14. Click and hold on Cell C3, drag to Cell D3, and release. Cells C3 and D3 are selected.
15. On Cell D3, click and hold the fill handle, and drag to Cell G3. Rows E3 through G3 are filled with dates, each one week apart.
16. Save the workbook as Time Sheet.

Working With Formulas And Functions

Sometimes, you won't know what data belongs in a cell.

If you've entered a column of numbers, and at the bottom you want a total, you have to calculate the total in order to fill that bottom cell. Then, if even one number in the column changes later, you have to add up the column all over again. But if instead of calculating the total yourself, you enter in that bottom cell an Excel *formula* that calculates the total, Excel will come up with the correct number to display in that cell. More importantly, if any number in the column changes, Excel automatically recalculates the total, so the worksheet remains mathematically correct no matter how the cell values change. That little trick is what spreadsheet programs were born to do, and it's the main reason folks use 'em.

A formula is just an equation. A formula can be as simple as 2+2, or it can be a complex equation that borrows values from other cells, plugs them into the equation, and produces a result. You enter formulas in cells, just like data. But when you look at the worksheet (or print it), you don't see the formulas—you see only the results they produce. In a cell containing the Excel formula "=2+2", the cell appears to contain the value 4.

Complex formulas usually include *functions*. A function is a shorthand way to express a mathematical operation that would otherwise require a lengthy formula entry. For example, the function AVERAGE can calculate the average of a set of numbers in a fairly simple formula. Without the AVERAGE function, you'd have to calculate averages with a complicated formula containing three separate operations: adding up the numbers, counting the amount of numbers, then dividing.

Simple functions such as SUM or AVERAGE are handy, but they're kids' stuff compared to the functions Excel includes for performing sophisticated number-crunching, such as statistical standard deviations or payroll calculations.

Many functions work best when coupled with *cell ranges*. A cell range describes a whole block of cells with just a single address or name, so a function can act on all of those cells at once. For example, the SUM function coupled with a cell range produces a sum of all the numbers in cells in the range.

In the next few pages, you'll learn how to phrase and enter formulas in cells, and how to use functions and ranges within your formulas.

Fast Track

Formulas enable you to test "what if" scenarios in your worksheets. In a "what if" scenario, you change one or more values in a worksheet that contains formulas to determine what would happen if the values really changed. For example, in a worksheet that uses formulas to calculate loan payments, you could selectively change the values provided for interest rate, term, or loan amount. Each time you change a value, the payment changes, as well, based on the new data.

Entering Formulas

Quite simply, you enter a formula in a cell by typing an equation preceded by an equals sign (=). The equals sign tells Excel to perform the equation and show its result in the cell, rather than simply showing the equation itself in the cell.

Fast Track

Any time you begin a cell entry with an equals sign, the Name Box on the left end of the Formula bar is replaced by a drop-down list of functions, so you can easily use (and get help with) common functions in your formula. See "Entering Functions" later in this chapter.

Like all equations, formulas are made up of two basic parts:

- *Values*—The values you insert in a formula—sometimes called *operands*—can be actual numbers (*constants*) or cell addresses. (A cell address in a formula is called a *cell reference*.)

- *Operators*—Characters that represent mathematical operations, such as + (plus) or - (minus).

As you type a formula, it appears in the Formula bar and in the cell, just like any other cell entry (see Figure 12.12). When you press Tab or Return to record the entry and move to the next cell, the formula result appears in the cell.

You also edit a formula much as you would regular data:

- When you single-click on a cell containing a formula, the formula result remains in the cell, but the formula itself appears in the Formula bar. Click in the Formula bar to place the edit cursor there, then make any changes you wish.

- When you double-click on a cell containing a formula, the formula appears in the cell (replacing the result), along with the edit cursor. You can then make any changes directly in the cell.

After editing a formula in the Formula bar or the cell itself, press Tab or Return to record the changes and move on to the next cell. Using the edited formula, Excel instantly recalculates and displays the new result in the cell.

Figure 12.12 You enter a formula—always starting with an equals sign (=)—in the Formula bar like any other data.

Adding Data, Formulas, And Functions **327**

Fast Track

To see the result of a formula before pressing Tab or Return, click on the Edit Formula button on the Formula bar (the equals sign). The Formula palette appears, with the formula result at the bottom.

While you edit in the Formula bar, the Formula palette recalculates its display of the formula result every time you make even a small change—you do not need to press Return or Tab to see the results. You can fiddle with the formula until you see the results you want in the Formula palette, then press Return or Tab to record the formula in the cell and move on.

For more about the Formula palette, see "Entering Functions."

Phrasing A Formula

Except for putting the equals sign at the beginning rather than the end, you phrase a formula pretty much as you would write an equation. Excel supports the operators listed in Table 12.3. If you're not familiar with computer-based math symbols, a few operators may not be what you expect. For example, the handwritten × used for multiplication is replaced in Excel by the asterisk (*), and the traditional division sign (÷) is replaced by the forward slash (/).

Using Cell References

When you use a cell reference in a formula, Excel automatically calculates the result by plugging the cell's data into the formula. For example, suppose Cell E13 has the value 10 in it, and in Cell G14 you enter the formula:

=5*E13

The result that appears in Cell G14 would be 50. More importantly, if one day the value in E13 changed from 10 to 7, the result in G14 would instantly be recalculated to 35. That's the power of cell references in formulas; they give your worksheet the power to update itself as cell information changes.

Table 12.3 Formula operators in Excel.

Operator	Action	Simple Example	Result
+	Addition	=2+2+3	7
-	Subtraction	=95-D4	The difference between 95 and the value in Cell D4
*	Multiplication	=3*4*2	24
/	Division	=6/2	3
^	Exponentiation (power)	=9^2	81 (Nine to the second power)

Fast Track

To make the data from one cell appear in another, simply enter a formula made up of nothing but the equals sign and the cell address. For example, to show the value of Cell H18 in another cell, enter this formula in the desired cell:

=H18

The value in Cell H18 appears in the cell containing the formula. If the value in Cell H18 changes, so will the value in the cell containing the formula.

You can type cell references directly into a formula, or you can click on cells to plug in their references while typing the formula. Once you enter the equals sign to indicate that you're working on a formula, click on any cell to copy that cell's address into the Formula bar. For example, in the Formula bar, you could start the formula "=177/". Then, leaving the edit cursor at the end of the formula, point to a cell whose address you want to plug into the formula, and click. An animated dashed line appears around the cell, and the cell's address appears at the end of the formula.

FYI: They Said You'd Need Algebra One Day...

In addition to phrasing simple formulas of the type shown in Table 12.3—formulas involving a single operator—you can also phrase complex, multi-operator equations in formulas, such as:

=((8+16)/2)*(G2^3)   (Result: The value in Cell G2 cubed, times 12.)

This is not the place to give you a crash course in algebra, and we're not the ones to teach it. (Sorry, Mrs. Gray...Ned was distracted by the girl in the row behind him—and Brian's just plain crummy at math.) But suffice it to say that Excel follows the standard algebraic rules for expressing complex equations. Any operations enclosed in parentheses are performed first, from left to right. Then the results of those calculations are used in completing the operations outside the parentheses.

In addition to observing parentheses, Excel follows the standard algebraic rules for operator hierarchy. The operator hierarchy determines the order in which operations are performed (in the absence of parentheses). Following the operator hierarchy, Excel performs all *negation* (the making of a negative number) first, then any exponentiation. After that, it does all multiplication and division operations in the whole formula (left to right), then all addition and subtraction (left to right).

Keeping Formulas Accurate When Cells Move

When you move a cell containing a formula, the formula does not change—it remains the same, letter for letter, in its new location. However, when you copy a cell containing a formula, any cell references in the formula change automatically.

You see, Excel assumes you don't really want to display the same results of the same calculation involving the same cells in two different places. It figures that when you copy the formula, you want to perform the same operation, but on different cells. So Excel automatically changes any cell references so that, in the new cell, the new cell references have the same *relative position* to the new cell that the old cell references had to the original cell.

For example, suppose the formula in Cell C8 adds up the two cells above it: C7 and C6. The formula in C8 would be =C6+C7.

If you copy Cell C8 to Cell D8, the formula changes so that its cell references refer to the two cells above D8: D6+D7. These cells have the same relative position to Cell D8 that the cells in the original formula had to Cell C8. In both cases, the formula refers to the two cells directly above the cell holding the formula.

To prevent a cell reference from changing when a cell is copied, you must type it in the formula as an *absolute address*, which includes a dollar sign ($) before both parts of the address. For example, the cell reference D9 is an absolute reference to Cell D9; if used in a formula, the reference won't change if the cell is copied. You can also type partial absolute addresses, in which one part can change, but the other remains constant. If you enter G$4, the column described by cell reference (G) may change if the cell is copied, but the row always remains 4.

FYI: *Auditing Worksheets Containing Formulas*

Using cell references and *ranges*, you can use cell data within formulas. And by using cell references that refer to other cells containing formulas, you can create complex worksheets containing formulas that calculate results based on results of other formulas, which may themselves be based on the results of still *other* formulas.

Of course, when you create such a worksheet, it's easy to mess it up. When formulas are so interdependent, making one little change in your worksheet or in one formula can invalidate multiple formulas or cause them to deliver inaccurate results. To avoid this, you can examine the relationships between formulas and the cells they use with Excel's *auditing* tools. To use the auditing tools, open the worksheet you want to audit, then choose Tools|Auditing to display the Auditing submenu. From the submenu, you can choose among the important auditing tools, or choose Show Auditing Toolbar from the bottom of the submenu to display the Auditing toolbar, from which you can perform all auditing activities.

The most useful auditing tool is Trace Dependents, which shows you which cells are referenced in the formula—*dependents* of the formula. To trace dependents, click on the cell containing the formula, then choose Tools|Auditing|Trace Dependents or click on the Trace Dependents button on the Auditing toolbar. In the worksheet, blue *tracer arrows* point from the cell you clicked on to any dependents. (If the cell is producing an error, a red tracer arrow appears.) To jump from the cell containing the formula to one of its dependents to check or edit the dependent's contents, double-click on the tracer arrow.

Defining Cell Ranges

A *range* is a rectangular block of cells. You use ranges with functions to enable the function to work on many cells without having to enter individual references for each cell in the formula. A range may be a single cell, a row or column, or any combination of cells that forms a rectangular block.

Whereas the immediate use of ranges is to refer to blocks of cells in formulas, note that ranges have other uses. In Chapter 13, you'll learn the value of defining certain blocks of cells—for example, a discrete table within a worksheet, a column heading, and so on—as ranges so you can manipulate them more easily.

You can describe a range by the addresses of its upper left cell and lower right cell, separated by a colon (:). For example, the block of cells selected in Figure 12.13 can

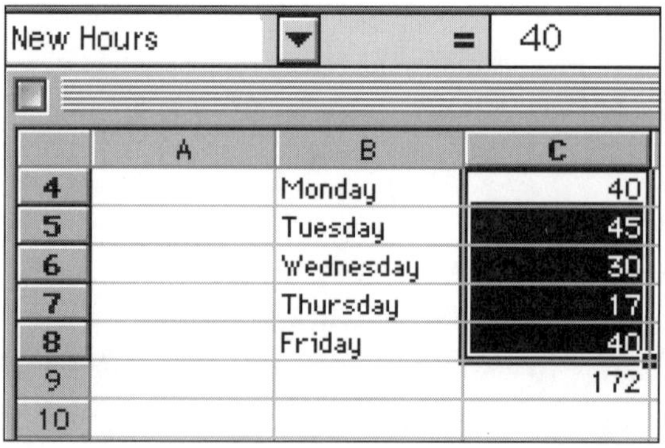

Figure 12.13 You can express a cell range with cell addresses or with a range name.

be described as C4:C8. But often, you'll find it more convenient to refer to a range by a name you have given it. When you give a name to a range and then use the name to refer to the range in a formula, the formula will still work properly even if you move the range to another area in the worksheet (the range's actual cell addresses change, but not its name).

To name a range, select the block of cells that make up the range. Click in the Name Box, which appears at the far left end of the Formula bar, and type a descriptive name for the range.

Fast Track

Just as you can enter a cell reference by clicking on a cell while editing a formula, you can also enter a cell range in a formula by selecting the range.

Position the edit cursor in the Formula bar at the point where you want to enter the cell range. In the worksheet, click and hold on the upper left cell of the desired range, drag to pull the animated dashed line until it surrounds the desired selection, and release. The cell range for the selection appears in the formula.

Entering Functions

A function is a quick way to perform a big operation in a formula. For example, consider a column of 10 numbers. You could put the column total in a cell by entering the formula:

=B3+B4+B5+B6+B7+B8+B9+B10+B11+B12

Or, using the SUM function and a range, you could get the same result by entering the formula:

=SUM(B3:B12)

Fast Track

In a function, you can refer to a cell range by name, if you have named it. For example:

=SUM(workhours)

A function includes two basic parts: the function name (SUM, COUNT, and so on) and its *arguments*, the values with which the function works (arguments appear in parentheses following the function name). In a formula, a function's arguments immediately follow the function name. For example, the following formula uses the

AVERAGE function to calculate the average of the following values (attributes): the numbers in Cell A5, all of the numbers in the range B2:C6, and the number 17:

=AVERAGE(A5,17,B2:C6)

While you're reviewing this example, observe three important facts about using functions:

- All arguments are enclosed within a set of parentheses.
- No spaces intrude within the function, its arguments, or the parentheses.
- Multiple arguments are separated from each other by commas.

Functions not only save time and effort in formula entry, but they also help those of us for whom algebra seems like neurosurgery. For example, when Brian wants a square root or a sample variance, he doesn't have to try to come up with the correct algebraic formula. Instead, he can just use the SQRT or VAR function, and let Excel worry about the math. (Of course, Brian never really wants a square root or sample variance—no one does. But he enjoys knowing Excel could give him one, in a pinch.)

Table 12.4 describes some of the more commonly used functions and their actions. Note that the values required by arguments for all functions in Table 12.4 may be supplied in either of two ways:

- The value may be typed directly into the formula; for example, =SQRT(81)
- The value may reside in a cell for which a reference is provided; for example, =SQRT(E15)

Table 12.4 Commonly used functions.

Function	Action
SUM	Computes the total of the argument values.
PRODUCT	Multiplies all arguments together.
AVERAGE	Computes the average of the argument values.
COUNT	Counts the number of numerical arguments (the number of numbers).
MAX	Shows the highest value among the arguments.
MIN	Shows the lowest value among the arguments.
SQRT	Computes the square root of its arguments.

Fast Track

Because SUM is such a commonly used function, Excel provides a quick way to use it. Select the cell in which you want the SUM to appear, then click on the AutoSum button on the Standard toolbar.

Excel guesses which cells you want to sum, and selects them. For example, if the current cell is at the bottom of a column of numbers, Excel assumes you want to sum the cells in the column and selects them. If Excel's guess is correct, press Return. If Excel's guess is wrong, select the cells you want to sum, then press Return. Either way, Excel pastes the SUM function into the cell and uses references to the selected cells as SUM's arguments.

Besides the functions described in Table 12.4, Excel offers many more, including some that don't really calculate anything, but rather display something special in the cell containing the formula. For example, the NOW function displays the current date and time and the TODAY function shows the current date only. These two functions require no arguments—you follow each with empty parentheses. For example, all you need to enter to display the current date and time in a cell is "NOW()".

There are many, many more functions, some designed for performing advanced engineering, financial, or statistical calculations. You phrase these just like you do any other function; the only trick is that you must understand something about the function's purpose in order to supply the necessary arguments. For example, the DB function calculates asset depreciation, and requires the following among its arguments: cost, salvage, life, and period. If you don't have the necessary financial background to know what those arguments represent, you can't phrase the function so that it delivers the proper result.

One way to get help with entering functions is to use the Formula palette (see Figure 12.14). As soon as you enter an equals sign in the Formula bar to start a formula, the Name Box changes to a drop-down list of commonly used functions. Choose any function from the list, and two things happen:

- The function (but not its arguments) appears in the Formula bar.
- The Formula palette drops down to help you phrase the arguments.

The Formula palette looks different for each function. At the very top of the palette, the name of the function you're working on appears (in Figure 12.14, we're working on the COUNT function). Beneath the name, one or more text boxes appear in

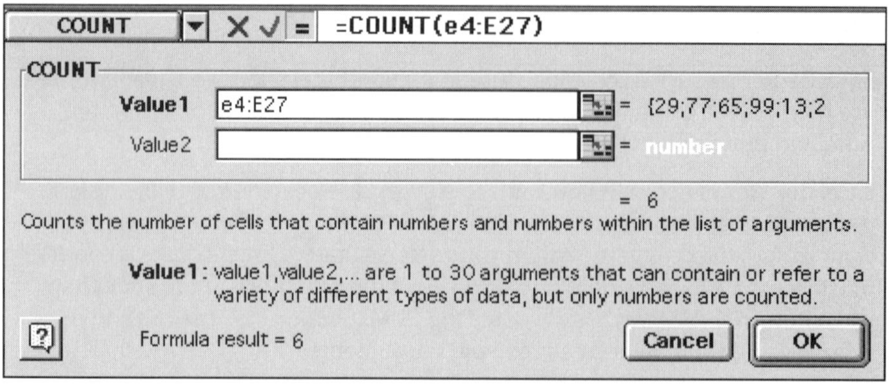

Figure 12.14 The Formula palette helps you enter your arguments.

which you can type your arguments. Also on the palette, you'll find instructions for phrasing the arguments, and at the very bottom of the palette, the result of the current formula appears. Following the instructions in the dialog, enter your arguments in the boxes provided, then click on OK. The arguments appear properly phrased with the function in the Formula bar.

Net Savvy

Besides helping you phrase formulas, the Formula palette also helps you insert *hyperlinks* into cells. A hyperlink in a cell, when clicked on by the viewer, opens a Web page. To learn more about adding active hyperlinks to Office documents, see Chapter 17.

If you drop down the Formula bar's list of functions and don't see the one you want, choose More Functions from the bottom of the list to open the Paste Function dialog (see Figure 12.15). You can also open the Paste Function dialog by clicking on the Paste Function button on the Standard toolbar or by choosing Insert|Function.

In the Paste Function dialog, choose a Function Category from the list, then choose a Function Name. A description of the function you've chosen appears at the bottom of the dialog. Click on OK to paste the Function Name into the Formula bar and begin supplying your arguments in the Formula palette or Formula bar.

Walk-Through: Ranges, Formulas, And Functions

Follow these steps to practice entering formulas and functions in Excel. If you have not yet performed the first Walk-Through in this chapter, do so first.

1. Open the workbook Time Sheet.

2. Click on Cell C9, then click on the AutoSum button on the Standard toolbar. An animated border surrounds the range C4:C8 to indicate that the values in that range will be summed.
3. Press Return. The sum of Cells C4:C8 appears in Cell C9.
4. Click on Cell C9 and look at the Formula bar to see the formula you created with AutoSum.
5. With C9 still selected, click on the Copy button on the Standard toolbar.
6. Click on Cell D9, then click on the Paste button on the Standard toolbar. The formula in C9 is copied to D9, with the cell references changed so that the formula now sums the range D4:D8.
7. Repeat Step 6 in Cells E9, F9, and G9.
8. Click and hold on Cell C9, drag to Cell G9, and release to select the range C9:G9.
9. Click in the Name Box on the Formula bar and type "WeekHours". The range C9:G9 is named "WeekHours."
10. Click on Cell G11 and enter "Total Hours Worked, Jul 7 - Aug 4".
11. Click on Cell G12, type "=SUM(WeekHours)", and press Return. The sum of Cells C9:G9—which are themselves column totals—appears in Cell G12.
12. Click and hold on Cell C4, drag to Cell G8, and release to select the range C4:G8.
13. Click in the Name Box on the Formula bar and type "DayHours". The range C4:G8 is named "DayHours."
14. Click on Cell G14 and enter "Average Hours Per Day, Jul 7 - Aug 4".
15. Click on Cell G15, then type "=AVERAGE(DayHours)" and press Return. The average of all of the values in C4:G8 appears in Cell G15.
16. Click on Cell G17 and enter "Longest Day Worked".
17. Click on Cell G18, then type "=MAX(DayHours)" and press Return. The highest value in C4:G8 appears in Cell G18.
18. Double-click in any cell within the DayHours range, change the value, and press Return. Everything is recalculated based on the new data. The column total changes, as do the total hours and daily average.
19. Save the worksheet.

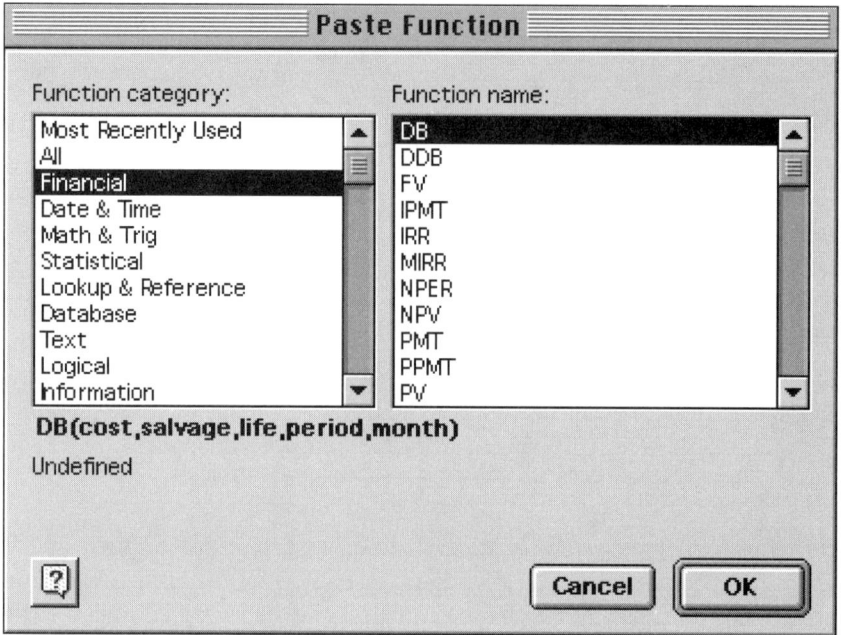

Figure 12.15 Choose from among many advanced functions on the Paste Function dialog.

Moving On

A cell, as you well know by now, is more than just a simple repository for a word or number—though it is that, too. A cell is a point of activity, a single container in which data resides, equations are performed by formulas and functions, and data is culled from other cells. In this chapter, you learned how to do all of these things in cells, and how to manage your entries with fills, spellchecking, Cut and Paste, and Replace.

Believe it or not, you've crossed the threshold. What you just survived is really the hardest part about using Excel—the rest is cake. In Chapter 13, you'll learn how to make your worksheet pretty, which mostly involves techniques that you probably already know from your experience with Word. (If you haven't already explored Word, don't worry—formatting a worksheet is easy in any case.) Give your logical side a rest, wake up your artistic side (some tea and good music helps), and move ahead to Chapter 13.

13

Formatting Workbooks

In Word and PowerPoint, content and style are one and the same—*how* you say something in either of those programs is usually as important as *what* you say (sometimes more so). But in Excel users often don't pay much attention to form. Many people use Excel simply to record information and produce calculations and analyses from that information, never worrying about the appearance as long as the results come out correctly. The worksheet is intended only to serve information to its user, not to communicate to someone else, and thus most formatting falls into the "optional" category.

Of course, Excel is not limited to such purely functional approaches. You can do a lot to dress up a worksheet, from controlling the page layout to adding headers and footers, choosing fonts, and even adding pictures—all of which you'll learn to do in this chapter. But perhaps because Microsoft recognizes that Excel users may be more attuned to data than to decoration, the formatting features in Excel are somewhat more limited than those in Word or PowerPoint. However, unless your formatting needs are extravagant, you'll probably find that Excel has all of the formatting capabilities you require. And unlike Word and PowerPoint, Excel's scaled-down ambitions keep its formatting features relatively easy to access and apply.

However, if you find that Excel does not provide you with sufficient formatting control to produce the type of document you want, then you should consider trying another tactic. Namely, think of Excel not as the program for producing your document, but as the medium for serving data or tables to another Office program, such as Word. Using Office's advanced integration capabilities (see Chapter 16), you can easily incorporate Excel data, tables, and charts (including formula results) into a Word document, where you can then format the stuff 'til the cows come home.

FYI: Templates And Formatting

If you use a template to create a new document (see Chapter 11), you won't need most of the stuff in this chapter—at first. Your template-based document comes with all of the formatting it needs.

However, as you work, you may decide that you want to change that formatting. More important, when you edit the data in a worksheet, you always run the risk of inadvertently changing the formatting. In either case, using a template is no replacement for knowing how to apply formatting in worksheets and cells—or how to fix formatting when Murphy's Law kicks in.

Fast Table Formatting With AutoFormat

Excel comes with a family of built-in *table formats*, which you can apply in a snap through the AutoFormat dialog. In a single step, AutoFormat applies all of the different types of cell formatting you'll learn to apply as this chapter progresses, including fonts, cell borders and shading, alignment, and more.

To format a table with AutoFormat, select the whole table, including any row or column headings. Choose Format|AutoFormat to open the AutoFormat dialog (see Figure 13.1). In the dialog, the list on the left shows the available table formats, and the Sample pane on the right shows you a sample of each type of formatting. Don't worry if the sample does not match your table in its organization, use of headings, and so on—the sample represents the *style* in which your table will appear, not its content or organization, which AutoFormat leaves alone.

Click on any table format to see its sample, and consider whether you like the way it looks. When you like what you see in the sample, click on OK.

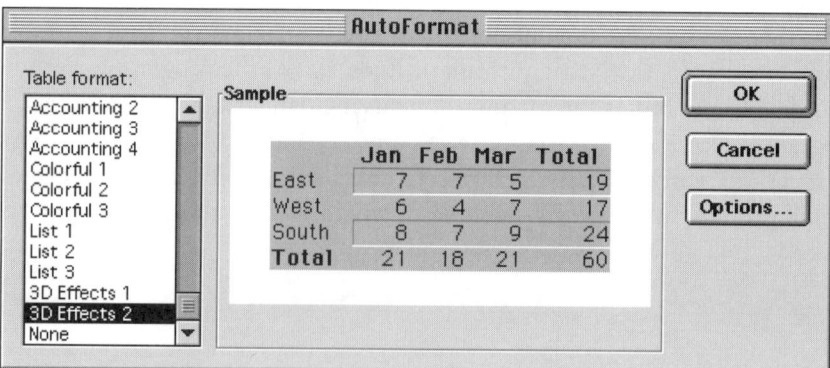

Figure 13.1 Choose a table format in the AutoFormat dialog to instantly format a block of cells.

If none of the table formats in the AutoFormat dialog is exactly what you had in mind, select a table format that is close to what you want, then do either (or both) of the following:

- Click on the Options button on the AutoFormat dialog to display the checkboxes at the bottom of the dialog (see Figure 13.2). The checkboxes list the six kinds of formatting you can have AutoFormat apply. Clear the checkbox for any formatting you don't want (the Sample pane changes to show the results).

- Go ahead and apply the table format that's closest to what you want, then fine-tune any formatting you wish, using the techniques you'll discover throughout the remainder of this chapter.

Formatting A Worksheet

You can apply to the data in cells many of the text-formatting options you may be familiar with from Word or PowerPoint, including selecting the font and font size, text attributes (such as bold, italic, or underlining), and more.

But unlike Word and PowerPoint, you usually begin not by selecting the data *per se*, but by selecting the cells containing the data. In Excel, formatting is attached to cells. Apply formatting to a cell, and you format the cell's contents. Apply formatting to an empty cell, and whatever you type in the cell takes on the formatting.

In the next few pages, you'll learn how to apply formatting to cells with the Formatting toolbar; you'll also learn about applying advanced formatting through the Format Cells dialog.

Using The Formatting Toolbar

You can accomplish most common formatting jobs with the buttons on Excel's Formatting toolbar (see Figure 13.3). If you don't see the Formatting toolbar, choose View|Toolbars, then click on Formatting.

To apply formatting from the toolbar, select the cells you want to format, then click on the desired button on the Formatting toolbar:

- *Font, Font Size*—Drop down the Font list to select a font (typeface) for the cell data, and drop down the Font Size list to choose the size of the type.

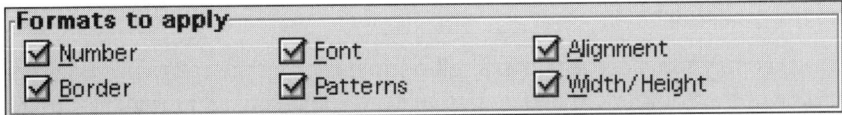

Figure 13.2 Click on Options on the AutoFormat dialog to display these checkboxes, which list the kinds of formatting that AutoFormat can apply.

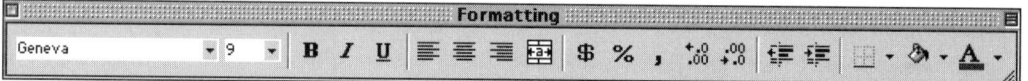

Figure 13.3 Take care of most cell formatting quickly with Excel's Formatting toolbar.

- *Bold, Italic, Underline*—Click on an attribute button (Bold, Italic, Underline) to apply a text attribute to the data. To remove attribute formatting, click on the button again.

- *Left, Right, Center*—Click on an alignment button (Left, Right, Center) to choose the horizontal alignment of the data. You can align data to the left side of the cell, to the right side of the cell, or center the data within the cell.

- *Merge And Center*—Select two or more cells and click on the Merge And Center button to combine the cells into one large cell and center the contents within. Note that if more than one of the cells you select has data in it, all data is lost except for the data in the top left cell of the selection.

- *Number Styles*—Click on any of the number styles (Currency, Percent, Comma, and so on) to change the number format of the data or the format's presentation style (see Chapter 12).

- *Indents*—Click on these buttons to increase or decrease the level of indention for your selected data within the cell.

- *Borders*—Click on the arrow on the Borders button to drop down a panel of options, each of which applies a border to one or more sides of the selected cells. The gridlines you see on your worksheet do not print; if you want borders to appear around tables or gridlines to appear within, you need to create those lines by applying borders.

- *Color*—Click on the Fill Color button to fill selected cells with a color, or click on the Font Color button to set the data in the cell in color. Note that each of these buttons has an arrow you can click on to drop down a list of colors.

Fast Track

You can apply Font, Font Size, attributes (Bold, Italic, Underline), and Font Color to a whole cell, or you can apply them to only a selected portion of the data within a cell. For example, if a cell contains two words, you can make one bold and the other not bold.

To format only some of the text in a cell, double-click on the cell to position the edit cursor there. Click, hold, and drag to select the characters you want to format, then apply the formatting from the toolbar.

Using The Format Cells Dialog

To apply advanced formatting options not available on the Formatting toolbar, select the cells to format, then choose Format|Cells. The Format Cells dialog opens. By choosing from among options on the dialog's tabs, you can apply any of the formatting available on the toolbar, and much more.

For example, on the Format Cells dialog's Alignment tab (see Figure 13.4), you can choose not only the horizontal alignment options available on the Formatting toolbar (Left, Center, Right), but also the *vertical* alignment of data within the cell, its position between the top and bottom of the cell. By choosing from the Vertical list, you can make the data rest at the bottom of the cell (Bottom), hang from the top of the cell (Top), or hover in the center (Center). Also on the Alignment tab, you can tilt data at any angle using the Orientation controls. Click on any point along the Orientation scale to tilt the data in all selected cells. This is a great way to create slanted column headings (see Figure 13.5).

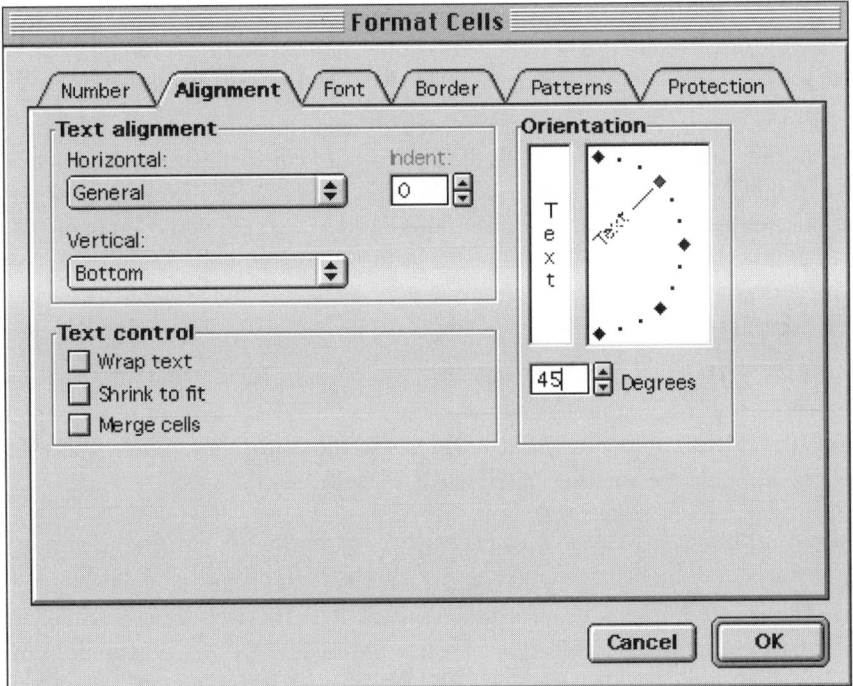

Figure 13.4 Choose advanced alignment options from the Format Cells dialog's Alignment tab.

Figure 13.5 The Alignment tab's Orientation scale enables you to tilt text to any angle.

On the Border tab (see Figure 13.6), click on any of the Preset buttons or the various individual Border buttons to add border lines around cells. For example, you can use the Outline border to draw a box around a block of cells, or click on both Outline and Inside to display a box around the block of cells and display the gridlines in between cells. (This is a good way to create a boxed table with gridlines inside.) You can also add and remove border lines by clicking on the sample in the center of the dialog in any spot where you want to add or delete a line. To change the line style of a border line, choose a Style from the list on the tab, then add the border line.

Finally, you can use the Patterns tab (see Figure 13.7) to fill in selected cells with color, a pattern, or both. To fill with a color, click on one of the color squares on the tab. To fill with a pattern, choose from the Pattern list. Dark colors and patterns can obscure text, so make sure you can still read the data in the cells through the color or pattern, especially after printing the worksheet.

Fast Track

Like Word, Excel features a Format Painter button on its Standard toolbar that lets you easily copy formatting from one cell or block of cells to another.

To use the Format Painter, format a cell or cells using any of the options on the Formatting toolbar or Format Cells dialog. Select the formatted cells and click on the Format Painter button (a little paintbrush is added to your Excel cell pointer to indicate that you're copying formatting). Point to the cells you want to format, then select them to copy the formatting from your previous selection.

Using Styles

A *style* is a prefab cell format, a way to apply number formatting and text formatting with a single operation. When you create a new document from a template, the template typically applies a variety of styles in the document. The regular blank Excel workbook also includes a few basic styles.

You can apply and modify a worksheet's styles from the Style dialog. Begin by selecting any cells to which you want to apply a style, then choose Format|Style. On the Style dialog (see Figure 13.8), the boxes under Style Includes describe all of the types of formatting. Choose a style from the list and review the Style Includes box to verify that the style applies the formatting you want. Click on OK to apply the style to the selected cells.

Working With Worksheets

You can add worksheets to a workbook or take them away. If you have used an earlier version of Excel, note that Excel 98 eliminates the old limit of 16 worksheets per workbook; you can include as many worksheets as available memory permits.

Formatting Workbooks 343

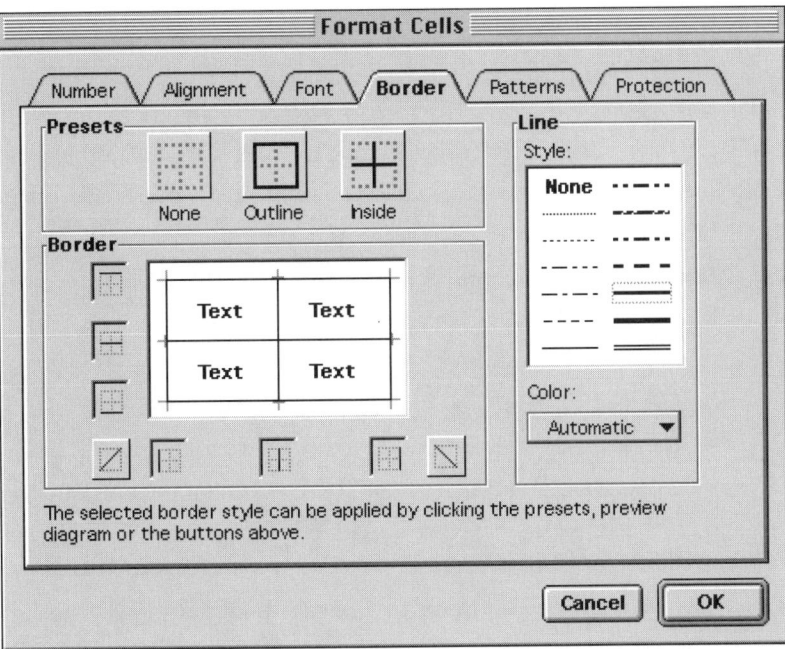

Figure 13.6 Use the Border tab to show boxes around cells (and blocks of cells), and gridlines in tables.

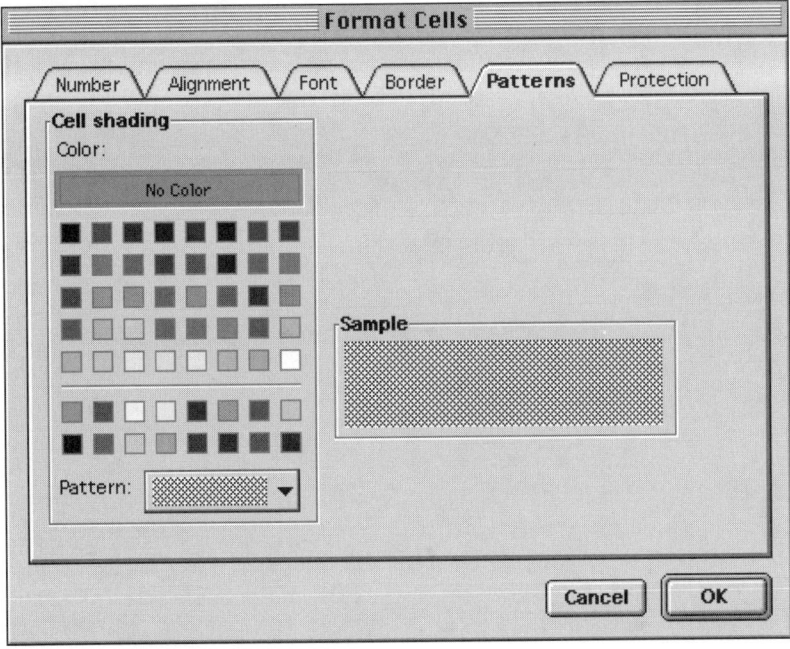

Figure 13.7 On the Patterns tab, choose a color square, a pattern, or both to shade a cell or block of cells.

Walk-Through: Cell Formatting

Follow the steps below to practice formatting cells. Note that this walk-through uses Time Sheet, a simple table created in Chapter 12. If you have not yet created Time Sheet, you might want to go back now and create this file before performing this walk-through.

1. Open the workbook Time Sheet.
2. Select the cell range B3:G9. The entire table is selected.
3. Choose Format|AutoFormat. The AutoFormat dialog opens.
4. From the list of Table formats, click on Colorful 1, then click on OK. The table is attractively reformatted.
5. Select Cells B4:B8 and click on the Bold button on the Formatting toolbar. The bold formatting is removed from the row headings.
6. Select Cells C3:G3.
7. On the Formatting toolbar, drop down the Font list and choose Garamond (or the typeface of your choice). The column headings are reset in Garamond, or the face you selected.
8. With Cells C3:G3 still selected, choose Format|Cells.
9. On the Alignment tab, click on the Orientation scale at the 2:00 position (45 degrees), then click on OK. The column headings are tilted by 45 degrees.
10. Save the worksheet.

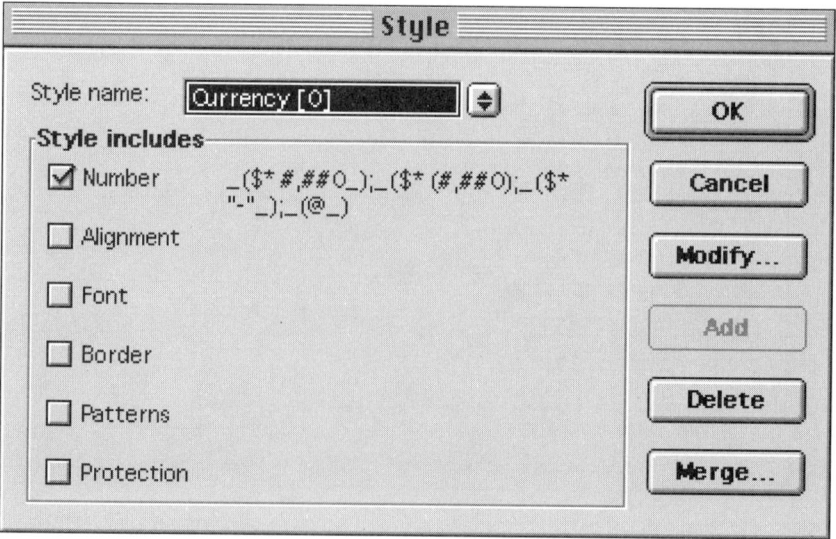

Figure 13.8 Choose Format|Style to format selected cells with a prebuilt style.

Formatting Workbooks 345

Sometimes working with worksheets requires that you first select one or more worksheets so that what you do next will be applied to the sheet or sheets you want to affect. While you're viewing a worksheet, it is selected—so the easiest way to select a single worksheet is to open it by clicking on its tab. To select multiple sheets, hold down the Command key while clicking on the tabs of any sheets you want to select. Each tab you click on changes color to indicate that you have selected the sheet.

FYI: Watch Out For Advanced Formulas

In Excel formulas (see Chapter 12), you can use cell references from worksheets and workbooks other than the one that contains the formula. This gives you the ability, for example, to calculate and display a total of subtotals that appear on multiple worksheets or to total up values from multiple workbooks.

Using cell references from other worksheets is not difficult to learn in and of itself. But doing so is necessary only in fairly elaborate projects, and it also opens a Pandora's box of advanced complications that exceed the scope of this book. For both reasons, we have not covered such cell references in this book.

However, if you've taken it upon yourself to learn this technique on your own, we must warn you about several possible perils where these cell references are concerned. Changing worksheet names, deleting worksheets, copying worksheets within a workbook, and moving or copying worksheets from one workbook to another are all very likely to foul up cell references that point beyond the worksheet in which the formula appears.

What to do? Here are a few suggestions:

- Enter your formulas last, after doing all of your naming, moving, copying, and other workbook manipulation.
- If you move, copy, rename, or delete any worksheet after phrasing your formulas, recheck your formulas carefully. (Excel's Auditing tools can help you make sure your formulas work properly.)

Naming A Worksheet

You have to give names to your workbooks, because files needs names. You're not obliged to name your worksheets—the defaults, Sheet1, Sheet2, and so on work fine—but in a workbook containing many worksheets, you may have trouble remembering what's on each sheet. In such cases you can give your worksheets descriptive names (see Figure 13.9) to help you quickly locate the sheet you want.

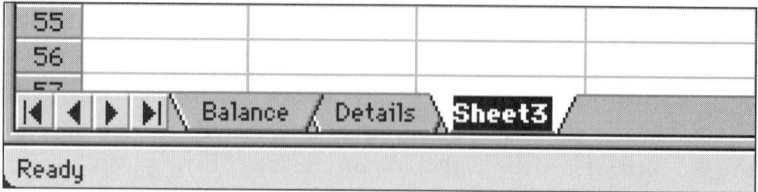

Figure 13.9 Double-click on a worksheet's tab to type a name for the worksheet.

To name a worksheet, double-click on its tab. The current name is highlighted, and whatever you type next replaces that name. Note that you can use any name you want to, but names must be unique—you cannot give any two sheets in a workbook the exact same name.

Inserting A New Worksheet

If you need a new worksheet in your workbook, and that worksheet contains content or formatting that's similar to another worksheet you've already worked on, you'll save yourself some time if you create the new worksheet by copying the existing one (see "Copying A Worksheet" later in this chapter).

However, when all you want to do is insert a new, blank worksheet, begin by selecting the worksheet you want the new sheet to go on top of in the stack. (In other words, when you insert a new worksheet, the sheet is inserted on top of the current sheet so that its tab appears to the left of the tab for the current sheet.) Don't worry if you insert the sheet in the wrong place; you can always delete it and try again.

To insert the worksheet, choose Insert|Worksheet. The worksheet appears and is automatically given a "Sheet" name. The number in the Sheet name will be one higher than the total number of sheets in the workbook; for example, if there are five sheets in a workbook, and you add a new one, the new sheet will be named Sheet6, regardless of what the other sheets are named. After inserting the new worksheet, you can rename it.

Fast Track

Instead of inserting a new blank sheet, you can insert a sheet based on any template to take advantage of that template's built-in content or formatting. To insert a new sheet based on a template, Control-click on a sheet tab in your worksheet, then choose Insert from the contextual menu that appears. The Insert dialog opens, showing the contents of your Templates folder. Choose a template to insert the sheet.

Deleting A Worksheet

You can delete any worksheets in a workbook, as long as you leave at least one—Excel will not permit you to delete all sheets in a book. (And why would you want to?) Keep in mind, though, that deleting worksheets is rarely necessary. When a workbook will be printed, you can easily prevent the printing of any extraneous sheets in the book, so there's no need to delete them. However, you may want to delete extra worksheets from workbooks you will present online, so that they don't confuse or distract viewers.

To delete worksheets, select all the worksheets you want to delete, then choose Edit|Delete Sheet. A message like the one in Figure 13.10 appears. The message is meant to protect you from accidentally deleting a sheet that contains valuable data (although the message still appears when you're just deleting blank sheets). Be very careful when you're deleting sheets that contain data, because Undo cannot restore a deleted worksheet—when it's gone, it's gone. (You have a measure of recourse by closing the document without saving, but then you lose any other work you've done.)

To confirm that you want to delete the sheet or sheets, click on OK.

Moving A Worksheet

Within a workbook, you can move any worksheet from one position within the stack to any other. The easiest way to do that is to drag the sheet from its current position and drop it in its new position. Note that moving a sheet has no effect on its name, content, or formatting.

Click and hold on the tab for the sheet you want to move, then drag it to its new position. Note that as you drag, you'll see the following:

- A little page icon follows along the drag, just to show you that you're moving a sheet.

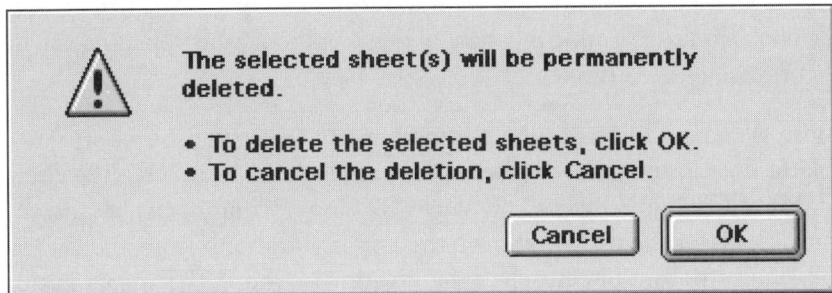

Figure 13.10 Excel checks with you before deleting a worksheet.

- A tiny black arrow pops up at each point where you drag between two sheets. The arrow shows you exactly where your sheet will be positioned if you release the mouse button.

When the tiny arrow appears between the sheets at the point where you want to move the worksheet, release the mouse button.

Copying A Worksheet

Within a workbook, you can copy a worksheet to create a new worksheet based on the content and formatting of an existing one. That's a great time saver when you have several similar worksheets within a workbook. After you make a copy, you can edit a copied sheet any way you like, with no effect on the original (and vice versa).

To copy a worksheet, point to the sheet you want to copy. Press and hold the Option key, then click and hold on the worksheet and drag it to the spot in the stack of worksheets where you want to position the copy. Release the mouse button, then release the Option key. Excel gives the copied sheet the same name as the original worksheet, but it's followed by a number in parentheses to indicate it's a copy. For example, the first copy you make of a worksheet named Balance is named Balance(2); if you make another copy, it's named Balance(3). You can change the copy names any way you wish.

Moving And Copying Between Workbooks

To move or copy a worksheet from one workbook to another, use the Move Or Copy dialog. Note that the dialog can also be used to move or copy worksheets within a workbook, but drag and drop is easier for that purpose.

To move or copy worksheets from one workbook to another, begin by opening both workbooks—the *source* workbook (the one you want to copy a worksheet from), and the *target* workbook (the one you want to move or copy to). You can open two work-books in Excel simply by opening one workbook, then opening the next without closing the first one.

Choose Window, and from the Window menu select the source workbook. Click on the tab for the worksheet you want to copy or move, then choose Edit|Move Or Copy Sheet. The Move Or Copy dialog opens, as shown in Figure 13.11. In the dialog, choose the target workbook from the list under To Book. Under Before Sheet, select the position—among the sheets in the target workbook—to which you want the worksheet moved or copied. If you want to copy rather than move the worksheet, check the Create A Copy checkbox at the bottom of the dialog.

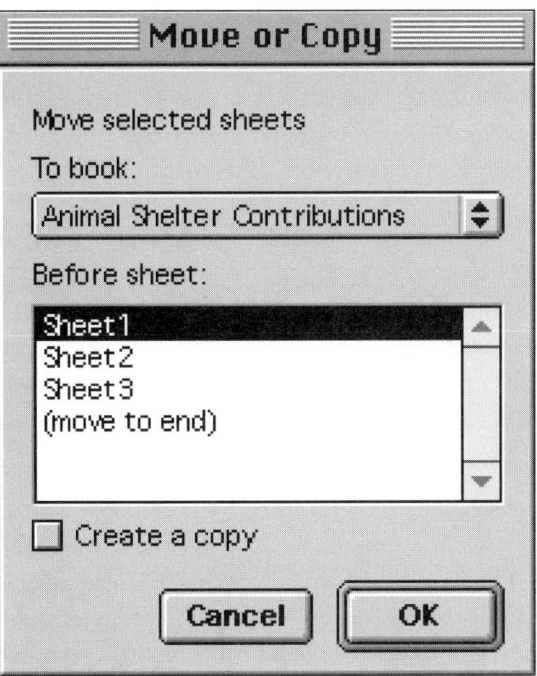

Figure 13.11 Open two workbooks, then choose Edit|Move Or Copy Sheet to move or copy sheets between workbooks.

When you've finished making selections in the Move Or Copy dialog, click on OK. The worksheet appears in the target workbook at the position you chose. Its name is the same as it was in the source workbook, but you can change the name in either workbook, or both.

Fast Track

You can move or copy sheets between workbooks quickly using drag and drop and the contextual menu. To copy a sheet, open both workbooks and drag the desired sheet by its tab from one workbook into the other. You can also access the Move Or Copy dialog, just as you did above, by Control-clicking on the source worksheet's name tab, then selecting Move Or Copy from the contextual menu.

Inserting And Deleting Rows, Columns, And Cells

Ideally, you will enter and position your cell data so that you never need to add or delete new rows, columns, or cells within a worksheet. But after working awhile on a worksheet, you may discover, for example, that you need to add a row or column to the middle of a table. Or you may decide that some elements on the sheet appear too close together or too far apart.

When there's not much data on the sheet, you can often solve such problems simply by selecting and moving blocks of cells, as you learned to do in Chapter 11. But when there's already a lot of data on the sheet, you may find it easier to insert or delete cells to solve your problem. When you insert cells, you push existing cells to the right or down, to make room for the insertion. That often changes the position—and thus the cell address—of other data in the sheet.

Inserting Cells

When inserting a cell, row, or column, you always begin by selecting one cell to determine where the new row, column, or cell will appear. The cell you choose—and all cells to the right or under it—will shift to the right or down to accommodate the new cell, row, or column. Here's a quick look at how to insert cells, rows and columns:

- *Cell*—To insert a cell, begin by selecting the cell that will appear to the right of, or under, the new cell. Then choose Insert|Cells to open the Insert dialog (see Figure 13.12). Click on Shift Cells Right to push the selected cell and the rest of its row to the right to make room for the new cell, or choose Shift Cells Down to push the selected cell and the rest of its column down. Click on OK to make the insertion.

- *Row*—To insert a row, begin by selecting any cell in the row that will appear under the new row. Choose Insert|Row, or choose Insert Cells and choose Entire Row from the Insert dialog.

- *Column*—To insert a column, begin by selecting any cell in the column that will appear to the right of the new column. Choose Insert|Column, or choose Insert Cells and choose Entire Column from the Insert dialog.

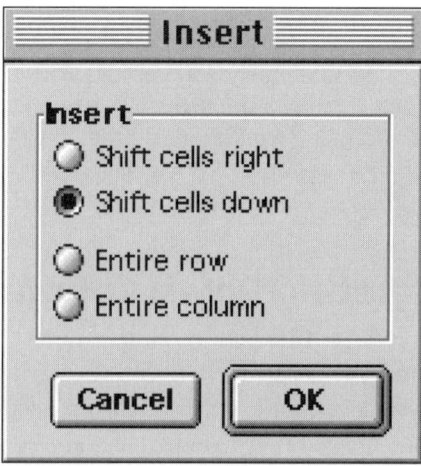

Figure 13.12 Add cells, rows, or columns with the Insert dialog.

Formatting Workbooks 351

Fast Track

You can also use contextual menus to insert cells. To insert a cell, Control-click on the cell adjacent on the right to where you want your new cell and choose Insert from the contextual menu to open the Insert dialog. To insert a row or column, Control-click on the row heading or column heading of the "following" row or column, then click on Insert on the contextual menu.

FYI: Insertions May Scramble Formulas

Inserting or deleting rows, columns, or cells usually changes the cell address of other data in the row or column where you made the insertion. If you've used formulas in your worksheet that contain cell references to that data (see Chapter 12), there's a chance that the references may be invalidated. If the cell references are wrong, the result of your formula will be, too—if it can produce a result at all.

If you've used only *relative* cell references in your formulas, there's a good chance that Excel will successfully adjust the references so that the formula still works properly after you make insertions or deletions—but that's not guaranteed. If you've used absolute addresses, they're very likely to be scrambled by insertions and deletions.

To prevent this problem, try to wait to enter your formulas until you're fairly sure you won't have to insert or delete cells. Any time you do insert or delete cells in a worksheet that contains formulas, check the formulas carefully. In a worksheet with complex formulas, Excel's Auditing tools can be a big help with testing and fixing formulas.

Deleting Cells

Before deleting anything, it's important to understand the essential difference between *clearing* cells, which you learned to do in Chapter 11, and *deleting* cells:

- Clearing a cell empties the data (and/or formatting) from the cell, but leaves the cell in place, and does not affect the position of other cells or data.

- Deleting a cell removes not only the cell's contents (if it has any), but also yanks the cell itself from the grid—like a brick from a wall—so that other cells must shift left or up to fill the gap.

To delete cells, begin by selecting the cell or cells you want to delete. (If you intend to delete an entire worksheet row or column, you need to select only one cell in the row or column you wish to delete.) Choose Edit|Delete to open the Delete dialog (see Figure 13.13). On the dialog, you have several options:

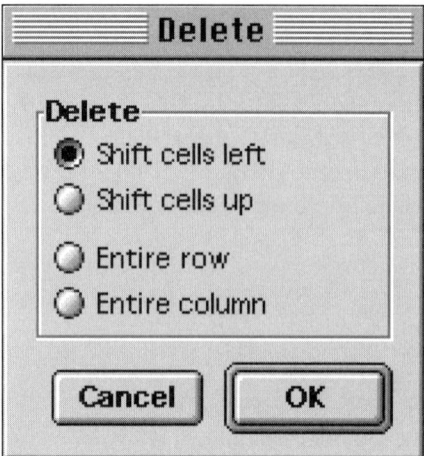

Figure 13.13 Use the Delete dialog to yank cells out of the worksheet (carefully).

- Choose Shift Cells Left to delete only the selected cells and shift other cells from the right to fill the gap.

- Choose Shift Cells Up to delete only the selected cells and shift up other cells from below to fill the gap.

- Choose Entire Row to delete the entire row or rows holding the selected cells, and shift the following rows up to fill the gap.

- Choose Entire Column to delete the entire column or columns holding the selected cells, and shift the following columns left to fill the gap.

Inserting Pictures Into A Worksheet

Although it's not done often, you can insert pictures in Excel worksheets using the same steps you use to add pictures to Word documents and PowerPoint presentations.

To insert a picture in a worksheet, choose Insert|Picture. You then have two options:

- Choose Clip Art to choose a picture from Office 98's Clip Gallery. (To learn more about the Clip Gallery, see Chapter 2.)

- Choose Picture to open a dialog from which you can navigate to and select a picture file on your hard disk.

Whichever method you use, when the picture opens in Excel, it does not go into a cell—it floats over the cells. You can then position it anywhere in the worksheet—even overlapping data in cells, if you wish—and edit its size and shape to best integrate it into your worksheet.

Before you can work with a picture's size and shape, you must first select the picture in the worksheet. A picture is automatically selected right after you insert it, and you can select a picture any other time simply by clicking on it. When a picture is selected, a border appears around it, and *handles*—tiny squares—appear on the border at each corner and on all sides.

To integrate the picture into your worksheet, first select the picture, then apply any of these formatting techniques:

- To position the picture in the worksheet, point to it so that the pointer becomes a four-pointed arrow. (If the picture is from the Clip Gallery, you may have to point to the edge of the picture to get the four-pointed arrow.) Click and hold the mouse button, then drag the picture to its new position.

- To change the picture's size (without changing its shape), point to a corner handle (the pointer becomes a two-pointed arrow), then click and drag inward (to reduce side) or outward (to increase size).

- To change the picture's height, click on the top or bottom handle and drag inward (to shorten) or outward (to lengthen). Be careful to adjust height and width equally, lest you destroy your picture's proportions.

- To change the picture's width, click on the handle on either side and drag inward (to make the picture more narrow) or outward (to widen the picture).

- To deselect a picture when you're finished working with it, press Esc or click on any cell.

Fast Track

In a worksheet, you can insert a link to a sound clip or movie clip, so that an online viewer can play multimedia from within your worksheet. You can also add a *background* to an Excel worksheet (Format|Sheet|Background), a picture that's repeated across the whole worksheet, behind all cell data.

Because these techniques are applied most often in creating Excel worksheets for online publication, you'll learn more about them in Chapter 17.

Formatting Pages

If you're familiar with page layout principles from Word, you need to change your mindset a little before Excel's approach will make sense to you. Oh, sure, the basic components of a page are the same—margins are still margins, headers are still headers. But unlike Word, Excel treats as optional, rather than essential, such issues as print formatting.

You see, despite Word's ability to produce documents for online publication, Word's design pretty much assumes that the document will eventually wind up on paper. That's why Word shows you page breaks—in both Normal and Page Layout view—and always formats text on screen the way it will appear between the margins in print.

Excel, on the other hand, treats page layout like an optional afterthought. While you're in Normal view, Excel shows all cell formatting—fonts, sizes, and so on. It also shows adjustments to row height and column width, which you'll learn how to perform next. However, except in the Print Preview, Excel doesn't bother trying to show how it will format your worksheet between the margins and from page to page. Excel doesn't consider such formatting relevant except when printing.

When you print a worksheet, Excel automatically ignores parts of the sheet that don't contain data. It then prints the rest of the worksheet using the page layout guidelines you define in the Page Setup dialog. If the data-filled area of your worksheet is wide and your page narrow, Excel may have to lop off the right side of your worksheet and print it on a separate page. In the Page Setup dialog, you can take steps to prevent that or to control exactly how Excel spreads the width of a worksheet to multiple pages.

Changing Cell Size

After you've entered and formatted all the data in your worksheet, you may decide that one or more rows or columns need to be larger or smaller to accommodate your data properly. The easiest and best way to adjust column width or row height is to simply move the borders between the row numbers or column letters. For example, if you point to the row numbers that appear along the left side of the worksheet and move the pointer slowly up and down, you'll see that as the pointer moves between row numbers, it changes to a black cross with arrowheads at its top and bottom. When the pointer looks like that, you can click and drag to pull up or down on the gridline between the rows, making a row taller or shorter. Similarly, if you point to a spot between column letters, a black cross appears; click and drag to make a column wider or narrower.

You can also adjust row height and column width by first selecting the row or column you want to adjust, then choosing from the Format menu. For example, select a column and then choose Format|Column|Width. In the Column Width dialog (see Figure 13.14), enter a width for the column. (The units for this measurement are truly strange. Microsoft defines column width by "the average number of digits 0—9 of the standard font" that will fit across the column—the standard font being the default font in Excel. The easiest course is probably to manually adjust the column width by dragging the borders around.)

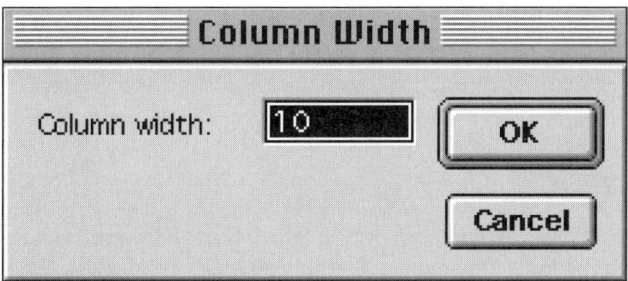

Figure 13.14 Use the Column Width dialog to resize a selected column.

Fast Track

The AutoFit option automatically adjusts row height or column width so that the largest value in the row or column fits perfectly. To AutoFit a row, choose Format|Row|AutoFit. To AutoFit a column, choose Format|Column|AutoFit.

Defining Page Size

After you've performed all of your cell formatting and made any adjustments to columns or rows, you need to define the page layout. Note that you should avoid working on the page layout until the other formatting is mostly complete, because the other formatting affects the size of your worksheet and data. Your principal task when defining the page layout is to make the final worksheet fit on a page the way you want it to.

Fast Track

You define page layout sheet by sheet. To define the page layout for a whole group of sheets at once, select the sheets before opening the Page Setup dialog.

To define the page layout for the current worksheet, choose File|Page Setup. The Page Setup dialog opens, showing the four tabs on which you define or modify the layout of the current page. The specific choices you can make on the tabs are described in the next few pages.

As you work on the page layout, observe that all four tabs of the Page Setup dialog have three buttons on the right:

- *Print*—Opens the Print dialog so you can print the worksheet to test the current page setup.

- *Print Preview*—Opens the Print Preview, an on-screen representation of how the worksheet will look in print, including how the worksheet will be split up into pages.

- *Options*—Opens the Options dialog for your printer, so you can change the configuration (for example, switch from draft to best quality on an inkjet printer—as always, your options will vary).

Fast Track

In the Print Preview, you can click on the Setup button to open the Page Setup dialog within the Print Preview itself. After you make changes to the Page Setup dialog and click on OK, the Print Preview instantly shows you the results of your changes. You can then click on Setup again to fine-tune the page setup, click on Print to print the worksheet, or click on Close to close the preview and return to editing the worksheet.

Page Tab

On the Page tab (see Figure 13.15), begin by choosing the orientation of your page. *Portrait* orientation organizes the worksheet's contents on a page that's taller than it is wide, like this book or the Sears building in Chicago. *Landscape* orientation, on the other hand, lays out the contents on a page that's wider than it is tall, like a bank check or a Denny's restaurant.

Whereas portrait is the most commonly used orientation for printing documents, many of the documents traditionally created in spreadsheet programs—such as

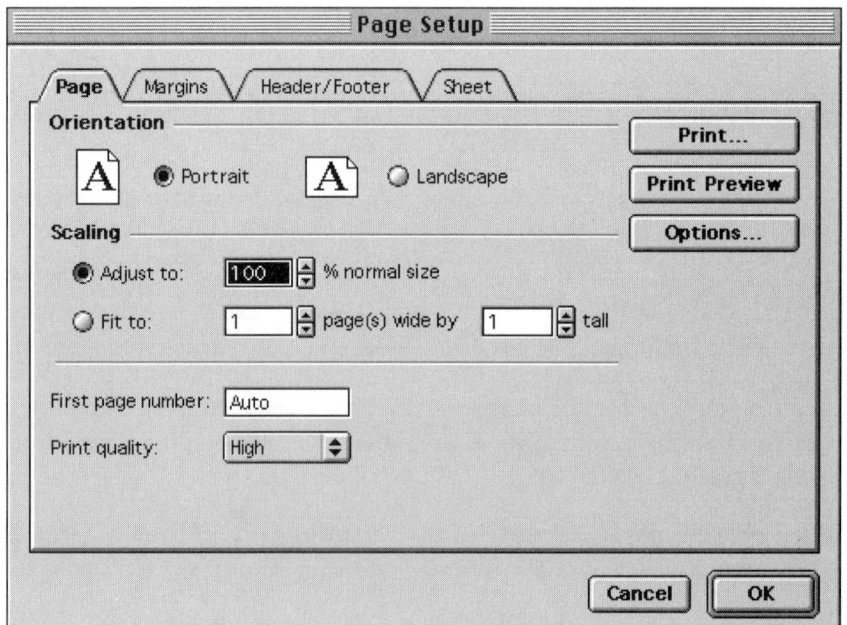

Figure 13.15 Choose the orientation of your page on the Page Setup dialog's Page tab.

balance sheets or other financial statements—are traditionally presented in landscape orientation. When a worksheet contains a wide table, landscape orientation is best because the extra width may prevent Excel from breaking some columns off onto another page.

The Scaling selections enable you to enlarge or reduce the size of everything presented in the worksheet, to better fit a worksheet's contents within a page or pages. For example, if a worksheet's contents are too wide to fit on a page at your chosen orientation, but you don't want some columns to be bumped to another page, you can change the value in Adjust To from the default (100 percent—full size) to a lower percentage. (Note that reducing the percentage too much may make some data too small to read easily.) The Fit To option enables you to fit worksheet contents to one or more pages without having to guess what percentage to use. For example, to instruct Excel to scale the worksheet contents so that the whole worksheet fits on a single page, click on the radio button next to Fit To and make sure that the number 1 appears in both lists following Fit To.

Click on the Options button to choose the paper size for which you want the printout formatted. If your printer supports different print qualities you may be able to select one from the list under Print Quality. (You can also control your printer options by clicking on the Options button.)

Margins Tab

On the Margins tab (see Figure 13.16), select the top, bottom, left, and right page margins in inches. When you open the tab, the current margins are shown in gray on the sample page in the center of the tab. When you change a margin, the new margin appears in black on the sample.

Note that you have two margins to set at the top of the page: the Top margin and the Header margin. The Top margin sets the amount of space from the top edge of the paper to the top of the worksheet content. The Header margin sets the amount of space from the top edge of the paper to the top of the header text (which you create next, on the Header/Footer tab). The Header margin is smaller than the Top margin, so that the header will print within the space allotted to the top margin. Similarly, at the page bottom you can set both a Bottom margin and a Footer margin.

After you set margins, it's possible that the worksheet content will not fill the entire space between the left and right margins, or between the top and bottom margins. When that's the case, Excel automatically aligns the worksheet to the left and top margins, leaving any blank space on the right and bottom. By clicking on the Center On Page checkboxes at the bottom of the Margins tab, you can float the worksheet to the center of the space between the margins, either in one direction or both.

358 Chapter 13

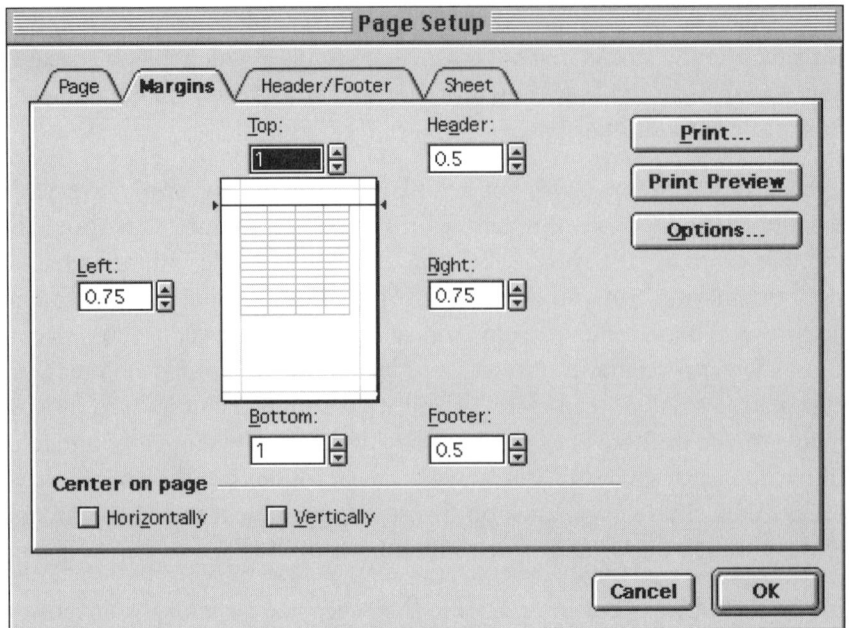

Figure 13.16 Choose your margins, and the position of the worksheet within them, in the Page Setup dialog's Margins tab.

Header/Footer Tab

On the Header/Footer tab (see Figure 13.17), you can define a *header* (text that appears at the top of every printed page) and a *footer* (text that appears at the bottom of every page). Headers are a great place to put page numbers, your name, and the worksheet title. (Excel uses the worksheet's name as a title in headers and footers.)

The easiest way to add a header or footer is to select from among the choices in the Header list or Footer list. When you select from either list, a preview appears on the tab (header at the top, footer at the bottom) to show you how your header or footer will appear on your pages.

If none of the headers or footers on the list matches what you want, click on Custom Header or Custom Footer to create your own. On the dialog that opens, you can define each portion of a header or footer separately: Left, Center, and Right.

Sheet Tab

On the Sheet tab (see Figure 13.18), you can choose from among a few final options that control how your worksheet prints.

Formatting Workbooks   359

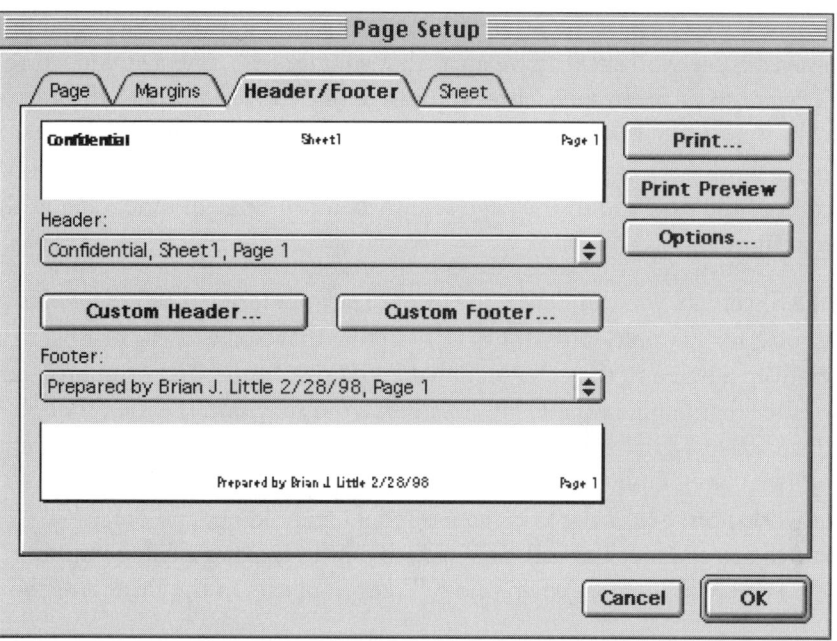

Figure 13.17   On the Page Setup dialog's Header/Footer tab, choose text to appear at the top and bottom of every page.

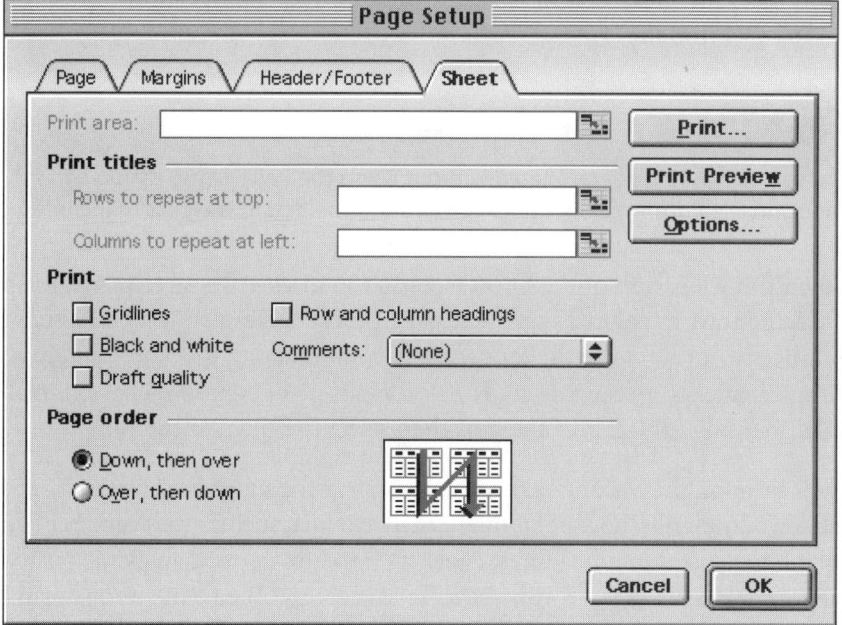

Figure 13.18   Define a few final print options in the Sheet tab of the Page Setup dialog.

By default, Excel limits the print area to regions of the worksheet containing data. However, some worksheets have areas that contain data, but that you won't necessarily want to print. In such cases, you can define the *print area* of the worksheet on the Sheet tab (note that you can only do this with *one*, not multiple, sheets selected). When a worksheet has a defined print area, Excel formats for printing only that portion of the data within the page setup when printing; all other data in the worksheet is ignored.

In the Sheet tab, you can define the print area by entering a cell range in the Print Area box; for example, enter B4:H11 to define that range as the print area. (If you have given a name to the cell range that contains your desired print area, you can also enter that name in the Print Area box.) You may find it easier, though, to click on the Collapse Dialog icon (the funky icon that appears at the far right end of the Print Area box). Doing so temporarily folds up the Page Setup dialog and shows your worksheet. Select the print area by clicking, holding, and dragging, just as you would to select a block of cells. Then click on the Expand Dialog button to return to the Page Setup dialog, where the cell range appears in the Print Area box.

Note that when you define a print area, a dashed box always appears around that area when you view the worksheet in Excel, to remind you where the print area is. To change the print area later, return to the Sheet tab and repeat the procedure. To remove the print area, clear the Print Area box on the Sheet tab, or choose File|Print Area|Clear Print Area.

Fast Track

You can also define the print area without using the Page Setup dialog by choosing File|Print Area|Set Print Area and then selecting the cells to include.

In the Print Titles area of the Sheet tab, you can instruct Excel to repeat the printing of selected rows or columns on every page. This enables you to enter a title for the worksheet in a row along the top—or in a column along the side—and repeat that title automatically on every page. To select the rows or columns, click on the Collapse Dialog button at the end of the box, then select the rows or columns.

Under Print on the Sheet tab, checkboxes appear for a number of worksheet elements that don't ordinarily show up in the printed product, such as the worksheet gridlines or the row and column headings; check a checkbox to print an element. If you have entered comments in your worksheet (see Chapter 12), use the drop-down list to print your comments either exactly where they appear on the worksheet or in a summary at the end of the worksheet.

Finally, under Page Order, you tell Excel how to deal with worksheet data when the data is still too wide to fit within the page—within the orientation, scaling, margins, and other selections you've made in the Page Setup dialog. You can choose either of these options:

- *Down, Then Over*—Instructs Excel to leave off the right end of the worksheet while printing all of the worksheet to the very bottom (on as many pages as it takes), then to begin printing the right end of the worksheet.

- *Over, Then Down*—Instructs Excel to print one page of the left side of the worksheet, then start printing the right portion on the next page, and move down in the sheet only after printing the whole width.

Walk-Through: Page Formatting

Follow these steps to practice page formatting. If you have not yet performed the earlier walk-through in this chapter, do so before performing this one.

1. Open the workbook Time Sheet.
2. Select the range B4:B8.
3. On the Formatting toolbar, drop down the Font Size list and choose 16. The font size of the row headings is increased to 16 points; they no longer fit completely within their cells.
4. With B4:B8 still selected, choose Format|Column|AutoFit selection. Column B is widened so that the table row headings fit properly.
5. Choose File|Page Setup. The Page Setup dialog opens.
6. On the Page tab, click on the Landscape and Fit To radio buttons.
7. On the Header/Footer tab, choose any Header and any Footer from the lists provided.
8. On the Header/Footer tab, click on the Print Preview button. The Print Preview opens.
9. On the Print Preview, click on Setup. The Page Setup dialog reappears in the Print Preview.
10. On the Page tab, click on the Portrait radio button, then click on OK. How does the sheet look now?

Moving On

In three chapters, you've learned everything that 90 percent of Excel users ever do, and a few more things, besides. In this chapter, you've learned how to shape, mold, and decorate a worksheet to make its data communicate more effectively—or at least more attractively.

What's left? Well, if you don't care about generating charts from your Excel data, performing a few basic database functions (like sorting lists), or creating forms to be filled out by others, then we guess there's nothing left. Jump ahead to Chapter 15, which deals with Outlook Express. Or make a salad, or go grocery shopping—it's really up to you. But if you're eager to move ahead to a few advanced Excel activities—and there's already plenty of milk and cheese puffs in the house—*Vamos, amigo o amiga!*

Organizing, Analyzing, And Charting Data

A decade ago, when hard disks were luxuries and spreadsheet programs were the only application anybody owned (besides WordPerfect and Flight Simulator), spreadsheet programs were all things to all users. People banged out not only financial statements in their spreadsheet programs, but they also generated reports, collected recipes, and even ran rudimentary database operations. Whole corporate databases were moved from mainframe computers to floppy disks so they could be managed in Lotus 1-2-3. (Nobody today really remembers why, but it was done.)

That period established a precedent that persists today: the *spreadsheet-as-database* paradigm. It's sort of like the *turkey-as-bacon* paradigm, only worse. In its time (the mid-'80s, the era of annoying buzzwords like "paradigm") the paradigm was a necessary evil. But given today's superior database programs, nobody needs to use a spreadsheet program for database work like sorting and plotting charts. So why does Excel still have all these database capabilities?

Well, as a practical matter, Access hasn't been brought over to the Macintosh—and it shows no signs of arriving on our Desktops any time soon. But more importantly, many people's database ambitions fall somewhere below a point where they justify learning a new program like Claris's FileMaker Pro. If you create an occasional simple table in a document, you use Word's table feature—you don't bother with Excel. Similarly, if you occasionally need to do a little simple database management, and the data is already in Excel worksheets, you don't have to steepen your learning curve by adding FileMaker to the hill—at least not until your database needs exceed Excel's capabilities.

In that spirit, this final chapter on Excel provides a tour of some of the "databasey" things Excel can do with data. You'll learn the basics of quickly producing charts (and maps), sorting and filtering lists of data from your worksheets, and creating forms for data collection. If after you finish this chapter, you feel you have data management needs that haven't been addressed in the Excel context, then you should consider purchasing a program outside the Office suite.

Creating Charts

Excel includes a Chart Wizard that takes you through a few simple steps to produce great-looking charts based on data already in your worksheet. You'll learn how to use this excellent tool in the next few pages.

Running The Chart Wizard

The Chart Wizard takes data in your worksheet (including formula results), plugs it into a predefined chart format such as a bar, pie, or scatter chart, and creates an attractive graphical representation of your data. The wizard can then deposit the charts into a workbook in either of two ways:

- *Embedded*—The chart appears anywhere in the worksheet, like a picture. You can adjust the position, size, and shape of the chart exactly as you would a picture, to integrate it into the worksheet layout in any way you wish.

- *Chart sheet*—The chart has its own sheet in the workbook—a *chart sheet*. You can open and print the chart sheet just like any other worksheet, but you can't add anything else to that sheet.

A chart is connected to the data from which it was created, so the chart changes automatically any time the data changes. Excel can create dozens of different types of charts, and within each type, you can change the appearance of the chart in many different ways. Figures 14.1 and 14.2 show just two examples.

Before getting started with charts, it's important that you understand a few basic terms that come up on the Chart Wizard's dialogs:

- *Series*—A data series is a set of cell values that make up the data you want to plot in a chart. A pie chart, for example, plots a single series—each cell in the series gets a slice of pie. A column chart (see Figure 14.1) plots at least two series—one plotted vertically against another plotted horizontally.

- *Axes*—Some charts, such as column charts, plot data against two axes: X (the horizontal axis) and Y (the vertical axis).

- *Labels*—Labels are text on the chart that identify series or data. For example, labels may appear along an axis to describe the data series that is plotted along that axis. The Chart Wizard can create labels automatically out of row and column headings in your table, and you can add or change labels to customize the chart.

- *Legend*—A legend is a text box adjacent to the chart that explains the way data is represented in the chart. When a chart calls for a legend, the Chart Wizard creates one automatically.

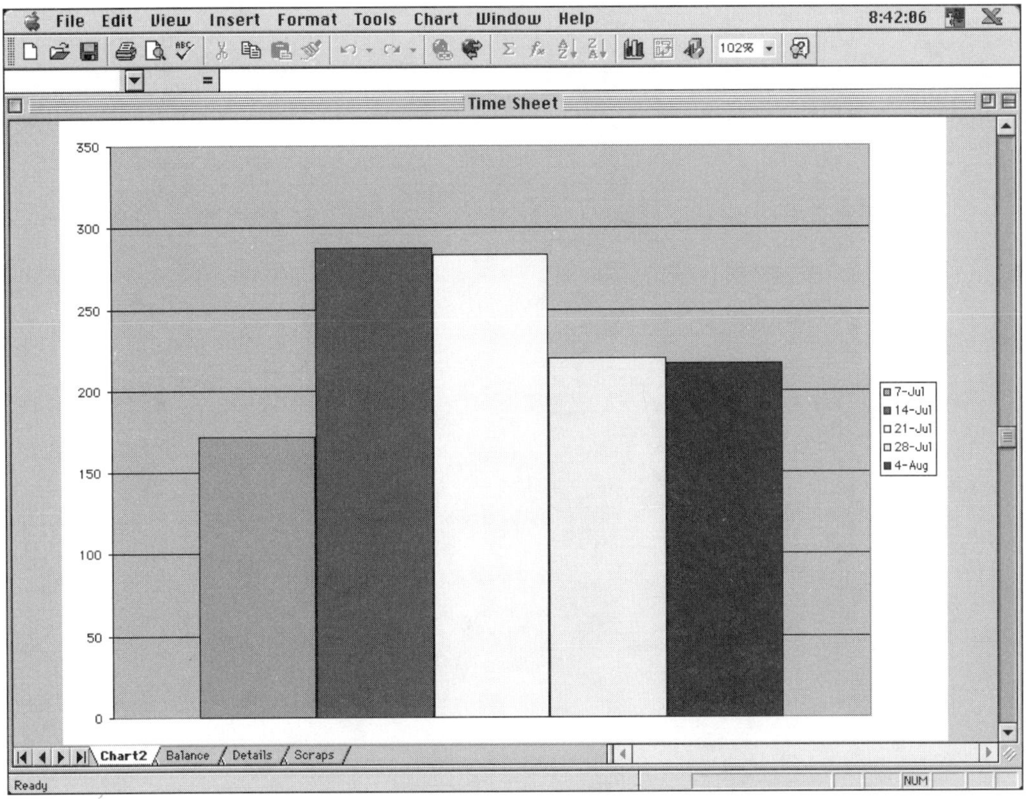

Organizing, Analyzing, And Charting Data **365**

Figure 14.1 The Clustered Column chart type is the default that Chart Wizard selects for comparing two data series.

Fast Track

In a big hurry? If using even the Chart Wizard seems like too long a process, you can create Excel's default chart (a basic column chart) in a chart sheet with a single key. Select the data to go in the chart, then press F11, and the chart appears in a chart sheet in the current workbook. You can then format and customize the chart the same way you would any other.

To create a chart with the Chart Wizard, begin by selecting the data you want to include in the chart. If you want to incorporate a table's row or column headings as labels in the chart, select them, too. However, avoid selecting portions of a table containing data that does not properly belong in the chart. For example, if your table has totals at the bottoms of columns, you may get a meaningful chart by selecting the table data alone, or by selecting the totals alone, but probably not by selecting both.

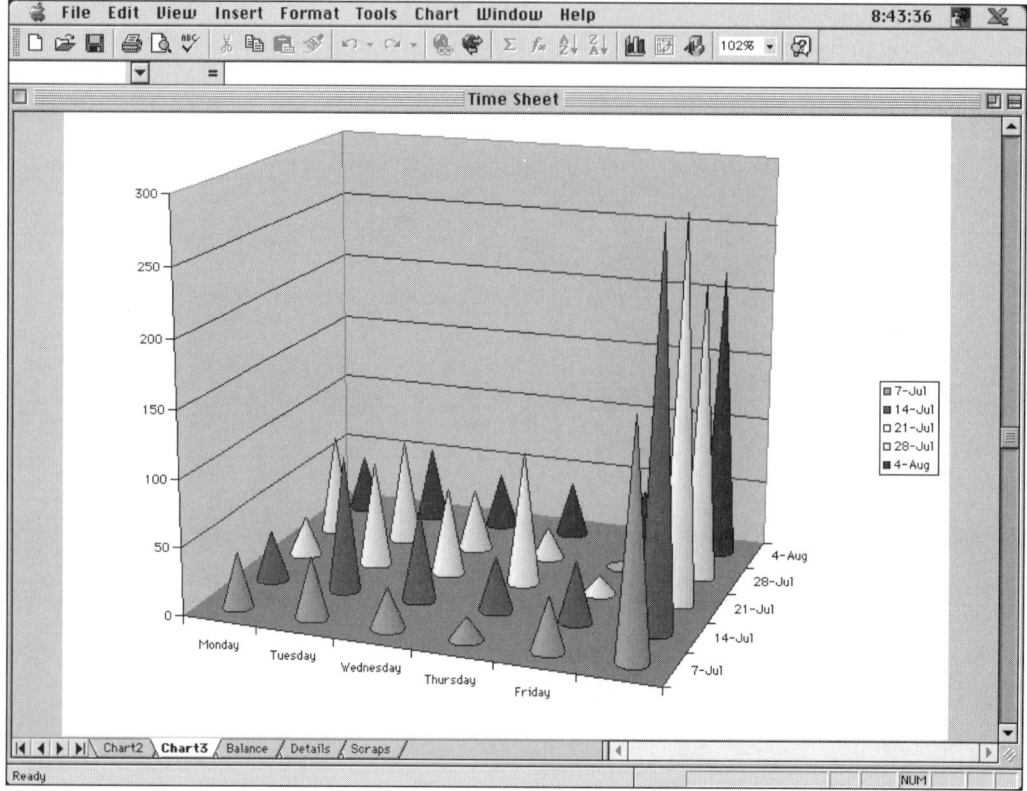

Figure 14.2 Chart Wizard's 3D chart types show trends and comparisons in three dimensions.

After selecting the data, click on the Chart Wizard button on the Standard toolbar. The Chart Type dialog opens, the first of the four Chart Wizard dialogs. As with any wizard, you move from dialog to dialog within the Chart Wizard by clicking on the Next button (to advance to the next dialog) or the Back button (to move back to a previous dialog). When you finish making your choices, click on the Finish button (on any of the Chart Wizard's dialogs) to produce the chart according to the choices you've made.

Over the next few pages, you'll learn how some of the choices you make on each of the Chart Wizard's dialogs affect the final chart. As you go, remember three things:

- You do not have to choose options on every tab, or every dialog, or even choose any options on any dialogs at all. The Chart Wizard has default settings for everything, so you can change what you want to and leave the rest alone.

- You can use the dialogs and tabs in any order, although it's best to choose a chart type (on the first dialog) before doing anything else. After that, you can jump around—and back and forth—all you like until you've changed all the settings you wish.

- After you finish the chart, you can easily change anything about it, as you'll learn to do in "Editing And Reformatting A Chart" later in this chapter. So don't fret if you're unsure of your choices in the Chart Wizard. Take your best shot; if you don't like the result, you can fix it later.

Chart Type Dialog

On the Standard Types tab of the Chart Type dialog (see Figure 14.3), select the chart type you want to create from the list provided, and then choose the particular chart sub-type by clicking on one of the pictures on the right. When you select any type and sub-type, a description appears in the lower right corner of the dialog. (For your reference, Table 14.1 describes each of the major chart types, each of which has at least two sub-types.)

Also in the lower right, you can click and hold the button with the very long name—Press And Hold To View Sample—to see a rough preview of your data plotted into the chart type and sub-type you've selected. The sample appears only as long as you hold down the mouse button. If you choose another type or sub-type, you can click and hold the button again to see a new sample.

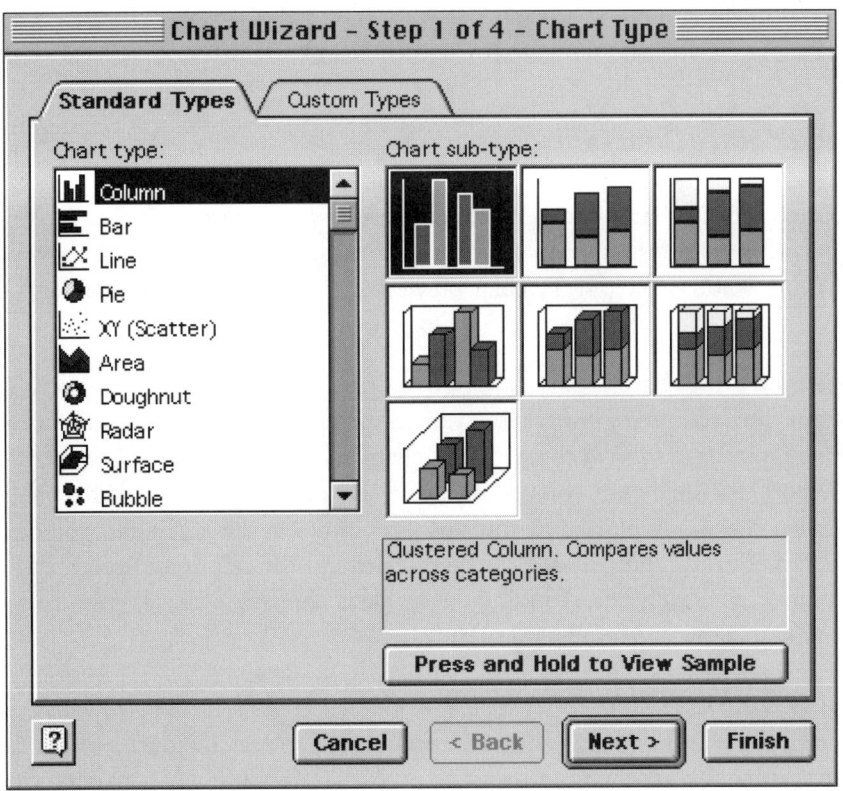

Figure 14.3 Choose the chart type and sub-type from the Chart Type dialog.

Table 14.1 Charts that Excel can make from your data.

Use This Chart Type	When You Need To
Column (Default)	Show changes in one or more series against changes in another (usually time).
Bar	Compare data values in one or more series.
Line	Show trends and projections in series.
Pie	Show each cell value's proportion of the whole constituted by the series.
XY (Scatter)	Show relationships among values in a series.
Area	Show the magnitude of changes over time.
Doughnut	Compare the size of values in multiple series.
Radar	Compare series values by showing each as a line radiating from a common center point.
Surface	Show optimum combinations between series.
Bubble	Show both relationships between series values and their relative proportions.
Stock	Show a series' high, low, and closing values.
3D Cone, Cylinder, and Pyramid	Show trends and comparisons in three dimensions.

Chart Source Data Dialog

The Chart Source Data dialog (see Figure 14.4) shows the data that has been selected for the chart's data series and labels. If you've carefully selected your data in the worksheet before starting the Chart Wizard, you probably don't have to change anything on this dialog. If the chart preview at the top of the dialog presents the data series the way you want, leave the dialog alone.

However, if the chart doesn't look right to you, the Chart Wizard may have chosen to plot the data by rows when you wanted data plotted by columns, or vice versa. Or you may have selected the wrong range of values for the data you wanted to plot. On the Data Range tab, you can adjust the data range used in the chart and choose whether the data is plotted by row or by column. On the Series tab, you can choose the individual cell ranges used for each series and the cell range used for the labels that appear on each axis. Any time you make a change on this dialog, the preview changes to show the results.

Chart Options Dialog

The Chart Options dialog, shown in Figure 14.5, offers a wide assortment of ways to fine-tune the appearance of your chart. For example, you can give it a title (from the Titles tab), choose whether (and where) to display the legend, and choose

Organizing, Analyzing, And Charting Data   369

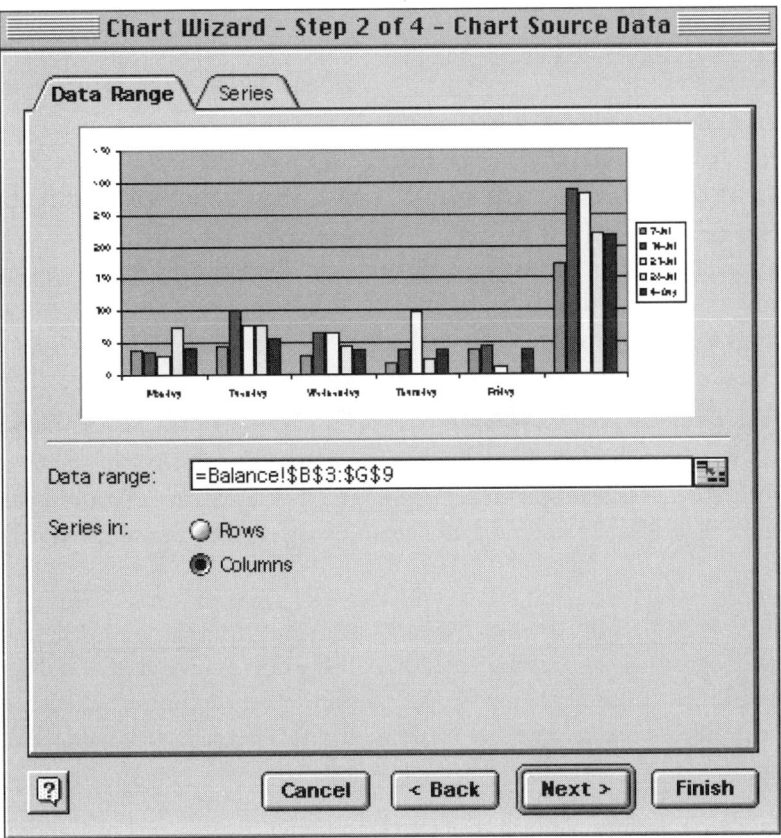

Figure 14.4 If you don't like the way the Chart Wizard plots your data, or you need to adjust the data selection, make changes in the Chart Source Data dialog.

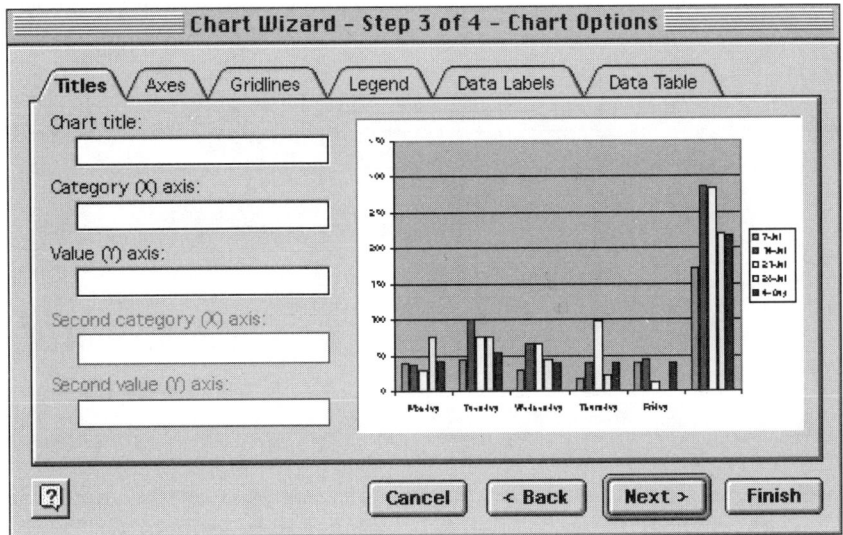

Figure 14.5 Choose all sorts of formatting options from the Chart Options dialog.

whether to label the data in the chart with the individual cell values upon which it is based (from the Data Labels tab).

Chart Location Dialog

On the Chart Location dialog (see Figure 14.6), you can choose whether to put the chart in its own chart sheet (As New Sheet) or embed it in a worksheet (As Object In). If you choose As New Sheet, you can type a name for the new chart sheet (in place of Chart1); you can also rename the chart sheet later, just as you can change the name of any worksheet. If you choose As Object In, you can choose any worksheet in the current workbook from the list.

Working An Embedded Chart Into The Layout

When you create an embedded chart, it appears in the worksheet floating above the cells, just like an inserted picture (see Chapter 13). You can position the chart anywhere in the worksheet and edit its size and shape to best integrate it within the layout.

The chart is automatically selected right after you insert it, and you can select a chart at other times by clicking on it. When the chart is selected, a border appears all around it, and *handles*—tiny squares—appear on the border at each corner and on all the sides. To integrate the chart within the worksheet layout, select it and then apply any of these formatting techniques:

- To position the chart, point to it, click and hold the mouse button, then drag it to its new position.

- To change the chart's size (without changing its shape), point to a corner handle (the pointer becomes a two-pointed arrow) and click and drag inward (to reduce the size) or outward (to increase the size).

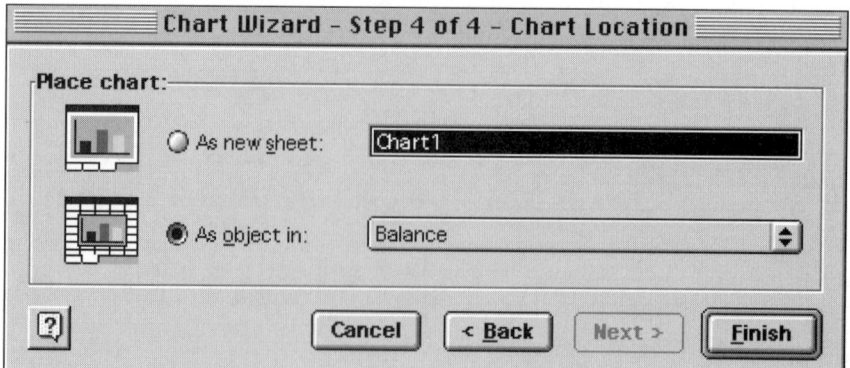

Figure 14.6 In the Chart Location dialog, choose whether you want the chart to appear in its own chart sheet or whether you want it to be embedded in a worksheet.

- To change the chart's height, click on the top or bottom handle and drag inward (to shorten it) or outward (to lengthen it).

- To change the chart's width, click on the handle on either side and drag inward (to make it more narrow) or outward (to widen it).

- To deselect a chart when you've finished working with it, press Esc or click on any cell.

Fast Track

Besides positioning and scaling the chart as a whole, you can also reposition individual chart elements such as the plot area (the area of the chart containing the values) and the legend. Select the whole chart, click on an element to display handles around that element, then position or size the element.

Editing And Reformatting A Chart

After creating a chart, you can change its appearance at any time by recalling any dialog of the Chart Wizard and changing the settings there. To recall a Chart Wizard dialog, select the chart, choose Chart from Excel's menu bar, and then, from the Chart menu, choose the name of the dialog you want to change: Chart Type, Chart Source Data, Chart Options, or Chart Location.

You can also fine-tune the formatting of any individual component of a chart—an axis, data series, legend, and so on—by double-clicking on it to call up a formatting dialog specific to that element. For example, if you double-click on the legend, the Format Legend dialog opens (see Figure 14.7), offering ways to adjust the borders, font, and other aspects of the legend's appearance. To change the font, border, or other formatting aspects of the whole chart, double-click on any empty spot within the box that contains the chart to display the Format Chart Area box. (There is a caveat with this—Excel forces any changes to stay within the defined area of the chart. This can produce some odd results when things get resized, so proceed with caution.)

Walk-Through: Creating And Formatting A Chart

Follow the steps below to practice creating and formatting a chart with the Chart Wizard. (This walk-through uses a simple table for charting, but feel free to use your own Excel tables and experiment beyond the boundaries of these steps.)

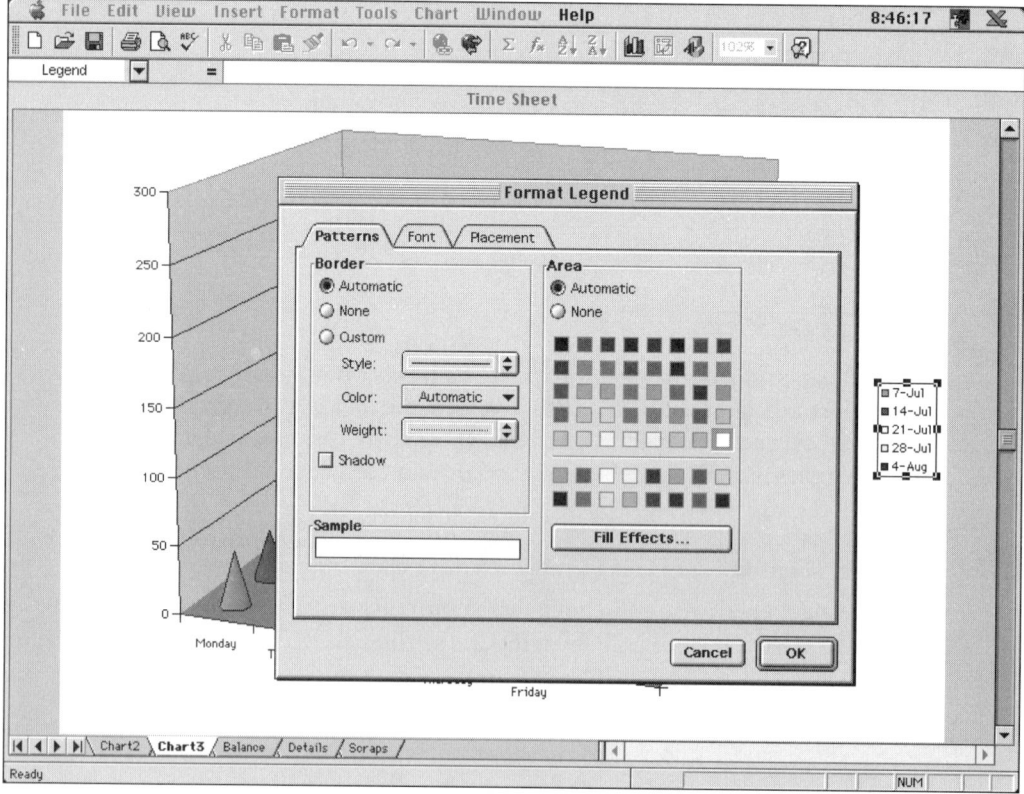

Figure 14.7 Double-click on any part of a chart to open a dialog for formatting that part.

1. Create a simple table with two columns: one containing text, the other containing number values. If you don't want to come up with your own table, enter this one:

   Apples   20
   Oranges   35
   Bananas   22
   Grapes   140
   Mangoes   3

2. Select the whole table.
3. Click on the Chart Wizard button on Excel's Standard toolbar.
4. In the Chart Types dialog's Standard Types tab, choose Pie.
5. Click and hold the Press And Hold To View Sample button until the sample appears. Evaluate the sample, then release the button.

6. Change the Chart Type to Bar and display the sample again. Decide whether you prefer Pie or Bar, make your selection, and click on Next.
7. On the Data Range tab of the Chart Data Source dialog, click on one of the radio buttons under Series, examine the preview, then click on the other radio button. Click on the selection you prefer, then click on Next.
8. On the Titles tab of the Chart Options dialog, enter descriptive text for a chart title, then click on Next.
9. In the Chart Location dialog, click on the radio button next to As Object In to embed the chart in the sheet containing the table.
10. Click on Finish. The chart appears in the worksheet, preselected.
11. Point to one of the chart's corner handles.
12. Click and hold, drag a little ways toward the center of the chart, and release. The chart shrinks.
13. Point to an empty area within the chart box, then click and drag to reposition the chart.
14. Double-click on an empty area within the chart box. The Format Chart Area dialog opens.
15. In the Patterns tab, drop down the Weight list and choose a heavy line. Then click on the checkbox for Round Corners and click on OK. A heavy border with rounded corners appears around the chart.
16. Choose Chart|Chart Type. The Chart Wizard's Chart Type dialog opens.
17. Choose a new Chart Type and click on OK. What do you think of the change?

Managing Data

What do we mean when we say "managing data"? We mean moving beyond the basic Excel job of putting data in cells and formatting it there to actually reorganizing the data based on particular criteria. Sorting and filtering data—the things you'll learn to do in this section—are database operations.

Note that you cannot perform most data-management activities on just any old Excel table or worksheet. A database must be created in Excel following a particular structure; without that structure, Excel can't use the data. Over the next few pages, you'll learn first how to create an Excel database, or *list*, and then how to manipulate that list.

Creating A Database (List)

A database is made up of *records* and *fields*. A field is a discrete piece of data—usually a single cell entry. A record is a set of fields that together make up a meaningful description.

For example, your first name is a field, as are your last name, street address, city, state, and ZIP code. Put all those fields together in a row, and you have a record about you. Put your record in a list of other rows, each of which contains a name and address record of somebody else, and you have a database. In the database, *fieldnames* describe fields across records. For example, we can group together all of the first names in all of the records in our database under the fieldname First Name.

In Excel, a database is commonly referred to as a *list* (perhaps to help distinguish a simple Excel database from a more complex database in a "real" database application). To create a database list in Excel, you must arrange the data in a table in a particular way, so that Excel can identify the fields, fieldnames, and records. In an Excel list, the top row contains the fieldnames—which function like column headings—and each row after the top contains a record. (Figure 14.8 shows a simple database—a list of customers and their outstanding payable balances—that we'll use throughout this chapter to illustrate database operations.)

To create a simple database list, begin by creating the top row of fieldnames. Note that the fieldnames must not have a numeric data format. If you enter a number or a date as a fieldname, you must change the format of the cell to Text (see Chapter 12). Also, be sure to enter the fieldnames in an uninterrupted row—don't leave any empty cells between the names.

In the row immediately below the fieldnames, enter the first record. The first record must immediately follow the fieldnames; leaving any blank rows in between fieldnames will invalidate the database. Enter the remaining records row by row, again

	A	B	C	D	E	F	G	H	I
1									
2		Payables Summary							
3									
4		First Name	Last Name	Street	City	State	ZIP	Current Balance	
5		Harry	Nils	98 Chestnut Hills	Ithaca	NY	10055	$571.00	
6		Stephen	Lovely	877 University City Blvd.	Thurmont	MD	39618	$951.00	
7		Fredo	Corleone	745 Red Fox Lane	Concord	NC	34982	$872.00	
8		Ziggy	Diablo	7 Eastway Drive	Charlotte	NC	27510	$1,632.00	
9		Susan	Woronicz	698 Airlie St.	Walkersville	MD	39617	$2,200.00	
10		Marty	Rodriguez	27A Highway 49N	Rock Hill	SC	11732	$24.00	
11		Helen	Carvel	21 Bat Cave Road	Old Fort	NC	34987	$1,409.00	
12		Nancy	Simons	1884 Banks Road.	Finger	TN	17548	$347.00	
13		Anthony	Samson	15644 North Tryon	Fairfax	VA	23910	$19.00	
14		Annie	Diaz	1173 Independence Blvd.	Chambersburg	PA	2175	$45.00	
15		Columbus	Burgin	1127 Aube Drive	Greenville	SC	11770	$500.00	

Figure 14.8 Enter your database list by rows, with the top row holding the fieldnames.

leaving no blank rows between records. (Note that although you must enter each field in a record in its correct column, you can leave some cells in a record blank if the record contains no entry for a given field.) When you're finished, you'll have a database that can be manipulated by Excel's data-management tools.

Observe that you can format the list any way you like, as long as you do not break up the table with empty rows or columns. The database tools ignore formatting—except for the number format of cells. For database operations to return reliable results, you must make sure that each cell uses the number format—number, date, text, and so on—you intended.

FYI: Tips For List Entry

When you're creating Excel database lists, try to follow these tips:

- Put only one database on a worksheet. (It's okay to put other kinds of tables and entries in the same worksheet, but only one list upon which you will perform database operations should appear in any one worksheet.) Technically, Excel permits you to enter multiple databases on a worksheet, but doing so can create problems when you use some data-management features.
- Between the database list and anything else on the worksheet—other cell entries, charts, and so on—leave at least one blank row and column. This helps Excel pick out what's part of the database and what isn't.
- Don't type any blank spaces at the beginning of a field entry.

Fast Track

When you have a lot of data to enter in a database, Excel can open a handy data form to collect your entries. To display the data form, first create a few rows—including the fieldnames row—of your database. Then click on any cell in the next empty row (the row where the next record belongs).

Choose Data|Form to open the data form, which has text boxes in it for each field in the database. Click on the New button to start a new record, then fill in the text boxes in the dialog, pressing the Tab key to jump from box to box. When you're finished, press Return to add the record to the list. The record is added, and the boxes in the data form clear so you can type another record. When you're finished adding records, click on Close on the data form.

Sorting Data

Sorting a database means changing the order in which records appear. Changing the sort order in a database can reveal important trends or other useful information in a database. For example, we could sort our payables database by the Current Balance field to see who our worst payers are or sort by the State field to see where we're owed the most.

The key to sorting is the *sort key*, the field by which the whole database will be sorted. For example, in our sample database, if we chose Last Name as the sort key, the records would be reordered so that they were listed alphabetically by last name. Besides choosing a sort key, you control the order by choosing *ascending order* or *descending order*:

- Ascending order lists the records from lowest to highest. For numbers, that means starting with the lowest value; for dates and times, the list begins with the earliest value; for text, the list runs alphabetically, from A to Z.

- Descending order does the opposite of ascending order, listing records from highest to lowest. For numbers, that means starting with the highest value, and for dates and times, the latest value. Descending text values go in reverse alphabetical order, from Z to A.

To sort the data, click on any cell in the column whose field will be the sort key, then click on the Sort Ascending button or Sort Descending button on Excel's Standard toolbar. Figure 14.9 shows the results of selecting Current Balance for the sort key along with the Sort Descending button.

Payables Summary

First Name	Last Name	Street	City	State	ZIP	Current Balance
Susan	Woronicz	698 Airlie St.	Walkersville	MD	39617	$2,200.00
Ziggy	Diablo	7 Eastway Drive	Charlotte	NC	27510	$1,632.00
Helen	Carvel	21 Bat Cave Road	Old Fort	NC	34987	$1,409.00
Stephen	Lovely	877 University City Blvd.	Thurmont	MD	39618	$951.00
Fredo	Corleone	745 Red Fox Lane	Concord	NC	34982	$872.00
Harry	Nils	98 Chestnut Hills	Ithaca	NY	10055	$571.00
Columbus	Burgin	1127 Aube Drive	Greenville	SC	11770	$500.00
Nancy	Simons	1884 Banks Road.	Finger	TN	17548	$347.00
Annie	Diaz	1173 Independence Blvd.	Chambersburg	PA	2175	$45.00
Marty	Rodriguez	27A Highway 49N	Rock Hill	SC	11732	$24.00
Anthony	Samson	15644 North Tryon	Fairfax	VA	23910	$19.00

Figure 14.9 Choose Current Balance as the sort key and click on Sort Descending to sort records from highest Current Balance to lowest.

Fast Track

Using the Sort dialog, you can sort one database by up to three different sort keys at once. To use the Sort dialog, choose Data|Sort, then choose one, two, or three sort keys from the lists provided on the dialog.

Filtering Data

Filtering culls from the database a particular subset of data you want to see, hiding the rest of the database from view. For example, if we wanted to see only the customers in our payables list who owe us more than $1,000, or just the customers in Illinois, we could use filters to show just those records.

The easiest way to filter in Excel is to use the AutoFilter facility. To use AutoFilter, click on any cell in the database list and choose Data|Filter|AutoFilter. In the list, a drop-down list arrow appears next to each fieldname (see Figure 14.10).

To select which fields to filter your records by, click on the arrow to drop down a list for a field, then select from the list. Choices on the AutoFilter lists include:

- *All*—Choose All to include all records in the selected field. In general, you use All to redisplay the whole database after having viewed it through a filter.

- *Top 10*—Choose Top 10 to open the Top 10 AutoFilter dialog (see Figure 14.11), from which you can choose to display a selected number of records containing the highest (or lowest) values in the field. Using the settings on the dialog, you can choose highest or lowest values, the number of records to include, and whether to show the highest/lowest entries by field value (Items) or by percentile (Percent).

Figure 14.10 Choose Data|Filter|AutoFilter to display arrows you can drop down to filter the list by any criteria.

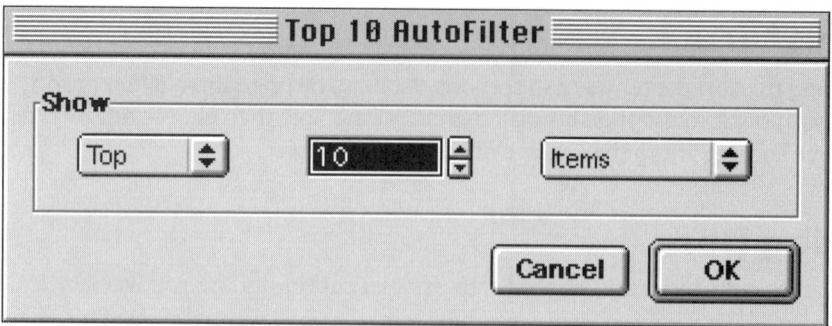

Figure 14.11 From any AutoFilter list, choose Top 10 to filter the list to only those records containing the highest or lowest values in the field.

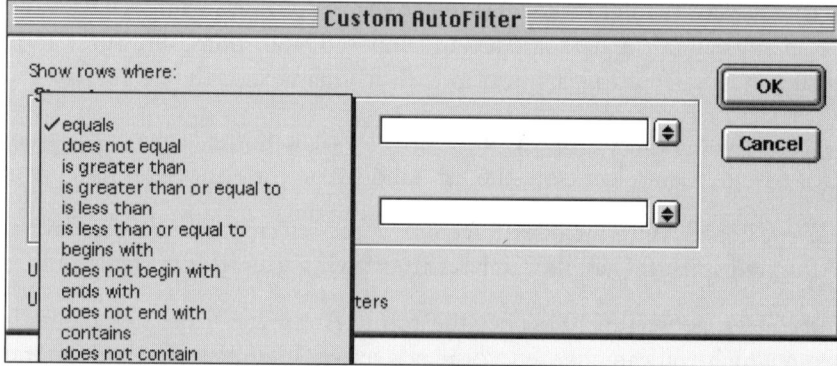

Figure 14.12 From any AutoFilter list, choose Custom to filter the list according to custom criteria you select on this dialog.

- *Custom*—Choose Custom to open the Custom AutoFilter dialog (see Figure 14.12), where you choose from drop-down lists to filter the database by a wide range of available criteria.

Just below the All, Top 10, and Custom choices on each AutoFilter list (as shown for the Last Name field in Figure 14.10), the complete list of entries for the selected field appears. Choose any entry to display just the records containing that field entry.

When you're finished filtering, remove the AutoFilter arrows by choosing Data|Filter|AutoFilter again.

Fast Track

By selecting from multiple AutoFilter lists, you can filter a database by more than one criteria. For example, in the payables list, we could drop down the AutoFilter list for the City field and choose MA, then drop down the Current Balance field, choose Top 10, and use the Top 10 dialog to choose the five highest items. The list would then show only Massachusetts customers, and of them, only those with the five highest balances.

Creating A Form

A *form* is a document designed for collecting data, like a tax form. Excel includes special formatting tools and other features to help you create forms. You can use these features to create attractive printed forms that users can fill out with pen, pencil, or a typewriter. But more importantly, you can create *online forms*—forms users can view and fill out from their workstations. When you create an online form, you can design it so that the user's entries are automatically copied to a database.

Formatting A Form

A form is just a worksheet like any other; create it and format it any way you like. When creating a form—whether for printing or for use online—you can also take advantage of Excel's special form formatting tools, accessible from the Forms toolbar (see Figure 14.13). To display the Forms toolbar, choose View|Toolbars|Forms.

The buttons on the Forms toolbar add and format elements one usually finds on forms, such as checkboxes, option buttons, and other *controls*. Some of the available controls apply exclusively to online forms—such as scroll bars or drop-down list boxes—but others, such as checkboxes, can be used in both printed and online forms. Controls float above cells, like pictures or charts. You can position them anywhere you want by clicking and dragging them, or adjust their size and shape by dragging their handles.

To add a control to a form, click on the button on the Forms toolbar for the control you want to add. You have two options for sizing the control:

- To insert the control at its default size and shape (which you can change later), point to the general area where you want the control to appear, then click.

- To insert the control in a specific size and shape, click and hold the mouse button, drag to create an outline of the size and shape you want, and release.

Figure 14.13 Use the Forms toolbar to add form elements to a worksheet.

Creating An Online Form

To create an online form, you create the form as you do for printed use, then save it not as a workbook, but as a new workbook template. (Before saving the template, delete any unused worksheets from the form so that they don't confuse or distract users.) To save a template, choose File|Save As, then drop down the Save File As Type list and choose Template.

In a typical scenario, you will save the template in a shared Office templates folder, so all users on the network have access to it. To use your online form, the user opens Excel, chooses File|New, and then selects the form template from the shared Templates folder. A new workbook based on the form template is created. The user fills in the form and then saves the workbook in a shared location, where you (or whoever is responsible for collecting form data) can open it to collect the user's answers.

If you want to supply online forms to Excel users with whom you do not share a network, you can provide the template file on diskette or attach it to an email message. The user returns the completed form to you—saved as a workbook—in the same way.

Choosing What The Controls Do

For many of the form controls—such as drop-down lists or checkboxes—you decide what that control does by setting options on the Control Properties for the control. For example, to create options a user can select from a drop-down list in the form, type the options in a cell range in another sheet of the workbook (other than the sheet containing the form). Add the list box to the form, then select it and click on Control Properties on the Forms toolbar. A Format Control dialog with the Control tab selected appears (see Figure 14.14). In Input Range, enter the cell range containing the list of options. When the user drops down the list, the selections appear.

Fast Track

To hide any worksheets containing list choices and other form underpinnings, choose Format|Sheet|Hide.

Controlling Where And What Users Enter

When users fill in your form, you want them to restrict their entries to the cells where you want the entries recorded. You may also want to restrict the type of data a user can enter—for example, in a part of the form where the user should enter a number, you can configure cells to refuse to accept a text entry. Both of these techniques help ensure that your forms collect reliable entries.

To restrict users to making entries in only certain areas of the form, you must *protect* the worksheet. Begin by selecting all cells in which users will enter data. (To select

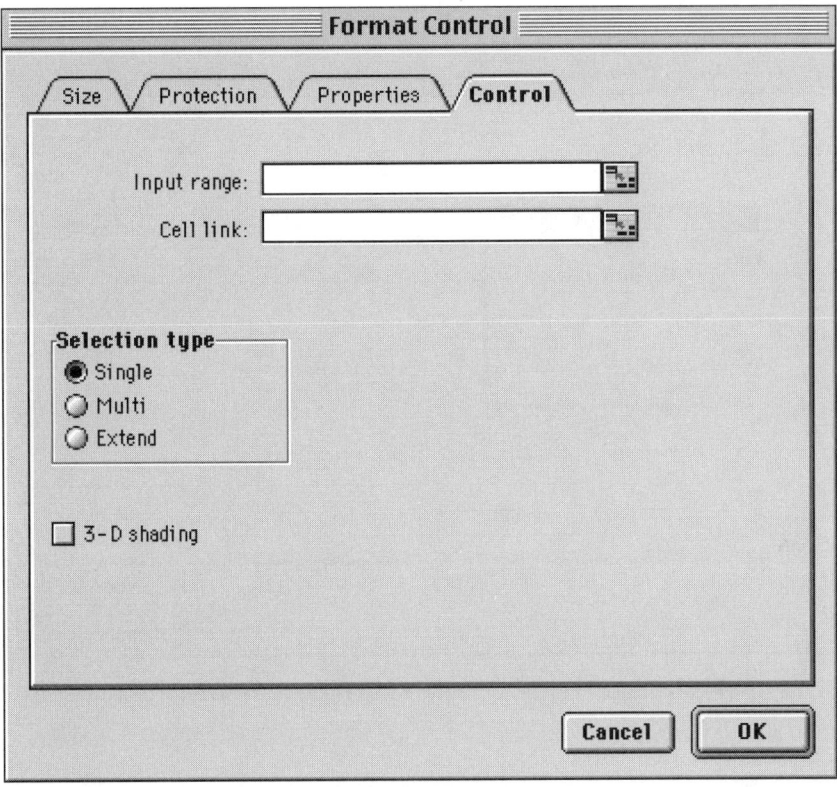

Figure 14.14 Click on a control in a form and choose Control Properties (on the Forms toolbar) to bring up the Format Control dialog.

noncontiguous blocks of cells, hold down the Command key while selecting.) Choose Format|Cells|Protection to open the Protection tab of the Format Cells dialog. Clear the checkbox next to Locked and click on OK to close the dialog. Then choose Tools|Protection|Protect Sheet to lock all the cells in the worksheet except those you selected and unlocked previously. All cells in the sheet other than those you just unlocked are now locked—they can't be changed.

To restrict users to entering only certain types of information in specific cells, first select the cells for which you want to apply restrictions, then choose Data|Validation, then choose the Settings tab of the Data Validation dialog (see Figure 14.15). From the list under Allow, choose the type of data to allow in the cell. Optionally, you can make selections in the data list and other options in the tab to limit the entry not only by the type of data, but also to a given set or range of acceptable values. To allow a user to leave the cell blank, check the checkbox for Ignore Blank. If you want to display a message when the user makes an invalid entry, fill in the Input Message and Error Alert tabs of the Data Validation dialog.

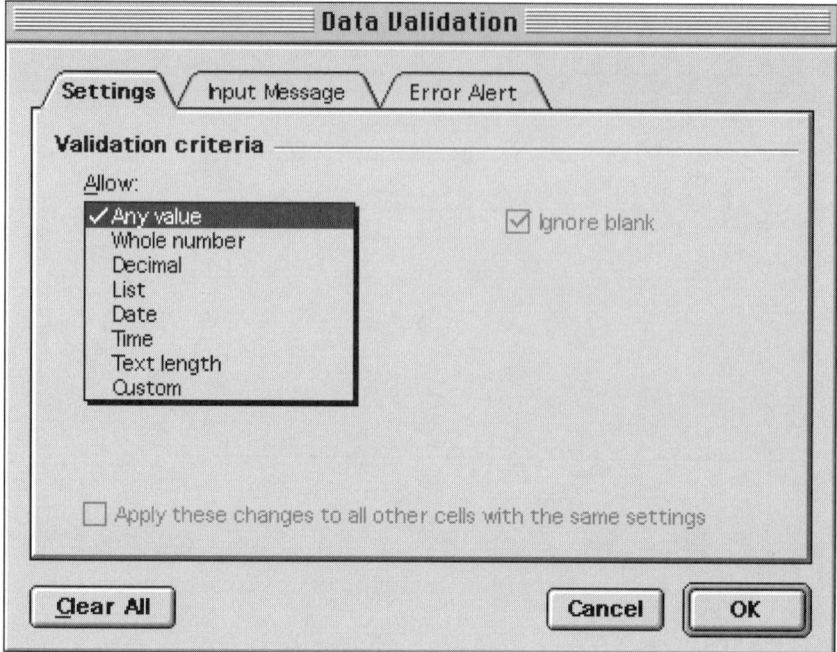

Figure 14.15 Select cells and choose Data|Validation to restrict the values a user can enter in the cells.

Fast Track

When you're creating an online form, you can add comments containing instructions for filling in any particular part of the form. When the user of the form points to that region, the comment appears. To learn how to enter comments, see Chapter 12.

Linking A Form To A Database

You can link a form to a database so that users' entries are automatically collected as records in the database. Use this when your forms will be served from a shared network drive, and when that drive is located on the same network as the database.

The easiest way to link a form to a database is to run the Template Wizard when you're saving the new form template. The Template Wizard is an Excel add-in that is not automatically installed when you set up Office. If you don't see an option for Template Wizard on the Excel Data menu, you need to install the Template Wizard With Data Tracking add-in (to learn how to install add-ins, see Chapter 11).

To use the Template Wizard after installing it, create the form workbook, but do not save it as a template yet. (If you have already saved the form as a template, choose

File|New, create a new workbook from the form template, then save that workbook under a new name and use it in this procedure.) In the worksheet containing the form, use the Labels button on the Forms toolbar to enter a label directly above or to the left of each cell that will collect data for the database. After labeling all the cells that will collect data, choose Data|Template Wizard to start the wizard, and follow the wizard's instructions to complete the link.

Walk-Through: Working With A Database

Follow the steps below to practice creating and manipulating an Excel database list. (The example provides a simple table for database practice, but feel free to create your own database and experiment beyond the boundaries of this example.)

1. In a blank worksheet, enter a simple database. Begin with a row of fieldnames and follow with at least seven records, one record to a row. You can create your own data, or copy the data shown in Figure 14.9.
2. Click on any cell in the first column, then click on the Sort Ascending button on the Standard toolbar. The records are sorted by the values in the first column, in ascending order.
3. Click on the Sort Descending button on the Standard toolbar. The records are re-sorted in descending order by the values in the first column.
4. One at a time, choose cells in other columns, click on Sort Ascending or Sort Descending, and observe the results.
5. Click on any cell in the list and choose Data|Filter|AutoFilter. A dropdown arrow appears next to each fieldname.
6. Drop down any AutoFilter list and choose Top 10 from the list. The Top 10 AutoFilter dialog opens.
7. In the center list on the dialog, choose 3 and click on OK. The list shows only the three records containing the highest values in the field whose AutoFilter list you selected.
8. Drop down the same AutoFilter list you chose in Step 6, then choose All. All records in the database reappear.
9. Click on any cell in the list and choose Data|Filter|AutoFilter. The AutoFilter arrows disappear.
10. Select the entire database list and see what you get if you create a chart with it.

Moving On

Show's over, folks—that's all the Excel information that any beginning/intermediate user needs or deserves. We hope you've come away with the understanding that although learning the whole of Excel is a tall order, learning just the pieces of Excel required to accomplish any individual task is pretty simple. The only really hard part to Excel is getting used to the way it does things, adapting yourself to its cell-centric world view.

You've finished with the major Office Applications, but there's more. Now you're ready to learn Outlook Express, so you can hit the wires and share your newfound knowledge with all and sundry. Suit up, strap in, and let's go!

PART V

Outlook Express

Communicating Via Outlook Express

Outlook Express is an unusual animal, different from the other Office programs in its appearance and behavior. In the Office 98 combo, Outlook Express is Ringo.

The other Office programs tend to have a single major purpose, centered on *creating* something—a newsletter in Word, a spreadsheet in Excel, a presentation in PowerPoint. Outlook Express is more scattershot, combining three usually discrete functions—email messaging, newsgroup messaging, and contacts management—into a single package.

Outlook Express is less about creating things than tracking things. Specifically, it is concerned with tracking your electronic communications. When future archaeologists dig up the relics of our culture and try to learn what our lives were all about, they'll base whole theses on the contents of our Outlook Express folders, and maybe any copies of *TV Guide* that survive.

Outlook Express not only organizes your communications, but it also maintains a list of those you communicate with—your contacts. And because it's so good at organizing this list, Outlook Express supplies this information to other Office programs upon request. For example, Word can use the contents of your Outlook Express Address Book to automatically address form letters or envelopes in a mail merge.

In this chapter, you'll learn how to use the primary functions of Outlook Express—email messaging, contacts management, and newsgroup reading. You'll learn not only how to send and receive email messages and newsgroup postings, but also how to organize and *filter* those messages according to rules you set up. If you already use another email client, you'll discover here how to import your accumulated information from that program into Outlook Express.

Installing Outlook Express

Because Outlook Express is so different in form and function from the other programs on the Office 98 CD, it's fitting that the chapter describing it is different, too. Installing the Office suite proper is relegated to Appendix A of this book. Outlook Express, though, requires some configuration before you can do anything with it, so it's best to start from the very beginning.

To get started, pop your Office 98 CD into your Mac. You'll find the Outlook Express installation program in the folder named Microsoft Internet. Double-click on Outlook Express 4.0 Installer to begin. A license agreement will appear—click on the Accept button to proceed. When the Installer window finally pops up, you can select three options from the drop-down menu in the upper left: Easy Install, Custom Install, or Remove (see Figure 15.1). We recommend the Easy Install.

Easy Install

Easy Install places both Outlook Express and a separate program called Internet Config on your Macintosh. To run Easy Install, simply click on the Install button, allowing the installer to do its appointed task, and proceed with your setup. Note that the OE installer may ask you about replacing some obscure-sounding Microsoft files—this is because Office 98 installs these same files. It is perfectly okay to allow the installer to overwrite them. We did, and it caused no problems.

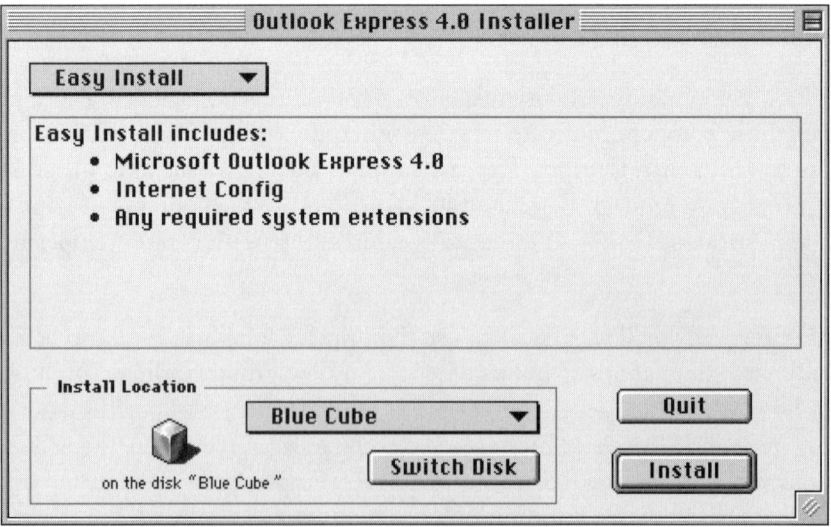

Figure 15.1 Use Easy Install to place Outlook Express and the handy Internet Config utility on your Macintosh.

Net Savvy

Internet Config creates a *global* Internet configuration for your computer. In English, this means any program you use to access the Internet that can access Internet Config (and nowadays, that's most of them) can automatically get your settings. No more manually entering your username, password, news server, and so on. As you gain Internet experience (or if you're already pretty knowledgeable), you'll find this an invaluable time saver.

Custom Install

The Custom Install option, selected from the drop-down menu in the upper left of the Installer window, allows you to install either Outlook Express or Internet Config, or both of them. Use this if you already have Internet Config installed, or if you don't wish to use it. To use the Custom Install, select it from the menu, then check those items you wish to install. When you're ready, click on Install, and read ahead a bit while the installer churns away. When it's finished, proceed with your setup.

Setting The Default Mail And News Client

If you used the Easy Install option (or if you already have Internet Config on your Mac), you'll be asked if you want to make Outlook Express your default mail and news client (see Figure 15.2). This means the installer will tell Internet Config to set its files to point to Outlook Express any time you need to use mail or get news-groups—which can affect programs ranging from Netscape Navigator to the Mac OS Internet Assistant. Because you're installing Outlook Express, it's reasonable to assume that you want it to be your default program for mail and news, so click on Yes. Click on No if you're installing Outlook Express only to evaluate it—you can change your Internet Config defaults later, if you wish. (See the Internet Config documentation for more on how to do this.)

Finish And Restart

If you installed Outlook Express only, you're now ready to go to work. Click on Quit and get ready to launch Outlook Express for the first time (see Figure 15.3). If you also installed Internet Config, it's a good idea to restart your Mac, because IC puts

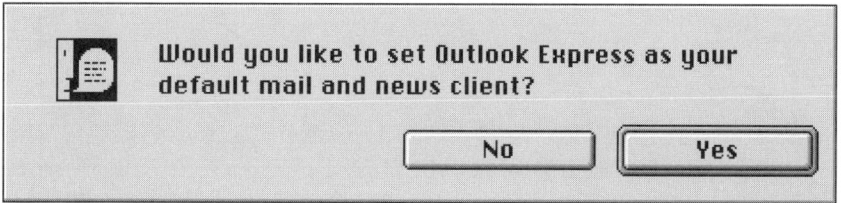

Figure 15.2 Selecting Yes makes Outlook Express your default mail and news program.

390 Chapter 15

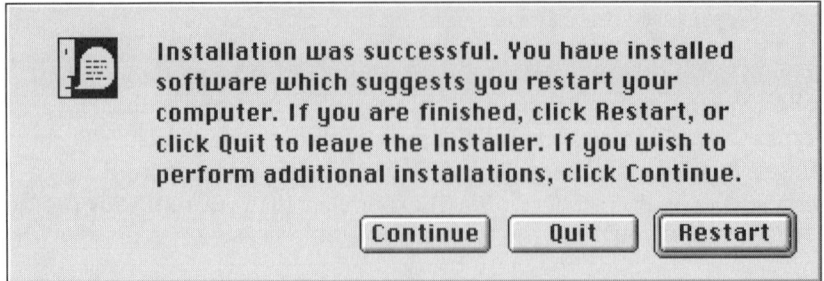

Figure 15.3 Select Quit to start immediately with Outlook Express, or Restart if you installed Internet Config.

some items in your System folder. Click on Restart, and when your Mac comes back to life, you'll find the Outlook Express folder and icon waiting for you. Now for the real meat of this chapter—configuring and using Outlook Express.

Opening Outlook Express

There are actually several ways to open Outlook Express. Which of these you have access to will depend somewhat on how your Macintosh is set up. The three starting options are the Outlook Express icon, the Microsoft Office Manager menu, and the Email icon.

The Outlook Express Icon

The most convenient method at the moment is to double-click on the Outlook Express 4.0 icon in the Finder (see Figure 15.4). Later on, though, you'll close that window, and you'll want a faster way to open the program than digging through folders. No problem!

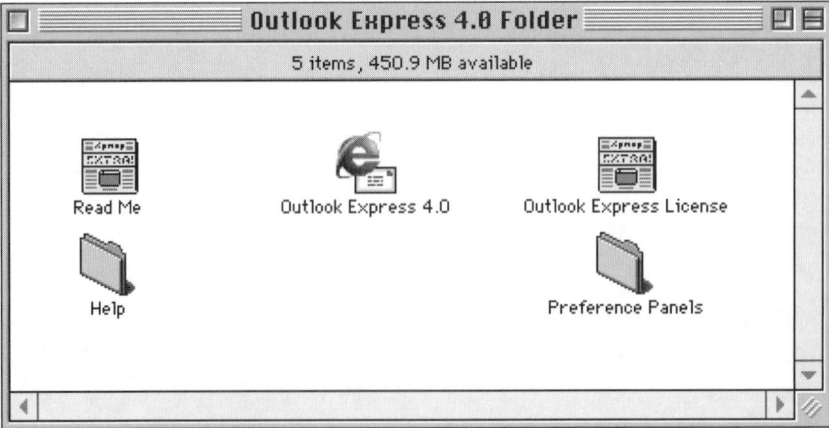

Figure 15.4 After you've installed Outlook Express, you'll find its folder open and waiting for you.

The Microsoft Office Manager Menu

Like all Office 98 programs, Outlook Express also opens from the Microsoft Office Manager menu. When you choose Microsoft Outlook Express, Outlook Express springs to life.

The Email Icon

Outlook Express also opens a third way—usually. New Macs using OS 8 or later come with an Internet Assistant. This assistant creates two icons on your desktop—one called Browse The Internet, the other called Email (see Figure 15.5). During installation, if you chose to make Outlook Express your default mail and news client, double-clicking on the Email icon on your Desktop now opens Outlook Express instead of your previous email client.

If you don't have an Email icon and you're using OS 8 or later, look for your Internet Assistant and run it (check your system documentation for more information). Having that little icon on the Desktop makes things much simpler!

Configuring Outlook Express

Regardless of how you do it, once you launch Outlook Express, the first thing you see is a question. Outlook Express wants to know if you'd like to import files from other mail programs. If you've used another email program and want to move your old mail over to OE, click on Yes. Otherwise, click on No, and skip the next few paragraphs.

Importing Mail

When you click on Yes, the Select Import Types dialog appears (see Figure 15.6). What you'll actually see in this dialog will vary, depending on what email programs Outlook Express finds on your Mac. Select the program(s) you want to import from by clicking to the left of the name. (At the time of this writing, Outlook Express allows you to import from Qualcomm Eudora, Netscape Navigator, Netscape Communicator, and Microsoft Internet Mail and News. Microsoft will undoubtedly extend Outlook Express's import capabilities as time goes on. Check the Microsoft Free Downloads page periodically to see if the translator you need is available.)

Figure 15.5 The Mac OS Internet Assistant creates this icon to launch your default email program.

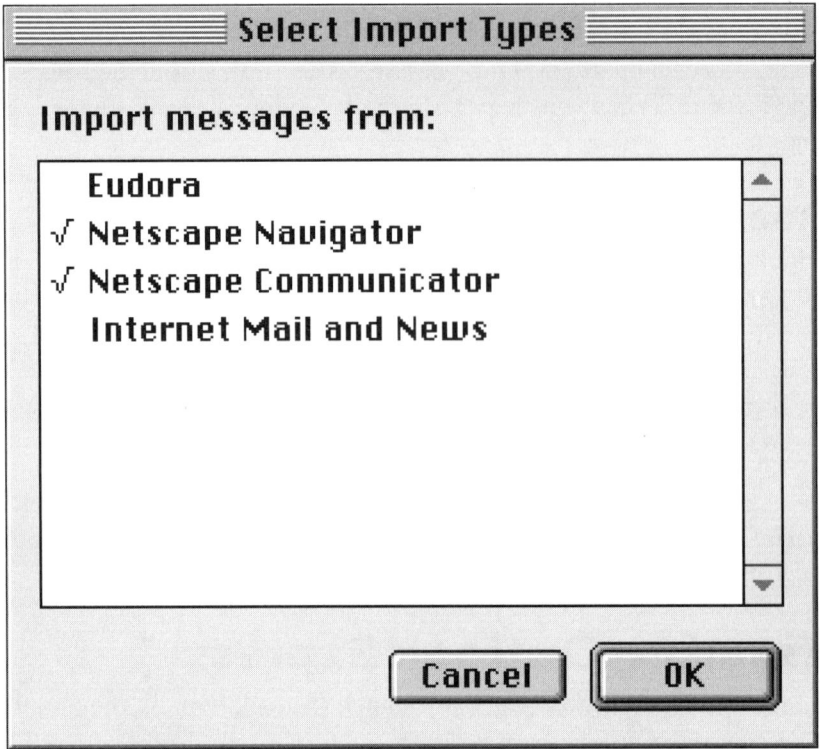

Figure 15.6 In the Select Import Types dialog, choose the name of your old email program to import your messages into Outlook Express.

Fast Track

If you're importing messages from Netscape Navigator or Netscape Communicator, the process can be a little slow (especially if you have lots of messages). To speed things up, launch Navigator or Communicator and open the Mail window. Then, one at a time, select your mail folders and choose File|Compress Folder. When you've compressed all your mail folders, quit the program, return to Outlook Express, and continue the import process.

Next, you will be asked to locate the folder where your old mail program's information is stored. Eudora users, for example, will be asked to locate the Eudora Folder (which is in the System folder). Netscape users will be asked to find the Netscape ƒ and Netscape Users folders (both of which are in System/Preferences). In the dialog, once you've navigated to the folder you need, click on it and then click on Select. Outlook Express will translate your old information and ask for other folders if necessary.

Once the import is complete, you are warned to be sure and verify that your mail has been sorted and filed into folders correctly. For now, don't worry about that—we'll get into sorting mail later in the chapter. If you ever need to import messages again, simply select File|Import|Messages to invoke the Select Import Types dialog again.

Setting Preferences

Next on the list is setting preferences for Outlook Express. We know what you're thinking: "Preferences? How can I prefer anything? I've never used the program before!" Not to worry. This is really your Internet account information, not your program preferences. The specific information you need should have been given to you by your Internet Service Provider (ISP) when you registered for service. If you're on an office network, ask the system administrator for the proper settings.

You'll need the following data: email address, POP server, SMTP server, news server, and authentication preferences. Make sure you have this in hand before proceeding. If you've previously used Internet Config, Outlook Express will read your settings from the Internet Config preferences file—just double-check what you see in the preferences fields.

If you have to enter the information manually, start with your email preferences. Select Edit|Preferences to open the Preferences dialog. If you did not previously have Internet Config installed, the New Account dialog opens. Enter a name for your account, select POP or IMAP for your account type (this should be included in the information from your ISP), and click OK. You're now ready to set up your email account.

Net Savvy

POP and SMTP are acronyms for the current Internet standard ways of sending and receiving mail—or *protocols*, in geek speak. POP, which stands for Post Office Protocol, is the software responsible for receiving your email and holding it at your ISP until you call for it. SMTP—Simple Mail Transfer Protocol—is responsible for taking the mail you send and pointing it in the correct direction.

Email Preferences

First enter your Account Information, including your full name, email address, and organization (see Figure 15.7). Your full name is the same one on your birth certificate (or the one you go by). Your email address is normally in the form lawman@dodgecity.com (or something along those lines). All email addresses have the @ symbol in the middle. If your entry doesn't have the @ symbol, then you're entering the wrong data. The organization entry is optional. It can be your school, business, or (if you're using this for personal mail) blank.

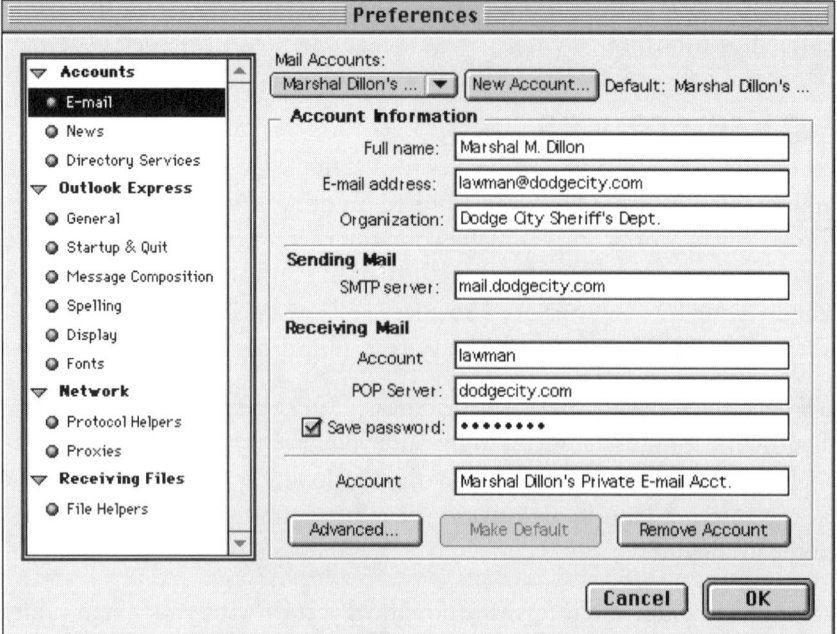

Figure 15.7 Use the Preferences dialog to enter vital information about your email account.

Now enter data about your SMTP server—it's the server you send mail *to*. You may see it listed in your ISP information as something like "mail server." It should appear like something along the lines of "smtp.mindspring.com" or "mail.well.com." Normally, there is no @ symbol involved.

Next, enter data about the server you get mail *from*—your POP server. The account will normally be the same as your email address, and your POP server data should look similar to your SMTP server setting—in fact, many companies use the same server for both sending and receiving mail.

If you are the only person who uses your Mac, and you're sure nobody else can access your copy of Outlook Express, go ahead and enter your password in the Next box, and check Save Password. On the other hand, if you work in an open office or on a machine used by more than one person, leave this box unchecked and blank. Outlook Express will ask you for your password each time you check your mail. (Note that for purposes of this discussion, we will assume that you've told Outlook Express to save your password. If you have *not* done so, you'll be asked for your password when connecting to your mail account. Just enter it, and proceed as usual.)

The Advanced button leads to a new batch of settings, all of which are beyond the scope of this book. As you learn more about email accounts, feel free to monkey about with these advanced settings, but be careful. The Remove Account option will delete all information about the currently displayed account—handy if you ever change ISPs, but otherwise something to avoid.

Net Savvy

Internet power-users tend to have more than one email account (Brian currently uses four). Outlook Express handles this with aplomb. Once you've finished setting up your primary account information, simply click on New Account, name your new account, select the account type, and click on OK. Then enter appropriate settings for your new account, use the Make Default button to set the account you prefer to use as your primary account, and move on.

News Preferences

Next up are your preferences for newsgroups, or Internet news, as newsgroups are sometimes called. Start by clicking on News in the left-hand pane of the Preferences dialog to display the News Preferences dialog (see Figure 15.8).

Fast Track

What are newsgroups? Essentially, they are open forums devoted to particular (or sometimes not so particular) lines of discussion. For example, subscribers to rec.pets.photos like to trade pictures of their cats and dogs, and readers of

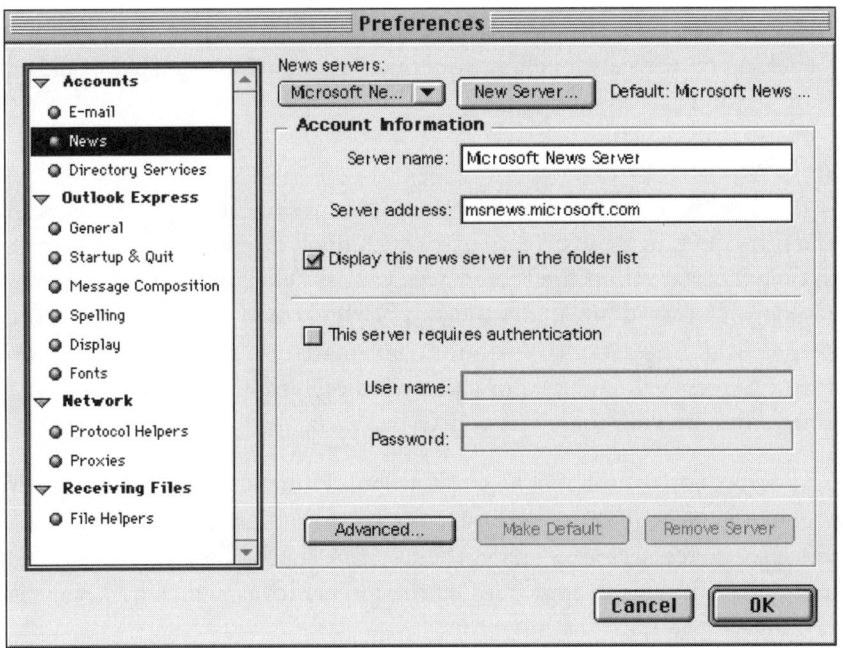

Figure 15.8 Set up your news server access in the Preferences dialog.

alt.tv.animaniacs enjoy talking about their favorite wacky cartoon show, Animaniacs (for the record, an exceptionally funny show). At last count, there were over 20,000 newsgroups to be found on the Internet, so you're almost sure to find one you like. See the "Reading Newsgroups" section later in this chapter to learn more.

Microsoft has thoughtfully provided its own free news server that you can access, creatively named Microsoft News Server. However, this server carries only newsgroups that are related to Microsoft products. To get access to *all* Internet newsgroups, you must use your ISP's news server.

First, click on New Server. Enter a name for this server (one you'll recognize easily) in the Account box, and click on OK. The name you entered will appear in the Server Name box. Now enter the server address. This will look kind of like the SMTP and POP server addresses—three words separated by periods. Normally, it will also use a name like NNTP or news, as in nntp.mindspring.com or news.earthlink.com.

If you're going to use this news server regularly (and presumably you are, because you're going to the trouble to set it up), check Display This News Server In The Folder List. This assures that you can reach your newsgroups conveniently from the main Outlook Express window.

If your server requires *authentication*, or a name and password, enter that data in the lower part of the preferences window. Your ISP's information packet should tell you whether or not authentication is required. Finally, click on Make Default to make this your regular server. Remove Server will delete the current server from your list, and clicking on the Advanced button, once again, opens up a list of higher-level settings beyond this volume's bailiwick.

Other Preferences

Two other settings merit attention before we move on. If you want to secure your mail a little more tightly, you can instruct Outlook Express to require a password each time it is started. In the Preferences window, click on Startup & Quit. Check the Require Password box under Startup Settings, then enter your password in the Password field. Enter it once again for confirmation in the Confirm Password box; Outlook Express will now ask for a password each time it's launched. Don't forget this password, because there's no way to bypass it.

Next, because you're probably new to Outlook Express, you may find it helpful for the toolbar icons to have labels, rather than just tooltips. Click on Display to open the Display Preferences area. Under the toolbars, check Show Text Under Icons. This will cause small labels to appear under the toolbar icons, which makes it easier to find things as you learn the program.

That's it. You're ready to receive and send email. There are tons of other preferences here, and we could write an entire chapter just on setting up Outlook Express to best fit your heart's desire. Suffice it to say that for 99 percent of OE users, the default settings are fine. If you ever need to change a preference at some later date, select Edit|Preferences to manually open the Preferences dialog, and change whatever isn't right. For now, though, click on OK, and let's have a look at Outlook Express.

Learning The Outlook Express Interface

To understand how Outlook Express helps you manage information, it helps to understand two basic Outlook Express terms:

- *Item*—Each useful chunk of information you work with in Outlook Express is called an "item." An email message is one item, as is one newsgroup message or one contact listing.

- *Folder*—Each type of item is stored in a different Outlook Express *folder*. There are folders for incoming mail, outgoing mail, draft mail, and so on. (These OE folders are not *bona fide* Mac OS folders; instead, they're a special way of organizing data that's unique to Outlook Express. You won't see these folders in the Finder.) Within Outlook Express's folders, you can create new *subfolders* for organizing the type of items the folder manages. You can also create your own folders.

The Outlook Express Window

When you open Outlook Express, notice the overall layout of the program window (see Figure 15.9). Whereas other Office programs have a document window, a series of toolbars above, and a status bar below, Outlook Express has a single window that holds all its elements.

The Outlook Express window is divided into four panes, or sections: the toolbar (at the top), the folder list (down the left side), the message list (top right), and the preview pane (lower right). In almost every window, you'll find some form of the toolbar and folder list—the exact contents may change, but the basic elements remain. The message list pane and the preview pane come and go, depending on what function of Outlook Express you're using. At the bottom of the window, you'll find the Outlook Express status bar.

Toolbar
The Outlook Express toolbar contains a series of buttons for all of the major operations you can accomplish in Outlook Express: creating new messages, replying to and forwarding messages, adding contacts, searching, connecting to various servers, and setting up preferences (see Figure 15.10). Buttons on the

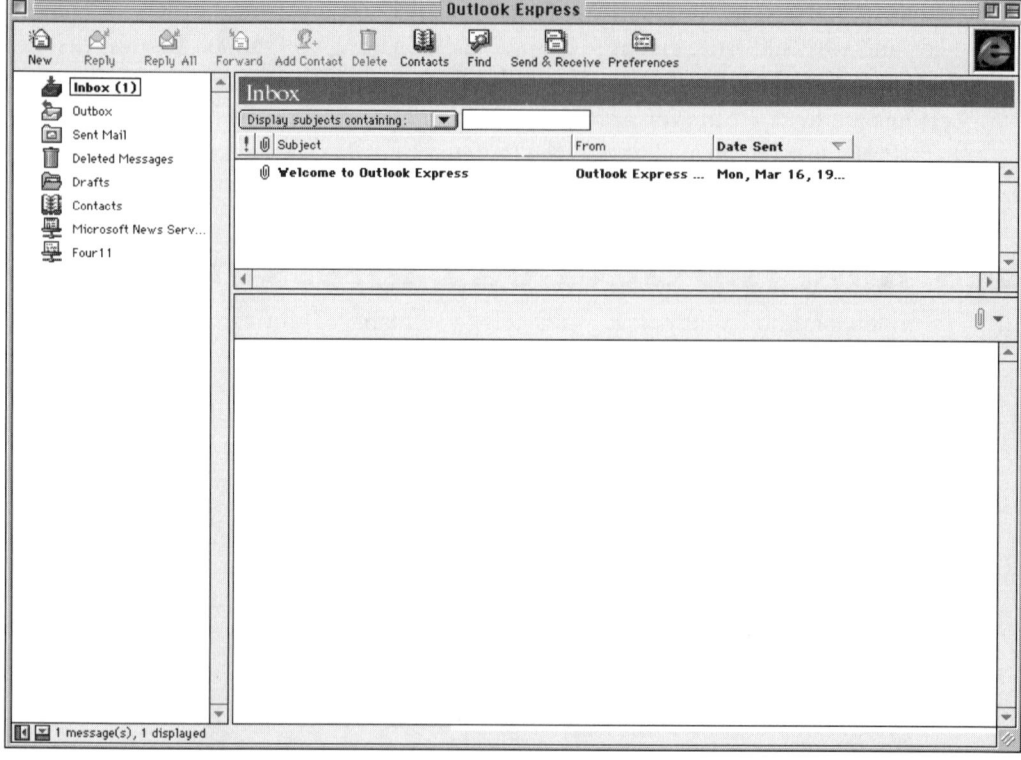

Figure 15.9 Outlook Express not only acts differently from other Office programs, it also *looks* almost entirely different.

Figure 15.10 The Outlook Express toolbar—the text labels are the ones you turned on while setting your preferences. (If you don't see all the buttons on your screen, widen the Outlook Express window a bit.)

toolbar appear dimmed if the function they invoke isn't available right at the moment. To learn more about what each button does, move the mouse pointer over each button and pause a moment. A tooltip will appear with the name of the button (most are pretty self-explanatory). The "e" logo on the right side of the toolbar is one you may recognize—it's the Internet Explorer logo. If you have Internet Explorer installed, clicking on this button automatically launches it. Otherwise, it's pretty useless.

Folder List
Down the left side of the Outlook Express window is the folder list. By default, Outlook Express comes with these folders: Inbox, Outbox, Sent Mail, Deleted Messages, Drafts, Contacts, Microsoft News Server, and Four11. Each of these

points to a different area of Outlook Express. The folder list, like the toolbar, is a constant—you'll see it no matter what you're doing in the main Outlook Express window. Unlike the toolbar, though, the icons in the folder list pane never dim. You can always click on any of them to switch to that area.

Message List
The top right area of the main Outlook Express window is called the message list. The message list shows—you guessed it!—a list of your messages. These can be email messages or newsgroup postings, depending on what area of Outlook Express you're using. The message list will change, or even disappear, depending on what function you've chosen from the folder list.

Preview Pane
The preview pane, in the lower right area of the Outlook Express window, displays a small portion of the item you've selected in the message list. Like the message list, the preview pane comes and goes according to your whims (or, more accurately, the whims of the programmers).

Status Bar
Finally, lurking quietly at the bottom of the Outlook Express window, is the status bar. This unobtrusive little strip serves two purposes. First, it tells you how many items are displayed in the current area and how many there are altogether. Second, the status bar holds two small buttons for opening and closing specific panes in the Outlook Express window; you'll learn how to use those buttons in the next few paragraphs.

Rearranging Things To Suit Your Tastes

The Outlook Express window is nothing if not flexible. You can resize, hide, and show the various panes according to your taste, or according to the amount of screen space you have available. There are three main ways to customize what you see in the window: opening and closing panes, resizing panes, and manipulating columns.

Opening And Closing Panes
The most convenient way to rearrange the Outlook Express window—and, coincidentally, the most helpful—is to close panes you're not using. For instance, if you're in the midst of reading through a batch of email messages, you're probably most interested in the message list and the preview pane. It would be nice to have some extra space to show your messages. If your message list is really long and you prefer reading messages in a separate window anyway, you may get the most benefit from just closing the preview pane.

There are two ways to accomplish each of these objectives. The first is the View menu. By selecting View|Folder List or View|Preview Pane, you can hide or show each of these panes. (Notice that you can also hide or show the toolbar. We recommend leaving the toolbar visible at all times, just because it's so useful.) The second, and more convenient, way to hide or show panes is via the Hide/Show buttons in the lower left corner of the status bar (see Figure 15.11). The leftmost button is the Hide/Show Folder List button. Click on it, and the folder list "rolls away" into the left side of the window, allowing the message list and preview pane to expand. Click on it again, and the folder list reappears. The next button is the Hide/Show Preview Pane button, and it produces a similar effect, rolling the preview pane away to give the message list more space.

Resizing Panes

The business of hiding panes is clever, but not very useful if you need more space *without* closing any panes. Outlook Express is flexible here, too. Each pane is separated from the others by a narrow gray bar. To resize any pane, first move the mouse over its bar (there are only two bars: one vertical, one horizontal). The mouse pointer will change into a double-bar/double-arrow. Now click and drag the separator bar in the direction you want to go (see Figure 15.12). When you release, the pane will be resized. Note that each pane does have a certain minimum size past which you can't drag its bar.

Manipulating Columns

The message list is usually further divided into columns, with names like Subject, From, and Date Sent. These columns hold various bits of information about each item in the folder you've selected from the folder list. To customize your view of these columns, place your mouse pointer over the line in the headers that divides each column. It will change to the resize pointer. Now click and drag the border left or right, to make the column narrower or wider (see Figure 15.13).

You can also elect to remove a column entirely. Select View|Columns to see a submenu of available columns. Those with checks are currently displayed. Select them to uncheck, and thus hide, them in the display. You'll also see three unchecked columns, which you can turn on or off as you prefer: The To column shows to whom each item is addressed, Size displays the size of each item in kilobytes, and Account shows the account that received the item.

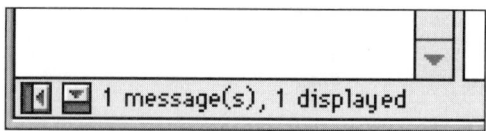

Figure 15.11 Use the Hide/Show buttons to "roll away" panes you're not using.

Communicating Via Outlook Express   **401**

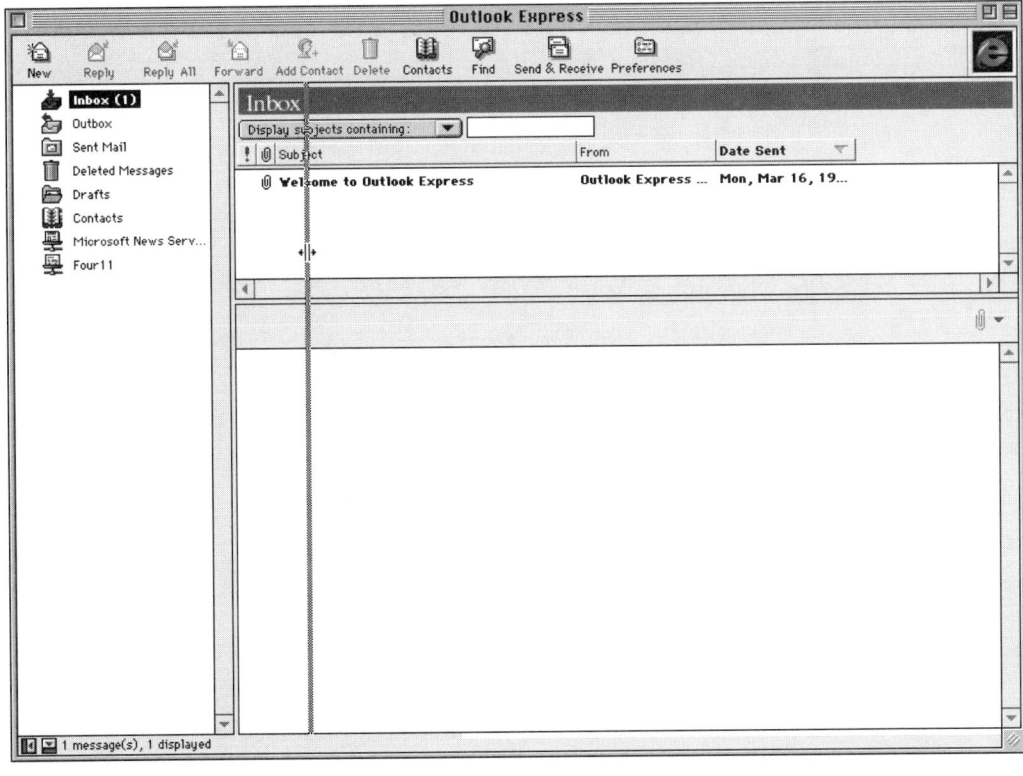

Figure 15.12 By dragging each pane's separator bar, you can resize panes to fit your needs.

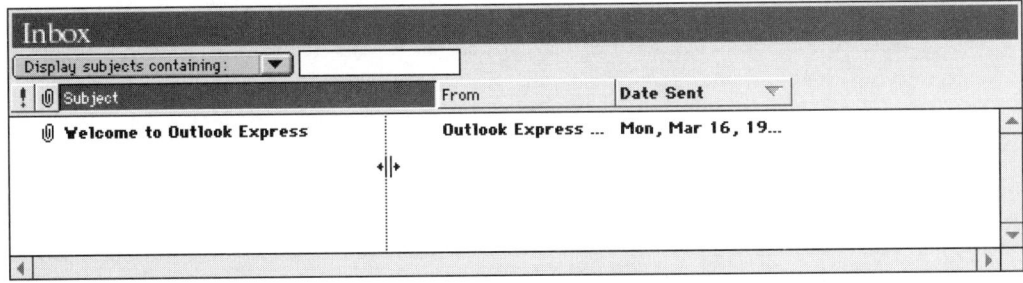

Figure 15.13 Drag separator lines between columns to resize each column.

Walk-Through: Getting Around

Go through the following steps once or twice to get familiar with the Outlook Express interface:

1. Start Microsoft Outlook Express. If you haven't run Outlook Express before, you'll be asked for your email account settings.

See "Configuring Outlook Express" earlier in this chapter for information on setting up Outlook Express.

2. Beginning with the Inbox, click on each of the icons in the folder list pane to explore the various areas of Outlook Express. Notice how the message list and preview panes change according to what you select.

3. Click on the Hide/Show Folder List button to hide the folder list. Do the same for the preview pane. Observe how the size of the remaining panes changes when one is closed.

4. Select View|Folder List to display the folder list again. Select View|Preview Pane to reopen that pane as well.

5. Click and drag the folder list pane's separator bar to make it narrower.

6. In the same way, expand the message list pane as far as possible. Experiment with resizing panes until the overall view pleases you.

7. Click on the Inbox icon. In the Inbox message list pane, resize the Subject, From, and Date columns so you can see all of the information in each column.

Working With Folders

Folders are crucial to working in Outlook Express. They are how you maintain your organization (and in some cases, your sanity) amid the flood of email messages, mail list digests, and newsgroup postings that inevitably accumulate as you use Outlook Express. That makes the whole affair sound a little overwhelming. Fortunately, thanks to Outlook Express's thoughtfully designed handling of folders, it isn't.

The minute you start Outlook Express, you already have five folders: Inbox, Outbox, Sent Mail, Deleted Messages (looks like a trash can, but it's a folder), and Drafts (see Figure 15.14). You can also create and delete additional folders as needed. Using these new folders, you can sort your mail into easily manageable batches, grouped by subject, time, source, or any other criteria you wish.

Figure 15.14 Outlook Express starts with five default folders, to which you can add your own.

Net Savvy

Some ISPs are beginning to offer IMAP folders, as well as POP mail accounts. This book focuses on POP accounts exclusively, as IMAP folders are not only uncommon at this point, but are also beyond the scope of this book. If you have an IMAP-based account, you can certainly use OE. In fact, Outlook Express works quite well with IMAP folders. Consult the OE help documents for more on using OE with IMAP.

Creating And Moving Folders

To create a new folder, start in the Outlook Express main window. Select File|New|Folder. The new folder appears in the folder list. Type a name for the new folder and press Return. The folder is now ready for you to use in sorting and storing mail.

You can also create a *subfolder* inside another folder. Select the folder in which you want the subfolder to appear. Select File|New|Subfolder. The top folder will "drop down" to contain the new folder. Name the new folder, and it's ready for use (see Figure 15.15).

You can move subfolders into other folders, as well. Simply drag them out of the original folder and drop them on the new folder. They will appear within the new folder immediately.

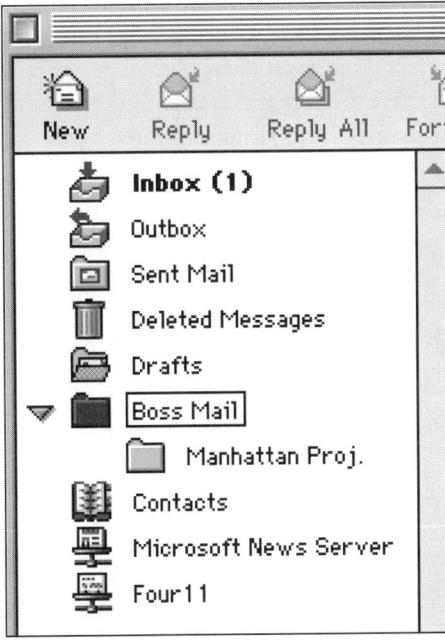

Figure 15.15 The user-created folder called *Boss Mail* contains a subfolder called *Manhattan Proj.*

Renaming And Deleting Folders

To rename a folder, click on its name in the folder list and type the new name. Press Return to accept the new name. To delete a folder, select it in the folder list. Then choose Edit|Delete Folder. If the folder was empty, it immediately disappears. If the folder contains items, you will first be asked to confirm that you wish to delete the folder. Click on Yes to delete, or No to cancel.

Note that you can't rename or delete any of the five default folders used by Outlook Express.

Placing Messages In Folders

To file a message inside a particular folder, first select the folder that currently contains the message. When the message appears in the message list, simply drag it out of the message list and drop it on the folder where you want it stored. It will be moved there immediately. To make a *copy* of the message in the new folder, while leaving the original in the first folder, follow the same procedure, but hold down the Option key as you drag the message. A copy will appear in the new folder, leaving the original unaltered.

Compacting Folders

Outlook Express actually stores your mail and news messages in a single file on your Mac. The folders are just a way to make it convenient for you to organize your messages. But as you move items around within folders, delete items, and just generally use the program, unused space can appear in the Outlook Express database file.

This expands the database file unnecessarily and can hamper the performance of the program. To prevent this, you should compact your mail folders periodically, especially if you've recently deleted a large number of messages from one. To do so, select Tools|Compact, then in the folder list, click on the folder you wish to compact. (Note that this option is only available if Outlook Express determines that a folder has free space to be compacted. Otherwise, the option appears grayed out.)

Now that you know how to handle folders, we'll look at actually working with mail messages. Keep folders in your mind, though, because it will soon be time to sort your mail, and you'll need folders then.

Walk-Through: Folder Handling

Follow these steps to create a folder and copy a message into it:.

1. If Outlook Express is not already open, launch the program or switch over to it.

2. Select File|New|Folder. A new, untitled folder appears in the folder list.
3. Name the folder "Boss Mail" by typing the name and pressing Return.
4. Select the Boss Mail folder.
5. Choose File|New|Subfolder. A new, untitled subfolder appears within the Boss Mail folder. Boss Mail "drops down" to show the new subfolder.
6. Name the new subfolder Manhattan Proj.
7. Click on the Inbox to show its message list.
8. In the message list, Option-click on "Welcome to Outlook Express," drag it to the Manhattan Proj. subfolder, and drop it. A copy of the welcome message is placed in the subfolder.
9. Click on the subfolder to show its message list. You should see a copy of the welcome message there.

Receiving And Reading Email

If you're comfortable with the Outlook Express interface, it's time to move on to actually working with email. There's a lot of ground to cover, but we'll start with the simplest activities and move on. The first thing to do is check your account for messages.

Receiving Messages

To check messages, you must first be connected to the Internet, either through your ISP or your network. (Using the TCP/IP control panel, you can set your Mac to connect to the Internet automatically when you check your mail—consult your system documentation for more information on this.) When you're connected, click on the Send & Receive button in the Outlook Express toolbar. Outlook Express jumps to it, checking your mail account (or accounts) for messages, and bringing a list of them from the server to your Mac (see Figure 15.16). (That's right—just a list. OE downloads the message *headers*, or the subject and other descriptive elements. When

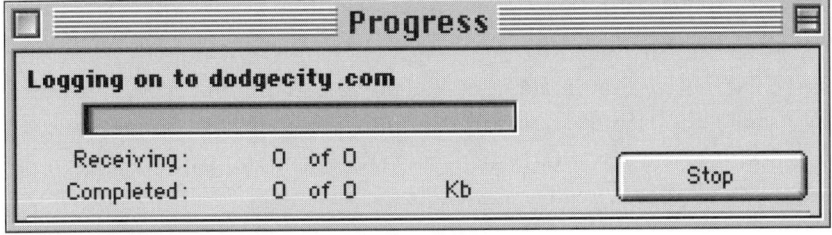

Figure 15.16 The Progress window, showing Outlook Express's status as it checks for new mail messages.

you click on a message in the message list to read it, OE goes back out to your mail server to retrieve the actual message body and any attachments.)

If you use multiple accounts, you can choose to retrieve messages from a specific account by selecting Tools|Send & Receive and then selecting the account you wish to check.

Reading Messages

After Outlook Express retrieves your message headers, it will place them in your Inbox. To see if you did, indeed, get new messages, check the folder list. After Inbox, if you see a number in parentheses, that is the number of unread messages waiting in your Inbox. Click on the Inbox to show its message list.

Items shown in the message list in bold type are the ones you haven't yet read. The next thing to do is actually read your mail (we find it's more enjoyable with a cup of coffee and some cookies…outfit yourself as you see fit).

At this point, you may be wondering how you're going to read mail if your mail account is *brand new*. Nobody could have sent you mail yet, right? Not quite. The Outlook Express Team at Microsoft has thoughtfully included a greeting for you. It's titled "Welcome to Outlook Express," and should be shown in your message list (this is the same message you copied in the previous walk-through, so it should appear as read).

To view the welcome message, click once on it in the message list. A truncated preview of the message appears in the preview pane. You *could* read it there, but all the scrolling you'd have to do to read the whole message would quickly drive you nuts. To see the complete message, double-click on it in the message list.

The message will appear in its own window, wide enough for you to read it without having to scroll sideways (see Figure 15.17). Note that this double-clicking trick can be done with almost any element of Outlook Express—try double-clicking on your Inbox in the folder list to open it in its own window. We told you the interface was flexible.

When you're finished reading a message, click on the window's Close box. In the message list, notice that if the item was previously in bold type, it is now in plain type (if you completed the last walk-through, you may have noticed this while you were working). You can use the listings here just as you would an open envelope to tell if you've already read a particular message.

Communicating Via Outlook Express   407

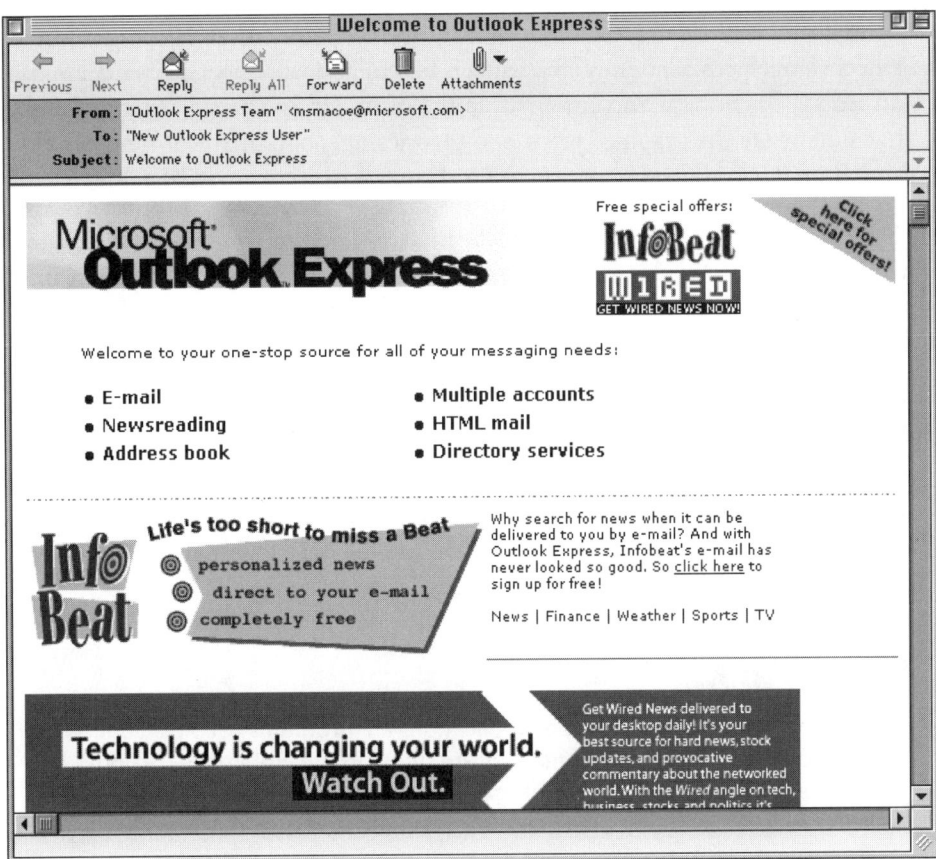

Figure 15.17 The Outlook Express development team at Microsoft sends its greetings, and a little more.

Net Savvy

International messages can sometimes throw Outlook Express a curveball. Normally, OE doesn't have a problem showing a message in the language in which it was sent. Occasionally, though, the program has a problem deciphering the mail. If this is the case, select the message in the message list and double-click on it. Select Format|Character Set, then select the language character set in which to show the message. This will force Outlook Express to display the message in a new character set, but will not change the message itself. (You must have foreign language support installed on your Macintosh to do this—see your system documentation for more information.)

Opening Attachments

Look at the message list again, paying close attention to the entry for the welcome message. Notice the little paper clip icon to the left of the message title? That paper clip indicates that there are *attachments* to this message. Just as you might put a disk in an envelope with a letter, you can attach files of almost any kind to email messages and send them along with your email to the recipient. In this particular case, the attachments are the graphics you see in the message, but an attachment can be anything from a Word document, to an Excel spreadsheet, to a database file.

To get a look at the attachments for this message, first open the message in its own window by double-clicking on it in the message list. When the message's window opens, click on the drop-down Attachments menu in the toolbar (see Figure 15.18). This menu shows a list of the attachments and, in parentheses, their file types. Select the one you want to view.

Provided that you have the right program on your Mac (JPEGView, in this instance), the attachment will open right up. Otherwise, OE will tell you that it can't find an appropriate *helper application*, and it will ask if you'd like to save the file for later. If you get this dialog, simply click on Yes, then use the Save dialog that follows to store the attachment away until you get the right program to view it.

Fast Track

What's a *helper application*? Helper applications are programs used by Outlook Express to open your attachments. They are set up in the Preferences dialog under File Helpers. Essentially, by interpreting certain characteristics of a file, OE recognizes it as "belonging" to a particular program, and uses that program to open it.

When you open the Preferences window, you'll see that OE is already set up to open a vast number of file types, literally from A to Z. If there's an attachment you can't open, it's probably because you don't have that helper installed on your Mac. If you're missing a particular helper application, it's likely that there's a program available from the Internet to help you. Use your Web browser to look for the program you need at **www.shareware.com** or **www.download.com**.

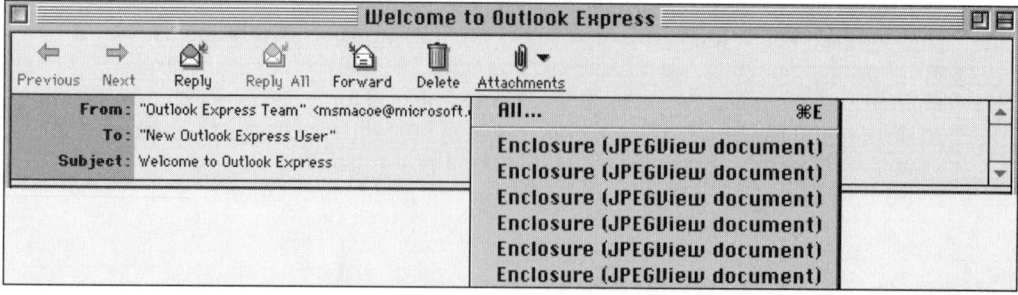

Figure 15.18 The welcome message's Attachments menu lists the graphics you see in the message window.

It is possible to set up new helper application links in the Preferences dialog, but that discussion requires knowledge beyond the scope of this book. Consult the Outlook Express help files or your system administrator to learn more about configuring new helpers.

Often, you'll simply want to save attachments for later viewing, without trying to open them first. To do so, simply select the message in the message list and choose Message|Save Attachments. From the submenu, choose either All (to save all attachments to the selected message), or select a specific attachment if there is more than one (see Figure 15.19). In the Save dialog that appears, pick a place to store your attachment(s), and click on Save.

Printing Messages

One of the truisms of the "paperless office" is that it's never really paperless. A primary cause is email, because no matter how secure computers are, lots of people feel even more secure having a "hard copy" of their email, to file and reference at a later date. Outlook Express provides you with a couple of options for printing your email.

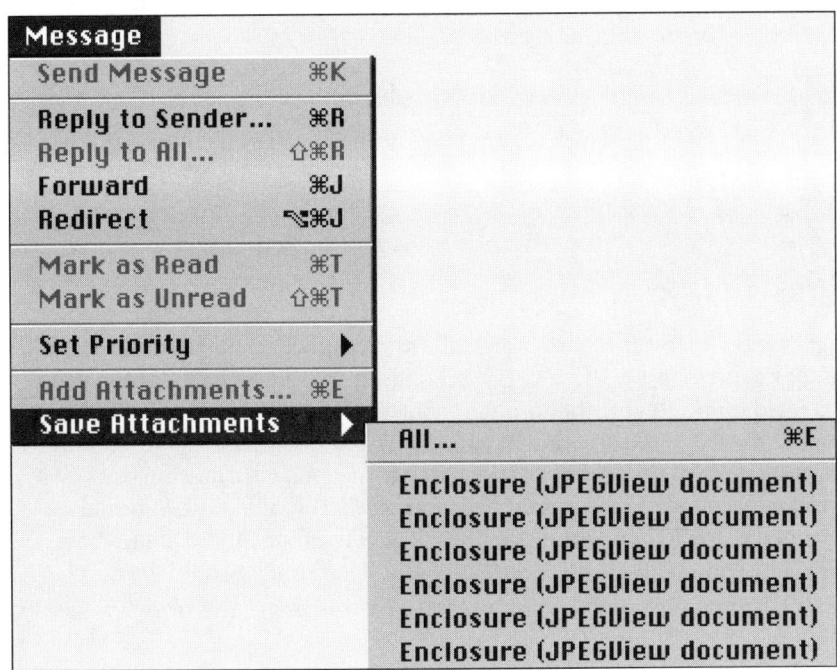

Figure 15.19 Like the Attachments menu, the Save Attachments menu lists each attachment; select one to save it to disk for later use.

In a message window, to print a copy of the message you're viewing, select File|Print, then click on the Print button. Depending on your printer, you may have a few options to select from in the Print dialog, but because most email consists of very little besides text (and perhaps a bit of formatting and, in rare cases, a graphic or two), there's really no need to do much fiddling.

Fast Track

To print a single copy of a message, simply press Cmd+Opt+P. Your mail will immediately be sent to the printer.

If you have a batch of messages to be printed, simply select the items in the message list by Shift-clicking on each one, then select File|Print. The lot of them will be sent to your printer in succession.

Saving As Text

Frequently, you'll want to copy information contained in an email message to another document—either as a direct quotation, or by reproducing and massaging the information. To open an email message in another application, Word, for instance, you'll need to save the message as a text file.

Open the message in its own window by double-clicking on it in the message list. Choose File|Save As, select a location for the file, type a name in the box, and click on Save. A copy of the message is now saved as a text file, which can be opened by almost any word processor.

Fast Track

There's an even faster way to move information from an email message in Outlook Express to, say, Word or PowerPoint. First, open both Outlook Express and Word (or whatever other program you need). Now open the target document in Word (the document into which you want to move the information). Leaving the Word document visible, open the message in question in its own window in Outlook Express, then click and drag to highlight the information you need to move. Move your cursor back over the highlighted area, where it will change to a hand. Click on the highlighted information, hold the mouse button down, and drag the information over to the Word window. Drop it there, and it will appear in your Word document.

This trick is functionally equivalent to the standard copy-and-paste routine, which you can also use. Just highlight your text in OE, press Cmd+C to copy it, then switch to your target document. Position the cursor where you want your copied text to appear, then press Cmd+P. Your text appears, ready to go.

Remember, though, that neither the drag-and-drop trick nor the copy-and-paste routine produces a separate, savable file of the text you selected. To do that, you must save your mail as a text file or try the next trick—clippings.

If you have the Clipping extension installed on your Macintosh (consult the system documentation for more on this), you can drag the highlighted text out to the Desktop, where it will appear as a clipping. The clipping can then be dragged and dropped into your target application at a later date. (This last trick is most useful for boilerplate, repetitive data that you use frequently and need fast access to.)

Deleting A Message

Obviously, you're not going to keep every message you receive in perpetuity. For one thing, it would take up too much space on your hard drive. For another, before too long, you'd never be able to find anything in your message list. So it stands to reason that you'll need to delete messages every so often. (Besides, if you're like us, you'll get a bunch of spam messages every day that you'll delete without even reading.)

Net Savvy

Spam is Internet lingo for junk mail, also called *Unsolicited Commercial Email (UCE)*. If you do much Web surfing, or post to newsgroups or mailing lists, you can expect to become the recipient of a fair amount of spam. Some ISPs offer anti-spam services, and there is commercial software available that purports to block out a large percentage of UCE. Outlook Express has a built-in tool, however, that proves quite useful for handling spam—it's called *rules*. You'll learn more about rules shortly.

In the message list, select those messages you wish to delete, then select Edit|Delete Message. The messages disappear from the message list, but they're not really deleted yet (surprise!). They've merely been moved to the Deleted Messages folder (the one in the folder list pane with a trash can icon) (see Figure 15.20).

On the one hand, you might find this annoying—after all, you told the program to delete the messages. Consider, though, that there will come a time when you're in a hurry. You've got 10 spam messages in your Inbox, and one critical assignment from the boss. In your haste, you select all 11 messages and delete them. Later, you realize your mistake, and nearly have a coronary wondering how you're going to tell the boss that you tossed her message. Relax! Outlook Express has you covered. In the folder list, select Deleted Messages, and the message list shows all 11 messages you deleted earlier. Simply find the boss's message and drag it from the message list over into the Inbox (see Figure 15.21). You're safe—the message is now stored back in your Inbox, ready for your attention.

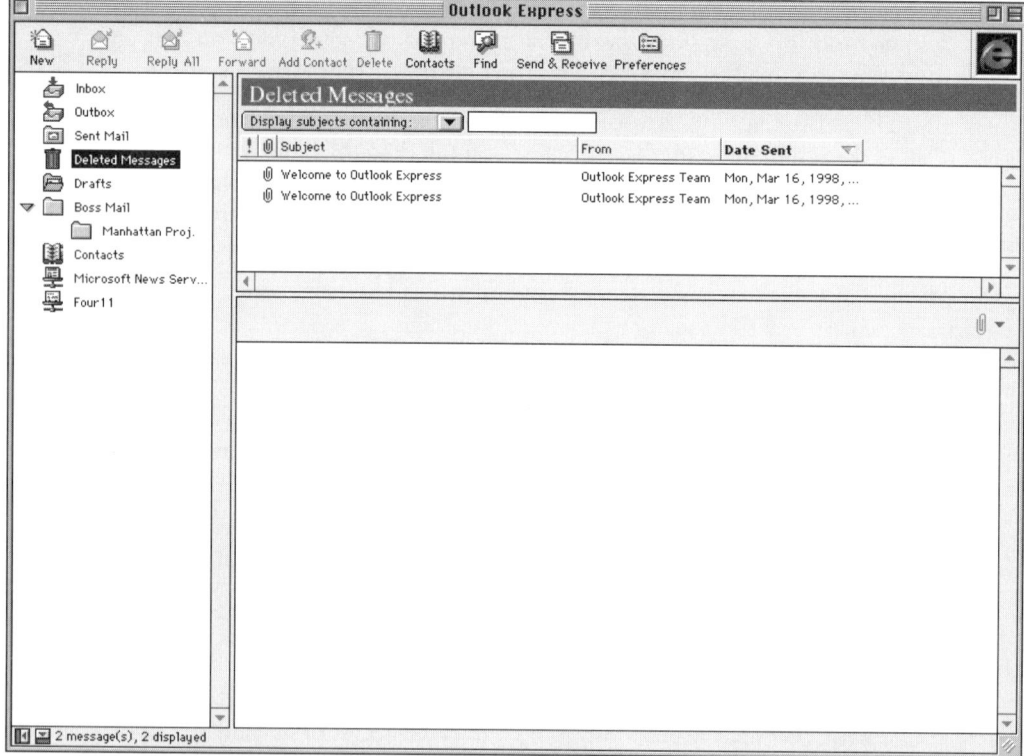

Figure 15.20 When you delete mail, it's actually held in the Deleted Messages folder (selected at left) until you specifically empty this folder.

To *really* delete the messages, select the Deleted Messages folder and choose Edit|Empty Deleted Messages. A dialog appears, asking you to confirm that you *really* want to delete your messages. Click on Yes—now the messages are gone for good.

Fast Track

Emptying the Deleted Messages folder gets old quickly. To have Outlook Express automatically empty it for you when you quit the program, select Edit|Preferences. Select Startup & Quit from the left pane, and on the right side, under Quit Settings, check Empty Deleted Messages folder.

Walk-Through: Handling Mail

Follow these steps to practice checking, reading, printing, and deleting email, as well as working with attachments.

1. Launch Outlook Express.

Communicating Via Outlook Express 413

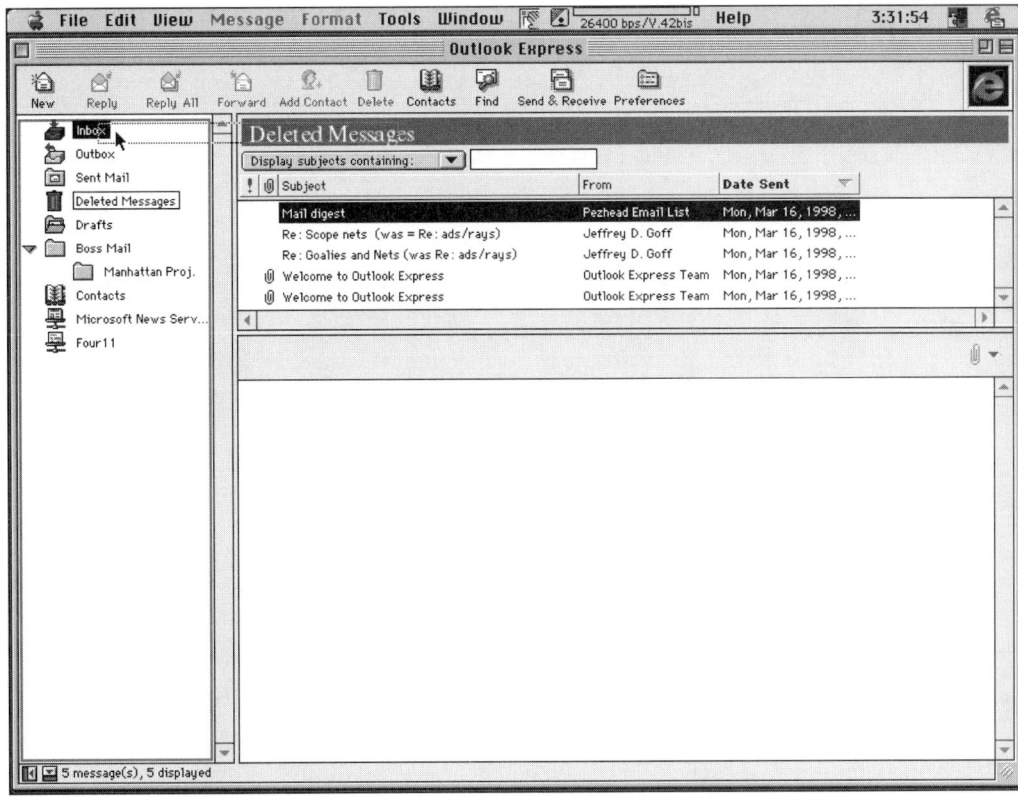

Figure 15.21 Rescuing an accidentally deleted message before it gets permanently trashed is simple.

2. Make sure you are connected to the Internet (or that your Mac is set to automatically connect when you check email).

3. Click on Send & Receive in the toolbar. The Progress window appears as OE checks your email account for new messages. If there are new messages, their headers are placed in your Inbox. Note the Inbox name to see if a number appears, denoting unread mail.

4. Click on your Inbox to show its message list.

5. Double-click on the Welcome To Outlook Express message to read it in its own window. Notice that it includes static and animated graphics, as well as links to the Internet.

6. Open the Attachments menu on the toolbar and select one of the graphics. If you have JPEGView installed on your Mac, the graphic will open. If not, you'll be asked if you want to save the graphic.

7. If you have JPEGView and you can view the attachment, close the JPEGView file and return to Outlook Express. If you do not have

JPEGView, you can either cancel the Save operation or save the graphic to another spot for later use.

8. Close the welcome message's window.
9. In the folder list, select Inbox.
10. Click on the welcome message, then click on Delete on the toolbar. The message disappears from the message list.
11. Click on Deleted Messages to show that folder's message list. In the list, notice the welcome message.
12. Drag and drop the welcome message out of the Deleted Messages folder and back into the Inbox. The deleted mail is rescued and usable again.

Sending Mail

Now that you've learned how to receive and read email, it's time to try sending some. We'll start with opening a new message, then walk you through addressing the messages, composing the body, attaching files, and finally sending the mail on its way.

Creating, Addressing, And Sending A Message

The first step in sending email is to create the message document. In the Outlook Express main window, click on the New button on the toolbar. This opens an untitled message window (see Figure 15.22).

At the top of the window, you'll see the toolbar for message handling. Directly below is a series of boxes for addressing your mail. In the Account box, OE lists your email account (or your default account, if you have more than one). If you have multiple accounts set up, choose the account you want to send this mail through by clicking on the down arrow next to your name and selecting the desired account. Directly to the right, use the next drop-down menu to set a priority level for your mail (this only affects mail that is *received* by someone using a program that recognizes prioritized mail—some do, some don't).

In the To field, type the email address of the person to whom you're sending the mail. If you're sending your message to multiple recipients, you can enter more than one address in this field, or use the CC and BCC fields. Simply separate each address with a comma or semicolon.

Enter appropriate addresses in the CC and BCC fields. CC and BCC mean the same thing in email as they do in paper mail. CC, which means carbon copy, indicates that you thought the recipient might like to know about the mail, but would probably not have a direct interest in it (because they're not listed in the To field).

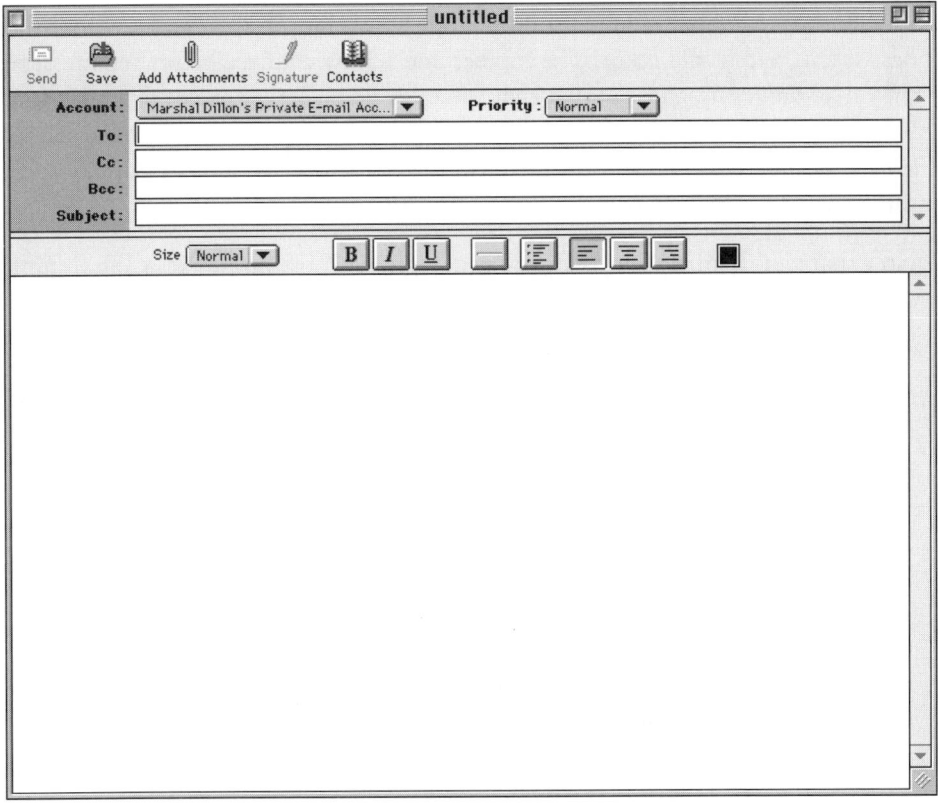

Figure 15.22 The default untitled message window is opened when you click on the New button from the main OE toolbar.

A BCC is a blind carbon copy. BCC is a bit more touchy—the recipient knows that you sent the mail, but that person is not told who else received a copy, or whether anyone else received one at all. Nor are other recipients told who is BCC'd on a piece of mail. It's often considered a little impolite to BCC mail, but use of this feature is up to you.

Fast Track

There are other ways to address mail more quickly. If you have Contacts set up (see "Working With Contacts" later in this chapter), OE will automatically fill in contact names that match your typing as you enter names in the To, CC, and BCC fields. When you see the correct one, type a comma or semicolon to accept it and move on. You can also drag a contact from the Contacts window to the To, CC, or BCC field. Finally, if you have another message or a text document open, simply highlight the email address you need and drag it to the appropriate field.

Finally, enter a subject. The bottom line on subject lines is this—make them short, descriptive, and to the point. The subject line is how your recipients see messages in their mail programs, and it's what they use to decide whether or not to read it (much like a newspaper headline). It's also how mail is filed for storage, so make sure the subject is something you and the recipient will recognize six months from now, if you think the mail will be kept.

Now that your mail is addressed, you can begin with the body. Press Tab to jump to the message body. Enter the text of your message, making it as long or as short as you like.

As you type, you'll find that Outlook Express automatically checks your spelling. Any misspelled or unknown words are underlined with a red squiggle. To manually spellcheck your finished message, select Tools|Spelling.

When you've finished entering your message, you're ready to send it (see Figure 15.23). Click on the Send button on the toolbar to begin the send procedure. The

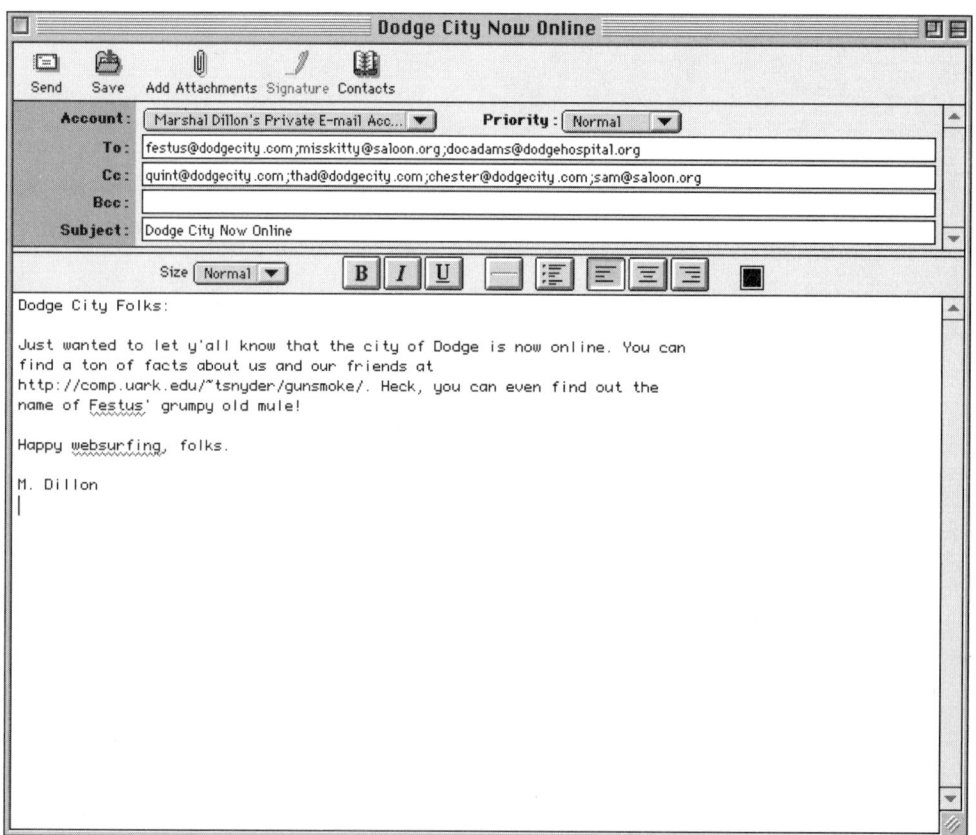

Figure 15.23 When your message is addressed and typed, you're ready to send it.

Progress window that appears will show you how far along Outlook Express is, and will disappear when the process is complete.

If, for any reason, you decide that you're not ready to send this mail yet, you'll want to save it for later. (We *strongly* recommend you do this before shooting out an angry reply to someone's message to you—reconsider, and if you still feel that way in the morning, send your mail. After all, once it's sent, email can't be retracted.) To save the mail, click on the Save button on the message window's toolbar. Your message will be saved, intact, to the Drafts folder (in the folder list). From there, you can open it later and edit it, send it, or delete it, as you see fit.

You may think that's all there is to email—just text and a zippy message to friends and family. With Outlook Express, though, there's much more.

Creating And Adding A Signature

A signature, in terms of email, is a block of standard text you can apply to the bottom of each outgoing message. Normally, a signature contains information like your name, position, email address, and business name. Business email is also often signed with the sender's phone number and business address, although this is less common with personal messages.

To create a signature, select Edit|Preferences. Choose Message Composition. In the lower right of the dialog, you'll see a large text box. Enter your signature here (see Figure 15.24). If you want OE to automatically tack this signature to the end of each message you send, check Automatically Add This Signature To All Messages. Otherwise, you can elect to add it manually to each message when you create the message. When you're done, click on OK.

Apply your signature manually by selecting Format|Insert Signature. The signature you entered in the Preferences dialog appears at the bottom of your message. Note that if you chose to have your signature added automatically, you will never actually see it attached to your message—Outlook Express attaches it automatically as each message is sent.

Formatting A Message

One of the most intriguing (and infuriating) features of Outlook Express is the ability to send HTML-formatted email. HTML (Hypertext Markup Language) is the language used to format text on the Internet, allowing you to create, among other variations, bold, italic, or colored text (see Figure 15.25).

The capability is intriguing in that it allows you to add zip to your mail messages, bolding or italicizing those items you think are important, highlighting something

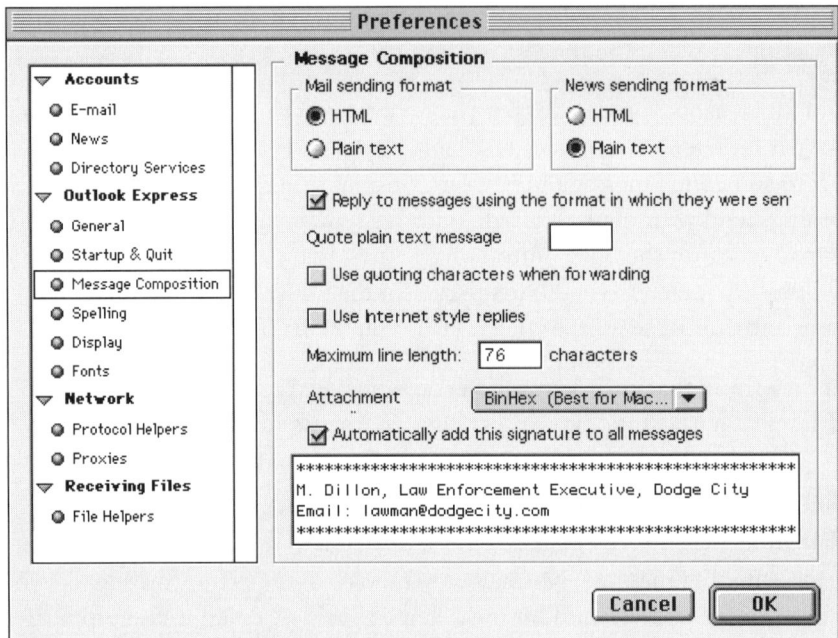

Figure 15.24 Use the Preferences dialog to create a signature to attach to your mail.

in red, centering certain lines, and so on. It's infuriating, though, because many—in fact, most—email users have email programs that don't interpret HTML formatting. For them, your beautifully HTML-formatted message will be gobbledygook, and they're likely to throw it in the trash without reading it.

Though we'll tell you *how* to add HTML formatting to a message, we can't tell you *when* to do it. If you're certain that each recipient of your message can read HTML-formatted mail, go for it. If there's the least doubt, however, stick with plain text. You can be sure they'll be able to read that.

Fast Track

To restrict your mail to plain text only, and thus ensure that you don't accidentally send HTML-formatted mail to someone, we recommend that you select Format|Rich Text (HTML) to turn this feature off. When you do so, the Formatting toolbar no longer appears in the message window, and your mail is sent as plain text.

To apply formatting to your messages, first enter your message as you normally would. When you're finished, open the Format menu and make sure that Rich Text (HTML) is checked. If it isn't, select it. After highlighting the text you want

Communicating Via Outlook Express   419

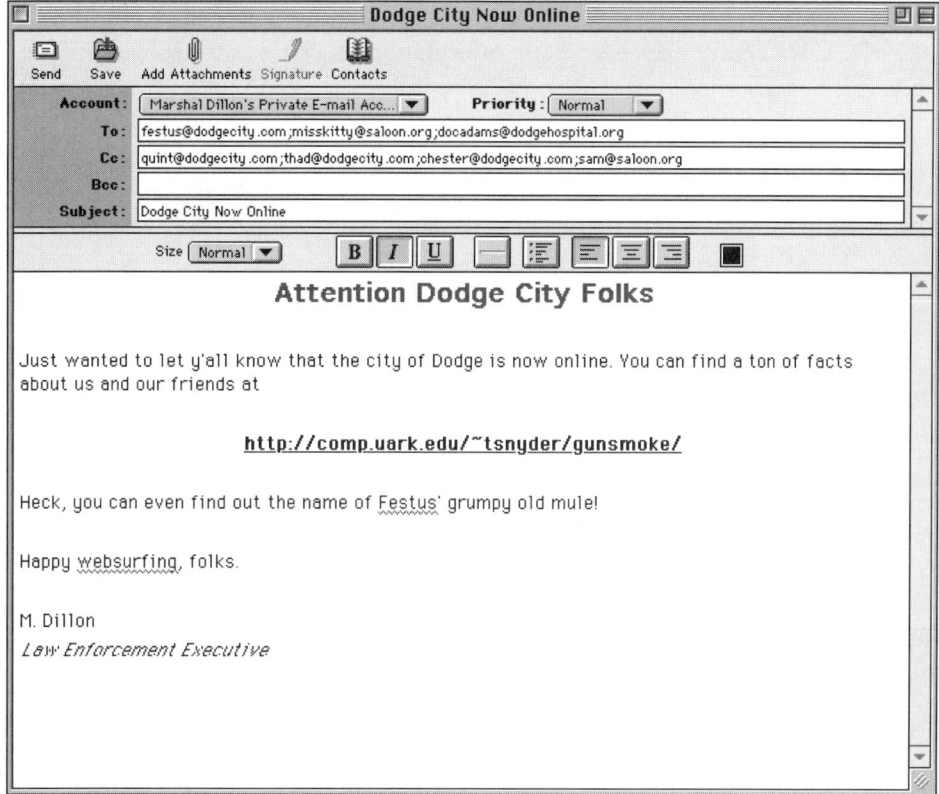

Figure 15.25   Now the message is spiced up with a hint of formatting—enough to add zip, but not so much as to be overpowering.

to format, you can perform any of the following actions by choosing from the message toolbar, immediately above the message body:

- To alter the size of the selected text, choose a new size from the Size menu.
- To bold the selected text, click on the Bold button.
- To italicize the selected text, click on the Italic button.
- To underline the selected text, click on the Underline button.
- To place a horizontal rule in your document, click on the Line button.
- To make the selected text into a bulleted list, click on the Bullet List button.
- To align the selected text to the left, center, or right, click on the appropriate alignment button.
- To change the color of the selected text, choose a color by clicking on the Color button, then selecting from one of the presets. You can also create a custom color

by choosing Other, then selecting a new color from the Color Picker (this is the Mac OS Color Picker—for more information on using it, consult your system documentation).

One more word of caution about using HTML formatting in your mail—it's like hot sauce. A little goes a long, long way. Use it to add punch, or to clarify, but be wary of making your mail so busy that it's hard to read.

Fast Track

Outlook Express currently has a bug in handling formatted mail saved as a draft. When you click on Save to place the message in the Drafts folder for later, the entire message is formatted to match the first line. For example, if your first line of type is bold, 18-point blue type, OE will change *all* of your type to bold, 18-point blue when you save as a draft. The bug is inconsistent, changing some types of formatting but not others. The moral is that you shouldn't apply formatting until you're ready to send your message.

Attaching Files

You've heard the old saying "a picture is worth a thousand words." Well, it's true—especially with email, where the words carry no emotional inflection, and there are no cues to be gained from the sender's facial expression or body language. Frequently, what you need to say will be more than what simple words (even HTML-formatted words) can express. Perhaps you need to attach a file containing a graph or picture, or even a sound or movie, to your message.

To attach a file, first have your message open in its own window in Outlook Express. Keeping the window open and visible, move to the finder and open the window that contains the file or files you want to attach (you can attach multiple files to the same message). When you can see the file's icon, click and drag it over the message's window. If you have a small screen, remember that you can shrink the message window as much as necessary to get to your files. It's worth the little bit of extra dragging, because this drag-and-drop method makes attaching files so much easier.

The file is now attached to your message. In the message window, a frame will appear below your message, separated by a heavy line. Below the line, you'll see the icon for the file you just attached (see Figure 15.26). Repeat this procedure for each file. You can also attach all your desired files at once by Shift-clicking on them in the Finder and dragging the batch of files over the message window. When their icons appear in the bottom of the message window, the message is ready to be sent with its attachments.

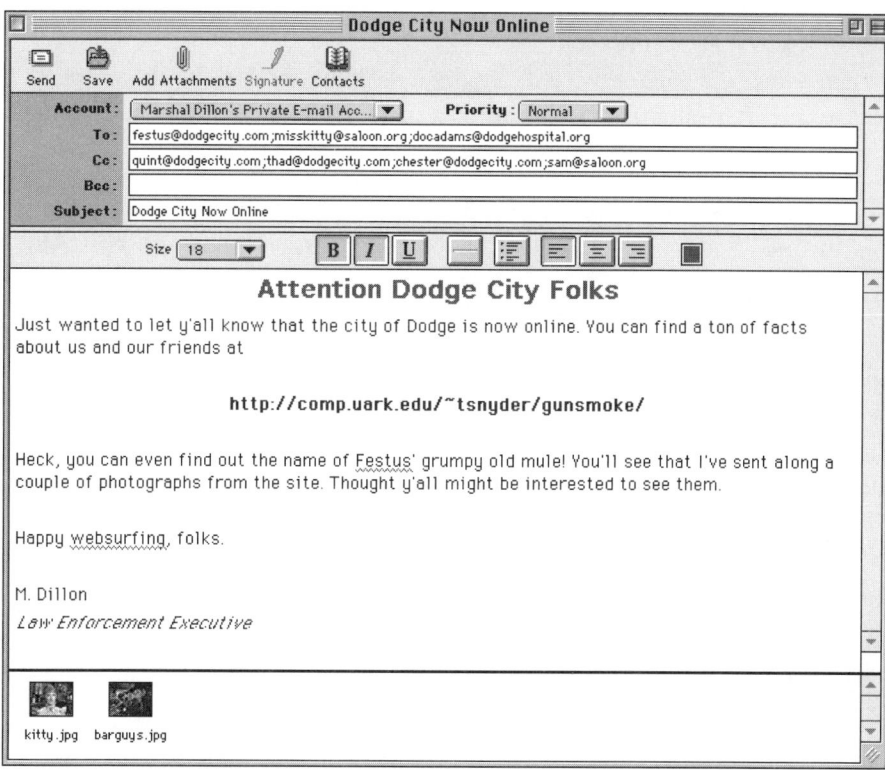

Figure 15.26 Attach files to your message by dragging and dropping them onto the message window.

If you change your mind later (before sending the message), you can unattach files by selecting them in the message window, dragging them to the Mac's trash can (the one on the Desktop), and dropping them over it. They'll be removed from your message immediately.

You can also attach files using the Add Attachments button from the toolbar in a message window. Click on Add Attachments to invoke the Add Attachments dialog. Using the dialog, navigate to where each file you wish to attach is stored, select it in the file list window, and click on Attach. The file now disappears from the file list window and its name appears in the Attached Files list at the lower left. (If you attach the wrong file by mistake, select it in the Attached Files list and click on Remove, or use Remove All to get rid of all selected files.)

When you've selected all the files you wish to attach, click on Done. You will be returned to the message window, where your attachments will appear at the bottom.

Replying To A Message

Often, a message you receive will require a response, or *reply*, to the sender. There are two primary options for replying to a message. First, either open the message in its own window, or select it in the message list.

To reply to the sender only, click on the Reply button. To reply to both the sender *and* anyone listed in the CC box of the original message, click on Reply All.

When you click on either button, a new message window appears, with the text of the original message quoted in the main text area. The To and CC boxes contain the addresses of those persons you're replying to. Add any other addresses to each field as appropriate, then type your reply in the main text area. When you're finished, click on Send Message. (To manually quote the text of another message, copy the text from the original message, then return to your new message. Position the cursor in the message body, then select Edit|Paste As Quotation. The text will appear with a ">" character to the left of each line, indicating that this text is quoted from another message.)

Net Savvy

Quoting is considered a standard procedure when replying to a message. Because people typically receive many email messages over time, it may be difficult for the recipient of your message to remember exactly what the two of you were talking about (especially if, like us, you're sometimes a little slow getting around to replying). Quoting the salient portions of the message to which you're replying helps the recipient recall their last comments to you. Don't overquote, though. Select and delete those parts of the message that don't pertain to what you're talking about.

Forwarding A Message

Often, you'll want to pass along an email message to other people. It may be a meeting schedule, an inventory update, or a letter from grandma you want the kids to see. Forwarding allows you to pass messages along, adding your own comments.

To forward a message, either open it in its own window or select it in the message list. Click on the Forward button or select Message|Forward. In the To, CC, and/or BCC fields of the new window that appears, enter the email addresses of the recipients you're forwarding the message to. Give your message a subject and add any comments you wish in the main text area (the text of the forwarded message will already appear there). Choose Send Message to forward the message to your recipients.

Fast Track

To forward a message without adding to it, use the Redirect function. With the message open in its own window, or selected in the message list, select Message|Redirect. Enter an address in the To, CC, and/or BCC fields, and choose Message|Send Message Now.

Walk-Through: Composing And Sending A Message

Follow these steps to compose and send a message to yourself (sure, it sounds a little wacky, but it's good practice).

1. Launch or switch to Outlook Express.
2. In the Outlook Express main window toolbar, click on New. A new message window appears. Your email account is selected in the menu at the top right.
3. In the To field, type your email address.
4. In the Subject field, type "Test Message to Me".
5. Click in the main text area and type yourself a short message. Make it about anything you like: chocolate, minor-league hockey, zebra finches…whatever.
6. Add a bit of formatting to the text by selecting parts of the text and clicking on the formatting buttons immediately above the message body. Experiment with the formatting until you're happy with it. You can overdo it if you like this time, because you're the only person who will read it. (This is the HTML formatting of mail we warned you about.)
7. Slide the message window over a bit so you can see your Mac's Desktop (you may have to rearrange windows a little).
8. Click on the Desktop and find a small file to attach to your mail (it can be anything, but keep it small).
9. Drag the file onto the message window in Outlook Express and drop it there. When you drag the file over the window, the window highlights. After you drop the file, its icon appears in a separate area at the bottom of the window.
10. Click in the message window to jump back to Outlook Express.
11. If you've created a signature, but not told Outlook Express to add it automatically, select Format|Insert Signature. Your signature is added to the message.
12. Make sure you're either connected to the Internet, or configured to connect automatically, and click on Send. Your message and the attached file are sent winging their way to your mail server. The message window closes, and you return to the Outlook Express main window.

13. Click on the Send & Receive button. This time, Outlook Express should find your test message waiting in your mailbox. The message header is retrieved.
14. Click on Inbox (1) to see your message in the message list.
15. Double-click on your message to open it in its own window. The formatted message appears, with the attached files listed at the bottom of the window.
16. To save the attached file, use the Message|Save Attachments submenu to select a save location.
17. Close the message window. Select the message in the message list and click on Delete on the toolbar to throw the test message away.

Organizing Mail

If you use email for any length of time, you'll accumulate a pile of messages. No matter how scrupulously you delete unneeded messages. No matter how quickly you follow up and discard mail. So of course, you need an effective way to sort and organize your mail. Fortunately, Outlook Express provides several tools for doing just that. You've already learned about folders and about storing messages in them. In addition, Outlook Express has a few other helpful methods of dealing with mail organization.

Searching For Messages

Outlook Express allows you to search saved messages for specific text. This can be useful if you're looking for a message on a particular topic, or if, for instance, you want to find mail that mentions a product or place.

Searching The Message List

If you know what folder your message is stored in, you can search that folder's message list. Click on the folder in the folder list to show its message list. You can search the list by message subject, by sender, or by recipient.

Click on the Display Subjects Containing menu immediately above the message list. From the menu, select Display Subjects Containing to search by subject, Display Messages To to search by recipient, or Display Messages From to search by sender.

In the text box to the right, enter the text you want to search for. As you type, the message list will be whittled down to just those messages matching your search criterion (see Figure 15.27). To redisplay the entire list, delete your search phrase from the text box.

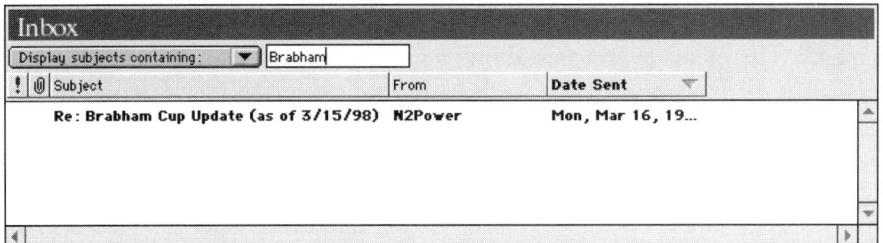

Figure 15.27 Use the Display Subjects Containing search to narrow down your message list according to subject keywords.

Searching All Mail Messages

You can also search through all messages in all folders. Be aware, though, that if you have accumulated a significant number of messages, this can take a while.

Choose Edit|Find to start the process. In the Find dialog, enter the text you want to search for (see Figure 15.28). Then choose the area of the message you want to search: From, To, Subject, or Body. If you don't check a particular search area, all areas of every message will be searched. Specifying a search area can significantly reduce search time. Select the All Folders radio button on the left to search all folders, or select Inbox to search only those messages in your Inbox. (If you have a message open, you can also elect to search only that message.) Click on Find to begin the search.

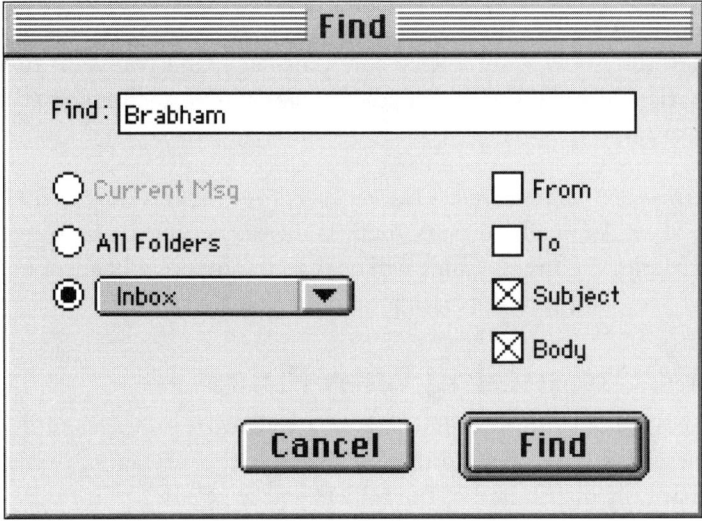

Figure 15.28 Use the Find dialog to perform extensive searches of your mail folders.

When the Search Results window appears, it contains a message list and message window. The message window allows you to sort through the messages matching your search criterion until you find the one you want. When you're finished, close the Search Results window. Note that the messages found are not moved from the folder that holds them—they are simply part of a compiled list. The original messages stay put.

Sorting The Message List

To sort your message list, click on the head of the column you want to sort by. For example, to sort your message list by message subject, click on the Subject column header. The default is to sort in descending order. To change this, click on the triangle in the right of the column header. The sort order changes to ascending. To change back, simply click on the triangle again.

Showing Unread Messages Only

In a folder that's very full of messages, it's often helpful for you to be able to see only those messages that you haven't yet read. Simply choose View|Unread Only to hide all of your previously read messages from view. To show them again, choose View|Unread Only again to uncheck it.

Marking Read And Unread

Sometimes, you might read a message and then decide you want it to continue to be designated as unread (perhaps to catch your attention). Conversely, there are times when you know exactly what's in a message, and you want to keep it, but have it marked as read. Each of these changes can be accomplished with a single menu selection.

To mark messages as read, select the messages you wish to mark and choose Message|Mark As Read. To mark them as unread, select the messages and choose Message|Mark As Unread. (This will change the message headers in the Message List to bold or plain text, depending on what you select.)

Automatic Organizing With Rules

Outlook Express also allows you to automatically sort messages into specific folders as they are received. In other words, you never see the messages in your Inbox—they are automatically distributed to the folders you select. If, for instance, you want all of your email from the boss put into a particular folder, you create the folder, then create a *rule* that tells Outlook Express to put all the mail you receive from your boss into the Boss Mail folder.

Setting Up Rules

To set up rules, first decide what the purpose of each rule will be. If you want mail meeting certain criteria to be filed in a particular folder, go ahead and create that folder before setting up the rule. Once you have your rules envisioned and your folders created, select Tools|Inbox Rules. On the Inbox Rules toolbar, click on New Rule to invoke the Define Inbox Rule dialog.

In the Rule Name box, give the new rule a name. For example, if you're still keen to file mail from your boss, call the rule "File Boss Mail," or something similar. Next, make sure Enabled (the checkbox is to the far right of the dialog) is checked.

In the Criteria section, set up the actual rule. Notice that you can specify three different criteria. (You can enable the second and third by clicking on their checkboxes. The first is always enabled.) Essentially, in using a rule, you are attempting to match a specific criterion to a specific portion of an incoming message. You can search the From, To, CC, BCC, Subject, or text portion of any message to see if it contains or does not contain, starts with or ends with, is or is not your specific search text.

Next, indicate when the actions you select should be performed. The most general setting is called If Any Criteria Are Met. To be more specific, you can choose If All Criteria Are Met. This is the more stringent test.

Finally, select an action or actions to perform if a message meets your criteria. If you select multiple actions, they are performed in order, starting with the first action you specify.

If you select Move Message or Copy Message, a list of folders appears. Select the folder you want the message moved or copied to. If you choose Reply, the Reply button appears. Click on it and enter the text of your reply message in the Reply Text dialog. When you're finished, click on OK to return to the Define Inbox Rule Dialog.

Selecting Forward or Redirect produces a text field, in which you can enter the addresses of people you want the incoming message sent to. Set Color brings up a color swatch. Click on the swatch to invoke the Mac Color Picker, where you can choose a color for the text. Mark As Read, Mark As Unread, and Delete Message perform exactly those actions they describe, and Play Sound produces a menu of sounds you can select from (this is handy if you're expecting a very important message—you can get an audio alert of its arrival).

Add Sender To Contacts adds the incoming message's From address to your Contacts list. Add Sender To Mailing List adds the From address to your Mailing

List, whereas Remove Sender From Mailing List deletes the From address. Alert produces an Alert button. Click on the button to invoke the Alert Text dialog. Here you can enter text to be displayed in a small alert dialog box when a message arrives (see Figure 15.29).

The last setting is a small checkbox at the bottom labeled Stop Applying Rules To This Message. You will probably want to leave this turned on, because it prevents two or three rules from applying to the same message, possibly refiling and redirecting it so many times that you can't find it later without a lot of trouble. Your rules should now be complete (see Figure 15.30).

When you're finished with this rule, click on OK to return to the Inbox Rules dialog (see Figure 15.31). Your new rule appears in the dialog's main area now. When you have multiple rules in this dialog, use the Increase Priority Of Rule and Decrease Priority Of Rule buttons to change the order in which your rules are applied to incoming mail.

Sounds pretty complicated, right? It really isn't. Try the next walk-through for a quick tour of rules setting—you'll be surprised how quickly you can automate your mail handling.

Changing And Deleting Rules

At some point down the road, your boss's email address may change, or you may decide to get rid of that rule altogether. In such cases, select Tools|Inbox Rules to open the Inbox Rules window. To delete a rule, first select the rule, then click on

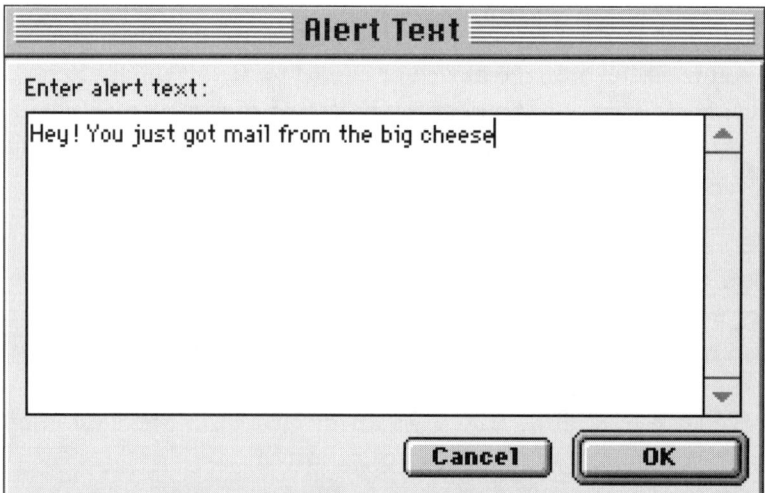

Figure 15.29 Using Inbox rules, you can instruct Outlook Express to pop up a small dialog (containing the text of your choice) when a specific message arrives.

Communicating Via Outlook Express **429**

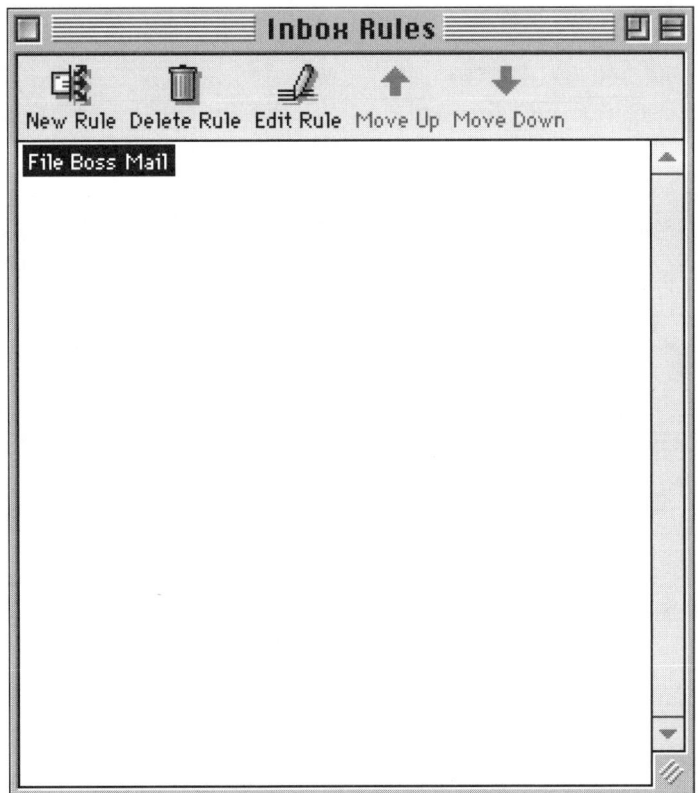

Figure 15.30 A completely configured Inbox rule, ready to be applied.

Figure 15.31 The Inbox Rules window shows your new rule.

the Delete button. You'll be asked if you're sure you want to delete the rule—click on Yes. Your rule is whisked away into the ether, never to be seen again (unless you recreate it).

To change a rule, simply double-click on it in the Inbox Rules window, change your criteria or actions, then click on OK. Your changed rule is immediately available.

Walk-Through: Setting Up Rules

Follow these steps to move incoming mail from a specific sender to the folder of your choice and to have OE notify you that this message has arrived:

1. Launch or switch to Outlook Express.
2. Select Tools|Inbox Rules. The Inbox Rules window appears.
3. Click on the New Rule button. The Define Inbox Rules dialog appears.
4. In the Rule Name field, enter "File Boss Mail".
5. Make sure Enabled is checked. Assume that your boss's email address is bigcheese@widgetcorp.com.
6. For the first criterion, select From, then Is.
7. In the first criterion's text field, enter "bigcheese@widgetcorp.com".
8. Select Execute Actions If All Criteria Are Met. For this example, you could select either All Criteria or Any Criteria. Both do the same thing, because you're only establishing one criterion.
9. For Action 1, select Move Message. A menu of your folders appears.
10. In the menu of folders, select the Boss Mail folder you created earlier in the chapter.
11. For Action 2, select Play Sound. A menu of sounds appears.
12. In the menu of sounds, choose Quack (or whatever tickles your fancy).
13. For Action 3, choose Alert. The Alert button appears.
14. Click on the Alert button. The Alert dialog appears.
15. Enter the text of your alert message in the dialog and click on OK.
16. In the Define Inbox Rule dialog, click on OK.
17. Close the Inbox Rules window. Your rule is now established and ready to go to work.

Working With Contacts

In the modern office, there is a massive amount of information to keep track of—letters, memos, inventory sheets, annual reports, coffee-duty rosters. The list could go on forever. Frequently, though, the bigger task is keeping track of *who* a particular piece of information came from. That's a *contact*, someone you deal with on a regular or semi-regular basis, whose name, address, and pertinent personal information you need to keep handy. (In fact, it's often someone you *rarely* correspond with—after all, information you don't often use is tougher to remember off the top of your head.)

It's also true that information is becoming more complex. For example, someone's address at 123 Main Street is pretty easy to recall. However, an email address—such as acu00bdl@uncsvm.uncs.edu—is distinctly more difficult (this one isn't real, but it's only two letters away from Brian's real work address, so they really can be this strange).

Outlook Express rides to the rescue. With its built-in Contacts facility, OE allows you to easily and speedily manage your contacts, and it can even provide that information to other Office applications on demand. According to Microsoft, Outlook Express is meant primarily for managing email contacts, which is probably true. But its capabilities are so useful that you may find yourself using it to manage all your contacts.

In addition, OE's Contacts facility provides access to Internet *directory services*, which let you look up people and businesses on the Internet, and allows you to set up mailing lists, or groups of email addresses.

To get started with Contacts, select Contacts from the Outlook Express folder list (or from the toolbar). The preview pane vanishes, and the message list is replaced by the contacts list. The toolbar also undergoes a slight transformation in order to handle contacts information. (Note that you can also open Contacts by clicking its button in the toolbar. This opens Contacts in its own window, which is arranged a little differently, but functions about the same. For now, use the folder list to select it. When you are more comfortable, go ahead and try Contacts in its own window.)

Note that the contacts list is divided into columns for Name, Email Address, and Company, and has a Display Names Containing field. You can organize, sort, and search the contacts list just as you did the message list earlier. (Because the search and organization procedures are so similar, we won't cover them again. Thumb back to the sections "Searching For Messages" and "Sorting The Message List" earlier in this chapter to learn how to use the capabilities.)

You're now ready to work with Contacts (see Figure 15.32).

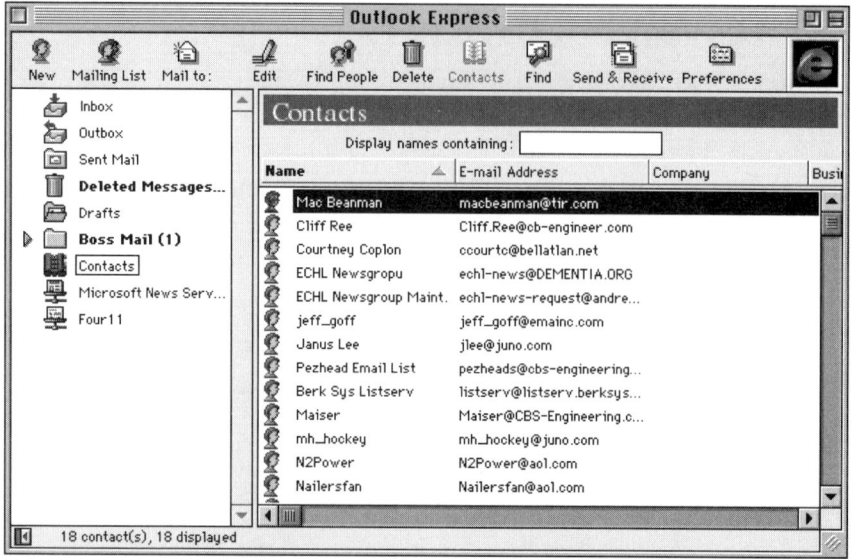

Figure 15.32 The Contacts area of Outlook Express.

Adding A New Contact

To add a contact manually, first click on New on the Contacts toolbar. This invokes the Contact dialog, where you'll enter your contact's pertinent information (see Figure 15.33).

Start with your contact's name, title, company, and department. Simply enter this information in the text boxes provided.

Under E-mail Address, click in the field and type an email address. A check will appear next to the address, indicating that this address is the default—the one to which mail will normally be sent. If your contact has multiple email addresses, click on Add to add a new field. Enter the next address in this field. If you need to remove an address, click on it in the list, then click on Remove. To change the default email address, click on the address you want, then click on Make Default.

Move on to the Address area (this time, the regular postal address). Enter the appropriate information. The default selection in the menu to the left of the Address field is Business. To enter your contact's home or another address, select Home or Other from the menu. The Address fields will clear, allowing you to enter new information. To see the Business address again, simply select Business from the Address menu.

For Phone Numbers, enter a single phone number in each field and select the phone number type from the adjacent menu. Each field can hold multiple numbers, just

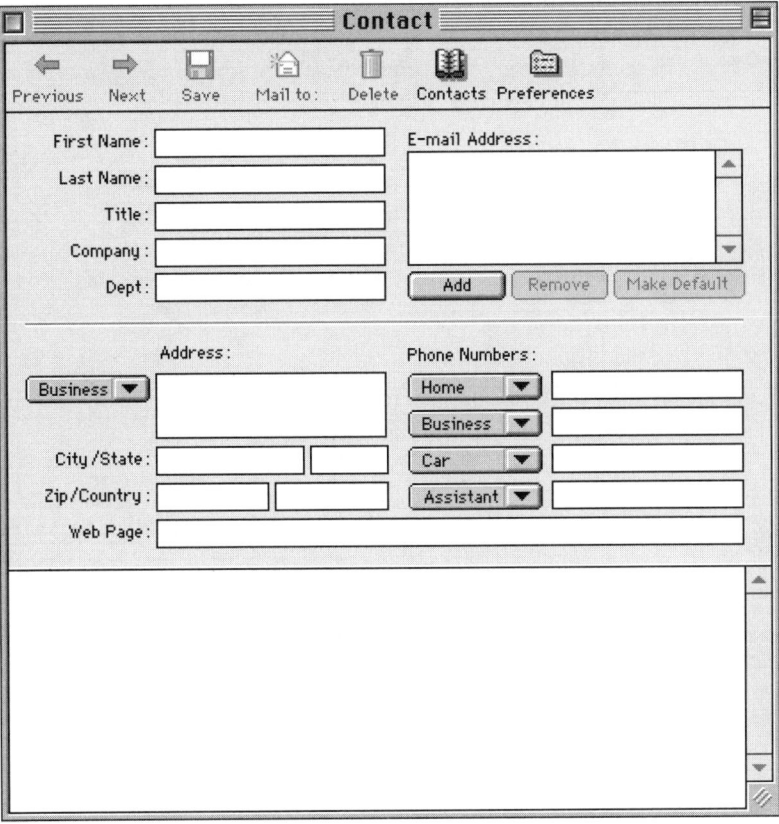

Figure 15.33 The empty Contact dialog, awaiting your information.

like the Address field. Enter a phone number in a field, then select a new designation from the menu adjacent. If there is already a number to match that designation, it appears in the box. Otherwise, you get a blank box to enter a new number. There are preset selections for Home, Home 2, Business, Business 2, Car, Assistant, Mobile, Pager, Fax 1, Fax 2, ISDN 1, and ISDN 2. (Ever wonder how we got along without so many ways to be in touch?)

In the Web Page field, enter the URL for your contact's Web page. Use standard URL format: "http://www.widgetcorp.com/bigcheese.html".

Finally, use the large text field at the bottom to enter any other pertinent information about your contact: birthday, spouse's name, favorite dessert...whatever. When you're finished, click on Save Contact on the toolbar, then close the window. Your contact will now appear in the Contacts window. See Figure 15.34 for a completed contact form.

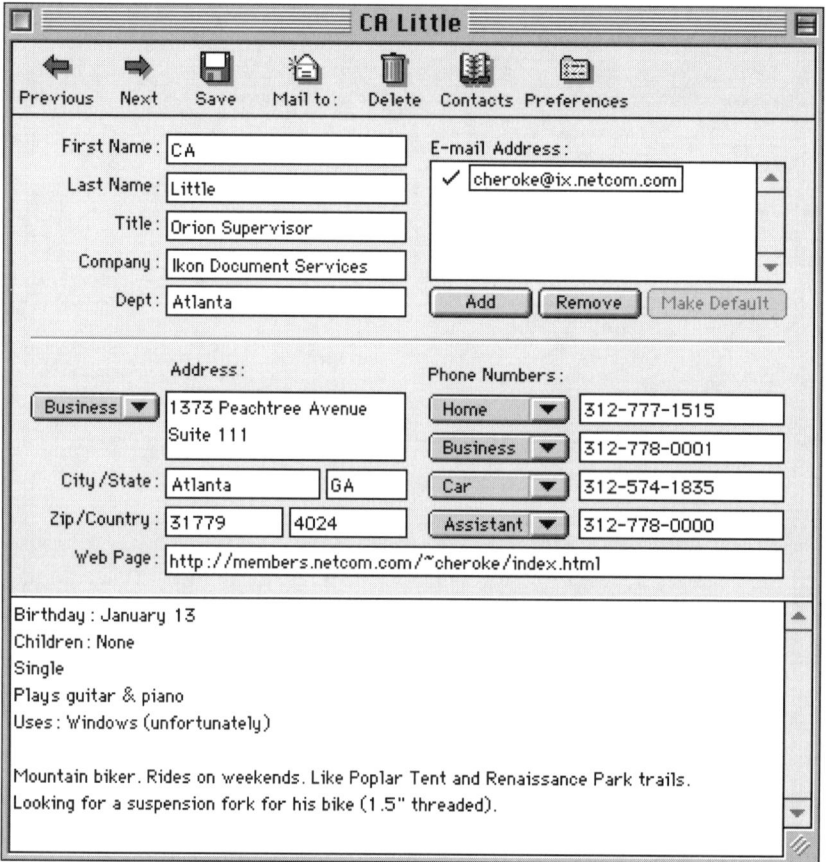

Figure 15.34 A completed information form for a manually added contact.

Adding A Contact From Email

Often, you'll want to add the sender of an email message to your contacts list. To do this, simply select the message item in the message list, then on the toolbar click on Add Contact. The sender's email address is automatically added to your Contacts. Depending on how the sender's mail preferences are configured, you can add other information as well, including the sender's name and organization. To complete the contact information, open the contacts list and double-click on the new item. Then fill in the data just as you would for any new contact. (Frequently, this last step isn't even necessary, because the main point of concern is the email address. How much other information you include is entirely up to you.)

You can also add contacts by using email addresses from a message body, or from any text file. Simply open the message in Outlook Express, or switch to the Finder and open a text file in a program like Word or SimpleText. Highlight the email address you want to add to Contacts, drag it over the Outlook Express window and drop it on the Contacts icon in the folder list. The address is automatically added to your contacts list.

Changing And Removing Contacts

To change a contact's information, first open the contacts list. Locate the item you wish to change in the list and double-click on it to open the item in its own window. Edit the information as you wish, click on the Save button, and close the window.

To delete a contact from your contacts list, choose the item in the contacts list and click on Delete Selected Item(s) in the toolbar. Confirm the deletion in the dialog that appears. The contact vanishes from your list, and you can continue working.

Sending Messages From The Contacts List

You can also use the contacts list to send messages to your contacts. First, open the contacts list. Select the person you wish to send a message to. To send the message to multiple recipients, Shift-click on each recipient in the list. Click on Mail To on the toolbar, and a new message window appears, with the selected contacts listed in the To field. Create and send the message as usual.

Importing And Exporting Contacts

In addition to importing your email from other applications, Outlook Express allows you to import your contacts or address book. To do so, select File|Import|Contacts. Select the program(s) you want to import from in the Select Import Types (if your old mail or contact management program isn't available, trying saving *from* that program as a tab-delimited file—consult the program's documentation for help with this). When you've selected the programs you want to import from, click on OK. Outlook Express will ask you to locate the old program's files. When you've found what OE is asking for, select it and click on OK. OE will import your contacts and place them in your contacts list.

Any group addresses you had in the previous program will be imported as mailing lists (which you'll learn more about shortly).

You can also export your Outlook Express contacts list to other programs as a text file. To do so, select File|Export Contacts. Choose a location for the exported file and type a name for it in the text box. When you click on Save, your contacts list is exported to a file. You can then open and manipulate this file in Word, Excel, or any other program that handles text files, which is especially useful when you want a printed copy of your contacts list.

Creating And Modifying Mailing Lists

A *mailing list* is a group of Outlook Express contacts to which you can send a single email all at once. More specifically, it's a group of email addresses. You use mailing lists to send a single message to a large number of people without having to enter each email address separately.

To create a mailing list, click on Contacts in the folder list. Then, in the toolbar, click on Mailing List. Contacts will open into its own window, and an icon for the new mailing list appears in the folder list as a subfolder for the Contacts icon (see Figure 15.35). Type a name for the new mailing list, then press Return. Make the name short but descriptive. The mailing list is created and is now available from the folder list. If you don't see the mailing list in the main Outlook Express window's folder list, click on the blue arrow next to the Contacts icon. This opens the Contacts icon by dropping it down to display the new mailing list.

To add contacts to your mailing list, select an item from the contacts list, then drag and drop it on the mailing list's icon in the folder list (see Figure 15.36). To create a

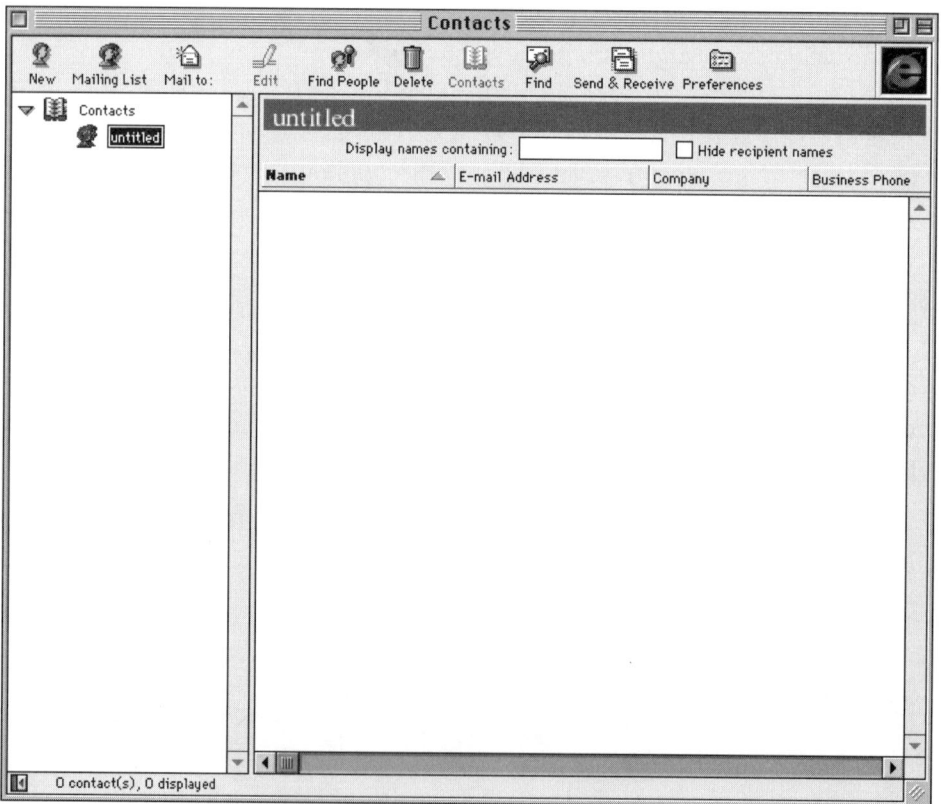

Figure 15.35 A new mailing list, awaiting a name and addresses.

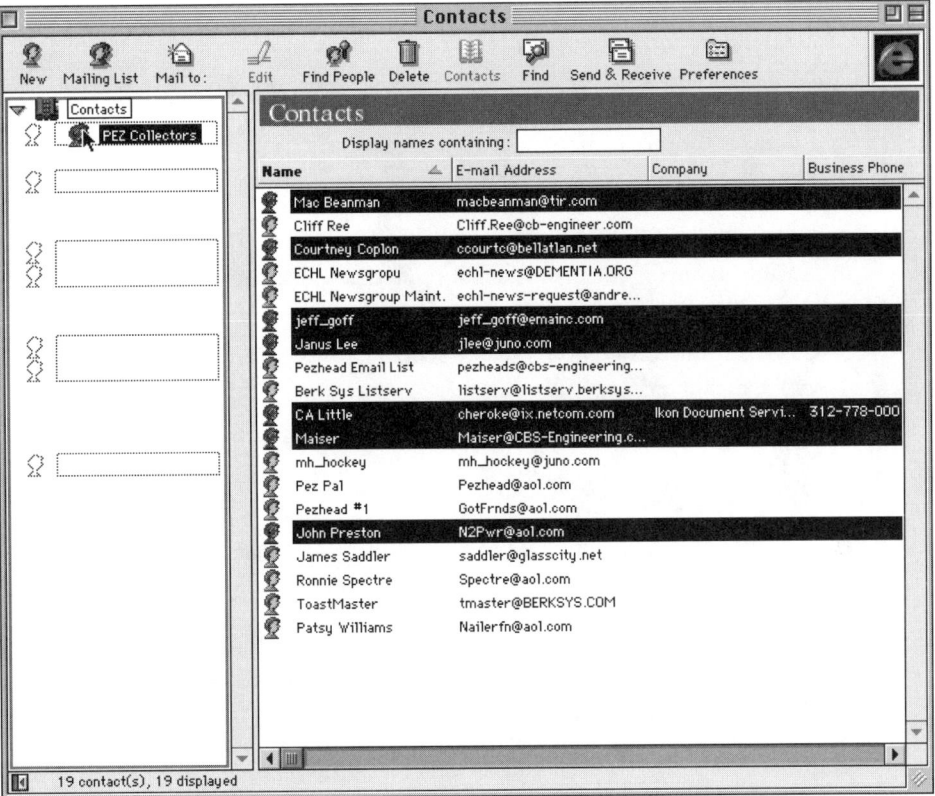

Figure 15.36 Adding contacts to a mailing list by drag and drop.

new contact in the mailing list, open the contacts list, then open the mailing list. Click on Create A New Contact on the toolbar and fill out the new contact's information just as you would when creating a new entry in the contacts list. When you're done, click on Save and close the window. The new contact is added to both the contacts list and your mailing list.

Removing a contact from a mailing list is also easy. Open the mailing list, select the contact to remove, and click on Delete in the toolbar. The contact is removed from the mailing list, but not from the contacts list. To remove an entire mailing list, select it in the folder list and click on Delete. The mailing list disappears, but the individual contacts remain in the contacts list.

Sending Messages To A Mailing List

To send a message to everyone on a mailing list, first select the mailing list's icon in the folder list. Click on Address A New Message To Selected Contacts on the toolbar, and a new message window appears, with the name of the mailing list in the To field. Create and send the message as usual.

Walk-Through: Using Contacts

Follow these steps to practice working with contacts and mailing lists.

1. Launch Outlook Express.
2. Click on Contacts in the folder list to open the contacts list.
3. Click on New on the toolbar to open a new contact listing.
4. Enter a name for your contact, along with company and title information, and an email address.
5. Click on Add, then enter a second email address (it can be fictional, because you're just practicing).
6. After you enter the second email address, click on it to select it, and click on Make Default. The first email address is unchecked, and a check appears by the second address.
7. In the Address area, enter a business address for your contact.
8. Now in the Address drop-down menu, select Home. The address fields clear.
9. Enter a home address for your contact.
10. Enter phone numbers in each of the four boxes provided. By default, you are entering numbers for Home, Business, Car, and Assistant.
11. Now in the Home Number field, click on the drop-down menu and select Home 2. The field clears.
12. Enter a second home number in the field.
13. Enter a Web page URL for the contact.
14. Enter any other information in the notes area at the bottom.
15. Click on Save to store your contact. Close the window.
16. Click on Inbox in the folder list.
17. Select a message in the message list and click on Add Contact on the toolbar.
18. Switch to the contacts list by clicking on the Contacts icon. Notice that the sender of the item you selected is now in your contacts list.
19. Open the contacts list in its own window by clicking on Contacts from the toolbar.
20. Click on Mailing List on the toolbar. A new mailing list icon appears under the Contacts folder.
21. Give the new list a name by typing the name and pressing Return.
22. Click on Contacts in the folder list to view your contacts list.
23. Select several contacts by Shift-clicking on them in the contacts list.

24. Drag the selected items to the new mailing list icon and drop them there. The selected contacts are added to your mailing list.
25. To see the additions to your mailing list, click on the mailing list's icon in the folder list.

Finding Email Addresses

Outlook Express is obviously a great tool for keeping track of people you correspond with. But there's more—OE also allows you to look for the addresses of people you *want* to correspond with, but haven't yet. This is accomplished by accessing *Internet Directory Services*.

At no extra charge to you, OE provides access to Four11, Bigfoot, Infospace, Infospace Business, Switchboard, and WhoWhere. Some of these may sound familiar if you've surfed the Net for a while. They're the same services you can access through a Web browser. OE, however, lets you search their extensive lists of email addresses without ever leaving your email program.

To use directory services, select Edit|Find People. In the Find People window, you'll see a list of directory services in the folder list (note that you can also search your contacts list from here—we've already covered searching within Outlook Express, so for now we'll stick to directory services). Select the service you want to search (see Figure 15.37).

Before continuing, make sure you're either connected to the Internet or have your Mac set up to connect automatically.

You can search for either a name or an email address, depending on what information you already know. Most likely, you'll be searching for a name, hoping to locate the person's email address. Enter a name in the Search For Name field, or an email address in the E-mail field. When you click on Find, Outlook Express connects to the directory service and returns a list of matches for the name or address you entered.

Sometimes the list can get quite huge (see Figure 15.38). Use the column headers and Display Names Containing field to sort and filter the results, just as you learned to do for sorting and filtering your message list.

Be aware that there are literally *millions* of people connected to the Internet, and some of them may not be listed with a directory service. You may have to search several, or even all, of the available directories to find someone. Even that's no guarantee—it's possible you'll actually have to call or write the person and ask for an email address.

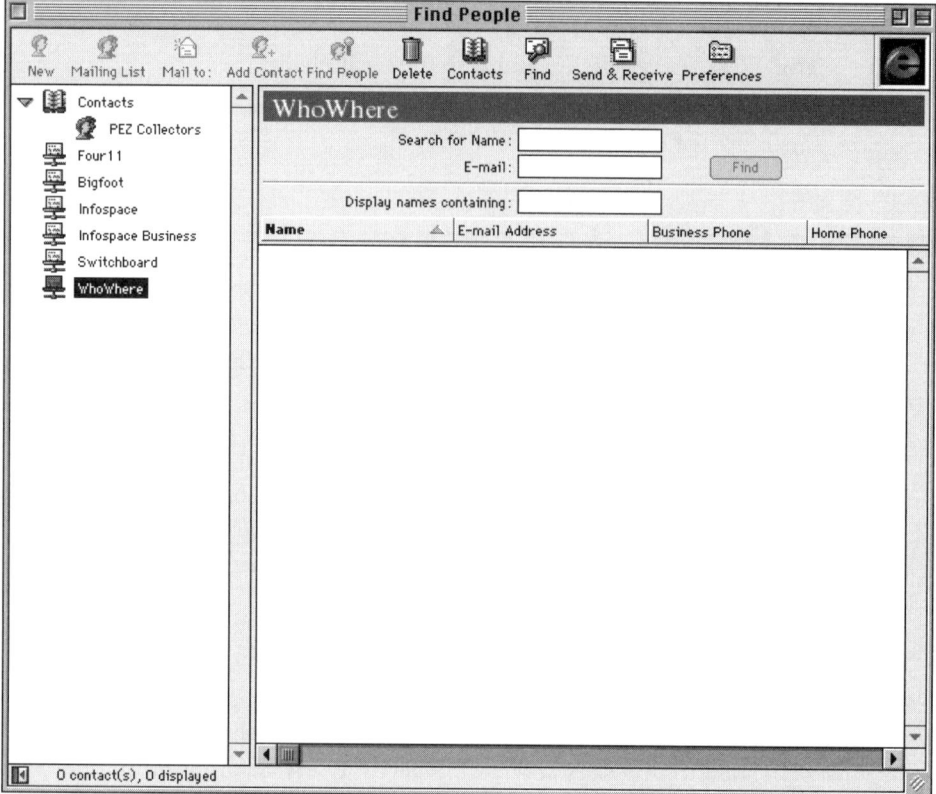

Figure 15.37 The Find People window allows you to use directory services like WhoWhere to search for people on the Internet.

When you locate the person you're looking for (or someone you think is the person you're looking for), add that person to your contacts list by dragging the entry in the search results and dropping it on the Contacts icon in the folder list. You can add the person to a mailing list in the same way.

Unless you're dead certain you've got the right person, courtesy dictates that you should send an inquiry to the address you located to make sure. You wouldn't want to go dropping a lot of unexpected email in an unsuspecting stranger's box.

Using Newsgroups

Newsgroups are the water coolers of the Internet—the places where people with similar interests gather to talk about things, exchange ideas, engage in debates (sometimes heated), and just generally shoot the breeze. Topics range from aardvarks to Z-scale model trains. Functionally, you can think of newsgroups as big bulletin boards, where everyone writes their comments on cards and sticks them to the board for everyone else to read. Some posts are random thoughts, but others follow an existing train of thought, or *thread*.

Communicating Via Outlook Express **441**

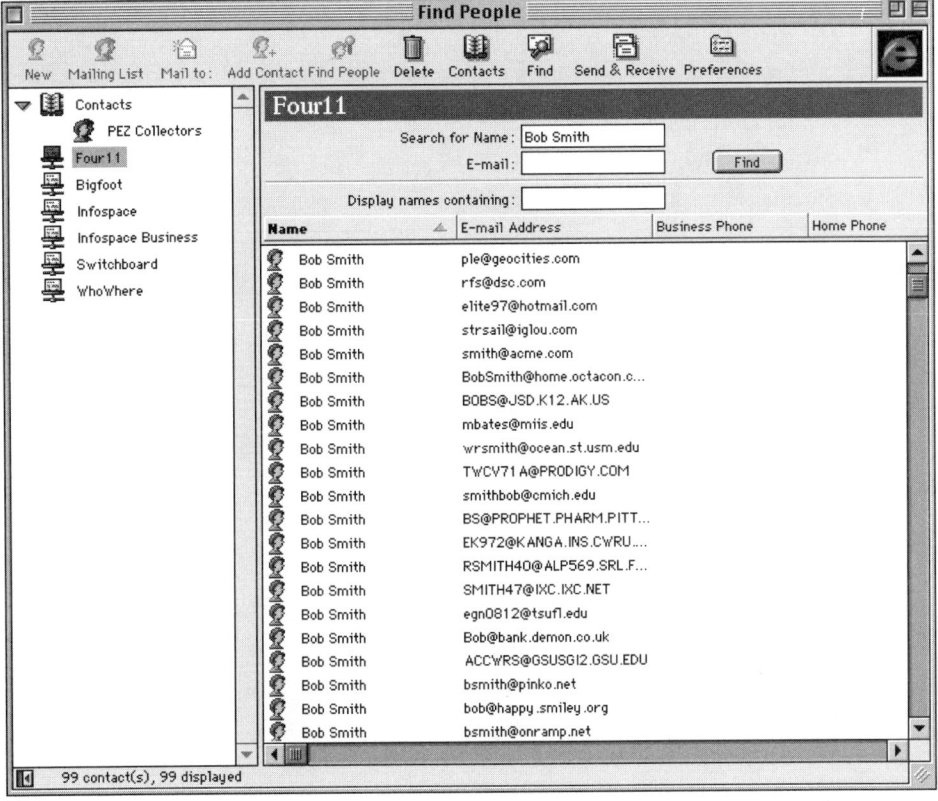

Figure 15.38 A search on Four11 for Bob Smith yields nearly 100 results—it's a good thing OE allows you to sort and organize the list!

Earlier in the chapter, you learned how to configure Outlook Express to connect to either the Microsoft News Server or your ISP's news server (or both), so we'll jump right in with actually showing you how to *use* newsgroups.

Netiquette: Or How To Avoid Getting Flamed

Before we jump into using newsgroups, a couple of caveats are in order. First, you are advised to *lurk* on a newsgroup for a while before posting a message. Lurking means reading messages, getting the general feel of the group, and understanding normal lines of discussion. You may think it sounds silly, but newsgroups develop a very specific culture and attitude, which you may or may not fit in with. When you've read enough, post your opinion about something, but keep it pertinent. A good start is a reply to what someone else has said.

Which leads to the second point: Be civil. That seems easy enough, but you must consider that in email, there are no facial expressions, no body language, and no tone of voice to help convey your message. Something said in jest, even when punctuated with an *emoticon*, or *smiley* (a colon followed by a right parenthesis—try it), can be taken as an insult.

The usual result of insults and off-topic posts is a *flame*, directed at you. Flames are heated (and frequently profane) messages. Depending on the newsgroup in question, they may be a simple request to keep the discussion on track, or they may question your intellectual capacity and your parentage. People on the Internet can be *very* blunt, so don't be surprised.

To help you learn more about netiquette (Internet etiquette), here's a list of helpful Web sites. Use the Internet Explorer included on your CD to surf over and take a quick read:

- Dear Emily Postnews at www.clari.net/brad/emily.html
- Netiquette Home Page at www.albion.com/netiquette/index.html
- Netiquette Primer at jade.wabash.edu/wabnet/info/netiquet.htm
- Yahoo!'s Beginner's Guides to Netiquette Links at www.yahoo.com/Computers_and_Internet/Internet/Information_and_Documentation/Beginner_s_Guides/Netiquette/

Finding Available Newsgroups

In order to read a newsgroup, you must *subscribe* to it. Essentially, this means you tell Outlook Express that you want to check a specific newsgroup for new messages each time you log on. The first step is to actually see what newsgroups are out there. Establish your connection to the Internet to get started.

When you set up your preferences, you should have set up a news server connection. If you have not done so, go back and set up the connection now. When you've set up a connection, its icon appears in the folder list. Click on that icon to connect to the news server.

To receive a list of all available newsgroups, select View|Get Complete Newsgroup List. Now go do the Sunday crossword over a cup of coffee. There are thousands of newsgroups available, so downloading the list can take a while. If you're using the Microsoft News Server, the download will be quick—that server only lists a little more than 700 newsgroups. When Brian downloaded the latest complete listing from Mindspring—his ISP—it showed more than 21,000 groups. You can imagine that the download took a while. When the download is complete, the news-groups list will appear in the right side of your window (see Figure 15.39).

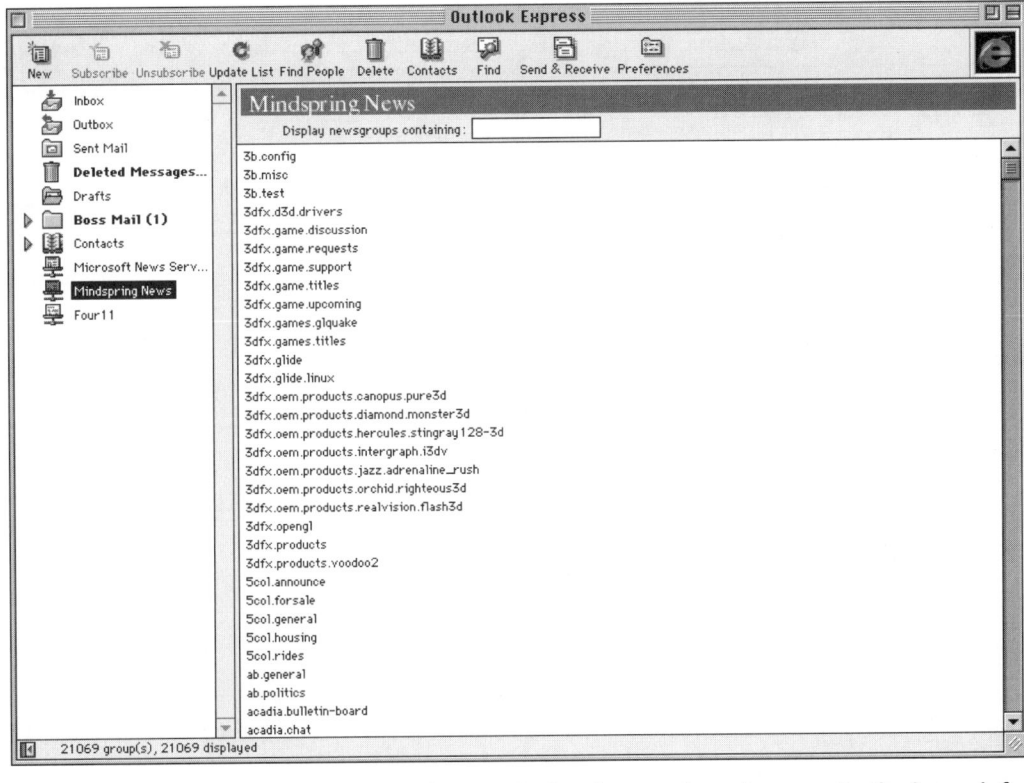

Figure 15.39 The full newsgroups listing. Notice the number of groups in the lower left.

Fast Track

From now on, when you want to see what new newsgroups are available, you don't have to download and search the entire list. Simply select View|Get New Newsgroups to see a list of the groups that have been added since the last time you checked.

Searching The Newsgroups List

By this point, you're probably wondering how in the world, out of 21,000+ newsgroups, you're going to find the two or three that interest you. Outlook Express makes it easy. In the Newsgroups List, you'll see a text box labeled Display Newsgroups Containing. Type in a word here to let Outlook Express narrow down the list for you (a newsgroup title is a pretty good indicator of that group's content).

For example, Brian likes cats (he has five—he doesn't have much of a choice about liking them or not), so he tried finding newsgroups related to cats. Entering the word "cat" in the Display Newsgroups Containing field reduced the 21,000+ list to just 157 entries (see Figure 15.40). Shorter, but still hard to wade through, especially because

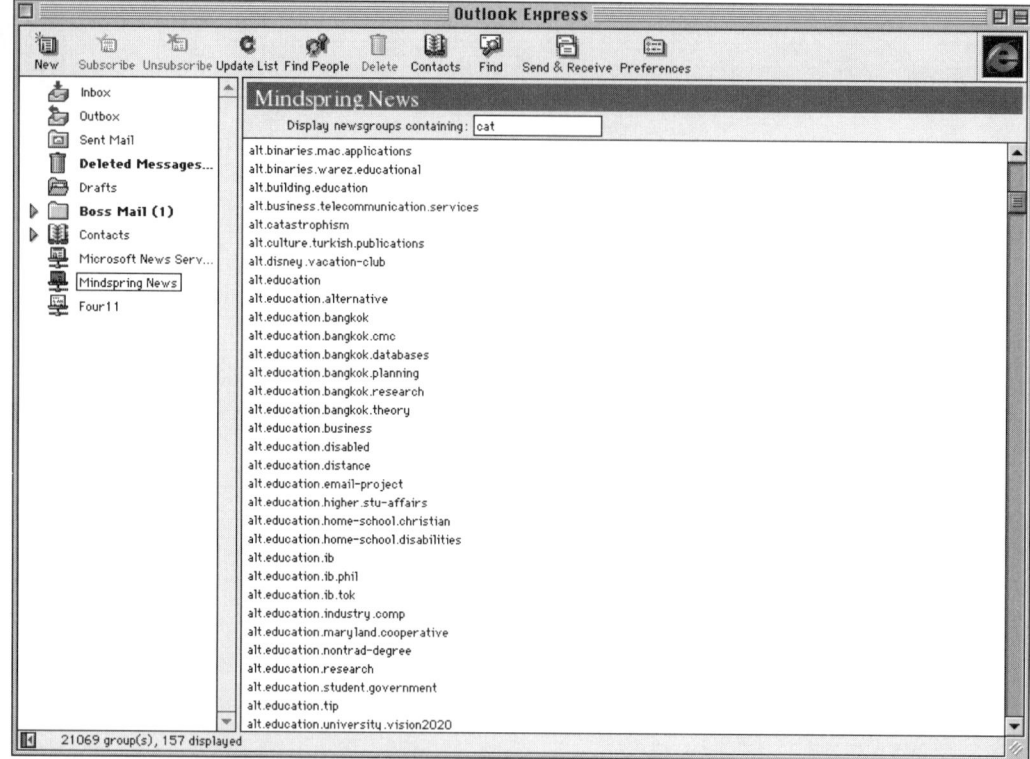

Figure 15.40 The first search keyword narrows the list of groups down quite a bit—but not enough.

it includes entries like alt.**cat**astrophism. To narrow it a little more, he changed the word to "cats," which produces an easily accessible list of eight groups, all pertaining directly to cats (see Figure 15.41). (Well, except the alt.tv.pizzacats entry, which is about this really *strange* Japanese cartoon show called Samurai Pizzacats. Don't ask—if you're really curious, try the Web page at **www.sci.kun.nl/thalia/funpage/ pizzacats/**. It's worth every minute.)

This search procedure is fast, too. You might think it would take a long time to scan all those thousands of groups, but we've found that the average search takes a matter of three or four seconds on a middling-fast Mac.

Subscribing To Newsgroups

Once you've found a group or two that sound interesting, you'll want to read them for a few days to see if you really like what you find (sort of like a trial subscription to *The Utne Reader*). To subscribe to a group or set of groups, select the group(s) in the group list, then choose Tools|Subscribe (you can unsubscribe later by selecting a group and choosing Tools|Unsubscribe).

Communicating Via Outlook Express 445

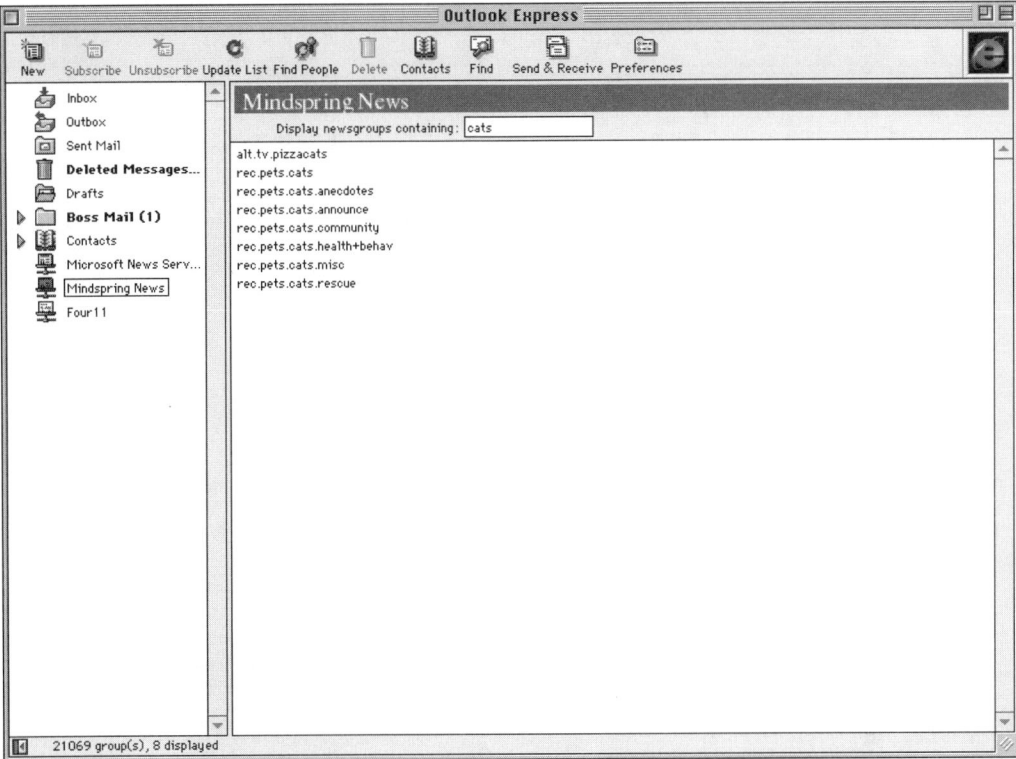

Figure 15.41 Making the search keyword just one letter more specific makes a world of difference!

When you have subscribed to a group, the group's name appears below the news server's icon in the folder list. When you connect to your news server, the name of each group is updated with a number in parentheses. This number, like the one attached to your Inbox, denotes the number of unread messages in a newsgroup.

Now that you've subscribed to a few newsgroups, you probably don't want to see the entire list every time you click on the server's icon in the folder list. To change this, select the server, then choose View|Subscribed Only. The newsgroups list condenses to just those groups you've subscribed to (see Figure 15.42).

Reading Newsgroups

When you've subscribed to a group, you're ready to begin reading messages. There are two ways to do this: in the main OE window or in an independent window. To view messages in the main window, select the group you want to read from the folder list by clicking on it once. The window now behaves as it does when you're reading mail: A list of postings appears in the message list area, and the messages, when selected, appear in the preview pane (see Figure 15.43).

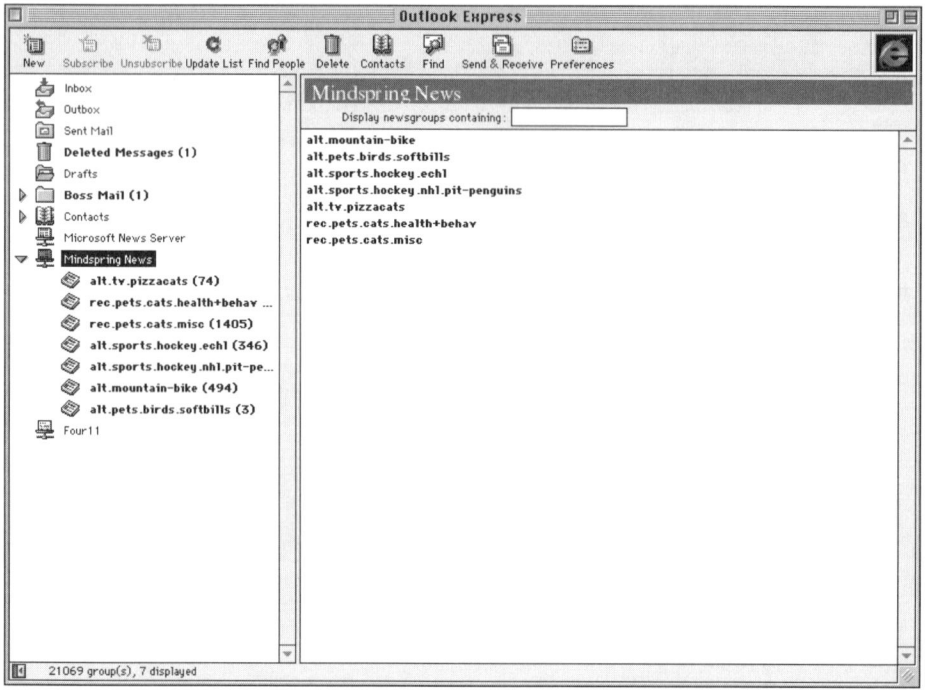

Figure 15.42 After you've subscribed to a few groups, switch the view to show only those groups you're subscribed to.

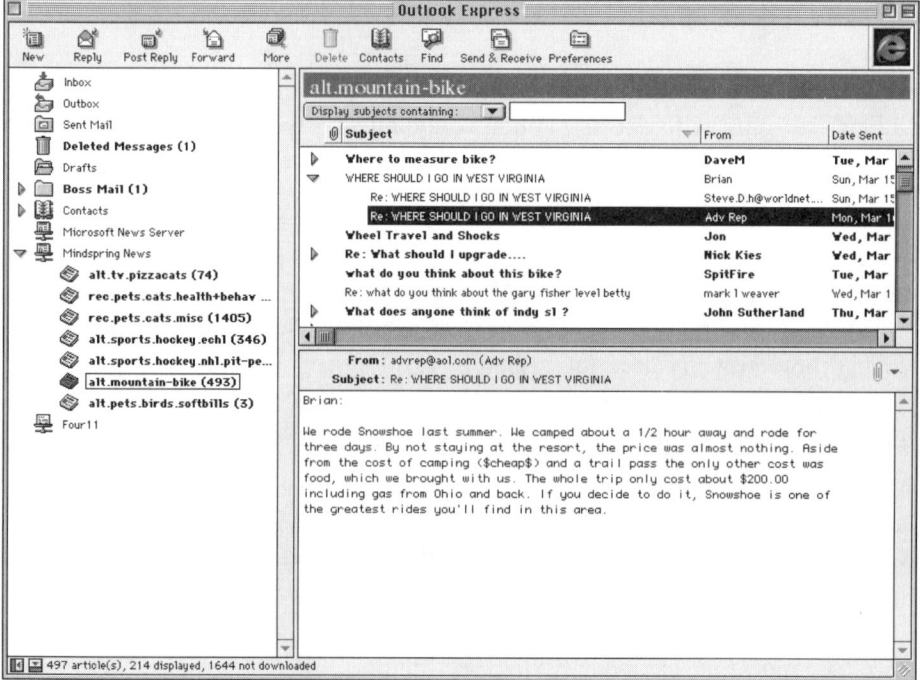

Figure 15.43 Reading a newsgroup message in the main Outlook Express window.

To view the newsgroup in an independent window, double-click on it from either the folder list or the newsgroups list. In the window that appears, the message list is on top, with the Message Pane below.

In either case, unread messages are listed in bold type. You can mark messages read and unread just as you do when using email. The triangles you see to the left of some messages indicate a *thread*, or a group of responses to the message you see in the list. To view the responses, click on the triangle. This opens the thread, and you can click on any of the messages to read them, just as you normally would (you can see an open thread in the message list in Figure 15.43).

To sort your message list and make things easier to find, you can click on the column headers in the list and use the drop-down menu above the list. To use the menu, select Display Subjects Containing or Display Messages From, then enter appropriate text in the text box. The message list will be shortened to just those messages matching your search criteria.

Using Newsgroup Rules

Much as you can use rules to sort and organize your mail automatically, you can use rules to help handle your incoming newsgroup messages. To create newsgroup rules, first select Tools|Newsgroup Rules to open the Newsgroup Rules dialog. Click on New Rule on the toolbar to invoke the Define Newsgroup Rule dialog.

Give the rule a name in the Rule Name field and make sure Enabled is checked. Under Criteria, specify which newsgroup(s) this rule applies to by selecting from the menu and entering text in the field. You can make the rule apply to All Newsgroups, or specify groups by names or keywords, just as you did when setting up rules for your Inbox.

Next, specify which messages in the group this rule applies to. You can specify by Subject, From (the sender's address), Date, or Number Of Lines. This last is useful for tossing really long messages that you don't have time to read through. Fill in the text box with appropriate information for the criterion you've selected. To specify multiple criteria, check the box next to the second and third criteria and make the appropriate selection. Then fill in the text box(es) as necessary.

Use the Execute Actions If menu to specify when your rule should be applied, just as you did with Inbox rules. Finally, choose one or more Actions for your rule to perform. You can elect to not show the message in the message list, to mark it as read, to set it to a specific color, or to download the entire message and file it in a particular folder. When you're done, click on OK to close the window.

Your new rule appears in the Newsgroup Rules window, ready for action. Just as with Inbox rules, you can manipulate the order of rules, edit them, or delete them as you see fit.

Posting Messages To A Newsgroup

Once you've lurked on a newsgroup for a while and you feel comfortable making your voice heard, it's time to post your first message. You can make this first post one of two ways—either as an original thought, or as a reply to someone else's comments.

Posting An Original Message

To post your own messages, first open the newsgroup by selecting it in the folder list. Click on New on the toolbar. The message window opens with your selected newsgroup in the To field. (You can actually add other newsgroups, but *cross-posting* the same message to multiple newsgroups is on a par with spam—we recommend you don't do it.)

Give your message a subject and enter the text of your message in the main part of the window. When you're finished and ready to send your message, click on Post on the toolbar. Outlook Express asks you to confirm the newsgroup you wish to post to—click on OK and your post is sent to the newsgroup for all to read (*post* is the method for submitting messages to a newsgroup—it's functionally the same as *send* in an email window).

Posting A Reply

Replying to someone else's message works in much the same way as posting an original message. First, find the message you want to reply to in the message list. Click on it once to select it, then click on Post Reply on the toolbar.

The original message appears in a new message window as a quote, and a line appears before it stating the identifier of the previous message and the sender. Enter your reply after this text. (Note that the subject line is already filled with "Re:" and the prior subject line—this helps to maintain the thread of discussion.) After you enter your reply, click on Post, then click on OK in the confirmation dialog to send your message.

Replying To An Author

Rather than posting a public reply to a message, you can send email to the message's author. This is the proper course of action if you have something private or personal to say, or if your response could be construed as a flame. It's usually considered bad form to take someone to task *personally* in a public forum.

To email your reply to a message's author, first open the message in its own window. When you click on Reply on the toolbar, the post appears as a quote in a new message window (this time, a standard email message window). The To and Subject fields are already filled in, so just enter your text below the quote and click on Send.

Walk-Through: Reading And Posting To Newsgroups

Follow these steps to learn how to read newsgroups and post your own messages:

1. Launch Outlook Express.
2. Make sure your Mac is connected to the Internet, or set to connect automatically.
3. Click on the Microsoft News Server icon in the folder list. The preview pane disappears and the message list shows the Microsoft News Server banner.
4. Select View|Get Complete Newsgroups List. Wait while the list downloads. It shouldn't take long. When the list is complete, a little more than 700 newsgroups will appear in the newsgroups list.
5. In the Display Newsgroups Containing field, type "test". The list of groups is truncated to two, both of which have the word "test" in their names.
6. Click to select microsoft.public.test. This is a newsgroup specifically for test messages like the one we're going to send.
7. Click on Subscribe on the toolbar. The newsgroup's name appears under the Microsoft News Server icon in the folder list.
8. Select microsoft.public.test in the folder list. The group's message headers are downloaded to your Mac. The group's name in the folder list changes to show the number of unread messages.
9. Scroll through the message list to have a look at the headers. Most are simple one- or two-word test messages. Occasionally, you find something useful for newsgroups *newbies*, or beginners.
10. Pick any message at random and click on it once to read it in the preview pane. Because most newsgroup messages are text, you can usually read them in the preview pane with no problem.
11. Click on New in the toolbar to open a new newsgroup posting window. Note that the Newsgroups field is already filled in with the name of the group you were reading, and the News Server selection is set to the server you were reading from.
12. Give the post an appropriate subject. "Testing MS Outlook Express for Mac" would be excellent.

13. Enter a few words in the main body area, something like "Testing a newsgroup post from OE for Mac".
14. If you feel really bold, sign your name to it and attach your signature, although it certainly isn't necessary.
15. When you're finished, click on Post, then click on OK in the subsequent confirmation dialog. You've just posted your first Internet news message.

Moving On

That's it for our tour of Outlook Express. In this chapter, you've learned how to send and receive email, read and post to newsgroups, handle your contacts, and automate your data handling in OE. There's more you can do with the program. Heck, we could write an entire book about using email and newsgroups (and people have done just that).

But for now, you've jumped in and had a little swim in the Internet waters. It's time to venture farther from shore by learning how to integrate the entire Office suite of programs—not just with each other, but with the Internet as well.

Pull your goggles down and take a deep breath—here we go!

PART VI
Getting It Together

Collaborating And Integrating With Office 98

16

Most of the time, Mac projects require one person and one program—but not always. A single project may require multiple files, each created with a different Office program. And it may require *input* (i.e., "interference") from collaborators, co-workers, and managers with approval power. (Ned once had a job where he routed proofs of publications to corporate directors for their scribbled comments before the publications went to print. By the time the last director signed off, he had to throw everything away and start over. The monthly newsletter was actually finished almost twice a year...but we digress.)

Consider the types of files that you might require at the end of a major study or research project. You might need an Excel worksheet to present data in a table, an attractively formatted, well-written Word document to describe the study and interpret its conclusions, and a PowerPoint show for presenting the study's conclusions to an audience. In fact, a particularly big project might demand several different documents from each program. It also might require contributions and edits from multiple workers collaborating on the study, each checking, commenting on, correcting, or expanding on each other's work to refine the final result.

In this and many similar scenarios, imagine being able to:

- Exchange, manage, edit, and print information among the files, so that you can create data, descriptions, charts, or other elements only once, in one program, and then use them in as many files in which they're needed.

- Collaborate on files, so that multiple Office users can contribute to and edit the same files, and everybody can keep track of who did what.

Well, you can. In this chapter, you'll learn about all of the ways Office helps you use programs and files "together"—whether that means "as one program," or whether it means "among multiple users."

Of course, you don't have to tell anybody about these capabilities. In many companies, the more people you get involved in a project, the longer it takes. (That's why at Microsoft, it takes huge teams of the best programmers in the world two years to finish a program, whereas the teenage geek next door can do the same job during two afternoon reruns of *Deep Space Nine*.) We can't tell you whether you *should* integrate or collaborate; we just want you to know that you *can*. The rest is up to you.

Exchanging Information Between Programs

In this book's parts on the various applications, we told you how to move or copy text from one Word document to another and how to move or copy data among Excel worksheets. Using some of the same techniques—and a few new ones—you can move or copy information between files in *different* Office programs.

Over the next few pages, you'll discover the various ways you can get more out of Office by creating something in one program and then moving it to others.

Moving And Copying Information

The easiest and most reliable way to move or copy data among programs is cut and paste and its cousin, copy and paste. Using these techniques, you can copy Excel cells to a Word or PowerPoint document, or copy Word or PowerPoint text to Excel cells, or copy a paragraph from Word into an Outlook message. The steps involved are essentially the same ones you use to move or copy data from Word document to Word document, or from Excel worksheet to Excel worksheet.

When you move or copy data from one file to another, the file containing the data you want to move or copy is known as the *source* file, and the file into which you want the data moved or copied is the *destination* file.

If you plan to move back and forth among programs several times to make multiple cuts or copies, you'll find it most convenient to begin by opening all of the programs and files you plan to use. While you're moving and copying data, you can jump from one program to another using the Applications menu or the Office Manager menu.

Making A Basic Copy Or Move

Begin by opening the file containing the information you want to move or copy. Select the data using the selection techniques supported in the source program. In the program's Standard toolbar, click on Copy (to copy data) or Cut (to move data). Next, switch to—or open—the destination program and file. In the destination file, click on the spot in the document, worksheet, slide, or message where you want to move or copy the data, then click on the Paste button on the destination program's Standard toolbar.

Fast Track

You can duplicate the actions of the Copy, Paste, and Cut buttons with menus or keystrokes. You can copy with Edit|Copy or Ctrl+C; paste with Edit|Paste or Ctrl+V; or cut with Edit|Cut or Ctrl+X.

Choosing The Format Of Pasted Data

Office programs use a "smart" method of determining the format of the data in the receiving program. For example, when you copy cells from Excel to Word or PowerPoint, the cells appear in the Word or PowerPoint document as a table—which is the logical, smart way to represent Excel data. Office determines these data formats automatically, but you can control the way the data appears in the destination document by using Paste Special instead of Paste.

To use Paste Special, perform the move or copy operation exactly as described in the last section, "Making A Basic Copy Or Move"—except do not click on the Paste button (or press Ctrl+V). Instead, in the destination application, choose Edit|Paste Special. A dialog like the one in Figure 16.1 opens. In the Paste Special dialog, a list shows all of the different formats in which you can paste the data (the list will differ depending on the source and destination programs and the type of data selected). To learn about each format, click on it; a description appears at the bottom of the dialog.

In the list on the Paste Special dialog, any option called an "Object"—for example, the top option in Figure 16.1 is "Microsoft Word Document Object"—has a special function. You can edit objects within the destination program using all of the menus

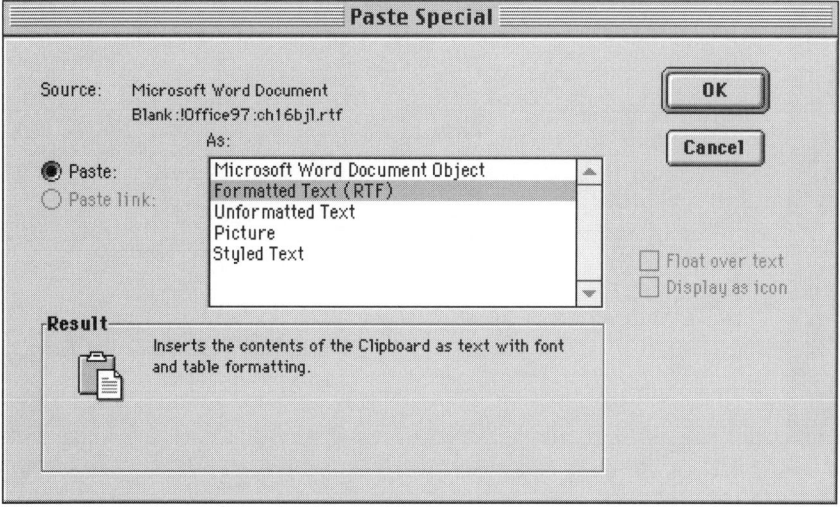

Figure 16.1 After copying or cutting, choose Edit|Paste Special to choose the format in which the data is to be pasted.

and tools from the source program. Pasting objects is a great way to apply the power of one program to special formatting tasks in another.

For example, suppose you copy a block of cells from an Excel worksheet to a Word document and use Paste Special to copy the cells as a "Microsoft Excel Worksheet Object." The cells appear as a table in Word but include all of their Excel formatting. When you click on the table in Word, handles appear around it so you can position it and edit its size and shape. When you double-click on the table, Excel's toolbars and menu bar appear within Word so you can edit the Excel table with all of Excel's features (see Figure 16.2), including formulas, functions, and all of Excel's formatting capabilities. When you click back in the document, Word's toolbars and menu bar return.

Linking Objects To Files

When you copy or move data as described previously in this chapter, the data is *embedded* in the destination file. Embedded data becomes a part of the destination file. You edit the data in the destination program just as if it had been created

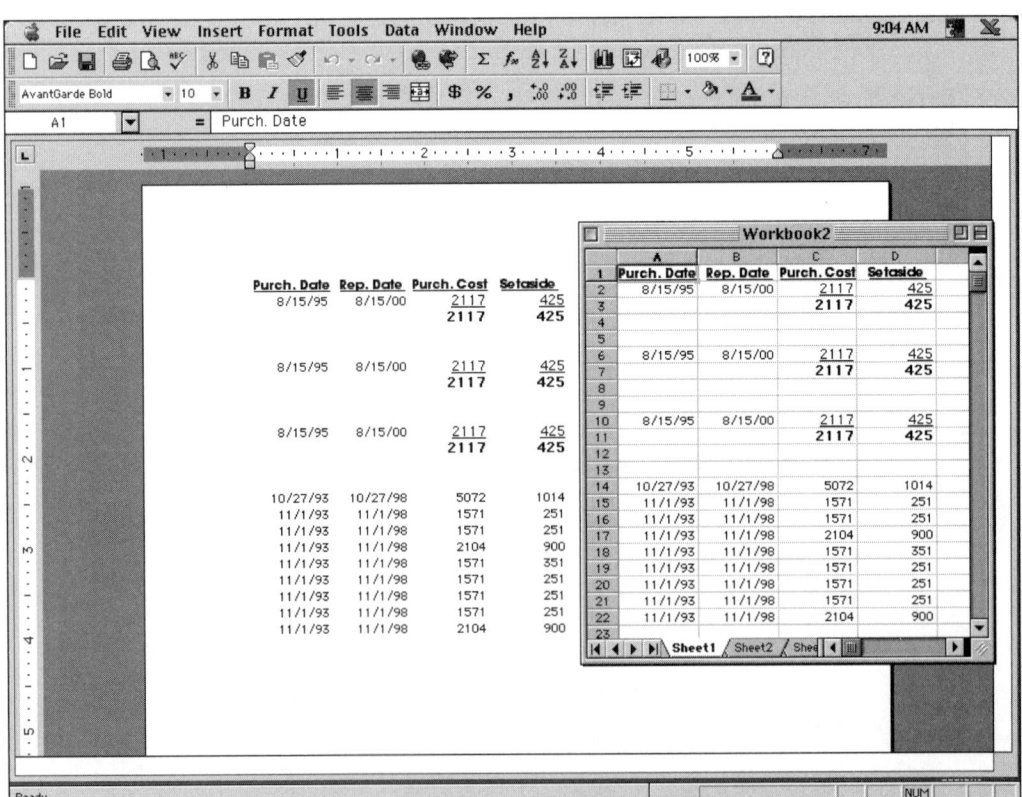

Figure 16.2 When you use Paste Special to paste an object, the object can be double-clicked to edit it in the program it originated from.

there, and the changes you make to the data have no effect on the data in the source document, and vice versa—even when you paste data as an object.

That's okay when data doesn't change. But in some circumstances, you'll want data in different documents to remain consistent, so that when it changes in one place, it changes everywhere it's used. That's where *linking* comes in.

Instead of embedding data, you can link data from one program or file into another. When you link, the data appears in the destination document when viewed on the screen and will appear in the printout if the document is printed. However, linked data is not actually a part of the destination file. Instead, a link has been inserted in the destination file, and that link points to the data in the source file. Whenever you open the destination file containing the link, it automatically contacts the source file, retrieves the data, and displays it in the destination document, as if it were actually there. But it's not.

Why link? Well, the main advantage of linking is that whenever the source data changes, the changes show up in every file to which that data is linked. For example, suppose you have an Excel worksheet showing sales data and a PowerPoint show that gives a monthly report on sales data. Every month, to give your presentation, you could copy the current month's sales figures from Excel to your PowerPoint show. But if those figures are linked to PowerPoint, rather than embedded, the figures change automatically in the PowerPoint show any time they change in the Excel worksheet. You don't have to do the work of copying the new data, and you can rest assured that the data in your PowerPoint show is accurate, if the data in Excel is.

Creating A Link
The easiest way to link data is to copy it, using the procedure described earlier for copying data among programs, and paste it in the destination document using the Paste Special dialog (Edit|Paste Special). On the Paste Special dialog (refer back to Figure 16.1), select the Paste Link radio button, then choose a format for the data and complete the paste operation.

You can create links in other ways besides Paste Special. On some of the dialogs you use to insert pictures, sounds, or other objects, you'll see a checkbox labeled Link To File. If you check that checkbox, the object you're inserting is linked into the current file; if you clear that checkbox, the object is embedded.

Maintaining Links
After creating the link, you edit and update the data in the destination file—and all other files linked to the same source data—by editing the source file, from within the source application. By default, any time you change the linked data in the source file, the changes appear in the destination file either immediately (if it is open) or the next time you open the destination file. However, you can change a link so that

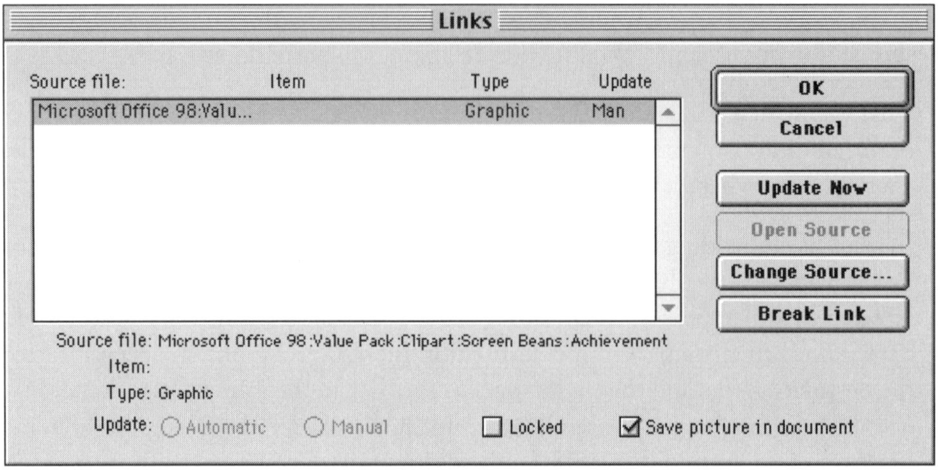

Figure 16.3 Choose Edit|Links to control how links behave.

up-dates don't happen automatically—and change other aspects of a link's behavior—by choosing Edit|Link in the destination program to open the Links dialog (see Figure 16.3).

In the Links dialog, you can click on a link in the list to select it, then make choices in the dialog that affect that link. For example, you can click on a radio button at the bottom of the dialog to change from Automatic to Manual updating. If you select Manual, the data in the destination file is only updated to match the source file when you open the Links dialog again and click on the Update Now button. Also on the dialog, you can click on the Break Link button. When you break a link, the last up-dated data remains in the destination file, and the source file will never update that data again. Also, you can edit the data in the destination file after breaking a link.

FYI: Be Careful When You're Moving Files Containing Links

The only tricky part to linking comes into play if and when files—either the source file or the destination file—move. The link in the destination file can access the data in the source file because the link specifies the path to the source file—disk, folder, and so on—and the file name of the source file. Move either file, and the link is broken—the data vanishes from the destination document.

To avoid this, try to keep the destination file and source file in the same folder. If you move them, move both—as long as they share a folder, the link will still work.

You can put the two files in separate folders, of course—but if you do, and you move either or both files, it becomes more difficult to keep the relationship the same so that the link still works.

If a link is broken for some reason, you can fix it by choosing Edit|Links in the destination program (see the "Maintaining Links" section), choose the link that's broken and click on Change Source to enter the correct path to the source file.

Fast Track

To jump quickly from the link in the destination document to the source data so you can edit it, Control-click on the linked data and choose Linked Object (instead of the word "Linked," you will see a description of the type of object— for instance Excel Worksheet Object). Then, choose Edit to edit the source data.

FYI: Drag And Drop To Copy

As an alternative to the cut-and-paste and copy-and-paste methods of moving and copying data among programs (and linking), you can use drag and drop.

To drag and drop data between programs, you must first size and position the program windows so that the data you want to move or copy—and the place in the destination file where you want to move or copy it—appear on screen simultaneously. To copy data, select it in the source document, drag it to the destination file, and drop it.

Although drag and drop works by exchanging data between programs, it can be inconvenient. Office programs often use full screens, so setting up for a drag-and-drop operation usually requires resizing and arranging windows. Also, when you drop, you may not be able to position the data in the destination program as accurately as you could with another method. Finally, Microsoft appears to have been a little spotty in implementing drag and drop—you can drag text from Word into an Excel cell, but you can't drag Excel cells back into Word.

Even given those caveats, drag and drop can be fast and efficient. The benefits often outweigh the small problems.

Using Special-Purpose Data Exchange Facilities

With copy, move, and linking, you can get data from one Office program to another pretty reliably. However, you will come across some special facilities in programs for performing common integration activities. These are described on the next few pages.

Creating A Worksheet Or Chart From Within Word

On Word's Standard toolbar you'll find the Insert Microsoft Excel Worksheet button. In effect, that button creates a new worksheet object in Word—which you can edit using Excel controls. You do this by making a mini-worksheet right from the button.

When you click on the button, a grid of squares opens (see Figure 16.4). Pull the pointer down and to the right to select as many cells as you want in the table (up to four rows by five columns), and click. The table appears in your Word document. Excel then opens to allow you to enter and format data. When you're finished, just close the worksheet, and your formatted table appears in Word.

Similarly, all from within Word, you can create an external worksheet file—actually a *datasheet* file, a sort of worksheet-lite—and generate a chart based on it for display in your Word document. In Word, choose Insert|Picture|Chart. The datasheet—containing sample data—opens in Microsoft Graph, and in your Word document, a chart based on the data appears (see Figure 16.5).

Using basic Excel cell-editing techniques, replace the sample data in the datasheet with your own data. After finishing the data, close the datasheet and format the chart as you would in Excel (see Chapter 14).

Fast Track

Instead of using Word's Chart facility (which is actually Microsoft Graph, a sort of lesser offshoot of Excel's chart engine), you may prefer to create the chart by

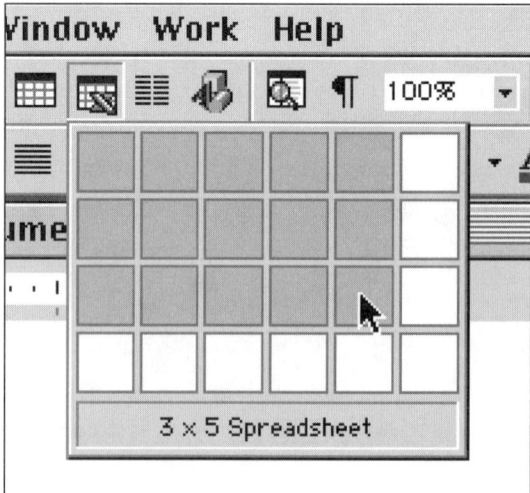

Figure 16.4 Click on Word's Insert Microsoft Excel Worksheet button to create an Excel object right in Word.

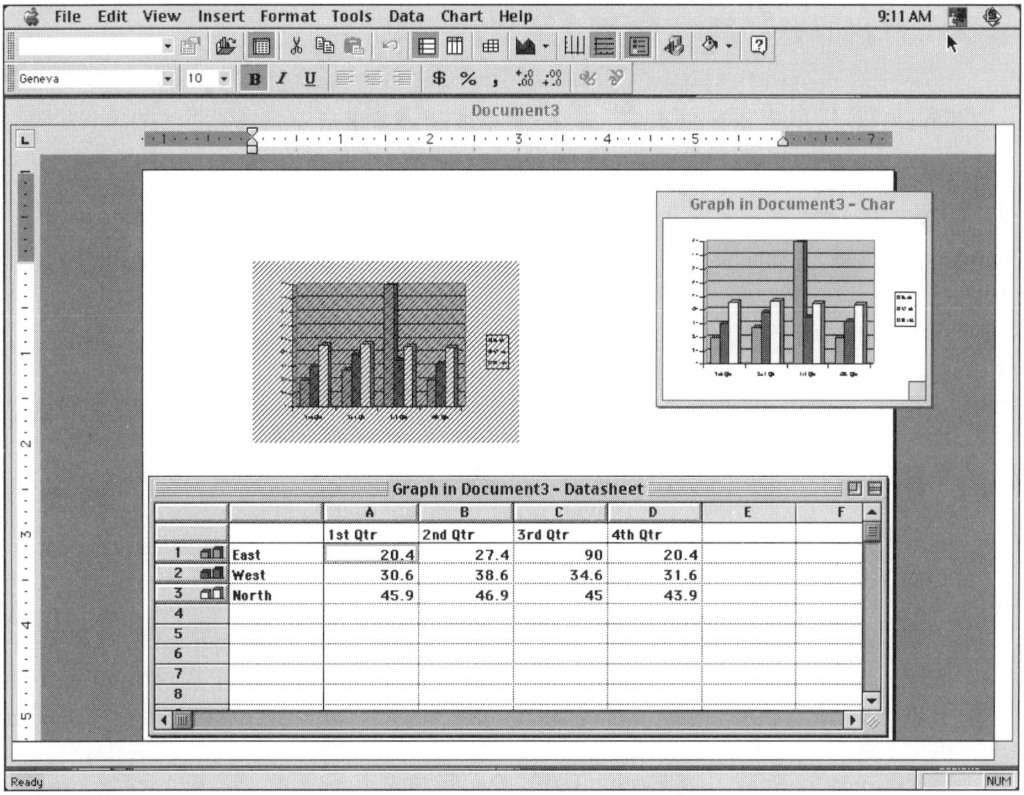

Figure 16.5 In Word, choose Insert|Picture|Chart to create a chart right in Word.

entering your data in Excel. Use Excel's Chart Wizard to create and format the table, then copy and paste the chart into Word. If you link the chart into Word (using Paste Special), it will be updated automatically any time you update the Excel worksheet.

Sending A File As An Email Attachment

In Word, Excel, and PowerPoint, choosing File|Send To opens a submenu from which you can choose to send the current file to a number of different destinations.

The most important option on the Send To menu, Mail Recipient, opens an Outlook Express new message window with the current Word, Excel, or PowerPoint file already in the message as an attachment (an icon for the file appears below the message body). You can address the message, add whatever body text you want to, and then send it off. This is a great way to distribute files to collaborators.

Collaborating On Projects

Word, Excel, and PowerPoint all include features that make it easy to allow multiple people to work on the same file and to keep track of all that activity. These features are described in the next few pages.

Tracking Changes

In both Word and Excel, you can *track changes*. Tracking changes means highlighting edits made to a document (Word document or Excel worksheet) in such a way that the author of the document can see exactly what's been changed and who changed it.

To use this feature properly, each contributor must choose Tools|Track Changes|Highlight Changes before making any changes to the file. (The steps for enabling tracking are the same in both Word and Excel, but the dialogs differ.) The Highlight Changes dialog opens (see Figure 16.6). In the dialog, the contributor must check the checkbox for Track Changes While Editing.

In Word's Highlight Changes dialog, the other two checkboxes determine whether the change highlighting shows up on the screen or in print. Some contributors may wish to track changes (so that others can see them) but they may not want to see their changes highlighted on the screen or in print as they're working. In Excel's Highlight Changes dialog, other items enable you to control which user's changes will be highlighted, and for which cell ranges.

As the file is worked on by various contributors, each new contributor's changes are recorded in a different color than everyone else's changes. New text added by

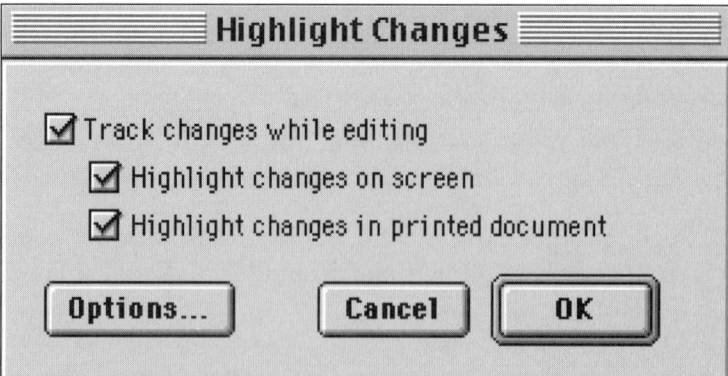

Figure 16.6 When you're collaborating on a file, choose change-tracking options on the Highlight Changes dialog (this figure shows Word's dialog for tracking changes).

a contributor appears in the document in the contributor's assigned color, and any deletions made by each contributor are crossed out by a line in the assigned color. By examining colored text and crossed-out text, the author can see what has been changed. If the author points to a change and lets the pointer rest there for a moment, a tip pops up with the name of the person who made the change and the approximate time and date the change was made.

In Word, after reviewing changes, the author can accept or reject changes in two different ways. First, the author must select the text containing the changes he or she wants to accept or reject (unless the author intends to accept or reject all the changes). Then the author has two choices:

- *Choose Tools|Track Changes|Accept Or Reject Changes*—This opens the Accept Or Reject Changes dialog (see Figure 16.7). On the dialog, the author can click on the Accept button or the Reject button to accept or reject changes in the selection, or click on Accept All or Reject All to accept or reject all changes in the document.

- *Control-click on the selection*—This displays a contextual menu (see Figure 16.8). The author can then choose either Accept Change or Reject Change from the contextual menu, or choose Accept Or Reject Changes to open the Accept Or Reject Changes dialog.

When the author accepts a change, highlighting is removed, crossed-out text disappears, and the change becomes permanent. When the author rejects a change, highlighted (added) text disappears, crossed-out text is restored, and the text reverts to its original state.

Track Changes works no matter how the document file is distributed, as long as each contributor remembers to choose Tools|Track Changes|Highlight Changes before editing. Each contributor can access the file separately from a shared network disk,

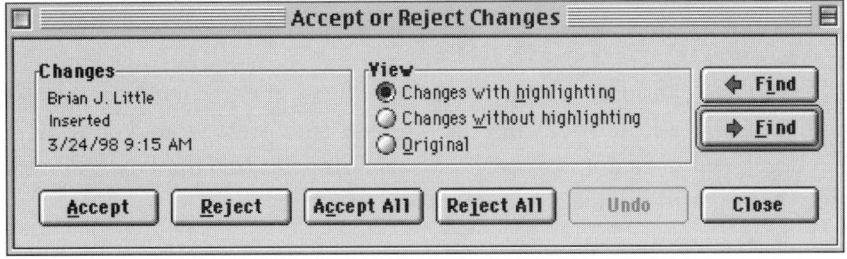

Figure 16.7 Use the Accept Or Reject Changes dialog to either make tracked changes permanent or undo them.

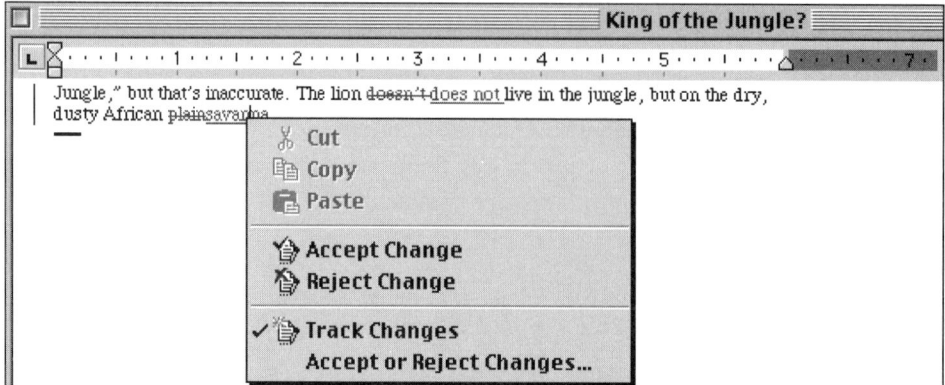

Figure 16.8 You can accept or reject changes by selecting the changes, Control-clicking, and choosing from the contextual menu.

or the file can be sent around to each contributor on diskette or as an email attachment. But all contributors must work on the same copy of the file for the changes to be consolidated so that the author can see them.

In general, the changes are preserved when the file is moved among recent versions of Word and Excel, even if the file is used in the Windows versions. That enables PC and Mac users using different (but recent) versions of Word or Excel to collaborate on a file. However, if the file is converted to a file format other than a recent Word or Excel format, edited, and then converted back to Word or Excel, all change tracking will be lost, and all changes made to the file by all contributors will be permanent.

Fast Track

Word, PowerPoint, and Excel each have a Reviewing toolbar that provides quick access to each program's reviewing tools. In any of the three programs, you can display the Reviewing toolbar by choosing View|Toolbars|Reviewing.

Adding Comments To Files

In Word, Excel, and PowerPoint, you can add comments anywhere in a file. A comment is like a little sticky note on the file. It appears when you want it to, for reference, but it does not ordinarily show up in print (or in a PowerPoint show during presentation) unless you want it to.

Comments are most useful in Excel for creating pop-up instructions in forms (see Chapter 14) or for making notes about cell contents. Comments are also valuable to reviewers of files in Word, Excel, or PowerPoint documents, because they provide a way to insert comments, critiques, complaints, kudos, queries, or any other input without affecting the actual, visible content of the document. What makes comments especially useful for this purpose is that comments show the name of the person who wrote them. A group of reviewers can all add comments to a file, and the author will know the source of each comment.

To enter a comment in any of the three supporting programs, select the on-screen object—some text, one or more cells, a slide, and so on—to which the comment refers. Then choose Insert|Comment and type the text of the comment.

When you're reviewing a file, comments display differently in each program:

- In Word, text to which a comment has been attached is highlighted in yellow. When you rest the pointer on the highlighted text, the comment appears.

- In Excel, a red marker appears in the upper right corner of the cell or range to which a comment is attached. When you rest the pointer on the cell, the comment appears.

- In PowerPoint, choose View|Comments to show all the comments in a presentation (even when you're viewing the show). Choose View|Comments again to hide the comments.

To delete a comment, click on it and press the Delete key.

Protecting A Document From Unwanted Changes

There may be times when you want others to review your files online, but not be able to change them. By choosing Tools|Protect in any Office program, you block changes to a file or to particular aspects of a file. Exactly which aspects of a file you can protect differs by program. Note that any protection you apply to a file affects you, too. However, you (and you alone) can unprotect the file by choosing Tools|Unprotect Document.

In Word, for example, when you choose Tools|Protect Document, the Protect Document dialog opens, as shown in Figure 16.9. In the dialog, if you choose Tracked Changes, anyone can make changes to the file, but all changes are automatically tracked so you have the power to accept or reject them—no one can turn change tracking off. If you choose Comments, anyone can insert comments in the document, but no other changes can be made—even tracked ones. If you select Forms, no changes can be made in the document except in *form fields* and sections you select; this option enables you to create online forms that users can fill in, but not change.

The Password option allows you to enter a password that you or anyone else can use to unprotect the document and make any kinds of changes. By using a password and then telling it only to selected reviewers, you give those reviewers the same level of

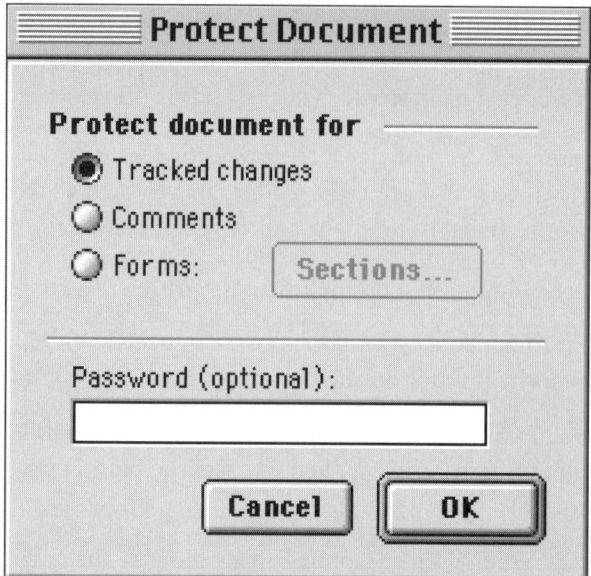

Figure 16.9 Protect a document to prevent others from making unauthorized changes.

editing control you have. As you enter the password, it appears in the dialog only as asterisks (*) so that no one can peek over your shoulder to discover it.

Note that the password is *case-sensitive*. If you enter "Archie" as the password, to edit the document a user must enter "Archie"—the entries ARCHIE, archie, or arCHie would all be invalid password entries.

Saving Multiple Versions

Word (and Word alone) includes a special facility for saving multiple, different versions of the same document. This *versioning* capability is an alternative to tracking changes. Instead of consolidating everyone's changes in one marked-up copy, each collaborator creates his or her own version. (Note that versioning is unique to Word 98, and is not supported by earlier versions; all contributors who want to view or create versions must have Word 98.)

This capability is very different from using Save As to create and work on various copies of one file (which you can do in any Office program). With versions, multiple files are not created. Instead, all changes to a file are tracked, and when a user saves a version, a record of those changes is saved in the file so that you can reconstitute that version on demand. Also, once a version is created, it cannot be changed—each version is "fixed." However, if you want to edit a version, you can change it from a version to a separate file that you can edit.

To save the current state of a Word file as a version, choose File|Versions. The Versions dialog opens, listing all other versions of the current file, the name of the person who created the version, and any comments that person typed to describe the version. Click on the Save Now button to create a new version, then type any comments you want to in the box that appears. After creating a version, close the Versions dialog and continue editing the current file, moving it forward from the version you just created.

To open and view an existing version, choose File|Versions, select the version in the list of Existing Versions, and click on Open. The version opens in a new window; the window's title bar shows the same file name as the current file, but it is followed by the date the version was created and the word "version."

To convert any existing version into a separate file that you can edit, open the version, choose File|Save As, and save the version with a unique file name.

Fast Track

To produce an automated comparison of a version and the existing, current incarnation of a file, save the version as a new file and close the version (but leave the main file open). Choose Tools|Track Changes|Compare Documents to open the Compare Documents dialog, then navigate to and select the newly created file in the dialog.

Moving On

Microsoft markets Office as a cohesive, tightly integrated family of applications that share data. But the majority of people who use Office—at least up to an intermediate level—use the programs exclusively independently and never exchange data among them or bind them together.

Whose Office vision is the right one? Well, if folks used the integration and collaboration tools described in this chapter, they'd save a lot of time and effort in the long run, because of all the duplication of effort and errors that could be prevented by a little smartly applied integration. On the other hand, there's something a little scary about hooking files together this way and letting everybody work on them—many users fear they're building a house of cards where a flaw in one document will cause a cascade of flawed linked documents or scrambled tracked changes.

The truth, as always, lies somewhere in between. Overzealous application of these features by inexperienced users can build up to a nightmare of links, highlight colors, and no one with the knowledge to sort it all out. But as you can probably see, a little smartly applied, carefully managed integration and collaboration is moderately safe, moderately easy, and moderately rewarding. It's a fair deal.

Where to next? Well, if you're not interested in putting your work online for others to see, or in hooking your documents to other resources online, your tour here is done. Thanks for stopping by. Write if you get work.

Of course, if you *are* online-inclined, move ahead to Chapter 17. There you'll discover that Office was made to participate in a larger world than one Mac, or one corporate network. Office wants to hook into the Internet, and in Chapter 17 you'll learn how to give Office the chance.

Office 98 And The Internet

17

It's a funny idea, merging the desktop, the corporate network, and the Internet. We're not completely sure anyone really asked for that to happen. But as you know by now, what Microsoft wants, Microsoft gets. And Microsoft wants to merge the desktop, the network, and the Internet so that we use it all as one big, seamless computer. Upcoming versions of Microsoft's applications will build on this theme with ever-increasing synergy. So here we go. Buckle up—it may be a bumpy millennium's end.

As part of its everything-is-one-big-computer strategy, Microsoft has built Office 98 with a variety of features that enable you to create documents designed not to be printed or shown in presentation, but to be published online—on a *server* computer from which others can access and read your work. You can publish an Office document on any of three basic kinds of servers: garden-variety corporate network servers, intranet servers, or Web servers. In each case, there are two formats:

- *Native*—The file is published online in its regular state, such as a Word file or PowerPoint file. A native Office file retains all of the features and formatting you apply in Office, but can be viewed only by those with the right hardware and software to open Office files. Native format is generally used on local Mac networks.

- *Web page*—The file is converted to the standard file format for the Web, Hypertext Markup Language (HTML), so that anyone with a Web browser and access to the Web server can read it, no matter what type of hardware or other software they have. This format is typically used for publishing on the Internet or on a corporate intranet.

Besides creating online content, you can give Office files the power to connect to and browse online content through Office's built-in support for hyperlinks and its Web toolbar. You can also enhance your online documents with special features that only an online document can use, such as animation and backgrounds. In this chapter, we'll introduce you to Office's online toolset.

Before you proceed, note that the material in this chapter makes two assumptions about what you already know. It assumes you have a basic understanding of:

- *The Office application(s) you intend to use for producing online documents*—If you want to create Web pages with Word, for example, you should already have read most or all of Part II of this book.

- *The Internet and the World Wide Web*—You needn't know anything about creating Web pages or other online documents to get started here, but this chapter does not provide a beginner's introduction to surfing the Web or using the Internet in general.

FYI: *What's An Intranet?*

The technology that enables users from anywhere to read Web pages over the Internet is mature and reliable, and lots of people already know how to use Web browsers. Recognizing that, many companies model their internal company networks on the Web. A local network that looks and acts like the Web is called an *intranet*.

Using the same standards and software used on the Internet, companies can publish internal information—training sessions, personnel records, employee handbooks, and so on—in Web-page format on the company's network server, then equip employee workstations with Web browsers so employees can read the pages. Many intranets are also connected to the Internet, so that employees can browse both local (intranet) and remote (Internet) Web pages from within their browsers.

If the online documents you create will be used only by others on your company network and if that network is set up as an intranet, you have the option of publishing your documents in Web-page format on the intranet. Technically, an intranet file is identical to a Web page, and the steps for creating either one are the same in Office.

Publishing Native Office Documents Online

When you publish an Office document online in its native format, you have complete control over what the user sees. The document retains all of its formatting, no matter how elaborate, and any fields or linked objects in the document update automatically. When precise appearances are important, that's a great advantage over a Web page, where you often must compromise formatting.

Of course, native documents come with a catch: When you publish a document as a Web page, anyone with any Web browser—on any type of computer in the world—can read it. To read a native Office 98 document, on the other hand, the viewer must have at least one of the following:

- Office 98 for Macintosh or Office 97 for Windows 95/NT.

- The Office 98 viewer program for the file type. For example, a Word 98 viewer is required for reading a Word document. You can acquire the viewers and distribute them freely to anyone who needs to see your stuff.

The most important part of choosing whether to publish your documents online in native format, therefore, is finding out whether your intended audience will be able to read your files. In the next few pages, you'll learn more about each of the ways people can read native Office files. If you decide to publish native documents, note that you can publish them either on a local network or on the Web.

- If you choose to publish files on a local network, contact your network administrator to learn how to publish them. In general, the network administrator need only copy the files to a shared disk your audience can access and then configure the files for sharing.

- If you choose to publish native documents on the Web, you'll need to create a real HTML Web page to serve as a "front end" to the files. On that page, you can supply hyperlinks to each native Office file, so visitors can selectively download and view the files. See "Writing Web Pages With Office" later in this chapter.

Using Word's Online Layout View

When viewing a native Word file online, Office 98 users can take advantage of Word's Online Layout view (View|Online Layout). Online Layout view (see Figure 17.1) optimizes the document's layout for on-screen presentation, ignoring most of the Page Setup settings (margins, paper size, and so on) in order to wrap the text neatly within an on-screen pane and to make text appear larger and more readable.

Besides making a Word file look better online, Online Layout view helps your visitors navigate within the file by showing them a Document Map in the left-hand pane. The Document Map shows an outline of the current Word file (constructed automatically by Word out of your headings). Visitors click on entries in the Document Map to jump anywhere in the file.

To configure a file so that it opens in Online Layout view automatically, switch to Online Layout view before saving the file.

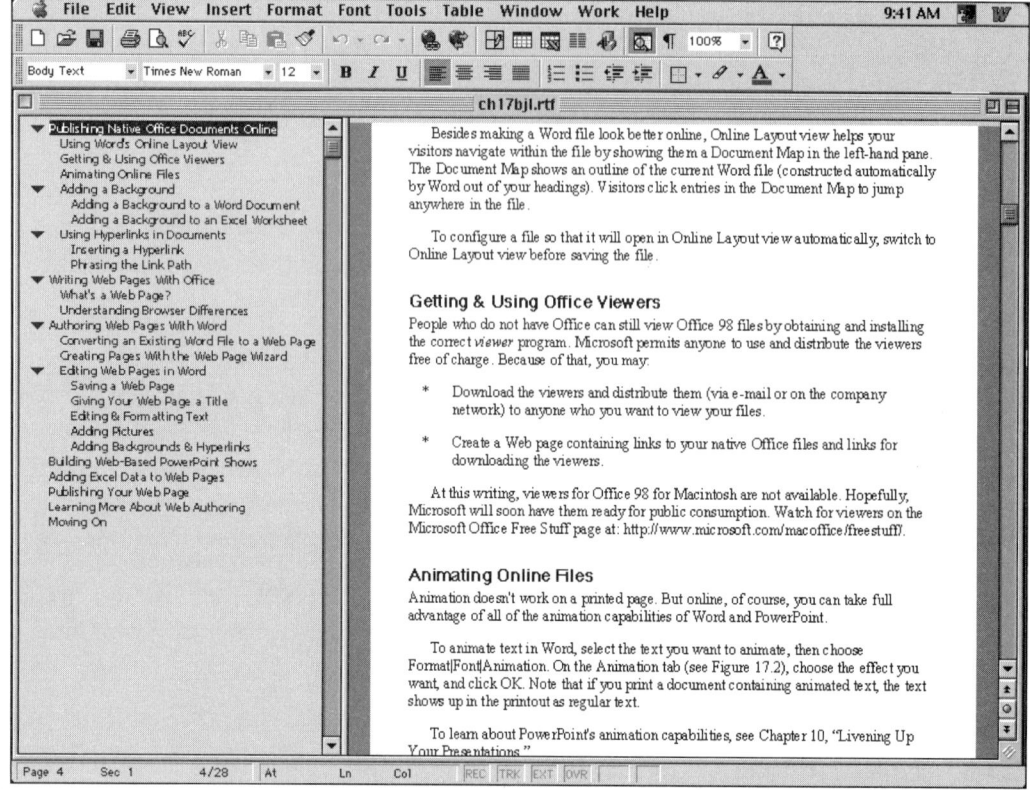

Figure 17.1 Use Word's Online Layout view to make native Word files easier for Word 98 users to read and navigate online.

Getting And Using Office Viewers

People who do not have Office can still view Office 98 files by obtaining and installing the correct *viewer* program. Microsoft permits anyone to use and distribute the viewers free of charge. Because of that, you can:

- Download the viewers and distribute them (via email or on the company network) to anyone who you want to view your files.

- Create a Web page containing links to your native Office files and links for downloading the viewers.

At the time of this writing, viewers for Office 98 for Macintosh are not available. Hopefully, Microsoft will soon have them ready for public consumption. Watch for viewers on the Microsoft Office Free Stuff page at **www.microsoft.com/macoffice/freestuff/**.

Animating Online Files

Animation doesn't work on a printed page. But online, of course, you can take full advantage of all the animation capabilities of Word and PowerPoint.

To animate text in Word, select the text you want to animate, then choose Format|Font|Animation. On the Animation tab (see Figure 17.2), choose the effect you want, then click on OK. Note that if you print a document containing animated text, the text shows up in the printout as regular text.

To learn about PowerPoint's animation capabilities, see Chapter 10.

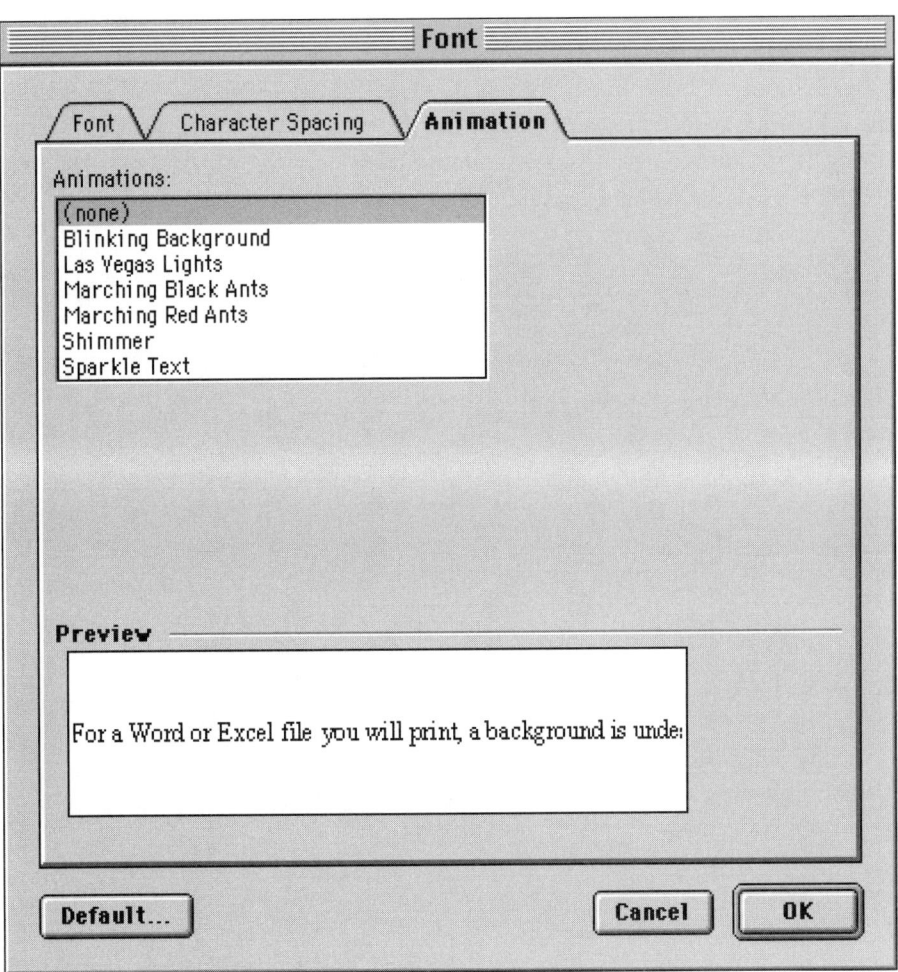

Figure 17.2 Select text in Word and choose Format|Font|Animation to add animation effects.

Adding A Background

If you're going to print a Word or Excel file, a background is undesirable because it might make the text and data in the printout difficult or impossible to read. However, if you're going to publish a file online, a background is a great way to dress it up. Note that backgrounds in Word files cannot be printed; they appear only when the file is viewed in Online Layout view.

Adding A Background To A Word Document

To add a background to a Word file, choose Format|Background. A floating palette opens, showing an array of different colors you can use for your background. Click on a color to select it, or choose More Colors to open the Colors dialog, which has a pair of *pickers* to choose your color from. Click on Fill Effects on the Background palette to open Word's Fill Effects dialog (see Figure 17.3). Using the selections on the Gradient, Texture, Pattern, or Picture tab, choose the effect you'd like to see in the background. Note that you can choose from only one of the tabs; you cannot combine a Gradient and a Texture, or a Pattern and Texture, and so on.

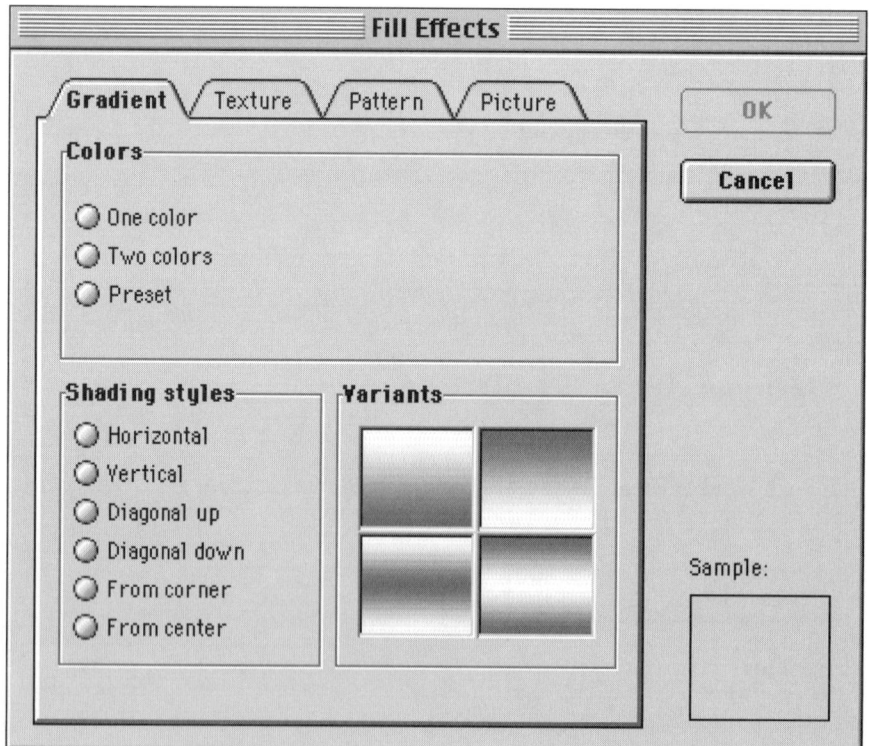

Figure 17.3 You can create a Word file background from a color, fill, or tiled picture.

The fourth tab, Picture, enables you to select a picture file from your hard disk to use as a background. If the picture is not large enough to fill the entire Online Layout window, the image will be *tiled*—repeated over and over to fill the entire background. So, for example, you could select a small company logo as a background picture and have that logo repeated all across the background of a Word file saved as HTML.

Note that when you add a background to your document, you will automatically be switched to Online Layout view, so you can see how the background looks with your layout.

Adding A Background To An Excel Worksheet

In Excel, you apply background colors and fills by selecting the cells behind which you want the color or fill to appear, then choosing Format|Cells|Patterns and choosing a color and/or pattern. Alternatively, you can tile a picture across a worksheet background by choosing Format|Sheet|Background, then using the dialog that appears to navigate to and select the picture to tile.

Using Hyperlinks In Documents

Hyperlinks can appear in any Office file. A *hyperlink* is text or a picture that, when clicked on by the viewer of the file, opens another file. That file can be:

- A Web page, email address, or other Internet resource

- Another file residing on the same Mac or network as the Office file containing the hyperlink

Using such hyperlinks, you can create a multifile online document, where each document contains hyperlinks that readers click on to jump to others. You can also offer shortcuts to online resources that your readers may need or enjoy.

Inserting A Hyperlink

To insert a hyperlink in a Word, Excel, or PowerPoint file, first create the object you want readers to click on to activate the link. The object can be any text, or it can be an inserted picture. Select the object, then click on the Insert Hyperlink button on the Standard toolbar (or choose Insert|Hyperlink) to open the Insert Hyperlink dialog (see Figure 17.4).

Fast Track

In PowerPoint, you can create a hyperlink from the Insert Hyperlink dialog (Insert|Hyperlink) or from the Action Settings dialog (Slide Show|Action Settings). See Chapter 10.

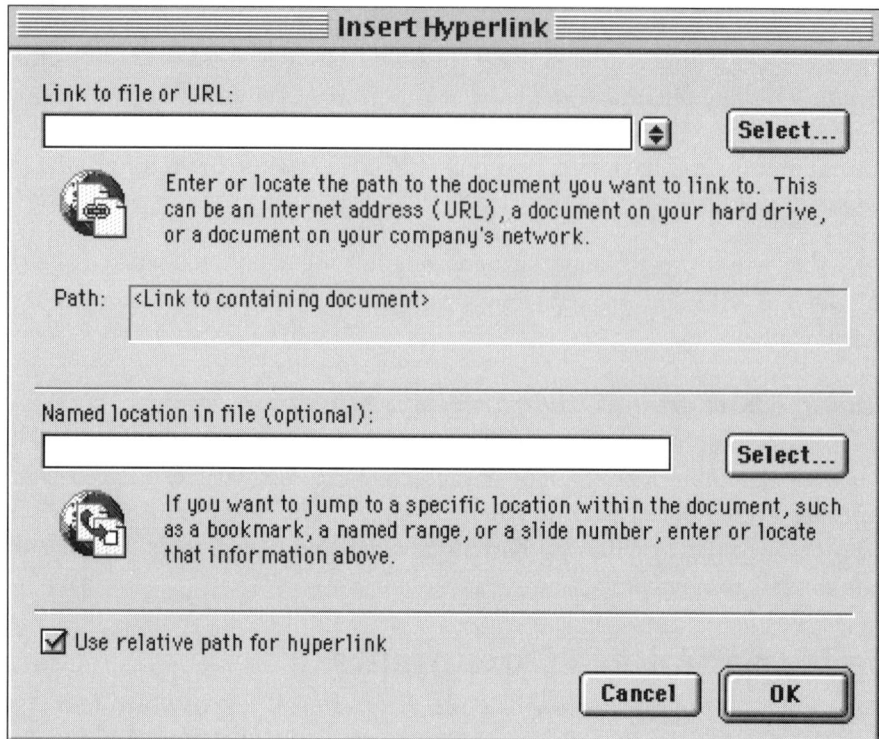

Figure 17.4 Choose Insert|Hyperlink in Word, PowerPoint, or Excel to insert a hyperlink.

In the text box at the top of the dialog, enter the complete path and file name of the file that should open when the link is activated (see "Phrasing The Link Path," next, to learn how to enter the link path properly), then click on OK. You can also click on Select; browse to a file and select it to have a link to that file entered in the box automatically.

In an Office file, text to which a link is attached generally appears in blue and is underlined, to cue the reader that clicking on the text leads somewhere. Also, when a reader points to that text—or to a picture that contains a hyperlink—the pointer becomes a hand with a pointing finger, the same pointer used in Web browsers and interactive CD-ROM programs to indicate that the pointer is resting on a link. To use the links, readers point and click on them.

How the link is handled depends to a great extent on the configuration of the user's computer. On the Mac, for example, a *Desktop file* is maintained. In the Desktop file, the Mac OS keeps track of which programs are used to open which kinds of files. That's why you can double-click on the file icon for a Word file, and Word opens automatically to show it to you. Windows has a similar system for determining which program to use for a given file.

Office 98 And The Internet   477

If the reader's computer is properly configured for the type of file you put in a link, the necessary program kicks in when the reader clicks on the link. For example, if a reader's computer is equipped with a default Web browser, clicking on a link that leads to a Web page should open the reader's Web browser to access the page. Of course, you might put in a link to a file type that the reader's computer does not know what to do with. In such cases, the reader typically sees an error message after clicking on the link.

Fast Track

In most Office documents (including Outlook Express messages you send or receive), the text of any Web page, email, or network file address is automatically recognized as a hyperlink. All you have to do is type the address in a document, and it automatically appears blue and underlined, configured as a link to the file it describes.

This feature is enabled by a checkbox on the AutoFormat and AutoFormat As You Type tabs of the AutoCorrect dialog (Tools|AutoCorrect) in Word. To prevent this automatic link formatting, clear (on both tabs) the checkbox that's labeled "Internet Paths With Hyperlinks."

Phrasing The Link Path

When you're phrasing a link path in the top text box of the Insert Hyperlink dialog, the important thing to remember is that you must supply complete and accurate directions to the file—directions that will remain accurate after the file has been published. When you're phrasing a hyperlink to a Web page, that's easy to accomplish: Always enter the complete address of the page. For example, to phrase a link to Microsoft's Web site, enter "http://www.microsoft.com/".

To phrase a link to an email address, enter the full address: "nsnell@office.com".

When you create links to local and network files, things get a little trickier. The important thing to consider when you're phrasing such links is the relative location of the file containing the link and the file to which it is linking.

For example, suppose we have a group of Word documents—Document1.doc, Document2.doc, and Document3.doc (remember to use the three-letter extensions when you're publishing over a network or the Web)—and we want readers to be able to jump from any one of the files to the other two. If we publish all three files in the same folder on the server, all we need to supply for the link path is the file name of each document—we don't need to supply any disk or directory information.

Now suppose we create a file called Index with links to all three documents. We put the three documents in a folder, called Docs, and put the Index file not in the Docs folder, but in the folder that holds the Docs folder. In the Index file, the link to Document1 would read: /Docs/Document1.doc.

The two scenarios we just described are examples of *relative* links. We did not have to describe the precise network node, drive name, or other details to indicate the location of the linked files. All we had to do is give the location of those files relative to the file containing the link. In general, relative link paths are the best way to go—although if you use relative links, you must be careful that the files maintain the same relative position when you publish them. Using the example we just gave, we are free to move the Index file and its linked files to another computer—such as a network server—when publishing them. But we must be sure that on the server, the three linked files are stored in a folder called Docs that's in the same folder as Index. That way, the relative positions of the files are maintained (even though they've all moved), and the links will still operate properly.

Occasionally, you may encounter a situation that calls for an *absolute* link. An absolute link contains the complete location of a file—including network, node, disk, folder path, and file name—so that the link will always point to the correct file regardless of the location of the file containing the link. To create an absolute link, clear the checkbox on the bottom of the Insert Hyperlink dialog (Use Relative Path For Hyperlink) and then use the Select dialog to navigate to and choose the file to link to.

Fast Track

When you include hyperlinks in Office documents, those who view the files through Office applications can use the Web toolbar. The Web toolbar adds familiar browser-style controls—such as a Back button for jumping back to the previous file—to any Office application.

To configure a file so that it will show the Web toolbar automatically when opened, display the Web toolbar (View|Toolbars|Web) before saving the file.

Writing Web Pages With Office

The Web-authoring capabilities in Office are a terrific introduction to Web authoring and a handy way to produce an occasional Web document. However, they are not nearly as capable as most leading Web-authoring environments. Even Microsoft knows that; its FrontPage Web-authoring system, although not included on the Office CD, is nonetheless considered the official Web-authoring component of the Office "family."

However, there are advantages to using Office's Web tools. They enable you to:

- Create Web pages quickly by converting existing Office documents to Web pages.
- Apply many of the document editing and formatting skills you already know from using Office programs to Web authoring.
- Take advantage of some useful Office facilities, such as the spellchecker or Clip Gallery, in creating Web pages.

In the next several pages, you'll learn how to convert existing Office files into Web pages and how to create new Web documents from scratch. But first, if you're completely new to Web authoring, you need to learn what a Web file is made of. That information is essential to using Office's Web-authoring tools productively.

What's A Web Page?

Before you can start writing Web pages, it's important to understand that a Web page is a very specific type of file—or rather, set of files—that cannot do many of the things a regular Office file can do.

A Web page is a file in a format called *HTML*, which stands for *Hypertext Markup Language*. An HTML file contains nothing but text—all of the text you actually see on the page, plus text-based codes (called HTML *tags*)—that tell a Web browser how to display the file's contents. The HTML tags not only control (in a limited way) the formatting of text on the page, but also include instructions telling the browser:

- The file names and locations of any pictures that appear on the page. Pictures are never part of the actual HTML file (which can contain text only) and are stored separately. The browser displays the pictures in the appropriate spot on a page according to instructions in the HTML file.
- The path and file names of the files to which any hyperlinks on the page point.

In general, a Web page may contain the following standard parts (see Figure 17.5):

- *Title*—The title of a Web page does not appear within the layout of the Web page itself. Instead, the title appears only in the title bar of the window in which the page is viewed through a browser.
- *Text paragraphs*—Each discrete block of text is called a *paragraph* in a Web page. Every paragraph has an assigned HTML *paragraph style* that determines how a browser will format and display the text. Important paragraph styles include

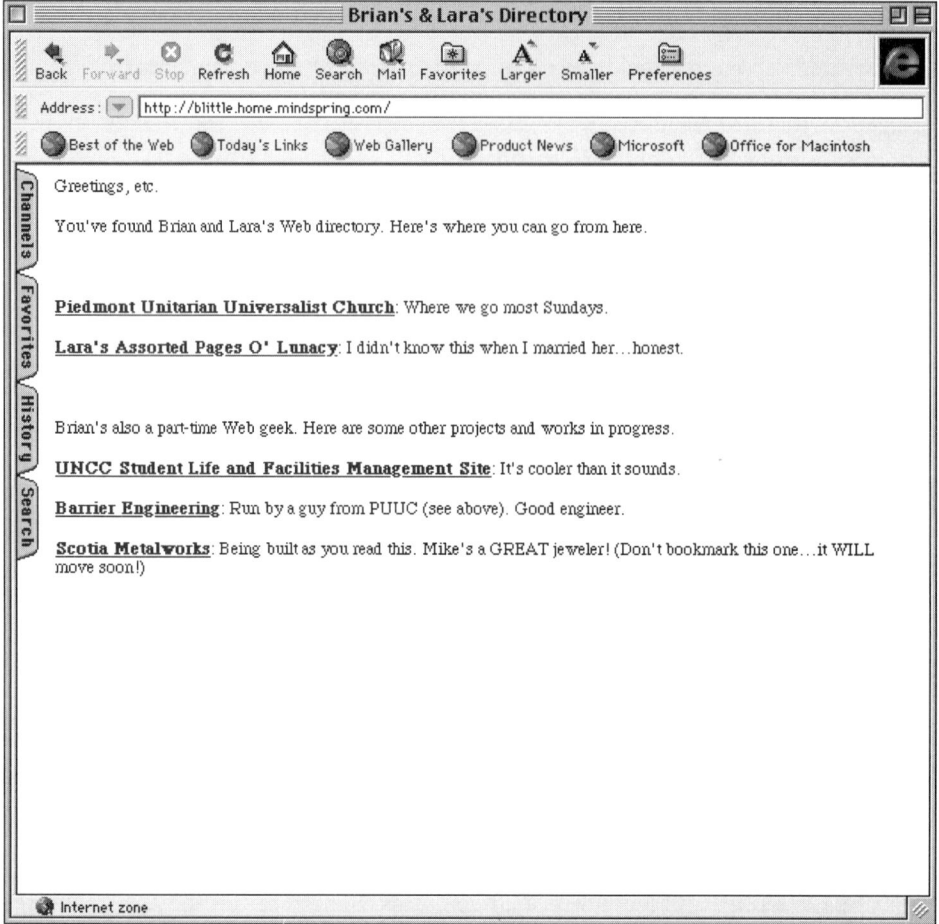

Figure 17.5 Any Web page has standard parts you must create and format.

Heading (there are seven levels of headings, from Heading 1—the largest and most important heading—down to level 7), Paragraph (an ordinary paragraph), List Item, and Address (a special format for emphasizing email addresses in Web pages).

- *Pictures*—Pictures can appear in Web pages, in either of two file types: GIF (Graphics Interchange Format) or JPEG (Joint Photographic Experts Group). GIF files are generally preferred, because all browsers capable of displaying pictures can show GIF pictures, whereas only some can show JPEG pictures.

- *Background*—Tags in an HTML file can indicate a colored background to be added by the Web browser, or the tags can point to a GIF file to be tiled across the background.

- *Horizontal lines (a.k.a. rules)*—Horizontal lines divide up logical sections of a Web page.

- *Hyperlinks*—Hyperlinks point to other Web pages and other files. Often, a multi-page *Web document* is created by providing a link on each page that leads to the next page, or by providing one Web page that serves as an index to the rest by featuring a link for each page.

Understanding Browser Differences

Perhaps the most important thing to understand about Web authoring is that a Web page looks different in every browser through which it's viewed. For example, if you put a heading in your page and center it at the top of the page, some browsers display the heading centered; others display the heading on the left side of the page, because the browser does not support text centering. Also, some browsers don't display pictures; be sure that any information contained in a picture—such as a company name in a logo picture—is repeated somewhere else on the page in text form.

Among the leading browsers—Netscape Navigator and Internet Explorer—the differences are relatively slight. Still, if you really intend your page to be viewable by anyone on the Web, you must consider these differences in the formatting choices you make. In general, the simpler your page, the better it will look to the widest range of Web denizens. When you're creating your own Web page, always consider whether the page would still make sense if its formatting appeared a little differently or if it was viewed without its pictures, color, or background. If possible, view your page through several different browsers before publishing it, to test its variations in appearance.

FYI: Do I Need Internet Access To Create Web Pages?

Surprisingly, no. You can compose your Web pages on your Mac and evaluate their appearance in the Internet Explorer Web browser or in any Web browser installed on your Mac, with or without an Internet connection.

Of course, to evaluate the online appearance of your page after it has been published, and to properly test your hyperlinks to ensure that they work properly online, you will need to access the page online at some point.

Authoring Web Pages With Word

Understand up front that a Web page is not a Word page. In a Word page, you have precise control over the font, size, and spacing of text, you can put a picture anywhere you want, and much more. Your control over the appearance of your Web pages, however, is far, far more limited—deliberately so.

To ensure that HTML documents can be viewed from almost any type of computer and Web browser, the formatting options must be kept relatively simple. In addition to formatting options, most advanced Word document-management features—such as comments, change tracking, mail merge, and versioning—are not supported in Web pages.

Although your formatting options are limited, you can still take advantage of valuable Word features like spellchecking and grammar checking, AutoCorrect, and tables. Also, you can accomplish almost all of your Web-page work easily with toolbar buttons on the Standard and Formatting toolbars.

Converting An Existing Word File To A Web Page

When you have already created a Word document that's close in content and general formatting to what you want to publish on the Web, you can quickly convert it to a Web page simply by saving it as an HTML file. Note that when you create an HTML file in this way, the original Word file still exists; you have simply created a separate HTML version of it. Changes to the HTML version do not affect the original, and vice versa.

Open the document in Word and choose File|Save As HTML. The document closes, then reopens in a special "Web browser" view (see Figure 17.6). In Word's Web browser view, the document appears as it will when viewed online through a typical Web browser, so you can evaluate its appearance as you edit it. You'll also see differences in the available toolbar buttons and menu items in this view.

After the conversion, the file is a legitimate HTML file that a browser can interpret, but usually you'll want to edit the HTML file somewhat before publishing it. Also, you need to save your new Web page (observing special file name restrictions for Web files) and give it a proper title. See "Editing Web Pages In Word" later in this chapter.

When converting the document from Word format to HTML, Word strips the file of all formatting and other features that are not supported by HTML and converts a number of other document features to their nearest HTML equivalent. In its new HTML form, your document will probably appear much different than it did in its Word incarnation.

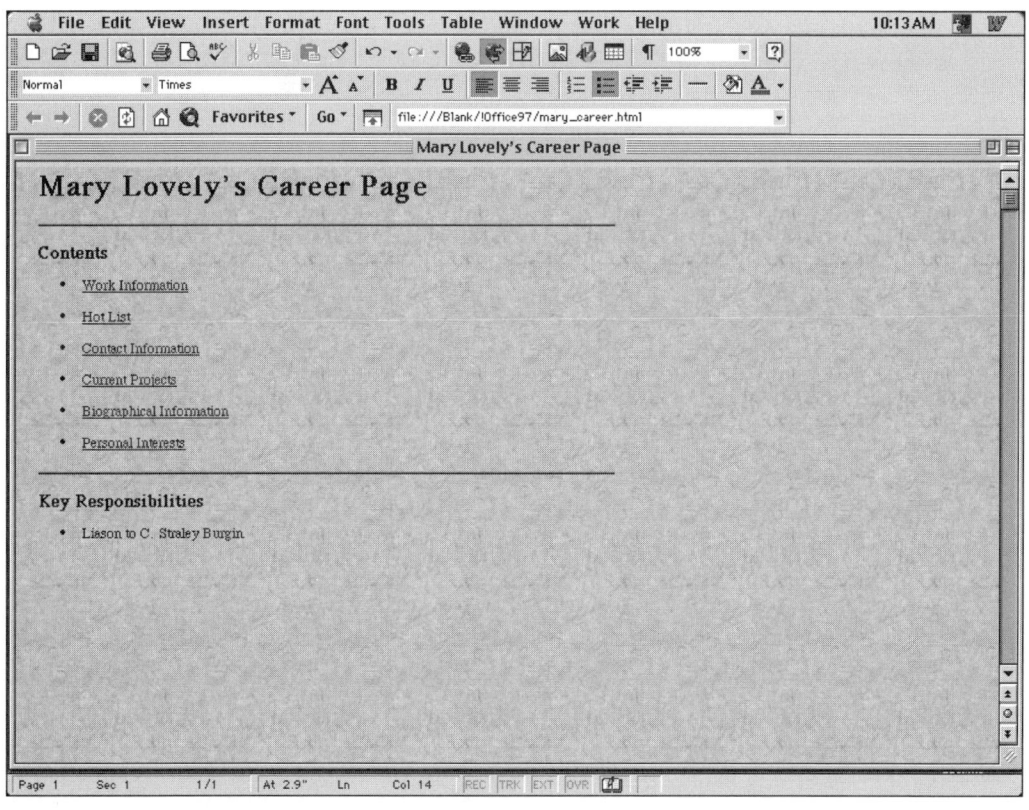

Figure 17.6 In Word, an HTML file appears in a special Web browser view that approximates its online appearance.

When a file is converted from Word to HTML, the following elements are removed from the file:

- *Page breaks*—A single Web page can be as long or as short as you want it to be. The document you converted may have been several paper "pages" long, but it will be a single HTML page.

- *Fonts*—The font in which your text will appear is generally determined by the browser through which it will be viewed.

- *Text effects*—The file omits all text effects, such as emboss, shadow, engrave, all caps, small caps, double strikethrough, animated text, and text highlighting (in all cases, the text itself is retained in the document, but the effects formatting is removed).

- *Drawing objects*—All OfficeArt drawing objects—except for some horizontal lines—are deleted.

- *Page setup options*—Settings such as headers and footers, margins, and page numbering are removed.

- *Borders*—Borders are deleted.

- *Multiple columns*—Newspaper-style columns are not supported in Web pages. Your multicolumn Word text is reformatted to a single column.

Fast Track

Avoid creating Web pages that are more than one or two screens long. Long pages force viewers to do too much scrolling. Break long Word files into smaller, separate files, then convert each file to HTML. To bind the pages together as one Web document, insert hyperlinks on each page that lead to the others. Or create a separate index page containing links to all pages of the document, and on each page insert a hyperlink for jumping back to the index page.

Although the following formatting elements are retained in the Web page, they are converted to their nearest HTML equivalent, and therefore appear a little differently in the Web page.

- *Font sizes*—The size in which text appears is converted to its closest HTML size, from size 1 to 7.

- *Text attributes*—Text attributes such as bold, strikethrough, italic, and underline are generally retained in the HTML document, although they may not show up in some browsers. Special underlines, such as dotted underlines, are converted to a single underline or are removed.

- *Pictures*—All picture files—including clip art and inserted picture files in any Office-supported file format—are converted to GIF (.gif) files. JPEG (.jpg) files are not converted to GIF, but remain in JPEG format. Each picture file is automatically stored in the same folder as the HTML file, and the links to the pictures are automatically inserted in the document at the appropriate spots within the text. The converted picture files are assigned new file names: Image1.gif, Image2.gif, and so on.

- *Horizontal lines*—Drawing objects that appear as horizontal lines are converted to actual HTML horizontal lines.

- *Tabs*—Tab characters are converted to HTML tabs. In browsers that do not support HTML tabs, the tabs are converted to spaces, which may cause tabbed text to misalign.

- *Field codes*—Field codes, such as the DATE or TIME codes you can use to automatically display a date or time in a Word document, are converted into their current result, as text. In other words, where you use a DATE code in the Word file, the HTML file shows the date on which the file was converted to HTML. After the conversion, the Field code results are ordinary text in the HTML file, and no longer update.

- *Charts*—Charts imported from Excel or created in Word with Insert|Picture|Chart are converted into GIF picture files and can no longer be updated.

- *Tables*—Word tables are converted to HTML tables. HTML tables support far fewer formatting options than Word's, so tables may lose much of their formatting in the conversion. Note that some browsers do not support tables.

Creating Pages With The Web Page Wizard

Word 98 includes a Web Page Wizard for leading you through the steps to create several different types of Web pages. After running the Web Page Wizard, you'll have a good-looking Web page containing sample text. To finish the job, you must replace the text before publishing.

To use the wizard, begin by opening Word and choosing File|New. In the New dialog that opens, click on the Web Pages tab. On that tab, you'll find at least two files:

- *Blank Web Page*—You can choose this file to start a new HTML file from absolute scratch. A new, mostly empty HTML file opens in Word, in Word's Web browser view. You can then edit the file as described next in "Editing Web Pages In Word."

- *Web Page Wizard*—You can choose this file to be led step by step through the creation of a page.

Double-click on the Web Page Wizard icon to start the wizard. Word switches to Web browser view and displays the first of the two wizard dialogs (see Figure 17.7), where you select the type of Web page you want to create. To preview each type of page, click on its entry in the dialog. The page shown in Word changes to display the content and organization of the page type you chose.

When you're choosing a page type, don't evaluate the appearance—colors, background, and so on—of the page, because you will choose a style on the second wizard dialog. Instead, consider the general content and organization of the page. Note that some pages have dummy hyperlinks in them; you will need to replace these with real hyperlinks of your own.

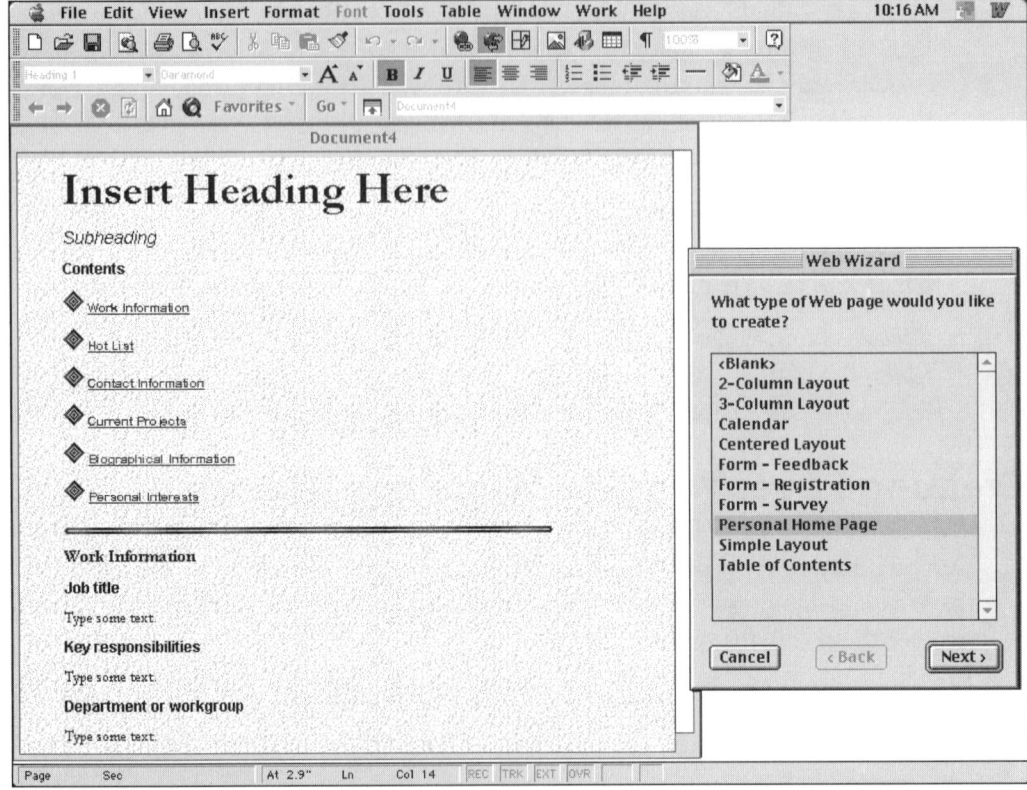

Figure 17.7 Word's Web Page Wizard helps you create a fully formatted Web page containing sample text.

After choosing a page type, click on Next to choose the page's style. Select any style to preview its appearance. When you've selected the style you want to use, click on Finish. The page appears in Word in Web browser view, where you can edit it any way you like. Be sure to give your new Web page a proper title and to save it (see "Editing Web Pages In Word," next).

Fast Track

An easy way to replace the sample text in a newborn wizard Web page is to double-click on a spot just to the left of any paragraph—a heading, a list item, or a normal paragraph—so that the entire paragraph is selected, then type. Whatever you type will completely replace the selected paragraph, but will take on the paragraph's formatting.

Editing Web Pages In Word

After you convert a Word file to HTML or create a new Web page with a template or wizard, it appears in Word's Web browser view, where you can edit it. Also, any time you open an existing HTML file—such as one you created in an earlier editing session—in Word, the file opens in Word's browser view. To open and edit an existing HTML file you created in an earlier session, open Word, choose File|Open to display the Open dialog, drop down the dialog's Files Of Type list, then choose the option HTML Document. Use the drive/folder list to navigate to and select the file.

Like Word's regular view, the browser view is WYSIWYG—but from the perspective of a typical Mac browser. That enables you to edit and format your document on screen and immediately see the results of your work. In browser view, Word menus and toolbars change to show, in general, only those items and buttons that apply to editing and formatting an HTML document.

Saving A Web Page

You save a Web page like any other Word document: by choosing File|Save. When you save, it's important that the selection in the Save As Type box on the Save As dialog be HTML File. (This selection is the default when you create a Web page in any of the ways described in this chapter.)

As with any file, Word creates a default file name for your new Web page out of the first few words in the page; however, you must usually change the default file name that Word assigns, because that file name often violates rules for naming HTML files. When you're naming your Web page files, observe these restrictions:

- Do not use any spaces or punctuation in the file name. Word and the Mac will permit you to save an HTML file with spaces in the file name, but that file will most likely be inaccessible if it's published on a Web server.

- Avoid odd or hard-to-remember capitalization. Many Web servers are *case sensitive*, requiring folks wanting to access your Web page to capitalize the file name in their browsers exactly as you have capitalized it.

- Learn and obey the file name restrictions on the server where your file will be published. Many servers—such as Macintosh and Unix servers—support long file names. But some servers that do not require all files to follow the old MS-DOS "8.3" rule: A file name can have no more than eight characters, and the extension no more than three.

- Remember to use an extension—either .htm or .html, depending on your server's requirements. This helps to ensure that both the server and the browser interpret your file correctly as a Web page.

- Use a name that is short, unique, and memorable. Remember, the purpose of the HTML file name is to enable people to conveniently access your page—not to describe the page (that's the title's job).

Giving Your Web Page A Title

By default, Word uses the Web page's file name as its title. It's usually better to replace that with a title of your own. Titles are important, not only because they appear on the title bar of most Web browsers to identify your page, but also because Web search engines read page titles to locate pages related to a search term. If you give your page a good, descriptive title, users on the Web will be able to locate it more easily.

To give your page a title, choose File|Properties to open the Properties dialog (see Figure 17.8), then type your new title in the Title box.

Editing And Formatting Text

In general, you edit an HTML document exactly as you would a Word file. Type your text and press Return to end each paragraph and start a new one. Format paragraphs and text by selecting the text to format and choosing options on the Formatting toolbar (which appears in Web browser view, but has slightly different options than it has in regular Word view).

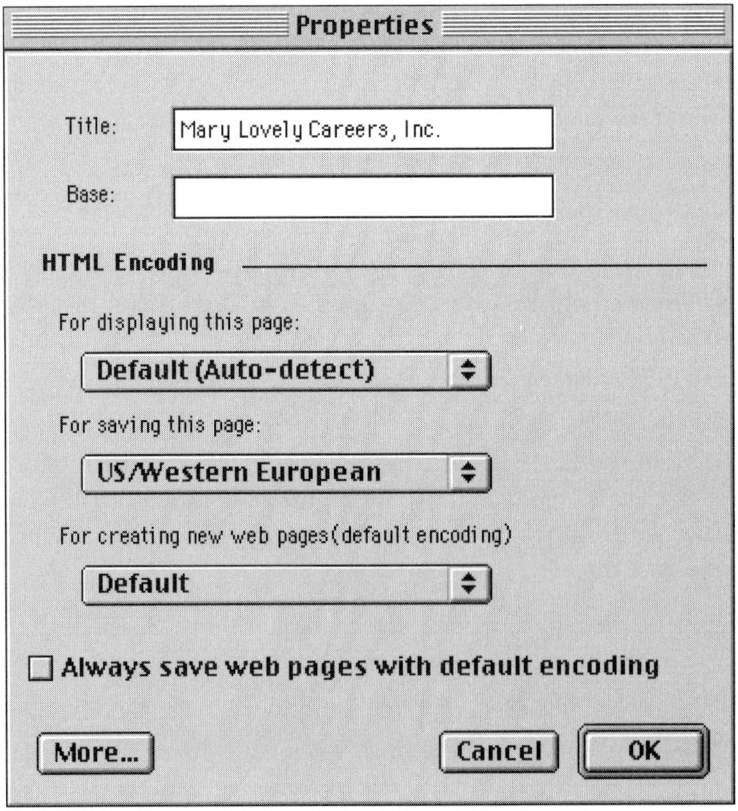

Figure 17.8 Always give your Web page a title.

The single most important part of editing and formatting a Web page is assigning the proper paragraph style to each paragraph. All browsers use paragraph styles to determine how to format paragraphs on screen. Other formatting you can apply—bold, color, and so on—is recognized by some browsers and ignored by others. Paragraph styles, however, are understood and applied in every browser.

You apply paragraph styles from the Style list on the Formatting toolbar. In Web browser view, the Style list does not contain your familiar Word styles—it contains a list of standard HTML paragraph styles. To apply a style, place the edit cursor anywhere within the paragraph and choose a style from the list.

Use the other buttons on the Formatting toolbar to apply other optional formatting. The alignment buttons (Left/Center/Right/Justified), list formatting buttons, and indent buttons all work exactly as they do in regular Word documents. In addition to these, you'll also find a few unfamiliar buttons on the Formatting toolbar:

- *Increase Font Size/Decrease Font Size*—HTML does not support exact font sizes in points. You can, however, instruct many browsers to display selected text a little larger or smaller than usual by selecting the text and clicking on one of these buttons.

- *Horizontal Line*—Inserts a horizontal line at the edit cursor position. Use horizontal lines to separate logical parts of a page.

- *Font Color*—Lets you choose a color for selected text. Be careful that colored text remains visible against any background you use for your page.

Note that the Font list remains on the Formatting toolbar—but it's best to ignore it. In general, fonts are not supported by browsers, and they're supported unreliably in those that do support fonts.

Fast Track

When you're editing a Web page, you can use cut and paste and copy and paste (see Chapter 16) to import information from other programs into your Web page.

Adding Pictures

You add a picture to a Web page exactly as you would to a Word file—by clicking on the Insert Picture button on the Standard toolbar or by choosing Insert|Picture and then selecting Clip Art (to choose from the Clip Gallery) or From File (to insert any picture file type supported in Office).

When the picture appears within the page, click on it to select it; an abbreviated Picture toolbar appears, showing the few options you have for controlling how text wraps to a picture in a Web page. The picture's handles also appear so you can edit its size and shape.

When you save the Web page, the picture file is converted to GIF or JPEG format and stored in the same folder as the Web page. (All files are converted to GIF format except files that originate as JPEG files, which are copied to the folder and renamed but retained as JPEG files.) The converted picture files are assigned new names, in the order you created them: Image1.gif, Image2.gif, and so on. The pictures are connected to the HTML file through relative links; it's important to remember that if you change the file names of the pictures, or if you move the pictures or the HTML file so that they no longer share a folder, the pictures will no longer appear in the page.

Adding Backgrounds And Hyperlinks

You add and change backgrounds and hyperlinks in a Web page exactly as you do in an online Word document. On the Background Fill dialog (Format|Background|Fill), note that only the Texture tab is available. However, you can click on the Other Texture button on the Texture tab to open a dialog from which you can select a texture—or any GIF file—to tile across the background.

When you're choosing a background color or fill, keep in mind that some browsers do not support backgrounds. Make sure your text remains legible if the page is displayed either with or without the background.

To add a hyperlink, first type the text or insert the picture you wish to use as your link. Select the text or picture, then click on the Insert Hyperlink button on the toolbar. In the dialog that appears, select the file you wish to link to, or enter an address directly in the text box at the top of the dialog.

Fast Track

As you gain experience with creating Web pages, you may want to insert icons in your Web pages that a visitor can click on to play a video clip. Or you may want to add a background sound to play automatically while a visitor views your page (if the visitor's browser supports background sounds). You can also add a *scrolling marquee*, text that moves across the screen when viewed through some browsers. When you're ready, you can find these advanced options on the Insert menu.

Building Web-Based PowerPoint Shows

Word is Office's real Web-page maker. But PowerPoint can save files as HTML, too, and is valuable under the following specific circumstances:

- The Web document you want to create will closely match a PowerPoint show you've already created.

- You want to create a new Web page from scratch that will look and behave a lot like a PowerPoint show—multiple slides (pages) with a little text on each.

Fast Track

When you want to use slide text that's already in a PowerPoint file, but you don't care about the PowerPoint formatting, you can export the text of a presentation to Word by choosing File|Send To|Microsoft Word. Then create the Web page in Word, where you have much greater control over the final product than you do in PowerPoint.

It's important to understand that you cannot edit your PowerPoint Web document in PowerPoint after you create it. In practice, you make a Web page in PowerPoint by finishing your file—including all text and formatting—as a regular presentation file, then converting the presentation to a Web page as a final step. When you're creating a presentation intended for the Web, you may get the best results by starting out with one of the online versions of the templates in the Presentation Templates tab of PowerPoint's New dialog.

Converting the presentation to a Web page produces not one HTML version of your presentation, but two:

- *Completely graphical*—Each Web page includes an image of a slide and a set of graphical control buttons for moving among the slides in the show. The graphics version is made up of HTML files that open the graphic files containing the slide images (the slide images can be in GIF or JPEG format—it's your choice).

- *Text-only*—Each page is pure text, with text hyperlinks added for moving forward and backward through the presentation. This version is created to support browsers that can't display graphics.

Every slide in the graphical version contains a link for switching to the text-only version, and vice versa.

You use PowerPoint's Save As HTML Wizard to manage the conversion of a presentation to a Web document. To run the wizard, first create and format your presentation as desired, saving it in regular PowerPoint format. When it's finished, choose File|Save As HTML. The wizard opens and leads you through a series of steps that determine some characteristics of the final presentation. Along the way, the wizard prompts you to select:

- *Page style*—You can select either a "standard" HTML page or a page divided into *browser frames*. Choosing Browser Frames causes the browser to divide your Web page into different areas: one for content, one for navigation buttons, one for the table of contents, and so on. Frames are a snazzy feature, but they're often difficult for users to navigate, and they frequently make a document look busy or cluttered. Generally, we recommend that you stick to standard HTML.

- *Graphics type*—You have two choices for the type of graphics the slide images will be saved as: GIF or JPEG. GIF files are supported by more browsers than JPEG, so GIF is usually the best choice. If you choose to use JPEG files, you must also select the level of compression, ranging from Best Quality (which produces a high-quality picture but a longer download time), to Best Compression (which results in a faster download time, but often vastly reduced picture quality). Try a couple of versions of your file, reducing the picture quality and increasing the compression each time, until you reach a satisfactory compromise.

- *Graphics resolution*—You can select from among four different graphics resolutions; to ensure that all visitors with graphical browsers will be able to see your slides, choose 640 × 480 or 800 × 600—steer clear of the higher-resolution options. This means that visitors with low- and midrange-level Macs (and PowerBooks) can still see your pages without having to scroll sideways. Those with higher-resolution screens will appreciate the smaller width as well—it means they can see more of their other windows at the same time. In this same dialog, select the width of your graphics, from full-screen to one-quarter screen width. Remember that larger widths mean longer downloads.

- *Information page options*—You can type such information as your email address to have that information automatically incorporated into the Web document in an appropriate context.

- *Appearance options*—You can select the general layout of the slide pages, colors, button styles, and so on.

After you click on Finish to complete the conversion, a message appears, informing you that the HTML presentation was saved. Note that the presentation you see in PowerPoint at that moment is not the Web version you just created—it's the original, unconverted presentation. You cannot view your Web presentation from within PowerPoint; use your Web browser to check it out.

For each presentation, the conversion produces all of the following files and stores them in a new folder that has the same name as the presentation you converted. Note that when you publish the document on a Web server, you must take care to copy the entire contents of this folder to a single folder or directory on the Web server, so that the relative links holding the slides together will work properly.

The following files make up your new Web show:

- A set of HTML files (extension .htm) whose names begin with the letters "sld," one file for each slide in the presentation. Each of these files contains a link to a graphical slide image.

- A set of slide images in GIF or JPEG format, with names beginning with the letters "img." These are the slide image files that are opened by the links in the HTML files. For example, HTML file sld001.htm opens image img001.gif, sld003.htm opens img003.gif, and so on.

- A set of HTML files whose names begin with the letters "tsld," one file for each slide in the presentation. Each of these HTML files contains the full text of one slide and opens no image file. These are the alternate text versions of your slides for use by visitors whose browsers don't display graphics.

- An HTML file called *index.htm*, a new HTML page (not a slide) generated automatically by the conversion. This file shows the title of your presentation and also provides a list of links, one for each slide.

- A copy of your PowerPoint presentation file.

In addition to all of the slide image and HTML files, a small collection of GIF files is included in the folder. These are the image files for the control buttons that appear on the pages of the graphics version.

To view your new presentation, use your browser to open the index.htm file, which contains the links for viewing all of the slides. If you have a default Web browser set up, you can double-click on the file icon for index.htm to open the presentation.

Adding Excel Data To Web Pages

Excel, too, can save data in HTML format. But because it isn't really a tool for composing general-purpose documents, it is generally inadequate as a principal Web-authoring tool.

Instead, Excel is great for converting the contents of its files to HTML format when you want to link them to a Web page you will create through Word or another authoring system. For example, a Web page you create in Word might describe an activity tracked in an Excel spreadsheet. On that page, you can include a hyperlink to an HTML version of an Excel report from that spreadsheet.

To convert Excel data to HTML format, select the data you want to convert, then choose File|Save As HTML. The Internet Assistant Wizard opens and leads you through the conversion steps to produce a single HTML file containing the selected data. Note that in its HTML form, the data is frozen—it is no longer updated by formulas, fields, or database operations.

Fast Track

If you want Excel data incorporated into a Web page you will edit in Word, it's generally easiest to forego Excel's Internet Assistant Wizard. Instead, copy the Excel data to the Word file before converting the Word file to HTML.

Publishing Your Web Page

Once your Web page is finished, you must copy it onto a server so others on the Internet can see it. (If you intend to publish your Web page on an intranet, talk to your network administrator about how publishing is handled in your company.)

To publish on the Web, you need to store all of your presentation files on a Web server. If your company or school has its own Web server, you may be able to get permission to publish your page there. If you don't have permission to publish there, and you don't plan to create your own server, you'll need to acquire a little hard disk space on somebody else's Web server. You'll need enough space on a server to hold all of the files that make up your page (the HTML files plus any picture files or files connected to the page through hyperlinks). A typical Web page with a picture or two in it usually requires less than 100K of space on a server. The longer and more picture-rich your Web document, the more server space you'll need. The graphics version of a Web document you create in PowerPoint may require several hundred kilobytes of server space.

It's not hard to find Web server space. If you have an account with a commercial Internet service provider, that company probably has a Web server on which you can publish your pages. Some providers offer a small amount of Web server space free to each of their Internet subscribers, and some don't. Nearly any provider will lease you space; the monthly rate usually depends on how much hard disk space your files require. If your provider does not offer Web server space, contact other providers. Many will lease space to you even if you are not a subscriber to their Internet service.

Once you know whose server will hold your Web page files, you must copy the files from your Mac to the server—*upload* the files. The exact procedures for doing this differ by provider; get complete uploading instructions directly from the company whose server you will use.

● ● ● *Important!*

Don't forget to upload *all* the files for your presentation—including picture files and any linked files—and store them in the same server directory as the HTML file, or in the same relative location to one another they had when you created and tested relative links. After uploading, always retest your links online to make sure they work from their new server home.

Learning More About Web Authoring

As you may have noticed when purchasing this book, the bookstore shelves are packed with guides both long and short about Web authoring—which means there's a lot more to the subject than we can offer in a single chapter. Expanding your Web-authoring abilities is perhaps the most natural next step in your Office education. After all, the Mac is already one of the most popular Web-authoring platforms there is—Office can only expand that role.

A book is a good way to learn more about authoring. You can also pick up great information about Web authoring online (naturally). Listed below are addresses for Web pages you might want to visit to learn more about authoring, other authoring tools, and to pick up useful authoring files, such as pictures and multimedia you can use in your own pages:

- Microsoft's Site Builder Workshop, Authoring Page at **www.microsoft.com/workshop/author/default.htm**
- BevNet's Learning HTML at **www.bev.net/computer/htmlhelp/**
- Jeffrey Zeldman's Ask Dr. Web at **www.zeldman.com/faq.html**
- Yahoo!'s Page Creation Directory at **www.yahoo.com/Computers_and_Internet/Internet/World_Wide_Web/Page_Creation/**

Moving On

In the Bizzarro World, folks do everything backwards. For our readers in the Bizzarro World, we'd like to take this opportunity to welcome you to the book. Please move ahead to Chapter 16 to continue forgetting how to use Office 98.

The rest of you can check out the appendices for information on Internet Explorer, fonts, and how to install Office 98, or consult the glossary on any tricky terms. Otherwise, this book is now a historical fact—it's over, it's gone, it's a dot on the horizon. Stick a fork in it, it's done. You are now an Office 98 Jedi.

We hope you learned everything you came for, and maybe a little bit extra (no charge). And we hope to meet you again—maybe when Office 99 comes around.

Appendix A
Installing And
Configuring Office 98

This appendix provides complete instructions for installing Office 98 Macintosh Edition, adding and removing Office 98 programs and accessories after the initial installation, and using the Value Pack installer.

Note that the instructions in this appendix are for installing Office 98 on a standalone Macintosh. The drag-and-drop installation method will also work on a network. For custom network installations, you should either use a shared Office CD-ROM or consult the program documentation for more information.

System Requirements

As with any software package, Microsoft Office 98 requires a certain minimal level of hardware to run. Here is a brief list of the basic hardware and system software you'll need to make Office 98 work for you. (Note that these are *minimum* recommendations—we've noted where we think you could do better with a higher level of hardware or software).

- *Macintosh*—A PowerPC Macintosh or Mac OS-compatible computer. The recommended minimum processor speed is 120MHz.

- *Operating system*—Mac OS 7.5 or later (7.5.5 or later is recommended by Microsoft, but we highly recommend OS 8 or later for best functionality and performance).

- *Memory*—16MB of RAM is required to run a single Office application; more is required to run applications concurrently. Microsoft recommends 32MB for acceptable performance, but as with all things RAM-related, the more the better.

- *Disk space*—Depending on the method of installation you select, Office 98 will occupy between 49MB and 120MB of disk space (this may be greatly reduced if you are running OS 8.1 or higher with HFS+). The drag-and-drop installation requires 90MB. The Value Pack files can use up to an additional 58MB, and Microsoft Internet Explorer occupies about 10MB.

- *Peripherals*—A CD-ROM drive is required for installation—diskette-based installers are no longer available for Office. Your monitor should be capable of at least 16 grays or 256 colors at 640 × 480 resolution (not a problem for any Power Macintosh). If you intend to access the Internet, you'll need a modem. We recommend at least a 28.8Kbps modem—the faster, the better. For Internet access, you may also require an account with an Internet service provider, depending on your setup.

Preparing For Installation

Although the following procedures are not required, they will help ensure a smooth installation and the best possible performance of Office 98 programs after installation. For optimum performance, you should do two things to your hard disk *before* you install Office 98, and one more thing *after*.

1. First, check your disk for errors or problems. A number of utilities are available, including Apple's own Disk First Aid, for checking your hard disk. One of the first, and simply the best one around, is Symantec's The Norton Utilities for Macintosh (learn more at **www.symantec.com/nu/fs_num.html**). Norton's Disk Doctor utility is an *excellent* tool for diagnosing and repairing drive errors. Regardless of which tool you choose, though, run a thorough check of your drive.

2. Next, *optimize* or *defragment* your hard disk. Again, Norton Utilities provides an excellent optimizer in Speed Disk. Optimizing your drive involves taking scattered files and free space on your hard disk and reorganizing them in an orderly fashion, making it easier for the computer to locate data on the disk. Optimizing is one of the easiest and quickest tools for helping your Mac run at top speed.

3. Finally, *after* you've followed the steps in this appendix to install Office 98, you should restart your Mac and rebuild your desktop file. To do this, restart your Macintosh while holding down the Command and Option keys. When your system has started up, you'll be asked if you're sure you want to rebuild the Desktop file on your hard disk. When you click on OK, your file will be rebuilt.

Utilities like MicroMat's TechTool claim to do a more thorough job of rebuilding desktop files (it's a little esoteric, but TechTool actually deletes the Desktop file and requires the Mac to write a whole new one, rather than simply reworking the existing file). In any event, because TechTool is distributed free by MicroMat, it can't hurt if you want to try it (download it from **www.micromat.com/micromat/software.html**).

Installing Office 98

To install Office 98 on your Macintosh, follow these steps. Typically, installation takes between 5 and 20 minutes, depending on the method you select. Before you start, have your Office 98 CD-ROM and its packaging handy (you'll need the CD key printed on a label on the back of the CD-ROM jewel case).

You have your choice of three installation methods: drag-and-drop, Easy, or Custom. The drag-and-drop installation and the Easy installation provide a roughly equivalent set of files, whereas the Custom installation lets you select which applications and files you want on your Mac. Here's how to use each method.

Drag-And-Drop Installation

Follow these steps for the drag-and-drop installation. This installation method provides you with Excel, Word, PowerPoint, and the most popular add-on components and files for these applications.

1. Start your Macintosh with extensions turned off (hold down the Shift key when your Mac starts up). You may need to use the Extensions Manager to turn off all extensions except your CD-ROM driver, depending on your setup. At a minimum, make sure all virus-protection extensions are disabled.

2. Make sure no other programs are running besides the Finder.

3. Insert the Microsoft Office 98 CD-ROM in your CD-ROM drive.

4. In the window that appears, you will see the Microsoft Office 98 folder. Next to it is a block of text that reads "To install Office, just copy this folder to your hard disk." Drag the Microsoft Office 98 folder over to your hard disk icon on the Desktop and drop it on the icon (see Figure A.1).

5. Office is installed in the folder Microsoft Office 98, at the top level of your hard drive. Open the folder and choose the application of your choice to get started.

Fast Track

If you wish to install Office on a subfolder within your hard drive, either open that folder into a Desktop window or use Mac OS 8's spring-loaded folders. Using spring-loaded folders, first drag the Microsoft Office 98 folder over your hard disk, and pause. After a couple of seconds, the hard disk icon will open. Now select the folder you want and drop the Office 98 folder on it. The Office 98 folder will be copied into the folder you dropped it on. You can navigate through multiple levels of folders easily and quickly using the spring-loaded feature. (For more information on spring-loaded folders, consult your system documentation.)

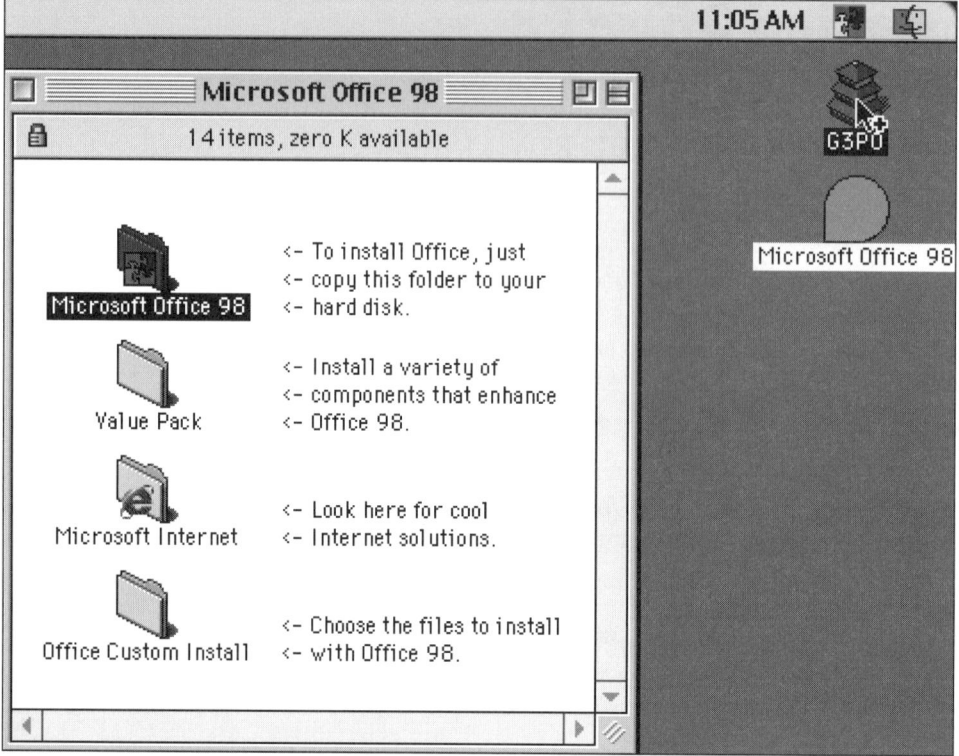

Figure A.1 The fastest way to install Office is to simply drag the Microsoft Office 98 folder onto your hard disk.

Easy Installation

Follow these steps for the Easy installation. This installation method provides you with Excel, Word, PowerPoint, and the most popular add-on components and files for these applications.

1. Start your Macintosh with extensions turned off (hold down the Shift key when your Mac starts up). You may need to use the Extensions Manager to turn off all extensions besides your CD-ROM driver, depending on your setup. At a minimum, make sure all virus-protection extensions are disabled.

2. Make sure no other programs are running besides the Finder.

3. Insert the Microsoft Office 98 CD-ROM in your CD-ROM drive.

4. In the window that appears, double-click on the Office Custom Install folder.

5. Double-click on Microsoft Office Installer. The Installer launches.

6. If you have previous versions of any Office applications installed, you will be asked if you wish to delete them when installing Office 98. Click on Yes or No according to your preference. First-time Office installers will not see this dialog.

7. When the Installer window appears, Easy Install is selected by default in the menu at the top left (see Figure A.2).

8. If you want to change the selected drive or pick a particular folder in which to install Office, use the Install Location menu. To change drives, pick one from the menu. To change folders (the default is the top level of your hard disk), choose Select Folder. Use the dialog that appears to select the folder you want Office to be located in. Click on it in the list window, then click on Select.

9. Click on Install.

10. In the dialog that appears, enter your name and (optionally) your organization, then click on OK.

11. Click on OK again to confirm your information, or Cancel to enter your name and organization again.

12. Enter your 10-digit CD key (found on an orange label on the back of your jewel case).

13. The Installer will now proceed with installation. When it's finished, click on Quit in the dialog that appears (or on Continue, if you're installing to another machine).

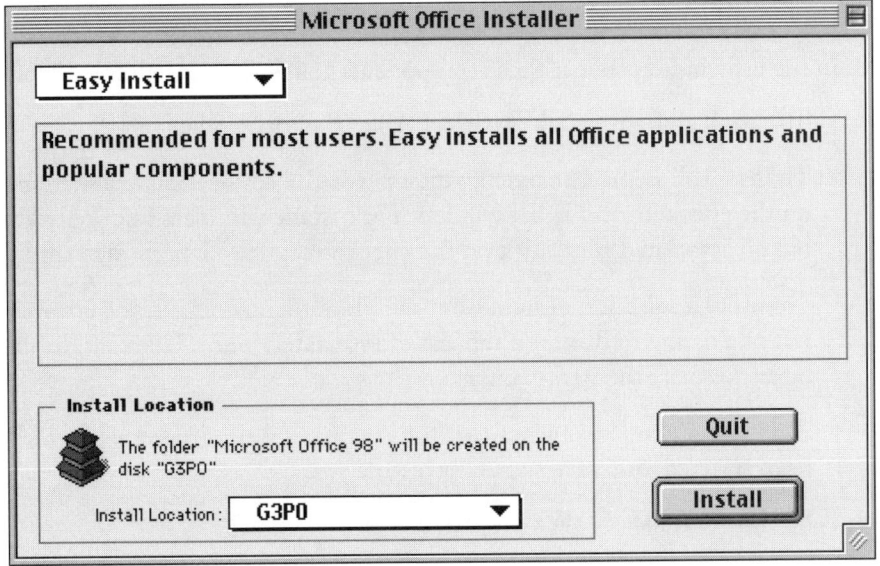

Figure A.2 By default, the Microsoft Office Installer selects Easy Install.

14. Restart your Macintosh.

15. You're now ready to run! Open the Microsoft Office 98 folder on your hard disk and choose the application you want to start with.

Custom Installation

Follow these steps for the Custom installation. This installation method allows you to select only those applications and add-ons you wish to install. You can install other components later, if you wish.

1. Start your Macintosh with extensions turned off (hold down the Shift key when your Mac starts up). You may need to use the Extensions Manager to turn off all extensions besides your CD-ROM driver, depending on your setup. At a minimum, make sure all virus-protection extensions are disabled.

2. Make sure no other programs are running besides the Finder.

3. Insert the Microsoft Office 98 CD-ROM in your CD-ROM drive.

4. In the window that appears, double-click on the Office Custom Install folder.

5. Double-click on Microsoft Office Installer. The Installer launches.

6. If you have previous versions of any Office applications installed, you will be asked if you wish to delete them when installing Office 98. Click on Yes or No according to your preference. First-time Office installers will not see this dialog.

7. When the Installer window appears, choose Custom Install from the menu at the top left.

8. In the list window, choose those components you wish to install (see Figure A.3):

   - To install all items, click on Select All at the top center.

   - To install all items associated with a particular application or function, click on the checkbox in the list window. For instance, to install not only Word, but all associated files, click on the checkbox next to Microsoft Word.

   - To install a selection of items, but not all of them, click on the arrows to the left of a listing to display a sub-list of associated items. Click on the checkboxes to select the items you want.

   - A dash in a checkbox means that the item has sub-items, some of which have been selected, others of which have not.

9. When you're finished, click on Install.

10. In the dialog that appears, enter your name and (optionally) your organization, then click on OK.

Installing And Configuring Office 98   **503**

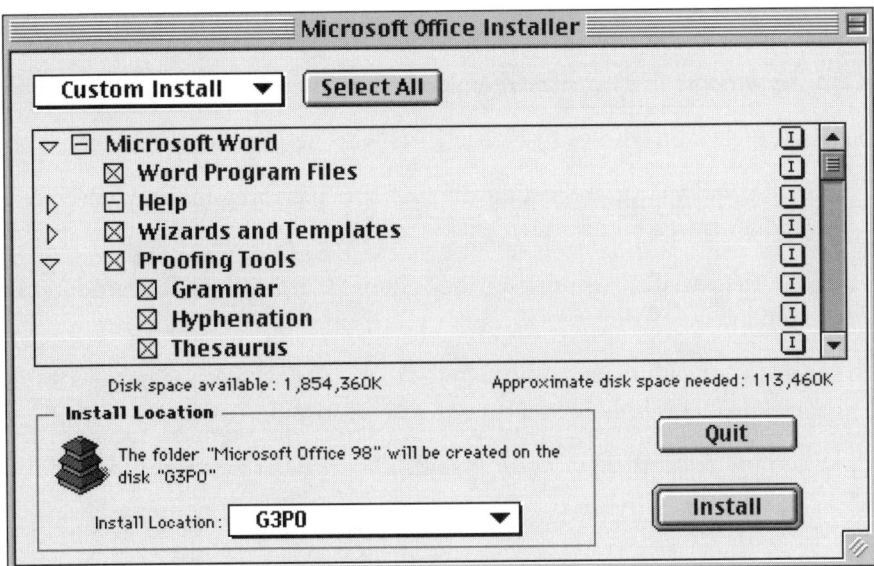

Figure A.3 Choose those items you wish to install in a Custom installation.

11. Click on OK again to confirm your information or Cancel to enter your name and organization again.

12. Enter your 10-digit CD key (found on an orange label on the back of your jewel case).

13. The Installer will now proceed with installation. When it's finished, click on Quit in the dialog that appears (or on Continue, if you're installing to another machine).

14. Restart your Macintosh

15. Office 98 now awaits your command. Open the Microsoft Office 98 folder, pick a program, and go to town.

Adding Components

Follow these steps to add components and files to an existing Microsoft Office installation. This method allows you to select exactly which applications and add-ons you wish to install.

1. Start your Macintosh with extensions turned off (hold down the Shift key when your Mac starts up). You may need to use the Extensions Manager to turn off all extensions besides your CD-ROM driver, depending on your setup. At a minimum, make sure all virus-protection extensions are disabled.

2. Make sure no other programs are running besides the Finder.

3. Insert the Microsoft Office 98 CD-ROM in your CD-ROM drive.

4. In the window that appears, double-click on the Office Custom Install folder.

5. Double-click on Microsoft Office Installer. The Installer launches.

6. A dialog will appear, indicating the Office is searching for previously installed components (see Figure A.4).

7. When the Installer window appears, choose Custom Install from the menu at the top left.

8. In the list of components, those items that you have not yet installed will be checked. Uncheck those you do not wish to install.

9. When you're finished, click on Install. The Installer gets right to work.

10. Click on Quit when the Installer finishes up, and you're ready to go.

Removing Office 98

Should you for any reason wish to uninstall Office 98, follow these steps. This method allows you to remove all Microsoft Office 98 program files. Your data files and any program files shared by other programs on your hard drive outside the Office suite will not be removed.

1. Start your Macintosh with extensions turned off (hold down the Shift key when your Mac starts up). You may need to use the Extensions Manager to turn off all extensions besides your CD-ROM driver, depending on your setup. At a minimum, make sure all virus-protection extensions are disabled.

2. Make sure no other programs are running besides the Finder.

3. Insert the Microsoft Office 98 CD-ROM in your CD-ROM drive.

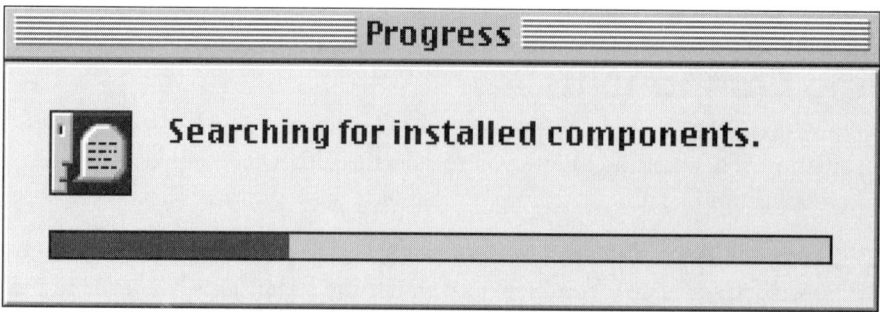

Figure A.4 When you launch the Microsoft Office Installer to add components, the Installer searches for any Office parts already installed.

Installing And Configuring Office 98 505

4. In the window that appears, double-click on the Office Custom Install folder.

5. Double-click on Microsoft Office Installer. The Installer launches.

6. When the Installer window appears, choose Remove from the menu at the top left.

7. In the Install Location area, select the drive from which you wish to delete Office.

8. There are no custom options for Remove. All Office program files will be deleted. Click on Remove to proceed.

9. When the Installer finishes its job, click on Quit. Office has now been removed from your hard drive. It would be a good idea to restart your Mac, although you don't have to.

Installing The Microsoft Office 98 Value Pack

The Office 98 Value Pack is a collection of templates, clip art, add-on components, and assorted other bits and pieces of programming that Microsoft thinks you'll find helpful. In fact, we think you'll find it helpful, too. If you have the hard drive space, we recommend installing the Value Pack, at least in part. Here's how:

1. Start your Macintosh with extensions turned off (hold down the Shift key when your Mac starts up). You may need to use the Extensions Manager to turn off all extensions besides your CD-ROM driver, depending on your setup. At a minimum, make sure all virus-protection extensions are disabled.

2. Make sure no other programs are running besides the Finder.

3. Insert the Microsoft Office 98 CD-ROM in your CD-ROM drive.

4. In the window that appears, double-click on the Value Pack folder.

5. Double-click on Value Pack Installer. The Installer launches.

6. In the Value Pack Installer dialog, select the items you wish to install (to install all items, click on Select All at the top center). Your options are fairly extensive (see Figure A.5):

   - *Assistants*—A baker's dozen of those annoying and/or occasionally helpful little animated help characters supplement Max the Macintosh. Some are a little weirder than Max. Some, like Bosgrove and the Genius, are more reserved.

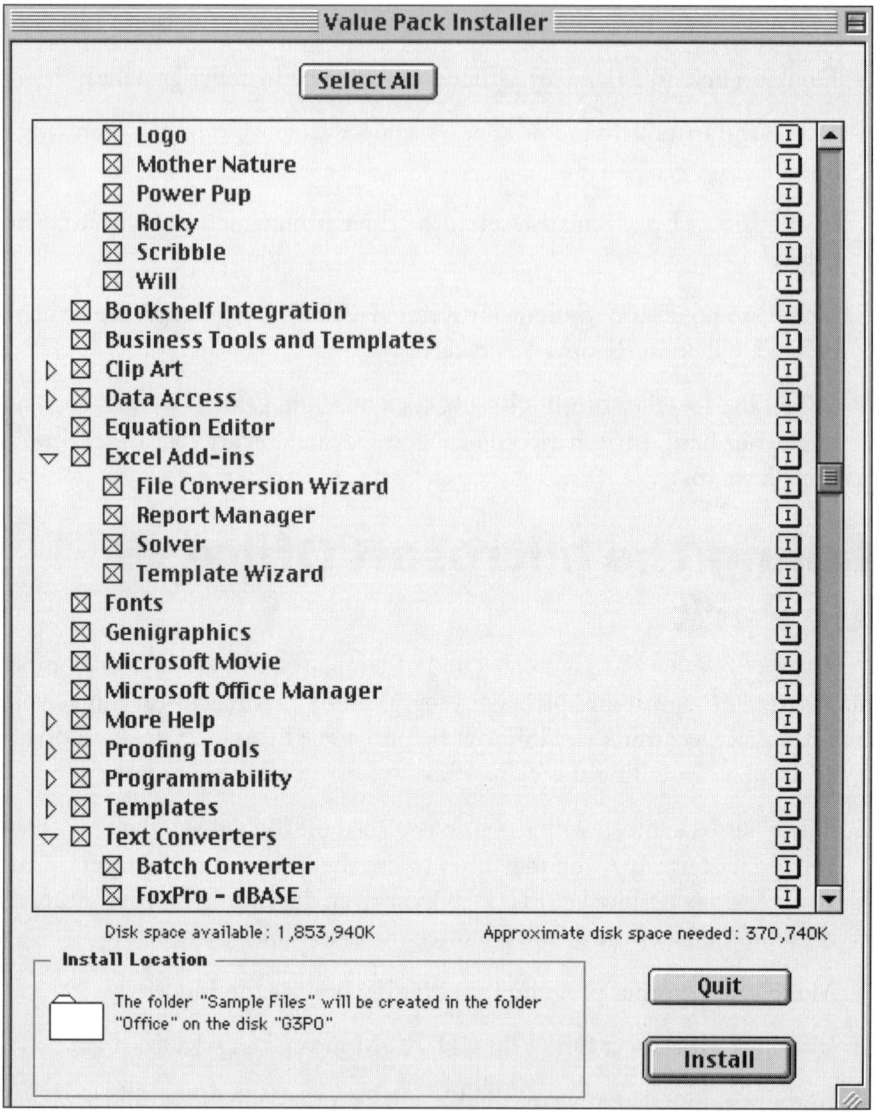

Figure A.5 The Value Pack includes a laundry list of helpful additions to Office 98.

- *Bookshelf Integration*—Allows your Office applications to work with Microsoft Bookshelf (if you have it installed).

- *Business Tools And Templates*—An assortment of 43 small-business tools and templates for the various Office applications.

- *Clip Art*—Pictures and movies for your Office documents (this is 150MB, so you might want to use it from the CD, not your hard drive).

- *Data Access*—Database drivers and utilities.

- *Equation Editor*—For placing mathematical symbols, equations, and notations into your documents (recommended for educators).
- *Excel Add-ins*—A variety of macros for common spreadsheet jobs.
- *Fonts*—Microsoft's library of TrueType fonts. These are placed in your Fonts folder and are available to all your applications.
- *Genigraphics*—The Genigraphics driver for PowerPoint.
- *Microsoft Movie*—Shared between the Office applications, this program allows you to add QuickTime movies to your documents.
- *Microsoft Office Manager*—*Highly* recommended. Places that handy little menu in the upper right of your Menu Bar.
- *More Help*—Supplemental help files.
- *Proofing Tools*—Installs Microsoft's Proofing Tools package for checking your work.
- *Programmability*—Adds macros for Word and Excel.
- *Templates*—An assortment of templates for Word, Excel, and PowerPoint.
- *Text Converters*—Additional converters for opening other programs' files in Word.
- *Unbinder*—A utility for splitting apart Binders created in Office for Windows. Office for Macintosh does not use Binders.
- *Word Speak*—An add-on that lets Word speak text aloud.

7. When you're ready, click on Install.
8. When the Installer has finished, click on Quit, and you are ready to work.

That's it—installation is complete. You've installed Office and the Value Pack just the way you want them. Although you don't have to, it wouldn't hurt to restart your Mac now, and don't forget to rebuild your Desktop.

Appendix B
A Brief Introduction To Internet Explorer

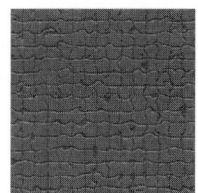

Among the Office programs, Value Pack files, and assorted other tidbits on the Microsoft Office 98 CD-ROM, you will find the installer for Microsoft Internet Explorer 4.0 for Macintosh. Internet Explorer is Microsoft's entry into the field of *Web browsers*, programs that allow you to view pages on the World Wide Web.

Internet Explorer isn't really part of the Office 98 suite—Microsoft just threw it on the CD to strengthen their claim that Office 98 is "ready for the Internet." Fact is, an in-depth discussion of Internet Explorer is fodder for a book all by itself (we can prove it—just check your local bookstore). So we're not really going to go into a lot of detail about the program.

What we will do here is tell you how to install it, what you get with the installation, and how generally to get started using IE (as it's commonly referred to). Microsoft has been kind enough to fortify its Web site with significant help resources, so if you have questions that we don't answer here (and you will), the Microsoft site can probably help you out.

FYI: Switching Browsers

At this point, those of you already familiar with the Web may be on the horns of a dilemma. If you're already using another browser (Netscape Navigator, for instance), should you switch to Internet Explorer? In a word, maybe. The answer is entirely dependent on what you'd like to do. There isn't any compelling technical reason to use the Microsoft browser. Although it does offer some neat tricks like channels, no thinking content provider is going to serve up content that only users of Internet Explorer can reach. In other words, if you can get it with IE, you can get it (perhaps another way) with Navigator.

Some people report improved stability with one browser or the other. Some say one browser handles certain types of data better than others. Some, like Brian, just don't like throwing all their eggs in one basket by using software from only one company. It all pretty much boils down to personal preference. Both browsers are free, and both will let you access better than 90 percent of the content on the Web. If you're already using Navigator, switching your bookmarks and other settings over might be more trouble than it's worth. If you're a new user, give IE a try. You can always check out Navigator later down the road.

Installing Internet Explorer

To install the Internet Explorer Web browser, follow these steps. (Don't worry about your hardware setup—if you can run Office 98 and connect to the Internet, you can use Internet Explorer. If you have any concerns, check the hardware and software requirements for Office in the Introduction.)

1. Start your Macintosh with extensions turned off (hold down the Shift key when your Mac starts up). You may need to use the Extensions Manager to turn off all extensions besides your CD-ROM driver, depending on your setup. At a minimum, make sure all virus-protection extensions are disabled.

2. Make sure no other programs are running besides the Finder.

3. Insert the Microsoft Office 98 CD-ROM in your CD-ROM drive.

4. Double-click to open the Microsoft Internet folder.

5. Double-click on Internet Explorer 4.0 Installer. The installer launches and presents you with a license agreement. Click on Accept.

6. Next, you'll see the dialog shown in Figure B.1. This is the main installer window.

7. If you have not yet installed Outlook Express, and you would like to do so, the best course is probably to use the Easy Install option from the menu in the top left (Easy Install is selected by default). This option installs the following software:

    - The Internet Explorer Web browser
    - Java support
    - A set of Web fonts (typefaces commonly specified using the <FONT> tag in HTML)
    - The Outlook Express mail and news client
    - The Microsoft Personal Web Server, for sharing your own Web pages

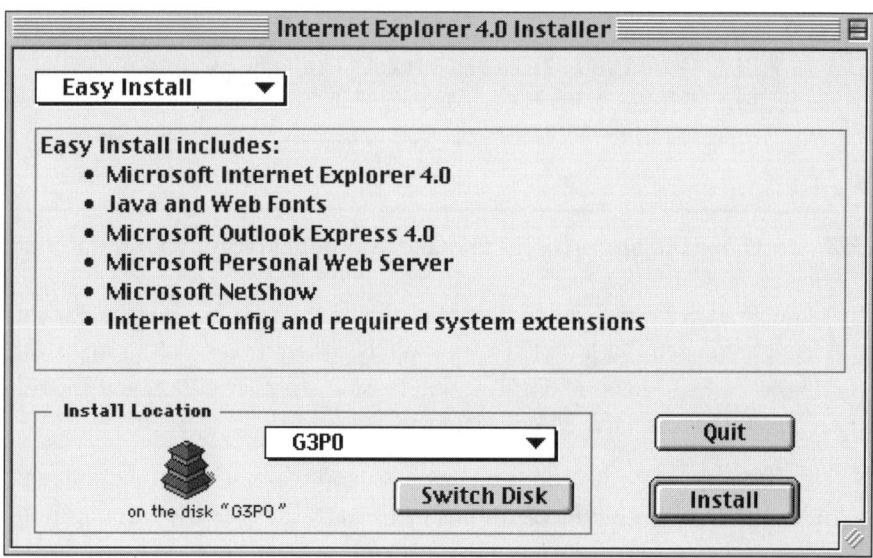

Figure B.1 The Microsoft Internet Explorer 4.0 Installer dialog, with Easy Install selected.

- Microsoft Netshow, a program for viewing Web multimedia files

- Internet Config, which sets up a global Internet preferences location (you can learn more about Internet Config in Chapter 15)

8. If you already have Outlook Express or Internet Config installed, you can select Custom Install and choose only those options you wish to install at this time. Note that the menu also contains a Remove item, should you wish to uninstall Internet Explorer.

9. From the Install Location menu, select the disk and/or folder you want to install IE to. To select a disk, simply choose it from the menu. To select a folder, choose Select Folder, and in the dialog that appears, navigate to the folder you want. Click once in the list to select it, then click on Select.

10. When you've chosen your installation options and selected an install location, click on Install.

11. If you have opted to install Internet Config (or if you already have it installed), then in the dialog that appears (see Figure B.2), tell the installer whether or not to make Internet Explorer your default browser. If you click on Yes, any time a Web browser is called for (for example, if you select Help On The Web or click on a URL in Word), Internet Explorer will be launched. If IE is the only browser you will have on your machine, it makes sense to click on Yes here.

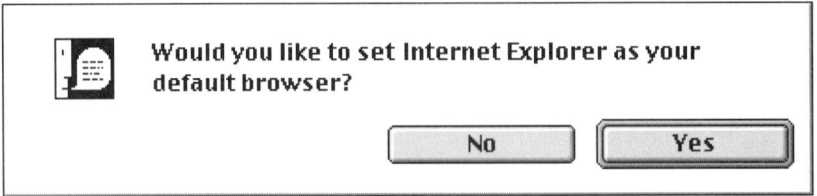

Figure B.2 You have the opportunity to make Internet Explorer your default browser.

12. Again, if you've opted for Internet Config or are already using it, *and* you have selected to install Outlook Express, you'll be asked if you wish to make OE your default mail and news client. If it will be your primary client, you should click on Yes. Otherwise, the choice is up to you.

13. The Installer now goes about its business, and when it's finished, informs you that you can either Quit, Continue, or Restart. Because the installer puts items in your System folder during most installations, you should choose Restart.

14. When your machine restarts, you should see the window shown in Figure B.3 on your Desktop (if you've chosen a custom installation, your window may look a bit different). Start up your connection to the Internet, then double-click on the Internet Explorer 4.0 alias to launch IE.

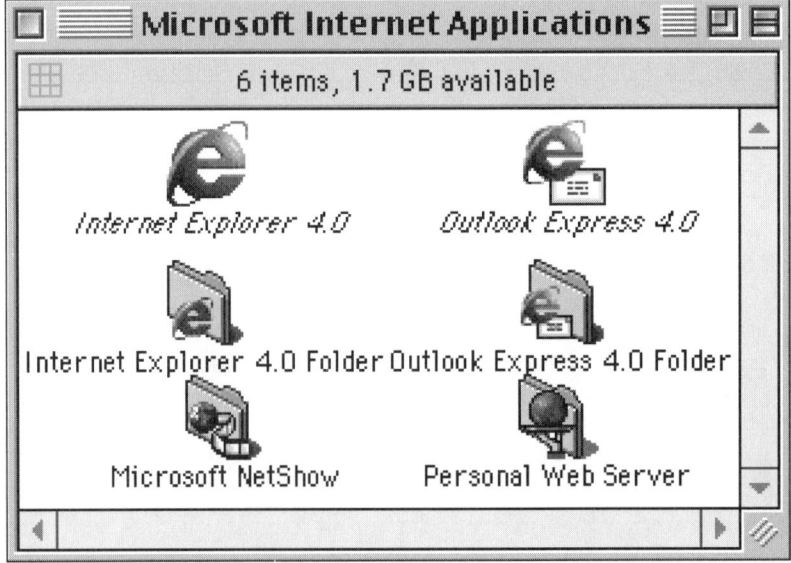

Figure B.3 The Desktop window created by the IE 4.0 installer.

Getting Around In Internet Explorer

If you've ever used a Web browser before, you can jump right in with Internet Explorer—the rest of this appendix won't be of much use to you. But if you're a newcomer—a *newbie*, in Internet lingo—keep reading. We'll point out the raw basics of Internet Explorer for you and tell you where to get more information.

When you launch Internet Explorer for the first time, you'll be taken to the Microsoft Internet Start page (see Figure B.4). Before we learn about Internet Start, though, let's examine the IE window in a little more detail.

Figure B.4 Internet Explorer takes you first to Microsoft's Internet Start page.

The Button Bar

At the top of the window, in the title bar, you'll see the Web page name—in this case, IE Welcome Page. Directly below this is the Button bar, containing all the buttons you need to navigate the Web and control IE (see Figure B.5). The Button bar holds the following buttons:

- *Back*—Takes you to the Web page you last visited in this session of browsing. Note that you must have visited more than one page for Back to work.

- *Forward*—If you've used the Back button to retrace your path, use Forward to step through the list of pages you've visited in the other direction. Forward is only enabled if you've already used Back.

- *Stop*—Halts the loading of a page immediately. Handy if you realize belatedly that you've entered the wrong page, or if a page is taking too long to load.

- *Refresh*—Reloads the page. Useful on pages with rapidly updating content.

- *Home*—Takes you immediately to the home page configured in the Preferences dialog or the home page set up in your Internet Config preferences. By default, IE comes set to jump to the Internet Explorer page. You can set this to any page you like by choosing Edit|Preferences|Browser/Search and entering the desired URL. If you use Internet Config, you can set a preference for your home page there.

- *Search*—Takes you to Microsoft's Web Search page, where you can access a variety of *search engines* to scan the Web for material on the topic of your choice.

- *Mail*—Opens your default mail and news client, if you have one configured (this may be Outlook Express, if you've installed it). Note that unlike Netscape Navigator/Communicator, Internet Explorer has no built-in mail and news functions.

- *Favorites*—Opens a window listing sites you've selected as your favorites (you can add pages to Favorites by surfing to them, then pressing Cmd+D). Microsoft has thoughtfully included a number of helpful links in Favorites, most of them related to using IE 4.0.

- *Larger/Smaller*—These two buttons increase or decrease the default font size for Internet Explorer.

Figure B.5 The IE Button bar.

- *Preferences*—Opens the IE Preferences dialog.
- *Explorer Logo*—Clicking on the logo jumps to Microsoft's IE home page.

The Address And Favorites Bars

Directly beneath the Button bar, you will see the Address bar (see Figure B.6). Here you can enter the address, or *Uniform Resource Locator (URL)*, of a Web page. As you type, IE scans a list of pages you've visited and attempts to fill in the URL for you. If you see that it has correctly entered the URL you want, simply press Return. If not, just finish typing your URL and press Return. (Note that when you start typing, the small arrow to the left of the box is enabled—click on this arrow to see a list of recently visited sites. You can select from this list to jump straight to a site.)

Sliding down another level, you will see the Favorites bar, containing buttons for Best Of The Web, Today's Links, Web Gallery, Product News, Microsoft, and Office For Macintosh (see Figure B.7). These buttons all link to pages created and maintained by Microsoft, many of which point to helpful information about the Web, information on using IE, and fun or cool links. These make excellent starting points for the IE newcomer.

Each of the three bars—the Button bar, the Address bar, and the Favorites bar—can be moved around in the top area of the page by clicking on the vertical bar that appears on its left side, then dragging. Experiment a bit with rearranging the top of your window.

You can also turn the three bars off by clicking on the View menu, then choosing a bar name to select or deselect it. Each currently displayed bar has a check next to its name in the menu.

The Main Window And Status Bar

The next area of the IE window is the main page area, directly below the Favorites bar. In this area, all the Web sites you access are displayed. Basic Web navigation is performed here by clicking on *hyperlinks*. Hyperlinks in text are usually blue, or another obvious color, and underlined. Pictures can also serve as hyperlinks. You can

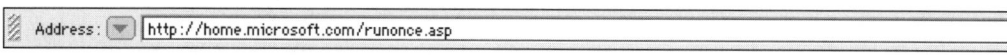

Figure B.6 The IE Address bar.

Figure B.7 The IE Favorites bar.

recognize graphic hyperlinks by your mouse pointer. When it moves over a link, the pointer changes to a hand with a pointing finger, and the *target* of the link (the site you'll jump to if you click on that link) will be displayed in the Status bar. The status bar, which is at the bottom of the window, is shown in Figure B.8.

The Status bar lets you know what's going on as you browse. If a page is loading, the bar reports what files are being loaded and what progress is being made. If your mouse is resting over a hyperlink, the Status bar shows the target of that link. One of the most common uses for the Status bar is to check to see if a page is finished loading. If the Status bar remains static for some time or reports slow progress, you can click on Stop in the Button bar and try loading the page again later.

The Explorer Bar And Channels

Finally, to the left of the IE window, you'll see the tabs of the Explorer bar: Channels, Favorites, History, and Search. Move your mouse over a tab to see what it contains, or move your mouse back out of a tab to close it (you can also "lock" a tab open, or close it again, by clicking on the tab name).

Channels are a specialized method of content delivery. In the Channels tab of the Explorer bar—shown in Figure B.9—you will find not only a link to Microsoft's Internet Explorer channel, but also links to more information about channels and to Microsoft's channel guide. Use these resources to learn more about channels and how to use them.

Clicking on the Favorites tab (see Figure B.10A) displays a list of sites currently in your Favorites list, much like clicking on the Favorites button on the Button bar. Clicking on the History tab displays a list of sites you've recently visited—click on a site to jump back to it (see Figure B.10B).

Finally, the Search tab displays a search box, as well as a clickable list of channels for IE provided by the search engine (see Figure B.11—the search engine varies, but in this instance was Excite). To use the search, type the subject you wish to search for in the text box and click on the Search button. The search engine will scan the Web for pages and sites matching your topic and will report back with a hyperlinked list of matches.

Those are the basic components of Internet Explorer. Naturally, there's much more you can do with the program—it's highly configurable. But more discussion of

Figure B.8 The IE Status bar.

Figure B.9 The Explorer bar's Channels tab.

program features is beyond the scope of this book. To learn more, visit **www.microsoft.com/ie/** for links to more extensive information on how to use and configure Internet Explorer.

Figure B.10A The Favorites tab, which is followed by...

Figure B.10B ...the History tab.

Configuring Your Own Start Page

When you first launched Internet Explorer, you were taken to the Internet Start page. If you've moved around since, reload the page from your history list or enter the URL **home.microsoft.com/runonce.asp**. The Internet Start page allows you to build a custom "home page," containing your own preferred links, news, and more. Here's how to set it up.

Entering The Basics

First, make sure you've got the page loaded in Internet Explorer. In the top left of the page, you can click on a button to add a link to the *Guide To The Internet*. For newbies, this is an invaluable resource, so click on the little checkbox.

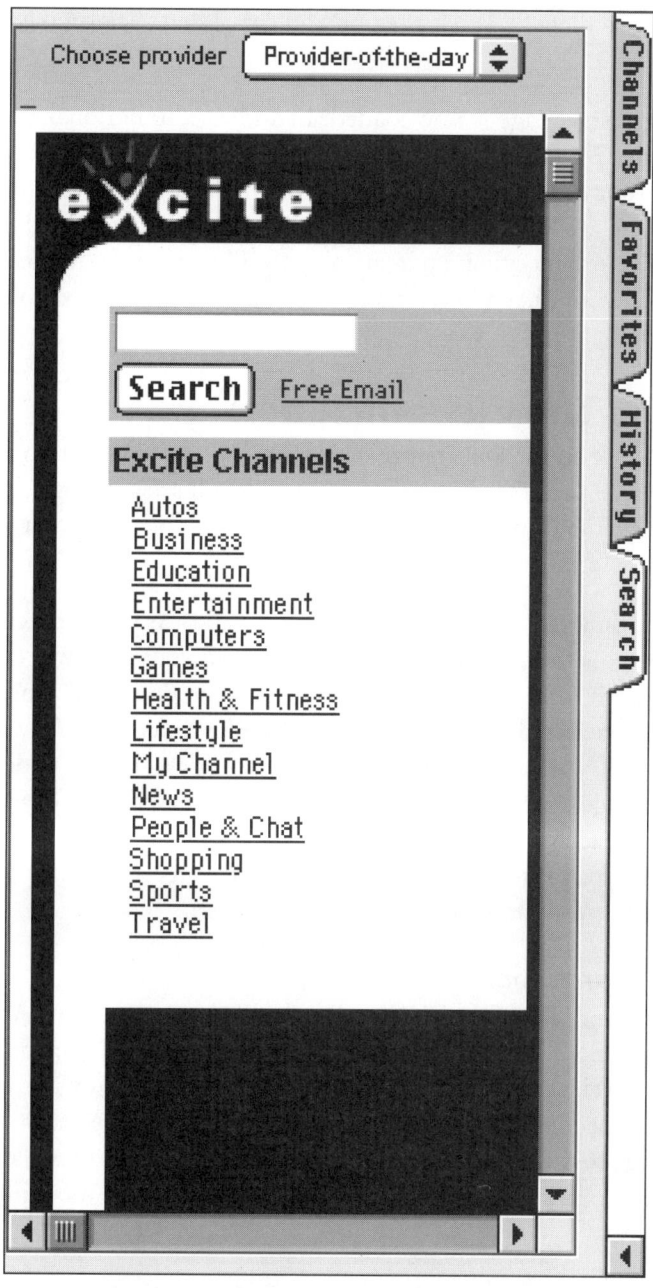

Figure B.11 The Search tab allows you to quickly hunt down a particular topic.

Next, look in the lower right area of the page. Here, you can enter your time zone, ZIP code, and city to get a custom weather forecast placed on your start page. Use the top menu to select your time zone, then type your ZIP code in the text box (if you're in the United States). If you're an international user (outside the U.S.), use the bottom two menus to pick a region and city. Then click on the Done button to move on.

Your personal start page is now loaded. In addition to national and international news and sites Microsoft thinks you'll be interested in, you can scroll down to see local news, your local weather forecast, and most importantly, a little green smiley. Actually, there are little green smileys all over the page. By clicking on one, you can customize the specific item it sits next to. The one we're interested in is shown in Figure B.12, and has a "Personalize this page!" caption next to it. Click on that little guy, and let's get to work on the meat of your start page.

Completing The Customization

When you click on the Personalize This Page link, you're taken to the Personalize Your Start Page page (see Figure B.13). Here you'll see a listing of the various items your start page can display. Those listed with checks *will* be on your start page. Those left unchecked *will not*.

Notice the estimated download time in the top right. As you add items to your page (or remove items from it), the time it takes to load your page will change. This bar provides a rough estimate for how long it will take to download your start page, with your currently selected items on it, using a 28.8Kbps modem. As with all things Internet related, your mileage may vary, but it provides a handy guide. The more you put on your page, the slower it will load. To speed load times, display fewer items. (Note that in each of the areas we're about to discuss, you can select more than one item. To keep load times reasonable, though, we suggest starting with just one item from each area. You can add more later if you like.)

Adding A Search Engine

Start the customization by picking your preferred search engine. At the time of this writing, the options were AOL NetFind, Excite, InfoSeek, Lycos, and Yahoo!. More experienced Web surfers will probably already have a favorite. For newcomers, we recommend selecting Yahoo!, the oldest and most easily used search engine, which provides links to a ton of sites about almost anything you can name. Other search engines provide links to more sites, and still others provide more information about

Figure B.12 Click on the little green smiley to start personalizing your page.

Figure B.13 Use this page to customize your Microsoft start page.

those sites, but Yahoo! strikes the best balance between usability, depth, and breadth. Click on the radio button for your search engine of choice, then check the Show On Start Page box in the Search header.

Getting The Latest News

Next, pick your preferred news service. By default, MSNBC News—the Microsoft/NBC joint venture—is selected (surprise, surprise). But you can also choose Slate (another Microsoft enterprise), the *New York Times*, NetGuide Events, Fox News, OnNow Web Events, and *Time*. Each of these specializes in a different flavor of news coverage, but for the best overall news reporting, we suggest you start with the *New York Times*. Click on your news service, then click on Show On Start Page.

Bloomberg TV, Fox News, and MSNBC all make video clips of their news stories available on the Web. By default, your start page will link to clips from all three services. For the moment, though, we'll stick with our recommendation for just one item in each area, so select a video clip service, make sure the others are deselected, select Show On Start Page, and move on. (Really, any of these services is fine. The fact is, unless there's something *really* compelling in a video clip, most people don't have time to wait for one to download. And if it's something really compelling, it will be available from all three services, right?)

Your Own Personal Stock Ticker

If you want regular updates on how your stocks are doing, you can get it right on your start page. In the box under Stock Quotes, enter the ticker symbols for your desired stocks, separating the symbols with commas. Pick one of the four major stock indices to get a quick snapshot of how it's performing through the day, make sure Show On Start Page is checked, and keep moving.

Tracking Sports News

You can also choose a sports news service. At the time of this writing, a whole slew of services was available: ESPN Top Story, Fox Sports, ESPN SportsZone, MSNBC Sports, AudioNet, CBS Events, OnNow Web Events, and Yack! Chat Guide. For the best general sports coverage, we find that ESPN Top Story is excellent. ESPN SportsZone offers similar news, with a little more depth to the stories. Select one and click on Show On Start Page.

Local News And Weather Updates

Next is the selector for local weather. If you've been following along, you should already see your ZIP code or region and city displayed here. Use this area to change your locality information if you move later. Also, you can elect to have temperatures shown in either Fahrenheit or Celsius by clicking on the appropriate button. Again, make sure the Show On Start Page box is checked.

Under Local Information, MSNBC Local News is your only option, so check it. You may also have a City Guide available from Microsoft's Sidewalk service. Check the menu—if you see your city, select it and click on City Guide. Otherwise, deselect City Guide. You can also have the various event-reporting services adjust event times so that they're accurate for your time zone. To so do, select your time zone from the Adjust Event Times menu. Make sure Show On Start Page is checked, then get ready to add your favorite links.

Adding Your Favorite Pages

In the Your Links area, you can add a list of your four favorite pages, which will then be displayed as clickable links on your start page. If you're an old hand at the Internet, you undoubtedly already have a list of favorite pages. For newbies, here's our list of the Top 10 best sites on the Net for information and fun (of course, this is exceptionally subjective, and we're not counting the Microsoft Office pages, because IE already links to them):

- *MacSurfer's Headline News (www.macsurfer.com)*—Provides all the latest Mac-related headlines, as well as links to and summaries of the contents of the top 10 or so major Mac news sites. If you can't find it here, it isn't news in the Mac world.

- *Apple Computer (www.apple.com)*—The latest and insanely greatest from Apple, including news about new models, software updates, and more. A must for the Mac-head.

- *MacAddict (www.macaddict.com)*—The Web site for what may just be the very coolest Macintosh magazine in the world. News, reviews, opinions, and unmitigated gall from some of the best Mac writers in the business.

- *The Evangelist (www.evangelist.macaddict.com)*—Guy Kawasaki's excellent pro-Mac site. We'll let him summarize. "The purpose of this Web site is to help people evangelize Apple, Macintosh, and Newton—and to make the world a better place! Here you'll find archived messages from EvangeList—our mailing list of good news about Apple, Macintosh, and third-party developers—plus links to other useful Web sites. If you'd like to join the EvangeList mailing list, please visit Apple's Public Mailing Lists page. We'd love to have you. We hope you'll find the information that we've compiled useful. Thanks for your loyalty and support. Semper fidelis!" We couldn't have said it better ourselves.

- *VersionTracker (www.versiontracker.com)*—Version Tracker keeps regularly updated lists of the latest software releases from a ton of Macintosh developers. If you like keeping your Mac software up to date, Version Tracker helps cut through the hassle.

- *Centre For The Easily Amused (www.amused.com)*—On a lighter note, the CEA maintains a frighteningly compete list of the top sites for silly entertainment on the Web. When you hear people decrying the flood of useless information on the Web, this is exactly the sort of thing they're talking about—visit this one first. Be sure to check out the Amuse-O-Matic 2000 while you're there.

- *eBay Online Auction Service (www.ebay.com)*—Online auctions are a growing field, and eBay is one of the biggest and best. Just click around the listings for a while—we can just about guarantee you'll place a bid on something.

- *The Icon Factory (www.iconfactory.com)*—As they put it, "Macintosh icons that don't suck." Gedeon Maheux and the crew at the Icon Factory have amassed a tremendous number of Mac icons, ranging from miniature computers to characters from Ultraman. If you want to customize the look of your Mac quickly and easily, drop by the factory and pick up a few things.

- *Bungie Software (www.bungie.com)*—Makers of the Marathon series and Myth: The Fallen Lords, some of the greatest games ever made for the Macintosh. If your friends ever tell you that you can't get great games for the Mac, tell them to visit Bungie.

- *MacMAME (www.emulation.net/mame/)*—This one you won't believe. Remember Frogger? How about Galaxian, Donkey Kong, Defender and, oh yeah, Pac-Man? If you remember the '80s at all, you almost certainly remember video arcades. MacMAME is a coin-op arcade emulator for the Macintosh. Using MacMAME, you can play all the great video games you remember (and some we'll bet you never heard of), right on your Mac. Think of how much you can save on the quarters alone.

That's our Top 10, serious and silly as it may be. You can enter four of these in the Your Links area of your start page, or you can pick some of your own, or just mix and match. Enter the address for your links in the Enter URL column and the name of the page in the Enter Site Name column. Make sure Show On Start Page is checked, then move on to the business section.

Getting Down To Business

In the business area, you can pick a service devoted to the latest business news. Current offerings include The EIU, *Forbes*, *Fortune*, Microsoft Investor, Money Insider, Bloomberg, MSNBC Commerce, OnNow Web Events, and the MS Investor Ticker. We suggest Bloomberg for excellent overall coverage. Make your selection, be sure Show On Start Page is checked, and continue on.

Internet And Computer News

Under Computers And Internet, you can select from a number of Web publications and news services devoted to news related to computers, high technology, networking, and the Internet. CNET, Forbes Digital, Internet Guide, CMPnet's TechWeb, Wired, ZDNet, Microsoft Site Builder Network, Computing Central, OnNow Web Events, and Yack! Chat Guide are offered. CNET provides quick and dirty tech news, updated throughout the day. Wired, though a trifle pretentious in our estimation, does offer excellent in-depth coverage of technological issues. Select one, make the now-standard check of the Show On Start Page box, and keep going.

Education And Reference

Pickings under this area are relatively slim. The Discovery Channel site, Discovery Events, and OnNow Web Events all devote some coverage to educational materials. Of the meager offerings here, we would select the Discovery Channel (don't get us wrong, it's a good site—we just wish there were more offerings under this heading). Check it, check Show On Start Page, and slide down the page one more level.

Entertainment News

If the people making headlines in Hollywood interest you, check out the Entertainment news options. Hollywood Online, MSNBC Entertainment, MTV, *People*, Warner Bros. Online, AudioNet Events, OnNow Web Events, Warner Bros. Online Events, and Yack! give you a slew of choices. To get the latest Hollywood scoop, combined with a fair mix of book, TV, and music news, try the *People* site. Check it and the Show On Start Page box. Keep going (we're almost finished).

Getting Healthy

Health news—from the latest dietary recommendations to the straight dope on fat—is available from five sources. Mayo Health O@asis, MSNBC Health, PHYS, NetGuide Events, and OnNow Web Events all offer at least a modicum of health-related news. Our favorite is the Mayo Health O@asis. Select one, make sure that the Show On Start Page box is checked, and scroll down again.

Home And Family

The Home And Family section offers a selection of sites geared toward family issues, parenting, family entertainment, and the like. Disney.com, Disney's Family.com, Parent Soup, MSNBC's Family Room, Warner Bros. Online, NetGuide Events, OnNow Web Events, and Parent Soup Events are offered as of this writing. Probably the most informative of these is the Parent Soup site. Make your selection and check the Show On Start Page box.

Lifestyles And Hobbies

In Brian's daily newspaper, *The Charlotte Observer*, the Lifestyles section seems to be a general catchall area for stories that just don't fit anywhere else. This area of the start page is no different. Current offerings include CarPoint, Epicurious Food, Forbes FYI, Third Age, *USA Today*, Women's Wire, OnNow Web Events, Third Age Events, and the Yack! Chat Guide again. We can't really make an accurate recommendation here, because this is based on your interests. We do, however, like the Epicurious Food site. Try any one that strikes your fancy (you can always change it later) and verify that Show On Start Page is checked.

Travel

You can see the end of the list from here. Travel sites give you a glimpse of the world and invariably instill a wanderlust that you have to either satisfy with a trip or spend a long time trying to quash. Feed that fire with Epicurious Travel, Expedia.com, Expedia.com Events, or NetGuide Events. We lean toward the Epicurious Travel pages. Make your choice and check that ubiquitous box.

Thing Of The Day

Things of the day have achieved an astounding level of popularity. The culprits, we think, are those calendars that offer you one of something each day of the year—a Dilbert cartoon, a quote, a golf tip, a recipe, a sniglet, or just some totally useless factoid. Jumping right on this bandwagon is the Thing Of The Day area, which offers a Merriam-Webster word definition each day, a selected hyperlink of the day, or a Quote of the Day. Personally, we like the Merriam-Webster selection—it at least pretends to be edifying. You can also check the box to display your daily horoscope. Select your astrological sign from the Your Horoscope menu to get the proper prediction. Make sure it will appear on the start page, and keep on rolling.

Microsoft Information

This section offers four options for keeping up to date on the latest offers and news from Microsoft. All four of these are worth having, so pick the ones you want, check the Show On Start Page box one last time, and scroll back up to the very top of the page.

When you reach the top of the page, check your estimated download time. It should be in the 35-second range—not bad for all the information you'll get. In the top right area of the page, click on Update, and your new custom start page will be created (see Figure B.14).

Pay Dirt

Wow! If you scroll down your new start page, you'll find that you've got a ton of information in front of you. Now, if you actually *read* all of it and follow all the links, you're either a very fast reader or have a *lot* of free time. But at least scanning this page will give you a passing acquaintance with the latest in current events. Remember that you can customize each individual area of your start page even further, by clicking on the green smiley in the header for that area.

The last thing to do is make this page your home page. Select Edit|Preferences. In the left area of the dialog, select Home/Search. Click on Use Default, then on OK. From now on, when you launch IE, your Web browser will open on your personal start page—with all the latest news and updates you requested.

One final note before we draw this appendix to a close. Underneath the Personalize This Page link on your start page, you'll see a link labeled Click Here For Internet Explorer Support. Use it—it allows you to register with Microsoft Support and get loads of helpful resources on Internet Explorer. Happy surfing!

Figure B.14 At last, your completed start page.

Appendix C
Mac OS, Fonts, And
Microsoft Office 98

Fonts remain, in spite of the efforts of industry giants like Apple, Microsoft, Adobe, Bitstream, and others, one of the most poorly handled aspects of computer operation. Though most other aspects of Mac system maintenance are both elegant and gracefully implemented, font management remains the ugly duckling. There are probably about a zillion technical reasons why font handling is so strange (this goes for both the Mac OS and Windows), but the upshot for you is that there are some things you need to know before fiddling with your Mac's font assortment.

Recognizing A Font

The first thing you need to know is what fonts look like on your Macintosh, so you can recognize them right away. Fonts are normally found in your System folder, inside the Fonts folder (see Figure C.1).

What you'll see inside the folder depends on your system setup. In general, though, you can expect to find four different categories of files:

- *Font Suitcases*—*Suitcase* is a term for a specific type of file designed to hold and consolidate fonts. Suitcase files can be recognized by their icon: a little suitcase with a big, oddly shaped "A" on it (see Figure C.2). Suitcases can hold both TrueType fonts and PostScript screen fonts (which you'll learn more about shortly). To view the contents of a suitcase, double-click on it in the Finder. A suitcase opens into a standard window, much like a folder, allowing you to move files in and out. In OS 8 and later, you can distinguish an open suitcase from an open folder by looking in the upper-left corner of the window—open suitcases will show a small suitcase icon.

Figure C.1 The Fonts folder is the usual storage point for your fonts.

Figure C.2 Three of the four most common files found in the Mac OS Fonts folder. From left to right, a loose PostScript screen font, a font suitcase, and a printer font.

- *Loose Font Files*—TrueType fonts and PostScript screen fonts can also be stored outside of suitcases, loose in the Fonts folder. Normally, their icon is a standard document icon with that big, oddly shaped "A" on it. Although you can store these files outside a suitcase, it's not recommended. We'll get to more on this shortly.

- *Printer Fonts*—Printer fonts are one half of the two-file PostScript font format (the other half is the screen font). Printer font icons vary widely—often they use a small printer, but Adobe favors a large, stylized "A." The easiest way to identify a printer font is to switch your window view to By Kind. Printer fonts will show "PostScript font" in the Kind column.

- *AFM Files*—With older fonts (and a very few new ones), you get what's called an Adobe Font Metrics (AFM) file. The name of these files usually has .AFM tacked onto the end. AFM files are pretty rare nowadays—you're not really likely to find one unless you get into serious publishing work.

Now that you can recognize the general file types found in the Fonts folder, it's important to know what they are and how they work (more or less). For that, you need to know about font types.

Types Of Fonts

There are two basic flavors of fonts: *PostScript* and *TrueType*. Each is set up differently, and there are both hardware and software considerations for using them. Things are going to get a little geeky for a few minutes, so stick with us. When you come out the other side, you'll be light-years ahead of where you are now with fonts.

PostScript

The more mature type of font, and the more technically sophisticated, is PostScript. PostScript is a computer language owned by Adobe, Inc. When your Mac talks to a PostScript-capable printer, the PostScript language allows the Mac to give highly accurate instructions about how each page should be printed. PostScript fonts use the PostScript language to describe the precise lines and curves involved in printing each letter of a font.

PostScript fonts usually come in two forms: Type 1 and Type 3. Type 3 is older and less common now. Normally, the two are indistinguishable (the differences are primarily technical). However, you may be able to tell a Type 3 font by its name (font authors will often tack T3 or T1 on the end of a Postscript font's name to tell you that it's PostScript) or by its icon. See the printer font icon in Figure C.2? If you look closely, it has a small "1" in the diamond sticking up out of the printer. That's a Type 1 font—a Type 3 font will have, amazingly enough, a 3 instead of a 1.

Regardless of the type, all PostScript fonts come in a dual-file format. That is, one font is actually composed of two discrete files—a screen (or bitmap) font and a printer font. (No matter what else happens, you must keep *both* of these files for a PostScript font to work.)

A *screen*, or *bitmap*, font is the portion of a PostScript font that can be stored in a suitcase. Normally, the suitcase will have the same name as the font (for example, the screen fonts for Optima will be stored in a suitcase named Optima). Inside a suitcase holding PostScript screen fonts, you will see files with the A-emblazoned document icon shown in Figure C.2. Frequently, a font's author will make it even easier to distinguish the screen fonts for PostScript fonts by attaching the tag .bmap to the suitcase's file name.

These files hold the data that instruct your Macintosh in the correct way to show each font on screen. In fact, you'll probably see multiple files with nearly identical names—the only difference being a number at the end, like 12 or 24. This is because PostScript requires special descriptions for different point sizes. For maximum flexibility in using your PostScript fonts, be sure to keep all the sizes of screen fonts shipped with your font.

Printer fonts (we discussed the icons for them a little while back) reside loose in the Fonts folder. These files hold the PostScript code for describing each character of a font to your printer. The name of a printer font is usually a truncated or otherwise-distorted version of the actual font name, and typically, there is a printer font for each version—bold, italic, roman, bold italic, and so forth. For example, the font Optima Bold would be associated with the printer font named OptimBol. Note that you should *never* rename a printer font—doing so will cause it to stop working correctly.

To print PostScript fonts, you must have a PostScript-compatible printer. Printing PostScript fonts on a non-PostScript printer produces jaggy, stairstepped type that is typically unreadable. In addition, you should never separate the screen and PostScript fonts—both must reside in the Fonts folder. If you remove the printer font, your type will appear jaggy. If you remove the screen font, the font name will not appear in your applications' font lists, and you will be unable to use that font.

Clear as mud? We figured. Take heart, though, because even people with *years* of experience in computer-based typography have a tough time understanding and explaining PostScript fonts. You can boil it down to this—*always* install *exactly* the files included on the disk for your PostScript fonts. Don't delete or move any files from the Fonts folder, and don't rename any of them, either. Stick to that practice, and everything should be peachy keen.

Let's wade out of the PostScript bog for a bit and into the relatively clear waters of TrueType fonts.

TrueType

TrueType, a technology developed by Apple Computer and later incorporated into both System 6.0 and Windows 3.1, is the newer, and arguably more popular, of the two major font formats. Unlike PostScript fonts, TrueType fonts have only one suitcase file and need only one description per face, instead of multiple sizes. This means that inside a TrueType font suitcase (often denoted with the tag .tt or .ttf attached to the suitcase name), you'll typically find four files: one each for the roman, bold, italic, and bold italic versions of the font.

Because you can store all four of these files in one suitcase, TrueType is considered a single-file format. You can distinguish TrueType fonts by their icons—the standard document adorned with a series of three graduated A's (see Figure C.3).

TrueType fonts, which can be printed on both PostScript-capable and non–PostScript-capable printers, can be printed effectively at almost any size. Unless you have specifically installed PostScript fonts on your Mac or installed a program that includes PostScript fonts, you'll probably find that your Fonts folder contains nothing but TrueType fonts. The core Mac OS fonts are TrueType, as are the fonts that install from the Office 98 Value Pack. In addition, fonts you download from the Internet are almost always available in TrueType format—PostScript may or may not be online.

At this point, you may be asking why TrueType hasn't completely supplanted PostScript in the font realm. After all, it has no weird files, it prints on anything, and it's available on both platforms. Well, that's all true, but there are a couple of

Figure C.3 The icon for a TrueType font file.

caveats. If you're preparing a file for output at a service bureau, most prefer to use PostScript fonts, because TrueType can be quirky when it's printed on expensive, high-end imagesetters. TrueType is also not quite as technically sophisticated as PostScript.

Choosing A Font Format

So how do you choose which font format to use? You may never have to. For most folks, the fonts that come with the Mac OS and in the Office 98 Value Pack are more than enough. In fact, some people may never venture beyond the basic three or four fonts they use regularly.

If you decide to purchase or download additional fonts for your Mac, though, there are two basic guidelines:

- If you plan to do mid- to high-level desktop publishing, especially if you plan to have a service bureau output your work, use PostScript.

- If you don't plan to do so, use TrueType. It's simpler to manage and will work fine for what you're doing.

We have run across the occasional quirky program that doesn't like TrueType fonts, but such programs are pretty rare. Usually, they're older versions of a program—if you find a situation like this, try upgrading your software.

Installing And Removing Fonts

If you've taken the plunge and acquired, either through purchase or download, some new fonts, you'll need to know how to put them on your system. It's pretty simple:

1. Make sure no other programs besides the Finder are running on your Mac.

2. Locate the files for your new font, either on your hard drive (if you downloaded them) or on the disk where they're stored (floppy, Zip, etc.).

3. Select the font files and drag them onto your System folder icon.

4. Drop the files there. A dialog will appear (see Figure C.4), asking if you want these items stored in the Fonts folder. Click on OK.

5. The font files are moved into your Fonts folder and are ready for applications to use.

Removing a font is just about as easy:

1. Make sure no other programs besides the Finder are running on your Mac.

2. Open the hard disk by double-clicking on its icon.

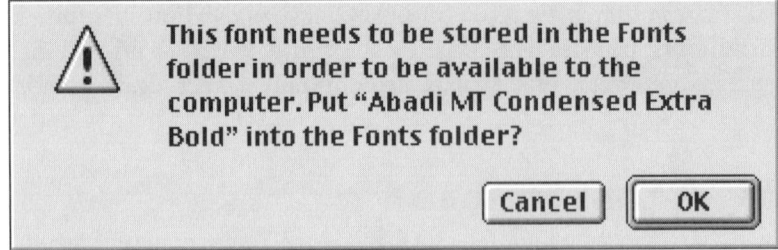

Figure C.4 When you drag a font onto your System folder, the Mac OS will query you to be sure you want the file put in the Fonts folder.

3. Open the System folder by double-clicking on its icon.

4. Open the Fonts folder by double-clicking on its icon.

5. If the font you wish to remove is TrueType, locate its suitcase and drag it out of the Fonts folder. If the font is PostScript, first remove the screen font suitcase, then drag the printer font out of the Fonts folder (if you're using a font that has AFM files, drag those out as well).

6. Close the Fonts and System folders. Your Mac is now ready to use—the fonts you removed will no longer be available.

Fonts And System Performance

When it comes to having a large number of fonts installed on your Mac, there's one very simple rule: The more fonts you have, the slower your applications will run. Many applications, particularly those like Adobe Photoshop and Adobe Illustrator, have to load specific information about available fonts each time you launch the program. Having a ton of fonts installed slows the launch process considerably.

Other programs, like Microsoft Word, use What You See Is What You Get (WYSIWYG) font menus, meaning that the name of each font is displayed in that font in the menu. If you have a lot of fonts installed, displaying the Font menu can take what seems like a lifetime. Finally, having many fonts installed increases the amount of memory required by the Mac OS itself.

There is also a technical issue with large numbers of fonts—you can only put 128 items in the Fonts folder. This means you can have 128 TrueType fonts or 64 PostScript fonts (at two files per font). It is possible to skirt this limitation, because multiple TrueType fonts can be placed in the same suitcase, as can multiple PostScript screen fonts. You can even mix TrueType and PostScript screen fonts in the same suitcase.

But we don't recommend it. For one thing, it makes your fonts harder to manage when you have to shuffle through multiple suitcases to find a particular font. Besides, if you're using more than 128 files in your Fonts folder, you're either using too many fonts in your document (which looks tacky and is hard to read), or you're doing fairly advanced desktop publishing. In the latter case, you should consider a professional font-management utility like MasterJuggler or Suitcase.

Remember also that fonts are not cross-platform. Whereas Arial Black on the Macintosh looks like Arial Black in Windows, they're two very different files. Mac users can't use Windows fonts, and vice versa. Each must acquire specific versions of a typeface, written for their particular platform.

The core point in all of this is simply that you should keep your Fonts folder lean and clean. Don't clutter it up with a lot of fonts, especially ones you use only once in a blue moon, and don't monkey around with the font files, recombining suitcases and shuffling screen fonts like a mad scientist building some gigantic Macintosh Font-kenstein. It'll only lead to trouble in the end. Keeping the Fonts folder simplified will greatly reduce your system maintenance headaches and will help keep your Mac, and Office 98, snappy and brisk.

One final note: There are certain fonts that your Macintosh uses for basic system displays and dialogs. These include Geneva, Chicago, Times, Charcoal, Monaco, and Courier. These should be left in the Fonts folder at all times (and, generally speaking, should not be used for printed work, because they're optimized for on-screen use).

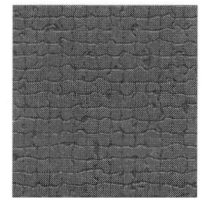

Glossary

address—1. A set of instructions that describes the precise location of a file or other resource, such as a Web page address or the path to a file on a network. 2. The precise row/column location of a cell or range in an Excel worksheet.

Address Book—A file of name and address information used for conveniently addressing email messages, envelopes, and letters.

alignment—The relative position of text or data within a document page or in a cell. An object can have both horizontal alignment (left, center, right, justified) and vertical alignment (top, bottom, center, justified).

Apple menu—A menu denoted by a small Apple logo on the far left of the Mac OS menu bar. Clicking on the logo opens the Apple menu, from which you can access a variety of programs, recently used files, and control panels.

application—A term generally applied to a computer program (or, more often, a set of programs) that accomplishes a specific task. Each major part of Office 98—Word, Excel, and so on—is an application, though each may also be informally called a program.

Applications menu—The menu on the far right of your Menu bar. The Applications menu is denoted by a program icon. In the Finder, you will see the familiar Mac OS logo. In Word, you see the W icon, in Excel the X icon, and so on. The Applications menu, when opened, displays a list of currently running applications. You can also use the Applications menu to hide the active application or hide other applications running in the background.

attribute—A type of formatting applied to text that does not change the font of the text, but still changes its appearance. Attributes include bold, italic, underline, and color.

background—A color, pattern, or picture that appears in a file behind any other content in the document, including text, data, and pictures.

Binder—An Office program for Windows that combines multiple files from different programs so you can edit and print them as a single project. Any Binder projects sent from Windows to the Macintosh must be unbound before use. Use the Microsoft Unbind utility on your Office 98 CD.

browser—See **Web browser**.

bulleted list—A list of items in which each new item is preceded by a bullet character.

button—A graphic on a toolbar or a rectangular button on a dialog that performs a function when the user points to it and clicks. Buttons in dialogs have labels on them that describe their function; the function of a toolbar button is suggested by its appearance, and also by the tooltip that appears when the pointer rests on a toolbar button. (See also **radio button**.)

cell—One box within a grid created by the intersection of rows and columns. Text and data are entered within cells in Excel worksheets and Word tables.

cell range—See **range**.

checkbox—A small square box on a dialog used to enable or disable an option. Each time you point to a checkbox and click, a check mark or "X" (depending on the program) is inserted or removed. When the check mark appears in the checkbox, the option is enabled.

client—See **server**.

clip art—A general term describing a collection of picture files (and sometimes also multimedia) that you can use freely in your documents.

Clip Gallery—An optional Office facility that organizes a library of pictures, sound clips, and video clips by subject, and helps you insert those files into Office documents.

comment—Text entered into a file, like a sticky note, to comment on the file; comments are not displayed or printed with the file in its final form.

Control-click—To point to an object and click on the mouse button while holding the Control key, displaying a menu of actions you can perform related to that object.

copy and paste—See **cut and paste**.

cut and paste—A Mac OS feature, supported by Office, that enables you to move information from one file or program to another (or from place to place within a file) by deleting it from one spot and then pasting it into another. A similar feature, copy and paste, allows you to copy information from one location, file, or program and paste it into another.

data—Information in a file. Data can take many forms—text, numbers, pictures, logical values, and so on.

database—A collection of data organized into records so it can be manipulated by database operations such as filtering and sorting.

default—A setting or action that a program uses automatically unless the user indicates an alternative.

default Web browser—A Web browser configured to open automatically any time an action requiring a Web browser is initiated. For example, if a hyperlink in an Office document leads to a Web page, clicking on that hyperlink opens the default Web browser.

Desktop—The area of the screen in the Mac OS that is open (when not covered by programs or open files and folders). Folders, files, and programs can be stored on the Desktop, and certain icons—such as your hard disk, the Trash can, and any mounted network drives—can reside only on the Desktop.

dialog—Within a program, a pop-up window on which you select options that control how a particular action will be carried out.

drag and drop—A Mac OS feature, supported by Office, that enables you to move information from one file or program to another (or from place to place within a file) by selecting it, then dragging it from one spot and dropping it in another.

drawing object—A simple line drawing created with the Drawing toolbar available in most Office programs.

drop-down list—A list of options in a dialog (and occasionally in a toolbar) from which you can choose an item. An arrow appears at the right end of all drop-down lists; you click on the arrow to drop down (open) the list so you can see all the options and select one.

edit cursor—A tall, flashing vertical bar that appears within text on screen, indicating the spot at which whatever you type will appear within the text.

email—1. Electronic mail, a system for exchanging messages through a computer network. 2. The messages exchanged through electronic mail.

extension—See **file extension** and **file name**.

field—A location in a form or database where a single piece of information resides.

field code—In a document, a code that accesses and displays information from another source, so that the information—not the field code—appears when the document is printed. Common field codes are DATE, TIME, and PAGE NUMBER.

file extension—On Windows machines, the three-letter suffix at the end of a file name, always preceded by a period (.) and usually phrased to indicate the type of file. For example, Word files generally use the extension .DOC, whereas Excel files generally use the extension .XLS. Although not necessary on the Macintosh, extensions are sometimes tacked onto file names to make it easier to tell at a glance what program created the file. You should also use them when you're sharing files with colleagues who use Windows-based machines.

file name—The name by which a particular file is identified. A file name can be nothing (although a blank file name is singularly unhelpful), or can run well over 200 characters in length in the latest Mac OS (32 characters is the max for OS versions prior to 8.1).

fill—1. A patterned background for a cell, table, or document. 2. In Excel, data entered automatically in a worksheet when you drag the fill handle of a cell containing data.

filter—In Excel, a setting that restricts the display of data in a database to a selected subset of the available data.

font—A particular typeface in which text is set to control its appearance.

font size—The precise size of text, measured in points (1 point = 1/72 of an inch).

footer—In a document, text repeated automatically across the bottom of multiple pages.

formula—In Excel, an equation stored in a cell to perform mathematical operations.

function—In Excel, a special operator used within a formula to perform complex equations and logical operations.

function keys—The row of "F" keys on extended Macintosh keyboards, usually including F1 through F15. Each key has a specific use within a program, and some keys play the same role in multiple programs. Often, a program will allow the user to assign specific functions to specific keys, as in Office.

handle—A small white or black square that appears along the boundaries of a selected object in a document. Clicking and dragging on handles alters the size and shape of the object within the layout of the document.

header—In a document, text that's repeated across the tops of multiple pages.

HTML—See **Hypertext Markup Language (HTML)**.

hyperlink—Text or a picture to which an unseen file address is attached. When you're viewing a document online, clicking on a hyperlink opens the file to which the hyperlink points. Hyperlinks are often referred to casually as links.

Hypertext Markup Language (HTML)—The standard file format for publishing pages on the Web.

Internet account—An account with an online service or Internet service provider through which you can access the Internet.

Internet Explorer—A graphical Web browser from Microsoft, included with Office 98.

intranet—An internal company network based on Web and Internet technology.

link—The set of instructions that connects a linked object to a location within a document. (See also **hyperlink**.)

linked object—A block of text, cells, a picture, or other data that is connected by a programming link to a document in which it appears. Although the object appears in the document, it remains technically separate from the document file.

local area network (LAN)—See **network**.

mail merge—A system for automatically generating pre-addressed form letters, envelopes, or labels by combining a database of names and addresses with a document containing field codes. Office supports mail merge by combining Word documents with Outlook's Address Books.

Menu bar—The thin strip across the top of your Macintosh screen that holds, at a minimum, the Apple menu, the Applications menu, and your standard Mac menus for File and Edit. The menu bar may contain other menus as well, depending on your system setup and your current applications.

multimedia—A general description for the creation and use of various kinds of media files: pictures, sound clips, video clips, and animation.

network—A group of computers interconnected so that they can share information. A network may be made up of computers all in one office or building (a local network or local area network), spread out to multiple cities (a wide area network), or made up of computers and interconnected networks—internetworks—across the world, like the Internet.

nonprinting characters—Characters you type that affect the appearance of a document, such as tabs and paragraph breaks, but do not themselves appear in the printed document.

number format—In Excel, a special formatting characteristic applied to data in cells to determine whether Excel is to treat the data as text, a number that can be used in an equation, a date, a time, or another format.

Office Assistant—In Office 98, a new, animated cartoon help facility that monitors your actions, offers tips, and responds to your questions.

Office Manager—An icon with a pull-down menu in the Macintosh menu bar that allows you to select and open Office applications. The Office Manager can be customized to include any programs or documents you wish.

OfficeArt—In Office 98, a set of tools for creating and conveniently inserting pictures in documents.

password—A secret word that the user must type to enable a selected feature or open a protected file.

picture file—A file in one of the many graphics file formats supported by Office programs. You can insert picture files in documents and format them there.

placeholder—In PowerPoint, an invisible box that holds one element in the layout of a slide, such as a list, a title, or a picture. Placeholders have handles so you can control their size and shape.

pointer—The on-screen icon that moves when you move your mouse or other pointing device. You move the pointer to on-screen objects and then click on the mouse button to perform an action on the object. The pointer usually appears as a black arrow, but you can customize it, and its appearance changes automatically under certain circumstances.

radio button—A small circle on a dialog that enables or disables an option. Each time you click on a radio button, you select it (fill it in, black) or deselect it (make it empty, white). When the radio button is black, the option is enabled.

range—In Excel, a specific rectangular block of cells described by an address or by a name you assign to the range.

select—To highlight a block of text, group of cells, group of list items, a picture, or other object so that the next action you take affects everything that's selected. You select objects by clicking on or dragging across them.

server—A computer that stores files and programs for the use of other computers that are connected to it through a network. Computers that connect to a server and retrieve information from it (and the software on those computers that controls the exchange) are called clients.

shortcut key—A combination of keyboard keys you can press to duplicate the action of a menu item or button in a program. Typically, you perform an action by pressing and holding the Command (or Option) key, pressing another specific key, then releasing both keys.

Standard toolbar—A toolbar that appears in all Office programs, containing buttons for basic operations such as creating, opening, and saving files. Although all Office programs have a Standard toolbar, each program's Standard toolbar is different.

table—Text or other data organized into rows and columns. Word, PowerPoint, and Excel each create a different kind of table.

template—In Word, PowerPoint, and Excel, a special preformatted file used as a shortcut in creating a file of your own, or to impose formatting consistency among a group of related documents.

toolbar—A row of graphical buttons appearing near the top of most program windows. You can click on the buttons to perform common tasks quickly.

tooltip—The name of a toolbar button, which appears momentarily when you point to the button and allow the pointer to rest on it for a moment. Tooltips help you locate and identify the buttons on a toolbar.

Uniform Resource Locator (URL)—A name for the address format generally used in Web browsers to identify resources on the Internet, such as Web pages.

URL—See **Uniform Resource Locator (URL)**.

view—A display configuration that shows the data within a program (and the program itself) in a particular way. Most Office programs allow you to switch among various views, each suited to a different type of work.

Web—Short for the World Wide Web (also known as the WWW), a group of server computers that store Web pages and other resources that can be accessed through the Internet and displayed in a Web browser.

Web browser—A program for interpreting HTML files to download and display Web pages stored on the Web or an intranet server. Netscapes Navigator and Microsofts Internet Explorer are two of the most popular browsers. Other popular browsers include Opera, Lynx, Mosaic, and MacWeb.

Web page—A document written and stored in HTML file format. A Web page is designed to be viewed through a Web browser.

Web site—A name used casually to refer variously to a Web page, a server on which a particular group of Web pages can be found, or a set of Web pages that together make up a multipage document.

window—The box within which a file listing or file appears in the Mac OS.

wizard—A program that helps you perform a complex task (usually within another program) by leading you through it step by step.

workbook—In Excel, a single Excel file made up of one or more worksheets.

worksheet—In Excel, a single grid of cells within which you create tables and other Excel objects.

zoom—The magnification level at which a program displays text or data in a file. Office programs allow you to increase or decrease the zoom to fit the type of work you're doing.

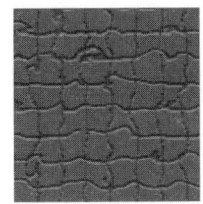

Index

A

Access, 363
Action buttons, PowerPoint, 246, 274-276
Action Settings dialog, PowerPoint, 273, 274
Add-Ins, Excel, 304
Add-Ins dialog, Excel, 304
Addition, Excel worksheet, 326, 327
Address, Excel, 290, 329
Address bar, Internet Explorer, 515
Add to Template checkbox, Word, 181
AFM files, 530
Align Bottom button, Word, 159
Alignment, paragraphs, 128
Alignment tab, Format Cells dialog, 341
Align Top buttons, Word, 159
Analysis ToolPak, Excel, 304
Animation
    online publishing, 473
    PowerPoint, 246, 265-272, 473
    Word, 473
Animation Order list, PowerPoint, 267
Animation tab, Font dialog, 95
Antonyms, Word, 196
Apple Computer Web site, 523
Applications menu, 19
Apply Design button, PowerPoint, 234
Apply To list, Word, 109
Area chart, Excel, 368
Arrow button, 38
Arrow keys, 24, 29, 314
Arrows, Word, 100
Artifacts, pictures, 148
Assistant. *See* Office Assistant.
Attachments, email, 407-409, 461
AutoComplete, Word, 187, 190
AutoContent Wizard, PowerPoint, 209-211

AutoCorrect
    Excel, 322-323
    Word, 184-185
        adding entries, 185-186
        AutoComplete, 190
        AutoFormat, 187-189
        AutoText, 189-191
        capitalization, 185
        spelling, 186-187, 191-195
AutoCorrect dialog, Word, 184, 188
AutoCorrect tab, Word, 184, 185
AutoFilter dialog, Excel, 377-379
AutoFormat
    Excel, 338-339
    Word, 187-189
AutoFormat As You Type, Word, 187-189
AutoLayout options, PowerPoint, 234, 256
Automatically Update checkbox, Word, 181
AutoRecover, Word, 58, 63
AutoSave, Excel, 304
AutoShapes list, 38
AutoText, Word, 189-191
AutoText tab, Show Toolbar button, 189, 190
AutoText toolbar, 189
AVERAGE function, Excel, 332

B

Back button, 46
Background
    Excel worksheet, 353
    PowerPoint, 240-241
    Web pages, 480, 490
    Word, 474-475
Background dialog, PowerPoint, 241
Background fill, PowerPoint, 240-243

Backspace key, Word, 53
Balloon Help, 28, 40, 44-48
Bar chart, Excel, 368
Bitmap images, 36, 150
Blind carbon copy, email, 415
Body text, 90
Body Text style, Word, 181
Bold button, 21, 94, 340
Boldface, choosing, 94
Bookmark, Word, 74
Borders
   Excel, 340
   Word, 162-166
Borders And Shading dialog, Word, 162, 163, 164, 165
Borders tab, Format Cells dialog, 342, 343
Break dialog, Word, 107, 124
Browse By feature, Word, 183
Browsers, 481, 509
   Internet Explorer, 509-526
   switching, 509-510
Browsing, Word, 183
Bubble chart, Excel, 368
Bullet dialog, PowerPoint, 227
Bulleted lists
   PowerPoint, 226-227
   Word, 130-134
Bulleted tab, Bullets And Numbering dialog, 133
Bullets And Numbering dialog, 132-133
Bullets button, Formatting toolbar, 132
Bullets and Numbering dialog, Outline Numbered tab, 134
Bungie Software (Web site), 524
Button bar, Internet Explorer, 514-515
Buttons, 21-22, 27

C

Capitalization
   AutoCorrect, 185
   changing in Word, 87-89
Carnegie Coach button, PowerPoint, 211
Cell ranges, Excel, 325, 330-331
Cell references, Excel, 326, 327-328, 345
Cells
   Excel, 290, 307
      absolute address, 329
      cell ranges, 330-331
      changing cell size, 354-355
      clearing a cell, 317-318
      comments, 313-314

      copying data, 320-321
      deleting, 351-352
      entering data, 314-324
      filling cells automatically, 318-320
      formatting, 339-345
      inserting, 350
      moving data, 320-321
      number of characters, 309
      number formats, 309-313, 317
      typing data in, 308-309, 326
Center aligned paragraph, 129
Center alignment button, 340
Center tab stop, Word, 135
Center Vertically button, Word, 159
Centre For The Easily Amused (Web site), 523
Change Case dialog, 87-88
Change Text Direction button, Word, 159
Channels, Internet Explorer, 516-517
Character formatting
   PowerPoint, 224-225
   Word, 176, 177
Character Spacing tab
   Font dialog, 95, 98-100
   kerning, 99-100
   vertical spacing, 99
Character-type style, 177, 178, 180
Chart Effects tab, PowerPoint, 269
Chart Location dialog, Excel, 370
Chart Options dialog, Excel, 368-370
Charts
   Excel, 364-373
   Web pages, 485
Chart sheet, Excel, 364
Chart Source Data dialog, Excel, 368, 369
Chart Type dialog, Excel, 367
Chart Wizard, Excel, 364-370
Chart Wizard button, Standard toolbar, 366
Checkboxes, 27
Check Grammar As You Type checkbox, Word, 192
Check Spelling As You Type checkbox, Word, 192
Clearing cells, Excel, 351
Clip Art tab, Clip Gallery, 36
Clip Gallery, 34, 36-37
   PowerPoint, 255, 256, 257-258
   Word, 255
CloseView control panel, 30
Closing (a document), Word, 62-63
Cmd+E, 129
Cmd+F, 29
Cmd+J, 129
Cmd+L, 129

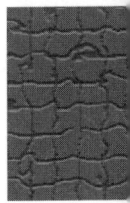

Cmd+N, 29
Cmd+P, 29
Cmd+R, 129
Cmd+S, 29
Cmd+Shift+Tab, 32
Cmd+Tab, 32
Cmd+Y, 200
Collapse box, 19
Color
    Excel, 340
    fill color, 162, 163
    PowerPoint, 236-239
    Word, 97, 142, 147
Color list, Font dialog, 97
Color Scheme dialog, PowerPoint, 236, 237
Colors And Lines tab, Word, 163-164
Column breaks, Word, 107
Columns
    Excel, inserting, 350
    newspaper-style columns, 484
    Outlook Express, 400
    saving as HTML and, 484
    Word, 122-127
Columns dialog, Word, 122
Column width, Word, 160-161
Command key, shortcuts with, 28
Comments, 464-466
    Excel, 313-314
Contacts, Outlook Express, 13, 14, 415, 431-439
Contents button, 45
Contents and Index dialog, 45-46
Contextual menus, 25, 26, 351
Continuous button, Word, 107-108
Contrast, Word, 147
Control-click
    contextual menus, 25
    Excel, 346
    Office Assistant, 43
    PowerPoint, 237
    on toolbar, 22
    Word, 196
Converting (a document)
    Excel, 299, 302-303
    MacLink Plus, 62, 67
    Word, 60-62
        earlier versions, 66-67
Copying
    among Office 98 applications, 454-456
    Excel
        between workbooks, 348-349
        cell data, 320-321
        workbook, 296
        worksheet, 348
    Word, 84-86, 88
        by saving, 58-59
        copying formatting, 200-201
        from document to document, 85-86
        within a document, 84-85
Copyright symbol, Word, 100
COUNT function, Excel, 332, 333
Crop button, Picture toolbar, 146-147
Cropping, 144, 146-147
Cursors, 53. *See also* Edit cursor.
Custom Animation dialog, PowerPoint, 266, 267
Custom Paper Size dialog, Word, 116
Cut button
    Excel, 320
    Word, 85
Cutting text, Word, 84-85, 88
Cylinder chart, Excel, 368

D

Database, Excel, 12, 13, 363, 374-383
Data series, Excel, 364
Dates
    Excel, 311
    Year 2000, 312
Decimal tab stop, Word, 135
Default setting, defined, 28
Default tab stops, 135
Delete dialog, Excel, 352
Delete key
    Excel, 316, 317
    tables, 160
    Word, 53, 83, 124
Deleting
    Excel
        cells, 316
        worksheet, 347
    Office Express folders, 404
    Outlook Express, email message, 411
    PowerPoint, 228
    Word, 53, 83
        highlighted text, 81
        restoring deleted text, 81, 82, 85
        in tables, 160
Del key
    Excel, 316
    Word, 53, 83
Deselecting text, 80, 83

Desktop file, 476
Dialog boxes, 20, 25-28
   defaults, 28
   similar in Office 98 programs, 4
Different First Page checkbox, Word, 113
Different Odd And Even checkbox, Word, 113
"Dingbat" fonts, 101
Display
   toolbars, 22-23
   Word, 68-73
      Full Screen, 72-73
      Master Document view, 70
      Normal view, 69
      Online Layout view, 70
      Outline view, 70
      Page Layout view, 69, 70
      Print Preview, 70-71
      Show/Hide, 71-72, 135
      toolbars, 79
      WYSIWYG, 7, 68, 487, 534
      Zoom, 71
Division, Excel worksheet, 326, 327
Document dialog
   Word, 108-110
      headers and footers, 106, 118-121
Documents folder, 32, 55, 56, 215
Don't Hyphenate checkbox, Word, 126
DOS, file names for, 57
Double-click
   for Document dialog, 109
   Excel, 316, 317, 372
   selecting text, 80
   on toolbar, 23
Doughnut chart, Excel, 368
Down arrow key, 24, 29
Drag and drop, 25
   copying info among applications, 459
   copying text, 86
   Office 98 installation by, 499
   opening a file, 67
   PowerPoint, 235
   toolbars, 23
Dragging, 25
Drawing toolbar, 34, 37-38
Drop-down lists, 26

E

Easy Access control panel, 30
eBay Online Auction Service (Web site), 523

Edit cursor, 52, 315
Editing
   Excel, 347-360
      cell data, 314-324
      chart, 371
      formulas, 326
   PowerPoint, 222-223
      Undo, 228
   Word, 83-89
      AutoCorrect, 184-185
      automated, 84
      capitalization, changing, 87-89
      copying, 48-49, 84-86, 88
      Cut and Paste, 84-85
      deleting, 53, 81, 83
      inserting, 84, 88
      moving, 84-85, 88
      overwriting, 84, 88
      replacing, 197-201
      tracking changes, 89-90
      Undo, 81-83, 84, 85
      view, 69
      Web pages, 486-490
Effects checkboxes, Font tab, 97
Effects tab, PowerPoint, 268
Email
   attachments, 407-409, 461
   blind carbon copy, 415
   Outlook Express, 7, 14, 405-430
      attachments, 407-409
      bug, 420
      deleting messages, 411-413
      forwarding mail, 422-423
      importing mail, 391-393
      newsgroups, 395-396
      organizing mail, 424-430
      preferences, 393-395
      printing messages, 409-410
      quoting, 422
      reading mail, 406-407
      receiving messages, 405-406
      saving as text, 410-411
      sending mail, 414-422, 423-424
Email address, Outlook Express, 393, 439-440
Email icon, Outlook Express, 391
Embedded chart, Excel, 364
Embedded data, 456-459
Em dash, Word, 100
Emoticons, 186
Eraser button, Tables And Borders toolbar, 160
The Evangelist (Web site), 523

Even page button, Word, 107
Excel 98, 11-12, 287-288
   absolute address, 329
   add-ins, 305-306
   Add-Ins dialog, 304
   address, 290, 329
   AutoCorrect, 322-323
   AutoFilter dialog, 377-379
   AutoSave, 304
   cell ranges, 325, 330-331
   cell references, 326, 327-328, 345
   cells, 290, 307
      changing cell size, 354-355
      clearing a cell, 317-318
      comments, 313-314
      deleting, 351-352
      editing data, 314-324
      entering data, 308-314
      filling cells automatically, 318-320
      number of characters, 309
      number formats, 309-313, 317
      typing data in, 308-309, 326
   chart, from within Word, 460-461
   Chart Location dialog, 370
   Chart Options dialog, 368-370
   charts, 364-373
   Chart Source Data dialog, 368, 369
   Chart Type dialog, 367
   Chart Wizard, 364-370
   clearing cells, 351
   closing workbook, 298-299
   comments, 464
   contextual menus, 351
   copying, 296
   copying data, 320-321
   creating new workbook, 288-297
   as databases, 12, 13, 363, 374-383
   dates, 311
   Delete dialog, 352
   deleting cells, 351-352
   earlier Excel versions and, 301-302
   exchanging files, 299
   features, 12-13
   filtering data, 377-379
   footers, 357, 358
   Format Cells dialog, 341-342
   Format Control dialog, 380
   Format Legend dialog, 371
   Format Painter, 342
   formatting, 337-361
      AutoFormat, 338-339
      worksheets, 339-345
   forms, 379-383
   Forms toolbar, 379
   Formula bar, 290, 307, 308, 326, 334
   Formula palette, 333
   formulas, 322-335, 345
   Full Screen mode, 281
   functions, 325, 331-335
   handles, 353, 370
   headers, 357, 358
   Insert dialog, 350
   inserting and deleting rows, columns, and cells, 349-352
   margins, 357-358
   Margins tab, 357
   moving and copying information among applications, 454-456
   moving data, 320-321
   naming, 295
      workbook files, 294
      worksheet, 345-346
   New dialog, 292
   number formats, 309-313, 315, 317
   Open dialog, 300
   opening workbooks, 299-303, 305-306
   Options button, 357
   Options dialog, 356
   page formatting, 361
   page layout, 351-361
   Page Setup dialog, 354, 356-357
   Paste Function dialog, 334
   pictures, inserting, 352-353
   Print dialog, 297-298, 355
   printing, 297-298, 305-306, 354
   Print Preview, 355-356
   Replace, 323
   Replace dialog, 323
   Save As dialog, 294, 295
   Save dialog, 503
   saving, 294-295
      as HTML, 493-494
   scrolling, 291
   selecting, 314-315
   sheet tab, 358, 369, 370
   similarities among Office 98 products, 4-6
   sorting data, 376-377
   spellchecking, 321-323
   Spelling dialog, 322
   Standard toolbar, 291, 313

Style dialog, 342, 343
Styles, 342, 344
tables, 157
templates, 291-294, 338, 346
time, 312
tracking changes, 462-464
Undo, 321
Web pages with Excel data, 493-494
wizards, 302, 304
    Chart Wizard, 364-370
    File Conversion wizard, 302, 304
workbooks, 288-289, 291
worksheets, 11-12, 288
    background, 475
    from within Word, 460-461
Year 2000 problem, 312
ZIP code number format, 313
Excel toolbar, Save button, 294
Explorer bar, Internet Explorer, 516
Exponentiation, Excel worksheet, 326, 327

F

Favorites bar, Internet Explorer, 515
Faxing, Word document, 76
Field codes, 121, 485
File formats, 62
    conversion, Word, 60-62
    pictures, 142-143, 148
    PowerPoint media objects, 258
    saving to another, 67-68
    Word, 66-68
File names
    for PC format, 57
    Web pages, 58
    Word, 52, 56, 56-58
Fill, PowerPoint, 240-243
Fill color, Word, 162
Fill Effects dialog, Word, 474
Fill handle, Excel, 318-319
Fills, Excel, 318
Film recorder, 250
Filtering, Excel, 377-379
Filters, 35
    Word, 60, 61-62, 67
Find And Replace dialog, Word, 73, 84, 197, 198
Flaming, 441
Floating, graphics, 143, 147-148, 149
Float Over Text checkbox, Word, 143
Folder list, Outlook Express, 398

Folders, Outlook Express, 397, 402-405
Font box, Formatting toolbar, 92
Font Color button, Formatting toolbar, 94
Font dialog, 95
    Animation tab, 95
    Character Spacing tab, 95, 98-100
    Color list, 97
    opening, 99
Font list, Formatting toolbar, 91, 92
Fonts
    AFM files, 530
    changing, 92-93
    choosing, 92-93, 533
    downloading, 92
    Excel, 339, 339-340, 340
    font suitcase, 529
    installing, 533-534
    kerning, 99-100
    loose font files, 530
    monospaced, 93
    PostScript fonts, 91, 92, 93, 253, 530-532, 534
    PowerPoint, 224
    printer fonts, 530
    proportional, 93
    removing, 533-534
    saving as HTML and, 483
    sizes, 92-93, 95
    system performance and, 534-535
    TrueType fonts, 91, 92, 93, 253, 532-533, 534
    Web resources, 92
    Word, 90-95
Font Size list, 92
Font Style list, Word, 96
Font suitcase, 529
Font tab, 96-98
    Effects checkboxes, 97
    Preview pane, 95
    Underline options, 96, 97
Footers
    Excel, 357, 358
    Word, 106, 118-121
        creating, 126-127
        margins and, 111
        multiple footers, 119-120
        page numbers in, 120-121
        pictures in, 140
        position of, 110
        rules in, 164
Format Cells dialog, Excel, 341-342
Format Control dialog, Excel, 380
Format Legend dialog, Excel, 371

Graphics   **551**

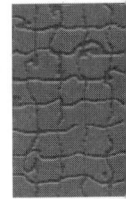

Format Painter
   Excel, 342
   Word, 201
Format Painter button, Standard toolbar, 201
Format Picture dialog
   Position tab, 149-150
   Wrapping tab, 150-151
Formatting, Web pages, 488-490
Formatting (graphics)
   PowerPoint, rearranging slide elements, 233-236
   Word, 144-147
      brightness, color, and contrast, 147
      cropping, 144, 146-147
      sizing, 136
      undoing, 146
Formatting (text)
   Excel, 337-361
      AutoFormat, 338-339
      changing, 315
      chart, 371
      forms, 379-380
      number formats, 309-313, 315, 317
      worksheets, 339-345
   Outlook Express, email message, 417-419
   PowerPoint
      character formatting, 224-225
      fonts, 224
      paragraph alignment and spacing, 225
   Word, 90-95
      advanced text-control options, 95-100
      alignment symbols, 137
      breaking pages and columns, 124-127
      Character Spacing tab, 95, 98-100
      columns, 122-124
      copying, 200-201
      finding and replacing text, 197-200
      Font tab, 95, 96-98
      headers and footers, 106, 118-121
      Layout tab, 112-114
      leaders, 137
      lists, 130-134
      margins, 110-112
      Page Setup dialog, 114-118
      paragraphing formatting, 106, 127-130, 137-138
      section breaks, 106-108
      Show/Hide, 71, 135
      special characters, 100-102
      styles, 176-183
      symbols, 100-103
      table, 156, 158-159
      tabs, 134-137

      templates, 110, 169, 170, 173-176, 182-183
   Web pages, 91
   wizards, 170-173
Formatting toolbar
   Bullets button, 132
   displaying, 79
   Excel, 339-340
   Font box, 92
   Font Color button, 94
   Font list, 91, 92
   Highlight button, 94, 163
   Numbering button, 132
   Outside Border button, 94, 163
   PowerPoint, 224, 225
   similar in Office 98 programs, 4
   Style list, 177, 178
   Word, 79, 80, 177, 178
Forms, Excel, 379-383
Forms toolbar, Excel, 379
Formula bar, Excel, 290, 307, 308, 326, 334
Formula operators, Excel, 327
Formula palette, Excel, 333
Formulas, Excel, 322-335, 345
From Edge box, Word, 110
Front Page, 378
Full Screen mode, Word, 72-73
Functions, Excel, 325, 331-335

G

Genigraphics, 251
Genigraphics Wizard, 251, 252
Get Data button, Mail Merge Helper dialog, 203
GIF files, 142, 143, 480, 484
Go To tab, Word, 73, 84
Grammar checker, Word, 191-195
Graphics
   bitmap images, 36, 150
   drawing pictures, 37-38
   imported files, 35-36
   OfficeArt, 34, 36-37
   overlapping, 155-156
   Web clip libraries, 37
   Web pages, 480, 484, 489-490
      PowerPoint-based, 492
   Word, 139-140
      borders, 162-166
      floating, 143, 147-148, 149
      pictures, adding, 140-153, 155-156
      shading, 162-166

tables, 156-161
text boxes, 153-155
Greek letters, Word, 100
Gutter box, Word, 110-111

H

Handles
    Excel, 353, 370
    PowerPoint, 235
    Word, 144, 145
Handout master, PowerPoint, 240
Handouts, PowerPoint, 244, 245
Hanging indent, 131
Hard breaks, 124, 125
Header And Footer dialog, Insert AutoText button, 121
Headers
    Excel, 357, 358
    Word, 69, 70, 106, 118-121
        creating, 126-127
        margins and, 111
        multiple headers, 119-120
        page numbers in, 120-121
        pictures in, 140
        position of, 110
        rules in, 164
Helper application, Outlook Express, 408
Help On The Web, 6, 7, 40, 46-48
Help option, similar in Office 98 programs, 6
Help topic, 46
Highlight button, Formatting toolbar, 94, 163
Highlight Changes, Word, 90
Highlight color, Word, 162
Highlighting text, 79-81, 83
History button, 46
Horizontal scroll bar, 24
HTML (Hypertext Markup Language), 417, 479
HTML files, 142, 143
HTML tabs, 484
HTML tags, 479
Hyperlinks, 490
    color, 515
    defined, 272, 475
    in Excel cells, 334
    inserting, 475-477
    phrasing the link path, 477-478
    PowerPoint, 246, 272-276, 475-477
Hypertext Markup Language (HTML), 417, 479

I

I-beam pointer, in Word document, 53
The Icon Factory (Web site), 523
Import converter, 67
Indenting
    Excel, 340
    paragraphs, 129-130
Indents And Spacing tab, Paragraph dialog, 130
Index button, 45
Inline picture, 148, 149
Insert AutoText button, Word, 121
Insert Clip Art button, Standard toolbar, 257
Insert dialog, Excel, 350
Insert Merge Field button, Mail Merge toolbar, 203-204
Insert mode, 84
Insert Picture dialog, Word, 141, 142, 143
Insert Table button, Word, 157
Insert Table dialog, Word, 158
Internet, 6-7. *See also* Email.
    browsers, 481
    computer news, 524
    education and reference, 524
    entertainment news, 525
    flaming, 441
    font libraries, 92
    health news, 525
    Help On The Web, 6, 7, 40, 46-48
    hobbies, 525
    home and family, 525
    lifestyles, 525
    local news, 522
    Microsoft Excel Free Stuff page, 294
    Microsoft information, 526
    Microsoft Word Free Stuff page, 173
    multimedia clip libraries, 37
    netiquette, 441-442
    news, 521-522
    newsgroups, 440-450
    online form, 381
    Outlook Express, 387-449
    PowerPoint online presentation, 248
    reference, 524
    search engines, 520-522
    sports news, 522
    stock news, 522
    templates, downloading, 173
    Top 10 best sites, 522-524
    travel information, 525
    viewers, Office 98 for Macintosh, 472

Modify buton, Style dialog **553**

weather, 522
Web authoring information, 495
wizards, downloading, 173
Internet Explorer, 509-526
    Address bar, 515
    Button bar, 514-515
    channels, 516-517
    Explorer bar, 516
    Favorites bar, 515
    getting around in, 513-517
    installing, 510-513
    Outlook Express, 7
    start page, configuring, 518-527
    Status bar, 515-516
Internet Setup Assistant, 43
Intranet, 470
Invoice template, Excel, 292
Italics, choosing, 94
Italics button, 21, 94, 340
Item, Outlook Express, 397

J

JPEG files, 142-143, 480, 484
Justified text, 114, 129

K

Keep Lines Together checkbox, Word, 125
Keep With Next checkbox, Word, 125
Kerning, 99-100
Keyboard, creating boldface or italics, 94
Kiosk presentation, PowerPoint, 247, 277, 278

L

Landscape orientation, 356
Layout tab, Word, 112-114
Leader characters, 137
Left-aligned paragraph, 128
Left alignment button, 340
Less Brightness button, Word, 147
Less Contrast button, Word, 147
Letter Wizard, Word, 172-173
Line And Page Breaks tab, Paragraph dialog, 124-126
Line button, 38
Line chart, Excel, 368
Line numbers, Word, 114, 125

Linking, Objects to files, 456-459
Link To File checkbox, Word, 143
List Files of Type menu, Word, 67, 68
Lists
    bulleted lists, 130-134, 226-227
    Excel, 374
    formatting, Word, 130-134
    nested lists, 226
    numbered lists, 130-134
    PowerPoint, 226-227
Lock Anchor checkbox, Word, 150
Loose font files, 530

M

MacAddict (Web site), 523
MacLink Plus, 62, 67
MacMAME (Web site), 524
Mac OS Setup Assistant, 43
MacSurfer's Headline News, 523
Mailing lists, Outlook Express, 436-437
Mail merge, Word, 9, 201-203
Mail Merge Helper, Word, 202-203
Mail Merge Helper dialog, Get Data button, 203
Mail Merge toolbar, Insert Merge Field button, 203-204
Margins
    Excel, 357-358
    printers and, 112
    Word, 110-112
Margins tab
    Excel, 357
    Word, 110, 112, 117
Master, PowerPoint, 239-240
Master Document view, Word, 70
Match Case checkbox, Word, 198
MAX function, Excel, 332
Media files, PowerPoint, 258-260
Meeting Minder, PowerPoint, 280, 281
Menu bar, 20
Menus, similar in Office 98 programs, 4
Merge And Center button, 340
Message List, Outlook Express, 399
Microphone, for PowerPoint sound recording, 261
Microsoft
    import converter, 67
    Typography page, 92
MIN function, Excel, 332
Mirror Margins, Word, 110, 111
Modify button, Style dialog, 182

554 Modify Style dialog, Word

Modify Style dialog, Word, 182
Monospaced fonts, 93
More Brightness button, Word, 147
More Contrast button, Word, 147
Mouse
    deselecting text, 80
    selecting text, 79-80
Mouse pointer, in Word document, 53
Move Object With Text checkbox, Word, 150
Movies, PowerPoint, 246
Moving
    among Office 98 applications, 454-456
    Excel
        between workbooks, 348-349
        cell data, 320-321
        worksheet, 347-348
    Office Express folders, 403
    Word, 85, 88
        from document to document, 85-86
        within a document, 84-85
MS-DOS, file names for, 57
Multimedia
    OfficeArt, 34, 36-37
    PowerPoint, 10, 11, 245-246, 255-260
    Web clip libraries, 37
Multiplication, Excel worksheet, 326, 327

N

Name Box, Formula bar, 290
Naming, Office Express folders, 404
Naming (a document)
    Excel
        workbook files, 294
        worksheet, 345-346
    Word, 52, 56-58
Native documents, online publishing, 469, 470-478
Nested lists, 226
Netiquette, 441-442
New dialog
    Excel, 292
    PowerPoint, 233
New Folder button, Word, 57
New Presentation dialog, PowerPoint, 212
Newsgroups, Outlook Express, 440-450
New Style dialog, Word, 180-181
Nonprinting characters, Word, 71, 72
Normal template, 176, 177
Normal view, Word, 69, 124
Note pages, PowerPoint, 243-245

Notes master, PowerPoint, 240
Notes Page view, PowerPoint, 244
NOW function, Excel, 333
Numbered lists, 130-134
Numbered tab, Bullets And Numbering dialog, 133
Number formats, Excel, 309-313, 315, 317
Numbering button, Formatting toolbar, 132
Number styles, Excel, 340

O

Odd page button, Word, 107
Office 98 (Mac), 3-4, 15
    adding components, 503-504
    application programs, 4, 7-14
    components, 4, 7-14, 503-504
    contextual menus, 25, 26
    cross-platform compatibility, 6
    customizing, 39-40
    data exchange among applications, 454-461
    dialog boxes, 4, 20, 25-28
    dialog defaults, 28
    dragging and dropping, 25
    drawing pictures, 37-38
    email. *See* Email.
    exchanging information between applications, 454-461
    "family resemblance," 4-6
    filters, 35, 60, 61-62, 67
    help, 40
        Balloon Help, 28, 40, 44-45
        Contents and Index, 45-46
        Help On The Web, 40, 46-48
        Office Assistant, 6, 40-43, 66
    importing graphics, 35-36
    installing, 499-503
    integrating and collaborating, 6, 453-468
    Internet. *See* Internet.
    linking objects to files, 456-459
    menu bar, 20
    Microsoft Web site, 67
    OfficeArt, 34-38
    Office Manager, 4, 6, 18-20
    online publishing. *See* Online publishing.
    opening and closing programs, 18-20
    Outlook Express, 4, 13-14, 387-449
    protecting a document, 465-466
    saving a document, 31-32
    scrolling, 24-25
    shortcut keys, 28-30

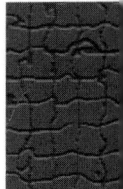

system requirements, 497-499
toolbars, 21-23
uninstalling, 504-505
Value Pack, 48, 170, 171, 293, 304, 505-507
viewers, 472
Web sites of interest, 48
WordArt, 34, 38-39
OfficeArt, 34, 148, 150
 Clip Gallery, 34, 35, 36-37
 formatting, 145
Office Assistant, 6, 40-43, 66
 customizing, 42-43
 hiding, 42
Office Installer, 170
Office Manager, 4, 6, 30, 31, 32
 customizing, 32-33
 enabling/disabling, 34
 opening Office programs from, 18-20, 31
 QuickSwitch, 32
Online documents, page layout, 106
Online form, Excel, 381
Online Layout view, Word, 70, 471-472, 474
Online presentation, PowerPoint, 248
Online publishing
 animation, 95, 473
 color, 142
 Excel worksheets, 353
 native documents, 469, 470-478
 Web pages, 469, 478-490, 494-495
Online template, PowerPoint, 213
Open button, Standard toolbar, 300
Open dialog
 Excel, 300
 PowerPoint, 231, 232
 Word, 64, 65, 67, 68
Opening (a document), 18-20
 Excel, 299-303, 305-306
 from icon, 64
 PowerPoint, 231-233, 242-243
 Word, 63-68
  All Files, 67
  with drag and drop, 67
  from earlier Word versions, 66
  from other word processors, 67
Options button
 Excel, 357
 Word, 57
Options dialog, Excel, 356
Orphan, 125
Outline Numbered tab, Bullets and Numbering dialog, 134

Outline view
 PowerPoint, 217, 221-222, 224
 Word, 70
Outlook Express, 4, 13-14, 387-449
 Address Book, 202
 configuring, 391-397
 Contacts, 13, 14, 415, 431-439
 email, 7, 14, 405-430
  attachments, 407-409
  bug, 420
  deleting messages, 411-413
  forwarding, 422-423
  importing mail, 391-393
  newsgroups, 395-396
  organizing mail, 4224-430
  preferences, 393-395
  printing messages, 409-410
  quoting, 422
  reading mail, 406-407
  receiving mail, 405-406
  saving as text, 410-411
  sending mail, 414-422, 423-424
 email address, 393, 439-440
 features, 14
 folders, 397, 402-405
 icon, 390
 installing, 388-390
 interface, 397-402
 mailing lists, 436-437
 newsgroups, 440-450
 opening, 390-391
 panes, 399-404
 window, 397
Outlook Express toolbar, 397-398
Output Options dialog, PowerPoint, 211
Outside Border button
 Formatting toolbar, 94, 163
 Tables And Borders toolbar, 163, 164
Oval button, 38
Overhead transparencies, PowerPoint, 248-249
Overtype mode, 84

P

Page Border tab, Word, 166
Page Break Before checkbox, Word, 125
Page breaks
 saving as HTML and, 483
 Word, 69, 70, 107, 124-127
Page formatting, Excel, 361

556 Page layout

Page layout
    Excel, 351-361
    Word, 105, 106-110
Page Layout view, Word, 69, 70, 111, 123, 144
Page numbers, in headers and footers, 120-121
Page Setup dialog
    Excel, 354, 356-357
    Word, 114-118
Page tab, Excel, 356
Panes, Outlook Express, 399-404
Paragraph, defined, 127
Paragraph dialog
    Indents And Spacing tab, 130
    Line And Page Breaks tab, 124-126
Paragraph formatting
    PowerPoint, 224-225
    Word, 105, 127-130, 137-138
        styles, 176, 177
        tables, 158-159
Paragraphs, Word, 128-130
Paragraph-type style, 177, 180
Paste button, 84-85
Paste Function dialog, Excel, 334
Patterns tab, Format Cells dialog, 342, 343
PCs, file names for, 57
Pen pointer, PowerPoint, 282
PgDn key, 24, 29
PgUp key, 24, 29
Pictures
    artifacts, 148
    Excel, inserting into a worksheet, 352-353
    Web pages, 480, 484, 489-490
    Word
        brightness, 147
        color, 142, 147
        contrast, 147
        cropping, 144, 146-147
        file formats, 142-143, 148
        formatting, 144-147
        in headers and footers, 140
        inserting, 140-141, 143-144
        positioning, 144, 147-153
        sizing, 146
        text wrap, 150-152
Pictures submenu, Word, 140, 141
Pictures tab, Clip Gallery, 36, 140
Picture toolbar, Word, 139, 140, 144, 146
Pie chart, Excel, 368
Placeholders
    PowerPoint, 214, 222, 234, 235-236
        animation, 265, 266

Play Settings tab, PowerPoint, 269, 270
Play Sound checkbox, PowerPoint, 274
POP, 393
Portrait orientation, 356
Position tab, Format Picture dialog, 149-150
PostScript fonts, 91, 92, 93, 253, 530-532, 534
.pot file, 233
PowerPoint 98, 9-10, 207-209, 274
    Action buttons, 246, 274-276
    Action Settings dialog, 273, 274
    adding, moving, and removing slides, 228-230
    animation, 246, 265-272, 473
    AutoContent Wizard, 209-211
    AutoLayout, 234-235
    AutoLayout options, 234, 256
    background, 240-241
    Background dialog, 241
    Bullet dialog, 227
    bulleted lists, 226-227
    character formatting, 224-225
    Clip Gallery, 255, 256, 257-258
    Color Scheme dialog, 236, 237
    color schemes, 236-239
    comments, 464
    Custom Animation dialog, 266, 267
    custom shows, 279-280
    editing text, 222-223
    features, 11
    fonts, 224
    Formatting toolbar, 224, 225
    Genigraphics Wizard, 251, 252
    Handout master, 240
    handouts, 244, 245
    hyperlinks, 246, 272-276, 475-477
    kiosk presentation, 247, 277, 278
    lists, 226-227
    Meeting Minder, 280, 281
    movies, 246
    moving and copying information among
       applications, 454-456
    multimedia, 10, 11, 245-246, 255-260
    narrating slides, 261-263
    New dialog, 233
    New Presentation dialog, 212
    note pages, 243-245
    Notes master, 240
    Notes Page view, 244
    online template, 213
    Open dialog, 231, 232
    opening existing presentations, 231-233, 242-243
    outline view, 217, 221-222, 224

Output Options dialog, 211
paragraph alignment and spacing, 225
pen pointer, 282
placeholders, 214, 222, 234, 235-236
presentation hardware and software, 252-255
presentation medium, 245-248, 276-278
Presentation Options dialog, 211
Presentation Style dialog, 211
Presentation Type dialog, 210
Print dialog, 245
printing
    notes and handouts, 245
    transparencies, 248-249
proto-presentation, 209
rearranging slide elements, 233-236
Record Narration dialog, 261-262, 263
Record Sound dialog, 260
Save dialog, 215
saving presentations, 215
    as HTML, 490-493
self-running presentation, 247, 276, 279
setting up and running electronic shows, 252-255
Set Up Show dialog, 277
similarities among Office 98 products, 4-6
slide master, 239
Slide Setup dialog, 280
slide show view, 219-221
slide sorter view, 218-219, 228
slide timings, 278-279
Slide Transition dialog, 271
slide view, 216-217, 221, 222, 224, 244, 257, 260, 263, 264
sound, 246, 255, 259, 260-264
speaker options, 280-282
spellchecking, 227
spelling, 227
Standard toolbar, 207, 208
Startup dialog, 231
tables, 157
tables and worksheets, 256
templates, 211-214, 221-222, 233
35mm color slides, 250-252
title master, 239
transparencies, 248-249
typefaces, 224
Web-based shows, 490-493
wizards, 209-211, 221-222, 233
Word document formatted for, 214
Zoom dialog, 216, 217
PowerPoint viewer, 253, 254, 280
.pps file, 233

.ppt file, 233
Preferences dialog, Word, 39, 40, 192, 193
Presentation Options dialog, PowerPoint, 211
Presentations tab, PowerPoint, 213
Presentation Style dialog, PowerPoint, 211
Presentation Type dialog, PowerPoint, 210
Preview pane
    Borders And Shading dialog, 163
    Font tab, 95
    Outlook Express, 399
Print button, 21, 297
Print dialog, 28
    Excel, 297-298, 355
    PowerPoint, 245
    Word, 74, 75
Printer fonts, 530
Printing
    Excel, 297-298, 305-306, 354
    Outlook Express, email messages, 409-410
    PowerPoint, 248-250
        notes and handouts, 245
        transparencies, 248-249
    Word, 74-76
        color, 142
        Page Setup dialog, 114-118
Print Preview
    Excel, 355-356
    Word, 70-71
Print Preview mode, Word, 111
Print What list, PowerPoint, 245
PRODUCT function, Excel, 332
Program window, scaling, 19
Proportional fonts, 93
Protecting (a document), Office 98, 465-466
Protocols, 393
PSPrinter Page Setup dialog, Word, 114-116
.pwz file, 233
Pyramid chart, Excel, 368

Q

Quadruple-click, selecting text, 81
QuickSwitch function, 32

R

Radar chart, Excel, 368
Radio buttons, 27
Ranges, Excel, 325, 330-331

Recent Documents subfolder, Word, 64
Record Narration dialog, PowerPoint, 261-262, 263
Record Sound dialog, PowerPoint, 260
Rectangle button, 38
Redo button
    Excel, 321
    Word, 82
Reformatting, Excel, chart, 371
Renaming, Office Express folders, 404
Replace, Excel, 323
Replace dialog, Excel, 323
Replace tab, Word, 197, 198
Replace Text As You Type checkbox, Word, 186
Reset Picture button, Picture toolbar, 146
Rich Text Format (RTF), 62
Right aligned paragraph, 129
Right alignment button, 340
Right tab stop, Word, 135
Row height, Word, 160-161
Rows, Excel, inserting, 350
RTF files, 62
Ruler, 111
    indentation, 130
    tab stops, 136-137
    Web pages, 481

S

Save As, Word, 59, 61
Save As dialog, Excel, 294, 295
Save button
    Excel toolbar, 294
    PowerPoint, 215
    Word, 55
Save Current Document As text box, Word, 59
Save dialog
    Excel, 503
    PowerPoint, 215
    Word, 55, 58, 59
Save File As Type, Word, 59, 61
Save File As Type list, Excel, 303
Save With Document checkbox, Word, 143
Saving (document), 52, 54-62, 63
    AutoRecover, 58, 63
    default setting, 31-32, 215
    Documents folder, 32, 55, 56, 215
    Excel, 294-297, 493-494
    Outlook Express, email messages, 410
    PowerPoint, 215, 490-493
    templates, 175, 294

Word
    conversion, 60-62
    copies of documents, 58-59
    from earlier Word versions, 66
    from other word processors, 67
    as HTML, 482-485, 487
    Save As, 59
Scaling
    Excel, 357
    picture, 146, 148
    program window, 19
Scatter chart, Excel, 368
Scroll bars, 24
Scrolling, 24-25, 29
    Excel, 291
    Web pages, 484
Scrolling marquee, 490
Search engines, 520-522
Section breaks, Word, 107
Section Start list, Layout tab, 113
Select Browse Object button, Word, 183
Selecting, Excel, 314-315
Selecting text
    PowerPoint, 221
    Word, 79-81, 83, 124
        tables, 159-160
Self-running presentation, PowerPoint, 247, 276, 279
Set Up Show dialog, PowerPoint, 277
Shading, Word, 162-166
Shading color, Word, 162
Sheet tab, Excel, 358, 369, 370
Shift+Right arrow, 81
Shift+Tab, 29
Shortcut keys, 28-30
Show/Hide, Word, 71-72, 135
Show Toolbar button, AutoText tab, 189, 190
Shut Down command, 62-63, 299
Sizing (picture), 146
Slide formatting. *See* Formatting (slides).
Slide master, PowerPoint, 239
Slide miniature, PowerPoint, 217
Slide Setup dialog, PowerPoint, 280
Slide show view, PowerPoint, 219-221
Slide sorter view, PowerPoint, 218-219, 228
Slide transition, animating, 271-272
Slide Transition dialog, PowerPoint, 271
Slide view, PowerPoint, 216-217, 221, 222, 224, 244, 257, 260, 263, 264
Smiley faces, 186
SMTP, 393
Snaking columns, 122

Templates   559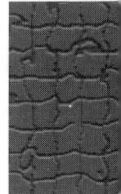

Soft page breaks, 125
Sort Ascending button, Word, 159
Sort Descending button, Word, 159
Sorting, Excel, 376-377
Sort key, 376
Sound
   CD as background, 263-265
   disk space for, 263
   microphone basics, 261
   PowerPoint, 246, 255, 259, 260-264
Sounds tab, Clip Gallery, 36
Spam, 411
Special characters, Word, 100-102
Special Characters list, 102
Special Characters tab, Symbol dialog, 101
Spellchecking
   Excel, 321-323
   PowerPoint, 227
   Word, 186, 191-195
Spelling And Grammar dialog, Word, 193
Spelling And Grammar tab, Preferences dialog, 192
Spelling dialog, Excel, 322
SQRT function, Excel, 332
Standard toolbar, 22
   Cut button, 85
   displaying, 79
   Excel, 291, 313
   Format Painter button, 201
   Open button, 300
   PowerPoint, 207, 208
      Apply Design button, 234
      Insert Clip Art button, 257
   Print button, 297
   Save button, 215
   similar in Office 98 programs, 4, 5
   startup dialog, 208
   Undo button
      PowerPoint, 228
      Word, 81-83, 84, 85
   Word, 79, 80
      Insert Table button, 157-158
      Paste button, 84-85
      Show/Hide, 71, 135
      Tables And Borders button, 139, 140, 160
      Zoom, 71, 144
Startup dialog, PowerPoint, 231
Status bar
   Internet Explorer, 515-516
   Outlook Express, 399
   Word, 73
Stock chart, Excel, 368

Style dialog
   Excel, 342, 343
   Word, 178, 179, 182
Style For Following Paragraph option, Word, 181
Style list, Formatting toolbar, 177, 178
Styles
   Excel, 342, 344
   Word, 176-183
      changing, 182
      creating, 177-182
      using, 177-179
Submenus, 20
Subtraction, Excel worksheet, 326, 327
SUM Function, Excel, 332, 333
Suppress Line Numbers checkbox, Word, 125
Surface chart, Excel, 368
Symbol dialog, Special Characters tab, 101
Symbols, Word, 100-103
Synonyms, Word, 196

T

Tab key, 29, 135
Tables
   choosing Excel or Word, 157
   Excel, 157
   Web pages, 485
   Word, 156-157
      border options, 163
      column width, 160
      creating, 157-158
      drawing, 160, 161
      editing, 159-160
      formatting, 156, 158-159
      row height, 160-161
Tables And Borders button, Word, 160
Tables And Borders toolbar, Word, 139, 140, 160, 163, 164
Tabs, 134
   HTML tabs, 484
   setting, 135-137
Tabs dialog, 136
Tab stops, 135-136
Templates, 52
   Excel, 291-294, 338, 346
   PowerPoint, 211-214, 221-222, 233
   Word, 110, 169, 170, 173-176, 182-183
      creating, 175
      editing, 175, 176
      Normal template, 176

560 Templates

    saving, 175
    using, 173-174
Text block, 79
    deleting, 81
    restoring, 81
    selecting, 79-81
Text boxes, 26, 153-155
Text files, 62
Text formatting. *See* Formatting (text).
Text wrapping, 150-152, 154
Thesaurus, Word, 196
3D cone chart, Excel, 368
Time, Excel, 312
Timing tab, PowerPoint, 268
Title master, PowerPoint, 239
TODAY function, Excel, 333
Toolbar buttons, 21-22
Toolbars, 21-23
    buttons, 21-22
    displaying, 22-23
    similar in Office 98 programs, 4, 5
    tooltips, 21, 22
    Word, 74
Tooltips, 21, 22
Track Changes, Word, 89-90
Tracking changes, 89-90, 462-464
Transparencies, PowerPoint, 248-249
Triple-click, selecting text, 81
TrueType fonts, 91, 92, 93, 253, 532-533, 534
Typefaces. *See* Fonts.

U

UCE (Unsolicited Commercial Email), 411
Underline, choosing, 94
Underline button, 21, 94, 96, 340
Underline list, 96
Underlining, Word, with zigzag, 193
Undo, Word, 179
Undo button
    Excel, 321
    PowerPoint, 228
    Word, 81-83, 84, 85, 146
Undo list, 82
Unsolicited Commercial Email (UCE), 411
Up arrow key, 24, 29

V

Value Pack, 48, 170, 171, 293, 304, 505-507
Vector graphics, 36
Version Tracker (Web site), 523
Vertical scroll bar, 24
Videos tab, Clip Gallery, 36
View. *See* Display.
Viewers, Office 98 for Macintosh, 472
View menu, 25

W

Web authoring, 495
Web browsers. *See* Browsers.
Web help, 6, 7, 40, 46-48
Web pages, 469, 478-479
    advanced additions to, 490
    background, 480, 490
    defined, 379-380
    file names for, 58
    formatting, 488-490
    page layout, 106
    pictures, 480, 484, 489-490
    PowerPoint, 490-493
    publishing, 494-495
    scrolling, 484
    text formatting, 91
    titling, 488
    with Web Page Wizard, 485-486
    with Word, 481-485
Web Page Wizard, 485-486
Widow, 125
Widow-Orphan Control checkbox, Word, 125
Window menu, 86
Windows, file names for, 57
Wizard dialog, Word, 171-172
Wizards
    Excel, 302, 304
        Chart Wizard, 364-370
        File Conversion Wizard, 302, 304
    PowerPoint, 209-211, 221-222, 233
        Genigraphics Wizard, 251, 252
    Web Page Wizard, 485-486
    Word, 170-173
        Letter Wizard, 172-173
Word 98, 7-8, 51
    advanced text-control options, 95-100

Word 98   561

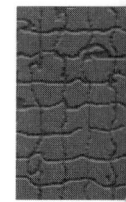

Align Bottom button, 159
Align Top buttons, 159
animation, 473
antonyms, 196
attributes, 93-94
AutoComplete, 187, 190
AutoCorrect, 184-185
AutoCorrect dialog, 184, 188
AutoFormat, 187-189
AutoRecover, 58
AutoText, 189-191
background, 474-475
Bookmark, 74
borders, 162-166
Borders And Shading dialog, 162, 163, 164, 165
browsing, 183
capitalization, changing, 87-89
Center Vertically button, 159
Change Text Direction button, 159
closing a document, 62-63
color, 97, 142
comments, 464
converting a document, 60-62
copying, 58-59, 84-86, 88
creating a document, 52, 54, 60
deleting text, 53, 81, 83
display, 68-73
documents in earlier versions, 65
entering text, 52-54
Excel worksheet or chart from within Word, 460-461
faxing a document, 76
features, 9
file names, 56
Fill Effects dialog, 474
filters, 60, 61-62, 67
Find And Replace dialog, 73, 84, 197, 198
fonts, 90-95
formatting, 90-95
   alignment symbols, 137
   breaking pages and columns, 124-127
   columns, 122-124
   copying formatting, 200-201
   headers and footers, 106, 118-121
   Layout tab, 112-114
   leaders, 137
   lists, 130-134
   margins, 110-112
   Page Setup dialog, 114-118
   paragraphing formatting, 106, 127-130, 137-138
   section breaks, 106-108
   tables, 156, 158-159
   tabs, 134-137
grammar checker, 191-195
Greek letters, 100
highlighting text, 79-81
inserting text, 84, 88
layout formatting, 106
line numbers, 114
mailings, 201-204
mail merge, 9, 201-203
Microsoft Word Free Stuff page, 173
Modify Style dialog, 182
moving, 88
   from document to document, 85-86
   within a document, 73-74, 84-85
moving and copying information among applications, 454-456
multiple documents, 65, 85-86
naming a document, 52, 56-58
New Style dialog, 180-181
nonprinting characters, 71, 72
Online Layout view, 70, 471-472, 474
opening a document, 63-68
   from earlier Word versions, 66
   from other word processors, 67
overwriting text, 84, 88
Page Border tab, 166
page design, 105-138
paragraph formatting, 106
pictures, 140-153, 155-156
PowerPoint use of Word files, 214
Preferences dialog, 39, 40, 192, 193
printing, 74-76
   Print Preview, 70-71
replacing, 197-201
ruler, 111
saving a document, 52, 54-62, 63
   from earlier Word versions, 66-67
   from other word processors, 67
   as HTML, 482-485, 487
selecting text, 79-81
shading, 162-166
similarities among Office 98 products, 4-6
Sort Ascending button, 159
Sort Descending button, 159
special characters, 100-102
Standard toolbar, 51, 52, 62
   displaying, 79

status bar, 73
Style dialog, 178, 179, 182
styles, 176-183
symbols, 100-103
synonyms, 196
tables, 156-161
    column width, 160-161
    row height, 160-161
Tables And Borders button, 160
Tables And Borders toolbar, 139, 140, 160, 163, 164
templates, 110, 169, 170, 173-176, 182-183
text boxes, 153-155
thesaurus, 196
tracking changes, 89-90, 462-464
typefaces, 90-95
Web pages with, 481-485
    editing, 486-490
wizards, 170-173
word count, 89
WordArt, 34, 38-39
Word count, Word, 89
Word Count dialog, 89
Workbooks (Excel), 288, 288-289, 291
    closing, 298-299
    creating, 288-297
    formatting, 337-361
    opening, 299-303, 305-306
    saving, 294-295
    templates, 291-294

Worksheets (Excel), 11-12, 288
    background, 475
    formatting, 339-345
    inserting new worksheet, 346
    inserting pictures, 352-353
    naming, 345-346
    printing, 354
Wrapping tab, Format Picture dialog, 150-151
WYSIWYG (What You See Is What You Get), 7, 68, 487, 534

Y

Year 2000, Excel dates, 312

Z

Zigzag underline, Word, 193
ZIP code number format, Excel, 313
Zoom
    PowerPoint, 216, 217, 218-219
    Word, 19, 71, 144
Zoom dialog
    PowerPoint, 216, 217
    Word, 19, 71
Zoom list, Standard toolbar, 291